Civil War Road Trip
Volume II

A Guide to Virginia & Maryland,
1863–1865

Bristoe Station to Appomattox

Civil War Road Trip
Volume II

A Guide to Virginia & Maryland,
1863–1865

Bristoe Station to Appomattox

MICHAEL WEEKS

The Countryman Press
Woodstock, Vermont

To my wife, Charlotte, for her patience, understanding, and love
and
To all those fighting to preserve America's history

Interior photographs by the author unless otherwise specified; all others courtesy of the National Archives.

Maps by Aaron Porter, © The Countryman Press

Book design and composition by Faith Hague

Civil War Road Trip, Volume II: A Guide to Virginia & Maryland, 1863–1865
978-0-88150-984-7

Published by The Countryman Press, P.O. Box 748, Woodstock, VT 05091
Distributed by W. W. Norton & Company, Inc., 500 Fifth Avenue, New York, NY 10110
Printed in the United States of America

10 9 8 7 6 5 4 3 2 1

CONTENTS

HOW TO USE THIS BOOK

THE TOURS

The sites presented in this book encompass all of the major campaigns of the Eastern Theater during the final two years of the Civil War. Certainly, there was a lot more action in this area around the capitals than could possibly fit into one book in detail. But if you were to follow each of the tours laid out here, you would see the sites of all of the area's significant action from the first campaigns following the battle of Gettysburg to the Confederate surrender at Appomattox.

Not all of these sites are preserved or are in pristine condition. As cities and towns grow, some of the sites are gradually being lost to progress. Thankfully, because the sites in this part of the country are so well recognized, there is almost always something to experience. Some of the sites are large or important, others less so. You will find enough information in this book for you to determine for yourself whether making the journey from one site to another is worth your time or not.

BREAKING IT ALL DOWN

Each tour in the book will take you along one of the Civil War's major campaigns, culminating in one or more major battles of the war. The trips are designed to be taken over a weekend or long weekend road trip. Of course, some tourists will take longer, whereas others can do it in half the time.

Road trips can (and should) be a very personal experience, and everyone goes about them differently. Some people might throw the map out the window and go where the road takes them, eventually winding up at their destination. Others plan every detail, forming an itinerary that prescribes every point of the schedule. Most people fall somewhere in the middle. Although some of the areas in this book are a bit off the beaten path, for the most part, you'll almost always be very close to food and lodging. There's also a lot of natural beauty in the places you'll be visiting, so even camping will be an option. In short, don't be afraid to wing it.

No matter how you take your trip, please remember one very important thing.

Getting out there and walking the fields where this history happened is essential—for you, for the local economies, and for preserving our country's history. However, the best thing you can do to not only learn about the Civil War but also create memories that will last forever is to stop and talk to people. Civil War history runs deep here, and being home to so much hallowed ground is a source of great pride. If you seek out conversations with the people who live and work here—from park rangers to the folks down at the local coffee shop—you will learn things that simply can't be put into a book. These experiences are guaranteed to give you a whole new perspective on the Civil War, American culture, and other things that can't possibly be predicted, so don't be afraid to go out there and discover for yourself what treasures await you in your journeys.

GETTING TO THE SITES

The classic gas station road map is a thing of the past. The modern road tripper, if relying on anything at all, is most likely to refer to a heads-up global positioning system (GPS), directions from MapQuest or Google, or their smartphones. The general driving directions to each site are within the chapters, but you will also find addresses and GPS coordinates for each site in appendix A.

LEARNING ABOUT THE CIVIL WAR

There is enough history in this book and at the sites themselves to ensure that you will learn a great deal during your tours. Still, you may want to read up a little before hitting the road. There have been so many books written on so many different aspects of the American Civil War that picking a good place to start can be a daunting task. There are books on the war as a whole, on individual campaigns, regiments, commanders, politics, technology, economics . . . the list goes on and on.

If you don't know much about the Civil War (which puts you in the majority), you have several great ways to learn. If you'd like to try and tackle a lot of material in one fell swoop, you can't do much better than Shelby Foote's three-volume set titled *The Civil War*. While Foote's work has had its critics, it has established itself as one of the best and most popular narratives on the war. If a single volume will do for you, James M. McPherson's Pulitzer Prize–winning work *Battle Cry of Freedom: The Civil War Era* is the standard. Finally, if both of those still seem to be a bit too much, don't hesitate to pick up *The Civil War for Dummies* by Keith D. Dickson. Hey, we all had to start somewhere, and the For Dummies series of books has proven to be a great first step for many.

If you're a more visual person, head to the library and check out the videos of Ken Burns's nine-part documentary *The Civil War*. Covering the war thoroughly in nine episodes is simply not possible, but this riveting series has inspired millions to further their knowledge not only of the war but of American history in general. Filled with great stories from great storytellers, Burns's film was an instant classic and is still worth watching today.

After you've finished visiting these places, hopefully you will come away with questions and will want to explore further. In each chapter you will find reading recommendations from the staff at the Abraham Lincoln Book Shop in Chicago. Established in 1938, the shop is one of (if not *the*) most respected bookstores in the country focusing on Lincoln and the Civil War, and its original owner was one of the founding members of the first Civil War Round Table. (There are now well over 300 Round Tables, and members from around the globe still visit the shop and sit at the original "round table.") These guys are the experts, and you can be sure that their recommendations will put you down the right path. You can find out more about the shop at www.alincolnbookshop.com.

If you do become hooked on this history, get on the Internet and find your nearest Civil War Round Table. These groups come in all different shapes and sizes, and usually the only requirement for membership is an interest in the Civil War. You will likely run into a mixture of scholars, amateur historians, reenactors, newbies, and everything in between, and discussing the war and having a good time are usually of equal importance. Not only will your knowledge increase, but you'll meet some great people along the way.

COMMANDS AND COMMANDERS IN THE CIVIL WAR

SCRATCHING BEYOND THE SURFACE of Civil War history can land you in a morass of names and terms that can quickly become confusing. The Union army promoted 583 men to the rank of general during the war, while the Confederacy had 425. That's a lot of names to remember, and when you begin to throw in brigades, divisions, and corps—none of which had a clear definition in this war—and further begin to attach numbers to them, it's easy to lose track of what's going on.

Once you get the hang of military structure, however, remembering who, where, and when for the different battles (as well as the politics behind the scenes) becomes much simpler. Soon you may even find yourself following a certain general through various campaigns, and maybe even picking a few favorites.

Here are a few things to remember about the military during the war, along with the most prominent leaders that were part of the Eastern Theater of the Civil War from 1863 to 1865. These are only a handful of the names that will appear over and over in your travels.

MILITARY STRUCTURE

»ORDERS OF BATTLE

Occasionally in your history reading, you will see an "order of battle," usually in an appendix, followed by a long list of various units and their commanders. At first glance, an order of battle can be overwhelming. After you've used them a few times, however, you will find them to be valuable references.

An order of battle is a representation of the command structure of an army and all of its subsets. In some cases, it can be done all the way down to the tiniest unit, whereas in others it is kept very general.

In appendix B, you will find abbreviated orders of battle for each of the armies discussed on your tours. They will help you keep track of who is in command of who, as well as where each unit lies in the army's organization.

» MILITARY UNITS

The various units an army uses are not always consistently defined. In fact, during the Civil War, it was the norm, not the exception, to stray widely from these standard definitions and to change them often. Just as the sizes of each army varied, so, too, did the sizes of the units, such as divisions and brigades, that made up that army.

Here is a very general breakdown of the various military units, in order from smallest to largest:

Regiment—Regiments are the building blocks of an army. When you hear the name "15th Alabama" or "2nd Wisconsin," these are almost always regiments. The size of a regiment usually numbered around 1,000 men, but would usually dwindle over the course of the war, sometimes into the low hundreds. Regiments were usually broken down further into companies. If you walked up to the soldier on the field and asked what unit he belonged to, he would almost always refer to his regiment.

Brigade—Put two to four regiments together and you have a brigade. While brigades, like regiments, usually have a numerical designation, they are often referred to by the commander or by some other nickname, particularly on the Confederate side—e.g., "Benning's Brigade." Brigade numbers hovered around 3,000 to 4,000 men, but like regiments, would often shrink over time, after which they were often shuffled or combined. (In this book, brigades on both sides will be referred to by the commander's name.)

Division—Divisions were usually made up of two to four brigades. Just like the brigades, they are usually referred to by their commander, and often the next level up (e.g., Heth's division of A. P. Hill's corps). Divisions varied widely in strength, but were almost always in the thousands. (Like brigades, in this book, divisions on both sides will be referred to by the commander's name.)

Corps—The corps structure is a little bit different than that of the other units. The idea of corps making up an army was a remnant of Napoleonic warfare, and neither army adopted it until the Civil War was well under way. Corps were usually made up of two to four divisions, and although still named after their commander, they are also commonly referred to by their number, often designated by Roman numerals. (In this book, Union corps will be designated by Roman numeral; Confederate corps will usually be referred to by their commander.)

Army—You probably think that this is the easy one. Well, not all armies are alike. Some armies used corps, some did not. In addition, one side in a battle may have several armies on the field. For example, during the siege of Petersburg, the Union Army of the Potomac and the Army of the James often acted in concert with one another, and corps from both armies fought side by side at times.

GENERALS: UNITED STATES OF AMERICA

Ambrose Everett Burnside

Born: May 23, 1824, Liberty, Indiana
Died: September 13, 1881, Providence, Rhode Island
West Point Graduation: 1847

Ambrose Burnside

Ambrose Burnside, a major general who would briefly serve as commander of the Army of the Potomac, was almost universally liked. However, before the Civil War was over, his name would be associated with a number of disasters (along with, of course, the distinctive facial hair he kept, now familiarly known as sideburns).

Although Burnside was originally destined to be a tailor, his father was able to secure a position for him at West Point. Postgraduation, he served mostly in garrison duty through the Mexican War and on the frontier, resigning in 1853 and moving to Rhode Island. After holding several positions (including one with the Illinois Central Railroad under George McClellan), Burnside was quickly in the heat of the action at the outbreak of the Civil War, commanding a brigade at First Manassas. He led a successful campaign to gain a toehold on the Carolina coast in early 1862, one of the Union's few early successes in the east.

In September 1862, he was leading the IX Corps of the Army of the Potomac at Antietam when his command had trouble overtaking a Confederate position on the opposite side of Antietam Creek. The crossing that his men labored over for so long has since been known as Burnside's Bridge. Still, less than two months later, Burnside was given command of the entire Army of the Potomac, accepting the assignment only after refusing twice and finally being ordered to do so. Only one month later, the army would suffer a bloody and disastrous defeat at the battle of Fredericksburg, for which Burnside would take much of the blame. Relieved of this command the following March, he was assigned to the west and successfully conducted the defense of Knoxville, Tennessee. He was eventually recalled to lead the IX Corps. There, Burnside's performance was questionable, and he continued to lose the respect of his peers. After the embarrassing episode of the Crater in Petersburg, another incident for which he unfairly shouldered a disproportionate amount of blame, Burnside was relieved of command. He later went into politics, serving three terms as governor of Rhode Island and then in the United States Senate, dying shortly into his second term at the age of 57.

Benjamin Franklin Butler

Born: November 5, 1818, Deerfield, New Hampshire
Died: January 11, 1893, Washington, D.C.
West Point Graduation: N/A

Benjamin Butler was good at a lot of things. He was a master politician. He may have been as good as an administrator as anyone in the Union army. He kept his troops happy. In practicing these skills, Butler also became very good at creating controversy and chalking up derogatory nicknames. One thing he was not good at was military command, but Ben Butler's stamp on the Civil War is unmistakable.

Butler was a self-made Massachusetts man. He earned his way through college, then passed the bar and became a very well-known criminal lawyer. First elected to the Massachusetts House of Representatives in 1853, Butler served as a delegate to the 1860 Democratic Convention in Charleston, South Carolina—where he voted to nominate Jefferson Davis for president on 57 consecutive ballots. Still, when the war broke out, Abraham Lincoln knew well enough the political value of appointing Butler the Union's first volunteer major general.

Butler's first command was at Fort Monroe at the tip of the Virginia Peninsula. Shortly after arriving, Butler shocked the Confederacy by declaring that slaves, considered property in the South, could therefore also be considered contraband of war. Slaves soon began flocking to Union lines for protection. Butler's next assignment was as military governor of New Orleans. Although the city arguably was operating more effectively under his command than it ever had before the war, Butler made few friends. After Confederate women began harassing Union soldiers a bit too much, Butler decreed that they would be arrested and considered "ladies of the town," earning him the nickname "Beast Butler." He also took very good care of his friends and supporters, as well as himself, allegedly pocketing large amounts of valuables and cash. This earned him the

Benjamin Butler

nickname "Spoons." Butler later commanded the Army of the James, which, under his poor military leadership, became bottled up on the Bermuda Hundred Peninsula outside Richmond. His final act in the military was a major blunder outside Fort Fisher in North Carolina. After the war, Butler returned to politics, serving as a U.S. congressman and as governor of Massachusetts—as a Republican.

Ulysses Simpson Grant

Born: April 27, 1822, Point Pleasant, Ohio
Died: July 23, 1885, Mount McGregor, New York
West Point Graduation: 1843

Coming from humble beginnings, failing at more than a few business endeavors, and developing an afflffi affinity for the bottle along the way, Hiram Ulysses Grant showed very few signs of amounting to much. Few could have predicted that the American Civil War would launch this obscure has-been of an officer from mediocrity to universal recognition as the Union's most vaunted military hero and, later, president of the United States.

Ulysses S. Grant

Grant was born in a small cabin along the Ohio River. His father had some influence with a local congressman, and he received an appointment to West Point, graduating in the bottom half of his class. He earned accolades while serving under both Zachary Taylor and Winfield Scott in the Mexican War, but afterward, his military career fizzled, mostly due to his alcoholism and the boredom of service in the Pacific Northwest. Resigning in 1854, Grant attempted several business ventures, all of which failed, and he eventually resorted to working for his brothers at a leather store in Galena, Illinois. When the Civil War began, Grant immediately offered his services but had a hard time finding any takers. It was not until two months after Fort Sumter that he was finally named colonel of the 21st Illinois Infantry.

After gaining a friend in Congress, Grant was appointed brigadier general. From that point on, his career skyrocketed. First was the capture of Fort Donelson, opening the Cumberland River and causing the fall of Nashville; his terms of surrender for the Confederates made him a household name as "Unconditional Surrender" Grant. His army received a close shave at the battle of Shiloh, but the Federals came out on top. Grant conducted a brilliant campaign resulting in the fall of Vicksburg, winning the

Mississippi River for the Union. He then moved east to Chattanooga, where a surprising victory proved enough for Abraham Lincoln to promote him to lieutenant general, the first since George Washington, and give him command of all Union armies. Rather than perform desk duty in Washington, Grant chose to stay with the Army of the Potomac, where Robert E. Lee had been embarrassing the Federals at every step. Grant's presence instantly changed the war in the east, where an aggressive but bloody war of attrition ultimately led to the Confederate surrender at Appomattox. Now an American legend, Grant was elected president in 1868, only seven years after he had been a clerk in Galena. His presidency would be troubled, mostly due to naïveté, and his final years brought great financial hardship. Grant therefore decided to pen his autobiography, finishing it in 1885 (with a little help from Mark Twain) while virtually on his deathbed. Not only did it bring his struggling family almost half a million dollars, but it is considered by some to be among the greatest military memoirs of all time.

Winfield Scott Hancock

> Born: February 14, 1824, Montgomery Square, Pennsylvania
> Died: February 9, 1886, Governors Island, New York
> West Point Graduation: 1844

Winfield Scott Hancock began the Civil War in Los Angeles, California, serving in the position he had the most experience in—quartermaster. When he finally did make his way east to fight, he quickly gained a reputation on the field for brilliant command, earning him the nickname "Hancock the Superb."

Hancock graduated from West Point at the young age of 19, but came out near the bottom of his class. He made it out just in time to see action in Mexico, and then served in various positions around the West until after the war was under way. George McClellan snatched his services at the first opportunity, and Hancock quickly became a mainstay in McClellan's Army of the Potomac. Commanding a brigade during the Peninsula campaign, he quickly distinguished himself as not only brave but also as a brilliant field general. He was given a division after the battle of Antietam, fought conspicuously well at Fredericksburg, and performed brilliantly at Chancellorsville, where he originated a defensive tactic that would soon become a textbook maneuver.

After being given command of the II Corps, Hancock would shine at Gettysburg, where as temporary commander of the army in George Meade's absence, he established the Union defensive position on Cemetery Ridge that would withstand multiple Confederate attacks on the second day of battle and Pickett's Charge on the third. It was during this charge that Hancock's star would peak, although he

Winfield S. Hancock

would leave the field with a serious wound that would keep him out of action until 1864. When he did return to his old II Corps, Hancock displayed neither the aggressiveness nor the brilliance that he had possessed before his Gettysburg wound, which continued to cause him great pain. While he performed well, and he and his II Corps were continuously called upon for the army's toughest assignments, hard campaigning was taking its toll. After a string of successive defeats, particularly around Petersburg, Hancock seemed to have lost his touch. When his wound became unbearable late in 1864, he finally relinquished command of his corps. Although he ran for president in 1880, he remained with the army until his death.

George Gordon Meade

Born: December 31, 1815, Cadiz, Spain
Died: November 6, 1872, Philadelphia, Pennsylvania
West Point Graduation: 1835

Although his name is associated with one great Union victory—Gettysburg—George Meade led the Army of the Potomac longer than anyone else, seeing it through its ultimate victory at Appomattox. Unfortunately, odd arrangements and circumstances put Meade in the shadows through virtually his entire command, and this is likely where it will stay.

Born in Spain to a wealthy American family, Meade graduated from West Point in the class of 1835, but was out of the army by the end of the next year, preferring to pursue an engineering career. He changed his mind again in 1842, rejoining the army's Corps of Topographical Engineers. Here he stayed, with the exception of some service in the Mexican War, until the Civil War broke out. Meade made good use of his engineering skills strengthening the defenses of Washington over the winter, but was given a field command at the opening of the spring campaign of 1862. He joined George McClellan outside Richmond just in time for the Seven Days battles in June, demonstrating his command capabilities on the field until he was wounded twice at the battle of Glendale. He was back commanding his brigade by Second Manassas in August, was awarded division command by the time the Antietam campaign began in September, and was given the V Corps shortly after the battle of Fredericksburg in December.

In late June 1863, Joseph Hooker vacated his position commanding the Army of the Potomac. It seemed that nobody wanted the job—Meade was fifth in line for the position—but finally, on June 28, he accepted. Had command remained vacant any longer, the army may have found itself in quite a quandary, as the battle of Gettysburg opened

NATIONAL ARCHIVES

George Meade

only two days later. Both sides took a beating, but Meade commanded ably and emerged the victor with Lee's withdrawal. After this, the army went into a mode of caution until the arrival of Ulysses S. Grant in 1864. In an odd arrangement, Meade remained in command of the Army of the Potomac. Grant, now commanding all Federal armies, felt he needed to remain in the field and set his headquarters with the army, looking over Meade's shoulder through the end of the war. Naturally, Grant earned all the accolades. Still, Meade retained several commands after the war, staying with the army until his death from pneumonia at the age of 56.

Philip Henry Sheridan

Born: March 6, 1831, Albany, New York
Died: August 5, 1888, Nonquitt, Massachusetts
West Point Graduation: 1853

Like Ulysses S. Grant, there were few who would predict that Phil Sheridan would someday be regarded as one of the Union army's most prominent generals. He only barely made it into West Point, and once there, he received a year's suspension for allegedly attacking a fellow cadet with a bayonet. When he did graduate, it was in the bottom third of his class. However, also like Grant, once Sheridan was given the opportunity, his success made him one of the Union army's most well-known personalities.

Sheridan spent the beginning of his military service on the frontier, receiving few opportunities until the Civil War broke out. Even then, he served as quartermaster for several departments until May 1862, when he was finally given his first command. Promoted to brigadier general, Sheridan fought tenaciously, first at the critical battle of Perryville and then again at the bloody battle of Stones River. Although his division suffered terribly at Chickamauga, they gained their revenge

Philip Sheridan

NATIONAL ARCHIVES

at the battle of Chattanooga, conducting a spectacular unauthorized charge that broke the seemingly impregnable Confederate line. This was done under Grant's watch, and when Grant moved east, he wanted Sheridan with him, giving him command of the Army of the Potomac's cavalry corps.

Sheridan did not possess great military skill, but he could think quickly on the field and had a remarkable talent for inspiring men. One of his first actions as cavalry commander was to take his entire corps to lure the Confederate cavalry into a fight in the open; one of the results was the battle of Yellow Tavern, bringing not only a Union victory over the vaunted Confederate cavalry but also the demise of its legendary leader, J. E. B. Stuart. The confident Union horsemen had become almost unstoppable, so when Grant needed to ignite a spark in the Shenandoah Valley, he called on Sheridan for the task. "Little Phil" led his army to significant victories in the Valley, where the Federals had previously had little success, and his amazing reversal of what should have been a decisive Confederate victory at Cedar Creek established his reputation as a star in the public eye. After the war, Sheridan eventually became commanding general of the U.S. Army, but died shortly after his promotion.

Gouverneur Kemble Warren

Born: January 8, 1830, Cold Spring, New York
Died: August 8, 1882, Newport, Rhode Island
West Point Graduation: 1850

One of many generals on both sides who began their military careers as engineers, Gouverneur Warren retained his skill to a degree unsurpassed by his peers. When he did make his mark on the battlefield, it was a brilliant moment that made him savior of the

Gouverneur Warren

Union army. However, by the time the war was finished, the depths to which his reputation had sunk were of equal magnitude. Warren graduated second in his class at West Point and went on to teach there while also serving as an engineer. When the war came, he was given a brigade, and fought at Gaines's Mill (where he was wounded), Second Manassas, and Antietam, eventually earning the rank of major general. Warren was soon named chief of engineers for the Army of the Potomac, and it was in this capacity that he served during the battle of Gettysburg. Warren was the man who recognized the strategic necessity of Little Round Top, and his quick action in arranging a defense there saved the day for the Federals.

After Gettysburg, Warren took over Winfield Hancock's II Corps and later the V Corps after Hancock returned from his Gettysburg wound. He soon earned praise for his action at Bristoe Station, and also for his lack of action at Mine Run, where his decision not to proceed with a massive Union assault was met with almost universal approval. Unfortunately, this would later translate into a reputation for being overcautious, particularly after Ulysses S. Grant arrived. Warren was repeatedly criticized, often unfairly, for his unwillingness to directly assault enemy works. At the battle of Five Forks, Phil Sheridan removed Warren from command because of oversights in the field that were largely his own. It would not be until 1879 that a court of inquiry cleared Warren of any wrongdoing at Five Forks and also found Sheridan's dismissal of him inappropriate. Warren remained in the army long after the war, returning to what he knew best—engineering.

GENERALS: CONFEDERATE STATES OF AMERICA

Pierre Gustave Toutant Beauregard

Born: May 28, 1818, St. Bernard Parish, Louisiana
Died: February 20, 1893, New Orleans, Louisiana
West Point Graduation: 1838

The first Confederate hero of the Civil War, P. G. T. Beauregard seemed made for the part. Handsome, an able general, and gaining early victories, Beauregard quickly became a household name in the South, but by war's end his work was limited severely, partly because of his own pomposity.

Beauregard distinguished himself during the Mexican War as part of General Winfield Scott's staff. He remained in the army afterward, and was assigned to the position of superintendent at West Point. A remarkable honor, the assignment came in January 1861, before the war but after some of the Southern states had already seceded. Remarkably, Beauregard accepted, but held the position only for a matter of days before he was relieved due to his Southern sympathies.

After he resigned his U.S. Army commission the next month, he went to serve the Confederacy and presided over the opening shots of the war at Fort Sumter.

P. G. T. Beauregard

As if this were not enough to earn Beauregard instant fame, three months later he was second in command at the great Confederate victory at First Manassas. He later went on to serve in the Western Theater, taking command at Shiloh after the death of Albert Sidney Johnston, but was bounced around the South afterward due to a combination of pretentiousness and a poor relationship with President Jefferson Davis. He eventually went back east to successfully defend Charleston, and was instrumental in saving Petersburg from being overrun in the last moments of Grant's Overland campaign in 1864. After the war, Beauregard went back to his native Louisiana, running the state lottery with fellow general Jubal Early until his death at the age of 74.

Jubal Anderson Early

Born: November 3, 1816, Franklin County, Virginia
Died: March 2, 1894, Lynchburg, Virginia
West Point Graduation: 1837

Robert E. Lee's "Bad Old Man," Jubal Early, who voted against Virginia's secession, was also one of its most devoted defendants during and after the Civil War. A hard and aggressive fighter, Early maintained an excellent reputation in the Confederacy until public opinion swayed against him following an almost hopeless campaign.

Early served in the U.S. Army for a time after his graduation, and then became a lawyer and politician. After Virginia decided to leave the Union, Early immediately

Jubal Early

enlisted to fight for his native state, and was in uniform at First Manassas, after which he was promoted to brigadier general. Time after time, Early's division could be counted on to do its duty, and though he was disliked by most of his men and his peers in the Confederate army, there was no doubt about his reliability on the field.

After the death of Stonewall Jackson in mid-1863, Lee had serious issues with his corps commanders; they were either not up to the task or, in James Longstreet's case, were wounded and taken out of action. However, Jubal Early stood out as a potential replacement. Beginning in late 1863, several opportunities arose to give Early temporary command of a corps. Early shined, and he was given a permanent corps command at the first opportunity. (He likely would have had one earlier, had he not rubbed most people the wrong way.) Just before the Petersburg campaign, Lee entrusted Early to leave the Army of Northern Virginia and take his corps to the gates of Washington, D.C. While he was not able to capture the capital, Early had shocked the Union. Unfortunately for him, the result was a new Union army built around Phil Sheridan, and Early's outnumbered men could not withstand Sheridan's size or his aggressiveness. The public and the government called for Early's ouster, and a reluctant Lee was eventually forced to accede. After the war, Early first went to Texas, then returned to practice law and assist P. G. T. Beauregard in overseeing the Louisiana State Lottery. Early never took the oath of allegiance, and was one of the Confederacy's staunchest defenders until his death.

Richard Stoddert Ewell

Born: February 8, 1817, Georgetown, D.C.
Died: January 25, 1872, Spring Hill, Tennessee
West Point Graduation: 1840

Richard S. Ewell was one of the Confederacy's most prized generals during the early years of the Civil War. By its end, however, Ewell had become such a liability that the Confederacy was exploring ways to gracefully remove him from command. The before-and-after Richard Ewell can be fairly easily explained; more difficult to answer is whether it could have made a difference in the outcome of the war.

Ewell left the U.S. Army in 1861 following a distinguished and decorated career. Made brigadier general in 1861 and major general by January 1862, Ewell fought hard under the command of Stonewall Jackson in the Shenandoah Valley and during the Peninsula campaign of 1862. However, less than two months later, Ewell lost a leg during the fierce fighting on the first day at Second Manassas. He went home to recover, and returned to the army in May 1863 to take over Jackson's corps following his death.

By all accounts, when Ewell returned to the army, he was a changed man. Some said that the obvious reason was his war wound. Others surmised that fault could be laid with Ewell's new wife, with whom he was absolutely smitten. Either way, the aggressive fighter that Richard Ewell had been was gone for good. In addition, he became more prone to losing his cool, a trait that concerned Robert E. Lee enough that he was compelled to order Ewell to control himself during the bloody battle of the Mule Shoe at Spotsylvania on May 18, 1864. Not helping matters was Ewell's propensity to become sick, and he was forced on several occasions to temporarily

Richard S. Ewell

relieve himself of command. When a case of dysentery attacked Ewell later in the Overland campaign, Lee used the opportunity to relieve Ewell from command and permanently assign his corps to Jubal Early. Ewell maintained charge of the Richmond defenses until the army's flight toward Appomattox, during which he was captured.

Ambrose Powell Hill

> *Born: November 9, 1825, Culpeper, Virginia*
> *Died: April 2, 1865, Petersburg, Virginia*
> *West Point Graduation: 1847*

During a short but brilliant military career, A. P. Hill distinguished himself on the field and rose quickly through the ranks. Although his performance near the end of his career is questionable (due to a still-debated severe illness that frequently kept him out of action and affected his judgment), Hill's importance to the Confederate cause may be best indicated by the fact that both Robert E. Lee and Stonewall Jackson invoked his name on their deathbeds.

Hill served in Mexico and also in the Seminole Wars in Florida and remained in the U.S. Army until just before the outbreak of the war, joining the Confederacy as colonel of the 13th Virginia Infantry regiment. Before long, Hill had advanced to the rank of brigadier general, and by the time the Peninsula campaign was over, he had been promoted to major general and commanded his own division. It was Hill's "Light Division" that did much of the heaviest fighting during the Seven Days battles.

A. P. Hill

Although by many accounts, Hill tended to rub people the wrong way (neither James Longstreet nor Stonewall Jackson were particularly fond of him), everyone knew that he and his division could be counted on, and he was eventually promoted to Lieutenant General. After the death of Stonewall Jackson, though, it was inevitable that Hill's performance would continually be compared to the late general's. It didn't help that Hill increasingly became unreliable—partly for his performance, but mostly for his lack of presence on the battlefield. A. P. Hill was killed in action on the outskirts of Petersburg, Virginia, as Union troops finally ended their 10-month siege. Only 39 at the time of his death, A. P. Hill was, and remains today, one of the Confederacy's best and most underappreciated commanders.

Robert Edward Lee

Born: January 19, 1807, Westmoreland County, Virginia
Died: October 12, 1870, Lexington, Virginia
West Point Graduation: 1829

It's difficult to find a bad word about Robert E. Lee. While there are many criticisms of his military decisions, his overall skill as a commander is rarely questioned, and you usually won't find any comments about his character or his honor. It is this combination that has made Lee a hero of the South and a symbol of the Confederacy itself.

Lee's lineage practically guaranteed that he would hold some important station in life. His father was Henry "Light Horse Harry" Lee, hero of the American Revolution and part of a family that included two signers of the Declaration of Independence. Although his father would eventually incur serious debt that would harm the family's well-being, youngest son Robert still earned a commission to West Point, graduating second in his class and having no demerits on his record. For the next seventeen years, Lee spent his time in the army as an engineer, overseeing much of the work on the fortresses being constructed along the Atlantic Coast. It was also during this time that he married Mary Custis, a direct descendant of Martha Washington. In the Mexican War he served under General Winfield Scott, and the two became very close. He was named superintendent of West Point in 1852, then served on the frontier in Texas. In 1857, his family moved into Arlington House overlooking Washington, D.C., and it was here that he made the decision to serve his state. On April 18, 1861, Lee declined an offer by Scott to command the Federal armies, and only days later accepted command of all military forces in Virginia.

After spending some time in the field and as an adviser to President Jefferson Davis early in the war, Lee became commander of the Army of Northern Virginia on June 1, 1862 after General Joe Johnston was wounded at the battle of Seven Pines. Lee's impact upon taking command was immediate. Over the next three years, Lee would continually defeat larger Union armies, frustrating the Union efforts until 1864, when General

Ulysses S. Grant arrived from the west. Grant was the first general to successfully keep Lee on the defensive, forcing him to move south and eventually into the earthworks surrounding Petersburg and Richmond. After a long siege, Lee attempted to lead his army to safety, but finally surrendered at Appomattox on April 9, 1865. Although the Civil War would continue for another two months, virtually everyone knew that Lee's surrender meant the end of the Confederacy. Lee went on to become president of Washington University, later renamed Washington and Lee University in his honor, and he remained in this position until his death at age 63. His legendary status is cemented in the South, and to this day his birthday is celebrated as a state holiday in parts of the old Confederacy.

Robert E. Lee

NATIONAL ARCHIVES

James Longstreet

Born: January 8, 1821, Edgefield District, South Carolina
Died: January 2, 1904, Gainesville, Georgia
West Point Graduation: 1842

During his lifetime, particularly after the Civil War, James Longstreet was a very controversial figure. While he clearly distinguished himself as one of the Confederacy's best generals on the battlefield, his comments and actions after the war earned him much grief in the South. In hindsight, though, the qualities of the general that Robert E. Lee referred to as "my old war horse" have brought him back into the limelight with the Confederacy's more recognized leaders.

During Longstreet's 19 years in the U.S. Army before the war, he served with distinction in Mexico and in several of the Indian Wars. Performing well at First Manassas and then particularly during the Peninsula campaign, Longstreet quickly became known as a reliable general. When given his own independent command, the results were not so praiseworthy; his performance in North Carolina was mediocre, and he failed to lift the siege of Knoxville, Tennessee, after the battle of Chattanooga. However, while under Lee's guidance with the Army of Northern Virginia (and at the battle of Chickamauga, where his corps moved by rail to reinforce Braxton Bragg), Longstreet proved himself to be a bold and aggressive general.

James Longstreet

At the battle of the Wilderness in 1864, Longstreet was severely wounded by friendly fire, under circumstances eerily similar to those that killed Stonewall Jackson a year before in almost the very same place. Longstreet was able to return during the siege of Petersburg, and remained until the surrender at Appomattox. After the war, Longstreet did the unthinkable by serving in the Grant administration and becoming a Republican. These acts, along with criticisms of both Lee and Jackson that came to light, essentially blackballed him from being celebrated as a hero of the war during his lifetime. He remained in public service, and was serving as a railroad commissioner in the Theodore Roosevelt administration when he died shortly before his 80th birthday.

James Ewell Brown Stuart

Born: February 6, 1833, Patrick County, Virginia
Died: May 12, 1864, Yellow Tavern, Virginia
West Point Graduation: 1854

Known for his daring exploits, J. E. B. Stuart's flair for the dramatic has made him one of the most entertaining characters of the Civil War. Although this daring would occasionally put himself (and, on occasion, the Confederate army) in grave danger, it also made him a legend in his own time. Stuart's accomplishments with the Virginia cavalry would earn him a place in the pantheon of the great Confederate generals.

Graduating from West Point only seven years before the war, Stuart spent most of his time in the U.S. Army on the frontier. When he resigned and pledged himself to the cause of the Confederacy, Stuart almost instantly distinguished himself, serving as part of the final actions that sent the Union army to flight at First Manassas. When it came to collecting intelligence—one of the essential functions of cavalry—Stuart may have been without equal. During the Peninsula campaign, while conducting a reconnaissance, he led his troopers on a famous "Ride around McClellan," completely encircling the Army of the Potomac while gathering critical information for Robert E. Lee. He made a similar ride during the Second Manassas campaign, raiding General John Pope's headquarters wagon and collecting valuable documents and information. (He also took Pope's jacket. Because Union troops had captured Stuart's signature plumed hat during a raid, Stuart wrote Pope a letter suggesting "an exchange of prisoners." Pope did not respond.)

In June 1863, Stuart overextended his mission and became separated from the Army of Northern Virginia for days. Usually serving as Lee's eyes and ears, he was not able to provide Lee the critical information needed as the Confederates moved north into Pennsylvania. Stuart was not heard from until late on the second day of the battle of Gettysburg, which may have turned out quite differently had he been able to at least stay in contact. He would receive much criticism for this, but otherwise, Stuart served gallantly. Later in the war, when the Union cavalry was finally able to show some initiative, they raided into the northern outskirts of Richmond, clashing with the Confederates at Yellow Tavern on May 11, 1864. Stuart was mortally wounded, dying the next day at the young age of 31.

J. E. B. Stuart

The Third Winchester battlefield, part of which has been successfully preserved by the Civil War Trust.

A WORD ABOUT HISTORIC PRESERVATION

AS YOU TRAVEL THROUGH VIRGINIA and visit these sites, you will find instances where landscapes and objects have remained virtually unchanged or pristine over decades or even hundreds of years. You will also come across some cases where historic sites are so unabashedly commercialized, disregarded, or destroyed that it may trigger embarrassment or even shame. Chances are that the more you visit these places, the more you will care about them, and the more you will want to see them survive.

Historic preservation is more complicated than we'd sometimes like to admit. In a perfect world, we would be able to save it all, and it's doubtful that anyone would object to that if it were possible. Unfortunately, it's not, and compromises have to be made. Frequently, the reason battles were fought where they were, were the resources and cities that were nearby, and those cities have continued to grow over the last century and a half. In addition, after the armies moved on and left their terrible aftermath to the local townsfolk behind them, people didn't always want to remember what happened. Pieces of battlefield were quietly covered and often quickly forgotten.

Today, the awareness and appreciation of historically significant sites is greater than it has ever been. In sensitive areas, federal, state and local laws, along with national and local organizations, protect important sites as best they can. However, not every inch can or will be saved. As it has been throughout human history, economics are often the first obstacle. If money is to be made by building a shopping center on a battlefield, whether it is important or not, someone is likely to try it. The result is often a site that is "memorialized" by some reference to its history. Subdivisions on battlegrounds are proudly named for the battlefield they destroyed, with streets named after the heroes who fought and died there. These developments happen on both large and small scale.

There have been wonderful success stories over the years. Gettysburg has fought off casino development adjacent to the battlefield several times, and parts of the battlefield are now being reclaimed to restore the 1863 landscape. For a time, a monstrous theme park threatened Manassas National Battlefield but was stopped largely through grass-roots efforts. Only years of public outcry finally persuaded Walmart from putting a superstore near the spot where Lee and Grant first clashed at the Wilderness. (For the record, Walmart is a major financial contributor to preservation efforts across the country, particularly in and around Petersburg, Virginia.) Unfortunately, the defeats outweigh the victories, and the outcome is final.

When a battlefield is lost, it is usually gone for good. These pieces of hallowed ground, as Lincoln put it so eloquently at Gettysburg, don't always seem as important today because the Civil War is history, not in any of our collective memories. However, this argument, that a piece of ground on which Americans shed their blood for cause and country is only history, is a false one. These places, all of them, are no less hallowed than the beaches of Normandy, the deserts of Iraq and Afghanistan, or Lower Manhattan.

By visiting these sites, you contribute enormously to their preservation. Historic sites inject out-of-town money into local economies, leading those locals to protect and improve their history. This attracts more visitors, and a circle of growth is formed that is not only a permanent generator of cash but preserves these places, and the memory of those who fought there, forever.

Besides visiting the sites, you can also look to some of the many groups dedicated to preserving these sites. The Civil War Trust, a nonprofit organization dedicated to battlefield preservation, has been one of the most significant contributors to these efforts. In your travels you will come across many sites saved by the trust; some are still in its care, whereas others have been passed to the National Park System and other organizations. Because of the trust's excellent reputation for wisely managing its finances, it is often able to provide unbelievable matching funding to aid its efforts. Finally, both Charity Navigator and GuideStar, two independent and trusted groups that evaluate charities for how well they spend donation money, have given the trust their highest ratings. You can find out more about the Civil War Trust at www.civilwar.org, where you will also find a wealth of resources on the war itself.

VISITING A CIVIL WAR BATTLEFIELD

IF YOU'RE LUCKY, when you visit a Civil War battlefield, all of the important features of the landscape, the movements of the armies, and the story of the battle are laid out for you. In most cases, though, even the best-interpreted historic sites can't tell you the whole story. Not all battlefields are the same, and the variables are endless. They may be as basic as who held the high ground or as complex as understanding the personal tendencies of a particular commander and how he saw the field at the time of the battle.

Fortunately, viewing a battlefield today and understanding what happened there 150 years ago can be relatively easy if you go in armed with just a few tips. In addition, smartphone apps and other gadgets are continually being developed that can help you better understand what you're looking at when you're looking at it.

Here are some helpful hints to keep in mind as you view these historic sites:

» PREPARING FOR THE VISIT

Obviously, the more you know about the battle before you go, the better you will understand what you're looking at. This could range from reading endless volumes on the battle and its context within a campaign, to simply remembering to take a map of the battlefield with you.

Some of the key things to consider finding out before you set out:

What time of year did the battle take place?

In general, most of the Civil War's major campaigns occurred in good weather, between April and October. However, this was not always the case. So when you are looking at the field, consider not only when the battle was fought and how conditions may have affected it, but also the time of year that you are looking at the battlefield yourself. If you're visiting during the summer, when all of the leaves are still on the trees, you probably won't have the same view that the soldiers did if the battle was fought in October. In fact, you may want to plan your trips for later in the year, when the lack of foliage might enable you to see any battlefield more clearly.

How much has the battlefield changed?

For a variety of reasons, battlefield preservation has not always been a high priority, and many battlefields have changed over the years. Sometimes these changes are man-made, as towns and cities expand in size and population. Other changes occur naturally; tree lines move and rivers take a different direction. Knowing the differences between the past and present appearance will prevent you from misinterpreting a battlefield because either Mother Nature or a landscape developer decided to make a change.

Where were the trees?

Particularly when it comes to the siege at Petersburg, the growth of forests where there were none previously can greatly affect how you view the battlefield. Visiting the battlefield today, you are surrounded by thick forest. During the siege, however, very few trees were present, and those that were present were soon cut down for firewood. A soldier on either side could often see for miles past the opposing lines, rather than just the couple of hundred yards that you will find today. Keep these changes in mind as you visit any battlefield.

» THE LANDSCAPE

Some principles of combat are almost as old as warfare itself. One of the most well known and well established is that, generally, holding the high ground puts you in a better position. This was as true in the Civil War as it was in ancient times, and as it is today. So when you take your first scan of the field, keep your eyes peeled for where the high ground might be. Don't limit yourself to looking only for a prominent hilltop; sometimes the slightest rises and ridges gave one army a tremendous advantage over the other. Not only does more of the battlefield become visible from these places, but the placement of artillery on high ground meant domination of a greater expanse of the area.

The slight ridges you find may be important for another couple of reasons. In some cases, slight changes in elevation were enough to conceal units of an army. At Antietam, for example, Union troops approaching the Sunken Road were not able to see what was really before them until they were only yards away from the Confederate lines, and they paid a heavy price for it. A good set of field glasses can also help out a lot in spotting these features from a distance (after all, that's what the generals used).

These ridges, as well as other natural and man-made features, often made excellent cover for an army as it defended its ground. Lying flat behind a small rise in the ground makes a very small target for an enemy marksman. Tree lines and forests also provided cover and concealment for a unit. (By the same token, trying to advance an army through a stand of trees is difficult, and how well this was done sometimes determined whether the enemy fought the entire force at once or in pieces as it emerged from the woods.) Of course, fences and walls—particularly those made of stone— have made enormous and infamous differences in the Civil War, not only providing excellent cover from which to fire but also serving as obstacles to an advancing army.

Finally, the importance of rivers, creeks, wetlands, and even the tiniest bodies of water made enormous differences in how campaigns were conducted and how battles were fought. The

Reconstructed Confederate earthworks provide a marked contrast to the remnants of the original works beside it.

Union army's inadequate maps of the North Anna River, which did not show tiny Long Creek, fooled the Federals into thinking they had captured an important river crossing when they hadn't even reached it yet. Just as important as these creeks are where and how the armies crossed them, either with or without supply wagons or artillery. During battles and campaigns, bridges and fords were key, as they could bottleneck an attacking force or trap an army.

The best way to get the lay of a landscape, of course, is to walk it. The driving tours created for many parks are great, but there is nothing like walking across terrain to give you the feeling of it. Walking the fields will also give you different views of the ground and may reveal features that are not easily discernible from a distance. In some cases, just the experience of a hike is enough to give you a good perspective on a battle. Hiking across the field at Cold Harbor or walking through the thick forests of the Wilderness will provide moments you will not soon forget.

» ENTRENCHMENTS AND FORTIFICATIONS

During the period of the Civil War you are about to tour, the importance of field fortifications came to the forefront. After two years of war, veterans had seen too many hopeless attacks against fortified positions. As soldiers learned out of necessity how to entrench quickly, direct assaults against fortified lines would soon be tossed out the window in favor of maneuver, geographic advantage, and cutting off supply lines. These fortifications would eventually result in the miles and miles of trenches dug during the siege of Petersburg, and ultimately to the horrible casualties of World War I as trench warfare became standard practice.

Most of the earthworks you see today are shadows of what they once were. While some have not been touched by man since the war, nature and erosion has reduced them in most cases to shallow lines of earth that sometimes seem only barely sufficient to provide any protection to a soldier. When they were originally created, however, just the sight of these earthworks was often effective in deterring an enemy attack.   You can see reconstructions of these works at a few places (notably the battlefield at Spotsylvania, Petersburg National Battlefield, and Pamplin Historical Park).

You might also come a few phrases in your travels that are unfamiliar. Before the war, the most well-respected military in the world was the French army, and many of the tactics and objects of this period came directly from Napoleonic warfare. These terms were often kept in their original language, so to prevent you from having to carry a French-English translation book with you, here are only a few of the more common ones:

Abatis: Interlaced and entangled tree branches, usually pointed in one direction, designed to slow down an attacking line.

Fraise: Sharpened branches or narrow tree trunks, buried in the ground at an angle facing the enemy, with the sharp end approximately chest high.

Cheval-de-frise: A log with spikes projecting through it, forming an X-shaped pattern; usually sitting on the ground, making it mobile, with the spikes approximately chest high. The plural is *chevaux-de-frise.*

» USING TECHNOLOGY

As you visit these sites, particularly the national parks, make use of every available resource they provide. One of the best features of the parks are the guided ranger programs; within an hour or two, through the ranger's knowledge (which is always considerable) or the questions that other visitors ask, you can learn things about the battlefield of which most people would not even conceive.

Of course, most of the time, you will not be able to get a personally guided tour of a battlefield. However, with the emergence of smartphones, you may have a guide at your fingertips. Several groups have now developed podcast tours of the better-known battlefields that will put you in exactly the right spot before they tell you what happened there. Apps (applications), the seemingly can't-live-without features that can be found for your smartphone, are continuously being developed to guide you through battlefields, providing information, photographs, and maps.

Your best sources for these tools:

National Park Service (www.nps.gov)—Podcasts are now appearing for many of the parks, and the orders of battle that are usually present are extremely valuable. Several of the parks also offer narrated driving tours of the park on CD.

Civil War Preservation Trust (www.civilwar.org)—The trust's mission of preservation is stretching to interpretation as a necessity, and you can find both podcasts and apps on its site. In addition, the trust's collection of maps, both modern (including animated) and historic, will soon become indispensable as you tour.

Civil War Traveler (www.civilwartraveler.com)—The organization behind the wonderful network of Civil War Trails signs that you will repeatedly run across on your tours, has numerous podcasts and accompanying maps on its website.

IMPORTANT THINGS TO REMEMBER

» Some of these battle sites are on private property. If you would like to see a site that is on private property and contact information is available, be sure to ask *before* you go trespassing through somebody's land. If you don't know, stay out.

» Some of the sites in this book are only seasonally staffed, and either reduce their hours in the off-season or close entirely. Other smaller sites (for example, town and county museums) may only be open one day a week or month throughout the year. If there's any chance that a site may not be accessible, be sure to call ahead and find out.

» All of these sites, including those overseen by the National Park Service, are desperately short of funding. Not only are they trying to remain open, but they also want to heighten the experience for the visitor and, with some luck, acquire and restore surrounding battlefield land. In addition, many sites are staffed by volunteers. When you visit, add a little to the donation box if you can and be sure to sign the guestbook so that when the time comes to ask for funding, it can be used to demonstrate that the site is bringing in people to support the local economy.

» Make sure that your vehicle is in tip-top shape. You don't want to get stuck with a broken-down automobile in a place where your cellular phone doesn't get any reception. Always plan for the worst—keep an emergency road kit with you, and make sure it includes first-aid supplies.

» As you make your journey, hopefully you will get to experience a few places with their own unique flavors, customs, and cultures. You may also come to some areas where you feel a little out of place, as if you don't belong. Although you should always follow your better judgment, do not be afraid to approach the locals and ask for directions, about the town, or where a good place to eat might be. They are just as friendly as you are, and will almost always be as eager to help as you would be if they visited your neck of the woods. In fact, you will find that most people are proud of the history that surrounds them and will share what they know with you. These conversations will be the highlights of your trip.

» Good shoes, water, sunscreen, and insect repellent. Keep these items with you and you'll be able to enjoy every site.

1

Interlude: The Bristoe and Mine Run Campaigns

IN THE FIELDS SOUTH OF THE COLLEGE TOWN of Gettysburg, Pennsylvania, two great but battered armies faced each other, each waiting to see what the other would do. It was the Fourth of July, 1863, but few were celebrating. Daylight had revealed the shattered, broken bodies of thousands of horses and men, wreckage of the most terrible battle ever fought on the continent. Both blue and gray uniforms were scattered across the large battlefield, and both armies decided that there would be no more fighting, at least not here and not today.

Robert E. Lee's Army of Northern Virginia, lessened by over 23,000 casualties, left Gettysburg that night under cover of darkness and rain, and began to move as quickly as possible to the south side of the Potomac River and the safety of the Shenandoah Valley. The Union Army of the Potomac, commanded by George Meade, began its pursuit on July 6, giving the Confederates a head start but also erring on the side of caution. Meade had seen what Lee could do with an army when cornered, and he, too, had lost more than 23,000 of his own men. This caution allowed the Confederates to cross the Potomac at Williamsport, Maryland, on July 14, eliciting loud groans from President Abraham Lincoln and his administration, which had already seen the Confederate army escape too many times for their taste.

While they maneuvered to gain position in Northern Virginia, both commanders had to deal with the issue of recovering from the great battle. Conscription helped to

The Railroad Embankment at Bristoe Station. The Confederates broke the Union line at this crossing.

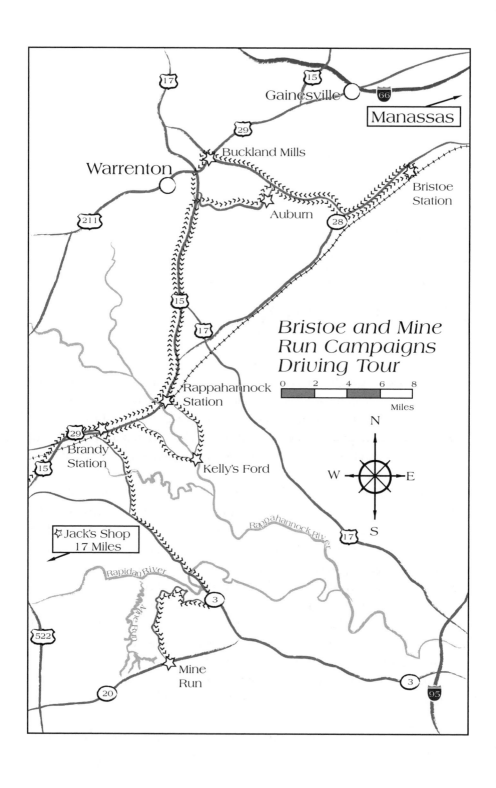

17

15

Gainesville

66

Manassas

29

Buckland Mills

Warrenton

Bristoe
Station

211

Auburn

28

15

17

Bristoe and Mine
Run Campaigns
Driving Tour

0   2   4   6   8

Miles

Rappahannock
Station

N

29

W   E

Brandy
Station

15

Kelly's Ford

S

Rappahannock River

☆ Jack's Shop
17 Miles

17

Rapidan River

Mine Run

3

522

Mine
Run

3

20

95

replenish both forces (particularly the Union), and men were also returning after recovering from wounds from earlier battles or illness. Desertion was a significant problem, though, for the Confederates, so much so that amnesty was offered to those who would return. Few did; letters telling of hardships at home took many rebel soldiers off the front line.

Indeed, Robert E. Lee faced tremendous pressure to not only repair and rest his weary and hungry army but also to bring relief to the people of Virginia. Over two years of war, the state had been ravaged, creating a vast wasteland. The reason for going to Gettysburg in the first place (and, earlier, to Antietam) was to try to feed his army with something other than the bounty of Virginia's already suffering farmers.

George Meade also faced significant pressure, but his was of a much different sort. There were many in Washington who, although he was the hero of Gettysburg, thought that he should be relieved from command for letting Lee escape yet again. Meade had seen his many predecessors fired for their timidity and did not want to suffer the same fate. He wanted to go after the Confederates. But he also held a healthy respect for the Army of Northern Virginia, and was not about to lead his own army into a fight it was not yet prepared for or, worse, into one of Robert E. Lee's traps.

This period of the war between Gettysburg and the arrival of Ulysses S. Grant in April 1864 is often overlooked, but the campaigns that occurred here—and those that did *not* occur—not only highlight the impact of Gettysburg on the war, but also reveal the reversal of the Confederate tide that had so dominated the Eastern Theater of the Civil War during its first two years. The sites you will see mark the Confederacy's permanent transition to the defensive and, for the Union, the emergence of a confidence that would carry them through the end of the war.

BEFORE YOU GO

» PLANNING YOUR TRIP

Only a few years ago, the sites related to these significant battles were not very accessible. Thanks to local and national preservation efforts, however, now at least pieces of all the major battlefields are available for all of us to enjoy. Although they are not major, heavily developed sites, the fact that they are out of the way of much of Northern Virginia's suburban sprawl make them great battlefield visits.

Most of your driving is going to be on state highways or county roads, and the countryside you will be driving through is beautiful, so be

BRISTOE AND MINE RUN CAMPAIGNS

Number of sites: 8
Total miles: 146
Estimated time: 2–3 days

sure to take your time and enjoy the ride. Make a few stops along the way, too, and enjoy some of the great small towns in the area.

Pay attention to the geography as you drive, particularly to the rivers and the handful of small peaks that rise from the landscape. Finally, keep your eye on the railroad—the former Orange & Alexandria Railroad that proved so critical during all of the campaigns in this area.

» RECOMMENDATIONS

Because the sites on this tour are relatively close together, you can probably set up in one location and stay there each night. There are a few hotels and inns in Culpeper, which is surrounded by many of the sites in this chapter (as well as many others). If you want more options for food and lodging than Culpeper offers, both Fredericksburg and Manassas are less than an hour from all of the sites.

THE CAMPAIGN TOUR

JACK'S SHOP

⟩ *Begin your tour 1 mile north of the town of Rochelle, Virginia, at the intersection of the South Blue Ridge Turnpike (VA 231) and Shelby Road.*

After the Confederates crossed the Potomac River and returned to Virginia on July 14, 1863, they spent several days recuperating in the Shenandoah Valley, then headed southeast through the gaps of the Blue Ridge Mountains toward Culpeper. The first of Lee's three corps, commanded by James Longstreet, arrived on July 24, with A. P. Hill's and Richard S. Ewell's corps following days later. By August 3, all of the Confederate infantry was south of the Rapidan River on both the east and west sides of the Orange & Alexandria Railroad, with Lee's headquarters set at Orange Court House.

Along with a restructuring of the Confederate cavalry, which divided J. E. B.

Stuart's horsemen into two divisions commanded by Wade Hampton and Fitzhugh Lee, the Confederate infantry was in for a major change. Throughout the war, the Confederates had not done well in the Western Theater, and right now the Army of Tennessee, commanded by Braxton Bragg, had just been driven out of the major railroad center of Chattanooga. Believing that the Western Theater was critical to the survival of the Confederacy, James Longstreet had proposed shifting troops there, and as it appeared that there may not be any fighting in the near future, he presented his proposal again. At the same time, Confederate president Jefferson Davis was begging Lee for troops to send to South Carolina, where the Federals had been pounding Charleston Harbor for weeks. It was finally decided, on September 6, that Longstreet would take his corps to join Bragg in Georgia, while two other brigades were sent to Charleston.

Longstreet arrived in Georgia on September 20, just in time to help the Confederates win the bloody battle of Chickamauga. However, without Longstreet, his "Old War Horse," Lee was left with only two corps. Worse, neither of the two commanders of those corps were James Longstreet. A. P. Hill had been promoted to corps command in June, and he did not perform well during the Gettysburg campaign. Richard Ewell was an excellent field general, but since losing his leg at the second battle of Manassas, it was evident that he was not the same leader he had been in the past. Both Hill and Ewell were capable commanders, but the loss of Longstreet, coupled with the death of Thomas "Stonewall" Jackson at Chancellorsville several months earlier, deprived Lee of his two best and most trusted lieutenants. Combined with the fact that his horses, both cavalry and artillery, were virtually without forage, this meant that Lee, despite his wishes, would not be directing an offensive movement.

Meanwhile, George Meade's Army of the Potomac began making its way south, crossing the Potomac River at Harpers Ferry and sealing the gaps in the Blue Ridge Mountains. Eventually settling in along the north bank of the Rappahannock River in late August, Meade focused his efforts on resupplying and resting his troops after Gettysburg, along with preparing his many new recruits for battle. Meade had seven infantry corps in late August, a total of 76,200 troops at hand, strung along the river from Kelly's Ford west to the town of White Sulphur Springs.

In between the Rappahannock and Rapidan Rivers, Confederate cavalry had been eyeing the Federals carefully while they fortified every ford and bridge. Further, Longstreet's departure had become known, although the number of troops he took with him was still unknown. Finally, Meade directed his cavalry, commanded by Alfred Pleasanton, to cross the Rappahannock River to conduct a reconnaissance in force on September 13. The Union cavalry was arranged in three divisions: H. Judson Kilpatrick's division would cross at Kelly's Ford, farthest east, with John Buford's division crossing at Rappahannock Station, and David Gregg's to the west. Gouverneur

Warren's II Corps would be standing by at Rappahannock Station in case infantry support was needed.

Having been alerted to the oncoming Federal movement by a local citizen (a former cavalryman), Stuart began to move his wagons south of the Rapidan River while preparing to meet the Federals. Although they put up some resistance, the overwhelming numbers of Union cavalry eventually drove the Confederates across the Rapidan River by late afternoon. Over the next few weeks, Meade would move his entire army across the Rappahannock River to the north bank of the Rapidan with the hearty encouragement of Lincoln and his general in chief, Henry Halleck. Setting up his headquarters at Culpeper Court House, Meade began to gather intelligence for an offensive that would get him over the Rapidan and around Lee's army.

As Meade boarded a train for Washington to meet with the president, Buford and Kilpatrick took their divisions of cavalry south to probe the Confederate line. Splitting at Madison Court House the next morning, September 22, Kilpatrick headed southwest toward Burtonsville, crossing the Rapidan River at Simm's and White's Fords. Buford turned south toward the town of Jack's Shop, splitting the brigades of George Chapman and Thomas Devin, intending to reunite and eventually cross the Rapidan at the town of Liberty Mills.

Detecting the Federal movement, Stuart, who had his cavalry collected in Liberty Mills, sent his horsemen, along with more than two brigades of infantry, northwest along the Orange Road to gather at Jack's Shop. From there they moved north, and soon found Chapman's brigade, along with Buford himself, heading toward them. The Union troopers lined up on both sides of the road behind a rail fence along a tree line and dismounted, preparing to hold until Kilpatrick could arrive with reinforcements. Although Stuart made several charges at the Union line, Buford's men held.

Where you now stand is at the point of first contact during the battle of Jack's Shop. As you face the Civil War Trails sign, Jack's Shop, now the town of Rochelle, would be to your rear, and it was from the road behind you that Stuart's Confederates approached. Buford, with Chapman's brigade, would be coming straight toward you from the front. Eventually, the action would move across your right and behind you toward Jack's Shop.

After several hours, the Federals' stubbornness was rewarded when Kilpatrick's division arrived after recrossing the Rapidan, hitting Stuart in his rear and left flank and turning his position rapidly. As Chapman's brigade and Kilpatrick's division pushed from two different directions, Thomas Devin's brigade also appeared, attacking Stuart from a third front and catching him in a crossfire. Stuart quickly began to withdraw his men, his rear guard continuing to beat off the Federal forces until he reached the safety of Liberty Mills on the south bank of the Rapidan.

Stuart had escaped, but Buford and Kilpatrick had gathered valuable intelligence.

It was now obvious that the Confederate line did not extend beyond Liberty Mills, and the fact that White's Ford was virtually unguarded indicated that a Federal crossing here would provide access to Lee's left flank. As a further bonus, the Union cavalry once again bested J. E. B. Stuart's weakening Confederate cavalry, suffering 120 casualties but inflicting 180 and holding the field.

BRANDY STATION

⟩ *Drive north on VA 231, then continue onto VA 687, for a total of 4.4 miles until you come to US 29. Turn right onto US 29 North and drive 21.7 miles to the ramp for Brandy Square. Turn left at the end of the ramp and drive 0.5 mile to State Police Road, headquarters for the Virginia State Police. Park in the public lot.*

While the Union and Confederate cavalry clashed at Jack's Shop on September 22, the view of the war from Washington, D.C., was changing by the minute. It was on this day that the first credible news of the battle at Chickamauga reached the capital. The magnitude of the Union disaster and the sudden vulnerability of the Federal forces around the critical railroad center at Chattanooga, Tennessee, necessitated a review of every front. Although they were both initially against the idea, Secretary of War Edwin M. Stanton convinced both Lincoln and Halleck that shifting some of Meade's troops west was necessary to counteract the sudden Confederate gains. Meade himself arrived in the capital later that day, and although he also opposed the idea, his pleas fell on deaf ears. It was decided that two of his seven infantry corps, the XI and XII Corps, would be shipped to Nashville and Chattanooga, and the first trains were on their way September 25. With his force greatly reduced, the pressure on Meade to advance also lessened, and many of the Union troops assumed that they would soon be preparing for winter camp, offensive operations presumably being over for the year.

Many Confederate soldiers south of the Rapidan had also come to that conclusion. But with the Federal advantage in numbers suddenly gone, Robert E. Lee was thinking of anything but settling down. Lee had been forced to yield the strategic initiative for months, and he had been looking for any opportunity to regain it. This was it. The Confederates would go on the offensive.

On October 3, Lee informed his corps commanders, Hill and Ewell, that they were going to attempt to turn the Union right. The Federals now held strong positions on high ground, but by moving west, around their right flank, Lee hoped to maneuver them off the Rapidan River line and possibly attack them from the rear. The success of the movement would depend on speed and secrecy, but Lee was confident that he could again outwit the Federals.

Unfortunately for the Confederates, the advantage they could have gained with stealth was quickly dashed. The Union line along the Rapidan was indeed on high ground, and the Federals used this to their advantage, erecting signal towers along the line that enabled them to see virtually all of the Confederates. The signal stations detected increased activity beginning October 6, and intercepted Confederate signals on the 6th and 7th that indicated an upcoming movement by the rebels. In addition to being in good position, all five Union corps, as well as its cavalry, was prepared to move at a moment's notice. It was evident that Lee was moving; what was not known was his objective.

At 7 AM on October 8, A. P. Hill's corps broke camp and began the Confederate movement. Using multiple crossings and passing around the Union right, the Confederates headed for Culpeper to get in the Federal rear. They did their best to stay low, out of the view of the Federal signal towers, and lit no fires along the way. This made for long marches in muddy conditions, and after a covert mission by the rebels to destroy one of the signal towers failed, the Federals had a fairly good idea of what Lee was trying to do. Meade conducted some exploration of the Confederate presence along the Rapidan, then withdrew his army north of the Rappahannock River on October 11, placing the Union right near White Sulphur Springs and the left just east of Kelly's Ford.

There was some neglect on the part of the Union army during the withdrawal. The previous day, the Union I and VI Corps, along with John Buford's cavalry division, explored south of the Rapidan River, looking for the Confederates. Later that day, all of the infantry corps received their orders to begin heading north, as did the other two divisions of Federal cavalry. Buford, however, did not get his orders until 7 AM on October 11 and found himself isolated south of the Rapidan. Forced to fight their way back across Morton's Ford, Buford's troopers fought off Fitz Lee's cavalry all the way north to the Rappahannock River. A heavy clash occurred in the town of Stevensburg, south of the river, but Buford kept moving. Eventually, the Federals would find the last of the Union V Corps, crossing at Rappahannock Station to join the rest of the infantry.

Buford knew this ground well, as did most of the horsemen on the field, both Union and Confederate. He also knew that the key to the battlefield ahead was a commanding rise known as Fleetwood Hill. He directed his cavalry to get to the top of the hill as quickly as possible and take up a defensive position. He would make his stand there, where only months before the Gettysburg campaign had opened with the massive cavalry battle of Brandy Station.

In the fields around this area you will find several interpretive signs telling of the battle of Brandy Station that occurred on June 9, 1863, as well as the Graffiti House, home of the Brandy Station Foundation. This was the largest cavalry battle ever to occur on the continent, and although the Confederates won the battle, it marked a clear turning point in the fortune of Union cavalry. The climax of that battle happened atop Fleetwood Hill, just as this one would. Unfortunately, though, most of the area of the October 11, 1863, battle is not preserved, although it is untouched enough to be easily interpreted.

Buford and Lee were not the only cavalry around Brandy Station. Also present was Judson Kilpatrick's Federal cavalry division, protecting the infantry as it made its way across the river. Kilpatrick's men had also been chased to this location, but their pursuers were the other half of the Confederate cavalry: Wade Hampton's division, under the personal command of J. E. B. Stuart while Hampton recovered from a wound received at Gettysburg.

Stuart emerged from the town of Culpeper, just to the west of Brandy Station, to find Kilpatrick in a defensive formation with artillery, prepared to receive an attack. Stuart approached the Federal position with caution, knowing that his 1,500 cavaliers were outnumbered by Kilpatrick's 4,000. For a while, the two units simply watched, waiting to see if the other would flinch. Suddenly, the rumblings of battle, Lee and Buford's clash in Stevensburg, reached the ears of both Stuart and Kilpatrick. They, too, had been at Brandy Station, and both of them, almost by instinct, ordered their commands to race for the heights at Fleetwood Hill.

From your position here in the parking lot of the Virginia State Police station, look to the south across Brandy Road (from which you turned into the property) and you will see a railroad, still in the position occupied by the original Orange & Alexandria. Kilpatrick's two cavalry brigades, commanded by George Armstrong Custer and Henry Davies, were moving through where you now stand north of the railroad. If you turn around so that you are now facing the police station, you can now see where Stuart's Confederates were taking their path, parallel to the Federals but about 0.5 mile to the north.

As Stuart and Kilpatrick moved toward the hill, they did clash along the way. Kilpatrick's route to Fleetwood Hill was shorter, and Stuart knew this, so he attempted to hit the Federals several times to slow them down, including in this area here, right between the paths of the two divisions. Stuart's attacks did slow Kilpatrick down, but unfortunately for the Confederates, his actions had other consequences that would not help their chances for victory that day.

❯ *Leave the State Police parking lot and turn left onto Brandy Road (SR 762). Drive 1.9 miles to Alanthus Road (VA 663) and turn left. Drive 1.2 miles to Fleetwood Heights Road (SR 685), then turn left and drive another 0.5 mile. Pull into the grassy area next to the interpretive signs.*

Although the crest of Fleetwood Hill is private property, be thankful that you can enjoy a vast amount of the battlefield here. The Civil War Trust has protected, and continues to grab, as much of the battlefield as possible. The land was slated only recently for an immense shopping and entertainment center, but through the actions of the trust, the Brandy Station Foundation, and other preservation groups, most of the land will remain untouched.

Looking to the east of your position here at the pull-off (toward the large hill with the house on top of it), you can see why every horseman in the area was racing for this spot. In an area full of rolling ground, Fleetwood Hill stands alone as the obvious high point for several miles. Immediately in front of you is the western slope of the hill; most of the action of October 11, 1863, would happen to your right, on the southern slope.

While Stuart and Kilpatrick had been triggered by the sounds of combat from Stevensburg, Buford and Fitz Lee had not had the same benefit. Although they were not far away, neither Buford nor Lee knew that the other two cavalry divisions were present because they had simply not made much noise. Thus, as Stuart slowed Kilpatrick's advance to Fleetwood Hill, he inadvertently pushed him directly into the path of Lee's Confederates just as they crossed the tracks of the Orange & Alexandria.

Lee was surprised by this sudden appearance of the enemy in his front and acted accordingly, hitting Kilpatrick's right flank. However, the presence of J. E. B. Stuart was just as surprising, so much so that Lee actually directed artillery fire at the other Confederate cavalry, thinking they must have been Union horsemen. Confusion reigned in all three divisions—Stuart and Lee's Confederates, as well as Kilpatrick's Federals—and the chaos was further heightened when artillery fire from the Union infantry's V Corps began to fall on the south slope of Fleetwood Hill.

The most important outcome of Stuart's pushing Kilpatrick into Lee's Confederates was the fact that the fourth cavalry division on the field, John Buford's Federals, had now been given time to occupy the crest of Fleetwood Hill. By the time Stuart and Lee had begun to coordinate their attacks, Custer and Davies had charged through the Confederates to take their position alongside Buford. The Federals now held with their infantry Fleetwood Hill, as well as the crossings at Rappahannock Station and nearby Beverly's Ford. Although Stuart's cavalry would hang around until dark trying to find a way to attack the Union position, the Federal cavalry was across the Rappahannock River by 8 PM, ending the action at Brandy Station.

In terms of casualties, the losses of both sides were about equal and fairly light. Even though the Confederates held the field, the Union felt good about its actions at Brandy Station. The entire Federal infantry had safely made it to the north bank of the Rappahannock, and Buford's escape from below the Rapidan to rejoin the Union lines had been magnificent. Although the campaign was not yet over, the Union army had once again avoided having the Confederates dictate the time and place of battle.

AUBURN

❯ *Turn right onto Fleetwood Road and drive to Beverly Ford Road (SR 676). Turn right on Beverly Ford Road and drive 0.2 mile to US 15/US 29 (James Madison Highway). Turn left onto US 15/US 29 and drive 15.1 miles to the exit for Meetze Road (CR 643). Drive 0.9 mile, then turn left on Old Auburn Road (CR 670). Follow Old Auburn Road for 4.3 miles; at this point, Old Auburn Road will split to your left to cross a small stream (Cedar Run), while the road that continues on to your front changes to CR 602. Pull off safely to the gravel area on the left side of the road near the historic marker.*

George Meade was now perplexed. Every indication was that the Confederate army had been trying to get around his right—that is, until Buford arrived with Fitzhugh Lee's cavalry on his tail. Meade had been under the impression that Lee's object was Culpeper, but the presence of Confederate cavalry south of the Rapidan River contradicted this. Meade was sure that Lee was somewhere between Culpeper and Brandy Station, and he adjusted his army accordingly, facing it slightly to the west but dangerously splitting his men across the Rappahannock River. He would send Buford's cavalry division toward Culpeper to scout out the Confederate position the next morning, and then wait for them to come to him for battle.

As for Lee, who was still in Culpeper the night of October 11, his idea of flanking the Federal right had not worked. Meade had brought his army north much more quickly than he had expected (although the loss of Confederate surprise early in the campaign didn't help). At this point, Lee had several options open to him. He could simply withdraw to his fortified positions south of the Rapidan; or he could also stop where he was, near Culpeper, and finally put his army into winter camp. Although he was still anxious to recapture the strategic initiative, neither of these options appealed to him. The Union army was still in a spot where the Confederates might still have a shot of outflanking its position if they moved very quickly. This is the option Lee chose: He would once again try to turn the Federal flank, this time via the town of Warrenton.

The next morning, October 12, the two Confederate corps headed toward Warrenton on separate paths 5 to 6 miles apart—Hill's corps crossing the Rappahannock at Waterloo Bridge and Ewell's crossing at White Sulphur Springs. The Confederate cavalry stayed to its front and right to screen its movements from the Federals, but that didn't prevent the troops from running into a brigade of Federal cavalry near Jeffersonton at around 10 AM. After the infantry was brought in the Federals were driven all the way to White Sulphur Springs, where it made another stand. The Confederate infantry again pushed them back and went into camp near the Rappahannock River by the end of the day.

After John Buford's cavalry expedition made it all the way to Culpeper with little Confederate resistance, Meade began to worry. Barely more than a year before, Lee had attempted virtually the same set of maneuvers over the same ground, and that campaign had ended in the second battle of Manassas—a Federal disaster. He did not want to be caught in the same position that general John Pope found himself in the previous August. When word of the Jeffersonton skirmishing finally reached his headquarters at around 9 PM, Meade realized that his right had been turned yet again. Within a short time, orders were sent to the Union corps commanders to get their armies up and moving. There would be no sleep tonight; the movements to block the Confederate advance had now turned into an escape.

During the early morning hours and late into the day on October 13, the Union troops wound their way north in two columns to maximize speed, trying to stay out of one another's way as they withdrew. Still, units became tied up at river crossings and other bottlenecks, and the Federals had to change the course of their march several times. Even Meade, who had intended to set his headquarters at Warrenton, eventually decided to move the army to the heavily fortified town of Centreville, where the Confederates would be very unlikely to attack.

Now that the army had switched directions, right became left and vice versa. The Union right column, consisting of three infantry corps and John Buford's cavalry division, was to the east, roughly following the path of the Orange & Alexandria Railroad. The I Corps, commanded by John Newton, reached Warrenton Junction (not to be confused with Warrenton) by 10 AM, then headed toward Bristoe Station, finally going into camp there at 3 PM. George Sykes's V Corps camped near Catlett's Station, not far south of Bristoe Station, around 5 PM. John Sedgwick's VI Corps followed the I Corps, finishing their march near Kettle Run, a small stream between Catlett's Station and Bristoe Station. It had been a hard march, but they were very close to reaching their goal of Centreville.

The Union's left column, the II and III Corps under the protection of both David Gregg's and H. Judson Kilpatrick's cavalry divisions, did not fare quite so well. Daniel French's III Corps moved slowly and ran into several delays, meaning that Gouverneur Warren's II Corps, following French, was delayed as well. The III Corps reached Three Mile Station around 11 AM, then made its way toward the crossing of Cedar Run at Auburn.

Confederate infantry, almost inexplicably, did not move much on October 13, and it would cost them greatly later in the campaign. Both Hill and Ewell's corps advanced only as far as Warrenton, then camped there in the early afternoon, stopping to rest and cook rations. Lee knew that the Federals had moved, but he did not know where.

The perfect tool for gathering this sort of information was cavalry, and few were better than what Lee had in J. E. B. Stuart. At 10 AM, Stuart sent Lunsford Lomax's brigade of cavalry along Cedar Run toward Auburn, while he personally led two other brigades toward Catlett's Station. Two more brigades, part of Fitz Lee's division, later followed Lomax toward Auburn.

Stuart found the enemy almost everywhere he went, and it was not lost on him that they all seemed to be in a hurry. What's more, they were also strung out along separate roads. He knew that if Lee were able to hit the Federals while they were in these positions, he would be able to inflict significant damage. After nearing Catlett's Station around 3 PM, Stuart turned west back toward Warrenton, heading along the north bank of Cedar Run toward Auburn and sending messengers to Lee with his findings.

Lomax's cavalry was already at Auburn, but it wasn't moving anywhere, at least not for the moment. It was now near 4:30 PM, and the Confederates were on a hill just south of the ford of Cedar Run at Auburn. From atop this hill, they could easily see the head of the Union left column heading straight toward them, David Birney's division of the III Corps. Lomax's cavalry dismounted in the woods south of the ford, placed artillery atop the hill, and waited.

French's corps, inexplicably, had no reconnaissance force in front of it. As his men headed north toward the ford at 5 PM, they were suddenly greeted with a heavy volley from the Confederate cavalry. Birney responded quickly, forming his division in a line across the road and moving through the woods, eventually pushing the Confederates out and over Cedar Run, where the rest of Fitz Lee's cavalry had recently arrived. Lomax had had plenty of time to withdraw his artillery safely, though, and before long the first battle of Auburn was over, with the Confederates heading west and camping on the Warrenton Road.

The roads forming the I-shaped intersection you are now parked at are the same roads that were present at the time of the battle. Country Road 670 (Old Auburn Road) and County Road 602 cross paths here, and the point where they cross Cedar Run is the location of the ford. As you face south (away from Cedar Run), Lomax's Confederates were in the woods around you, and you won't miss the obvious hilltop to your front. The road that splits off to your left comes from the south; this is Rogues Road (CR 602), which the Union III Corps used to approach the crossing. Birney's Federals eventually pushed their way toward your position here, and after the threat had gone, the entire III Corps began crossing Cedar Run at the ford.

〉 *You are about to begin a 2.5-mile circle around the Second Auburn battlefield. Cross the bridge over Cedar Run, then turn left onto Old Auburn Road (CR 670). Drive 0.7 mile, bearing left at the intersection with Old Dumfries Road, then pull over to the right near the intersection with Marshall Gardens Court to your left.*

After Fitz Lee withdrew from the fight at Auburn and went into camp, he was under the impression that the Confederates were safe. He had received the dispatch from Stuart's cavalry asking for infantry to come up and passed it on, and it was obvious that the Confederate army, resting in Warrenton, had nothing to fear from the Union infantry, quickly moving north toward Centreville. So after doing its duty and keeping the army safe, Lee's cavalry division rested along the Warrenton Turnpike, content with the day's work.

There was one Confederate unit, however, that was still in some danger—a lot of danger, actually. J. E. B. Stuart, heading back toward Warrenton, had reached Auburn around 6 PM to find the Union III Corps in his path as they crossed Cedar Run. Further, the II Corps was still in line behind the II Corps. In short, Stuart found his cavalry stuck between the left and right columns of the Federal army, with no way around them to reach the safety of Warrenton.

Stuart moved his men as quickly and quietly as possible into a small valley just east of the crossing and running north to south. Here they waited for the Federals to finish crossing, but it would not be that night. French's III Corps did not finish crossing until 1 AM, and Gouverneur Warren's II Corps, held up by French's slow advance, camped south of Cedar Run, stretched along the road to Three Mile Station. Aided by the noise of a light rain, overcast conditions, fog, and no moon, Stuart's men hid in the valley overnight, remaining as silent as possible and lighting no fires. Artillery was hidden but readied to be rolled out and faced to the west at a moment's notice. The Confederates remained in line of battle, just in case the Federals did detect their presence. Because even with all of the factors helping conceal them, two full brigades—close to 2,000 men, along with their horses and artillery—were hidden only 400 yards from the Union troops at Cedar Run. One mistake might render Stuart's cavalry finished.

There is some debate as to the exact location of Stuart's hiding spot of October 13 and 14, but where you are now standing may be nearest the most likely place. To your left is a private lane called Marshall Gardens Court, located in a small valley and fitting most of the descriptions left behind by Stuart and others at the battle. Some historians believe the correct site is farther east, near modern-day Pembridge Lane, but Adrian Tighe, in his book on the Bristoe campaign, presents a convincing argument that Marshall Gardens is closer to the true location.

> *Continue forward 0.4 mile to Dumfries Road (CR 605) and turn left. Drive 0.6 mile to Rogues Road (CR 602) and turn left again and follow the road 0.9 mile back to the crossing at Cedar Run. As you turn left onto Rogues Road, notice the significant rise to your left, Coffee Hill. Note also that looking to your right, toward Culpeper, will give you a commanding view that stretches for miles.*

With his right column on time but his left far behind schedule, Meade was forced to adjust the line of march of both the II and III Corps for the next day, October 14. French's III Corps, now in camp around Greenwich, would continue on its path northeast toward Centreville, while Warren's II Corps would now head east toward Catlett's Station, getting itself out from behind the slow-moving unit in front of them. Meade's orders were designed to get both corps away from the Confederate army, which he now knew was in Warrenton, as quickly as possible.

When Gouverneur Warren received his orders at 2 AM, he was relieved. He had felt isolated in his position at the rear of the army and wanted to get out of that position as soon as he could. Less than two hours later, his lead division, John Caldwell's, crossed Cedar Run and took up a position on a large hill immediately in front of them. They set themselves facing west toward Warrenton and the Confederate army, mounting three batteries of artillery and completing their dispositions by 6 AM. Soon after, Warren's other two divisions crossed Cedar Run and went east toward Catlett's Station. The Federals on the hill felt relatively safe, as their position provided commanding views to the north and south as well as the west. Little thought was given to the possibility of any Confederates looming to the east. Although reports that the Confederate infantry was moving were filtering in, the Union soldiers were relaxed and began to make their breakfast and coffee.

Just to the east, J. E. B. Stuart's cavalry began to hear picket fire from the direction of Warrenton. Stuart, without any other information, could only surmise that the Confederate infantry would be attacking the Federals there at any moment. The sun was also coming up, and he knew that his hiding place would soon be detected. It was time to move.

At 6:30 AM, Stuart ordered his artillery—seven guns—rolled up the west side of the small ravine the men had been hiding in, and they began firing on the unsuspecting Union soldiers. Caldwell's Federals immediately dropped what they were doing—giving the small rise its new name of Coffee Hill—and ran to the other side of the slope for protection. It was not long before they had their own artillery turned around to face east and began shelling the Confederates. Alexander Hays's division, taking the road just south of Stuart's position on its way to Catlett's Station, stopped and turned north to face the enemy, although the Confederates couldn't see Hays's men. Acting quickly, Stuart ordered one regiment to hold off Hays while the rest of his division mounted up and raced across Cedar Run and out of danger. Although they had to go the long way around Warren's corps, by 7:30 AM, Stuart's cavalry was out of danger. Although the second battle of Auburn, also known as the battle of Coffee Hill, was a relatively small action, it was yet another dramatic moment for J. E. B. Stuart's horsemen.

You will not be able to get to the top of Coffee Hill (at least not at the moment), but you will not need to reach the summit to realize its importance. The steep drive around the western face of the mountain will demonstrate why holding this prominence was so critical, and why the Federals chose this as a position for defending their troops as they withdrew toward Centreville. You will find that there are several roads to the top, but they are all privately owned, so please do not trespass. There has been talk of creating a small park to commemorate the battles of Auburn, but planning is still very much in the early stages, and it will be some time before any interpretation of the battlefields appears.

BRISTOE STATION BATTLEFIELD HERITAGE PARK

> *Keep following the circle you just made, continuing on Old Auburn Road (CR 670) for 1 mile until reaching Dumfries Road. This time, turn right on Dumfries Road (CR 605) and drive 4.7 miles to Nokesville Road (VA 28). Turn left onto VA 28 and drive 4.3 miles to Bristow Village Boulevard. Turn right and drive 0.1 mile and turn left onto Bristow Station Drive, then drive 0.4 mile to Iron Brigade Unit Avenue. To your left will be the parking area for Bristoe Station Battlefield Heritage Park.*

All five Union infantry corps would get an early start to their marches. Newton's I Corps, already close to Centreville, would be there by noon, and Sedgwick's VI Corps was only a few hours behind. George Sykes's V Corps left Catlett's Station at 4 AM, but were held up when they had to wait for the French's III Corps to cross Broad Run in front of them. Warren's II Corps still brought up the rear, reaching Catlett's Station around 11 AM, and then turning northeast to follow the tracks of the Orange & Alexandria Railroad toward Bristoe Station.

George Meade did not want his five corps spread too far apart. Indeed, the concept of dividing an army into corps, a remnant of Napoleonic warfare, was that each corps was large enough to function on its own, yet mobile enough to support another if necessary. For that reason, as Sykes waited for French to take his corps across Broad Run, he received orders from Meade to wait until Warren's II Corps was within sight before beginning his own crossing. So the V Corps waited impatiently on the lower bank of Broad Run while the II Corps made its way up the Railroad.

In contrast to the previous day, the Confederate infantry was moving quickly. October 13 had seen the Confederates resting while Meade pushed his army northward as quickly as possible. October 14 would now be the Confederates turn to race, hoping to catch the Federals before they reached the safety of Centreville or even perhaps the defensive ring around Washington, D.C. Ewell's three divisions began their march at 4 AM, while Hill's were on the move by 5 AM. There was some confusion on the march. Robert Rodes's division was held up at Auburn by Caldwell's Federals, who remained

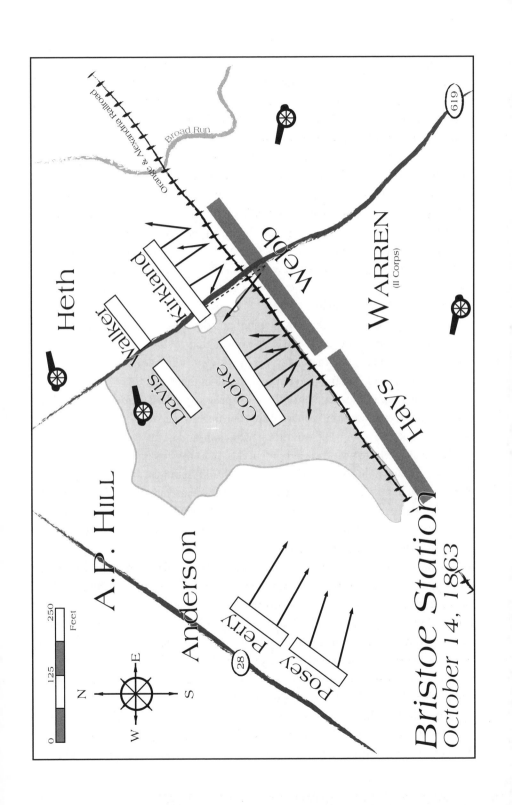

Bristoe Station
October 14, 1863

on Coffee Hill until almost 10 AM, while Warren's remaining two Union divisions headed for Catlett's Station. Richard Anderson's division went northeast to Greenwich based on a false report of Union infantry there, then doubled back, only to find itself in the way of part of Ewell's corps that was also ordered to Greenwich. When things were finally sorted out, Hill's corps, with Henry Heth's division in the lead, would head for Bristoe Station, where the Orange & Alexandria crossed Broad Run. Ewell's corps would follow for a short time and then move east in a parallel fashion to where the railroad crossed Kettle Run just south of Bristoe Station.

It was not until noon that the Union III Corps finished its crossing of Broad Run at Milford, on the north bank near Bristoe Station. As soon as the last unit of French's corps was across, Sykes's V Corps began its own crossing. The men could wait for Warren's II Corps from the other side of Broad Run. The entire V Corps was across by 1 PM. Shortly after, Sykes received word from an aide that Warren was within sight, moving up the railroad. That was good enough for George Sykes, and his men began their march toward Centreville.

To this day, it is not exactly known who that aide saw—it may have been some of David Gregg's Union cavalry—but it is known that he did not see the II Corps. Warren's men, still behind the rest of the army, were still at least 3 to 4 miles away, with not only Broad Run but also Kettle Run still in their path.

Also not seen by any member of the V Corps were the lead elements of A. P. Hill's corps, Henry Heth's division, who were approaching a large, clear hill only 1 mile west of the Broad Run crossing. Hill was riding with Heth, and he saw a golden opportunity before him. The entire V Corps was bottlenecked in a crossing, one of the most vulnerable spots for any military unit to be in. Both Hill and Heth were anxious to score a hit, possibly bagging a large part of the Army of the Potomac. Heth directed his artillery to take a position atop the high ground and to the left, while his infantry emerged from the surrounding woods and formed a line across the road to Bristoe Station.

Bristoe Station Battlefield Heritage Park, part of the Prince William County parks system, has several trails that will take you through the rich history of this critical ground. In addition to the 1.3-mile trail that leads you through the battle of October 14, 1862, a separate trail will guide you through the August 27, 1862, fight at Kettle Run on the same piece of land. Also present are several Confederate cemeteries remaining from various Confederate encampments here before both battles. Brochures for the walking tours are available online and at the park, although you may want to print out your own just to be on the safe side. Also available online is a podcast that will guide you through the various stops on the tour.

When the first shots from the Confederate artillery hit the tail end of the V Corps, it was a complete surprise. Although some of the Union artillery set up and returned fire, beginning a protracted artillery duel, most of the infantry simply scrambled to get out of the way of the incoming shells. The end result was that the Federals on the other side of Broad Run were soon out of sight. By the time Heth's infantry was moving north along the railroad toward Milford, the last elements of the union V Corps were already leaving.

Walking the trail at Bristoe Station Battlefield Park will soon bring you to the top of the hill from which the Confederates began their movement and their bombardment. When you reach the house on the hill (soon to be a visitor center) look to your left toward the woods beyond the road. This is the general direction in which the Confederates were headed—toward the V Corps, making their crossing at Broad Run. The ground was not wooded at the time, and they would have had a clear view for their artillery to direct their fire effectively.

When Heth's division formed its line, John Cooke's brigade formed to the right of the road and William Kirkland's to the left, with Henry Walker's brigade behind Kirkland as support. As the men moved toward the Federals they could see at Milford, their right flank and rear were exposed to Bristoe Station, as they were moving alongside the Orange & Alexandria Railroad. The line was long, approximately 1,300 yards, making it difficult to maneuver in any direction but the way they were going. Shortly after they started moving, however, word came that Federal infantry was appearing on their exposed right. Heth halted the advance, refused his right flank (i.e., turned the right end of his line 90 degrees), and sent the 46th North Carolina out as skirmishers to investigate what was happening.

What was happening was the sudden and unexpected emergence of Gouverneur Warren's II Corps. Hill, in his eagerness to attack the seemingly vulnerable Federal column, had not done a reconnaissance of the area, and had no idea that other Union troops were in the area, let alone an entire corps of almost 11,000 soldiers. When the first Confederate artillery was heard shortly after 1 PM, Warren, who had been riding in the rear, rushed to the head of the column. Heath's brigade of Alexander Webb's division was the lead Federal unit, and the only one that had made its way across Kettle Run at the time. Warren had been worried about an attack, and had been marching in line of battle, with the 1st Minnesota infantry regiment acting as skirmishers on his left. He now sent the entire column ahead double-quick, still 2 to 3 miles from Bristoe Station.

The first contact happened at 1:30 PM in the thick woods to Warren's left, just to the west of the railroad embankment, when the 1st Minnesota skirmish line ran into the Confederate skirmishers of the 46th North Carolina. Soon the 59th New York was sent to aid the Minnesotans, and the Confederate skirmishers were pushed back to their main line. Webb, meanwhile, ordered Heath's and James Mallon's brigades to rush to Bristoe Station and take up a position behind the railroad embankment there, facing northwest toward the Confederate line.

As you learn about the Civil War, you will come across several battles in which a railroad embankment made a significant difference in the outcome of a battle. These embankments made a perfect protective breastwork for a defensive position. In some cases, they were also tall enough to virtually conceal an entire unit of an army. Here at Bristoe Station, the embankment of the Orange & Alexandria helped conceal the movement of the entire Union II Corps from A. P. Hill's view.

In the 10-minute span during which Henry Heth's Confederates were halted, Cooke protested to Heth that his right was exposed to the railroad. Heth responded that Davis's brigade, who had been supporting the artillery, would be moved to support Cooke's right, and that Anderson's division, directly behind Heth's, would also soon be forming there. With the matter put to rest, Heth soon resumed the march, but was now trying to wheel his entire massive line to the right to face the railroad embankment. As you follow the trail down the hill toward the railroad, you are following the general path of the Confederates as they wheeled toward the Union line.

Heth's correction would not happen soon enough for the Confederates. Heath's and Mallon's Union brigades began firing as soon as they reached the embankment. Soon, two batteries of artillery, ten cannon, were set on the high ground behind the embankment to add to the Federal firepower. The fire coming from the embankment was constant; both brigades had formed a double line, with the line in the front firing and the line in the rear reloading. Almost immediately behind Webb's two brigades came two more from Hays's division. The amount of lead coming from the Federal line was massive, and the embankment provided near-perfect protection. In fact, most of the Union casualties that would come at the battle of Bristoe Station would be in the short periods while soldiers were rushing toward the cover of the embankment.

Just as Owen's brigade had taken its place along the Union line, the Confederate infantry was just reaching the crest of the hill where the first Confederate artillery had been placed. On the other side of the crest was 600 yards of open ground, sloping downward toward the railroad embankment. One Confederate battery had been placed in front of the crest, against the protests of its commander, only 400 yards from the Union line. While Anderson's division attempted to hurry through the woods to take up the right side of the line, Cooke's and Kirkland's brigades rushed down the hill to a small rise 50 to 100 yards in front of the embankment. Both units paid a very heavy price. Both Cooke and Kirkland were soon wounded, and the rest of the soldiers were being quickly cut down. The new commander of Cooke's brigade, Col. Edward Hall of the 46th North Carolina, knew that they could not stay in their present position, so he ordered a charge along the line. Although in some places the Confederates were briefly able to make a dent—Mallon was mortally wounded in the open space where the road crossed the embankment—the attacks, without the guidance of Cooke

The Confederate view of the battlefield at Bristoe Station, near the location of McIntosh's Battery.

and Kirkland, came piecemeal, and by 3 PM both brigades were heading toward the rear, having taken heavy casualties.

When you get to the bottom of the hill, you will be very close to the railroad embankment. The point at which the trail turns right—close to both the road and the railroad—was some of the most heavily contested ground of the battle. As you follow the trail along the railroad, you are walking through the ground the Confederates were desperately trying to break through, while the Union soldiers were all behind the safety of the embankment to your left.

As you make the loop in the trail and come back to the crest of the hill, you will reach the spot where the Confederate artillery—David McIntosh's battery of seven guns—had been placed to support the faltering infantry assault. McIntosh's protests that his guns had been placed too far forward fell on deaf ears, and as the retreating Confederates ran past them, several Federal units saw an opportunity. Quickly, five of the seven guns were captured and brought back behind the Union line.

❯ *From the parking lot, turn right onto Iron Brigade Unit Avenue and drive 0.1 mile to Bristow Road (VA 619). Turn right and drive 0.5 mile to the railroad crossing. After you cross the tracks, safely make a U-turn and return to the tracks, pulling over on the right just before the crossing.*

The embankment of the former Orange & Alexandria Railroad, still in use, is at the center of the picture.

This railroad crossing, where the Bristoe Station Road intersects with the railroad, was the point of the only significant Confederate breakthrough. As you look at the area, take caution and be aware of any and all movement, rail or auto, as you explore the crossing.

You do not have to leave the crossing to view the Union position. Looking up and down the tracks here will show you virtually the entire Federal line. It will also show the protection offered by the embankment that allowed the Union army to pour fire into the advancing rebels. Also evident here is the reason why the Confederates broke the line at this point. Here at the crossing, the embankment naturally disappears to allow the road to pass through. Without the protection of the embankment, the Federals could not as easily defend this part of the line. Still, with flanking fire coming from both sides, the Confederates were not able to hold their breakthrough for very long.

Although Anderson's and Jubal Early's divisions soon arrived, by 4 PM the entire Union II Corps was on the field and under the shelter of the embankment. Also present by 4 PM was Robert E. Lee, and the rest of the Confederate army was not far behind him. Although Warren's preparedness had paid off with a very successful defense, he knew that he was still in some trouble. A courier was sent to George Sykes, telling him what had happened and that he would need support from the V Corps to be able to leave his position south of Broad Run.

By 5 PM, the firing had died down and darkness was coming quickly, but more

Confederates were arriving. Sykes received his message around this time, and George Meade, already in Centreville, only now received first word of the battle. Furious that Sykes had not waited for Warren, he ordered the V Corps as well as French's III Corps back to Broad Run to aid Warren's escape. It was not until 8:30 PM, under cover of darkness and in complete silence, that the II Corps began to withdraw across Broad Run. It would be 4 AM before Warren's men would finally stop marching near Blackburn's Ford, just north of Manassas.

Warren had only barely escaped. To be sure, he had conducted the battle flawlessly. But the fact that the II Corps had not been destroyed also had a lot to do with Confederate failure—not only here at Bristoe, but for the entire campaign. The most glaring, of course, was Hill's failure to scout the area before attacking. Even a simple reconnaissance would have detected the presence of the Federals. Also contributing was the 10-minute halt ordered by Henry Heth after Union activity was discovered on the Confederate right. These 10 crucial minutes were just enough for the first two Union brigades to get into place behind the railroad embankment. Finally, the virtual lack of movement of the Confederate infantry on October 13 cannot be ignored. Had Lee's men maintained their pursuit of the Union army, which Meade had kept moving relentlessly, the Confederates would have had a much better chance to isolate at least part of the Federal forces and bring them to battle on their own terms. In the end, the fight at Bristoe had cost the Confederates 1,380 soldiers, men that they could not spare this late in the war. Although the Union had suffered 540 casualties of their own, the Federals' victory was not only in number but also in their escape.

The next day, October 15, A. P. Hill's skirmishers went forward at daylight to find that the Union Army of the Potomac had disappeared. Later in the day, as Hill, Ewell, and Lee toured the field, Hill tried to explain his actions, fully shouldering responsibility for attacking too quickly and not conducting a proper reconnaissance. After enduring this in silence for some time, the usually reserved Lee delivered one of his harshest reprimands of the entire war. Although accounts vary as to the exact wording and tone of Lee's rebuke, it was simple and devastating: "Bury these poor men, and let us say no more about it."

BUCKLAND MILLS

⟩ *Drive forward on Bristow Road for 0.8 mile to Nokesville Road (VA 28). Turn left, then immediately turn right onto Vint Hill Road (VA 215). Drive 9.2 miles to Lee Highway (US 15/US 29) and then turn right. Drive 0.4 mile to the church parking lot on the right and pull in next to the Civil War Trails marker.*

By the morning of October 15, the Army of the Potomac was securely behind Bull Run, stretching in an arc that would detect virtually any Confederate approach.

George Meade, from his headquarters in Centreville, was not yet feeling a sense of relief. When he left the Confederate army at Bristoe Station the day before, he knew where almost all of Lee's army was. Now, though, Lee could have taken his infantry anywhere. Meade's defenses at Centreville were sound enough, but he would feel much better knowing the location of the Confederates and what their intentions were. Accordingly, he sent his cavalry out several times over the next few days to try and locate the rebels.

He needn't have worried at all. After the mess at Bristoe Station, Robert E. Lee knew that his campaign was over. He could not keep his army here any longer; his supply line was already stretched thin, and his ill-fed and ill-clothed men had already endured a hard campaign. Still, he would make the most of what he had. Over the next three days, while J. E. B. Stuart's cavalry demonstrated along the Union line to hold the Federals in place, Lee kept the Confederate infantry busy tearing up the Orange & Alexandria Railroad. With the railroad tracks mostly to the left of the Federals, Stuart kept busy mostly on their right, distracting them from the Confederates' work. By the time the Confederates were finished, the entire railroad from Manassas Junction all the way to the Rappahannock River, the most readily available supply line the Union army would have for any movement south, had been destroyed.

Under constant pressure from Washington to attack the Confederates, Meade finally ordered his men to advance on October 18, but the movement was postponed because of bad weather. The same weather did not stop the Confederates. Beginning at 1 AM, they began to move south toward the Rappahannock, and by day's end all Confederate infantry was either across or near the river. Stuart's cavalry was left behind to stall any Federal advance. Receiving intelligence that Judson Kilpatrick's cavalry division would advance from the town of Groveton in the morning, Stuart positioned his command at Broad Run, near the town of Buckland Mills, to intercept them.

Stuart's intelligence was correct. The next morning, Kilpatrick's division mounted up at Groveton and then headed west down the Warrenton Turnpike. At 8 AM, first contact was made near the town of Haymarket, and the Federals pushed the Confederates back, eventually reaching the strong defensive position at Broad Run. Kilpatrick ordered the 7th Michigan cavalry, part of George Armstrong Custer's brigade, to head upstream and find a ford that could bring them to the rear of the Confederate position.

During the two hours that Stuart and Kilpatrick faced off at Broad Run, Stuart received an urgent dispatch from Fitz Lee, who had his own cavalry division near Bristoe Station. Lee proposed a bold plan with long odds that, if successful, might trap Kilpatrick's entire division of cavalry. It was exactly the kind of plan that Stuart loved, and he enthusiastically agreed to it.

Stuart was to slowly pull back from his position at Broad Run, letting the Union cavalry pursue him down the Warrenton Turnpike all the way past the town of New

Baltimore. This would string Kilpatrick's division thinly along the turnpike. At the same time, Lee would bring his own division from the south through Auburn, coming up behind and to the left of the Federals. If it worked, Kilpatrick's division would be sandwiched between the two Confederate divisions with no escape.

At the bridge over Broad Run, Kilpatrick took the high ground on the right of the turnpike to position his artillery, then ordered Custer to charge across the bridge with his entire brigade. The charge was successful, and Custer pushed Stuart's horsemen back for a mile, stopping there to rest his men and eat and, reportedly, refusing to go farther until his men had had their breakfast. Henry Davies's brigade took over the chase, pushing Stuart's three brigades west to New Baltimore. In no time, there were almost 3 miles between Custer's and Davies's brigades.

The bridge here is in the same place as the original, crossing Broad Run with the Warrenton Turnpike, also following its original path. If you turn your back to the road, you will be facing Lee's troopers as they advanced toward Custer's brigade.

Receiving reports that some cavalry had been sighted in the direction of Auburn, which Kilpatrick assumed were Federal reserve units coming to reinforce him. Still, to be on the safe side, he sent the 7th Michigan to scout toward Auburn just as Custer's men decided to resume their movement down the turnpike. After moving a little over a mile, the Michigan troopers ran into Lee's entire division and reported to Kilpatrick that they were most definitely not Federals.

Lee was disappointed that he had lost the element of surprise; he had expected Kilpatrick's entire division to be far down the turnpike by this time, and had not anticipated Custer's stopping for breakfast. Still, the woods and hills here effectively screened the size of his force. Custer turned his division to face south along the turnpike and began to move slowly through the woods.

❯ *Turn right out of the church parking lot, then make a U-turn at Buckland Mill Road. Drive 6 miles on Lee Highway to Colonial Road (CR 605). Turn right on Colonial Road, and then pull into the commuter parking lot on your left. Drive to the back of the lot.*

When Lee was ready, he fired his artillery at Custer's probing Federals. This was the signal for Stuart, who had taken a position atop a small rise called Chestnut Hill. Stuart immediately lined up all three of his brigades across the Warrenton Turnpike and charged the surprised Davies. Knowing that he was in trouble, Davies waited until the Confederates were 50 yards from his line, fired a final volley, and turned around to withdraw, quickly and in good order. When the second Confederate charge came, however, Davies entire brigade began racing down the turnpike back toward Groveton.

The hill adjacent to the parking area at the far end, stretching to the other side of the turnpike, is Chestnut Hill. From here you can see that it is not only an excellent defensive position, but is also large enough to conceal the true strength of Stuart's command before they sprang on the Union cavalrymen.

Almost as soon as Custer's brigade began to move, Lee opened up on him with his entire division. Not long after, Davies brigade was seen racing toward them down the turnpike, with Stuart's division right behind them. By the time Davies had passed them, Custer's line had collapsed, and all of Kilpatrick's cavalry was headed for the bridge at Broad Run. Unfortunately for them, Lee's Confederates got there first, and all remaining hope for an orderly retreat were lost. Union horsemen escaped through the woods, on foot, across streams, and in any other fashion they could to get back to the safety of the Federal line.

John Newton's I Corps of infantry had been ordered to Haymarket that day, getting there around 6 PM. Their arrival could not have been more timely, as elements of Custer's and Davies's brigades came streaming back in pieces. Newton advanced several infantry units to help the cavaliers reach safety, and although the Confederate cavalry chased the fleeing Federals for 3 miles, they came to a grinding halt when they confronted Newton's men. A few small charges were mounted, but Stuart withdrew his men around 10 PM and headed for Rappahannock Station on the orders of Robert E. Lee.

By the time the stragglers were rounded up, the Confederates had collected almost 250 Union soldiers, along with 28 wagons, including Custer's headquarters wagon. In his report on the affair, Stuart referred to the fight as the "Buckland Races," and the battle is more commonly known by that name today (at least in the South). Although both Kilpatrick and Custer filed reports that spun the battle into a virtual victory, they could not hide the embarrassment that the division had suffered. Kilpatrick's command would remain in Haymarket until October 31, recovering from the "races."

KELLY'S FORD

〉 *Turn right out of the parking lot and drive to US 15/US 29. Turn right onto US 29 and drive 14.8 miles, keeping left as the Lee Highway splits off after 0.9 mile. You will enter the town of Remington; turn left on CR 651, Freeman Ford Road, and follow CR 651 for 5.1 miles to Kelly's Ford Road (CR 620). Turn right and drive 0.3 mile, crossing over the Rappahannock River and pulling into the parking area after the bridge.*

Elsewhere on October 19, away from the Confederate infantry crossing the Rappahannock River and the Federal cavalry being routed toward Haymarket, the five infantry corps of the Union Army of the Potomac emerged from its line along Bull Run. The infantry quickly discovered two things: the Confederate Army of Northern Virginia was long gone, and the Orange & Alexandria Railroad had been rendered completely useless. Over the next few days, intelligence gathering would reveal the Confederate position below the Rappahannock, and George Meade's army slowly and gradually made its way south toward the river while beginning the massive project of rebuilding the railroad. By October 30, it was clear that the Confederates had taken up a very strong position on the river, and that they intended to stay there.

Robert E. Lee's soldiers were under the same impression. Although no orders had gone out, most of the soldiers and officers were convinced that they would go into winter camp here along the Rappahannock, just as they had the previous winter. The weather was growing cold and wet, discouraging active campaigning. The Confederates held Kelly's Ford, Beverly's Ford, and Freeman's Ford, and they were picketing as far north as Waterloo Bridge. Further, at Rappahannock Station, they had taken fortifications (previously built by them but then altered by the Federals) on the north bank of the river and strengthened them. With their weakest point being the right flank at Kelly's Ford, a strong position at Rappahannock Station would force the Federals to divide their army if they were going to try to cross the river in force.

The railroad bridge of the Orange & Alexandria had crossed the river at Rappahannock Station, but Union troops had destroyed it on their way north during the Bristoe campaign. But the railroad was still intact south of the river, and because it was the single point of supply for Lee's army, he made Rappahannock Station the center of his line. A. P. Hill's corps took up their position along the river to the left (west) of the ford, while Richard Ewell's corps formed the right.

Lee knew that if the Union army attacked Kelly's Ford, he could not hold it. The high ground at the ford was on the north bank, wooded and commanding the open fields on the south bank. So he formed a stronger fallback, relying heavily on the fortified position at Rappahannock Station.

North of the river, propelled by continuing pressure from General in Chief Henry Halleck in Washington and a desire to bring the Confederates to battle, George Meade searched for a plan. After proposing several plans to Halleck, all of which were rejected, Meade finally settled on an agreeable strategy on November 5. It would involve splitting his army into two parts, just as Lee had wished, plus an attempt to turn the Confederate right, just as Lee had predicted. However, Lee assumed that the weakness of Kelly's Ford meant that the Union troops would make that their primary crossing point. Further, he had great confidence in the fortifications at Rappahannock Station. Meade had other ideas.

On November 7, John Sedgwick, commanding the right wing of the army, would take the V and VI Corps from Warrenton to Rappahannock Station, a distance of 16 miles. William French would command the left wing, moving the I, II, and III Corps from Warrenton Junction 17 miles to Kelly's Ford. Speed would critical. Sedgwick would lead a direct assault on the position at Rappahannock Station. French, with the easier portion of the operation, would take Kelly's Ford as quickly as possible and, instead of moving southwest against the Confederates, would head west along the south bank of the Rappahannock River to aid Sedgwick in capturing Rappahannock Station. Reunited, the combined force would then confront the Confederate army at Brandy Station, finally bringing the large, decisive battle that Meade, Halleck, and Abraham Lincoln wanted.

French's wing of the army left promptly at 5 AM that day, and by noon was at Mount Holly Church, only 1 mile north of Kelly's Ford. Their movement to that point had gone undetected, having been screened by the high bluff on the north bank of the Rappahannock. The Confederates at Kelly's Ford—Robert Rodes's division of Ewell's corps—had seen Federal cavalry across the river regularly for weeks, and not expecting anything different today, had only one regiment, the 2nd North Carolina infantry, at the ford. Artillery had also been placed in a tree line to the west.

When Rodes was told at noon that Union infantry was suddenly seen alongside their cavalry, he rushed to Kelly's Ford and brought up as many men as he could, placing them in the woods to the west and calling for reinforcements. Their orders were simple: Stall the Union advance until the rest of the division, then other reinforcements, could be called up. Rodes, like the rest of the Confederates, expected most of the Federal army to cross here, and he wanted as many men in front of them as he could get.

French massed his artillery on the bluffs of the north bank of the river, concentrating their fire on the 2nd North Carolina, pinned down in two lines of rifle pits around the ford. He then selected a brigade from his own III Corps to lead the assault, along with the 20th Indiana infantry and the 1st and 2nd U.S. Sharpshooters. The sharpshooters moved down to the riverbank first, picking off as many of the Confederates as they could, then wading across the cold river as quickly as possible. Although the Federals were easy targets and took many casualties, they eventually got through the river and hit the Confederate left, working their way down the rifle pits. The rest of the infantry soon followed them, capturing many of the rebels. The Federals suffered a scant 42 casualties to the Confederates' 330.

By 3 PM, David Birney's entire division of the III Corps was across, and a pontoon bridge was laid to aid the rest of the infantry. Rodes, obeying Lee's orders not to attack, held his position firmly, expecting a Union assault at any moment. But it did not come. The entire III Corps was across the river by dark, and the Confederates, seeing the Union army massing, strengthened and reinforced their line with Edward "Allegheny" Johnson's division. A. P. Hill was also ordered to reinforce the position, while Early's division, in its strong works at Rappahannock Station, would be able to hold. Robert E. Lee had been expecting this, and he prepared to attack the Federals' position at Kelly's Ford with his entire army the next morning. It would be several hours before he realized that Kelly's Ford was not the primary Union target.

As you drive across the ford and turn your back to the river, you can see the broad expanse where the village of Kellysville used to be. The Confederates were lined up along the river to your left and right, but were quickly driven from this position to the safety of the other Confederate units in the woods in the distance. By nightfall, French's III Corps would fill the fields in front of you, while the Confederates began to line up their troops to your right center, preparing themselves for the advance they were certain would come.

RAPPAHANNOCK STATION

> *Reverse your trail and head back toward Remington. Turn right out of the parking lot and drive 0.3 mile to CR 651. Turn left on CR 651 and drive 4.7 miles to US 15/US 29. Turn left and drive 0.1 mile; on your left will be a Civil War Trails marker in a gravel parking lot.*

Robert E. Lee, an experienced engineer during his army career before the war, thought the defensive works at Rappahannock Station about as good as any he'd seen, and that they could be manned by only one or two brigades and still hold. Richard Ewell agreed. Jubal Early, part of whose division would be manning the works on November 7, did not share their opinion—he thought it, at best, a temporary position—but there was no debate that the position had its advantages.

A full mile of defensive works stretched around the bridgehead on the north bank of the river. Only 100 feet west of the tracks of the Orange & Alexandria Railroad was a massive, enclosed earthen redoubt, with an even larger one 400 feet farther to its left. This second redoubt had an open side, sloping 500 feet toward the Rappahannock River, while the riverbank behind the first redoubt had a steep drop behind it. The two redoubts, both elevated positions, were connected by a line of rifle pits, and additional lines extended to the east, west, and southwest of the forts. Although the rifle pits to the southwest angled to a degree that they could not see very far to the north, they afforded good protection to the rear of the redoubts, as well as a pontoon bridge that spanned the river. Although the far right of the line—adjacent to the railroad—was somewhat vulnerable, the position also had the advantage of the railroad embankment as cover. On the south bank, artillery positions were set up to further protect the works and the bridge. Perhaps best of all, the ground in front of the position was open for over a mile. Any Union force attacking the position would have a long way to travel without shelter before it reached these works.

When John Sedgwick arrived with the Union right wing at Rappahannock Station early in the afternoon and stared across the large open field toward the Confederate works, he, too, thought them very strong. But like Jubal Early, he also saw weaknesses in the position. He had been prepared to storm the works directly, but Sedgwick altered the plan. He placed the VI Corps, temporarily commanded by Horatio Wright

Site of the Confederate pontoon crossing at Rappahannock Station.

while Sedgwick commanded the wing, to the right (west) side of the railroad, and George Sykes's V Corps to the left.

From the Confederate works, Harry Hays's famed Louisiana Tigers had four of its five regiments manning the position, along with two cannon in each redoubt. When the Federals first appeared, they were confident they could hold the position. Jubal Early was notified that the enemy was approaching, and soon afterward learned that Kelly's Ford was under attack as well, and that reinforcements were being rushed there. At 2 PM, Hays finally saw what he was up against when the Federals emerged from the tree line across the field. Hays called for his last regiment, placing one in the rifle pits to his right, one in the redoubts, and the remaining three in the extensive rifle pits to his left. His brigade of 900 men was about to face two full corps of the Union army, 30,000 strong.

Your position here at the interpretive sign puts you near the Confederate front. Although there are remnants of the original earthworks, they are currently all either on private or inaccessible property. However, that will change within the coming years. An ambitious plan for an interpretive park is planned for part of the battlefield that will, hopefully, include trails, interpretive signs, and possibly even water access to the Rappahannock River. The park would not only interpret the action of November 7, but would also include the fighting that occurred in August 1862, which preceded the battle of Second Manassas.

If you face the sign, to your left (away from the road) and just behind the tree line is the railroad, still in the same location as it was during the battle. To your front, as you look down the road that splits to the left, are the Confederate redoubts, none of which are currently visible. The Union army would have been coming from behind you, with the V Corps to your left rear across the railroad tracks and the VI Corps to your right rear.

Sedgwick began his advance at 3 PM. The assault began with the V Corps swooping down on the rifle pits on the Confederate right, quickly driving the Confederates there into the redoubts and establishing a position along the river, right at the rebels' point of weakness along the railroad. From this position on the riverbank, Federal sharpshooters were able to prevent the artillery positions on the south bank from being placed, thus taking out a major portion of the Confederate defenses. Meanwhile, the VI Corps rushed toward the works and then stopped behind a low rise in front of the Confederate rifle pits, approximately 250 yards away. With their position established, the Federals brought in their artillery and began pounding away.

By this time, both Jubal Early and Robert E. Lee were on the scene. Convinced that the attack here was a feint to distract the Confederates from the Federal crossing at Kelly's Ford, Lee authorized Robert Hoke's brigade of North Carolinians to join Hays in the works, bringing the total Confederate strength to 2,000 men. They crossed the pontoon bridge at 4 PM and took their places alongside the Louisianans in the rifle pits on their left.

With sundown fast approaching and the situation at a stalemate, Sedgwick realized that he could only do so much damage with his artillery. His men would have to assault the works, and they would do it in the dark. David Russell's division of the VI Corps, already in an advanced position, would lead the attack, with the 6th Maine in front, supported by the 5th Wisconsin. The infantrymen fixed bayonets for what they knew would be an ugly fight. Not stopping to shoot, the two regiments led the others toward the Confederate line, taking heavy losses but forcing most of the Confederates out of the rifle pits facing north. As for the other rifle pits—those angled toward the west and southwest—they could barely see the advancing Federals, much less shoot at them. What's more, with the darkness and smoke, the Confederates had a very difficult time seeing any of the Federal units that followed the first two brigades. Within a short time, both redoubts were overrun. The fighting was fierce, becoming hand to hand, and control of the redoubts changed several times.

❯ *Turn left out of the parking lot and drive 0.3 mile. After you cross the Rappahannock River, pull over to the side of the road.*

While the Confederates concentrated on defending the redoubts, Sedgwick ordered another two regiments to silently approach the far left of the Confederate position, the last of the rifle pits near the riverbank. In the darkness, the Federals were able to come within 25 yards of the rifle pits before they charged. They quickly overwhelmed the rebels, capturing the rifle pits and moving quickly to capture the pontoon bridge, preventing any escape of the Confederates on the north side of the river. Seeing this, most of the Confederates in this area quickly surrendered. It was not long before control of the bridgehead was securely in the hands of the Union.

The Confederate pontoon bridge was located near the location where US 15 crosses the Rappahannock River. If looking from the bridge (and take extreme caution if you choose to do so), looking downstream to your right you will see the current railroad bridge. Note the sharp drop in the terrain along the north bank; this would have been directly behind the two redoubts.

Remarkably, from the south bank, Lee and Early could gather little from what they saw. Not only did they have the darkness and smoke to contend with, but also distance, as well as an acoustic shadow, a natural phenomenon that prevented them from hearing what was going on. In fact, they knew so little that Lee, still convinced that the assault here was a feint, returned to his headquarters at Brandy Station to plan the next day's attack. Early eventually figured out what was happening, and quickly worked to secure the south bank. The pontoon bridge was burned, and reinforcements were brought up to fill the earthworks.

Lee received the news at his headquarters later that night and was forced to cancel his plans for the next morning. Rather than attack at Kelly's Ford with their whole army, the Confederates would be forced away from the Rappahannock entirely, eventually moving to their former camps below the Rapidan, the same camps they had occupied before they began the Bristoe campaign.

For the Union Army of the Potomac, it was a major victory. In a daring night attack on an extremely strong enemy position, it had inflicted 1,672 casualties, as well as captured the four Confederate guns in the redoubts. Having lost only a quarter of that number, 419, the Federals, only a few weeks after being pushed back almost to Washington, D.C., were now dictating the terms of combat.

MINE RUN

> *From the bridge, continue on Remington Road 0.5 mile, then turn left onto US 15/US 29 South (James Madison Highway). Drive 4.3 miles on US 15/US 29 to Alanthus Road (VA 663) and turn left. Drive 0.1 mile, turn left onto Brandy Road, and then immediately turn right onto Carrico Mills Road (still VA 663). Drive 5.9 miles on Carrico Mills Road to Germanna Highway (VA 3). Turn left onto Germanna Highway and drive 10.3 miles to Constitution Highway (VA 20). Drive 4.7*

miles on Constitution Highway, then turn left onto Gold Dale Road (SR 611) and drive 3.2 miles. Turn right onto Old Plank Road (SR 621 and drive 0.5 mile; pull into the church parking lot on your left.

Just after midnight on November 8, the Confederates began receiving their new marching orders, and aided by a hazy dawn, almost all of them were off the line facing French's wing at Kelly's Ford before daybreak. French had been expecting an attack, but when one of his divisions advanced to find empty Confederate camps, he knew that he had been given the slip. French took his wing west along the Rappahannock to join Sedgwick, and the reunited army, as planned, began its pursuit of the Confederates. By 2 PM, the Federals found them—in ready battle formation near Brandy Station, having taken up a strong defensive position as the rest of the rebels made their way south toward the Rapidan River. Meade was too late. The Army of Northern Virginia had escaped again.

Overnight, Lee moved his army across the Rapidan and set his defensive line, stretching 18 miles southeast along the south bank of the river. The left flank was in the area of Liberty Mills, while the right side of his line was refused, turning straight south from the Rapidan along a small creek called Mine Run. Ewell's corps made up the right side of the line, while Hill's corps took the left.

For several days, including a short conference in Washington, Meade considered his options. He wanted to wait until the Orange & Alexandria was repaired, at least to Brandy Station, but with the momentum on their side after the victory at Rappahannock Station, pressure was building from within the army to keep moving. It was obvious that a frontal assault along the river would be very difficult against the strong Confederate defenses, and the Confederate left was quite a distance away from his supply line. Intelligence was also coming in that indicated that the lower fords of the Rapidan River, past the Confederate right, were only lightly guarded. It was also discovered that the Orange Plank Road and the Orange Turnpike, two major arteries behind the Confederate lines, were relatively unobstructed.

On November 23, Meade presented his plan of attack to his corps commanders: They would attempt to turn the Confederate right. Three columns would cross the Rapidan—Warren's II Corps at Germanna Ford, French's III Corps and Sedgwick's VI Corps at Jacob's Ford, and Sykes's V Corps and Newton's I Corps at Culpeper Mine Ford. From there, the columns would move west on the Orange Plank Road and the Orange Turnpike toward Robinson's Tavern, surprising the Confederate right and rear and taking their army apart in pieces. The action was set for the next day, November 24; due to the secrecy required, Meade had told almost no one of the plan. Still, his corps commanders loved it.

Unfortunately for the Federals, a heavy rain made the roads impassable for two days, and it was not until the early morning hours of November 26 that the army began to move, and things did not exactly go as planned. The rain of the previous days had left the river swollen at Jacob's Ford, rendering it almost impassable, and the pontoon bridge that they had brought with them was too short, requiring a trestle to be built across the river. Although the II Corps had reached Germanna Ford by 9:30 AM, and the V Corps was at Culpeper Mine Ford at 10:30 AM, the III Corps was far behind schedule. Meade, upset with the lack of foresight by French, told the other two columns to wait for French.

It wasn't long before more trouble arose. It was realized that the south bank at Jacob's Ford was far too steep for wagons or artillery, so these elements of the III and VI Corps were rerouted to Germanna Ford. By the end of the day, only three of the five corps—the II, III, and V—were on the south bank of the Rapidan. Meade could have gone farther, but the prospect of placing his army in the thickly wooded area known as the Wilderness after dark—the same Wilderness in which Joseph Hooker had gotten his army entangled at Chancellorsville six months before—discouraged further movement. Meade changed his orders, directing the army to unite at Robinson's Tavern the next morning, from where they would head 6 miles to Old Verdiersville, squarely in the Confederate rear.

The Confederates, though, would not allow this to happen. Although the Federals' movements during the morning were obscured by fog, it was not long before Confederate signal stations detected their movement. Lee had anticipated a movement of some kind, but as of yet, he was still unsure of whether Meade would be attacking him here or would attempt to move for Richmond. Preparing his army for either contingency, Lee ordered Ewell's corps (under the command of Jubal Early, with Ewell ill) to advance east along the Orange Turnpike and the Raccoon Ford Road, while Hill's corps would use the Orange Plank Road. The rebels began their movement that evening, readying themselves to meet the Union army in battle the next day.

November 27 would be a confusing day for both armies. The unforgiving Wilderness, along with the poor condition of the roads, meant that each unit had limited options as to where they could move, as well as limited visibility. This meant that both armies, traveling on the few navigable roads (the Orange Turnpike and the Orange Plank Road), had set themselves on a collision course without knowing it. Both Lee and Meade were playing chess without being able to see all of the pieces, even their own.

Farthest south, on the Orange Plank Road, J. E. B. Stuart, still commanding Wade Hampton's division in his absence, ran into David Gregg's Union cavalry division just west of New Hope Church. Both sides fought dismounted because of the thick woods, and both were only concerned with holding their positions until infantry support could arrive. The Confederates arrived first, around 2:30 PM, with the lead elements of Henry Heth's division of Hill's corps quickly taking the high ground. About 30 minutes later, the Sykes's Union V Corps came up to relieve Gregg, and they quickly pushed Heth's skirmishers off the hill.

Standing with the road to your right and the church to your left, you are facing the Confederate line. The small rise to your front is the ground over which the skirmishing took place.

It had taken Sykes ("Tardy George," as he had been nicknamed at West Point) six hours to move 3 miles. Meade knew that Newton's I Corps was not far behind him, but the location of two of his other three corps—the III and VI—was a mystery. He did know the location of Warren's II Corps, and he knew that they could be in trouble. Waiting for further information, Meade ordered Sykes to hold the high ground west of New Hope Church until he could ascertain the condition of the rest of his army.

〉 *From the church parking lot, pull out to the right onto Old Plank Road and drive 0.5 mile to Gold Dale Road. Drive 3.2 miles on Gold Dale Road; just before the intersection with Constitution Highway, pull into the paved area on your left.*

The first action of the day had occurred here at Robinson's Tavern, the objective of all of the Union corps and Meade's unification point. 100 yards west of the tavern, the skirmish lines of Harry Hays's brigade—the Louisiana Tigers—and Samuel Carroll's brigade of Alexander Hays's division, II Corps, traded shots at 11 AM. Hays commanded Jubal Early's division, while Early temporarily commanded Ewell's corps. Hays put two brigades south of the turnpike and one to the north, waiting until the next division in line, Robert Rodes's, would come up quickly. While he waited, Gouverneur Warren brought the rest of his II Corps to the front, taking advantage of the delay and grabbing the high ground.

When Rodes did come up, he and Heth both saw the Union troops massing atop the hill and thought it best to wait for the final division from their corps—Johnson's—to come up. On the other side of the field, George Meade had now arrived. The Federals held a good defensive position, and the Confederate numbers were growing, so he held an attack until Warren could be reinforced by the III Corps, which all expected would be arriving shortly.

Robinson's Tavern is still near the intersection, but it has been moved and now sits approximately 200 yards north of its former location. Interpretive signs at the intersection discuss the campaign as a whole. As you face the signs, the high ground to your front was the Federal line, and it was also near here where the first shots were fired. You are facing west, toward the Confederates.

Just as they were doing at New Hope Church, 3 miles to the south, both sides traded the occasional volley, not advancing but expecting reinforcements soon. At both locations, both armies would remain in these positions until sundown, neither making any significant movement. Robert E. Lee was with A. P. Hill at New Hope Church, and for his part, he still could not tell whether the Union army was attacking him or if they were feinting, with Richmond their primary objective. As for George Meade, he was still missing the III and VI Corps of his army. It was the action of the III Corps, as well as the only Confederate division left, Johnson's, that would determine the day.

> *Pull out to your left and cross through the intersection; Gold Dale Road is called Zoar Road from this point. Drive 2.5 miles on Zoar Road (SR 611), then turn right onto Indiantown Road (SR 603). Drive 1.2 miles to the intersection with Russel Road; turn right onto Russel Road, then turn around and come back to the intersection.*

William French's III Corps got off to a good start, beginning their march promptly at daybreak and moving down the Jacob's Ford Road toward Raccoon Ford Road and Robinson's Tavern. It was not long, though, before a series of miscommunications, bungles, and sheer negligence would lead to an embarrassing day for the Union army.

The lead division for the III Corps that day was David Prince's, and it was only a mile into the day's march that the troops reached a fork in the road at the Widow Morris's farm. Both roads led to the tavern. The route to the right, though much more direct, was also more likely to be blocked by the Confederates. The road to the left was a winding path, much longer than the other, but would probably be free of the enemy. Already behind schedule, Prince elected to send cavalry to reconnoiter the path to the right, while he sent a courier to Warren by way of the left fork. It was soon confirmed that Confederates were, indeed, present on the right fork.

Wondering why they had halted, French and his staff pushed their way to the front of the column. French and Prince were already not on good terms; French blamed the previous day's delays solely on Prince, and Prince was not fond of his commander's behavior in general. French seemed to be exhibiting generally poor behavior this day, too, when he appeared to be more than slightly intoxicated. Evidence of this may be found in the fact that French first established his headquarters at the home of the Widow Morris, and then sent an aide to the front to find out what the delay was. The aide quickly covered the distance to the front—all of 300 yards of it.

At 9:20 AM, French sent a dispatch to General Meade, updating him of his situation. He told Meade that he was at the Orange Turnpike and was waiting for the II Corps. This was blatantly false, as French was at a dead halt a good 3 miles from the turnpike. A perplexed Meade, who received the dispatch at 11:30 AM, responded frankly,, "What are you waiting for?" reiterating that French's orders said nothing about waiting for Warren, nor stopping at the turnpike, and that he was to proceed directly for Robinson's Tavern, where the II Corps was waiting for him.

By the time Meade received the dispatch, French still had not made up his mind, although intelligence had been gathered from both forks of the road by 10 AM. In that time, he could have covered the distance to Robinson's Tavern already. Finally, just before 2 PM, French ordered Prince to take the road to the right, the direct route to the tavern. Prince deployed the 1st Massachusetts infantry as skirmishers, while placing artillery and one brigade in a clearing south of the Morris farm.

This intersection is the fork in the road that stopped the III Corps in its tracks. Facing south at the intersection, the property on your left was the site of the Morris Farm, where Prince deployed and French set his headquarters. Today, the entire site is private property, so remain in your car and do not trespass.

❭ *From the intersection, turn left onto Indiantown Road and drive 1.2 miles to Zoar Road. Turn left on Zoar Road and drive 0.2 mile; pull into the parking area near Zoar Baptist Church on your left.*

South of the III Corps' inactivity (and the forced inactivity of the VI Corps stuck behind them), the Confederate division of Edward Johnson headed east down the Raccoon Ford Road toward the Orange Turnpike and Robinson's Tavern. He had been ordered by A. P. Hill to join the rest of his corps there, Hays's and Rodes's divisions, and was about to deploy on Rodes's left when, at noon, he received word that his rear guard, George Steuart's brigade, was under attack. Rushing to the rear, he found Steuart holding his ground, although he could not do much with the thick woods of the Wilderness in front of him. Johnson responded promptly, recalling his division and lining up his men along the Raccoon Ford Road facing northeast and east, toward the Payne farms, at the road's intersection with the Jacob's Ford Road. Johnson deployed skirmishers, but with only a few small farm clearings cut out of the thick Wilderness, little information could be gathered.

As David Prince began to move his division down the Jacob's Ford Road toward Johnson's line, he abruptly received orders to halt. French had changed his mind; he had decided to take the fork to the left instead. Prince went to French's headquarters tent, pleaded his case, and the march was back on. He was also permitted to use Joseph Carr's division as support, if necessary, when Johnson's Confederates were encountered. Moving to the front to gauge the situation, Prince soon realized that Johnson's line overlapped his own, and he asked Carr for support. Carr refused, saying that he had been ordered by French to hold his position. Again, Prince asked for a clarification from French, and an aide soon arrived, authorizing Carr to support of Prince's advance.

With things seemingly sorted out, Prince again began to advance at 4 PM—and was again ordered by French to halt, this time to allow Carr's division to deploy on his left. At the same time, French gave Carr a bewildering order—to link the left of his line to the right of the II Corps, still miles away at Robinson's Tavern.

Finally, patience gave way—not on the Union side, but the Confederate. Johnson had had a full four hours to gather intelligence, place his troops, and make his plans, and now his plans were to attack. He was greatly outnumbered (although he could not have known by how many), but one of the effects of fighting in the Wilderness was that it greatly negated the impact of numbers. Johnson's division had four brigades, totaling 5,300 men, and in front of him, though mostly ineffective, were 32,000 Union soldiers.

Johnson advanced and found no Federals on his left, so he ordered his two left-most brigades, Leroy Stafford's and John Jones's, to wheel left. It was not easy to perform a maneuver such as this in the Wilderness, and many of the attacks came piecemeal as a result, but the Federals' slow movement allowed the Confederates to mostly remain intact. Carr's division was soon being hammered by the two brigades, as well as James Walker's, the famous Stonewall Brigade, on their right flank. It was not long before Carr's division was routed. Fortunately for the Federals, the remaining division from the III Corps, David Birney's, came up from the rear quickly and stemmed the tide of the Confederates.

On the Confederate right, Steuart's and portions of Walker's brigades met much heavier resistance from Prince's division, with the lines at times only 200 yards apart.

The well-blazed trail at Payne's Farm, site of the heaviest fighting of the Mine Run Campaign.

The fight went back and forth here, charge and countercharge, until nightfall, when the two sides were simply played out.

The walking trail at Payne's Farm, only recently developed, will take you through the heaviest part of the battle. Interpretive signs have been installed along the 1.5-mile trail to guide you through the fighting. It is a difficult battle to interpret—much of the fighting was in thick woods, and most of the trail goes through the same—but the signs are very well done, and you shouldn't have too much trouble. Parts of the trail path itself are still being developed and are a bit rough, but the ground is level and the trail is well marked. If you do decide to take the hike, be prepared with water and insect repellent.

By the time the fight was over, the Federals had suffered 952 casualties to the Confederates' 545. More important, Johnson's division, aided by the communication breakdown of the III Corps, prevented the Federals from coming down on Hill's left and rear at Robinson's Tavern. Meade's entire movement had been compromised. Instead of uniting his army at Robinson's Tavern, he fought on three different fronts over the course of the day. Not only were all traces of a surprise attack gone, but Robert E. Lee was now sure that Meade was not heading for Richmond. Meade was looking for a fight, and if that's what he wanted, Lee was not going to give him the luxury of choosing the battleground.

Overnight, Lee pulled the Confederate army west behind Mine Run, a small creek running north to south. In the darkness, the Confederates immediately began to fortify their positions, digging earthworks and creating obstructions in front of their lines. It was a long, rainy, and cold night, but the rebels worked tirelessly to improve their lines as best they could.

The Union army, in their various locations, all woke up on November 28 to find that the Confederates had again disappeared from their front. The I, II, and VI Corps moved west, where they soon found the Confederate line, already becoming a formidable set of works. The Federals began deploying in battle formation, but the movement took hours, hampered by heavy rains and the thick Wilderness.

By the time the line was ready, Meade was not. The Confederate position was remarkably strong. Mine Creek itself, which would have to be crossed, was flooded with the recent rain. Beyond the creek lay a 1,000-yard slope to the Confederate line, an open field with abatis and other defenses obstructing the way to heavy earthworks. Behind those earthworks was the entire Army of Northern Virginia, along with all of its artillery. Ewell's corps had taken the Confederate left, while Hill's corps was on the right, and the line stretched across both the Orange Turnpike and the Orange Plank Road. There would be no attack that day. All the while, the Confederates took every second of the Union army's delay to improve their works.

Overnight, Meade conferred with his generals. It seemed that the only feasible option was to attempt to turn the Confederate right. Warren's II Corps would lead the assault there the next morning, along with a division borrowed from Sedgwick's VI Corps and cavalry. While the other corps would demonstrate along the line to hold the Confederates in place, 18,000 Union soldiers would try to get around or through the right flank of the Confederate line.

That night, Lee ordered J. E. B. Stuart to find out what he could about the Federal movements. It was not long before he found out that the II Corps was headed for the Confederate right flank, but at daybreak on November 29 he was still behind enemy lines. Warren, his men already on the march, found out that Confederate cavalry was in his rear and halted his movement just as he had reached Mine Run at 1 PM.

After finding out that the Confederates in his rear were a small force, Warren resumed his advance, eventually pushing past Mine Creek and beyond their right flank. Although he could see that there were few Confederates in his path, darkness was quickly approaching and he was forced to suspend the advance for the day. Commanding his men to light extra campfires to show their strength, Warren reported the Confederate weakness on their right to Meade.

With this information, as well as information from John Sedgwick that the Confederate right was also very lightly guarded, Meade ordered an assault on both flanks for the next morning. Warren was given two more divisions, both from the III Corps, while Sedgwick had command of the V Corps to add to his own VI Corps. The I Corps and the remaining division of the III Corps would demonstrate in the center. Warren would attack promptly at 8 AM; at the same time, Sedgwick would open with his artillery, beginning his infantry assault at 9 AM.

Over the course of the extremely cold night—Union pickets were relieved every 30 minutes to prevent any of them from freezing to death—the Federal soldiers could hear the Confederates, only 600 yards away, continuing to dig and improve their works. They were moved into their battle lines at 3 PM, and from that time on, could only wait. A. P. Hill, knowing that the Federal numbers were growing on his flank, shifted many of his troops here to meet the oncoming assault, all of which could be heard clearly in the cold, still night.

When the sun came up on November 30 and the improved defenses on the Confederate right were revealed, virtually every soldier of the Army of the Potomac had one thought on his mind: Fredericksburg. It had only been a year since, in freezing weather just like what they encountered now, Union troops had been thrown repeatedly against a virtually unassailable defensive position like this, and no one who was there could ever forget the bloody repulse or the cries of the wounded who were left in the field, many of whom died not from their wounds but from hypothermia. The similarities were not lost on the Confederates, either, as they loudly urged the Federals to come and attack them.

Warren had been at Fredericksburg, too, and when he saw how vastly improved the Confederate position had become overnight, he grew extremely concerned. He estimated an eight-minute run from the Union position to the Confederate line, and quickly concluded that covering that distance, particularly with obstructions but no shelter, was likely to bring the same disastrous results as the assault at Fredericksburg. Meade, who was with John Newton's I Corps, could not be consulted, and it was almost 8 AM. Finally forced to make a decision when the Union artillery opened up on the Confederate left, Warren rushed a message to Meade saying that he was calling off the assault.

When George Meade heard the sound of artillery on his right but nothing from his left, he headed back to his headquarters. There he found one of Warren's staff members with the message that he did not think the assault could succeed, and that he would not attack unless ordered. Meade was shocked, replying, "My God! General Warren has half my army at his disposition!" but suspended the attack. The order reached John Sedgwick, who thought his own assault would succeed, just in time, and Meade rode to Warren's position to inspect it for himself. Finding himself unable to sway Warren and seeing the position for himself, Meade canceled the attack order, prompting a collective sigh of relief from the Union soldiers and disappointment on the part of the Confederates.

That night, at a council of war, it was decided that the Federals would withdraw from their position on the evening of December 1. That same day, Robert E. Lee had decided to again try to seize the initiative by attacking the Union line, but by the next morning the Union soldiers were already gone, headed north of the Rapidan River. Lee, who desperately wanted another victory under his belt, angrily stated, "We should have never permitted those people to get away."

There are remnants of the Confederate defensive position, but they are all on private property. Several roads on the west side of the run roughly trace the Confederate position, but the line is heavily wooded and there is not much to be seen.

After the two armies left each other at Mine Run, both camps settled in for the winter, and it would remain relatively quiet along the Rapidan River for several months. In Washington, D.C., however, the action did not stop. The aftermath of the Mine Run campaign, just like every other campaign that had not destroyed the Army of Northern Virginia, would have its heroes and goats. Gouverneur Warren fell into the hero camp for most; his decision to suspend the attack and not waste the lives of his men was seen as courageous. George Meade, who backed Warren's decision and did not regret it, did not have the same public or political support, and he took a large amount of criticism for coming away from the affair empty handed.

The Union army did suffer one notable loss over the winter: John Buford. The brave cavalry commander who had made his auspicious debut at Second Manassas and had shone ever since had contracted typhoid fever during the fall. Shortly after Mine Run he was confined to a hospital bed in Washington, where he died at the age of 37.

In mid-January 1864, Meade returned to his home in Philadelphia for what was supposed to be a brief furlough but developed into a case of pneumonia. In his absence, John Sedgwick was placed in temporary command of the Army of the Potomac. During that period, Benjamin Butler, a very good politician who was made a general at the start of the war (as many politicians were), proposed a joint operation with the Army of the Potomac. The plan was designed in part to relieve Confederate pressure on Union-held New Bern, North Carolina, but there was certainly an element of glory in it for Butler as well. The plan was for the VI Corps to feint across the Rapidan, drawing Confederate forces their way, while Butler took his own army up the peninsula of the James and freed Union prisoners in Richmond. Sedgwick found many flaws within the plan, but under pressure from Henry Halleck, participated. The result was the battle of Morton's Ford on February 6, 1864, a near disaster for the Federals.

By the time Meade returned to Washington on February 13, much had changed. Although it was not yet official, Ulysses S. Grant, the highly successful and aggressive commander from the Western Theater, would be given the rank of lieutenant general, commanding all Union armies in the field. Speculation was therefore rampant about replacing Meade—probably with Grant's good friend, William "Baldy" Smith. Secretary of War Edwin M. Stanton, however, assuaged Meade's fears, telling him that the administration had confidence in him but that some of his generals had to go. Meade replied that he would not object to any of Stanton's proposals. However, when he received the list, he strongly objected to one change: the relief of John Sedgwick. Ben Butler had blamed his failed operation on Sedgwick and used his political power to shift responsibility his way. When asked about why the operation had failed, Sedgwick replied with a very detailed, unflinching, and undeniable list of problems with the campaign plan. (Butler had also failed in his portion of the campaign, in almost exactly the manner that Sedgwick had predicted.) Because they had supported Butler, Abraham Lincoln, Henry Halleck, and Edwin Stanton had taken Sedgwick's reply as a criticism of themselves.

Although Meade had to fight hard, he was able to retain Sedgwick. Other changes, though, were coming. The I and III Corps, both of which had taken heavy losses, particularly at Gettysburg, would be dismantled and distributed among the other corps. Both commanders, John Newton and William French, who would not be able to shake charges of his drunkenness at Payne's Farm, were relieved. V Corps commander George Sykes was also relieved, providing a spot for Meade to retain Warren as a corps commander. With Gettysburg hero Winfield Hancock having recovered from his wounds, he would naturally return to his old II Corps, while Warren replaced Sykes. Perhaps the biggest question, however, was answered when Grant decided to keep Meade as commander of the Army of the Potomac. However, Grant would not be taking a desk in Washington. He would make his headquarters with this army, so critical to Union victory. Immediately, Grant's and Meade's respective staff began planning for the spring campaign.

The Confederates were also planning for the spring, but they had other large issues to contend with. As it had been from almost the beginning of the war, the primary issue was that of supplies, and in particular, food. Union control of the Mississippi River, which came with the fall of Vicksburg last July, meant that no beef west of river would make its way to the hungry soldiers. This and other shortages, as well as letters from home telling about the suffering there, led many Confederate soldiers to simply leave the army to tend to their families.

The winter of 1863/64 was a long one on both sides, necessarily so after Gettysburg and a very active fall. It would also prove necessary for the campaign to come, the longest and bloodiest campaign of the entire war.

The Bottle: Benjamin Butler and the Bermuda Hundred Campaign

IN THE UNITED STATES ARMY, the rank of lieutenant general had not been used very often until the Civil War. The first lieutenant general had been George Washington. Winfield Scott, veteran of the War of 1812 and hero of the Mexican War, had been awarded the rank of brevet lieutenant general in 1856, long after his glory days. And that was it. The United States had not needed such a high-ranking officer since its inception. The Civil War, however, if any war ever did, merited the return of such a rank. The problem was that no individual officer had distinguished himself enough to be made worthy of it, commander of all armies in the field. That finally changed with the emergence of Ulysses S. Grant, who was officially promoted to lieutenant general on March 12, 1864.

Before the rank had been officially awarded, Grant had already given a great deal of thought to how to win the war. For months, he had been bouncing ideas off fellow generals and weighing the merits and pitfalls of various strategies. Soon, several points became very clear. First, the army was scattered across too many fronts. Consolidating the forces into only a handful of departments would direct more force at the most critical strategic points and ensure that every available man was on the front line.

Parker's Confederate Battery held this position on the Howlett Line, part of Richmond National Battlefield.

Second, there had been very little coordination between the different theaters of war, and this needed to change. Coordinating efforts east and west to apply pressure at all points simultaneously would give the Confederates two options—either give up some of those points, or stretch themselves so thin as to be unable to hold any of them. Either way, the comparatively inexhaustible resources of the Union would eventually prevail.

With these in mind, Grant devised a grand strategy that he hoped would finish the conflict. Five offensives would be conducted simultaneously. The two primary offensives would be watched by all eyes north and south: the Army of the Potomac's campaign to defeat Robert E. Lee and capture Richmond and the Union drive to capture Atlanta, Georgia. The other three offensives were supplementary to the first two, but still critically important. Nathaniel Banks would move his forces east from New Orleans to capture the vital Confederate port at Mobile, Alabama. In the Shenandoah Valley, Franz Sigel would take a Union force to not only clear out the Breadbasket of the Confederacy but also cut the railroad lines feeding Lee's Army of Northern Virginia from the west. Finally, Benjamin Butler would take the newly formed Army of the James and move along the south bank of the James River toward Richmond.

In an April meeting with Grant, Butler proposed a plan to base his operations at Bermuda Hundred, a small peninsula at the confluence of the James and Appomattox Rivers measuring only 30 square miles. It was a good position, being only 16 miles from Richmond and having deep water to the east, meaning that supplies could easily be brought in by ship once a foothold had been secured. In addition, the defenses at Richmond were much weaker on its south side, and the Federals would have a relatively easy approach. After Butler made his case, Grant had two questions: Could he capture and hold Richmond if reinforced, and could he take it by surprise? Butler answered yes to both, and Grant ordered him to be ready to move in time with the other offensives.

In the history books, the Bermuda Hundred campaign is often forgotten, and if it isn't, it is only casually mentioned as a significant Union failure. At the time, however, Grant considered the movement along the James critically important, eventually hoping to link the Army of the Potomac with the Army of the James outside Richmond. There are some historians who argue that had the campaign been properly conducted, the entire siege of Petersburg that resulted from Grant's campaigns in the east would have been avoided. Others argue that although Butler did not achieve all of his objectives, the overall result of his campaign was positive. Far from a footnote, the Bermuda Hundred campaign is a key piece to understanding the Civil War in the Eastern Theater.

BEFORE YOU GO

» PLANNING YOUR TRIP

Very few of the sites on this tour are perfectly preserved, but there is certainly enough left that the battles can easily be interpreted. The roads and railroads present during the campaign are still here, and some parts of the ground remain virtually untouched. Furthermore, there is a fairly good amount of interpretation about the campaign, thanks in large part to the Chesterfield County Historical Society of Virginia and the Chesterfield Heritage Alliance. The sites under their care are extremely well preserved and well interpreted.

> **BERMUDA HUNDRED CAMPAIGN**
>
> **Number of sites:** 9 (plus one optional)
>
> **Total miles:** 44 (71 with optional stop)
>
> **Estimated time:** 1–2 days

Some of the areas you will visit are in suburban neighborhoods, some in the middle of busy intersections and some in isolated locations. Be prepared for everything and use care as you tour the sites, and take particular care regarding traffic. Also, it would probably be wise to bring insect repellent with you, as some of the significant sites are near now still waters that have become large breeding grounds for mosquitoes.

» RECOMMENDATIONS

Staying in either Colonial Heights or Chester is your best bet. Numerous hotels and motels lay along the interstate in these two stops between the larger cities of Richmond and Petersburg. If you're looking for something beyond the standard chain restaurants, you will probably have to venture north or south; otherwise, you should be able to find everything you need here, and all of the sites will be within minutes of one another.

IN DEPTH

William Glenn Robertson—*Back Door to Richmond: The Bermuda Hundred Campaign, April–June 1864*

Herbert M. Schiller—*The Bermuda Hundred Campaign*

"Was Butler 'bottled up'? Robertson says no; Schiller says yes. Read them both, and decide for yourself."

—*Tom Trescott, Abraham Lincoln Book Shop, Chicago*

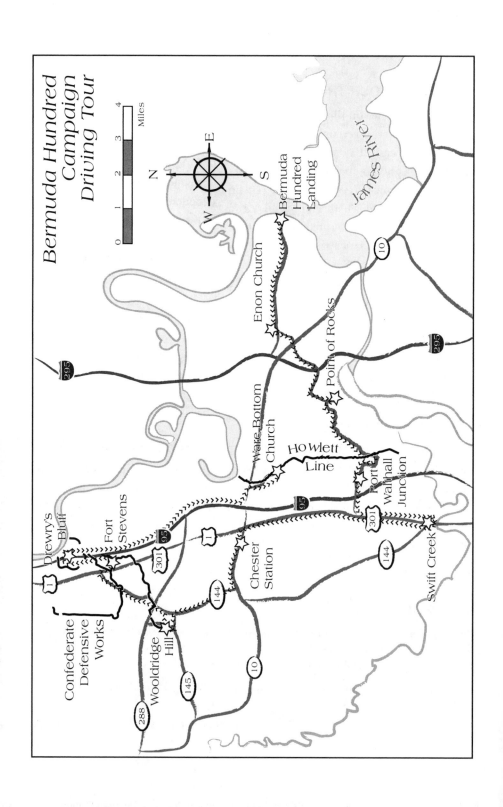

Bermuda Hundred
Campaign
Driving Tour

Miles
0 1 2 3 4

N
W · E
S

James River

Bermuda Hundred Landing

Enon Church

Point of Rocks

10

295

Wate Bottom Church

Howlett Line

Fort Walthall Junction

301

95

Drewry's Bluff

Fort Stevens

95

301

1

Chester Station

1

144

Confederate Defensive Works

Wooldridge Hill

144

145

288

10

Swift Creek

144

295

THE CAMPAIGN TOUR

BERMUDA HUNDRED LANDING

⟩ *Begin your tour at the far eastern end of Bermuda Hundred Road. This is approximately 3 miles west of the intersection of Bermuda Hundred Road and North Enon Church Road.*

Benjamin Butler, although already well-known as a Union general, had never commanded soldiers in the field. He was a master politician, and his influence was such that not only was he able to maneuver himself into positions of great power, but replacing him as commander of the Army of the James would be a very touchy situation. Grant came up with what seemed like the perfect solution. He assigned William "Baldy" Smith, who he knew well from the Western Theater, to shadow Butler, bringing his 20,000-strong XVIII Corps with him. Butler had proven himself extremely capable when it came to the administrative pieces of command. With Smith at his side, it seemed like a perfect match, at least on paper.

In addition to the XVIII Corps, Butler was also given Quincy Gillmore's X Corps, 10,000 men who had been assigned to garrisons in the not-so-hotspots of Florida, Georgia, and South Carolina. The troops began to gather in Yorktown and Gloucester, Virginia, in early April to prepare for the offensive. The mere presence of the Federals

Bermuda Hundred Landing at the confluence of the James and Appomattox Rivers.

(aided by a few Union deceptions about their intent) was enough to fuel rumors of a direct march on Richmond, prompting much speculation on exactly what the Union forces under Grant were going to do.

On the assigned date—May 4, the same day that Grant moved toward Lee in the Wilderness—the Army of the James was loaded onto barges and other transports to make the short sail around the Virginia peninsula to the new Union base at Bermuda Hundred. However, trouble began brewing even before the men boarded the boats. For one thing, Quincy Gillmore had not yet arrived, taking his time in Hilton Head, South Carolina, to be sure that all of his troops were properly directed. Although he did land at Gloucester on May 4, the absence of a commander for the X Corps greatly complicated not only preparation for the mission but also cooperation with the other units. Further, it turned out that before too long, Baldy Smith realized that he did not like Benjamin Butler. Butler would constantly be coming to Smith for military advice (which, in fairness, was the plan), and although Butler deferred to Smith's judgment in almost every case, Smith resented taking his orders from a political general and not a military man. Before long, the awkward command structure of the Army of the James—two strong-willed corps commanders with large egos under a politically appointed general—would prove to be its undoing.

As planned, the boats did launch on May 4, although the X Corps caused quite a holdup. That evening, the boats stopped at the end of the peninsula under the shelter of the massive guns of Fortress Monroe. They resumed their sail the next day, escorted by a flotilla of navy gunboats, including five ironclads. On their way up the James River, garrisons were dropped at Wilson's Wharf, on the north bank of the James, and Fort Powhatan, on the south bank. These strongholds would ensure unbroken communication between the Army of the James and Fortress Monroe. After making a final stop at City Point to take out a Confederate signal station, Butler's 30,000-man army disembarked at Bermuda Hundred Landing at around 5 PM. The unloading went on well into the night, and the soldiers went into bivouac around the landing as they came off the transports.

Your view of the water to the east is of the confluence of the James and Appomattox Rivers, and the small peninsula you stand on is Bermuda Hundred. The landing site was directly in front of you, and although you can't get all the way to the water today, it is easy to imagine numerous transports unloading tens of thousands of men in blue at this spot. The reasonably open ground around you was the brief campsite for the Army of the James, and by the next morning, the troops were on their way toward Richmond.

> *Turn around and drive 3 miles west back toward the intersection with North Enon Church Road. Pull into the parking lot for the church on your left.*

After all of the Federal troops were ashore, the Army of the James marched west on the Bermuda Hundred Road. At the intersection before you, the two corps of the army split. Gillmore's X Corps kept marching due west toward Ware Bottom Church, where the Federals would establish the northern part of a line that would stretch from the James River south to the Appomattox River. Smith's XVIII Corps turned left here, marching on to a well-known formation known as Point of Rocks, overlooking the Appomattox.

POINT OF ROCKS

❯ *From the church parking lot, turn left and drive south on Enon Church Road for 2.7 miles. You will reach Dodd Park; turn left at the second entrance to the park and drive 0.2 mile to the parking area for the playground.*

By 8:30 AM on May 6, the XVIII Corps had already established its base at Point of Rocks. A high bluff alongside the Appomattox River provided a good view of the surrounding area. In fact, it was also an ideal place for a Confederate signal station, which the Federals quickly seized for themselves. Here they anchored the left end of the Union line, which would stretch north from this strong formation north to connect with the X Corps.

A trail here at Dodd Park will take you through Point of Rocks, and will show you some well-preserved examples of the Union earthworks. The trail is one-way, but it emerges at one of the other parking areas of the park, so getting back to your vehicle isn't such a long walk should you choose to take it.

PORT WALTHALL JUNCTION

❯ *From Dodd Park, turn left onto Enon Church Road and drive 1.8 miles to Ruffin Mill Road. Turn right onto Ruffin Mill Road and drive 1.4 miles. You will see a large truck stop/travel center on your right; pull into the parking lot.*

To the north, the men of the X Corps, a bit behind their more organized companions, were still on their way to Ware Bottom Church. Once there, they began to fortify their position, extending north to the James River and south to join with the rest of the army. At 2:30 PM, Butler wired the War Department in Washington to let them know that not only was the army right on schedule, but that it had encountered virtually no Confederate opposition. The Federals had hoped that their approach would be a surprise, but they had not anticipated that they would be virtually unchallenged in their landing. Things were going almost too well.

To this point, the campaign could not have gone better for the Federals, but the suspicions of Butler and most others in the army were correct. The Confederates had solid information regarding the Union position and the size of the force that had landed. In fact, messages regarding the Union army possibly appearing south of the Confederate capital had been sent to Richmond since mid-April. The trouble, though, was that no matter how much information the two commanders in the area, generals George Pickett and P. G. T. Beauregard, passed on, nobody seemed to pay any attention to it.

Pickett, who had been part of the infamous charge that had been so costly to the Confederates at Gettysburg, had been in charge of the Department of North Carolina, not very far south of Richmond and Petersburg. This department had a critically important assignment: protecting the Weldon Railroad, which brought supplies from the port of Wilmington, North Carolina, directly north through Petersburg and Richmond and eventually to Robert E. Lee's Army of Northern Virginia. Long concerned about the defenses south of the capital, Pickett had been forwarding reports of Union activity to Richmond for weeks. Eventually, the recipient of most of those messages, Braxton Bragg, suspected that Pickett was crying wolf and paid little attention to his messages.

On April 15, Bragg relieved Pickett, replacing him with the South's first hero of the war, the well-known and flamboyant Pierre Gustave Toutant Beauregard. The victor at First Manassas had been successfully keeping the Union out of Charleston Harbor for the better part of a year. He immediately began reconstructing his new department, rolling several smaller departments into the larger and newly named Department of North Carolina and Southern Virginia. Beauregard would place his headquarters at Weldon, North Carolina, while Pickett remained at his location in Petersburg. Beauregard, seemingly the only commander who appreciated not only the danger to the capital but also the value of the railroad center at Petersburg, urged Pickett to continue reporting on the Union army's movements on the peninsula.

Pickett's reports were remarkably accurate, and the size of the Army of the James had been confirmed well before they left their jump-off base at Yorktown. Still, few gave them much credence. Even Robert E. Lee, who did not command this department but obviously held great weight in determining the Confederate army's actions, considered the operations on the peninsula simply a diversion.

When Pickett reported the Union movement up the James River on May 5, Beauregard told him to hold as best he could with his available force—including the citizens of Petersburg, if need be—while he gathered troops from North Carolina. Eventually gathering a force of 1,400 men, Pickett wired Richmond five times to warn them of the Union presence. Not receiving a reply, Pickett sent a sixth telegram asking whether the previous five were ever received. They had been, but no one had paid attention. Finally, Robert Ransom, commander of the Department of Richmond, did send some troops to Drewry's Bluff, a strong fortification on the James River, but too far from Pickett's position in Petersburg to do him any good.

Beauregard and Pickett anxiously spent May 6 attempting to gather more men to defend Petersburg, making some progress as Ransom sent more troops south, including Bushrod Johnson's brigade to move from Drewry's Bluff to Port Walthall Junction, a rail split approximately halfway between Richmond and Petersburg.

Shortly after he had informed Washington of his success, Butler ordered Baldy Smith to send a brigade west in an effort to find the Confederates. Smith chose Charles Heckman's brigade of 2,700 men, which left the base at Point of Rocks around 4 PM. Under orders not to bring on an engagement, Heckman advanced westward toward the Richmond and Petersburg Railroad. Eventually coming to a clearing on a plateau, the Federals looked across a long field toward the tracks at the other end. There, they finally encountered the enemy, formed in a sunken road approximately 300 yards east of the railroad. Not knowing the strength of the Confederate force, Heckman formed a line from Ashton Creek, to the north, stretching south to a tree line at the south end of the Dunn plantation.

Heckman advanced with understandable caution at 5 PM. The railroad between Richmond and Petersburg was critical to the Confederates, and if troops were present to protect it, there were probably a good number of them. Opening with artillery and sending his line forward, Heckman soon found the firing getting hotter and darkness coming. Mindful of his orders not to bring on an engagement and not making much progress, he withdrew.

The Confederates across the field, Bushrod Johnson's, were only 600 in number. By midnight, that number would increase, with the rest of Johnson's brigade arriving, followed shortly by Charles Hagood's brigade. The Confederate strength at Port Walthall Junction was now over 2,600 men.

Back in the Union camps, Smith was eager to attempt the movement again the next day, but with greater force. Readily taking Smith's advice, Butler ordered the movement, further ensuring that the operation would involve both Smith's and Gillmore's corps. Their objective would be to destroy the vital railroad, as well as feint southward toward Petersburg.

On the morning of May 7, Hagood's Confederates left their defenses began moving north on the Old Stage Road (today's Woods Edge Road, in front of you) to reconnoiter the Federal position. They soon ran into a small cavalry force moving ahead of the Union column from the X Corps, which was moving south on the same road. Although the Union cavalry was soon scattered, once the infantry came forward, Hagood withdrew to his defenses along the railroad.

Meanwhile, Charles Heckman's brigade returned to the Dunn plantation, where it had fought the previous day. These troops were a diversion from the primary force, the other three brigades moving down the Old Stage Road. Johnson sent two of his Confederate regiments across the fields at the Dunn plantation to meet Heckman. At the same time, the main Federal force of nearly 8,000 moved far beyond the left of the Confederate line. Around noon, the Confederates soon found themselves in a crossfire between Union troops approaching from the north and the east.

By 2:30 PM, the left side of the Confederate line along the railroad was under heavy pressure, and by 3 PM was preparing to withdraw. As the Union gained ground, one regiment, the 24th Massachusetts, began to try to tear up the railroad. Unfortunately, the men had never done this before, and they did not do a very good job of it, having not brought the tools necessary for the task.

By 4 PM, the Federals had the field. Through confusion on the field, though, the Federals began to withdraw from the ground they had gained. Union general William Brooks later denied giving the order to withdraw, but that is exactly what they did, heading back behind the Union defenses having done minimal damage. The Confederates, outnumbered three to one, had once again gotten away with driving away a potentially very dangerous Union force while taking very few casualties.

Believe it or not, here in the parking lot of this large truck stop, you are now standing on the battlefield at Port Walthall Junction. Most of the fighting of May 6 happened where you are now and where you can see the large interstate cloverleaf. The May 7 battle also covered this area, but the fighting along the railroad, where the heaviest action occurred, is west of the interstate, out of view. You will pass this area of the fighting on your way to your next stop, Swift Creek. You can follow Ruffin Mill Road to this area by turning right out of the parking lot and driving to the railroad crossing, but there is no good place to stop and look, so if you choose to do this, please keep driving as you view the area.

SWIFT CREEK

⟩ *From the travel center parking lot, turn right onto Ruffin Mill Road and drive 1 mile. Along the way, you will drive through the area of the May 7 battle, and will cross the old Richmond & Petersburg Railroad. After 1 mile, turn left on Jefferson Davis Highway (US 1) and drive 1.9 miles to the intersection with Harrowgate Road. Turn left at this intersection, then pull into the large parking lot for the Colonial Heights Baptist Church on your right. Drive to the interpretive signs and leave your vehicle.*

Although George Pickett now had 3,500 veteran infantrymen at Port Walthall Junction, he was still far from comfortable. The telegraph to Richmond was dead, cut during the battle at the junction, and reports of cavalry south of Petersburg (Augustus Kautz's Union horsemen, attacking the railroad) continued to float in. Pickett therefore ordered the troops at Port Walthall Junction south to Petersburg.

By 3 AM on May 8, all of the Confederates in the area were south of Swift Creek,

A view toward Swift Creek ravine from the Union position.

which runs only a few miles north of the city. The creek provided a very good natural defensive position, and the rebels formed their line just south of it, stretching from Brander's Bridge on the west, across the Richmond-Petersburg Turnpike, and terminating near Fort Clifton, a strong earthwork on the Appomattox River. One regiment was left on the north bank near the turnpike. By the end of the day, the continuously arriving reinforcements bolstered Pickett's force to 5,000 men and 18 pieces of artillery.

As for the Army of the James, Benjamin Butler was beginning to worry. Based on his discussions with General Grant, the Army of the Potomac was due to sweep south and join him at his position within days, but there was no sign of them. Rather than aggressively sweep into Petersburg or even Richmond, Butler sensed that the army was in danger and began strengthening its defenses. Other than time spent improving earthworks, May 8 would be a fairly light day for the Federals.

To his credit, Butler did not want to sit idly, and he ordered an advance back to the Richmond-Petersburg Turnpike for the next morning. He knew that he outnumbered the Confederates six to one, and he wanted to take advantage of these numbers while he still could. Baldy Smith would take five of his seven XVIII Corps brigades, hit the railroad at Port Walthall Junction, then turn south toward Petersburg. Quincy Gillmore would take the X Corps to the turnpike, then turn north and hit the railroad near Chester Station.

Smith was on the move at 5 AM May 9, moving cautiously and reaching the railroad near midmorning. Meeting little resistance, Smith turned south toward Petersburg, keeping one division on the railroad and the other on the turnpike. The XVIII Corps reached the area near Swift Creek around midafternoon, pausing briefly to assess the situation.

From your position here at the interpretive signs, you can easily see why the Confederates chose to place their defensive position here, although most of the battlefield is now covered with sprawl. As you face Jefferson Davis Highway (previously the Richmond-Petersburg Turnpike), look to your right at the intersection with the stoplights. This intersection was once the site of Arrowfield Church, a prominent landmark during the battle of Swift Creek (which is alternately known as the battle of Arrowfield Church). From where you stand, you can notice the sharp slope that begins near the intersection to your right and continues all the way down to the bridge over Swift Creek to your left. Any Federal attempt to approach Petersburg would mean advancing down this long slope, crossing the creek, and then climbing back up the other side.

〉 *Leave the parking lot for Colonial Heights Baptist Church and return to Jefferson Davis Highway. Turn left onto the highway and drive 0.2 mile. Just before you reach the bridge over Swift Creek, you will see the Swift Creek Mill Theatre on your left. Pull into the parking lot for the theater.*

Here, along the stretch of the old turnpike that you just drove on, is where most of the battle of Swift Creek was fought. Early on, Johnson Hagood, in charge of the Confederate defense, had pulled his troops from the north bank of the creek, knowing that they would be swallowed. However, near 4 PM, Hagood received orders from Richmond to reconnoiter northward toward the capital to determine the size of the Union force.

To Hagood—and every other Confederate who was present—it was a ridiculous order. The Confederates were well outnumbered, and any advance up the open northern bank of Swift Creek would be quickly repulsed. Forced to follow the order, Hagood chose the 11th South Carolina to cross Swift Creek and advance up the turnpike. The Federals held their fire until the Confederates were within 50 yards, then released a volley of musketry. Soon the 21st South Carolina was also on the north bank, doing what it could to rescue its companion regiment from the mess it had been thrown into.

Neither side came away from the engagement unscathed; the Union took 139 casualties to the Confederates' 138. All of these, though, were wasted, as the Federals did not attempt to cross the bridge and the rebels, of course, needed no more information on the size of their adversary than they already had.

While you are here, take a stroll down toward the creek and enjoy the view. Parts

Along Swift Creek at the site of Swift Creek Mill.

of the old millrace are still intact, and the waterfall created by the dam here, along with the natural scenery, is quite a nice surprise in the middle of the surrounding sprawl.

⟩ *From the theater, turn left onto Jefferson Davis Highway and drive 0.9 mile to Ellerslie Avenue. Turn left on Ellerslie Avenue and drive 1.2 miles to Conduit Road, then take another left and drive 1.6 miles. On your right, at Brockwell Lane, you will come to a school, along with signs for Berberich Park. Turn right on Brockwell Lane and drive to the end of the street, where you will find a parking area for Berberich Park and Fort Clifton.*

Although most of the action of May 9 was contained to the area north of Swift Creek, there was additional fighting here on the Appomattox River. Fort Clifton, a massive Confederate earthwork, is contained within the parkland in front of you. While Butler's troops advanced on the turnpike, the U.S. Navy's gunboats attempted to clear Confederate opposition from the Appomattox River. As they approached Fort Clifton, the fort's guns opened a heavy fire on the Federals, and before long, the Union boats headed downriver to safety.

Fort Clifton is well preserved but not well interpreted, except for a couple of scattered markers. Before you go exploring, please note that there are no trail maps, let alone noticeable trails through the fort itself. It is very much in its natural state, which has its advantages and disadvantages. Expect to see some significantly built earthworks as you venture in; just be prepared to wander for a bit, occasionally wondering if you have seen parts of the fort several times. Also expect to encounter a few somewhat rough spots in the trail, as well as swarms of mosquitoes. As long as you're prepared, though, Fort Clifton is worth exploring.

CHESTER STATION

❭ *From Berberich Park, return back down Brockwell Lane to Conduit Road, then turn left and drive 2.1 miles to Temple Avenue, where you will merge onto I-95 North. Drive 7.1 miles on I-95 North to exit 61B for West Hundred Road (VA 10). Drive 1.3 miles on West Hundred Road; you will see a large YMCA facility on your left with a Civil War Trails marker in front. Pull into the parking lot and park near the sign, then get out of your vehicle.*

Benjamin Butler, Baldy Smith, and Quincy Gillmore had now been together for nearly a full week, and their relationships, along with the command structure of the Army of the James, continued to deteriorate. A case in point occurred on the night of May 9, when Butler devised a plan to further threaten Petersburg, then presented the plan to Smith and Gillmore. Neither had any comment—until Butler left the room. Gillmore almost instantly proposed his own plan to Smith, who added more details, and the two generals sent the new plan directly to Butler. Around 9:30 PM, just as he had decided to cancel his own plan based on information received from Grant, Butler received the brand new plan from his subordinates. Exasperated, Butler sent a note to his two corps commanders, rejecting their plan and asking why they could not have presented it to him in his presence.

That night, learning that Grant was approaching, Butler decided to withdraw his troops from Swift Creek and head north toward the southern defenses of Richmond. Most of Gillmore's X Corps would move south to assist the XVIII Corps retire safely, while the 67th Ohio infantry remained near Chester Station at the junction of the Richmond Turnpike and the Chester Station/Bermuda Hundred Road. The rest of the brigade, Joshua Howell's, was a full mile away.

As the main body of Union troops was preparing to withdraw from Swift Creek, Robert Ransom, commanding the Confederate defenses at Richmond, ordered two brigades southward to reconnoiter the Union strength at Port Walthall Junction. It was not long before the Confederates approached the junction and ran into the Ohioans. Upon learning of their presence, Ransom ordered his men to stop while he gathered reinforcements.

VIEWING THE BERMUDA HUNDRED CAMPAIGN

Multimedia applications have made understanding just about everything a little bit simpler, and the Civil War is no different. Since some of the battles of the Bermuda Hundred campaign are difficult to picture through the sprawl, you may want to consider watching simulations of the battles online before you take your tour. The Chesterfield Historical Society has created animated maps of the movements of the campaign as well as most of the major battles. Viewing these maps, superimposed over features that you will recognize from today's landscape, may help you envision what really happened where that old gas station is now. Go to http://chesterfieldhistory.com to watch the very short animations of the battles, and your visit will be much improved.

After sending news of its distress, the 67th Ohio was joined by two other regiments, the 169th New York and the 13th Indiana. Although they were still outnumbered, the Federals would now at least have a chance to stall the Confederates until more help arrived.

Use the Civil War Trails sign at the location to help you orient yourself, which can be difficult within this busy, traffic-heavy area. As you face the road (Bermuda Hundred Road), the junction with the Richmond Turnpike (now Jefferson Davis Highway) is the major intersection to your far right. The two Confederate brigades would approach the junction by two routes: the road in front of you, from your left to your right, and southward down the Jefferson Davis Highway.

The three Union regiments formed a line crossing both roadways to protect the junction. To the far right of the Union line was the 169th New York, along with two cannons placed directly on the turnpike. Between the turnpike and the Bermuda Hundred Road (in the area to your front right, across the road) was the 67th Ohio. Near your location, stretching across the Bermuda Hundred Road, was the 13th Indiana.

Leave your location at the sign and start walking down the sidewalk to your right. In a short distance, you will come to a monument to the battle. Behind this monument, and still standing, is the Winfree farmhouse. The 13th Indiana set its two guns in the yard of the house.

Turn around to face the road again, and then look to your left. The Confederates approached on the Bermuda Hundred Road from this direction, as well as from the turnpike, at approximately 11 AM. While the Federals repulsed several assaults, the line was beginning to break when more reinforcements arrived from the south. Now receiving serious resistance, Ransom decided to withdraw from the fight. Also contributing to the end of the fight was the breakout of a wildfire, sparked by the hot firefight and the extremely dry conditions. A flag of truce was produced while both sides attempted to rescue the wounded from the flames. At 4:20 PM, Gillmore ordered his units to retire to their lines at Ware Bottom Church, while Ransom's Confederates made their way back to Drewry's Bluff.

WOOLDRIDGE HILL

⟩ *Turn left out of the YMCA parking lot onto West Hundred Road and drive 1.2 miles to Chester Road. Turn right on Chester Road and drive 1.8 miles to Centralia Road (VA 145 West), then turn left. Drive 0.4 mile to Hopkins Road, then turn right and drive another 0.2 mile. There will be a small cemetery on your left; pull into the gravel area here.*

On May 10, before the action at Chester Station had opened, P. G. T. Beauregard finally arrived in Petersburg to take personal command. Reorganizing the forces he now had in the department, Beauregard was able to relieve George Pickett of the burden of command at Petersburg. Having done as much as anyone could under the circumstances, Pickett transferred his command and soon collapsed, finally giving in to the strain of the last few days.

That night, Braxton Bragg asked Beauregard to bring his forces north. A new threat to Richmond was appearing from the north—a massive raid by Philip Sheridan's cavalry, headed straight for the heart of the capital. The citizens of Richmond were in a near panic, and Bragg felt it more important that Beauregard's troops join those of Robert Ransom at Drewry's Bluff. Despite his please that he should deal with the Federals in front of him, Beauregard replied that his men would march by the next evening, then proceeded to gather still more men from other areas of his department.

May 11 found the Union soldiers again improving their earthworks, further fortifying their position so that their line could be held by fewer soldiers. Doing this, of course, left both the Richmond & Petersburg Railroad and Turnpike open to the Confederates. As the Federals worked with spade and shovel, large columns of Confederates marched north only 2 to 3 miles to the west, unopposed.

That night, with the rebels still marching north in a heavy thunderstorm, Benjamin Butler laid out his plans for the next day. The Army of the James would again be moving. Three divisions—two from Smith's XVIII Corps and one from Gillmore's X Corps—would move north on the Richmond Turnpike, and would continue moving north until they could force the rebels into their defenses. Smith's remaining division would establish a base on the Appomattox to keep any Confederates in that area aware that there was still a Union presence there. Gillmore's two remaining divisions would perform double duty as the army's rear guard and reserve force, keeping an eye on Petersburg. Finally, Augustus Kautz would launch another cavalry raid far in the Confederate rear to do what damage he could.

Butler's army moved at 4 AM on May 12, Butler riding at the front with Smith. The lead division, Godfrey Weitzel's, reached the turnpike at 9 AM and headed north. Smith formed a line a mile and a half in length to move up the turnpike, ready to meet any resistance encountered. Moving through heavy forest, the line was slowed by the terrain and Confederate skirmishers harassing the front of the Union column.

After a mile's march, near Proctor's Creek, the Federals encountered a line of Confederates. Not knowing the enemy's strength, Smith asked Butler to order reinforcements from Gillmore. Butler did so, but they would not arrive until late in the day. With the rain still pouring, the Federals stopped where they were.

The next morning, May 13, Butler sent Smith ahead through the clearing in front of him, while Gillmore moved west in an attempt to outflank the Confederate right. Smith crawled forward at a snail's pace, only to find that the Confederates had long since vanished, pulling back overnight. Smith resumed the advance, but soon reached another clearing with another Confederate line behind it. Again, Smith told Butler that he couldn't take the position without more information, and again, Butler deferred to his judgment.

Gillmore, meanwhile, used a roundabout route through Chesterfield Court House, eventually coming to a strong position near a branch of Proctor's Creek known as Wooldridge Hill. It was the anchor of the Confederate right, and the rebels, facing east, had no idea that a large Union force was approaching them from the rear. Gillmore quietly had his artillery unlimber while he sent the 3rd New Hampshire up the western face of the hill. Upon reaching the crest, the New Hampshire men completely surprised the Confederates. Although they eventually realized that they were only facing one regiment and launched a vicious counterattack, the Confederates, who quickly abandoned their works, enabling Gillmore's men to occupy the entrenchments.

Some of the original entrenchments from the Confederate defenses at Wooldridge Hill still exist, but they are all on private property. As you face the roadway, which runs north–south, you are standing roughly in the middle of the Confederate line, on the eastern side of the small ridge known as Wooldridge Hill. The line ran along where the present road is, facing east, as you are now, toward the Richmond & Petersburg Railroad, only a short distance away. The 3rd New Hampshire would have come from your right rear, with other Federal units eventually coming up from your rear also.

Both Gillmore and Smith would advance again the next day, May 14, and would eventually reunite north of the earthworks that began here at Wooldridge Hill and stretched to the east. Now forming a line 2 miles wide, the Federals slowly advanced until they came upon another fortified Confederate position. As the rain continued, the Union infantry made several advances, but it was soon realized that the troops were not prepared for a general assault. The Federals dug in, waiting for the next fight.

DREWRY'S BLUFF

⟩ *Turn left out of the cemetery back onto Hopkins Road and follow it around the curve for 0.4 mile, staying with it as it becomes Old Lane. Turn left on Chester Road and follow it for 2.5 miles; this road will also change names as you go—Perrymont Road, then Chester Road again, and finally Bellwood Road. When you reach Fort Darling Road, turn left and drive 0.4 mile to the entrance to the Drewry's Bluff Unit of Richmond National Battlefield Park. Turn right and drive to the parking area.*

The line taken by the Federals, first at Wooldridge Hill and then along the rest of its length, was only the outer line of the Confederate defensive works south of Richmond. Falling back slowly in the face of the Federal advance, the Confederates eventually retired to their main defensive line, the northern anchor of which was Fort Darling, a heavy fortification along the James River at a site known as Drewry's Bluff. From Fort Darling, the line made its way south to another heavy fortification, Fort Stevens, then turned to the west. The line covered both the railroad and the turnpike and was exceedingly strong. Further, there were now, perhaps, enough Confederates present to actually hold it.

At 3 AM on May 14, Beauregard found his way to Fort Darling, the Confederate command center, after making a wide circle around Butler's army. Later in the day, Beauregard would meet with Ransom, whose division was here, as well as President Jefferson Davis, who rode down from Richmond to see the situation himself. Although anxiety in Richmond over the Federal cavalry raid had eased, the immediate situation was still delicate, as Robert E. Lee and Ulysses S. Grant had been fighting ceaselessly since May 5 at the Wilderness and Spotsylvania.

P. G. T. Beauregard, while certainly a talented general, had been taken to task in the past for his sometimes rather outlandish battle plans. It would be the same here at Drewry's Bluff, at least in the eyes of President Davis. Beauregard had earlier called Chase Whiting's force from Wilmington, North Carolina, north to occupy Petersburg. Beauregard now wished to trap the Federals between the Confederates to the north and Whiting, coming up from the south. Davis, however, was not impressed. Although he wanted to attack the Union force, his orders were to wait until Whiting made his way around Butler's army to Drewry's Bluff, thereby increasing Beauregard's chances of success. Whiting couldn't be at Drewry's Bluff any sooner than May 18, so Beauregard attempted to find a way of getting him there sooner—which just happened to involve hitting the Federals in the rear, which is exactly what he wanted to do in the first place.

The result of Beauregard's scheming was a long series of conflicting and confusing orders to Whiting on May 15. Whiting sat nervously in Petersburg trying to figure out what to do and repeatedly asking for clarification. Meanwhile, Beauregard, now in command, positioned Ransom's and Hoke's divisions into a line facing the Federals to the south, with Fort Stevens at the center. Although there was some skirmishing between the two lines, for the most part, the action on May 15 was limited to both sides staking their positions and the Federals attempting to fill a large gap between their right flank and the James River.

That evening, Beauregard gathered his commanders to finalize the next day's plans. They would not wait for Whiting. They would attack now, with Whiting trapping the Federals where they were and hopefully crushing the Army of the James.

A 1-mile trail will take you to and from Fort Darling, which sits very well preserved atop Drewry's Bluff. While the unit receives more visitors interested in the 1862 battle of Drewry's Bluff, in which a naval battery repulsed several ironclad warships making their way upriver toward Richmond, the fort itself is quite impressive. Although very little combat occurred around the fort during the May 16 battle, this was the primary headquarters for the Confederate high command during the battle. The area usually has few visitors, so enjoy the solitude and the great view of the James River from high atop the bluff.

FORT STEVENS/HALF-WAY HOUSE

⟩ *From the Drewry's Bluff Unit, turn left onto Fort Darling Road and drive 0.4 mile to Bellwood Road. Turn right onto Bellwood Road and drive 0.5 mile, then left onto Jefferson Davis Highway (US 1). Drive 0.4 mile on Jefferson Davis Highway to Norcliff Road, then drive 0.2 mile to the intersection with Pams Avenue. Pull into the parking area for Fort Stevens Park.*

Overnight, a heavy fog rolled onto the field between the lines. It was perfect timing for the Confederates. Beginning at 2 AM, Robert Ransom's division moved into two lines to the east of Fort Stevens, occupying the ground in front of the Federal right. Hoke's division occupied Fort Stevens and the works extending to the west. At 4:45 AM, with all the pieces in place, the Confederates quietly began moving south through the fog toward the Union line. The plan was for Ransom's division to surprise and break the seemingly vulnerable Union right, while the left would be held in place by Hoke's division.

In front of the Union right—the side occupied by Smith's XVIII Corps—was approximately 650 yards of open ground, gradually sloping up toward the Union position. Although virtually impossible to see, Union pickets detected Ransom's advance and quickly fell back into the main line. When the pickets had cleared out of the way,

The preserved earthworks at Fort Stevens Park.

Smith's men rose and unleashed a volley into the fog, with nothing to guide their aim but slight sounds.

The quiet soon transformed into a fury. Confederate artillery came into play almost as soon as the battle was joined. They had been able to get close to the Union line before they were fired upon, but with the thick fog, as well as telegraph wire stretched across the field to trip and slow an advance, the rebel formations were soon broken. The Federals poured lead blindly into the fog, firing as fast as they could.

In the confusion, Ransom's second line found the Federal right flank. This flank had been protected, but Charles Heckman's brigade, who had held the position, vacated the spot prematurely when it was thought the right was exposed. Heckman's movement not only really exposed the Union right flank but also opened the Old Stage Road, which provided the Confederates with easy access to the Union rear—if they could find it in the fog. (Heckman would soon be taken prisoner, himself lost in the fog.) The rebels wheeled right and began rolling up the Union line, advancing through four regiments until finally stopped by the 98th New York, who turned to the east and faced the Confederates directly.

By this time, just before 6 AM, the Confederate advance had stalled, with Ransom's units hopelessly disorganized by the fog and out of ammunition. The lull, however, was short, as the men of Hoke's division began their advance on the Union center. Charles Hagood's brigade, occupying Fort Stevens where you now stand, and Bushrod

Johnson's brigade to the west moved forward, hoping to prevent Union reinforcements from moving to their right.

Hoke's entire line was thin, as it had the protection of earthworks, which Ransom's attackers did not. This could have boded very well for the Federals, who had actually been ordered to attack. Gillmore's X corps had been set for a 6 AM assault, but before it could get under way, he reported that his men were under attack. There were Confederate skirmishers to their front, but it was hardly the overwhelming force that Gillmore imagined. Still, by 7 AM, he reported that he had been assaulted three times, and asked Butler whether he should continue with the planned attack. Butler left the decision up to Gillmore, who chose to stay put. Had he attacked, it is likely that he would have met some success, or at least been able to relieve the pressure on the Federal right.

As it actually happened, though, Hagood's and Johnson's brigades, on each side of the turnpike, were steadily pounding away at William Brooks's division of the XVIII Corps. Brooks's men were holding their, ground, though, just to the south of Fort Stevens. To their right, though, John Turner's X Corps division was having a hard time preventing a gap from forming between their two divisions. Not long before the fog lifted at 7:45 AM, Baldy Smith, who was worried about his right and the army's escape route, ordered Brooks to withdraw.

The men of Brooks's division were not pleased with giving up ground that they were holding well, but they fell back as ordered. At the same time, Turner's right flank—now greatly exposed—began to come under heavy pressure. Smith soon saw the mistake and tried to countermand his orders, but it was too late. Turner's division, followed by Alfred Terry's to his left, were eventually overwhelmed and overrun, forced to withdraw from their now-exposed positions. By 9:30 AM, Gillmore reported that his entire line was falling back. The entire Federal line, though it had fought well, was moving rearward.

Fort Stevens Park is a hidden gem, a set of well-preserved earthworks in the middle of a quiet neighborhood that has only infrequent visitors. Hagood's men filled this fort during the Confederate attack, and eventually advanced down the turnpike when Brooks's division began to withdraw. There is some interpretation here, but the real prize of the park is the fort, still in great shape after all these years.

> *From the park, head back west on Norcliff Avenue 0.2 mile to Jefferson Davis Highway, then turn left and drive 1.3 miles. At the intersection with Wonderview Drive, pull into the parking lot for the Half-Way House.*

This is the Half-Way House, so named because it sits approximately halfway between Richmond and Petersburg on the Richmond Turnpike. This building served as Benjamin Butler's and Baldy Smith's headquarters during the Second Battle of Drewry's Bluff, and would also become the rally point for the Union army after the battle.

The Half-Way House, Butler's headquarters during the battle at Fort Stevens.

By 2 PM, most of the Federals had made their way south to the Half-Way House, with only a few units unaccounted for. At 2:15 PM, Butler ordered an advance to attempt to recover some of the wounded that had been left behind, but his men soon ran into resistance.

With the day lost, Butler decided that the only appropriate course of action was to withdraw behind his entrenchments at Bermuda Hundred. After all, the Army of the Potomac, which should have made its way south by now, would need a solid base of operations when it arrived. It was also possible that the Confederate force under Beauregard could join Robert E. Lee's Army of Northern Virginia and seek to annihilate Butler's army. He ordered an immediate movement back to Bermuda Hundred, and his men were back in the trenches by 9 PM.

Beauregard, who had been anxiously awaiting word from Chase Whiting, did not pursue the Federals, fearful that he might drive them into the works. He still wanted to catch them between the two Confederate forces. However, it was not to be. Whiting, who had met some resistance at Port Walthall Junction, settled into an artillery duel with the small Union force. Insistent that the defense of Petersburg was his first priority, and that he never heard the sound of battle to the north, Whiting decided to withdraw his forces south of Swift Creek, despite repeated messages from Beauregard to join him. It is still unclear whether Whiting, who was known to have issues with the bottle, may have been intoxicated, or whether he was simply suffering from exhaustion, having borne the same heavy load that George Pickett had before him. Regardless, it resulted in a lost opportunity for the Confederates.

There is no doubt, however, that the Confederates were the victors. The Federals suffered approximately 3,000 casualties, almost half captured, and also lost five pieces of artillery in the fight. To boot, they also lost possession of the Richmond-Petersburg corridor. The Confederates had taken 1,000 casualties, and although they had let an opportunity slip through their fingers, they could only be pleased with the result.

The Half-Way House is now a well-established restaurant, still sitting on the old turnpike and serving passersby much as it did in the old days. If you can, try to arrange your day to have lunch or dinner here; you will have to plan carefully, however, as the restaurant does close between the two meals and does have somewhat irregular hours.

WARE BOTTOM CHURCH AND THE HOWLETT LINE

Battery Dantzler

⟩ *Turn left onto Jefferson Davis Highway (US 1) and drive 2.2 miles to West Hundred Road (VA 10 East). Turn left on West Hundred Road and drive 1.2 miles, then turn left onto Bermuda Triangle Road. Drive 0.4 mile, then follow the road around to the left onto Battery Dantzler Road. Pull into the parking area for Battery Dantzler Park just after the turn.*

The next few days at Bermuda Hundred would be defined mostly by digging. May 17, 18, and 19 saw the Federals, now safely behind their entrenched line, strengthening their already formidable works, while the Confederates formed matching works across from them. Although skirmishing did occur between the lines, for the most part, the Union med stayed where they were.

Ben Butler and P. G. T. Beauregard did both face one common adversary. Now that Beauregard had Butler under control, it was thought that he could easily spare troops to be sent to Lee's Army of Northern Virginia. Beauregard's force—reaching a final total of 19,000 infantry, 1,000 cavalry, and four battalions of artillery—was a far cry from what it had been only two weeks earlier. Now, it would be plucked away from him, piece by piece.

While the source of Beauregard's trouble was success, Butler's was inaction. Over the course of several days, news of Butler's repulse at Drewry's Bluff was coupled with Franz Sigel's defeat at New Market in the Shenandoah Valley and Nathaniel Banks's disaster along the Red River in Louisiana. Ulysses S. Grant, whose own campaign had been moving more slowly than expected, considered that perhaps if he could bring Butler's idle troops north, they could help him hammer Lee into submission more quickly.

On May 18, the Confederates began constructing a large battery overlooking the

James River, eventually mounting eight pieces of heavy artillery in the works. Their position was strong enough to deter the Union Navy from advancing any farther up-river than they already had. The battery was originally known as the Howlett House Battery, named for a large house that stood near it. It was soon renamed Battery Dantzler in honor of a fallen Confederate. The Howlett name, however, stuck, and the Confederate earthworks that stretched from this point all the way south to the Appomattox River would come to be known as the Howlett Line.

Battery Dantzler is still in fairly good shape, and a short walking trail from the parking area will take you right to the overlook of the James River. Several interpretive signs will guide you through the fortification and its importance, as well as that of the Howlett Line. Be aware that although the small park contains several short trails, there are some that seem to make their way down to the riverbank, a rather steep climb— or fall. Therefore, use caution if you venture from the well-traveled path.

Parker's Battery

> Turn right out of the Battery Dantzler parking area and drive 0.2 mile to Old Stage Road. Turn left here and drive 0.6 mile to Ware Bottom Spring Road, then turn left. Pull into the parking area for the Parker's Battery Unit of Richmond National Battlefield Park.

With his troop numbers dwindling and knowing that the trend would continue, Beauregard knew that he would need to shorten the entrenchments in front of the

BOTTLED UP AT BERMUDA HUNDRED

Shortly after the Army of the James was driven back into its works at Bermuda Hundred, Ulysses S. Grant asked Quartermaster General Montgomery Meigs and Chief Engineer John Barnard to visit the army and report on the situation. Discussing their final report with Barnard shortly afterward, Grant asked why Butler could not venture west and cut the Richmond & Petersburg Railroad. Pulling out a pencil, Barnard sketched Bermuda Hundred, along with the Howlett Line, and remarked that the peninsula was similar to a bottle, and that the Confederates had effectively corked it with their defensive position. Grant repeated the analogy in his final report on the campaign, saying that the Army of the James was "as if it had been in a bottle strongly corked." Grant later regretted having made the comment, but the phrase has stuck with historians ever since. To this day, any history of the campaign, large or small, is virtually guaranteed to lead to the comment that Benjamin Butler's army had been "bottled up" at Bermuda Hundred.

A well-preserved portion of the Confederate fortifications exists at Howlett Line Park.

Federals so that his reduced force would be enough to man the works. On the morning of May 20, Beauregard sent two divisions against the northern part of the Union line around Ware Bottom Church, which was still occupied by Gillmore's X Corps. The Confederates were able to push the Union pickets out of their advanced line near the church. Gillmore launched a successful counterattack, regaining the line, and the fight over the smaller works went on throughout the day. This battle, known as Ware Bottom Church, was essentially a draw, with the Confederates losing 800 men to the Union's 700. However, the rebels were able to occupy and solidify the former Union picket line overnight.

This line—which would become the Howlett Line—was exactly what Beauregard needed. The works were already strong; they only needed to be reversed to face east, and the Confederates began doing this immediately. Over the next few days, the line became stronger and stronger until it was virtually impregnable. Stretching only 3 miles between the two rivers that formed the Bermuda Hundred Peninsula, it essentially sealed Butler behind his earthworks.

Parker's Battery saw action during the battle of Ware Bottom Church, which was located only a short distance east. The Confederates would not solidify their position here until after the battle, and William Parker's veteran "Boy Company" would not take its place here on the line until July. However, this is an excellent place to see the strength of the Howlett Line, extremely well preserved and well interpreted. A very short trail, approximately a quarter of a mile long, will take you through the battery and part of the line on either side, telling the stories of both the Howlett Line and Parker's Battery.

Ware Bottom Church Battlefield Park

> *Turn right out of the parking area onto Ware Bottom Spring Road, drive 0.1 mile, and then turn right on Ramblewood Drive. Drive 0.6 miles to Old Bermuda Hundred Road, then turn right and drive 0.1 mile. Ware Bottom Church Battlefield Park will be on your right; carefully pull in and park, being mindful of the traffic.*

Chesterfield County has wholly embraced the critical Bermuda Hundred campaign as all its own, and has done an exceptional job of interpreting and preserving what's left of that campaign. This site, which covers a good portion of the area between the lines during the battle of May 20, promises to be the crown jewel in the county's collection. Although the site is not yet interpreted, it contains the longest unbroken sections of the Howlett Line still in existence. The land was only acquired in 2003, and eventually a parking area and interpretive trails will be added to the site. While it may not be fully accessible as of this writing, when it is, it promises to be something great.

Howlett Line Park

> *When possible, turn around so that you are now driving east on Old Bermuda Hundred Road. Just east of the sign for Ware Bottom Church Battlefield Park is Lawing Drive. Turn right on Lawing Drive and drive 0.5 mile to Woods Edge Road (SR 620). Turn Left on Woods Edge Road for 0.2 mile, then turn right onto Howlett Line Drive. You will drive for 0.3 mile on Howlett Line Drive; as you make your way, notice the massive Howlett Line appearing on the right side of the road. You will eventually come to Howlett Line Park on your right. Carefully pull over and climb the short stairway to the park.*

This park is a great example of what makes Chesterfield County's historic sites so special. Howlett Line Park is simply a redoubt along the original line, and like other parks, contains well-preserved earthworks and interpretive signs. What sets this park apart from the rest is the interpretation. It's beautifully simple. While you will find a detailed synopsis regarding the history of this portion of the line, you will also find several signs spread around the works explaining the most basic facts about earthworks. It's a fair criticism that many historic sites like this one lose the forest for the trees, throwing names and dates at visitors while assuming they know all about traverses, embrasures, and powder magazines. That mistake isn't made at this or any of the other related sites in Chesterfield County. There are several other earthworks and fortifications within the county's park system, and they can be found on the Chesterfield Heritage Alliance's website. If you have some extra time, be sure to visit these other sites—no matter your level of knowledge, you're bound to pick something up.

With the completion of the Howlett Line, the Union Army of the James was essentially neutralized. The Confederate works were simply too strong. The Federal works eventually became equally strong. Before long, Grant would indeed extract troops from Butler's command, and it would not be until the Army of the Potomac reached the outskirts of Richmond that the Army of the James was freed up enough that it could make the first Union assault on Petersburg on June 9.

It is indeed true that Benjamin Butler did not accomplish what he or Grant had hoped—the capture of Richmond. However, Butler had been able to keep parts of the Confederate army away from Robert E. Lee for a short period, and during the span of time that the campaign covered, while Grant and Lee tangled in the Wilderness, at Spotsylvania, and at the North Anna River, it made a noticeable difference. He had also established a solid base of operations near Richmond and Petersburg, which would become very useful to Grant's army when it arrived.

In terms of days, that arrival would not be long in coming. To the soldiers of the Army of the Potomac and the Army of Northern Virginia, however, it would be an eternity. On May 4, the same day that Butler's men boarded their transports at Yorktown, Grant led his Union army across the Rapidan River. The next day would see the first shots of some of the bloodiest and most intense fighting in history, and it would not stop until the armies had reached Richmond.

OPTIONAL STOP: FORT POCAHONTAS

> NOTE: To reach Fort Pocahontas, the site of the battle of Wilson's Wharf, you will need to drive to Sherwood Forest Plantation, the former residence of President John Tyler. The Tyler family still owns the land surrounding the plantation, and although the fort is open to the public from time to time for special events and to groups by appointment, it is not regularly accessible.

From Howlett Line Park, turn around and drive north 0.3 mile on Howlett Line Drive to Woods Edge Road (SR 620) and turn right, then drive another 0.3 mile to Ramblewood Drive. Turn right on Ramblewood Drive and drive 0.2 mile to Golf Course Road, turning left and driving another 0.2 mile to Old Bermuda Hundred Road. Turn right on Old Bermuda Hundred Road and drive 0.6 mile to West Hundred Road (VA 10 East). Turn right on VA 10 and drive 9.2 miles. At Jordan Point Road (VA 106/VA 156), turn left and drive 4 miles, crossing over the James River.

Turn right at John Tyler Memorial Highway (VA 5) and drive 12.8 miles. You will see signs for Sherwood Forest Plantation on your way. Once you reach the area, pull into the plantation site.

Before landing his main force at Bermuda Hundred, Benjamin Butler established several small garrisons along the James River to aid communications with Fort Monroe. One of these was at Wilson's Wharf on the north bank of the James. The troops there were from Edward Wild's brigade of United States Colored Troops—black soldiers. Wild was an abolitionist who strongly believed in the fighting ability of black soldiers. After he lost his left arm at the battle of South Mountain, Wild recruited several regiments of black soldiers while he recovered at his home in Massachusetts.

Approximately 1,100 strong, Wild's men quickly established a strong fortification at Wilson's Wharf, calling it Fort Pocahontas. Before long, rumors spread that these black soldiers were committing unspeakable (and unrealistic) atrocities among the citizens of the area. Matters were not helped when Wild, who was already actively freeing and recruiting slaves in the area, had a local planter with a reputation of cruelty flogged by his men, aided by a few of the man's former slaves.

Unable to ignore the public outcry, President Jefferson Davis felt that he needed to eliminate the garrison, even though it had virtually zero military value. On May 23, Davis's military adviser, Braxton Bragg, ordered Fitzhugh Lee to take 2,500 cavalrymen and wipe out the Union force. Lee's horsemen moved that afternoon and marched overnight, reaching Wilson's Wharf around 11 AM on May 24.

Lee had been told he would meet little resistance, but it was obvious, after viewing the fort, that he had been misinformed. It was a very strong position, and although the Federals were outnumbered, they could easily defend the fortification against Lee's cavalry. In addition, a Union gunboat, the USS *Dawn,* was anchored alongside the fort, able to add the weight of its heavy artillery to any defense.

Lee split his army into two wings. One remained near the west side of the fort to act as a diversion, while a larger body of dismounted horsemen moved into a wooded ravine east of the fort. After about an hour of skirmishing, Lee produced a flag of truce and asked for the fort's surrender. Lee's terms were tactfully vague, but they were clear enough. Black soldiers who surrendered would be treated as though they were prisoners of war—meaning that they would be returned to their former slave owners. The fate of white officers commanding the black soldiers went unstated, but Wild knew that they could be charged with inciting a slave insurrection. He immediately refused the surrender.

While Wild's decision might seem like an easy one, it was not. On April 12, barely a month before, a very similar situation had taken place at Fort Pillow, along the Mississippi River in Tennessee. After the commander there refused surrender, the Confederates, under famed cavalryman Nathan Bedford Forrest, overran the fort. Numerous reports soon emerged that many of the black soldiers had been killed while trying to surrender. The action was soon known as the Fort Pillow Massacre, and it was fresh in the mind of every man within the earthen walls of Fort Pocahontas.

Lee was also faced with a difficult decision. His aides, who had delivered the terms of surrender to Wild, confirmed what he already knew—that the position was too strong to be taken. However, he had been sent to Fort Pocahontas on political grounds, and to withdraw his force without serious engagement in the face of a garrison of black soldiers would not be acceptable. Lee felt he had no choice but to attack.

When the fighting resumed, the Confederates east of the fort charged across open ground toward the fort. Although the combination of the musketry from the fort and the artillery from the *Dawn* took a terrible toll, the Confederates made it to the walls of the fort and jumped into the ditch at the base of the walls. There they became pinned down, taking canister fire from the artillery in the fort. Before long the rebels were forced to withdraw, taking more casualties during the retreat than during the assault.

When the dust had settled, the Confederates had lost approximately 200 men, while the Federals had taken 46 casualties, only six of them killed. (A few of the Union troops were taken prisoner; several were shot along the way back to Richmond, while one was returned to bondage.) Both Lee and the Southern press downplayed the defeat, inflating the number of soldiers at the fort, saying that white troops were present, and even that several other Union gunboats were in the river. When all was said and done, however, the battle at Fort Pocahontas marked the first episode of sustained combat between black Union troops and the Army of Northern Virginia, and the result was a decisive victory for the Federals.

Fort Pocahontas is still in very good shape today. The land is privately owned, though, and opportunities to see it are unfortunately limited. The fort sits on the former estate of President John Tyler, and while his home, Sherwood Forest, is regularly open for tours, the grounds where the fort sits are not. However, the fort is open annually on the anniversary weekend of the battle for a major reenactment, and occasionally for other special events. Tours of the fort can also be arranged for groups of ten or more. Hopefully, in time, the public will have better access to this historic ground. For now, though, you will have to time your visit carefully.

SEDGWICK

ERECTED TO COMMEMO...
THIS SPOT WHERE
MAJ. GEN. JOHN SEDGWICK ...
COMMANDING SIXTH ARMY ...
WAS KILLED IN ACTION ON THE ...
OF THE 9TH OF MAY 186...

6TH. ARMY CORPS

The Overland Campaign, Part I: The Wilderness and Spotsylvania

As COMMANDER OF ALL UNION ARMIES in the field, it would have been more than acceptable, and probably expected, that Lieutenant General Ulysses S. Grant stay in the capital at Washington, D.C. After all, the Civil War was a big war, and controlling all of the pieces on the chessboard effectively would require knowledge of all Union military operations. However, for a man in a position of power, trying to do anything in Washington, D.C., was difficult. The incessant political scheming and backbiting, interference from the Congress, and a constant stream of favor-seeking visitors would be a constant distraction from the task of winning the war.

Grant also realized that overseeing every minute detail of the war would be impossible. So when he created his grand strategy for winning the war, he assigned the moving parts of his plan to subordinates—Nathaniel Banks in the deep South, Franz Sigel in the Shenandoah Valley, and Benjamin Butler south of the James River. Responsibility for the major Union effort in the west, the Atlanta campaign, had to be given to someone that Grant trusted completely, and he had that person in William Tecumseh Sherman. That left what was arguably the most critical part of the plan, the destruction of Robert E. Lee's Army of Northern Virginia. Although George Meade

---

A large monument marks the spot where Union VI Corps commander "Uncle" John Sedgwick was killed at Spotsylvania.

had already commanded the Union Army of the Potomac longer than any of his many predecessors, Grant was unsure that he was up to the task. At the same time, no other general had demonstrated that he could take on Lee and win.

Given these two major dilemmas, Grant killed two birds with one stone. He would not disrupt the command structure of the Army of the Potomac; George Meade would remain its commander. However, it was obvious that leaving Meade to his own devices would not do, particularly as far as the Lincoln administration was concerned. So General Grant would not take his office in Washington. His office would move with the Army of the Potomac, where he could carefully observe events and make command decisions on the spot rather than from behind a desk, surrounded by the political theater of the capital. Meade would still have free reign to command the army itself as he saw fit, with Grant managing the rest of the war and merely serving in an advisory capacity.

Well, that was the plan. Grant soon came to two stark realizations. The first was that the modus operandi of the Army of the Potomac, and of its commanders, was extreme caution, very unlike the hard-charging fighting that Grant had experienced in the west. The second was that he had severely underestimated his new adversary. Although he admonished his subordinates for their reverence and awe of Lee's methods, before long, Grant soon gained a healthy respect for the Confederate general's ability to command an army.

The first three weeks of what would be called Grant's Overland campaign in May 1864 would present hard lessons for both armies, as well as the citizens who watched from afar. The fighting would be incessant. The amount of blood spilled would be nearly beyond comprehension. The casualty lists would be appalling. And the two great generals who commanded these armies would come to realize that this would now be the standard. There would be no rest until the matter was settled, one way or the other. As Grant stated in a message to Lincoln shortly after the bloodbath at the Wilderness, there would be no turning back.

BEFORE YOU GO

»PLANNING YOUR TRIP

Between the two battlefields at the Wilderness and Spotsylvania Court House, there is a lot to see, particularly within the boundaries of Fredericksburg & Spotsylvania National Military Park. Miles of trails await, as well as several podcasts, videos, and guided tours. Add the fact that two other major battlefields of the Civil War— Fredericksburg and Chancellorsville—are in the same area, and you may soon find yourself having to make some choices. No matter what your plans are, make sure to give yourself enough time to see the battlefields properly.

The battlefield at Spotsylvania can be a confusing one, particularly for a first-time visitor. Not only did the locations of the battles cover a large area, but the two armies slugged it out here for almost two weeks. As you tour the battlefield, keep a map (or two or three) with you so that you can track the action. And don't be afraid to ask for help. Although the Spotsylvania Unit does not have regular staffing, rangers are at the interpretive shelter from time to time, and of course can always be found at the Chancellorsville or Fredericksburg visitor centers.

THE OVERLAND CAMPAIGN, PART I

Number of sites: 12

Total miles: 73

Estimated time: 3–4 days

» RECOMMENDATIONS

Fredericksburg is the logical place to stay for this tour, as it is really the only significant city near the battlefields. Having said that, the area covered by the Wilderness and Spotsylvania battlefields is large, so if you happen to run across a bed & breakfast more centrally located to the area, go for it, although you may have to travel a bit for a meal.

Also, don't forget that I-95 has several exits south of Fredericksburg that could put you in a very good location for your tour, particularly when it comes to viewing Spotsylvania Court House or as you move south to the North Anna River with the armies. Just as in Fredericksburg, you will find an abundant variety of hotels and restaurants.

IN DEPTH

Noah Andre Trudeau—*Bloody Roads South: The Wilderness to Cold Harbor, May–June 1864*

Earl J. Hess—*Trench Warfare Under Grant and Lee: Field Fortifications in the Overland Campaign*

Gordon C. Rhea—*The Battle of the Wilderness, May 5–6, 1864; The Battles for Spotsylvania Court House and the Road to Yellow Tavern, May 7–12, 1864*

"Trudeau's narrative of the overall campaign is superb, as are Rhea's studies of the specific battles. Hess goes into great detail as to how the campaign was fought."

—*Tom Trescott, Abraham Lincoln Book Shop, Chicago*

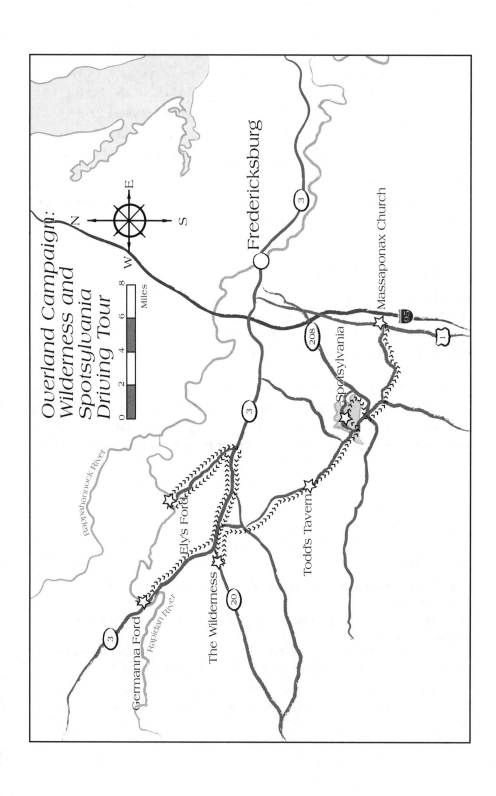

Overland Campaign:
Wilderness and
Spotsylvania
Driving Tour

Miles

0   2   4   6   8

N
W   E
S

Rappahannock River

Rapidan River

Germanna Ford

Ely's Ford

The Wilderness

Todd's Tavern

3

20

3

208

Fredericksburg

3

Spotsylvania

Massaponax Church

95

1

THE CAMPAIGN TOUR

GERMANNA FORD

❭ *Begin your tour at the Germanna visitor center, 2062 Germanna Highway, Locust Grove, Virginia. The visitor center is on the south side of the highway next to the campus of Germanna Community College. The river running just to the west is the Rapidan River.*

Both the Union Army of the Potomac and the Confederate Army of Northern Virginia had been in their winter camps since they faced off at Mine Run in November. Although there had been limited action during the lull, with the exception of the fight at Morton's Ford on the Rapidan in February, both armies had for the most part stayed put. But while the soldiers settled into the boring routines of winter camp, the two commanders of these mighty hosts were quite busy preparing for the spring campaign.

While the decisions to be made were somewhat limited, Robert E. Lee had plenty to worry about, and many of those worries had nothing to do with the Federals. The Confederate States of America, which had several times resorted to conscription to bring men to the army, expanded the draft to ages 17 to 50, while eliminating the possibility of substitutions. It didn't help much, as most of these men were already in the field. Further, supply continued to be a problem that worsened by the day, and Lee could not feed the men and horses that he already had.

Besides manpower and logistics, the rebels faced a potential command crisis. While most Union commanders in the east usually stayed far behind the lines, the Confederate style of leadership brought the high command, including even Lee himself, onto the battlefield and into the thick of the fight. This had created inspired moments of genius and courage, but it had also cost the Confederacy some of its best generals. The death of Stonewall Jackson at Chancellorsville was the most glaring example, but there were certainly others, and there was no denying that the army's talent pool was dwindling. Of his three corps commanders, only James Longstreet, his "Old War Horse," thoroughly had Lee's confidence. A. P. Hill had been an aggressive and brilliant divisional commander; corps command was another matter. Richard Ewell, too, had been an exceptional leader, but after losing a leg at Manassas (and, many said, after he had married), he was not the same.

When Lee learned that Ulysses S. Grant would be his new opponent in the east, he instantly noticed changes in the army on the other side of the Rapidan River. It was growing, and it was definitely more active. Scouts brought reports of increased activity at fords and crossings. Other intelligence brought news of increased troop movement elsewhere, including the development of a new corps, or possibly even an army, commanded by Ambrose Burnside at Annapolis. By the time May 1864 came, Lee's army of 65,000 was barely half the Union contingent across the Rapidan. The Confederate defenses at Mine Run were strong, but they were also not able to move anywhere. So Robert E. Lee, who had proven himself nearly undefeatable when he was able to aggressively seize the initiative, was forced to sit at his Brandy Station headquarters and wait to see what opportunities the Union army might offer him.

In the Union camps, things were quite different. After Grant settled on his grand campaign, the Federal ranks north of the Rapidan swelled to almost 120,000 active troops. Supply wagons and trains flew in and out of the camps with earnest speed. Even though Grant had clearly stated his intention to stay hands-off as Meade commanded the Army of the Potomac—and he stuck to his word, at least through the beginning of the campaign—all knew that a new sheriff was in town.

Those in the Union high command did not have nearly as many mysteries about the Confederates as the latter had about them. The Federals knew where they were, they knew how many of them were present, and they had a pretty good idea of where they were going—nowhere. Unfortunately, they also knew that they could not attack the rebels where they were, perched behind the Mine Run defenses. They would have to make the first move, and would have to predict how Lee would react. Union generals spent most of April forming and finalizing every conceivable way to bring the Confederates out into the open for a fight.

While Lee had seen most of his lieutenants grow with him, April gave Grant an opportunity to assess his own commanders for the first time. He had heard good things, but he also knew the Army of the Potomac's reputation for caution. The army was currently made up of three corps. The shining star of their three commanders was undoubtedly Winfield Hancock, only recently returned from a serious wound at Gettysburg. He would command his old II Corps. Another hero of Gettysburg, Gouverneur Warren, commanded the V Corps. Warren was young, outspoken, and showed much promise, and Grant liked him instantly. The veteran of the group was VI Corps commander "Uncle" John Sedgwick, steady and reliable in a fight and loved by his men.

There was also an additional corps that would prove to be a major complication, giving Grant his own command crisis. The reports that Lee had heard were true: Ambrose Burnside was indeed forming a new corps in Annapolis, the IX Corps, and it was headed for the Rapidan. However, Burnside, the former commander of the Army of the Potomac who had overseen the disastrous battle of Fredericksburg in 1862, outranked all of the other generals present, including George Meade. To solve the problem, the IX Corps was not given to the Army of the Potomac but was instead an independent command, reporting to Grant directly.

There was another new commander from the west. Philip Sheridan had also earned a reputation as a reliable, hard fighter, and Grant wanted him in the east. He had never commanded cavalry before, but he was nevertheless put in charge of the army's horsemen—not all of whom were thrilled. Sheridan would have to prove himself.

Like Sheridan, the Union troops viewed their new commander with skepticism. Grant was from the west, where, at least in the soldiers' minds, the fighting had been easier. He had not faced a general such as Robert E. Lee before. The soldiers took Grant's reputation for hard fighting and winning with a grain of salt. He would soon learn what real war was, they surmised. Confederate opinions were mostly the same, with one notable exception. James Longstreet had been best man at Grant's wedding, and knew that the Confederates were now facing a different animal. As he put it to Lee, Grant would "fight us every day and every hour until the end of the war."

More eager than anyone to start, Grant, in concert with the other parts of his grand offensive, set the army's march for just before midnight on May 3. Cavalry and engineers went ahead to secure the two points where the army would cross the Rapidan River. Hancock's II Corps would cross at Ely's Ford and take the road to Chancellorsville, while Warren's V Corps would use Germanna Ford and head toward Wilderness Tavern, followed by Sedgwick's VI Corps. Burnside and the IX Corps would cross at Ely's Ford after all of the Army of the Potomac had crossed. If everything went as planned, the Confederates would be taken by surprise, and once the Union army had concentrated south of their defenses at Mine Run, they would have no choice but to come out and fight.

The movement was well executed, but it really didn't matter. The Federals, watching south of the Rapidan for any sign that the Confederates were onto them, saw nothing unusual. However, they could not see behind Clark's Mountain, where most of Lee's men were already stirring. Some historians have elevated Lee's ability to predict the movement of Union armies practically to the level of telepathy. The truth is that he was an outstanding general, but he also guessed wrong on plenty of occasions. Here, though, on the Rapidan, he had already correctly predicted the movement of the Federals, and was ready for them. The stage was set for a collision of giants that no one could have predicted: Lee vs. Grant and the opening shots of the Overland campaign.

That campaign began here at Germanna Ford. It's a bit difficult to get to the location of the ford itself. From the Germanna visitor center, there are several trails that make their way down to the river; local fishermen often use these to get at the Rapidan's catch. The folks inside the center can help you get down to the river. (Take some time while you're there to learn about Germanna's very interesting history; the stretch of highway running by you, used by everyone from ancient Native Americans to Daniel Boone to Washington, is one of the most historic roads in the country.) The ford is located just downstream (north) of the existing bridge over the Rapidan, only a few hundred yards, and is easily discernible. You can also do a drive-by on the bridge to see it, but pulling over at this part of the highway is difficult, so only do so as a last resort.

ELY'S FORD

❭ *From the Germanna visitor center, get back onto Germanna Highway (VA 3) and turn right, then drive east for 10 miles to the intersection with Ely's Ford Road (CR 610). Turn left onto Ely's Ford Road and drive 4.8 miles. You will see a sign for a boat launch at Hunting Run Reservoir on your right; pull into the gravel parking area and drive down toward the river. Be careful of other drivers, as they may be putting their boats into the river.*

This is the location of Ely's Ford, crossing point for the Federal II and IX Corps. The crossings both here and at Germanna Ford, although they met some delays, were virtually unopposed by the Confederates. After cavalry had secured the crossing and engineers had laid pontoon bridges across the river, the II Corps began crossing, somewhere close to 5:30 AM on May 4. Soon a second bridge was added to ease the movement. The situation was similar at Germanna Ford, where the V Corps began their crossing at 7 AM. Behind them, the VI Corps waited—impatiently—as Warren's men made their way across and began their march southeast toward Wilderness Tavern, while Hancock took his men south-southeast from Ely's Ford to what was a terribly familiar sight to many of his men—Chancellorsville.

It is a bit difficult to discern Ely's Ford today, but it is approximately here in the location of the boat launch. The small island you see across from you was present when the Federals crossed in 1864, although it was a bit more prominent.

CHANCELLORSVILLE

❭ *From the boat launch, turn left back onto Ely's Ford Road and drive 4.7 miles. Just before the intersection with Germanna Highway, you will see a National Park Service parking area for Chancellorsville; pull in and park here.*

In May 1863, the Army of the Potomac, then led by Joe Hooker, had stolen a march on Robert E. Lee, approaching his rear at Fredericksburg virtually without detection. Once Lee realized what was happening, he orchestrated a number of movements and divisions of his army that resulted in a stunning victory at the battle of Chancellorsville, still regarded by many as Lee's masterpiece.

One of the hallmarks of that battle was its location in the Wilderness, an area west of Fredericksburg characterized by its densely thick undergrowth. Years before, iron was found to be plentiful in the area, and furnaces popped up everywhere. To fuel those furnaces, numerous trees were cut down, and the forest that replaced it had not yet fully matured. The result was a brushy mess so thick that in many spots one could not see anything more than 50 yards ahead. Trying to maneuver an army through the tangled mess was a nightmare for the Federals in 1863, and their plan was to escape the Wilderness as quickly as possible to avoid the same trap.

Lee had also learned from his experience in the Wilderness. He knew that the dense brush virtually negated the difference in the size of the two armies. The fact that he was outnumbered two to one would not matter, as long as he could catch the Union army before it left.

The ruins you see before you are those of the Chancellor House, the center of what was called Chancellorsville during the battle in 1863. The house was burned down during that battle, and by the time the Federals returned the next spring, it looked pretty much as you see it here. The open fields around you are somewhat close to what they were then, making this crossroads a good place for the Union II Corps to reform once it crossed Ely's Ford. From here, the men were to proceed west to advance with the rest of the army out of the Wilderness and toward the Confederate line. They had just finished an overnight march, however, and were worn out. The Union II Corps would camp here at Chancellorsville on the night of May 4.

FREDERICKSBURG & SPOTSYLVANIA NATIONAL MILITARY PARK— CHANCELLORSVILLE VISITOR CENTER

❯ *From the Chancellorsville parking area, turn right, then right again onto Germanna Highway (VA 3). Drive 0.8 mile to the entrance for the Chancellorsville visitor center for Fredericksburg & Spotsylvania Military Park on your right.*

Although behind the lines during the battle of the Wilderness, Chancellorsville still played a role in the battle, and the visitor center here should be your first stop. Neither the Wilderness nor the Spotsylvania battlefields have visitor centers, so this will be your best chance to talk to the park rangers and ask questions. You can also pick up the park's brochure, which contains a handy driving map.

While you're here, ask if any interpretive programs are going on during your visit. The park usually has regularly scheduled tours and programs, particularly during the summer, and you will occasionally find that even during the off-season, there may be some extra staff on hand, and the park may offer something it is normally not able to. (Luckily for the rest of us, most of these folks love what they do, and sometimes they just can't stay away.)

WILDERNESS TAVERN

❯ *From the visitor center, return to Germanna Highway (VA 3) and turn right. Drive 4.6 miles west on Germanna Highway to the intersection with Constitution*

Highway (VA 20). Safely reverse direction here by U-turn and drive 0.3 mile. Pull into the parking area on your right for Wilderness Tavern.

The ruins you see here are those of Wilderness Tavern. The tavern sat at the intersection of the Germanna Plank Road (now Germanna Highway, VA 3) and the Orange Turnpike (now Constitution, VA 20, where you made your U-turn). The roadbed of the old Orange Turnpike is still easily discernible here, and you can see where it angles off to the southwest, eventually picking up at VA 20 and continuing on. (This is a private drive today, so please stay off it.) The remains you see here are from the only building at the once-bustling intersection to survive the Civil War. It was not until 1978 that a fire finally took this last piece of Wilderness Tavern.

Wilderness Tavern was surrounded by several farms, again making a good rally point for the Union army—in this case, Warren's V and Sedgwick's VI Corps, both of which crossed at Germanna Ford and were making their way to this location down the Germanna Plank Road. The V Corps was in the lead, with the VI Corps stuck behind it, waiting in frustration.

Meade and Grant were both mindful of the dangers of the Wilderness, and wanted to leave the area. However, Lee's army, as far as they could tell, was still a good distance to the west. The Confederates would have no good reason to leave their exceptionally

The ruins of Wilderness Tavern overlook the old roadbed of the Orange Turnpike.

strong position at Mine Run. Furthermore, Union cavalry had been sent down the major roads to the west—the Orange Plank Road, the Orange Turnpike, and Catharpin Road—to ensure that the Confederates were not approaching. Having made a grueling late-night march, near 3 PM on May 4, the V Corps collapsed into the fields around Wilderness Tavern and made its camps, while the VI Corps, which had not been able to progress very far past Germanna Ford, camped along the Germanna Plank Road.

As the Federals bedded down on the night of May 4 in the midst of the Wilderness, they did not realize that they had many eyes watching them. One of the primary functions of cavalry was to gather intelligence, and no one had mastered the craft better than Confederate cavalry commander J. E. B. Stuart. All day, Stuart had had patrols tracking all of the Union movements, and for the most part, his men remained undetected. Therefore, by the evening of May 4, Robert E. Lee had a pretty good idea of where the Federals were. What he could not yet determine, though, was whether they were moving toward him at Mine Run or toward the city of Fredericksburg to establish what would be a very strong supply base. Either way, Lee's course of action was now clear, at least to him. This was the opportunity he had been waiting for to seize the initiative once again, and he prepared his army to march east. Once again, almost exactly one year after the battle of Chancellorsville, he would attempt to ensnare the Union Army of the Potomac in the Wilderness.

GRANT'S HEADQUARTERS

> *From Wilderness Tavern, very carefully pull out of the parking area and to the right onto Germanna Highway (VA 3). Drive 0.5 mile to Fox Gate Drive, then make a U-turn back onto Germanna Highway, now heading west. Drive 0.8 mile to Constitution Highway (VA 20, formerly the Orange Turnpike). Turn left and drive 0.4 mile. Pull into the gravel parking area on your right for Grant's headquarters.*

The small area in the woods here is roughly the area where General Grant set his headquarters tent when he arrived around 10 AM on May 5. During the next two days, however, he and the other commanders spent most of their time at the Lacy House, known as Ellwood, across the Orange Turnpike. There isn't a lot to see here, at least yet, but perhaps most useful is an interpretive sign showing a nice aerial shot of the area, which lets you know exactly where you are in relation to the Lacy House, the Orange Turnpike, Wilderness Tavern, and Saunders Field.

You will notice a home and some outbuildings adjacent to the area just before you pull in. This land, which certainly contained part of Grant's headquarters command, is in the process of being acquired by the Park Service through the work of the Civil War Trust and other battlefield groups. For now, though, it is private property, so please do not trespass.

ELLWOOD

❯ *Carefully pull out of the parking area for Grant's headquarters onto the highway and drive 0.2 mile. On your left will be the entrance for Ellwood. Pull in here and park. The house is usually open for tours on the weekends, but the grounds are open every day. If you choose to visit on a day when the house is not open, be sure to obtain a free parking permit from the Chancellorsville visitor center.*

Union expectations for May 5 were to be facing west toward Mine Run by sundown. Hancock's II Corps, from its point at Chancellorsville, would march south, then west on Catharpin Road. Warren's V Corps would move south on an old farm road, then head west on the Orange Plank Road from a point called Parker's Store. Sedgwick's VI Corps would follow, and all three corps would form a line and wait for Burnside's IX Corps. When the army was reunited, it would advance west toward the Confederates' position.

Critical to this plan was ensuring that all of these roads to the west were clear. That responsibility fell to Sheridan's cavalry corps. The corps was made up of three divisions. One of his commanders, David M. Gregg, was an old pro at leading cavalry and

The flag of the Union V Corps still denotes the Lacy House as Gouverneur Warren's headquarters during the battle of the Wilderness.

had been with the Army of the Potomac for most of its significant battles. The other two, like Sheridan, were new to the mounted arm. Alfred Torbert had been with the Army of the Potomac almost since its inception, but as an infantry commander. James Wilson had served in the west, mostly as an engineer.

George Meade assigned his cavalry's tasks accordingly, giving what he thought was the most critical task—guarding the army's supply wagons—to the experienced Gregg. Torbert was to support him, and both divisions would also look out to the east for Confederate activity. Meade, of course, assumed that the enemy was far from the Federals, and with this in mind, he tasked Wilson's division with covering the army's approaches to the west.

On May 4, Wilson did a thorough job of inspecting these roads, but also made a mistake that an experienced cavalry commander would not have. Riding out to a point far to the west, Wilson easily came to the conclusion that there were no Confederates close to the Union army. Then he rode back. No pickets were left anywhere to the west of the Army of the Potomac, leaving the Federals with no warning system were the rebels to march from the west.

Lee, having received Stuart's information, had decided to do exactly that. Lee would take the two corps he had east to hit the Federals while they lounged in the Wilderness. Richard Ewell's corps would use the Orange Turnpike, while A. P. Hill's corps would move on the Orange Plank Road. James Longstreet's corps, only recently arrived from the Western Theater, was still in Gordonsville, southwest of the rest of the army. He would follow Hill's trail, and upon his arrival, the two corps would be in position to crush the unsuspecting Union left. By sundown on May 4—well after Wilson had conducted and completed his reconnaissance—Hill and Ewell were in camp on their respective roads, only a short distance west of the Union camps. That night, they were given their orders for May 5—engage the Federals in the Wilderness, avoiding a general assault and holding them in place until Longstreet could come up.

When Hill and Ewell received these orders, they were actually closer to the home before you, Ellwood, than most of the Union high command was. With the exception of Gouverneur Warren, whose V Corps was already here and who took the house as his own headquarters, Meade, Grant, and the other commanders were elsewhere in the Wilderness. However, by 10 AM on May 5, Ellwood had become the Army of the Potomac's nerve center. The home and the yard around were soon filled with tents, troops, and aides running about. Throughout the two days in the Wilderness, Ellwood would be where everything on the Union side of the line originated.

Ellwood was a working farm, and served as a country house for the Lacys, the same family that owned the sprawling mansion of Chatham in Fredericksburg. Although certainly a fine house, it is quite humble, particularly when compared to its companion. Rescued, restored, and cared for by the Friends of Wilderness Battlefield, the home is open for tours on the weekends. Although the tour is self-guided, there are plenty of guides to tell you the home's stories and answer questions. There are also several very good exhibits here regarding the Wilderness, and Warren's headquarters room has been restored to something resembling its original appearance.

Also on the grounds is one of the oddities of the Civil War. It was near Wilderness Tavern, just down the road, that Stonewall Jackson's arm was amputated after he was wounded at Chancellorsville. Jackson's personal chaplain was Beverly Lacy, brother to J. Horace Lacy, who owned Elwood during the war. Following the amputation, Jackson was moved south to Guinea Station, where he died a week later. The arm, however, stayed, and Reverend Lacy buried it here in the Lacy family cemetery. It is still here, complete with its own marker.

As you proceed through the rest of the Wilderness battlefield, you will find that the story of the battle will keep returning to three locations: Saunders Field, your next stop; the intersection of the Orange Plank Road and Brock Road; and here at the Lacy House. After all, this was the first chance that Grant had to observe the eastern army in action, and he would learn a great deal from the experience. Although not much combat could be seen from here, what happened on the grounds around the Lacy House are a critical piece of the story of Grant and the Army of the Potomac.

WILDERNESS BATTLEFIELD

Saunders Field

⟩ *From Ellwood, pull out to your left onto the Orange Turnpike. Drive 1.1 miles, then pull into the parking area for Saunders Field on the right.*

The V Corps left its camps around Wilderness Tavern before 5 AM on May 5. Heading just a mile or so down the Orange Turnpike (VA 20, running right by your position), Warren's men would turn off the pike onto a narrow farm road that led southwest through the Wilderness to Parker's Store, a point on the Orange Plank Road. Samuel Crawford's division led the procession, followed by James Wadsworth's. Next in line to leave was Charles Griffin's division. It was about an hour after sunrise that Griffin prepared his men to move, and was about to call in the pickets he had placed to the west so they could rejoin the rest of the unit. Just before they came in, however, a small group of Confederates appeared on the Orange Turnpike in the distance. Upon hearing the report, Griffin rode west to Saunders Field, one of the Wilderness's rare clearings, to take a look for himself, then sent a message to Warren at the Lacy House.

You are now standing in the center of Saunders Field. For the most part, the field looks just as it did in 1864, with roughly the same dimensions. The Orange Turnpike,

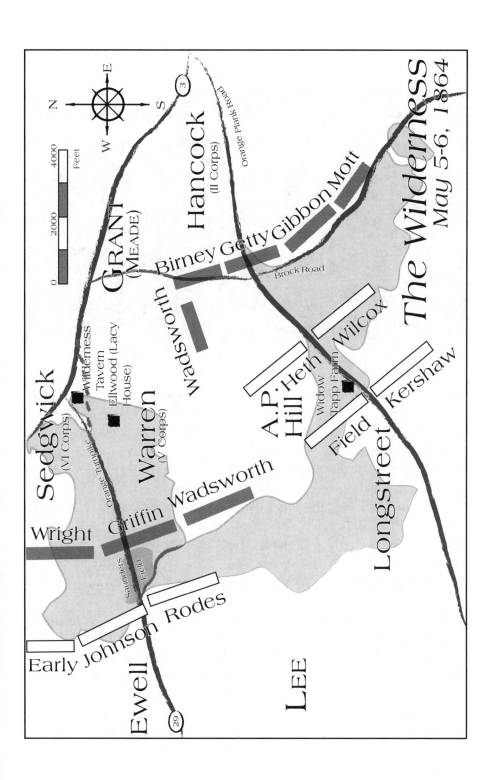

The Wilderness
May 5-6, 1864

A view from the commanding Confederate position at Saunders Field.

now Constitution Highway/VA 20, ran through the middle of the field just as it does today. Also still present, as you face away from the roadway, is the large swale to your left, running roughly north–south. The field itself is longer from east to west, with the ground on the western side of the swale sloping upward toward the tree line. It was on this high ground to the west, perpendicular to the road, that the Confederates first appeared and would eventually form their defensive line.

The Confederates seen that May 5 morning were Edward "Allegheny" Johnson's division, the van of Richard Ewell's corps. Johnson immediately set his men to building earthworks on this high ground, stretching across both sides of the turnpike and into the woods on each side. Robert Rodes's division was right behind him and fell in to support Johnson. Under orders not to bring on an engagement, Ewell's men dug in and waited.

Warren's initial messages to George Meade was that Lee seemed to be engaging in some kind of diversion on the Orange Turnpike with cavalry, and that his V Corps would not be stalled in their movement. Griffin's division, in the meantime, would advance from the east through Saunders Field to determine exactly what was in front of him, and would hold his position at least until the VI Corps arrived from its march down the Germanna Pike.

This seemed to suit Meade just fine, but his new boss, Ulysses Grant, was a bit more aggressive than that, and also happened to be standing over Meade's shoulder. At 7:15

Remnants of the still-formidable earthworks of Richard Ewell's Confederate Corps.

AM, with Grant's review and approval, Meade ordered Griffin to attack immediately. Strategically, the purpose of this was to break up any Confederate position before it had time to strengthen. It also sent another indirect message, intentionally or not, to every man in the Army of the Potomac, and perhaps the Army of Northern Virginia as well. The days of exhaustive exploration of the enemy's position that had habitually preceded Union assaults in the east (and which usually prevented their occurrence) were over. The Federal army's objective was to destroy the Confederate army. No one wanted to fight in the Wilderness, but if that's where Lee's men were, then so be it.

At 7:30 AM, Warren began to prepare for his attack, and by 8 AM he was at the front. The Wilderness was not making coordination an easy task. Sam Crawford's division was already well to the south at the Chewning Farm, while Wadsworth's division was still on the farm path, a mile-wide gap separating the two divisions. There would be no cross-country march through the dense Wilderness; the two forces would have to reverse course to rejoin Griffin. Furthermore, Crawford had found an excellent elevated position at the Chewning Farm. This would not be pertinent information, except that from this position, he could clearly see the Orange Plank Road to his south—along with A. P. Hill's entire corps marching on it, the rebels' left flank invitingly exposed. From this position, the Federals could split the suddenly present Confederate army in two, destroying it in detail.

However, unconfirmed intelligence was coming in too quickly for the Federals to

MISSED OPPORTUNITY

A. P. Hill's corps had a very specific objective in mind—the intersection of the Brock Road and the Orange Plank Road. Shortly before reaching the intersection, the Confederates arrived at a large clearing at the Widow Tapp Farm. It was a perfect place for Lee to place his headquarters.

Shortly after their arrival, as Lee, Hill, and cavalry commander J. E. B. Stuart were sitting underneath a tree, a group of Union soldiers appeared at the north side of the clearing, only 200 yards away. Lee froze, Hill stood, and Stuart started for his horse. After a very tense few moments, the soldiers disappeared back into the woods, having missed a prime opportunity to bag three of the Confederacy's best and highest-ranking commanders.

decipher. Meade was still on his way to the Lacy House, and Grant would not arrive until 10 AM. What he heard upon his arrival troubled him greatly, and unfortunately, it had little to do with the Confederates. Warren, who had said almost three hours ago that he was going to attack, had not. Meade was worrying about his army's flanks, particularly the II Corps, who he had lost communication with. After ordering George Getty's division of the VI Corps to hurry to the Brock Road/Orange Plank Road intersection, Meade issued orders for the rest of the VI Corps to hurry. 11 AM passed, then noon, and still there had been no fighting. Grant, who had pledged that he would stay out of affairs and let Meade run his army, quietly went about to whittling a stick as generals and their aides flew about him.

Finally, around 1 PM, Warren's corps was ready to attack. Wadsworth's division lined up to the left of Griffin, extending into the woods of the Wilderness. Most of Crawford's division was to his left, although Crawford had left part of his force at the Chewning Farm, not wanting to give up the prime real estate. Warren, who had been justifiably worried about his right flank to the north, had been trying to stall until John Sedgwick's VI Corps arrived, but it had already taken too long. Instead of charging with two corps, he would have two divisions.

Throughout this long waiting period, Rodes's Confederates were given plenty of time to improve their field works. After hours of digging and fortifying, they were more than ready to receive anything the Federals could throw at them.

While you are here at the parking area, visit the exhibits at the Wilderness shelter, then take the path (to your left, as you face away from the highway) and begin making your way up the slope toward the tree line. You are approaching the Confederate position. You will soon notice the slope, which while not exhaustibly steep, is certainly enough to give a defender inside the tree line, as you look up the path, a distinct advantage. You will also make your way over the swale in the field, where during the fight many men would try to find shelter from the heavy fight that would happen here. Noting the monument to the 140th New York infantry on your way up, continue up the path until you get to the tree line.

Before you step into the tree line, turn around and look back across the field. It becomes a bit easier, from this position, to appreciate the task that the Union soldiers had before them. Saunders Field, almost 800 yards long, is a lot of open ground to cover uphill and under heavy fire. Looking along the tree line to your left and right, the Confederates' line was perpendicular to the roadway, along and just inside the tree line. You can find their position easily by walking just a few yards into the woods, where remnants of their earthworks remain. Time has eroded them into something quite a bit less formidable than they were on May 5, 1864, but even what is left should give you a fairly good idea of the protection they afforded the rebel soldiers.

The first Confederate volley hit Griffin's Federals as soon as they stepped out of the tree line, across the field from you, at 1 PM. On this side of the turnpike, the north side, was Romeyn Ayres's brigade. Most of Ayres's men were either driven back completely or found themselves trapped in the swale running across the field. Two notable exceptions are the 140th and 146th New York infantry regiments, which were both able to make it across the field to the Confederate line. Before long, though, they, too, were forced to recross Saunders field and return to their lines.

As you look into the forest, try to guess how far you are able to see before everything gets lost in the trees and bushes. (Better yet, if you have someone with you, have them go into the woods for a short distance.) Here, in relative silence and with nothing going on around you, you will probably still find that it is difficult to see very far. With that in mind, realize that the woods here in the Wilderness have changed a lot over the last century and a half. At the time of the battle, visibility was actually much worse than it is now, with men often unable to see more than 50 yards in front of them. Add confusion and the smoke of thousands of weapons, and fighting a co-ordinated battle becomes nearly impossible.

You will find signs here for the Gordon's Flank Attack trail. It is a 2-mile loop that begins and ends at the parking area. The trail is well marked, the terrain is easy, and the path underneath your feet is good. Gordon's flank attack did not occur until the evening of May 6, but while you're here, you may want to walk the trail, which takes you through just about the entire northern front of the battle. It may also further help you appreciate some of the difficulties of fighting in the Wilderness. Supplementing the signs along the trail, brochures are available at the Wilderness shelter.

Confederate Defense Line

> *From the parking area at Saunders Field, pull out to the right and drive 0.2 mile. Turn left onto the park road, Hill-Ewell Drive, and pull over to the left.*

While Ayres's Union brigade charged north of the turnpike, Joseph Bartlett's moved through Saunders Field to the south. Despite the strong Confederate line, the right side of Robert Rodes's line—the south end, near your location—was not well protected. It was Confederate general John Jones's brigade that held this part of the field, and when Bartlett's men advance, they overlapped the Confederates right and were able to outflank them. After Jones was killed early in the fight, his brigade broke, and the Confederates were driven rearward for nearly three quarters of a mile.

Behind Jones line, however, was Cullen Battle's Confederate brigade. When the Federals came to a clearing, they attempted to reform their lines, which by this time had become hopelessly disorganized by the Wilderness. Shortly, they began receiving heavy fire from their right rear. At first, they thought it was friendly fire, not knowing that the Union had not been able to budge the Confederates north of the pike. Once they realized that they were well out in front of the rest of the Union army, Bartlett's men began to fall back, first in an orderly retreat and then in a rout as they realized that they were being surrounded. Many of the Union soldiers were captured. Although the troops had achieved a significant breakthrough, no other Federal units were near enough to support it.

Here on the south side of Saunders Field, you can see some very well-preserved remnants of the Confederate defensive line that Ewell's corps had constructed. As you observe their strength, keep in mind that you are looking at how formidable they are after 150 years of erosion. Beginning at the battle of Mine Run and through the end of the war, field fortifications such as these became increasingly important, and it was not long before both sides—but particularly the Confederates—had mastered the craft. After the initial earthworks were created, the soldiers would spend any lulls in the fighting further improving these works until they were virtually unassailable. The increase of this practice, as well as the skill with which the men performed it, would heavily shape how the rest of the Civil War was fought in the east.

Higgerson Farm

❯ *Pull back onto the park road and continue on for 0.8 mile. The road that you are now driving on was the farm road that the Federals had used to make their way south through the Wilderness. Pull into the parking area on your right.*

While Charles Griffin's Union division charged along the Orange Turnpike, James Wadsworth's division did the same, farther to the south. When the charge began, the right side of Wadsworth's line was nearly linked with Griffin's left. However, as Bartlett's brigade broke through and crumpled the right side of the Confederate line, Wadsworth's rightmost brigade drifted to the left, and the two divisions were soon

Looking west down the former Higgerson Farm Lane.

separated in the dense forest. That brigade was the Union's famous Iron Brigade, led by Lysander Cutler.

Richard Ewell realized quickly that he had a major problem on his hands. Not only was the Confederate right collapsing, but an entire additional Union division was to his south. To face the threat posed by Wadsworth's Federals, Ewell moved John Brown Gordon's brigade through the woods to his right in an attempt to slow the Union drive. Gordon soon came upon the Iron Brigade and charged them, breaking their line in the center. However, Gordon was now isolated from the rest of the Confederates, and between Cutler's and Bartlett's Federals, his men were fast becoming surrounded on three sides. Making a snap decision, Gordon decided to split his brigade in two and advance down Cutler's line in opposite directions. It worked, and before long, the Iron Brigade, for the first time in its history, was broken, streaming for the rear.

Just to the south of them was Roy Stone's Union brigade. Like Cutler and Bartlett, Stone was able to advance quickly, with little opposition in front of him. The brigade soon came to where you are now—the clearing at the Higgerson Farm. The Federals streamed past the Higgerson House and into the trees on the opposite side. As they passed the house, Mrs. Permelia Higgerson defiantly mocked the Union men, predicting that they would soon be coming back across her fields in the other direction.

Shortly after they cleared the field, Stone's men became stuck in a large swampy area. Gordon's Confederates, who had already sent the Iron Brigade rearward, now turned its attention to these Federals, firing at them from their front and their right. It was not long before Mrs. Higgerson's prediction came true, and Stone's brigade, like Cutler's, was headed rearward. The Confederates pursued the Union men all the way back to the Lacy House, where they finally pulled up and returned to their lines.

There is a short trail here that will take you to the ruins of the Higgerson House. The trail is an easy one; just don't get confused about which direction you're heading. The trail is not clearly marked, and several other paths seem to start near this point. The path defined by two lines of trees is the former Higgerson farm lane, and this is the path you should take to the house site. It is a one-way trail, but the walk to the site is well under a quarter-mile in length.

Chewning Farm

> *Continue down the park road for 1.1 miles, then pull into the gravel area for the Chewning Farm. As you drive, note the earthworks on your left along the roadway; these are remnants of the final Confederate defensive line.*

While the other two divisions of the V Corps, Griffin's and Wadsworth's, attacked, most of Samuel Crawford's division stayed here at the Chewning Farm. After Griffin and Wadsworth were repulsed, Crawford, now isolated, was forced to fall back as well, leaving the position here, which could have been so valuable to the Federals, up for grabs. The Confederates would eventually gain the ground and keep it.

There is a quarter-mile, one-way trail to the site of the Chewning House, which no longer stands. Just like at the Higgerson House, the walk is short, but the terrain can be a bit more difficult in parts. It cuts through a cornfield, and depending on the last time a vehicle used the path and drove through the mud, it could be a bit rough. That aside, the walk up to the high ground near the site of the house is worth it. Interpretive signs there will orient you and will explain the major opportunity lost here when the Federals did not exploit their position. Had Crawford's division not been ordered to move, it's likely that the Confederate army could have been split in half and defeated one piece at a time.

By 2:30 PM on May 5, the Union assault by the V Corps was over. No ground had been gained, and at all points, the Federals had been bloodily repulsed. A furious Charles Griffin rode to the Union headquarters at the Lacy House and exploded. His division had driven the Confederates for a great distance, but with their right exposed (because the VI Corps did not get into position), their left exposed (because

Wadsworth's division could not keep up), and no support available for their break-through, many of his men had lost their lives in a wasted, uncoordinated effort. Warren held the same opinion, although he held his tongue: The attack had been conducted too hastily. George Meade likely felt the same way, as evidenced by his reaction. Normally, the volatile Meade would certainly have lost his temper. However, when Grant suggested that Griffin should be arrested for his insubordination, Meade quietly turned to Grant and said that it was okay, and suggested that Griffin was just a bit temperamental. There would be a long way to go before Grant and the Army of the Potomac understood each other.

Eventually, John Sedgwick's VI Corps would come up on Warren's right, and the Union line would extend well into the woods north of Saunders Field, while Warren's stretched to the south. Although the Union line around Saunders Field would conduct several advances over the next two days, particularly in the woods to the north, all were repulsed. This pattern would define the rest of the fighting on the northern front of the battlefield until John Brown Gordon's flank attack late on May 6.

The Union entrenchments at the Wilderness are a fair distance to your east. If you would like to view them, there is a park trail that makes its way along its length. In addition, another trail begins here at Chewning Farm and follows the old Parker's Store road. Both of these trails are one-way and a few miles long, so be well prepared if you choose to take them. They will certainly give you a unique and seldom seen view of the Wilderness battlefield.

Parker's Store Site

⟩ *Continue 1.5 miles on the park road to its intersection with the Orange Plank Road (CR 21). On your way, you will pass a pullover for the Widow Tapp Farm; you will return to the farm site later in your tour. Turn right on the Orange Plank Road and drive 2.5 miles to the intersection with Windy Acres Lane (CR 611). Go; the location of the store was on your left just past the intersection. There is no simple place to stop here, and the site is not preserved, so find a good place to stop for a moment, then turn around back toward the intersection when it is safe to do so.*

This is the site of Parker's Store, the object of the V and VI Corps' march. Although the Union infantry never made it to this point, the Federal cavalry under James Wilson camped here on the evening of May 4 and fought Confederate cavalry fiercely around the intersection the next morning. Later that day and throughout the next, Parker's Store served as a primary fallback area for the Confederates, and a large field hospital was set up in the surrounding fields.

Nothing remains of the store today, and the site is on private property, so please do not trespass. Traveling to the Parker's Store site is worth the drive, however, for two reasons. First, it will give you a sense of the distance from the Federal position to this important point. Second, your drive back toward the battlefield will follow the march of A. P. Hill's corps on the morning of May 5, setting up your tour of the other significant area of the Wilderness battlefield—the intersection of the Orange Plank Road and the Brock Road.

Hill, riding with Robert E. Lee at the front of the column, reached Parker's Store around 8 AM on May 5. Two miles to the east was a large clearing at the Widow Tapp Farm. Lee set up his headquarters here, only a mile west of the intersection, the Confederates' primary objective.

Brock Road/Orange Plank Road Intersection

⟩ *From the intersection at Parker's Store, drive east 3.2 miles. Pull into the parking area on your right just before the intersection.*

Henry Heth, leading the foremost division in Hill's column on the Orange Plank Road, began to run into heavy resistance as the Confederates approached the intersection with the Brock Road around noon. Heth stopped the column and lined up his division across the road, preparing to advance in force and take the critical junction.

The critical intersection of Brock Road and Orange Plank Road at the Wilderness.

Had he known exactly what he was facing just that moment, he probably would have kept moving.

Union headquarters, by this time, had confirmed reports of a strong Confederate presence on the Orange Plank Road. This presented several major problems. One, of course, was that most of the Confederate army was now most definitely present. Perhaps the greatest problem, though, was that Winfield Hancock's II Corps, which had left Chancellorsville early that morning, was now in grave danger of being separated from the rest of the Union army.

George Getty's Union division had outdistanced their VI Corps counterparts marching on the Germanna Turnpike, and having reached Wilderness Tavern at 7:30 PM, had been resting for almost three hours. Meade ordered Getty to rush to the Brock Road intersection and hold it, while sending a simultaneous message to Hancock (whose whereabouts were unknown) that he was in danger of being isolated. While Getty's men were sent south on the Brock Road at the double-quick, Getty himself, along with his staff, rode ahead to the intersection.

Upon reaching the crossroads, Getty could easily see the Confederate column approaching from the west, and it was not long before the small band of Union men was taking long-range fire. In a moment borne of brilliance, desperation, or probably both, Getty and his staff stood squarely in the middle of the intersection, resisting the temptation to run for cover. In fact, Getty went so far as to begin pointing and waving his arms, just as if he was trying to move his troops into position.

It was just enough. Heth stopped just short of the intersection, and within minutes, Getty's lead brigades appeared and began to line up along the Brock Road, facing west toward the Confederates. The Federals had taken the critical intersection. Now all Getty's division had to do was hold it—against an entire rebel corps.

At 11:40 AM, as the drama was unfolding at the crossroads, Winfield Hancock finally received his orders from headquarters to head for the intersection and rejoin the Union army. His II Corps, which had stuck to its schedule well, was already 2 miles west on the Catharpin Road. Hancock reversed his march, then rode ahead to the intersection to join Getty, who had been holding off the Confederate attackers with great determination. It would not be until 2:40 PM that the first elements of the II Corps would reach the Orange Plank Road and begin digging in to help defend the position.

You are now just to the west of the intersection of the Orange Plank Road, which you drove in on, and the Brock Road, just to your left as you face the interpretive signs here. Resist the temptation to walk down the road to the intersection; both of these roads are still extremely busy, and cars tend to move rather quickly. In front of you is the head of a half-mile loop trail with a nice, soft path on even ground. If you take the trail, you will reach the intersection soon enough.

These woods around the intersection saw some of the heaviest, most terrible, and most gruesome fighting of the entire Civil War. Apart from the heavy contest for the intersection itself, the Wilderness added an entirely new dimension to the horrors of war. As was the case in the woods around Saunders Field, the forest here does not have the same appearance that it did in 1864, and the visibility today is much better than it was then. The dense undergrowth meant that as men advanced through these woods, all sense of organization was abandoned. They crept cautiously, as death was seemingly around every tree and bush. As they made their way through the Wilderness, the soldiers around them appeared, to many, to fall at random and without warning.

To add to the hellish nature of the fight here, conditions at the time of the battle were extremely hot and dry. This meant that the many muzzle flashes and artillery rounds making their way into the surrounding woods were prone to starting fires that were quickly beyond control. Wounded men who had been left on the field were often helpless, left to succumb to the flames. Many tried their best to drag themselves to safety, while others, seeing no hope, took their own life rather than be burned alive. In several cases, units of both armies would drop their weapons to assist each other in rescuing their fellow men from such a terrible fate and would then resume combat. These fires broke out continuously through two days of fighting, and no one present would ever forget the desperate cries of the wounded or the terrible stench of death at the Wilderness.

While Hancock's II Corps was still getting into position along the Brock Road to the south of the intersection, orders reached Getty at 3:45 PM to attack. Getty, who had a reputation for resolutely following any order he was given, prepared to advance, while Hancock did what he could to support him. Getty's men drove Heth's Confederate skirmishers through the woods, but soon found that rebels seemed to be taking advantage of every one of the Wilderness's numerous dips and ridges. The Federals were hit hard only a few hundred yards after advancing, and although they were able to push the Confederates back, they could not break their line.

The Federals would repeat their assault several times, but they were repulsed each time. By 5 PM, Heth's Confederates were outnumbered by a great deal, and in fact faced the same odds that Getty did upon his arrival—a single division, Heth's, facing an entire corps—Hancock's II Corps, augmented by Getty's division. By 7 PM, Lee, who had been hoping to wait until James Longstreet's corps could arrive, was forced to put in his last reserves, having already beaten back seven separate Union assaults.

By the time the fighting died down with the darkness on May 5, the Confederates had held their position, but just barely. While Hancock pulled his men back to the Brock Road and entrenched along the west side of the road, Hill's corps, for the most part, slept where they fell in the Wilderness. Fighting continued sporadically through the night over the same ground that had been contested all day, the half-mile or so of the woods west of the Brock Road.

A monument to the Vermont Brigade commemorates their valor during the fight for the Brock Road/Orange Plank Road intersection at the Wilderness.

As you walk along the trail, along with a monument to Lewis Grant's famous Vermont Brigade, which suffered heavily in these woods, you will find numerous markers telling the story of the fight here on both May 5 and May 6. Most of the fighting of both days happened in the woods around you, while a good deal also occurred north of the Orange Plank Road. As the trail nears the Brock Road, you will see the little that is left of the Union entrenchments. By May 6, these works would be much more formidable; what you see today are mere shadows of what once was. (There are other places on your tour where you will see examples of completed earthworks.) Finally, as you complete the trail, you will come to the intersection itself, the object of so much ferocious fighting in May 1864.

Widow Tapp Farm

❯ *From the parking area at the crossroads, carefully pull out onto the Orange Plank Road to your left. Drive 1.2 miles to the parking area for the Widow Tapp Farm on your right.*

The evening of May 5 was a sleepless one for Robert E. Lee. He knew that Longstreet's corps was on its way, but he needed it now. The two corps that he did have on the field, Richard Ewell's and A. P. Hill's, were far apart, a distance magnified by the challenges of the Wilderness. Further, Hill's men were almost completely fought out, and the Federals would be coming in force in the morning. Longstreet, when he arrived, was to take Hill's place, while Hill shifted left to fill the gap in the Confederate line. But when would he show?

Ulysses S. Grant had already determined his plans for the next day, and there were no surprises. Now that all of his armies were in place—Ambrose Burnside's IX Corps had arrived late in the day—he had the ability to crush the Confederate forces before him with a coordinated attack. The V and VI Corps would resume their attack along the Orange Turnpike, pitting their five divisions against Ewell's three. The main attack, though, would be along the Orange Plank Road, where Hancock's entire II Corps, Getty's division of the VI Corps, and Wadsworth's division of the V Corps would push through Hill's division. In addition to the Federal forces attacking from the Brock Road, the two largest divisions of Burnside's IX Corps would attack from the area of the Chewning Farm to the north. Seven Federal divisions would be countered against the two that Hill had available. Although they had taken a severe beating on May 5, all of the Union high command expected a banner day on May 6.

Along the Orange Turnpike, Ewell surprised the Federals by launching his own attack at 4:45 AM. Having massed artillery on the turnpike and extended the left side of his line to match the addition of the Union VI Corps, the Confederates only briefly advanced from their own lines before they were pushed back. Those lines, however, were very formidable, so when the Federals counterattacked, they were sent reeling back to their own positions. It was not long before Warren, fearing a repeat of the previous day's slaughter, called off his assault, and Sedgwick did the same shortly afterward, having no support on his left. Sporadic fighting would occur north of Saunders Field throughout the day, but little was gained.

A. P. Hill's Confederates at the Orange Plank Road were not nearly as well prepared as their comrades in Ewell's corps. Someone in the corps, perhaps Henry Heth or possibly even Hill himself, had made the decision to let the Confederate soldiers sleep wherever the battle left off for them, and the men remained scattered about the Wilderness throughout the night. The reasoning behind this decision was that the men needed rest, and Longstreet's corps would be up soon enough to take their place. There is no question that these soldiers had earned such a reward, but battle does not usually permit such a luxury. The result of the decision was that the Confederates did not have a defensive formation of any kind formed in the early morning hours, and the price paid would be high.

A Union signal gun to begin the attack on the Orange Plank Road was fired at 5 AM. Hancock's II Corps and George Getty's division advanced along the road, while James Wadsworth's division advanced from the northeast. With the Confederates completely out of formation, the Union advance was nearly unstoppable. Those rebels who did hear orders to retreat were fortunate; many did not, and they ended up as prisoners. As the Confederates farthest from the attack received word about what was happening, they attempted to form defensive positions, but the amount of fleeing soldiers running through their front and then through their ranks made this almost impossible. As Getty and Hancock moved westward, Wadsworth swooped southwest and rolled up any Confederates north of the road who tried to form a line of resistance.

From the parking area here at the Widow Tapp Farm, as you look along the Orange Plank Road, you are facing the Union advance. From this point, you are approximately 1 mile from the Brock Road intersection, where the Union advance began. The tree line directly across from you, along the road, is about a quarter-mile to your front, three-quarters of a mile from the Brock Road. By the time the Federals reached the opposite side of the clearing here at the Widow Tapp Farm, it was just about 6 AM. The Union soldiers that appeared to your front would have been Wadsworth's men; his movement to the southwest essentially pushed Hancock and Getty south of the Brock Road.

You can also see a few cannons right in front of your position. This is the position taken by William Poague's Confederate battery. Poague, along with a few rallied remnants of the breaking Confederate units, began firing in desperation from this position, with Lee watching anxiously by their side as the Union soldiers entered the

Confederate artillery at the Widow Tapp Farm, Wilderness Battlefield.

clearing. Poague's 12 guns were only enough to slow the Federals, but as it turned out, it was all they needed.

Just as things began to look truly desperate for the Confederates, the lead units of James Longstreet's corps appeared on the Orange Plank Road. With his men moving quickly but confidently as what was left of Hill's corps streamed past them, Longstreet set Joseph Kershaw's division in a line south of the road and Charles Field's division north. The line formed just behind a very slight ridge, just to screen the movement from the Federals. To maximize the effect of a breakthrough, Longstreet stacked the two divisions, creating a very compact and powerful advancing column.

What happened next is one of the truly remarkable moments of the Civil War. Robert E. Lee, the rock-solid commander who never seemed to break a sweat, was, by most accounts, starting to show signs of desperation before Longstreet's men arrived. When Lee noticed a line forming around him, led by a commander he did not know, he rode up to the officer and asked what brigade it was. General John Gregg, who had recently joined from the Western Theater, replied with what must have truly been music to Lee's ears. It was the famous Texas Brigade, part of Longstreet's corps. Lee's loss of composure went from near panic to near delirium as he began to shout the praises of Texas and her fighting men.

The east end of the Widow Tapp Farm, where Robert E. Lee attempted to lead James Longstreet's Confederates to the rescue.

However, as the brigade advanced, someone—and accounts vary as to who it actually was—noticed that Lee, whose blood was now up, was riding with the men, intent on leading the charge himself. The Texans stopped in their tracks, first pleading with him to return to the rear, then refusing to advance any further until he did. Eventually, through some tactful words from Gregg and Longstreet and, allegedly, one soldier grabbing the reins of Lee's famed horse, Traveller, the general commanding was guided to the rear and to safety.

There is a 0.5-mile loop trail leading through the Widow Tapp's field. It is a very easy walk over soft, mown grass. There are several interpretive signs along the way that point out the Tapp House, some well-defined earthworks left over from the battle, and finally a spot with several monuments commemorating the famous "Lee to the rear" moment. You will be following in the path of Field's division as they advanced toward the Union line.

Of course, the mere appearance of a fresh Confederate corps did not guarantee the Confederates a victory here—in fact, far from it. As the Confederates got to the woods and then began to push their way through the Wilderness, the fighting devolved into very much the same confused patterns as before. The fighting here was against James Wadsworth's Union division, and they were not about to give up the ground they had fought so hard for. After several hours of hard fighting, both Field's Confederates and Wadsworth's Federals began to pull back, having had enough for the moment.

Wadsworth, of course, was not supposed to be alone north of the Orange Plank Road. Ambrose Burnside's IX Corps divisions were expected to be to his right, ready to swoop down on the Confederate flank. But the IX Corps was nowhere to be found. Its assignment was to be at Wilderness Tavern at 4 AM, where it would then be led to its position near the intersection. However, the men did not begin to reach the tavern until after the fight had already started. The two divisions who were to participate in the attack—Robert Potter's and Orlando Willcox's—were ordered by the officers at the Lacy House to hurry to their position. Inexplicably, with the heavy sounds of battle coming from his front, Burnside stopped his corps to have breakfast along the way, resuming the march at 7:30 AM. Shortly afterward, the men began scuffling with Confederate reserve units and stayed near their position until 9 AM. Later in the day, they would advance to join the II Corps along the Brock Road, but this critical piece of the morning Union attack would remain out of the fight.

By 8 AM, the battle along the Orange Plank Road had returned to its stalemated status, with both sides exhausted but with their lines remaining close to each other. Commands on both sides of the line and of the road were confused and intermingled, and Hancock was doing his best just to observe the battle, let alone direct it. George Getty, who had so defiantly claimed the intersection the previous day, was wounded south of the Orange Plank Road. After another two hours, the battle had died down to sporadic firing. Both sides had reached the point of exhaustion. After five hours of see-sawing hard combat, it would take a brilliant move to be able to claim victory on this field.

Longstreet's Wounding

⟩ *From the Widow Tapp Field parking area, pull out to your left onto the Orange Plank Road. Drive 0.9 mile and pull into the parking area on your right. On your way, you will notice a large monument to Union general James Wadsworth on the left side of the road; if you choose to view it, make sure to watch the traffic and slow your car. If you do wish to stop and take a closer look, you should probably make a U-turn further down the road, come back, and carefully pull over next to the monument.*

Over the course of the two days of fighting at the Wilderness, the Union high command had been trying to account for all of the Confederate units. The biggest mystery, of course, had been Longstreet corps, which showed up early on May 6. Richard Anderson's division from A. P. Hill's corps was also still unaccounted for, as was George Pickett's, all of which was miles away defending Richmond and Petersburg. With the whereabouts of these and other units unknown, Federal officers were concerned with where and when they may unexpectedly appear.

The commander with the most reason for concern was Winfield Hancock, whose II Corps held the left of the Union line, dangling in the open on the Brock Road. There had been several false alarms beyond Hancock's left flank, but none of them had panned out. Cavalry fights had broken out to the south down the road at Todd's Tavern, but none of the fighting had threatened his line. By the time the midmorning fight along the Orange Plank Road had died down, Hancock was too busy with matters on the field in front of him to keep looking for a flank attack that would never come.

As it turned out, the Federals should have been looking not to the south, down the road, but southwest, through the Wilderness. The Orange & Alexandria Railroad, before the war, had planned to extend a line from Fredericksburg westward to Orange Court House. The path for the track had been cleared and graded, but the track itself was never laid. This path essentially created a narrow road almost parallel with the Orange Plank Road a quarter-mile to the south. Both armies had it on their maps, but only the Confederates would use it to their advantage.

During the lull in the fighting around 10 AM, Lee sent a small detachment of engineers to scout out the path. Not only was it clear, but several ridges, running roughly north–south, emanated from the path through the Wilderness. They created perfect avenues through which an attacking force could approach the Union left flank virtually undetected.

Longstreet's aide, G. Moxley Sorrel, was selected to lead the assault, and three fresh brigades were chosen from the Confederate reserves, all from separate divisions. Sorrel led the soldiers down the path, then halted the men and turned them to their left so that they were facing north. At 11 AM, the Confederates began quickly and quietly moving through the ravines. By the time the Union units on the left realized what had hit them, it was too late, and one by one, they began to break for the rear. As Sorrel led his flanking attack, Longstreet simultaneously attacked from the front with Field's division to attempt to hold the Federals in place, keeping them from slowing the momentum of the Confederate assault.

Pushing northward through the Wilderness, Sorrel's soldiers soon approached the Orange Plank Road. James Wadsworth attempted to line up his Union division to hold the road, but it was no use, and his men also fell back. As Wadsworth tried to rally them, his horse inexplicably bolted for the Confederate line and he was shot in the head. He was picked up by the Confederates, and died at their field hospital at Parker's Store several days later. A large monument along the Orange Plank Road has been placed near the spot where he fell.

Noon found the Union army left in a state of complete disorder, and the Confederates were ready to exploit their gains. James Longstreet had just performed a miracle, not only showing up at the perfect time but executing brilliantly on the battlefield. All of this would only magnify the tragedy of what happened next.

Micah Jenkins's brigade of Field's division, Longstreet's corps, was about to lead the next, and possibly final, wave of the Confederate attack. They were poised for an overwhelming and crushing victory over their Union foes. Longstreet, enjoying perhaps his finest of many fine moments as a commander, rode with Jenkins at the front, moving eastward down the Orange Plank Road. When they were half a mile from the Brock Road, firing erupted on their right, and it was answered immediately on their left. The firing on the right came from William Mahone's Confederate brigade; the firing on the left came from the 12th Virginia Infantry, wearing dark uniforms that gave the appearance of a Union uniform. The two units had begun a friendly-fire fight, and the Confederate generals were right in the thick of it.

Jenkins was hit first, in the head; he would soon die on the field. Joseph Kershaw, also riding at the front, rushed ahead to attempt to stop the firing. Before he could, Longstreet was shot in the neck. He began to choke on his own blood as it spurted from the wound. His staff surrounded him and called for his surgeon, certain that the wound was fatal. He was taken to Parker's Store, and although he raised his hand to let his troops think he was all right, he was not, and they knew it.

All the momentum that the Confederates had held dissolved instantly. The entire corps, already disorganized by its routing attack through the Wilderness, was in a frazzle. Next in line to command the corps was Richard Anderson, who had not been on the field all day. The Confederates had no choice but to pull back and regroup, delaying any further attack on the Union line.

Hancock, meanwhile, took the sudden stop in the Confederate assault to rally his men and reform his lines. Receiving reinforcements, Hancock strengthened the line along the Brock Road, expecting another attack at any moment. The men improved their earthworks—the same works you saw along the trail at the Brock Road intersection—and prepared for the worst.

At 4 PM, Lee was finally ready. Distraught over the loss of his best general, he knew that this might be the Confederates' best chance to complete their victory in the Wilderness. Around 4:15 PM, the rebels finally saw the Union position, and it was daunting. The breastworks, made of felled logs and earth, were chest high. Abatis and other obstructions lay in front, and all of the brush in front of the works had been completely cleared.

When the Confederates reached the clearing in front of the Union line, they were instantly hit with a massive volley of musketry and canister fire. Although the two lines stood toe to toe for thirty minutes, the rebels could make no headway—that is, until the Union works caught on fire. With a section of the Federals works so engulfed in flames that the defenders had to fall back, the Confederates (Micah Jenkins's former brigade) exploited the small gap, rushing into it and climbing over the Union line. The breakthrough only lasted fifteen minutes, though, as the gap was almost directly in front of the Union artillery, and other Federal units on either side plugged the gap and extinguished the fire.

CASUALTIES— WILDERNESS

Confederate: total: 10,800 (estimated)

Union: killed, 2,246; wounded, 12,037; missing or captured, 3,383; total: 17,666

Total Casualties (estimated): 28,500

The fighting along the Orange Plank Road and Brock Road was over by 6 PM. To the north, at Saunders Field, Confederate general John Brown Gordon led a daring flank attack that completely crumpled the Union right, but the attack came too late in the day, and the assault was stopped by the growing darkness. (Gordon had wanted to launch his assault much earlier, but had been denied permission by Richard Ewell and Jubal Early. The trail you saw earlier at Saunders Field will take you along the route of that attack.)

Gordon's flank attack was over just after 7 PM, and although additional firing occurred through the night, particularly north of Saunders Field, the battle of the Wilderness was over. The Confederates were the clear victors; however, they had still lost approximately 11,000 men—a sixth of their army that they could not replace easily. Furthermore, they had lost James Longstreet, who would eventually recover from his wounds and return after a lengthy recovery period.

For the Union, it had been two days of terrible loss. The final casualty total was 17,666, including a staggering 209 officers killed or mortally wounded. Grant, however, saw the battle as a draw. In his eyes, the Confederates had gained no advantage. Still, he learned two primary lessons from the fight at the Wilderness. The first was that he had sorely underestimated the aggressiveness of both Robert E. Lee and his men. The second was that he had greatly overestimated the abilities of his own commanders. Grant would leave the Wilderness with a better, but not complete, understanding of both of these.

Perhaps the most important lesson was learned by both armies. The introduction of Ulysses S. Grant into the Eastern Theater would change the war here. Both sides, Union and Confederate, saw tenacity in the new commander that had previously evaded the Army of the Potomac. What they could not know was that virtually the entire Overland campaign, only three days old, would be fought on these new terms.

TODD'S TAVERN

❭ *Pull out of the parking area to the right and drive 0.4 mile to Brock Road. Turn right on Brock Road and drive 4.7 miles. Pull into the parking area with the interpretive signs on your right.*

Late in the day on May 6, many wondered what would be next for the Army of the Potomac. Past practice would have virtually guaranteed a withdrawal north across the Rapidan River. Robert E. Lee still considered that the Federals might withdraw to

Corbin's Bridge, since rebuilt, saw action during the battle of Todd's Tavern.

Fredericksburg, pulling him out of his works and facing him on grounds more advantageous to the Union. Many guessed, but few knew where the Federals were going.

After a night of reflection, Grant had made his decision. To remain in the Wilderness and fight Lee in his defenses would be futile. Retreat, though, was never an option. Grant's objective was not to win battles. It was to destroy the Army of Northern Virginia, and although the Federals had suffered heavily, so had the Confederates, who could not afford losses as readily. The Wilderness may not be the right place, but if it were up to Grant, the two armies would meet again in battle very soon.

At 6:30 AM on May 7, Grant issued orders to Meade to prepare the army to march south that night. The troops would use two roads, almost parallel and close enough that the force on one road could support the force on the other if necessary. The objective would be to get between Lee and the Confederate capital at Richmond, pulling the Confederates out of their earthworks. The next logical place on the map was 10 miles to the southeast at the town of Spotsylvania Court House.

Union corps commanders were not told their objective until 3 PM, and the soldiers were not told at all. Union cavalry, meanwhile, had the important mission of clearing the lines of march, making sure that the infantry could move quickly and beat the Confederates to Spotsylvania Court House. This meant controlling the two routes, the Brock Road for the V and II Corps and a combination of Catharpin Road and Piney Branch Church Road for the VI and IX Corps, all the way to Spotsylvania. If the roads were clear, the V Corps could occupy the town by the morning of May 8.

Along the Brock Road, about 5 miles south of its intersection with the Orange Plank Road, was Todd's Tavern, and it was clear to all that when the Confederates detected the Union movement south, the tavern would be the most likely place they would try to stop it. There had already been plenty of cavalry action around Todd's Tavern during the battle of the Wilderness because of its intersection with Catharpin Road. What's more, when the day opened on May 7, the crossroads was held by J. E. B. Stuart's cavalry. Phil Sheridan's horsemen would have to drive them out.

Fitzhugh Lee's division of Confederate cavalry, 3,500 strong, sat at the intersection, with Wade Hampton's and "Rooney" Lee's divisions just to the west on Catharpin Road at Corbin's Bridge, stretching over the Po River. Sheridan sent David Gregg's cavalry division to hold the Confederates at the bridge while Wesley Merritt's headed for the crossroads. (Merritt was temporarily commanding the division while Alfred T. A. Torbert, who had been dealing with a very painful abscessed spine, was recovering from surgery.)

Two of Merritt's three brigades, commanded by Thomas Devin and George A. Custer, approached the tavern from the north along Brock Road late in the morning. Custer, in the lead, found Confederate skirmishers quickly, but was able to drive them backward until he reached Lee's main defensive line, just to the north of the intersection. By this point in the war, cavalry tactics had already begun to change significantly from its traditional use. Improvements in weaponry had made cavalry charges often wasteful and sometimes suicidal. To remedy this, cavalry was often found fighting as infantry, particularly when on the defensive, dismounted and behind breastworks. Lee's Confederates did this at Todd's Tavern, erecting a log breastwork squarely across Brock Road and firing dismounted toward the approaching Federals. Custer's first charge, made on horseback, was easily repulsed.

You are now near the site of the old tavern, which lay in the fields next to you. Turn your back to the signs and face the Brock Road. Custer's brigade, with Devin's following, would have been coming down the road from your far left. Also to the left but just north of the intersection in front of you would have been Lee's defensive line. At the time of the battle, the ground was fairly wide open, as you see it today. Because a position here was more difficult to defend, Lee eventually pulled his troops back approximately a mile to a more wooded area, near the intersection of Brock Road and Piney Branch Church Road. Lee's withdrawal, and the Union pursuit, would move across your front, from left to right. It would also be slow, delaying the Federals as long as possible while the Confederates, who now realized what the enemy was up to, raced toward Spotsylvania Court House.

> *Pull out of the parking area to your right onto Brock Road and turn right immediately onto Catharpin Road. Drive 2.3 miles, crossing a small bridge. After driving across, make a U-turn at a safe point and return to the bridge. Pull over, if it is possible to do so safely; otherwise, let a drive-by viewing suffice.*

This is the site of Corbin's Bridge. If you drove past the bridge and made your U-turn, you are now looking north-northeast. You are on the Confederate side of the line, looking toward the Federals.

After Merritt's cavalry had made its way past Todd's Tavern, Phil Sheridan sent a brigade of cavalry led by Col. J. Irvin Gregg (not to be confused with his cousin, division commander David M. Gregg) toward Corbin's Bridge down the now-open Catharpin Road. Gregg's men encountered Wade Hampton and Rooney Lee's cavalry divisions here at the bridge, commanding high ground on the west bank. Gregg wisely pulled back from the bridge, forming his own defensive line and repulsing several charges by the Confederate cavalry.

> *From Corbin's Bridge, drive 2.3 miles back to Brock Road, then turn right. Drive 2.2 miles on Brock Road; Piney Branch Church Road will enter Brock Road from your left rear. Again, there are not many places to pull over safely, so if you can't, keep driving.*

CAV IN THE FAMILY

You may have noticed a few names repeatedly popping up while reading about both the Union and the Confederate cavalry commanders.

On the Union side, Brig. Gen. David McMurtrie Gregg commanded his own division of cavalry from the Chancellorsville campaign in 1863 until nearly the war's end, when he resigned abruptly. During much of that time, one of the brigades under his watch was led by his cousin, Col. John Irvin Gregg. Another cousin, Andrew Gregg Curtin, was governor of Pennsylvania during the war and held heavy influence with President Lincoln.

As for the Confederates, you may have noticed another familiar name. Maj. Gen. William H. F. "Rooney" Lee was indeed one of Robert E. Lee's sons. Born at Arlington (Robert E. Lee's former estate and now the famous national cemetery), Rooney Lee was wounded and captured at the battle of Brandy Station in July 1863, and after being exchanged, was given his own cavalry division in 1864. His cousin Fitzhugh Lee, Robert E. Lee's nephew, was with the Confederate army from the first battle of Manassas. He was one of the Confederacy's most talented cavalrymen, commanding a division and eventually the entire cavalry corps of his uncle's Army of Northern Virginia through the Confederate surrender at Appomattox. Fitz Lee would later be elected governor of Virginia.

Just north of this intersection is where Fitzhugh Lee made his final line. At 3 PM, Federal cavalry—this time Merritt's third brigade, commanded by Alfred Gibbs's brigade—again made a charge at the Confederates, and again they were repulsed. The fighting became extremely heavy here, with both sides dismounted and fighting in the woods around you. Near 4 PM, logs in Lee's defensive works caught on fire, forcing him to fall back and reform his line, but the Confederates were able to hold until dark. The Union troopers soon withdrew to Todd's Tavern to rest for the night.

At 8:30 PM that evening, May 7, the Army of the Potomac began to move. A massive traffic jam slowed the army to a crawl, but the men picked up the pace after Ulysses S. Grant, at the head of the Union column, turned south on the Brock Road. The Union soldiers were instantly electrified; they would not be retreating. They were headed for Richmond.

It was not until 1 AM that Grant and Meade reached Todd's Tavern, finding all of the beds occupied by sleeping cavalrymen. When Meade realized that Sheridan had not cleared the road to Spotsylvania Court House, he was furious. He and Sheridan were never on good terms, and their relationship would deteriorate rapidly after this night. Sheridan's failure to comprehend the importance of his assignment would guarantee that it would be the Confederates, not the Federals, who won the race to Spotsylvania. For now, though, with Sheridan bivouacking miles away, Meade, along with Grant, found a patch of open ground and grabbed what little sleep they could.

SPOTSYLVANIA COURT HOUSE BATTLEFIELD

Alsop Farm Site

> *From the intersection at Piney Branch Church Road, continue south on Brock Road for 0.6 mile. Turn left onto Gordon Road (CR 627) and pull into the parking lot for Goshen Baptist Church on your left.*

As the fighting peaked in the Wilderness on May 6, although there was some pitched cavalry combat, the Union army had readily conceded control of the Brock Road to the Confederates. So when the Federals clearly wanted the road back in their own hands on May 7 at Todd's Tavern, Robert E. Lee had all the intelligence he needed. Although he still did not know Grant's intentions, everything indicated that Lee would have to pull his army south. After first issuing orders to his chief of artillery, William Pendleton, to cut a road through the Wilderness, he sent word to his corps commanders that they would march that night after dark.

Richard Anderson, who had succeeded James Longstreet as commander of the Confederate I Corps, had been ordered to begin moving south at 3 AM on May 8. Fortunately for the Confederates, Anderson did not follow his orders to the letter. The

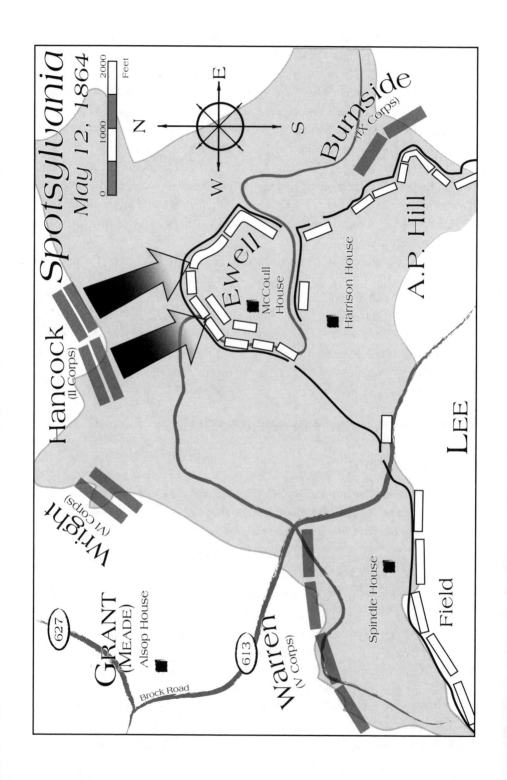

Spotsylvania
May 12, 1864

Feet
0   1000   2000

N
W   E
S

Hancock
(II Corps)

Wright
(VI Corps)

Ewell

McCoull House

Harrison House

Burnside
(IX Corps)

A.P. Hill

GRANT
(MEADE)
Alsop House

Brock Road

627

613

Warren
(V Corps)

Spindle House

Field

LEE

woods around his position were still ablaze, and the stench of the rotting and burning corpses of horses and men was almost too much for his men to bear. The new commander made a decision to move at 10 PM on May 7, five hours ahead of his assigned jump-off time. It would prove to be a critical decision.

The Federal corps, when they were able to move at all, were not able to do so as cleanly. Gouverneur Warren's V Corps reached Todd's Tavern at 2 AM on May 8 and kept pushing forward toward Fitzhugh Lee's Confederate line across the Brock Road. Union cavalry had been ordered directly by Meade to renew the assault, but was making little progress. After the weight of Warren's infantry was added to the fight around 3:30 AM, the Confederate cavalry began falling back, again slowly, to buy its infantry time.

Although Warren's progress was slow, it was far ahead of the rest of the Union army. John Sedgwick's VI Corps did not reach Chancellorsville, far from the front, until daybreak. Ambrose Burnside's IX Corps did not even begin its march until 8 AM. Winfield Hancock's II Corps was following Warren's path, and did not reach Todd's Tavern until 1:30 PM on May 8.

At 8 AM on May 8, the Union advance had reached the point where you now stand. If you exit your vehicle and stand in front of the church facing the road, you are looking at the former site of the Alsop Farm. At the time of the battle, the Brock Road forked around the farm. The gravel road continuing away from you from this position is what remains of the fork that ran to the east, while the Brock Road, to your right, continued on its present path. (This gravel road is on private property today, so do not trespass.) The two roads came back together only a mile to your southeast at what was then the Spindle Farm.

Although Fitz Lee's cavalry put up a short fight here, it would eventually move farther down the road to the Spindle Farm. Warren would send two divisions in pursuit. John Robinson's Federals would take the east fork here at the Alsop Farm, while Charles Griffin's took the west. Although they did not realize it at the time, when Warren's men reached the fields at the Spindle Farm, they would initiate the first major combat of what would be one of the war's most terrible battles, the battle for Spotsylvania Court House.

Block House Bridge

⟩ *From the church parking lot, pull out to your right, then turn left on Brock Road. Drive 1.2 miles on Brock Road, then bear right onto Block House Road and continue another 1.1 miles. Turn right onto Robert E. Lee Drive (CR 608) and drive 1.1 miles. You will come to a small bridge crossing the Po River, downstream of your previous crossing at Corbin's Bridge. Like Corbin's Bridge, there is no good place to pull over, so drive past the bridge, make the first safe U-turn, and then return to the bridge. Pull over only if it is safe to do so.*

Because of Richard Anderson's early start the previous evening, they had already reached this point, known as Block House Bridge, by 7:30 AM on May 8. It had been over nine hours of hard marching, but the Confederate infantry had a considerable jump on the Federals.

There is a misconception that the Confederates won the race to Spotsylvania Court House. Unfortunately for the Union, this is only partially true, and the actual events of the day further highlight the poor communication between commands in the Army of the Potomac. As David Gregg's and Wesley Merritt's cavalry divisions fought their Confederate counterparts, Phil Sheridan sent his third cavalry division, James Wilson's, on a roundabout route directly to Spotsylvania. Wilson had no opposition, and easily entered Spotsylvania Court House at 8 AM on May 8. Sending one brigade north to hit Fitzhugh Lee's cavalry in the rear, Wilson occupied the town with ease.

Shortly after Anderson reached Block House Bridge, citizens informed him of both Fitz Lee's fight at the Spindle Farm and Wilson's occupation of Spotsylvania Court House. Anderson made his second game-changing decision of the march, taking his lead division, Joseph Kershaw's, and splitting it in two. Two brigades went to aid the Confederate cavalry (now being commanded by J. E. B. Stuart, who had reached the field) at the Spindle Farm, while the other two headed directly for Spotsylvania Court House. Anderson would also send three brigades from his next division, Charles Field's, to the town, attempting to trap Wilson's Federals by approaching from a different direction.

Realizing that Confederate infantry was now present in force, Wilson recalled the brigade he had sent north back to the town. Before long, he realized that he was being surrounded. No other Union units were even remotely close to Wilson, and he knew that his cavalry would not be able to hold the town, so he withdrew his division to the northeast along the Fredericksburg Road (an extension of the road you are presently on). Spotsylvania Court House was now open to Field's troops, and they quickly occupied it. Anderson's early march, along with the decision he made here near the Block House Bridge, assured the Confederates that even though they did not exactly win the race to Spotsylvania Court House, they would hold the prize.

Spotsylvania Exhibit Shelter

⟩ *After you have made your U-turn, from Block House Bridge, continue 1.1 miles to Block House Road. When you come to the intersection, notice the church on your right; this was the former location of the Block House, for which the bridge and the road were named. Turn left on Block House Road and drive 1.4 miles, then turn right onto Grant Drive, the park road for the Spotsylvania battlefield. Drive 0.1 mile to the exhibit shelter on your left and park.*

This exhibit shelter serves as the National Park Service's information center for the Spotsylvania battlefield. Here you will find information on the battle itself, along with the park's many interpretive trails and roadways. If you are here during the summer, you will probably find a park historian here at the shelter, ready, able, and willing to answer any questions you have about the battle. In addition, on summer weekends, there are usually guided tours of the battlefield. If you are able, plan ahead and take one of these tours. Information about the tours and their times can be found online and at the park's Chancellorsville visitor center.

As mentioned at the beginning of the chapter, the battle here, because of both its size and the amount of time the armies spent here, can quickly become confusing, and you may find yourself either trying to remember things you already saw or backtracking across ground you've already covered. Although there was almost constant combat here for almost two weeks, there were essentially four major assaults here at Spotsylvania, occurring on May 8, 10, 12, and 18. Remembering those dates as you make your way through the battlefield may help clarify your understanding of the battle.

Laurel Hill and Spindle Field

> You have several options for visiting Laurel Hill. The ideal way, of course, is to walk the Laurel Hill trail, a 1.2-mile loop trail that begins here at the Spotsylvania Exhibit Shelter. The trail will take you along both the Union and Confederate entrenchments, as well as through the Spindle Field and past the ruins of the Spindle House. However, several spots are accessible by vehicle, so if you cannot walk the trail, you can do so by car. From the Spotsylvania exhibit shelter, pull out to your right onto Grant Drive and drive 0.2 mile, driving through the intersection with Brock Road and continuing as the road changes to Hancock Road. You will come upon a grassy opening on your left with a preserved part of the Union earthworks; carefully pull over here.

It was about 8:30 AM when John Robinson's Union division approached the fields around the Spindle House. Reaching the tree line in front of you, Warren, with Robinson, could see J. E. B. Stuart's cavalry posted on the other side of the field atop a rise known as Laurel Hill. Warren knew two things. First, the Union high command was not very pleased with his performance at the Wilderness, thinking that he had been far too cautious. Second, the longer he allowed the Confederates to dig in atop Laurel Hill, the stronger their position would become. With these in mind, he ordered Robinson to send two brigades to attack Stuart's cavalry, then went back to hurry the rest of his V Corps to the front.

What Warren did not know was that J. E. B. Stuart was no longer alone. His troopers had done an admirable job slowing the Union advance along the Brock

A view of Spindle Field from the Confederate position at Laurel Hill.

Road. His men would finally find some relief with the arrival of the reinforcements sent by Richard Anderson's infantry. As the fresh troops approached, Stuart cautioned them to remain quiet, and then positioned the infantry and artillery to form a line along the crest. The artillery was massed next to Brock Road while the flanks of the line were angled inward slightly, creating a deadly converging fire in the Spindle fields. The concealed Confederate deployment was completed just as Robinson's Federals arrived at the west side of the field.

The two Union brigades confidently advanced across the Spindle fields. Stuart allowed them to get close to the Confederate line, and then unleashed a devastating fire from both infantry and artillery. The Federals were shocked, but held their line as Robinson sent in the rest of his division. Charles Griffin's division followed close behind, advancing toward Laurel Hill on Robinson's left. Although one Union regiment was able to make it nearly to the Confederate line, the Federals were all eventually forced back to their line. (That regiment was the 7th Maryland Infantry; walking the Laurel Hill loop trail will bring you to a monument marking the furthest point of their advance on May 8.) Robinson was wounded during the assault and would lose his leg.

At 10:15 AM, Warren, with the rest of his V Corps up and now arrayed north of

Brock Road as well, renewed the assault. During the lull, however, the Confederates were also able to reinforce their own line, adding a brigade and an entire battalion of artillery—25 guns—on their right flank. Although they were now charging with three divisions, the Federals were again repulsed with heavy losses, and were busy digging their own entrenchments west of the Spindle Field by 11 AM. Meade would order Warren to conduct another assault at noon, but Warren replied that he simply could not do it.

Everyone in the Union high command knew that the more time the Confederates were given, the more difficult it would be to knock the Confederates out of their works. Meade ordered Sedgwick's VI Corps to hurry to Laurel Hill to join the V Corps in a joint attack. They arrived at 2:30 PM, exhausted after rushing to the sounds of battle, and extended the Union left. Meade and Grant were both on the field now, which created a command problem. With two corps commanders, the general commanding, and the commander of all Federal forces present, numerous confusing and conflicting orders were being sent. Warren asked for clarification of the command situation repeatedly, but Meade paid little heed. It would not be until 6:20 PM that the Federals were ready to again renew the assault.

Meade directed his men forward, but of course, by this time, the strength of the Confederate line had more than doubled. Richard Anderson's entire corps was on the line, leaving only a small force behind at Spotsylvania Court House, as it was evident that no Federals would be coming back. In addition, Richard Ewell's corps was also now well on its way, having reaching the Block House Bridge at 6 PM. As darkness quickly approached, the Federals focused their assault on the Confederate right, which they now overlapped considerably, hoping to outflank the entire line. However, just as they began their advance, Ewell's men swung into their position on that flank, arriving in time to again repulse the assault. All along the line, the Union assault had failed, and although some skirmishing went on as late as 3 PM, most of the Federals began to entrench.

In front of you is one of the more well-preserved examples of the Union line, complete with traverses. Unless you are here in the late fall or winter, you can probably not see the Spindle fields very well, but it is the clearing just past the trees in front of you. (Please do not climb the earthworks here to try to get a better view!) The Federals would hold this line for most of their time at Spotsylvania, launching further assaults on what would eventually become the Confederate left. Proceeding down Hancock Road, you can see more remnants of the line on your left, but none of the other sites have interpretation or are as accessible by vehicle.

⟩ *Make a U-turn when possible and return 0.1 mile to Brock Road, turning right. Drive 0.5 mile, first on Brock Road, then bearing left onto Block House Road. As you drive, notice the Spindle fields to your right, as well as the elevated position on the far side of the field. This was the well-defended and well-placed location of the Confederate line. Turn right onto Pritchett Road (CR 685) and drive just a short distance, pulling over when possible.*

On your right is what remains of the Confederate earthworks at Laurel Hill. You may notice that the works here are much more substantial than the Union defenses on the other side of the field. As the Confederates were on the defensive during most of their time here, they spent considerable time improving these earthworks until they were virtually impregnable by a direct assault.

Throughout this time at Spotsylvania, it would be Anderson's corps that would man these works, repulsing major attacks on May 10 and 12 that would coincide with other Union assaults on the line. Each time, the Confederates inflicted heavy casualties on Warren's V Corps, and several times ventured from the works to follow up their attacks, although they never advanced their line from this position. It was the fighting at Spindle Field, however, that defined the fighting at Spotsylvania on May 8.

Sedgwick Monument

⟩ *From here, you will be returning to the Spotsylvania Exhibit Shelter. Turn around and return to Block House Road and turn left, then drive 0.5 mile to Grant Drive. Turn right and drive 0.1 mile to the shelter. After you park, exit your vehicle and walk back toward the Brock Road to the large stone monument.*

Over the night of May 8/9, the Confederates entrenched further, adding traverses, logs, and abatis to their defenses, as well as clearing the fields of fire in front of them by cutting down any obstructive trees and other growth. Their line was arrayed with Anderson's corps on the left, running from the Po River to the Brock Road, and Ewell's on the right, picking up at the Brock Road and running approximately a half-mile to the Harrison House. A. P. Hill's corps, when it arrived, would form to Ewell's right and run all the way to Spotsylvania Court House.

Hill would not be with them. With increasing frequency, Hill was becoming too ill to hold his command, and this time it was enough to necessitate a temporary replacement. Jubal Early, who had earned a reputation as a cantankerous and difficult man but also an exceptional leader and field commander, would take command of the corps, holding it throughout the battles at Spotsylvania. Responsibility for the division he had commanded in Ewell's corps would fall to John Brown Gordon, who was also conspicuously proving himself a very capable general.

Because of the terrain to the northeast of Anderson's line, Ewell's position took on a very unusual and somewhat problematic shape. The ground was commanding, and all agreed that it should be held. However, it also created an enormous salient, or bulge, in the Confederate line. Any salient has the disadvantage of being exposed to enfilading fire, and those men left in a salient, extended in front of the line, are vulnerable to capture, particularly if the bulge is cut off from the main line. In the case of the Army of Northern Virginia, the salient contained Ewell's entire corps. Because of its size and shape, this area of the line was dubbed the "Mule Shoe," a name that would soon become infamous. Although none of the Confederates was thrilled with the Mule Shoe, all conceded that it was more important to deny the Federals use of this high ground.

The Federals also dug in, with the V and VI Corps following the shape of the Confederate defenses. Hancock's II Corps was still at Todd's Tavern, guarding against a suspected attack on the Union right, while Burnside's IX Corps was still behind the rest of the army. As the V and VI Corps worked on their fortifications, they were repeatedly harassed by fire from Confederate sharpshooters. Of particular interest to the sharpshooters was a Union battery of the VI Corps, placed at the Brock Road.

It had been decided that May 9 was to be a day of rest for the men of John Sedgwick's VI Corps; after all, they had been marching and fighting almost non-stop for five days. They would improve their earthworks, as well as receive rations and ammunition. After issuing orders to this effect, Sedgwick was informed of the Confederate sharpshooters. After his chief of staff, Martin McMahon, half-jokingly told him that he would not be going near the battery position, Sedgwick ordered skirmishers out to clear the sharpshooters out of the woods.

At 8 AM, Grant visited Sedgwick at his headquarters and had a brief chat with the general, who was in an unusually upbeat mood considering the carnage of the past few days. After Grant left, Sedgwick went to the front to inspect his lines, and soon found several problems with the line that needed correction. Around 9:30 AM, continuing his inspection near the Brock Road, he was joking with his soldiers when he noticed that several of them were instinctively ducking and weaving the occasional sharpshooter's bullet that whizzed by. Sedgwick began to kid his men for their behavior, taunting them that they were afraid for no good reason. He explained that the Confederate sharpshooters were much too far away to do any damage, remarking that "they couldn't hit an elephant from this distance." Almost immediately upon uttering those words, a bullet hit "Uncle" John Sedgwick just below his left eye, killing him instantly.

News of Sedgwick's death spread quickly. He had been well loved by his men, and many felt the loss acutely. Grant, in particular, was stunned, remarking that the effect of Sedgwick's death was greater than the loss of an entire division. The news eventually reached Confederate officers as well, many of whom were equally saddened, having served with him prior to the Civil War in the old army. James Ricketts was next in line to command the VI Corps, but he knew that it was Sedgwick's wish for Horatio Wright to take command of the corps in the event of his death, and Ricketts graciously stepped aside in favor of Wright.

The large stone monument here to John Sedgwick, complete with the insignia of the VI Corps at the top, marks the approximate spot where he fell. Several interpretive markers in the area tell the story of Sedgwick and his death. Also, if you were not able to get a good view of the Spindle Fields or Laurel Hill earlier, this position is a good one from which to view the field looking toward the Confederate position, atop the ridge in the distance.

Elsewhere on the field on May 9, the Union II Corps finally left its position at Todd's Tavern, heading west and then south in pursuit of A. P. Hill's Confederates. They would reach Block House Bridge by nightfall, where Hancock would decline to attack over the bridge in the darkness. Although there was only some combat here the next day compared to the rest of the battlefield, the events here would have a direct effect on other events of May 10.

To the east of the Mule Shoe, Burnside's IX Corps was approaching Spotsylvania Court House from the Fredericksburg Road (today's Courthouse Road). At 7:15 AM, the men had reached the Gayle Farm, only 1.5 miles from Spotsylvania Court House. The only things between Orlando Willcox's Federals and the town were elements of Fitz Lee's cavalry and the Ni River. Willcox drove Lee across the river easily and took up a position in a sheltered farm lane halfway up the opposite bank. After skirmishing for hours and receiving additional reinforcements, the IX Corps did not advance any farther than this position. At 1:15 PM, Willcox saw, in the distance, Early's corps occupying the town. For various reasons—poor maps, poor communication, and poor leadership (Burnside was not even on the field)—the Federals had not capitalized on a prime opportunity to take Spotsylvania Court House. The Confederates breathed a huge sigh of relief, as they fully expected the Union troops to advance and take the town easily.

Upton's Farm Road

〉 *Return to your vehicle at the Spotsylvania Exhibit Shelter and pull out of the parking area, this time to the left. Drive 0.6 mile on Grant Road and pull into the parking area on your right.*

The Union assaults of May 10 would begin early. At Laurel Hill, Warren began probing the Confederate lines at daybreak while pounding the Confederate position with artillery, to little effect. At 11 AM, he launched a general assault of his entire V Corps across the Spindle Fields, but his men were again repulsed along the length of the line.

While Hancock's II Corps remained at Block House Bridge, Horatio Wright sent a message to headquarters reporting that many of the Confederates in front of him—along the western leg of the Mule Shoe—were pulling out, possibly to assist in attacking Hancock's isolated position. Grant immediately saw an opportunity. If Lee was moving to crush the II Corps, then he must be weakening his line in other places, as it seemed was happening in front of Wright.

Grant wanted the Confederates to think that the Federals still intended to attack at Block House Bridge, or they would replace their troops on the line. He directed Hancock to leave one division behind as a show of force, and then withdraw the II Corps to join Warren at Laurel Hill to launch an assault there. Hancock elected to leave Francis Barlow's division, who had already crossed the bridge, as the bait. After Hancock left with his other divisions, Barlow waited nervously to see what the Confederates would do. Confederate attacks began at noon, and Hancock rushed back to tend to his stranded division. Finally receiving permission to withdraw at 2:30 PM, Barlow's men began to pull back to recross the bridge. The Confederates, assuming that a retreat was occurring, lunged forward and attacked. The fighting became very heavy, but the Federals held, repulsing the rebels three times.

Barlow would continue to fight until 5 PM. However, even though he had done his job and kept the Confederates in place, they were not who Grant thought they were. They were Early's men, and had been in front of Burnside's corps. The Confederate position at the Mule Shoe had not been weakened in the slightest.

Grant continued to plan his attack, certain that an assault along the Confederate line would reveal a weakness somewhere. Orders were issued for a 5 PM attack. Before that could happen, though, Warren and Hancock launched an unsuccessful attack at Laurel Hill, and reports came in regarding Confederates behind the Union right. Although these reports turned out to be false, it was enough to push the Union assault back to 7 PM.

Waiting anxiously through all of these developments and delays was a young brigade commander, Col. Emory Upton. Only 24 years old, Upton was extremely ambitious and loved nothing more than combat. He had proposed an attack upon the Confederate line that not all of his superiors were convinced would work, but now was the perfect time and place to try it. Rather than attack across the entire line, Upton wanted to take a large force and direct its entire weight against a single weak point in the Confederate line. Rather than stopping to fire and reload, his men would race across the open field to the enemy's position, holding their fire until they had reached the rebel works. With a breakthrough achieved quickly, the force would then turn in opposite directions and proceed down the Confederate line to widen the gap, while other Federal units, poised to exploit the gap, would rush in and establish their position.

With Grant giving his approval, Meade asked Horatio Wright to pick 12 regiments for the attack, while Confederate engineers discussed the best place for the point of attack. They quickly settled on a small salient on the west leg of the Mule Shoe held by George Doles's Confederate brigade. The field in front of the salient was flat, and a small stand of thick woods stretched to within 200 yards of the Confederate line, giving the Federals a good place to form their ranks under cover before making their short dash across the field. The breakthrough would be exploited by Gershom Mott's division of the II Corps, while Burnside's IX Corps would attack from the other side of the Mule Shoe to prevent Confederates from rushing to the breach.

Upton, of course, would lead the assault. When receiving word that his plan would be enacted, then seeing the list of crack regiments that would be under his command, his confidence went through the roof. As an added incentive, he was told that if the assault didn't work, he was to come back. If it did, he would be rewarded with a promotion to brigadier general.

In the area where you are now standing, Upton gathered his men—approximately 5,000—and provided very specific instructions to each of his 12 regiments. One regiment was to first proceed through the woods, driving off any Confederate pickets present. The rest of the force would then proceed through a narrow farm lane through the woods to the jump-off point for the attack. The men would form in four lines. The first would contain three regiments, two of which would be directed squarely at a Confederate battery just to the right of the salient while the third regiment began to move to the left. The second and third lines would follow the first to widen the gap, while the fourth would wait in the woods to await developments. The instructions for all of the men were the same: no speaking as they moved through the woods, no yelling during the attack, no stopping during the run across the field to help wounded comrades, no firing until they were in the Confederate earthworks. The men in Upton's force were the best of the best, all veterans and all well-disciplined, and there was little worry that they would not carry out their orders to the letter. With the plan of attack made, the men made their way down the farm lane and into the woods across from what would forever after be known as Doles's Salient.

Here at the parking area, a trail follows the path of the farm road through the woods and directly to the location of the salient. If you are able, take this trail. It is a one-way trail, so you will have to double back, but it is also fairly short—about 0.5 mile total—and will not take very long. The trail does go down through a small ravine and back up, so there will be some climbing in both directions, but the dirt path is clear and cared for. Once you reach the edge of the woods, you will find a monument to both Upton's regiments and the Confederate brigades who fought in the action. From here, the trail crosses an open field to the location of the salient, where interpretive signs tell the story of Upton's assault.

If you cannot or do not wish to take the trail, Doles's Salient is along the park road, and will be the next stop on your tour.

Doles's Salient

> *Pull out from the parking area and continue on Grant Drive, which then becomes Anderson Drive, for 0.5 mile. Pull over at the interpretive signs on your right.*

Gersham Mott, whose II Corps division was the unit that was to exploit Upton's breakthrough if he were successful, was placed under the direct command of Horatio Wright, commander of the VI Corps. From the beginning of the day, Mott had received numerous conflicting orders, and by the time the assignment for the assault on Doles's Salient was received, Mott's division, which had only 1,500 available men, was strung out to the east, as one of his orders was to bridge the gap between the VI and IX Corps. Of all the botched orders for the day, though, perhaps the most important one was one that he never received.

Mott was never informed that the 5 PM assault had been pushed back, so his division stepped off promptly at the appointed time. His position was near the Brown House, near the northern end of the Mule Shoe. Therefore, to reach Doles's Salient, Mott would have to march across the front of almost half the western leg of the Mule Shoe with his left open to the Confederates the entire time. As soon as they came within firing range, Mott's men began to receive a terrible fire from first Confederate

Looking east toward the center of the Confederate Mule Shoe from near Doles's Salient.

artillery, then musketry, and it was not long before he was forced to return his torn division to the Brown House.

Although no one was left to support Upton's attack, the day was growing late with little to show for it. Meade moved the assault up, and at 5:55 PM, Union batteries opened to soften the Confederate line, the main result of which was that Richard Ewell became suspicious that the Federals were up to something, and he prepared his corps to receive an attack. At 6 PM, Upton received word to hold, then was ordered forward by Meade at 6:35 PM. Through all this activity, however, there was one critical omission. No one had told Emory Upton that Mott's division had already attacked, and no one had arranged for any other Union units to support Upton should he break through the Confederate line.

Turn your back to the road and face the field. Walking forward just a bit on the path (the same one that begins at the last stop), you will see remnants of the Confederate earthworks that formed the Mule Shoe. With darkness coming quickly, Upton's first line came rushing out of the woods just slightly to your left shortly after Meade's order to attack was issued. It had been estimated by Confederate engineers that the Federals would take about one minute to reach your present position from the wood line. The first volley slowed, but did not stop, Upton's first line, and his men kept forward, clearing the abatis and other obstructions in front of them. Just in front of your position, the Federals took a second volley, then stormed over the works and opened fire. Just as planned, two regiments went to the right—your left—to silence the Confederate battery, while the third regiment went down the line in the other direction. The fighting was some of the fiercest of the war, with men using muskets as clubs, bayoneting, and using every available implement during their hand-to-hand struggle.

Within minutes, however, the second Union line, with Upton at the lead, came across the field to widen the gap, followed shortly by the third. With the area now intermixed with both friend and enemy, the rebels around Doles's brigade were hesitant to fire into the melee. The Confederate battery was silenced, and the Federals continued to move down the line, taking each part of the line piece by piece. Ewell rushed to the area, directing his units and eventually ordering a countercharge by Robert Johnston's brigade.

Upton's Federals performed magnificently, capturing many Confederates, but without support, the attack eventually lost its momentum. With the only exception of his fourth line, which went in on its own account, none of the Union units observing the attack had been ordered to go in, and none did. Slowly, the Confederates began to push the sides of the gap back until it had closed completely, and the Union troops were forced to fall back to the woods. Many of the rebels who had been captured (including Doles) simply ran back to their positions in the Mule Shoe.

By 7:30 PM, the attack at Doles's Salient was over. The Federals had lost approximately 1,000 of the best soldiers of the VI Corps. The Confederates had lost quite a few themselves (estimates range from 1,200 to 1,500), but they had held their position. Remarkably, many in the Union high command placed the blame on Mott, whose division was taken away from him. As for the soldiers, a great deal of them could not help but think that if "Uncle" John Sedgwick had been in command, none of this mess would have happened.

As for Emory Upton, he had earned, and soon received, his stars.

Reconstructed Entrenchments

> *From Doles's Salient, continue 0.6 mile, keeping right on Anderson Drive. Park at the dead end.*

Following the fighting of May 12, the Confederates abandoned the Mule Shoe and formed a new line in this location. As the interpretive signs here will tell you, the Federals launched an attack on these works on May 18. For now, though, carefully examine the reconstructed set of earthworks here.

When touring Civil War battlefields today, when you see earthworks, they are almost always similar to what you see on the left and right of the reconstruction: a small line of earth that, in some cases, is only barely discernible from the surrounding landscape. However, when the battles at Spotsylvania and those afterward were fought, the troops were contending with what you now see before you. By late 1863, having learned terrible lessons at Fredericksburg and Gettysburg, soldiers knew that charging against entrenched positions such as this one were nearly suicidal. Accordingly, men on the defensive quickly learned to construct some form of earthworks to protect themselves. Depending on the amount of time they spent there, the earthworks could range from simple dirt constructions to log and rail barricades such as what you see here, complete with abatis and other obstructions in front and often even a head rail to protect the men as they fired their weapons. Traverses, perpendicular extensions along the line, also quickly became common, as they provided the best way to hold off a flank attack.

As you tour the battlefields, to complete your picture of the battle, be sure to remember that these types of works were what the soldiers were attacking or defending. This becomes particularly important here at Spotsylvania, especially as you tour the terrible fighting of May 12—the battle for the Mule Shoe.

McCoull House and Ramseur Monument

> *From the parking area, drive 0.3 mile on Anderson Drive, then bear right onto Gordon Drive for 0.1 mile. Turn left onto the park road and drive 0.2 mile to the site of the McCoull House.*

Site of the McCoull House at the center of the Mule Shoe, Spotsylvania.

May 11 brought heavy rain, and soldiers took advantage of the weather to take what rest they could. Planning at the headquarters of both armies continued. Upton's attack the previous day, though ultimately unsuccessful, proved that similar assaults could work, if properly conducted. With this in mind, Grant forged a strategy for the next day, May 12, which would bring about what was quite possibly the fiercest combat of the war.

The Union army would concentrate its force at a single point on the Confederate line, just as Upton had. This time, though, it would be the entire II Corps, the Army of the Potomac's largest and best corps, which would make the attack. The point of attack would be the northern tip of the Mule Shoe. By taking the tip of the giant salient, the legs could not stand. The other Union corps would attack in their front and hold the Confederates in place, preventing them from reinforcing Ewell's corps, which held the Mule Shoe. Warren's V Corps would attack at Laurel Hill again, holding Anderson's Confederates in place, while Burnside's IX Corps would attack the eastern part of the line to hold Early's men. Wright's VI Corps would be held in reserve to lend support where needed.

To get into position, Hancock's II Corps would have to move to the attack position, the Brown House north of the Mule Shoe, from its current position near Laurel Hill. After a reconnaissance of the Confederate left confirmed their position, Hancock's men would withdraw successfully at 9 PM, moving behind the V and VI Corps undetected. The only other Union movement necessary was that Burnside's men moved to their right, bringing them closer to the rest of the Federals.

These two actions had unintended consequences that, as it turned out, could have been devastating to the Confederates. Lee saw the movement on his left and right and came to the conclusion that the Federals, having lost a great many men and finding the Confederate works unassailable, were retreating to Fredericksburg. He ordered his commanders to be on the alert that the Union army might be withdrawing, and if it was, to attack with everything they had.

Lee also ordered a massive shift in his artillery. Worried about the position of the Mule Shoe, the Confederates had initially placed Edward "Allegheny" Johnson's veteran division of Ewell's corps at the tip, along with 30 guns. Having made up his mind that the Federals were moving out, Lee ordered the cannons removed from the position and moved to the army's right. Late in the day, Johnson discovered while inspecting the lines that his artillery had been removed. Shocked, he protested, but his pleas fell on deaf ears.

Had those 30 pieces of artillery remained at the tip of the Mule Shoe, the events of the next day, May 12, would likely have been quite different. Instead, Winfield Hancock's corps of 20,000 men would be charging Johnson's position with no Confederate canister or grape flying at them. Lee had unwittingly made a very costly mistake.

You are now standing in the middle of the Mule Shoe. The McCoull House, as you can see by the outlined bricks, stood here. Remarkably, the McCoull family remained in the house during the battles at Spotsylvania, hiding in the basement during combat. Also occupying the house was Richard Ewell, as its central location made a perfect place for his headquarters.

As you stand at the rail fence and face the house site, the tip of the Mule Shoe is to your left front, about 400 yards through the trees. Turning to your left, you can see an open field, with a park road in the near distance. This is the location of Doles's Salient, where you had stopped earlier. You will find a path mown through the field here leading to and beyond a fairly large monument. The monument commemorates the actions of Stephen Ramseur's brigade during the combat of May 12, which swirled in the woods and fields all around where you now stand. Much of the area to your left front was more open

A monument to Stephen Ramseur's Brigade, which helped stem the tide of the Union attack at the Mule Shoe.

than it is today. Take the short walk to the Ramseur monument if you can, if for no other reason than to get an idea of the terrain across which the fighting occurred.

The Bloody Angle

❭ *From the McCoull House parking area, drive 0.2 mile back to Gordon Road, then turn right onto Gordon Drive. Keep to the right and follow Anderson Drive, then Grant Drive, for 0.5 mile and park in the area on your right.*

Hancock's men began to reach the Brown House at around 12:30 AM on May 12, and almost immediately Confederate pickets in front of the tip of the Mule Shoe detected their presence. Word quickly went back to Allegheny Johnson, who sent an aide, then went himself, to Ewell to get his artillery back to its original position immediately. Ewell said that Lee had had his mind set, but was eventually convinced to order them back. A copy of the order was forwarded to Lee, who immediately grew concerned, and further stressed that the guns be returned by daylight. The order was received at 3:30 AM, giving the artillerymen 20 minutes to move the cannons from Spotsylvania Court House to the tip of the Mule Shoe. It would not happen.

The attack had been set for 4 AM, but the morning blackness, along with a dense fog hanging over the field, compelled Hancock to delay the attack slightly. At 4:35 AM,

Memorials commemorate various units at the Bloody Angle, Spotsylvania.

Artillery marks the northern tip of the Mule Shoe. The initial Union attack came from across these fields.

the lead unit, David Birney's division, quickly and quietly made its way toward the Mule Shoe, with Francis Barlow's division on his left and only slightly behind. The Federals ran right past the rebel pickets, many of whom had been sleeping in their rifle pits, and hit the Confederate line, breaking up the abatis in front as quickly as possible. All semblance of orderly advance was already gone as Hancock's 20,000 men hurled themselves at Allegheny Johnson's 4,500.

It took some time for the Union men to push the abatis to the side, and it was enough for the Confederates to begin to mass to meet them. Instead of being greeted by a wall of fire, however, they instead heard only clicks and snaps. The heavy rains of the previous day and the current heavy fog had rendered much of their gunpowder too wet to fire. It was enough to allow the Federals to get past the abatis, descend the small ravine, and climb to the top of the earthworks. There, after following the same instructions that Upton had given his men two days before, they unleashed their first volley.

The results were devastating and decisive. The Union attack crushed the northern tip of the Mule Shoe, and Confederates were shot down or captured by the score. Barlow had hit the Mule Shoe at a small protrusion later known as the East Angle, with Birney overcoming the works to his right at the West Angle. General Johnson, as well as two of his brigade commanders, Robert Johnston and George Steuart, were quickly captured and sent to the rear. One by one, the Federals went down each leg of the salient, moving from traverse to traverse, with the Confederates fighting them desperately the entire time. For those who survived the fighting in the Mule Shoe on May 12, it was almost universally agreed that this was the most vicious hand-to-hand fighting of the entire war.

By 5 PM, Hancock reported to Grant that his men were inside the second line of Confederate works, and that they had captured over 2,000 prisoners. But the strength of the attack was now becoming a problem. In capturing over a half-mile of the Confederate line, the Federal success had certainly been amazing. However, 20,000 Union soldiers were now squeezed into a formation less than a half-mile wide, and their attack was beginning to lose momentum. Further, other units were now being rushed to the front by Richard Ewell and Robert E. Lee, and Confederate artillery was now making an appearance. Although the Federals had already overrun several pieces, the rebels had shot their own horses to prevent the enemy from taking them back to their own lines. The guns that hadn't been captured were now turned on the Union men, and they were used to great effect.

On the western leg of the salient, elements of Robert Rodes's were next in line after Johnson's division had been virtually destroyed. Rodes ordered Stephen Ramseur's brigade in, and they countercharged the oncoming Federals just to the west of the Mc-Coull House. John Brown Gordon also sent two of his brigades in toward the east leg, although the Confederate lines disappeared as quickly as the Union lines had in the confusion.

Ambrose Burnside's corps added their weight to the attack on the eastern face of the salient, and with success of the other Federal units, Robert Potter's division was able to briefly take some of the lines in its front. However, the fight here was not what the Union soldiers were hoping for, and Burnside was not able to fully exploit the chaos in his front. Failing to connect with Hancock's men on their right, the IX Corps soon found itself stalemated.

By 6 AM, Hancock was asking Meade to send the VI Corps to his aid. It was a similar situation to Upton's attack on May 10; the breakthrough had been successful, and now it needed to be reinforced. However, only Thomas Neill's division was at the Brown House, while the other corps' other two divisions were still far from the field. Neill sent his brigades toward the West Angle, where the Confederates were now slugging it out toe to toe with the Federals. The death struggle between the two armies here would more properly rename this position the Bloody Angle.

The mile-long trail at the Bloody Angle is an easy walk, much of it paved and the rest on soft grass. Although there are several hills, they are not overly taxing. The park service has created a seven-stop walking tour here that you can follow. Also, if you follow along the tree line to your right (which roughly corresponds to the position of

From the Union line, the elevated Confederate position at the Mule Shoe, as well as the low ground in front of the Bloody Angle, is easily discernible.

the Mule Shoe itself), you will soon come to the tip of the salient, the point at which Hancock's men first hit the Confederate line. Continuing just a bit farther will bring you to the East Angle.

The focus, of course, is the Bloody Angle, where there are several monuments to the units that fought here so desperately on May 12, 1864. Walking the trail will give you an idea of why the fight concentrated here. The ground in front of the angle takes quite a dramatic dip, and many of the Union soldiers tried to use this to their advantage, taking what little shelter they could. The Confederates, on the other hand, had an ideal position for firing on many of the Federals in this area. The earthworks on this part of the line changed possession many times, with the enemy troops often using opposite sides of the same breastwork as they mauled each other.

By 10 AM, after David Russell's Federal VI Corps division and several brigades from the Confederate corps of Anderson and Ewell were brought into the fight, there were six Union brigades firing into the Bloody Angle, defended by four rebel brigades. The fight around the Mule Shoe had grown into a bloody stalemate all around, and Grant, who surmised that Lee had to have weakened his line at other points, ordered a renewed attack at Laurel Hill. He knew that the chances of success there were slim (and he turned out to be quite correct, as Warren's men were cut up badly), but the soldiers around the Mule Shoe needed any relief they could be given, no matter how small.

While more units were poured into the fight, both Lee and Grant desperately looked for a way to break the stalemate. Lee eventually came to the conclusion that the Mule Shoe had to be abandoned, and he set men to work preparing a secondary line at the base of the salient. Grant ordered Burnside to renew his assault on the east face of the salient, but he met little success.

By 6 PM, Grant finally gave up on the IX Corps, telling them to dig in and await developments. The II and VI Corps were ordered to strengthen the positions they had. With darkness, the fighting died down but did not stop, and the two sides kept up the fight throughout most of the night. It was not until 3 AM on May 13 that the Confederates, with their new defensive line prepared, withdrew from the Mule Shoe. The battle had gone on without a stop for over 20 hours.

Shortly after dawn on May 13, those Federals still in the field reported that Lee's men were gone, and that they had possession of the Bloody Angle. By 10:30 AM, reconnaissance had revealed the details of Lee's new line, and it was as strong as any the Confederates had ever held. It did not matter; no one on either side was able to continue the struggle.

> CASUALTIES—
> SPOTSYLVANIA
> COURT HOUSE,
> MAY 7–21
>
> **Confederate:** killed and wounded, 6,519; missing or captured, 5,543; total: 12,062
>
> **Union:** killed, 2,725; wounded, 13,416; missing or captured, 2,258; total: 18,399
>
> **Total Casualties: 30,461**

The casualty counts vary greatly. The official losses for the Federals came to 6,820, but some historians place that total closer to 9,000. The Confederates had lost about 8,000, including 3,000 captured, mostly early in the fight. They had also lost the salient, but that was acceptable. The loss in manpower, however, was something they could not afford.

Harrison House

⟩ *From the parking area at the Bloody Angle, pull out to the left and follow Grant Drive, then Anderson Drive, for 0.5 mile. Bear left onto Gordon Drive, then pull over at the designated parking area.*

Robert E. Lee's headquarters at Spotsylvania was at the Harrison House, located just south of the Mule Shoe. When the Confederates reformed their line over the night of May 12 and 13, their new line—to be their final one at Spotsylvania—was placed just on the ridge behind (south of) the house. In the field across from you, you can see the remains of the house itself; the only pieces left are parts of the chimney, left after the home burned down well after the battle.

East Angle Trail

❭ *Turn left on Gordon Drive and drive 0.6 mile. Pull into the parking area on the left.*

The trail here follows along the eastern leg of the salient, wrapping around to the tip of the Mule Shoe. There are several markers along the trail here, so if you did not walk the trail from the stop at the Bloody Angle, you can further explore the Confederate salient from here. The battlefield here has many great trails to follow, so do follow along this one if you have the time.

Heth's Salient

❭ *Pull out of the parking area and continue for 0.4 mile on Grant Drive, which will then become Burnside Drive. Pull into the parking area on your right.*

At about 2 PM on May 12, during the fight for the Mule Shoe, Grant once again ordered Burnside's IX Corps forward, hoping that the Confederates had weakened their right to reinforce Ewell's corps. His target was a massive bulge at the eastern base of the Mule Shoe occupied by Henry Heth of Early's corps. However, as Burnside was preparing to advance, Early could see the left flank of the Union IX Corps dangling in front of him, tantalizingly open. He arranged to send two brigades against Burnside's flank.

Both sides' assaults occurred simultaneously. While Burnside's artillery enfiladed the southern part of what would be known as Heth's Salient, Early's two brigades formed in the woods just south of Burnside's left. The Federals were able to break through the Confederate line at the salient, but were forced to withdraw because of the rebel attack, which was rolling up their left flank. Within 30 minutes, both attacks were called off, with Union and Confederate units alike taking heavy casualties for little gain.

When the latter reformed their defensive line overnight, Heth's Salient remained as part of the line, an odd protrusion from an otherwise straightforward defensive position. Over the next few days, Grant explored an attack on the Confederate right, which had so far remained mostly out of the fight. Heavy rain, however, prevented either army from doing much of anything. On the evening of May 13, the Union V and VI Corps, after almost a week of futility, finally abandoned their position in front of Laurel Hill, pulling behind the II and IX Corps and emerging on the Union left, extending it well east of the Fredericksburg Road and eventually south across the

Massaponax Church Road. To correspond with the Union movement, Lee moved Richard Anderson's corps from Laurel Hill to extend the Confederate right.

On May 18, after having had to sit through several days of rain and having had time to develop and change his plan several times, Grant launched another assault on the Confederate line. The previous night, the II and VI Corps swung back around to the Union right, placing themselves in front of Ewell's corps. While the Confederates weren't expecting an attack on their left, their entrenchments made them more than happy to receive one.

In addition, Burnside's IX Corps was placed near their original position, assigned to attack the point where Ewell's and Early's corps connected, which happened to be just north and west of Heth's Salient. As Burnside's men advanced toward the point, their left was exposed to the Confederates in the salient, and they were soon caught in a crossfire. The II and VI Corps, advancing against Ewell's entrenchments, were easily repulsed, and the attack, which had begun at 4:30 AM, was officially called off by Meade at 8:45 AM—even though it had really been finished for some time.

The area of Heth's Salient is much more wooded than it was during the time of the battle, and it is a bit difficult to picture the action of either May 12 or 18. You will find a monument to the 17th Michigan Infantry and its sacrifice on May 12. (The anchor is the insignia of the Union IX Corps.)

Gayle Farm

❭ *Follow the park road 1 mile to its intersection with Courthouse Road. Turn left on Courthouse Road and drive 0.8 mile. Make a U-turn in the median and, if safe, pause a moment to observe the valley below.*

You are now viewing the Ni River Valley. The road you are on, Courthouse Road, was the Fredericksburg Road at the time of the battle. Your position here is near the former site of the Gayle Farm, where the IX Corps formed during its advance toward Spotsylvania Court House on May 9. The town is 1.5 miles to your front. Benjamin Christ's brigade crossed the Ni early on May 9, taking a position halfway up the slope you see opposite you, but unfortunately for the Federals, it did not press its advantage.

SPOTSYLVANIA COURT HOUSE

❭ *Continue through the median and drive 1.1 miles on Courthouse Road. The road will split here; turn left and follow Courthouse Road another 0.7 mile. Pull into the public parking area just before the T intersection.*

You are now in Spotsylvania Court House, the original object of both armies before they began their monumental battle just to the northwest on May 8. Take a few

Zion Methodist Church in Spotsylvania Court House served as both headquarters and hospital for the Army of Northern Virginia.

moments to walk around the immediate area of the intersection here. Across the street from you is the courthouse itself, one of the few buildings present at the time of the battle. To your right, at the T of the intersection, is what used to be Sanford's Tavern, which served as Jubal Early's headquarters while the Confederates occupied the town. The town jail, erected in 1855, was here during the battle, and is now open as a tourist attraction. Just across the street is the Spotsylvania Court House Museum, formerly the Old Berea Christian Church.

Zion Methodist Church

❭ *From the parking area, pull to your right, then turn left onto Courthouse Road (SR 208). Drive 0.5 mile and pull into the parking lot for Zion Methodist Church on your right.*

As the Union and Confederate lines shifted to the south and east, Zion Methodist Church became a hospital, observation post, and temporary headquarters for the Confederates. A. P. Hill first used the church, then Robert E. Lee as he and Grant tried to read each other's mind regarding their next intentions.

MASSAPONAX CHURCH

⟩ *From the parking lot, drive straight out of the lot onto Massaponax Church Road*
(CR 608). Drive 4.9 miles on Massaponax Church Road and pull into the parking lot
for Massaponax Church on your left, just before the intersection with Jefferson Davis
Highway (US 1).

After the assault of May 18 had failed, Ulysses S. Grant was convinced that remaining at Spotsylvania Court House would be an exercise in futility. The Confederates would not leave their strong defensive positions to fight. There was only one way
to draw them out, and that was to again resort to maneuver.

One of Timothy O'Sullivan's famous photos of the Union high command from the
upper level of Massaponax Church. Grant is leaning over the bench, looking over
George Meade's shoulder.

On May 20, Grant issued orders for the various corps, and at 10 PM that night, the Union II Corps left its works and began heading south. The army would move around the Confederate right, compelling Lee to leave his works here and again fall back toward the Confederate capital at Richmond.

A landmark for most of the army as it made its way south was Massaponax Church. The original building, since added onto, stands before you. At 11 AM on May 21, Grant and Meade arrived, riding ahead of Warren's V Corps, and made the church their headquarters. During the afternoon, the generals and their respective staff met on the church grounds, sitting on pews dragged out from the church. Photographer Timothy O'Sullivan, who was traveling with the army, climbed to one of the church's upper stories and captured a series of now-famous pictures that have been continuously reprinted in history books for 150 years. The images of the meeting are remarkable— no poses, no arrangements, just the Union high command actively planning the next part of the Federal campaign, the movement to the North Anna River.

4

The Overland Campaign, Part II: The North Anna, Cold Harbor, and the Race to Petersburg

ROBERT E. LEE HAD SEEN that the Union army would move south, though he never suspected that it would move as far as it did. He had earlier ordered Richard Ewell's corps down the Telegraph Road, the most direct route, to meet the Federals there, expecting to battle them again somewhere close to his lines at Spotsylvania Court House. Lee was expecting reinforcements (John Breckinridge's force was on its way from the Shenandoah Valley), and would be ready for the Federals if they wanted to fight.

It would not be until midday on May 21, 1864 that Lee realized that the Union was not just shifting its army; its men were on the move. Winfield Hancock's II Corps, which had left at 10 PM the night before, was at the town of Milford, 20 miles southeast of Spotsylvania Courthouse, by noon. The Federals had not used the Telegraph Road. They had moved far to the east, toward Massaponax Church, then southeast to Guinea Station, to avoid having to cross the Ni, Po, and Matta Rivers, all of which were swollen with the recent heavy rains. Lee could not pursue them, however, because there were still enough Union troops in his front to prevent his pulling out of his works without being mauled. Although Hancock was precariously extended from the rest of the army, the Federals had stolen a march on Lee.

A bridge across Totopotomoy Creek, looking toward the Union position.

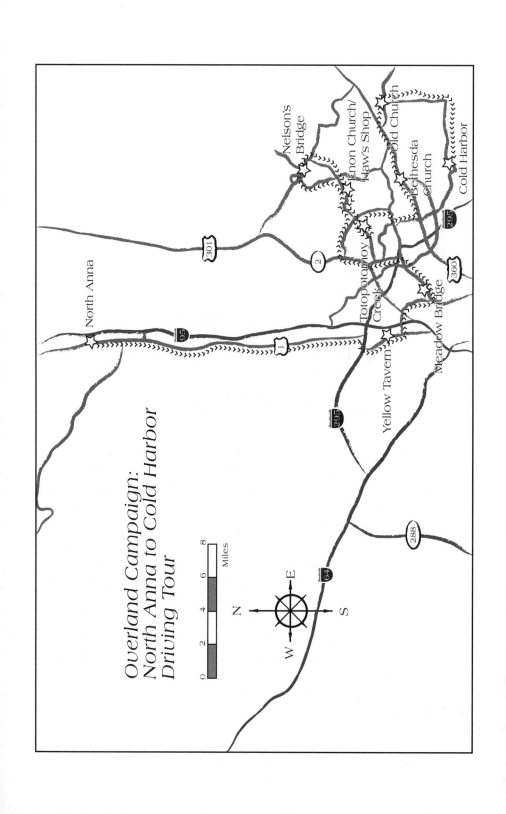

Overland Campaign:
North Anna to Cold Harbor
Driving Tour

Miles
0   2   4   6   8

N
W   E
S

North Anna

301

95

1

2

Nelson's
Bridge

Enon Church/
Haw's Shop

Old Church

Bethesda
Church

Cold Harbor

295

Totopotomoy
Creek

360

Yellow Tavern

Meadow Bridge

295

288

64

Hancock's isolation was by design. Ulysses S. Grant had sent the II Corps ahead, hoping to bait Lee into attack, but it did not work. By evening, the rest of the Union army was on its way south, following the same path to the east that Hancock had used. With Confederate cavalry swarming about, the men would spend a nervous night on May 21/22, wondering whether the Confederates were onto them or not.

Lee was not able to get his men moving until 7 PM on May 21, but when they did move, they moved fast. The Telegraph Road was open to them, a route leading due south. The last of the Confederates were out of Spotsylvania Court House by midnight. By 8:30 AM on May 22, Lee, riding at the head of Ewell's corps, was crossing Chesterfield Bridge over the North Anna River, with the rest of his army making its way over the river by noon and digging a new defensive line.

Union pickets had detected the Federal movement on the Telegraph Road, but remarkably, none of the reports reached headquarters. A stunned Grant, realizing that Lee had now moved south of him, decided to head straight for the enemy at the North Anna. The army would rest and reunite on May 22, and would move the next morning down the Telegraph Road, directly toward the Confederate line. Meeting only light resistance from rebel cavalry, the Federals would reach the North Anna by noon on May 23.

The Union and Confederate armies had been fighting almost nonstop since May 5. Both the Wilderness and Spotsylvania Court House had taken a toll on both sides, but both were also now being reinforced. There would be no letup here at the North Anna on May 23, and the two armies would fight several major rolling battles before they settled (for only a short time) northeast of Richmond on June 3. Neither Union pressure nor Confederate resistance would give way as the opposing forces wrestled each other southward over the North Anna, along Totopotomoy Creek, and finally to the battlefield at Cold Harbor.

BEFORE YOU GO

» PLANNING YOUR TRIP

Keep your walking shoes on for this one. Although all of the sites can be toured easily by car, there are also great trails at almost every stop, many of them leading you to some extremely well-preserved earthworks and other remnants of the battle. Some of the trails can run a bit longer than some of the other park trails you've visited so far, but the walks at North Anna Battlefield Park, Totopotomoy

THE OVERLAND CAMPAIGN, PART II

Number of sites: 9 (plus one optional)

Total miles: 90 (168 with optional stop)

Estimated time: 3–5 days

Creek, and Cold Harbor are well worth taking the time. They are shaded walks on good paths and are worth making time for.

Something else to remember, though—particularly in the areas northeast of Richmond—is that these grounds are near some prime mosquito grounds. Insect repellent will be a necessity here. If you stick to the other basics (good hiking shoes, hiking socks, and water), and come prepared for the hike, you'll have a great experience.

There is an optional site tacked onto this tour—the cavalry fight at Trevilian Station. The battle happened after Cold Harbor and was one of the larger cavalry fights of the war, but the site is a bit isolated from the rest of the tour. Still, if you have time, try to see it. It was quite a dramatic battle, including "Custer's first last stand," and the Trevilian Station Battlefield Foundation has created a great driving tour to show it off. The battlefield is closer to the North Anna battlefield than the other end of the tour at Cold Harbor, so if you choose to tour the site out of order rather than make the drive back, you're forgiven.

» RECOMMENDATIONS

The tour in this chapter links the end of the tour in the previous chapter with the tour of the siege of Petersburg in chapter 7. If you do have the time, link this tour with one or both of the others. Just be sure to give yourself enough time to enjoy the sites without rushing yourself through them.

Some hotels are available along the interstate in the vicinity of the North Anna battlefield, but you may want to base yourself in Richmond and make the quick drive up to the sites. There are certainly more options in this area. That said, if you plan on taking the trip to Trevilian Station (and you should), it might not be a bad idea to find somewhere to stay for at least the first night of your tour.

Also remember that you will spend a good deal of time in and around Richmond, and while you can certainly immerse yourself in just the history of the Civil War here, there is also plenty of other history in the area, from Jamestown to Patrick Henry to Edgar Allan Poe. There are also plenty of other activities that might be more family-friendly. Virginia Beach is less than two hours away from downtown Richmond, Colonial Williamsburg is a treat for everyone, and the plantations along the James River are spectacular. Finally, just a stone's throw from the North Anna battlefield is King's Dominion, a massive theme park that might serve as a good day break from touring the sites of the war.

THE CAMPAIGN TOUR

NORTH ANNA

Mount Carmel Church

❭ *Begin your tour at Mount Carmel Church, at the intersection of Jefferson Davis Highway (US 1) and Jericho Road (VA 658) in the town of Ruther Glen, just west of I-95 exit 104.*

The designated point where the Union Army of the Potomac would meet up was Mount Carmel Church, 3 miles north of the Telegraph Road crossing of the North Anna. The II and V Corps showed up shortly after 10 AM on May 23, and soon Hancock and Gouverneur Warren were comparing notes about their incorrect maps. After some discussion about the proper routes to take, they came up with a solution that seemed to eliminate the guesswork from their intended march. Warren's V Corps

Mount Carmel Church served as Union headquarters during the battle at the North Anna River.

would head west to cross the North Anna at a ford known as Jericho Mills, and Horatio Wright's VI Corps would follow . Hancock's II Corps would continue south on the Telegraph Road (today's Jefferson Davis Highway, US 1), crossing the river at Chesterfield Bridge, just as the Confederates had. Ambrose Burnside's IX Corps would also move upriver to the west, seeking an intermediate crossing between the two points.

Later in the day, George Meade and Ulysses S. Grant would arrive at Mount Carmel Church, setting their headquarters here and remaining behind the lines for the entire battle. The center building of the church complex, marked 1793, was the building present during the Federals' stay here. As at other churches used for such purposes, pews, pulpits, and alters were used desks and places to rest, while the generals and their staff busily went about the work that typified a military command center. The Union high command would maintain its headquarters here until the army left on May 26.

Long Creek

⟩ *From the roundabout in front of the church, turn right onto Jericho Road, then take the next immediate right onto Jefferson Davis Highway (US 1). Drive 2.6 miles until you reach a small bridge along the highway. Carefully pull over to the side of the road, making sure that you are well outside of any traffic.*

On the south bank of the North Anna River, the Confederates, although they continued to strengthen their line, were mostly looking forward to a day of rest on May 23. Their defensive position covered Chesterfield Bridge and the Telegraph Road, as well as the bridge of the Richmond, Fredericksburg, & Potomac Railroad, just downstream to the east. In addition, A. P. Hill's corps (he had recovered from his illness and retaken command of his troops, sending Jubal Early back to his division) was posted to the west, covering Ox Ford and Jericho Mills, the two primary crossing points of the river upstream from the bridges.

Besides the fact that the south bank of the river provided an excellent defensive position, there was another critical feature here. This was the location of the vital Hanover Junction, where the RF&P Railroad, running north and south, joined the Virginia Central Railroad, running from the west along the south bank of the river. The Virginia Central hauled the bounty from the farms of the Shenandoah Valley through Charlottesville and Gordonsville, while the junction provided goods coming from there a direct route to Richmond. The RF&P Railroad, of course, was a perfect direct supply line for Lee's army, bringing food, supplies, and soldiers from the capital. The continued operation of both railroads was a necessity for the Confederacy.

Just north of the river, left over from earlier positions constructed at Chesterfield Bridge, was a small, three-sided redoubt facing north, just to the west of the Telegraph

Road. It was manned by only John Henagan's brigade, part of Joseph Kershaw's division of Richard Anderson's Confederate corps. They were the only rebel soldiers north of the river, but their redoubt was strong, and in front of them lay 600 yards of open field. The position felt comfortable enough that Henagan's men took the time to bathe in the river, a luxury they had not been able to partake of for quite some time. While they were in the water, Confederate cavalry thundered by them, across Chesterfield Bridge and onto the south bank. The rebel infantry quickly exited the river, dressed, and manned the redoubt.

Pursuing the Confederates—Wade Hampton's cavalry—were Alfred T. A. Torbert's horsemen. Torbert, back only shortly after surgery, was commanding the few Union cavalry that had not gone with Phil Sheridan on a daring raid to Richmond over the past two weeks. Torbert found a strong defensive position at what he thought was the North Anna River, and then prepared to hold his position, waiting for the infantry to arrive.

The problem, though, was that Torbert had not reached the North Anna River. He had reached Long Creek, which you are now overlooking. As you can see, it is not a small creek, and could be mistaken for a river—particularly if there is only one waterway on your map, as was the case with Torbert. However, compared to the North Anna (which Torbert could not see yet), it was indeed a creek. In any case, the steep banks you see here provided a good defense for the Union troopers as the two sides began a short artillery duel.

In the early afternoon, Hancock's II Corps began to approach the position, and he, too, using the same faulty maps as Torbert, thought he had reached the North Anna River. Hancock sent a message to headquarters at 2:35 PM, stating that he had taken the river, and shortly sent another message saying that he already pushed three brigades across. It was not until 3:30 PM that the mistake was realized, and Hancock prepared to assault Chesterfield Bridge—and, by necessity, Henagan's Redoubt.

Henagan's Redoubt

〉 *Continue south on Jefferson Davis Highway (US 1) for 0.2 mile, then turn right onto Oxford Road (SR 689). Drive 0.3 mile. On your right, just before the road enters a large clearing, you will see an old road trace. Pull over here.*

Upon hearing of the II Corps' position, Grant ordered Hancock to take both the Chesterfield Bridge and the RF&P Railroad Bridge to the east. Hancock soon learned from an escaped slave that he was not just facing a rear guard, but that the entire Army of Northern Virginia was in front of him. Letting headquarters know that the Confederates were present in force, Hancock put John Gibbon's division east of the railroad, Francis Barlow's to his right west of the railroad, and David Birney's on the far right, with Robert O. Tyler's division as a reserve. At 5:30 PM, the Union artillery opened, and as the Confederate guns responded, the Federals moved forward.

Robert Anderson, whose corps was in the immediate area, sent Joseph Kershaw's division to hold the Federals at Chesterfield Bridge while Charles Field's men went to the railroad bridge. Henagan's men, though, were left isolated on the north bank. Birney sent first a single brigade forward to approach the front of the redoubt, then two others around to the sides of the earthwork. At 6:30 PM, the brigades—3,000 men—stormed Henagan's Redoubt, and although they met stiff resistance and a 10-foot wall, they eventually overran the position. Those Confederates who were able to escape found their way across the river, and the Federal II Corps occupied the north bank of the North Anna. Kershaw's men, after several hours of trading shots across the river, were eventually able to partially burn the railroad bridge.

Chesterfield Bridge crossed the North Anna slightly upstream of the current crossing of US 1, and although the bridge is gone, there are remnants of Henagan's Redoubt left. The road trace where you're now parked is what's left of the original Telegraph Road. If you place this to your back and look straight ahead, you will be looking south down the road, and the redoubt will be slightly to the right of your view. The redoubt is almost impossible to see, as you'll have to view it from a distance (the earthwork is on private property) and through some thick woods. The first Union brigade would have come from behind you down the road, while the other two would have swept across the open fields on either side of you, one from the right and one from the left.

Jericho Mills/Noel's Station

⟩ *From your position at the old Telegraph Road, make a U-turn and drive 0.3 mile east to Jefferson Davis Highway. Turn right on Jefferson Davis Highway (US 1) and drive 1.9 miles. You will cross the North Anna River shortly after your turn. Continue to Verdon Road (SR 684) and turn right, then drive 5.9 miles to Noel Road (SR 746). Drive 0.2 miles on Noel Road; you will come to an open area with power lines running overhead. Pull into the dirt road on your left.*

At the same time Grant ordered Hancock forward, he also ordered Gouverneur Warren to take the V Corps across the North Anna at the ford at Jericho Mills, establishing a solid foothold on the south bank. By the time he received the order, Warren was always making his way across, although the steep banks at the ford and the high river were causing a problem for his men and, especially, his artillery. After his first two regiments were across, he sent them forward as skirmishers to find out if the enemy was present.

It didn't take very long. After brushing aside a very small group of Rooney Lee's cavalry, they had soon advanced far enough to find the Confederates forming a line behind the embankment of the Virginia Central Railroad. The Federals rushed up the rest of their front brigade while A. P. Hill sent for Cadmus Wilcox's division, which was a full 3 miles away. While the Confederates waited, Warren directed the rest of his divisions over, forming an arced line that would put both of his flanks squarely on the river, facing south.

Lysander Cutler's division, though, was tardy getting into position, and before the Union position was complete, the Confederates charged the Union right at 6 PM, just where Cutler was supposed to be. The Confederate artillery, which had been concealed, was rolled up and brought into action, 16 guns in all, but did not last long, however, as the Union guns on the north bank, which had a more commanding position, knocked them out of the fight. Cutler, however, was helping place artillery overlooking a gulley on the south bank, instead of guiding his division to its proper place.

The rebels attacking the Union left were repulsed, while those attacking the center held firm. As for those attacking the Union right, there was absolutely nothing in their way. Now taking flanking fire from the right and rear, the Union line was in danger of collapsing. Cutler, though, who knew the gun placement, rallied his men to the side of the guns, which now had a clear line of fire at the Confederates. Using double loads of canister, the three Union batteries, along with renewed infantry fire from their front and left, was enough to send the enemy back to the railroad, with the Federals in pur-

BIG BOOTS TO FILL

Robert E. Lee felt ill on May 23, and by May 24 was suffering badly with a case of dysentery. Still, he insisted on being in the field and directing matters. This is a direct result of his wariness about his current set of lieutenants; had Stonewall Jackson or James Longstreet been around, he certainly would not have hesitated to leave the army in one or the other's hands.

Lee's illness also put him, by all accounts, in a very bad mood. A case in point was when he met A. P. Hill on May 24, the morning after the fight at Jericho Mills. Hill, who was repeatedly (and unfairly) measured against Jackson, suffered perhaps the most scathing rebuke he ever got from Robert E. Lee. "General Hill, why did you let those people cross here?" Lee said hotly, invoking his favorite epithet for Union soldiers. "Why didn't you throw your whole force on them and drive them back as Jackson would have done?"

A. P. Hill had his faults as a general, particularly as a corps commander, but had there been a better one in the Confederate army, he would have been replaced. His most glaring weakness (as it would later be for Jubal Early, in the court of public opinion) was that he was not Stonewall Jackson.

suit. Although A. P. Hill would call for additional units as reinforcements, they would come too late, and the fight was over before dark. The Union soldiers went back to their new line guarding Jericho Mills, while the rebels stayed behind the railroad.

It was a fierce fight, and a swift one, and gave the Federals a much-savored decisive victory, which had been all too infrequent in the Eastern Theater. The Confederates, meanwhile, had lost a good number of veteran soldiers in what turned out to be a poorly planned and coordinated attack.

Almost all of the land associated with the fight at Jericho Mills is now private property today. However, where you are now standing is only slightly south of the thick of the battle. If you exit your vehicle and look northward down the clearing, you will be looking toward the right flank of Warren's V Corps position, just to the right and beyond the woods. Cadmus Wilcox's division came from behind you and advanced roughly in the direction you are now facing, and then came back across the fields toward you after it was repulsed. Their position south of the Virginia Central Railroad, which was on your right as you drove along Verdon Road, is just behind you.

North Anna Battlefield Park

〉 *Turn around on Noel Road and drive 0.2 mile back to Verdon Road (SR 746). Turn left on Verdon Road and drive 2.9 miles to the entrance for North Anna Battlefield Park on your left. Turn left into the park, then follow the park road 0.4 mile to a parking area with a picnic area, interpretive signs, and the trailhead for the battlefield.*

On the evening of May 23, Lee gathered his staff and generals and held an open forum on what to do next. The prevailing sentiment, even in Lee's mind, was that a retreat was probably in order. The strong Federal foothold at Jericho Mills put the Union troops in a very good position to attempt to flank the Confederates out of their current position, strong as it was. The biggest problem with retreat, however, was the exposure of Hanover Junction, which would most certainly be cut by the Federals as soon as they got the chance.

Fortunately, one of Lee's staff—engineer Martin Smith—had done his homework. During the day, Smith had studied maps of the area and had ridden around the south bank for hours inspecting the terrain. Smith's findings, together with Lee's tactical mind, would create one of the most brilliant defensive positions ever seen—a masterpiece, even for Robert E. Lee.

At Ox Ford, the crossing of the North Anna just about midway between Chesterfield Bridge and Jericho Mills, a high bluff stretched about a half-mile along the river. To the left of that bluff, an old stage road ran to the southwest, also on elevated ground, all the way to the Little River. The road could provide an extremely strong defensive position. To the right of the bluff, another ridge stretched to the southeast

Trailhead at North Anna Battlefield Park.

toward Hanover Junction, ending near an impassable swampland. In essence, a line formed along these ridges would form a giant V shape, with the point of the V at Ox Ford and the two wings stretching southeast and southwest. The far right of the line would also be turned directly southward to protect Hanover Junction.

Besides the position's having strong natural advantages, Lee instantly saw tactical opportunities as well. At the very least, the Confederates would hold a strong, entrenched position on high ground, and with the lines inverted, they could move troops from one position to another with relative ease. It was also very likely that the Federals, seeing the rebels withdrawing on both flanks and abandoning the Chesterfield Bridge, would think that they were in retreat. Grant had already shown his aggressiveness, and if he followed his own playbook, he would pursue those retreating units. By doing so, part of the Union army would likely cross at Chesterfield Bridge on the east and Jericho Mills on the west, splitting into two around Ox Ford. If one part needed to support the other, the men would have to cross the North Anna River twice—first crossing back to the north bank, then traveling along the river and recrossing back to the south bank. If all went according to plan, the Federals would advance as one mass, breaking themselves on the wedge that was Lee's formation, enabling the Confederates to possibly defeat them in detail. It could be an excellent opportunity for Lee to regain the initiative he had so long been seeking.

Beginning at 10 PM, the Confederates quietly began moving into position along

The Confederate works at North Anna Battlefield Park are some of the best preserved in existence.

their new line. A. P. Hill's corps stayed on the left, facing the Union V and VI Corps and stretching over the bluff at Ox Ford. Anderson's corps made up the center of the line, overlooking most of the line on the V's eastern leg. From his right, Ewell's corps formed an angle around Hanover Junction. All of the men, as soon as they reached their new positions, began entrenching, which by now they had practically elevated to an art. John Breckinridge's force from the Shenandoah Valley, as well as George Pickett's division, recently arrived from Richmond, were held in reserve.

The North Anna Battlefield Park, administered by the Hanover County Parks Department, covers much of the line held by Hill's corps on May 24. The trail here is very well kept, and the interpretive signs along the way are outstanding. The woods here are very thick, so it can be difficult to interpret the battle at times, but the earthworks are in an outstanding state of preservation. There are a full 2 miles of trails here, but various shortcuts and cross paths can shorten your hike to just a mile, if you'd like. The county was also recently able to double the size of the park, so more trails and interpretation will be added in the future.

When Grant received his intelligence report on the morning of May 24, he came to the very conclusion that Lee had hoped. The Confederates must be retreating, and they should be pursued. By this time, Burnside's IX Corps was just north of Ox Ford. Hancock's II Corps was to his left at Chesterfield Bridge. To Burnside's right, at Jericho Mills but still north of the river, was Wright's VI Corps, which was to cross and join Warren's V Corps, still holding its position from the previous evening. Grant issued orders to each of his corps, with the intention of crossing the North Anna River by the end of the day.

The first to move was the V Corps, which advanced south all the way to the Virginia Central Railroad by 6 AM, meeting almost zero Confederate resistance. Warren also sent Sam Crawford's division, along with the 1st Pennsylvania Reserves in the lead, east along the south bank of the river in an attempt to aid Burnside's crossing at Ox Ford. On the way, the Pennsylvanians ran into a unit of crack Confederate sharpshooters organized from William Mahone's division. Mahone had seen the Federals coming and decided to stall them at Quarles's Mill, a small ford halfway between Jericho Mills and Ox Ford. Pinned down, Crawford's forces sent word to Burnside that they were meeting resistance and that Confederates were in his area.

Shortly afterward, around 8 AM, Hancock advanced skirmishers from the Union II Corps across Chesterfield Bridge, sending his divisions across behind them and forming a defensive line in the open fields south of the bridge. Confederates could be seen in the trees across the clearing, but it was assumed these were only elements of the rear guard. As part of the crossing, Hancock also sent three regiments toward Ox Ford, west of his position, to assist Burnside's IX Corps. These three regiments also ran into resistance well before they reached the ford.

As it turned out, the only soldier in the IX Corps that did not know that the Confederates were in their front at Ox Ford was Ambrose Burnside. Across the ford, on the south bank, was a 200-foot bluff, with artillery and earthworks atop it. Orlando Willcox, who was to lead the crossing, informed Burnside of this, but Burnside, under heavy scrutiny from his superiors for his performance in the Wilderness and at Spotsylvania, was determined to make an attempt. Just as the crossing began, however, Burnside almost simultaneously received messages from Crawford and from Hancock saying that they were trying to help him, but that Confederates were blocking their paths. Burnside finally called off the assault.

He then came up with a plan that might have proved very valuable had he been facing a rear guard. Burnside decided to send Robert Potter's division to Chesterfield Bridge to cross there and head west toward Ox Ford, while Thomas Crittenden's division would do the same at Quarles's Mill and approach from the east. With Willcox advancing with the other two divisions, the Confederates would be caught in a pincer and crushed. Grant immediately approved the plan and added Crawford's division to join Crittenden's advance from the west.

Potter reached Chesterfield Bridge in the early afternoon, but was hit hard with Confederate musketry only a quarter-mile into his march to the west. Crittenden, meanwhile, was able to cross at Quarles's Mill around 2 PM, filing into the earthworks that Crawford's men had built to protect themselves from Mahone's sharpshooters. At 3 PM, Crittenden's lead brigade, James Ledlie's, left the works and began to make its way east to Ox Ford.

Lee's trap was working to perfection. With the exception of Orlando Willcox's IX Corps division at Ox Ford, the Union army was split into two parts south of the river, with the entire Confederate army between them. Hancock's II Corps—the army's best—was isolated to the east and would be a prime target. It was creating and exploiting situations such as these that had made Lee and other generals over time legendary. Unfortunately for the Confederates, there were no generals like Robert E. Lee on the field—including Lee himself.

According to his personal surgeon, Lee had not slept more than two consecutive hours since the battle at the Wilderness on May 5, 20 days before. In the days leading up to the battles at the North Anna, Lee had appeared extremely weak, and even had to resort to inspecting his lines from a carriage rather than on horseback. Although he was back in the saddle in the early morning on May 24, trying to hide his weakness, before long he was simply too ill to command. Angry, frustrated, and helpless, Lee suffered through the day battling a crippling bout of dysentery. (Some have speculated that Lee actually suffered a heart attack during this time; although this is possible, it can never be proven.) He was now confined to his tent, and while a tremendous chance to deal a crushing blow to the enemy was well within the army's reach, none of his lieutenants was able to step up and take the aggressive initiative that Lee had made his hallmark.

That is not to say that the Confederates did not damage the Union army. Around 3 PM, Hancock was still probing the Confederate lines in front of him, advancing his brigades one at a time, claiming Confederate rifle pits and picket lines as he went, taking enough casualties to hurt but not enough to stop advancing. Little did he know that he was headed straight for Anderson's and Ewell's corps, even though several prisoners told him that he was doing just that. It was not until 5 PM that Hancock began to suspect Anderson's entire corps was in front of him, only 250 yards to the south. A Confederate charge by Stephen Ramseur confirmed it, and although the fight lasted until dark, the Union II Corps was forced to withdraw and entrench.

On the western part of the Confederate line, where you are now, the soldiers of A. P. Hill's corps waited anxiously for Federals to appear in their front. As the day went on, it seemed increasingly unlikely that that would happen. They had not counted, though, on Union Brig. Gen. James Ledlie.

Ledlie had no military experience. His appointment was a political one, and his first test leading troops was at Spotsylvania, where he performed embarrassingly poorly. What he would do here at the North Anna, however, had nothing to do with inexperience or incompetence. Ledlie was just dead drunk.

After leaving Quarles's Mill, Ledlie's brigade came to an open clearing about 1 mile to the east. Across an open field, 800 yards away, was a bluff, atop which were the unmistakable signs of Confederate earthworks. Ledlie had reached the position of William Mahone's division, near the apex of the Confederate V formation.

Ledlie formed his brigade into two lines, with the formation's left on the North Anna River. Filled with ambition and liquid courage, he decided to charge the Confederates. He sent a message back to Crittenden stating his intentions, to which Crittenden immediately replied not to do such a thing. By the time the courier rushed back, however, Ledlie had already made his preparations.

Mahone's soldiers, across the field, looked with wonder at this Union brigade. It seemed almost unbelievable to them that the Federals would actually attempt to charge heavy earthworks and artillery across a large open field. The rebels were not about to stop them, though, and soon the Confederates were shouting encouragement at the Yankee soldiers, pleading with them to assault their position.

At 6:45 PM, the Confederates got their wish. Ledlie stepped his brigade into the field and advanced as its enemy licked its chops and waited. A heavy rain began to pour almost instantly, and the Union lines were breaking apart even before rebel fire hit them. When it did, though, at close range, Ledlie's brigade was shredded. James Ledlie's brigade would suffer 450 casualties that day. Shortly after the fight, he made his way back to Crawford and Crittenden in their earthworks and remarked that he was too sleepy and tired to command.

Remarkably, James Ledlie would suffer no consequences for his actions on May 24, and even received command of a division only a few weeks later. This gross negligence on the part of the Union high command would lead to even greater tragedies.

As you make your way along the trail, you will see a number of signs devoted to explaining (or trying to explain) what happened on May 24 with Ledlie's brigade, as well as events elsewhere on the field at the North Anna. As you near the river and Ox Ford, you will be walking along Mahone's position, and the Federals would have been coming from your left, although the open fields have now been forested over.

That night, Grant ordered his engineers to build pontoon bridges near Jericho Mills, bringing the V and VI Corps back to the north

> ## CASUALTIES— NORTH ANNA, MAY 23–24
>
> **Confederate:** killed, wounded, missing, or captured: 2,517
>
> **Union:** killed, wounded, missing, or captured: 2,623
>
> **Total Casualties: 5,140**

bank of the river and east to join the rest of the army. The IX Corps would be responsible for holding the north bank at Ox Ford. The next day would bring on an exploration of the Confederate lines, and soon it would be plain to Grant, and painfully aware to Lee, just how close the Union Army of the Potomac was to being heavily damaged.

YELLOW TAVERN

⟩ *From the parking area at North Anna Battlefield Park, drive 0.4 mile back to Verdon Road (SR 684) and turn left. Drive 2.5 miles on Verdon Road to Jefferson Davis Highway (US 1). Turn right onto Jefferson Davis Highway and drive 1.4 miles to Kings Dominion Boulevard (VA 30 South), then drive 0.6 miles and take the ramp onto I-95 South. Drive 14.6 miles south on I-95 to exit 83B, then merge onto East Parham Road (VA 73). Drive to the intersection with Brook Road (US 1), and then turn right and drive 0.3 mile. Pull over in one of the parking lots just before reaching Telegraph Road.*

On the evening of May 24, after the dust had settled, one of the Union army's most valuable assets returned from an extended absence. Nearly bursting with pride, Phil Sheridan regaled Grant and his staff with tales of his cavalry's exploits over the last two weeks, their near-scrapes and their daring victories. Some historians discount Sheridan's great raid as more hurtful than helpful, leaving the Army of the Potomac with almost no cavalry for 16 days, and there is no question that the Federals could have used cavalry on many occasions during that time. However, no one could say that Sheridan did not cause quite a stir in both the Union army and the Confederacy as a whole.

Confederate legend J. E. B. Stuart is remembered where he fell on the Yellow Tavern battlefield.

It all began on May 8, the day of the first fighting at Spotsylvania. Sheridan and George Meade, who had never seen eye to eye, had had 12 hours to simmer since the fight at Todd's Tavern that had blocked the

Union's path to Spotsylvania Court House. In Meade's eyes, Sheridan had neglected his duties by not opening the road. Sheridan was equally incensed, angry not only that Meade had taken command of his cavalry without telling him, but also that he had been, in Sheridan's opinion, misusing his horsemen. Around noon, Sheridan entered Meade's tent in a rage, and the double explosion could be heard all throughout the headquarters camp. The fierce shouting match went on for some time, with Sheridan eventually storming out.

Shortly after the altercation, Meade went to Grant and told him of the affair. No doubt expecting Grant to see his side, Meade related that Sheridan said he could whip J. E. B. Stuart's vaunted Confederate cavalry, if only Meade would let him. Grant's response was not what Meade had wanted to hear. "Well, he generally knows what he is talking about," he replied. "Let him start right out and do it." By 1 PM, Meade had issued orders to Sheridan to attack Stuart's cavalry, using whatever means he saw fit.

When the Civil War broke out, there was no question that the Confederate cavalry was not just superior to its Union counterparts, both east and west. The disparity was so wide as to be embarrassing. Much of that had to do with Stuart himself, whose daring and flashy raids tended to capture headlines across the country. Gradually, though, the Federals began to catch up. John Buford's resistance at Second Manassas in August 1862 was the beginning of it, and the Federals had ridden well at Kelly's Ford in March 1863 and fought fiercely at the war's largest cavalry battle, Brandy Station, three months later.

As the confidence of the Union cavalry was growing, the Confederate mounted troops were declining. This had little to do with its horsemen, who were as spirited as ever. Horses, however, were a different matter, and it was difficult to keep Stuart's large number of cavalry mounts well fed and healthy. Before long, the scales were about even between the Union and Confederate troopers.

Sheridan, who had never commanded cavalry before his post at the head of the Army of the Potomac's horsemen, brought a fresh outlook, one that many of his peers did not agree with. Sheridan thought that the Federals' current use of cavalry— guarding wagon trains, scouting, screening movements—was work that anyone could do, but that would wear down horses quickly. He began to question the conventional practices, eventually reaching the conclusion that the cavalry could be just as valuable to an army as its infantry or artillery, truly equal to its counterparts. Although he struggled with some of the most basic functions of cavalry (the clearing of the road to Spotsylvania being a good example), Sheridan desperately wanted to show others what he thought he could do with his horsemen. He now had his chance.

Spending the rest of May 8 planning, the Union cavalry—the *entire* Union cavalry, all three divisions—began to move south from Spotsylvania early the next morning. Sheridan's column of 10,000 men was kept compact, but stretched 4 miles in length, with Sheridan at the front. They were not in a hurry; in fact, their pace, as they left, was almost inviting the Confederate cavalry to attack, which was exactly the idea. The Federals would head for Richmond and eventually join Benjamin Butler's Army of the James south of the city. There they would resupply and ride back. But Richmond was not the true objective of the raid. What Sheridan really wanted was to draw the Confederate cavalry into an open battle and then attempt to destroy it.

It was only a matter of hours before J. E. B. Stuart relayed the news of Sheridan's column to Robert E. Lee, and by 2 PM the first fighting came on, with a Confederate brigade harassing the Union rear guard. The Federals pressed on. Eventually, Stuart and Fitzhugh Lee were part of the pursuing force, and over the next two days, Sheridan's column was continually harassed as it made its way south.

By the next morning, the Union column had made its way east, near Beaver Dam Station on the Virginia Central Railroad, and then began to move south on the Mountain Road, angling southeast toward Richmond. Stuart, who knew that he was outnumbered, saw an opportunity. Taking the Mountain Road all the way to Richmond gave the Confederates the inside track. Fitzhugh Lee could move straight south on the Telegraph Road and beat Sheridan to Richmond, ambushing him just before he approached the outer defenses of Richmond. After getting some rest, the Confederates broke camp at Hanover Junction at 3 AM on May 11 and headed south down the Telegraph Road. Sheridan, expecting to receive that ambush at any moment, kept his troops moving steadily and cautiously toward Richmond, where the Mountain Road eventually joined with the Telegraph Road at an old, run-down shack called Yellow Tavern.

Even at the time of the battle, Yellow Tavern was only barely standing, and it is now long gone. It was, however, very near where you now stand, on the east side of Brook Road just south of where the Telegraph and Mountain Roads meet Brook Road, the road you drove in on. The arrangement of the roads is the same as it was in 1864; Telegraph and Mountain Roads combined to form Brook Road, which continues into the city of Richmond. The exact location of the tavern is unknown, but most of the battle took place at various points to the north.

❯ *Continue north, bearing right onto Telegraph Road. Drive 1.2 miles on Telegraph Road until you reach a dead end. Turn your vehicle around and park in the dead end.*

This is the old Telegraph Road, now the backbone of a nice suburb of Richmond. Turn your back to the dead end. The road used to go through the dead end behind you, continuing on for miles, but I-295 has now cut the road off. The Confederates, who would win the race to Yellow Tavern, came down the road from behind you.

The area between the Telegraph Road and the Mountain Road, about a mile to your right (west) at your current location, was wooded at the time of the battle. Fitz Lee directed the three regiments of Lunsford Lomax's brigade to line up along Telegraph

Road, facing west. Williams Wickham's brigade formed along a ridgeline between the two roads running east–west through the forest, facing south. From these two positions, if the Federals maintained their path down the Mountain Road, their left would march right past Lomax, while Wickham was in a good position to strike their rear.

The ridge that Stuart selected for Wickham's brigade is just behind you—just north of the interstate. Lomax's troopers would have lined up along the road in front of you, facing to your right, from your position here south to a small creek bed, a tributary of Turner's Run.

❯ *Drive back down Telegraph Road 0.4 mile to a point just before the intersection with Maryland Avenue.*

Turner's Run flows just along the base of the ridge where Wickham's Confederates formed. What you see here is a tributary of Turner's Run that loops back around from the main stream. Lomax's left flank was placed on this shallow creek, waiting for the Federals to pass in its front so the rebels could maul their left flank.

It didn't happen. Sheridan had been expecting just such an attack, and had been marching in a formation that allowed him to quickly turn his column in virtually any direction and quickly form a line of battle. Heavy skirmish lines were placed in front and flank to detect any Confederate presence, which is exactly what they did at Yellow Tavern.

Around 9 AM, Sheridan shifted his lead division, Wes Merritt's, to face east-northeast while still along the Mountain Road. Thomas Devin's brigade continued down the road toward Yellow Tavern, while George A. Custer's and Alfred Gibbs's brigades stayed along the road. Sheridan wanted to delay the main assault until his other two divisions were up, but Custer and Gibbs probed, pushing cautiously through the woods. They were eventually held up by Lomax's line, but Devin's Federals, coming up the Telegraph Road from Yellow Tavern, took Lomax in the left flank. Suddenly being attacked from two sides, Lomax had no choice but to fall back along Telegraph Road. He would eventually extend the Confederate line, forming to Wickham's left on the ridge behind Turner's Run.

During the later stages of the battle, the Federals would line up across Telegraph Road at a point just in front of you. Custer's brigade, with another brigade on each flank, would be on the road itself, thundering through where you now stand and making its way toward the Confederates on the ridge.

❯ *Continue another 0.1 mile on Telegraph Road, and then turn left on Virginia Avenue. Drive 0.6 mile on Virginia Avenue, taking care as you cross Brook Road. Turn right on Mountain Road and drive 0.3 mile. Mountain Road veers off to the left here, while Greenwood Road continues straight ahead. Pull over in one of the parking lots on the right at this intersection.*

You are now at the intersection of Mountain Road and what is now Greenwood Road. Greenwood Road is actually in the former location of what used to be the old Brook Turnpike, later replaced by Brook Road to the east. Greenwood Road is the road extending to your right, while Mountain Road is stretching out in front of you.

It was along Mountain Road that Sheridan's Federals approached the intersection where you are now standing. In the initial morning assault, Custer's brigade lined up along the road in front of you, with its left roughly on the intersection, and advanced through the trees toward Lomax's line behind you. Gibbs's brigade would line up to your left, also along the road.

During the afternoon assault, while Stuart's Confederates were all on the ridge north of Turner's Run, George Chapman's brigade of James Wilson's division formed its line in the area behind you. Chapman was on Custer's left flank, west of Telegraph Road, while Gibbs's brigade was on Custer's right.

❯ *Continue north on Greenwood Road 0.8 mile to Francis Avenue. Turn right on Francis Avenue and drive 0.5 mile, and then turn right on Virginia Central Parkway. Drive another 0.5 mile to Battlefield Road. Turn right on Battlefield Road, following it for about 0.4 mile. (There will be a point where the road crosses Francis Avenue, taking a quick jog to the right, then left again; stick with it and keep heading south.) When you come to the cul-de-sac, turn around, and be careful to park somewhere on the street where you will not disturb the residents, as you will be in the middle of a suburban neighborhood.*

It may be a bit difficult to pick out of the landscape, but you are roughly on the ridge where Wickham's Confederates formed their line. Turn and face toward the interstate. Lomax's brigade, after it was driven from its position along the Telegraph Road, would line up to your left, east of the road. Turner's Run, although changed over the years and almost impossible to see from this point, is only a few hundred feet in front of you.

Although Lomax's brigade had been driven back, J. E. B. Stuart was sure of success. The Confederate position here was strong, with a creek in front of it and atop high ground. At 3 PM, he sent a message to Braxton Bragg in Richmond, saying that he was confident, and that he hoped to see Confederate infantry, which Bragg had arranged, appearing soon in the Union rear, catching the Federals between the two forces.

Sheridan, meanwhile, had been waiting for the rest of his cavalry corps to come up. After Wilson's division came, Sheridan formed a new line across the Telegraph Road.

Chapman's brigade, from Wilson's division, would form the left, while Gibbs took the right, both brigades dismounted. Custer, meanwhile, along with the 1st Vermont Cavalry of Chapman's brigade, would form the center, remaining on horseback and charging up the Telegraph Road, where the Confederates had placed a strong artillery position.

> *Continue back up Battlefield Road 0.2 mile to Francis Road and turn right. Drive 0.2 mile to Telegraph Road, and then turn right again, driving 0.1 mile. The J. E. B. Stuart memorial will be on your right.*

Stand along the road with the Stuart monument to your right, facing south. You are now looking down the Telegraph Road, which would have continued through the interstate to the position you had visited previously. It is quite a bit easier to discern the ridge from the surrounding terrain here than in your previous location. The Confederate artillery, along with Stuart, would have been very near where you are standing. Wickham's Confederates were lined up to your right, while Lomax's were to your left.

At 4 PM, as the Union artillery opened, so did the heavens, releasing a heavy rainstorm. Stuart, from his position here along the ridge, could see the Federals forming and brought up the 1st Virginia Cavalry from the reserves to guard the critical artillery position here along the Telegraph Road.

Custer's horsemen came in a fury, racing up the road from your front and crashing into the Confederate line right here on the Telegraph Road. The 6th Virginia Cavalry, from Lomax's brigade, countercharged from your left, and heavy hand-to-hand fighting broke out all around your current position. On your right, Chapman's brigade also had some initial success, but like Custer, was stopped and eventually driven back by a Confederate countercharge, this time by the 1st Virginia Cavalry.

As the Federals were heading rearward, Private John Huff of the 5th Michigan Cavalry spotted a Confederate general conspicuously wearing a feathered hat. Huff, an award-winning marksman, aimed and fired. J. E. B. Stuart slouched over, hit in the stomach. Within minutes, the entire Confederate line was crumbling, and the rebel horsemen, shocked at the loss of their leader, began streaming to the rear.

Stuart was taken to Richmond for care, but it was obvious to all that he would not survive. He insisted on seeing his wife, who he luckily had seen only the day before, as she was visiting a relative a bit farther north. By the next evening, Stuart was dead, and all of Richmond was in mourning.

The loss at Yellow Tavern was a tough one for the Confederates. They had taken many casualties, and had also lost not only many mounts but the artillery they had atop the hill. Further, they had suffered a humiliating defeat, crushing the illusion of their invincibility, and had lost their beloved general.

For Phil Sheridan, Yellow Tavern, if nothing else, proved that he could whip the Confederates, and whip them good. His men had fought a good fight and the result was decisive. Union cavalrymen, whose confidence had already been growing, now truly felt that they could take the Confederates anytime and anywhere, particularly with their new general. The man who had never commanded cavalry before, and who had been met with skepticism by many, had gained the complete trust and confidence of his soldiers—and had brought them to within 7 miles of Richmond.

The massive whitewashed monument here is on or near the spot where Stuart received his mortal wound. Besides being one of the more tangible remains of the battle of Yellow Tavern, the monument is impressive but humble. Climb the stairs to the top to read the inscription, and walk to the back of the monument, where you will get a better idea just how commanding a position the Confederates had on May 11.

MEADOW BRIDGE

Richmond Outer Defenses

> *From the J. E. B. Stuart monument, turn around and drive 0.2 mile to Virginia Central Parkway. Turn left on Virginia Central Parkway and drive 0.5 mile to Brook Road (US 1). Turn left on Brook Road and drive 3.8 miles. On your right will be a shopping center; turn into the shopping center just before the tire center, then drive just past it. On your left, you will see an elevated grassy area at the edge of a large parking lot. Pull in next to this area on the side nearest to the tire store.*

A nicely preserved section of the Richmond Outer Defenses, near the spot where Sheridan's troops passed through prior to the battle at Meadow Bridge.

Regardless of the death of J. E. B. Stuart, the mere presence of 10,000 Union cavalrymen at the outskirts of Richmond was enough to send a major wave of panic through the capital. With Sheridan to the north and Benjamin Butler's Army of the James operating to the south, the Confederate government was desperately trying to arrange and bolster its defenses. A home guard, made up of government clerks and a unit from the Tredegar Iron Works, was formed and rushed north to meet the Federals. For a few days, it seemed as though the entire city, including the government, had lost its head.

Sheridan considered rushing into the city, but decided against it. He knew that he would never be able to hold the city, and as impressive a spectacle as it might have provided, it was also quite risky. Ultimately, he decided to follow his original plan, heading east to join Butler at Bermuda Hundred, where he would resupply and return to the Army of the Potomac.

That didn't mean that Sheridan wasn't willing to put a little scare into the Confederates, though. Yellow Tavern was only a short distance north of the outer defenses of Richmond, which he knew were weakly defended—if at all—from a dispatch captured hours before. South of the outer defense works was a middle defensive line, with a still stronger one closer to the city. A military road ran to the east between the outer and middle defensive lines. Not only was it the quickest way for his men to get to Bermuda Hundred, but being inside the Richmond defenses, even if only slightly, would serve to prolong the chaos in the city. At 11 PM, Sheridan started his already excited troopers south toward Richmond on the Brook Turnpike, passing through the Confederate outer defenses, then turning east at Brook Church on the Military Road.

The heavy and well-preserved earthworks you see here were part of Richmond's outer defensive line. Even though surrounded by a shopping center, the area is landscaped enough that it blocks out most of the intrusions around you. (Just the fact that someone thought to preserve these earthworks is proof positive that preservation and development can happen hand in hand.) If you walk up to the works, you will find several interpretive signs telling of the history that this section of the works saw (although the story of Sheridan's relative walk through the defenses is a bit one-sided), as well as the importance of this position along the Brook Turnpike, a major thoroughfare to Richmond. The signs also tell the too-little-known story of Gabriel's Insurrection, which, had it been successful, would have been the largest slave revolt in U.S. history, and would have begun just a few hundred yards to the north.

Meadow Bridge

> *Leave the shopping center and return to Brook Road. Turn right onto Brook Road and drive 0.7 mile to Azalea Avenue. Turn left on Azalea Avenue and drive 1.7 miles, then turn left onto Meadowbridge Road (SR 627). Drive 0.8 mile; pull into the gravel area on the right with the interpretive sign just past the railroad crossing.*

Fitzhugh Lee had been with the Confederates at Yellow Tavern, and had been right next to his beloved commander when he was mortally wounded. Lee was an excellent commander himself, but the loss of Stuart hurt him deeply. Besides the business of striking a blow for Stuart, he also had the very important task of stopping the Federal advance. He was not about to let Sheridan and his horsemen get away without a fight.

Lee knew that Sheridan would not just turn around to the north; James Gordon's Confederate cavalry brigade, which had been harassing his rear for days, would stop him. There were no good roads to the west. It seemed that the only route Sheridan could take was the Military Road, and once on that road, he could not maneuver through the Confederate middle defenses a mile and a half to the south, or to the north, which was flooded by the swollen Chickahominy River and Brook Run. He would have to keep moving east along the Military Road and would be forced to cross the Chickahominy at Meadow Bridge. That was where Lee would trap him. Before midnight on the night of May 11, the day of the Yellow Tavern fight, Lee's men camped at Meadow Bridge. After destroying the bridge that took the Military Road over the Chickahominy, they waited for the Federals to arrive.

At 3 AM on May 12, James Wilson's Union cavalry, leading the column, reached Brook Church and turned left onto the Military Road (the same place that you turned onto what is now Azalea Avenue). Soon after, a soldier in blue appeared and offered to show Wilson the way around the Confederate defenses. Wilson was suspicious, but played along for a short time. After a short time, one of Wilson's staffers asked a local farmer for a confirmation of their location. The farmer pointed out where the Confederate middle defenses were—armed with heavy artillery and only 200 yards away. The spy was executed on the spot, and Wilson's division began to form a defensive line facing south on a rise known as Strawberry Hill.

Wesley Merritt's division, which had been right behind Wilson's, was still on the road. Merritt had noted what had happened to Wilson and reconnoitered ahead. He found a heavy Confederate presence only a short distance in his front, with the Meadow Bridge destroyed. Meanwhile, the third Union division, David Gregg's, was being pressed from the rear by Gordon's still-pursuing Confederates. Just like that, the Union cavalry was caught in a trap, facing the enemy on three sides with a swamp to the north.

Sheridan quickly decided that there was only path to escape and another day's fight: crossing the Meadow Bridge. Just south of the road's crossing of the Chickahominy was a railroad bridge, which was still intact. It would not be an easy crossing, particularly under fire, but if the Federals could get a foothold on the other side, they might be able to get the rest of the cavalry across. With Wilson and Gregg's divisions fully occupied, Wes Merritt's division would stop Fitz Lee's Confederates, and the task of getting across the railroad bridge would fall to George Custer's brigade.

You are now standing near where Merritt's forces gathered early on May 12. Use the Civil War Trails sign to orient yourself, and then turn around so that your back is to the sign. To your right front, now obscured by trees and partially covered by Richmond International Speedway, is Strawberry Hill, where Wilson's cavalry formed against the Confederates behind the middle defenses. Looking down the road to your right, you are looking toward Gregg's division, which formed a line across the road facing west to meet Gordon's cavalry. To your left, down the road and to your left in the trees, is where Fitz Lee's cavalry had burned the bridge over the Chickahominy. The bridge for Meadowbridge Road runs south of the tracks; the former bridge was to the north of the tracks. From your position at the sign, walk over to the railroad tracks and carefully look northwest along the railroad. They eventually cross the Chickahominy less than a half-mile from your current position, running parallel to Meadowbridge Road.

The Federals' easiest task was to clear the Confederates from the middle defenses, though they did not realize it right away. Wilson's artillery had set itself on Strawberry Hill, but they men were soon persuaded to abandon their position. While they were in the process of doing so, Sheridan rode up. Although Phil Sheridan has his critics as a tactician, he had few equals in either army, if any, when it came to motivating and inspiring his men. After a few words about how Wilson's men were facing a bunch of government clerks from Richmond, the men replaced their weapons and doubled their fire, quickly scattering the makeshift force from the works.

Gregg's division had a much tougher fight. Forming a line a quarter-mile east of Brook Church, his left anchored on a stream and his right on high ground. Gordon's Confederates approached the position, but it was obvious that Gregg's 10 regiments, on the defensive, would easily be able to tear up his three. After asking for reinforcements from Richmond, Gordon received artillery around 9 AM and began dueling with Gregg's guns. An hour later, Gordon received infantry support, and he launched an assault against the Union right, where Gregg's artillery was placed. The Confederates made two charges, but both were repulsed. They gave it one last try on the other Union flank, but Gregg shifted his weight to the left and repelled this attack as well. Gordon, who led this attack, was wounded in the arm; he would last six days before dying in Richmond on May 18.

The third and most important front was Merritt's, where Custer faced the difficult prospect of making his way across the Chickahominy on the railroad bridge. Custer waded sharpshooters across the river, then dismounted the 5th Michigan cavalry. A signal was given, and the sharpshooters concentrated their fire on Fitz Lee's men to keep them from firing at the bridge, where the Michigan men were carefully making their way across the span from railroad tie to railroad tie. Once they had crossed and gained a foothold, the 6th Michigan joined them, and they steadily began to drive the Confederates back far enough that engineers could construct a new bridge along the road for the rest of the cavalry to cross the river. As was the case in many cavalry battles towards the end of the war, the Federals were armed with seven-shot Spencer repeating carbines. This was a technology that the Confederates, stuck with revolvers or their muzzle-loading rifles, were not able to easily acquire. These weapons helped make the difference here, as they did in many other battles.

By 4 PM, the engineers were able to complete the bridge, and Merritt reinforced Custer's men on the east bank of the Chickahominy. Soon the outnumbered Confederates were being pushed away from the river, with Sheridan's dismounted cavalry charging and routing the rebel line. The danger was over; Sheridan had not only led them out of a trap, but had brought them consecutive victories over the rebel cavalry.

Once the rest of the Federal cavalry had crossed, the makeshift bridge was burned and the men continued their march to the east. They would reach Mechanicsville that night around 7 PM, stopping for the night, and would travel to Bottom's Bridge the next day, May 13, where they were forced to stop and rebuild the bridge. On May 14, Sheridan's raid ended when his cavalry corps finally reached Bermuda Hundred, the base of the Army of the James.

After resting and feeding his men, Sheridan made his way back to the Army of the Potomac, rejoining it on May 24 at the North Anna River. His raid, when looked at separately, had been an absolute success. He had terrorized the Richmond populace; he had taken only 625 casualties, to the Confederates' 800; and he had defeated the enemy's cavalry in the open field twice, dealing a double blow to their morale by killing their legendary commander. However, many argue that Sheridan's absence deprived Grant's army of cavalry when he needed it most. At least parts of the attacks made on May 10, 12, and 18 may likely have never been made had Union cavalry been able to scout the Confederate positions, particularly at Laurel Hill, where thousands of casualties were incurred. In addition, J. E. B. Stuart's eventual replacement at the head of the Confederate cavalry corps, Wade Hampton, would prove more than capable.

Whatever arguments might be made, by the end of the Civil War, Sheridan's use of cavalry would prove revolutionary. He would eventually render many traditional cavalry tactics obsolete and even influence the use of mechanized armor, such as tanks, in later wars. It is often said that J. E. B. Stuart, unquestionably a master of cavalry, represented the youthful exuberance of the Confederacy. With this, Sheridan's first expedition, it might also be said that Stuart's death at the hands of the Federal horsemen represents a changing of the guard for the mounted arm.

NELSON'S BRIDGE

⟩ *From the Meadow Bridge pullover, pull out to the left and drive east 1.7 miles to Atlee Road. Turn left on Atlee Road and drive 2.2 miles to US 301 North (Chamberlayne Road/VA 2), and then turn right. Follow US 301 for 7.5 miles to River Road*

(SR 605). Turn right on River Road and drive 4.7 miles, then turn left on Nelson's Bridge Road (SR 615). Drive 0.4 mile to the bridge; cross the bridge, make a U-turn, and pull over just before you re-cross.

Union probing of the Confederate lines at the North Anna River on May 25 brought clarity to the army's situation. Lee's defensive strategy had been brilliant, and the Federals had almost marched into a massive trap. Grant now had enough information to know that once again, the Confederates had put themselves behind an unbreakable line of earthworks, and they had no plans to go anywhere. Gathering his generals that night for a conference, he gathered their opinions about the army's next move. There were three feasible options. The first was to bring Benjamin Butler's Army of the James from Bermuda Hundred to join the Army of the Potomac. Butler's troops were doing very little anyway, and Grant would not stand for soldiers standing idle when he could use them here. The second option was to repeat the flanking maneuver he had used to leave Spotsylvania Court House, when he had successfully extracted his men overnight and stole a march around the Confederate right. The third option was to surprise the rebels and move around their left flank, blocking their escape route to Richmond.

Although the first option was quickly ruled out, there was no doubt that Grant needed those troops, so William "Baldy" Smith's XVIII Corps was ordered to leave Bermuda Hundred and join the Army of the Potomac. The third option, the surprise movement around Lee's left, had strong support in the conference, but Grant ultimately ruled it out, as it would take the army too far away from its supply base. It was decided that the troops would pull out after dark on May 26, moving around the Confederate right, to cross the Pamunkey River at Hanovertown, forcing the rebels to move south to protect their capital.

One additional move was made, and although only administrative, it would hopefully serve to clear up some of the confusion that had plagued the Federals. Ambrose Burnside's IX Corps, which had operated independently and reported directly to Grant, was officially moved to the Army of the Potomac. Burnside would now report to Meade rather than Grant.

With Sheridan's return to the army, the Federal cavalry would take an active role in the movement. Early on May 26, a second straight day of unrelenting rain, two of Sheridan's divisions, David Gregg's and Alfred Torbert's (regaining his old division from Wesley Merritt), rode down the north bank of the Pamunkey River to crossing points at Littlepage Bridge and Taylor's Ford, well north of the actual planned crossing points but hopefully enough to confuse the Confederates. The third, James Wilson's division, demonstrated on Lee's left, trying to convince the Confederate commander that an attack or movement on that flank was imminent.

Lee, still ill but trying to sort out information from his tent, was in an unfortunate position that was becoming all too familiar. His army was safe, to be sure, but he was again forced to wait for the Federals to make the first move. He knew that their activity level had picked up, but he could not decipher their intentions. The Union cavalry activity on his left, along with several repulsed probes by his Confederates, convinced Lee that the enemy was preparing to attack his left. Still, unsure, he sent engineers south to prepare for the army's possible withdrawal to the South Anna River.

After dark, the Federals began to withdraw from their lines. It was as risky a withdrawal as they had ever attempted, given that they had to cross the still-swelling North Anna without being detected, but by sunrise on May 27, the entire army was moving east around the Confederate flank. While some cavalry continued to screen the two crossing points they had claimed the day before, others rode ahead to claim the army's crossing points near Hanovertown. The infantry proceeded on two paths. Wright's VI Corps led one column, with Hancock's II Corps behind, to Dabney Ferry. Warren's V Corps led the other, with Burnside's IX Corps trailing, to New Castle Ferry. Though slowed by the mud and rain, the Federals had stolen yet another march on Robert E. Lee.

The next morning, Lee was told not only of the Federal departure, but that the Union cavalry and infantry were already crossing the Pamunkey well south of him at Dabney Ferry. (The infantry had not yet reached that point, but it was still troubling news.) Looking at the maps, and knowing that a Federal crossing at Hanovertown gave Grant many options, Lee decided to move his men south to Atlee's Station along the Virginia Central Railroad. From this point, Lee could meet almost any possible movement that Grant could make. Wasting no time, the Confederates were moving south by 10 AM, each corps taking a separate road.

Having secured their crossing point at Dabney Ferry and built a pontoon bridge for the infantry, Torbert decided to do a little additional work that would save the Union army a lot of time. He had already secured one Hanovertown crossing, but on the way, they had passed another crossing, Nelson's Bridge, 2 miles upstream. The bridge itself had been burned, but it was still a prime spot for the army to get across the Pamunkey. Securing that bridge would give the Federals a crossing much closer than New Castle Ferry. Torbert ordered Custer to send two regiments to the critical intersection at Haw's Shop, 3 miles inland, and two others to the site of Nelson's Bridge.

In front of you is the site of Nelson's Bridge. It was here that the VI and II Corps would cross, while the V and IX Corps crossed at Dabney Ferry. With each column having shifted their line of march, it would save nearly every Union soldier 2 miles, and would also save the Federals critical time in their race south.

〉 *Drive forward across the bridge 0.4 mile to the intersection with River Road (SR 615). Pull over just before the intersection in a safe place.*

Stand facing the intersection with your back to Nelson's Bridge. The road crossing in front of you is the old Hanover River Road, and you are looking roughly southwest. To your right, about 5 miles northwest, is Hanover Court House. Fitzhugh Lee had sent James Gordon's former cavalry brigade, now under the command of John Baker, from this direction. They would proceed across your front to your left. It was from this direction that two of Custer's brigades were approaching from Hanovertown to clear Nelson's Bridge.

Now turn 90 degrees to your left, facing northeast up Hanover River Road. Approximately a mile in your front is where Custer's men first met the lead elements of Baker's Confederates, who put resisted strongly as they backed their way toward your position. If you look down the open field to your left, the tree line in the distance is approximately where Baker's dismounted Confederates dug in and formed a line across the road. Custer's men, putting one regiment north of the road and one south, attempted to push through the Confederate line, but they were repeatedly stopped.

Soon, reinforcements would be thrown in on each side, each with the design of surprising and routing the other's rear and flank. Fitz Lee sent Bradley Johnson's men to aid Baker, and it was decided that Johnson would move south—now to your right, down the road at your intersection—then turn north, hitting the Federal left.

What they did not know, though, was that Custer had two additional brigades on the field. Torbert saw a similar opportunity from his side of the fight, and had the manpower to pull it off. Custer's other two regiments had already secured the intersection at Haw's Shop. After ordering two regiments from Thomas Devin's brigade to assist in the fight along the River Road, Torbert ordered Custer's men to turn north on a farm road that would bring them behind the Confederate position—the same road that Johnson's Confederates were traveling on.

Once Devin's regiments joined the Union line along Hanover River Road, Baker was forced out of his position, steadily falling back toward you across the fields to your front. At nearly the same time, on the farm road, Johnson's Confederates met Custer's men— and Custer himself—head on, and moved back quickly, heavily outnumbered. Custer, not wanting to give the rebels time to retreat in an orderly fashion, sounded the charge, and the two Michigan regiments with him easily scattered Johnson's command, pursuing them for several miles, and then turning back to where Baker was still putting up a fight.

By this time, Baker's line was approximately in your position here south of Nelson's Bridge. Baker learned only too late that Johnson was no longer protecting his left flank. The Confederates broke for Hanover Court House to their rear (and your rear), many of them falling captured to the pursuing Union horsemen. Torbert, however, soon called off the pursuit to tend to the cavalry's first priority, securing Nelson's Bridge. Still, the fight for Nelson's Bridge on May 27 brought yet another confidence-building victory for the Union cavalry.

ENON CHURCH

> *From the intersection, turn left onto River Road (SR 605) and drive 0.8 mile to Gould Hill Road (SR 645). Turn right on Gould Hill Road and drive 2.1 miles. Turn left onto Williamsville Road (SR 615), then drive 0.4 mile to Studley Road (VA 606). (This intersection was the former location of Haw's Shop, which by this time in the war had already become a dilapidated shack.) Turn right on Studley Road and drive 1 mile. Immediately after a farm field on your right, you will see a small church. Pull in next to the interpretive sign and monument.*

After a hard day's march, the Confederate infantry stopped only a few miles short of Atlee's Station. The rebels were in a good position to counter whatever move the Federals might make, but with the cavalry presence now reported at Hanover and Nelson's Bridge, Robert E. Lee now had a pretty good idea of what the Union army intended to do. He issued orders for all of his men to rest, and then move out at 3 AM on May 28 to finish the march to Atlee's Station. The ultimate goal was to occupy high ground well known by many of the men from the Seven Days' battles of 1862: the

The battle of Enon Church raged in these fields. Oak Grove is the large white house in the distance on the right.

ridge running between Beaver Dam Creek, to the south, and Totopotomoy Creek to the north.

There was one burden that Lee was able to unload from his mind that night. Richard Ewell's performance, particularly at Spotsylvania Court House, had been troublesome. Although he made no egregious tactical blunders, Ewell's temperament had gotten out of control to the point that Lee had to tell the general to calm down during the attack on the Mule Shoe on May 12. By almost all accounts, Ewell was not the same commander that he was before he lost his leg at Manassas in 1862. Now, this night, Ewell reported that he had dysentery, and was forced to relinquish command of his II Corps. Ewell's illness solved two problems at once. First, Lee could gracefully remove him from command. Second, Lee now had an opening for Jubal Early, who had shown much promise taking A. P. Hill's III Corps during his illness, to a permanent corps command. Early was moved up the ladder. A bonus development was that Stephen Ramseur, a promising young brigade commander, could be given Early's old division.

Union infantry, with the exception of one division of the VI Corps, would not cross the Pamunkey River until May 28. Most of the men had gotten a good night's rest, for once, with all of the units except the IX Corps stopping before sundown the night before. They were up early the next day, with the rest of the VI Corps heading for Nelson's Bridge, where pontoon bridges were erected. The VI and V Corps, at Dabney Ferry, were both moving across the river by 9 AM.

Although Grant's withdrawal from the North Anna had been nearly flawless, there was a hole in the plan. Because of their separation, the Union army had little knowledge of where the Confederates now were. This was a job for cavalry, in the traditional sense, and Sheridan quickly began to organize an expedition to find the rebels. Sheridan also noted that he needed to further secure the intersection at Haw's Shop, now being held by only one regiment. David Gregg was asked to secure the crossing, and he sent Henry Davies's brigade, along with three regiments from Col. John Gregg's brigade—altogether, 3,500 horsemen.

Lee, also seeking more information about Federal activity, asked his new commander of cavalry, Wade Hampton, to move toward Haw's Shop. Hampton, who would accompany the force, chose Williams Wickham's Brigade, Thomas Rosser's famed Laurel Brigade, and John Chambliss's brigade. Fitz and Rooney Lee would also accompany the expedition of 4,500 cavalrymen.

Exit your vehicle and face the monument and Civil War Trails sign. Behind you is Enon Church. Added onto since its founding, the original building, the center portion, still stands, and was a landmark of the battle. Far across the field in front of you, on the same side of the road, is a white house known as Oak Grove, the home of John Haw's family. The road to your right, now Studley Road, was once the Atlee Station Road. The Federal cavalry would be coming toward you from your front, while the

Confederates would arrive from your rear. When the two collided here around Enon Church, it would be the start of a long and fierce cavalry battle.

Just before 10 AM, Davies set his headquarters up in the area of Oak Grove and sent a regiment of Federal cavalry west on the Atlee Station Road as a scouting party. The Federals advanced to Enon Church and formed a line north of the road, then send one company farther down the road to investigate. These men soon ran into the lead elements of Hampton's column, led by a similar scouting party of Wickham's brigade. The Federals fell back here to Enon Church, where they were able to hold the scouting party with ease. However, once the rest of the Confederate brigade came up, the line quickly withdrew to Davies's headquarters at Oak Grove.

As Davies watched the scene, the rest of his brigade was just coming up to the Haw House. When the 1st Pennsylvania cavalry arrived, Davies ordered it to countercharge. The Federal countercharge on the Atlee Station Road shocked the Confederates, who were forced to hurry back to Enon Church, where they dismounted and formed a defensive line until the rest of Hampton's men arrived.

Davies moved quickly to establish his own defensive line, just east of Enon Church, right in front of your position. The line consisted of four regiments, one south of Atlee Station Road and three to the north. When Wade Hampton arrived, he immediately countered the Federal formation, overlapping both flanks with Wickham's brigade on the right and Rosser's on the left. The Confederate line was behind you, west of the church, and was formed mostly within the woods you see today, extended well below the road and far to the north.

The two lines traded fire from 11 AM to almost 4 PM. Over that time, both sides would send in small sets of reinforcements. Davies line held firm, although it was definitely weakening. Hampton, meanwhile, had a strong position and was not about to leave it. This, however, did not ease the fighting. The Federals charged the Confederates several times in an attempt to break the stalemate, and the Confederates countercharged with roughly equal loss. All of this action happened around your position here at the church, much of it in the woods to your left and right.

At 4 PM, Davies received some much needed help. Most of the Federal infantry had completed its crossing, and Alfred Torbert took his cavalry division to Haw's Shop to assist. The lead brigade was Custer's, and he quickly dismounted his men and formed two lines across the road, two regiments on each side. Pushing forward, Custer's men began to take severe casualties as they neared the front.

Just before Custer's arrival, Rooney Lee had put Chambliss's brigade on the Confederate left. Lee, running into heavy elements of dismounted cavalry, mistook the Federals as infantry rather than dismounted cavalry. Troubled by this nondevelopment, Lee went to Hampton and asked for permission to withdraw his men, which Hampton quickly granted. When the Federals on the north end of the line saw the

Confederates falling back, they immediately went forward in pursuit. Chambliss's withdrawal meant that Rosser's brigade, to his right, suddenly had his left flank exposed, and he was also forced to fall back, extending the domino effect to Wickham's brigade on the southern end of the line. The Union men pressed forward on the entire line. The Confederate withdrawal was orderly, at first; however, not all of the units received the order, leaving parts of the line with no option but to surrender or run (mostly for the units to your right rear, in the forest south of the road). This became contagious, and the Confederate cavalry was soon on the run.

For the Union cavalry, it would turn out to be the hardest fight of the campaign. Casualties on both sides were about equal, 378 Confederates and 329 Federals. The Federals held the field, but Hampton had picked up the information he needed about the whereabouts of the Union army, which Sheridan was not able to do. Further, the Confederate horsemen were impressed with their new commander, beginning to fill the void that came about with the loss of J. E. B. Stuart. The Union cavalry had begun to think that the Confederate cavalry force was now broken; this was thoroughly disproved here at Enon Church.

TOTOPOTOMOY CREEK

⟩ *From the Enon Church parking lot, pull out to your right on Studley Road and drive 2.7 miles. On your left, you will see the Totopotomoy Creek Unit of Richmond National Battlefield Park. Park in the lot and walk over to the interpretive signs.*

While the Confederates finalized and strengthened their line south of Totopotomoy Creek on May 29, the Union army continued their search for them. The battle at Enon Church was only a clue. With the entire Army of the Potomac now west of the Pamunkey River, Grant directed his infantry corps to send a division each on separate roads west, fanning out to determine the whereabouts of Lee's Confederates. Sheridan's cavalry, after the fight the previous day, was allowed to rest behind the lines at Old Church.

Lee's arrangement was nearly perfect. Not only did Totopotomoy Creek provide a strong natural defensive barrier, but the makeup of his lines covered every major route heading toward Richmond. A. P. Hill's corps was on the left, anchoring its flank on the Virginia Central Railroad. To his right was John Breckinridge's force from the Shenandoah Valley, covering the Atlee Station Road. On Breckinridge's right, Jubal Early's corps turned south at almost a 90-degree angle, facing east with his right flank across Shady Grove Road and close to Beaver Dam Creek. Richard Anderson's corps was kept in reserve. The only other road through the area, Old Church Road south of Beaver Dam Creek, was covered by Confederate cavalry. Lee was ready for anything the Federals could throw at him.

Francis Barlow's II Corps division won the prize for being the first to find the Confederates. Heading west on Atlee Station Road and passing through the previous day's battlefield, he soon came upon rebel skirmishers. Pushing forward and closer to the creek, Barlow realized that Breckinridge's men were in force on the other side, and he formed his lines across Rural Plains, the Shelton estate, to await further orders.

Not long after Barlow's discovery, Charles Griffin's V Corps division crossed to the south bank of Totopotomoy Creek, where they soon found skirmishers from Early's Confederates along the Shady Grove Road, who were in line to the west. Eventually falling back to their crossing point, near the Via Farm, Griffin also awaited instructions. By the time night came, preparations were made for all four of the Union corps to form along the Confederate Totopotomoy Creek defenses and, hopefully, find a way around them.

The Totopotomoy Creek Battlefield unit, only formally opened in 2011, is a significant addition to Richmond National Battlefield Park. Other than the grounds at Cold Harbor, this is the best remaining example of Grant's Overland campaign protected by the park, filling a critical gap in that campaign's history. The home here, Rural Plains, dates from 1723 and was the home of the Shelton family. It was in the parlor of the home that Sarah Shelton was married to Patrick Henry, the famed orator and Revolutionary. During the combat of May 1864, the Shelton family sought pro-

Rural Plains, home of the Shelton family, sat in the line of fire at Totopotomoy Creek. Famed Revolutionary War orator Patrick Henry was married in the house's parlor.

tection in the basement of the house. The home remained in the family continuously through 2001. Although the home itself requires some structural repair, it, as well as the grounds around it, will be improved over the years.

The trails here will take you through much of what's left of the original Shelton farm, including remnants of Barlow's Union earthworks, scattered throughout the grounds. The short version of the trail is approximately 1 mile, but a longer route will take you all the way down to Totopotomoy Creek. Walking this part of the trail to the creek will make it obvious why the Federals did not launch a major attack here. A bridge across the creek reveals a creek with sharp banks, and with Confederate earthworks on the opposite side, a direct assault would have been costly. The trail down to the bridge is a bit more rough than the other section (particularly on your climb back up), but it is worth the effort. (There are interpretive signs along the way, and a park brochure will also guide you through the area.)

If you wish, you may continue along the trail outside of the park boundary to the Confederate earthworks. The trail on this side of the creek is still rougher than what you came across, with a few taxing climbs, but the reward of your efforts is an excellently preserved sample of the Confederate line.

At the time of the battle, the forest you are walking through along the trails was not here. It was the Shelton wheat fields, offering no protection to the Federals as they constructed their main line (Stop 6 on the trail) or their advanced line (Stop 4) on May 30, after the rest of Hancock's II Corps arrived, one division on each side of Barlow. To the right of Hancock, keeping along the northern bank of Totopotomoy Creek, was Wright's VI Corps. To Hancock's left, Burnside's IX Corps was forced to squeeze between the II Corps and Warren's V Corps, which had already established its position near the Shady Grove Road.

While other events took place on the field on May 30, particularly at Bethesda Church and Matadequin Creek, elements of the II Corps charged down the slope to Totopotomoy Creek and, for a moment, were able to get across. However, these assaults were meant to hold Breckinridge's Confederates in place and probe the enemy's line, not to attempt to break through. Similar attacks would be repeated on May 31 as the action moved still farther south to the crossroads at Old Cold Harbor.

〉 *From the parking area at Totopotomoy Creek Battlefield, turn right onto Studley Road and drive 0.6 mile to Rural Point Road (VA 643). Turn right and drive 1.6 miles on Rural Point Road to Heatherwood Drive; turn left on Heatherwood Drive and enter the parking area.*

This is the site of Polegreen Church, a major landmark of the time as well as a significant piece of history. The church became the meeting location for many of Virginia's dissenters with the colony's views on religious freedom, which of course developed into one of the seeds that would feed the American Revolution. There is a lot to experience in this small but beautifully designed park, so be sure to take at least a quick walk around the church site and interpretive memorials.

When Jubal Early formed the defensive line for his Confederate II Corps, he placed his left near Polegreen Church, then ran south along the road you drove in on, then known as an extension of Shady Grove road. On May 30, John Gibbon's division of the Union II Corps was able to advance and take the position around the church. Like the fighting at the Shelton estate, the fighting here was mostly meant to hold elements of Early's corps in place.

Before the Federals left this part of the line on June 1, an artillery duel broke out between the lines. One of the casualties was Polegreen Church, which had been standing for over 120 years. Today, you can see the three-dimensional outline of the space the church occupied. You can also see, running along the north side of the church, a fairly well-preserved line of entrenchments. These were likely Confederate earthworks, as they seem to face north, but like many other earthworks in this part of the country, they may have been altered and used by both sides.

BETHESDA CHURCH

⟩ *From Polegreen Church, return to Rural Point Road and turn left. Drive 0.5 mile on Rural Point Road to Pole Green Road (SR 627). Turn left on Pole Green Road and drive 1.8 miles. Turn left onto Walnut Grove Road (SR 615) and drive 0.9 mile, crossing US 360 and parking in the school parking lot on your left after the intersection.*

Robert E. Lee and Ulysses S. Grant had in common a valuable asset as field commanders: They could recognize opportunity when it arose. In fact, on several occasions throughout their battles over the last year of the Civil War, Grant and Lee could often be found heading for the same point on the battlefield, looking to exploit a strength or weakness. The fighting around Bethesda Church on May 30 is an example of that.

With Lee again strongly entrenched, Grant decided that the Federals' best prospect would be to press the Confederate right and, if necessary, maneuver farther to the south to endanger that flank. The V Corps was already in place to perform such an exercise, so on May 30, Warren was ordered to advance his corps, along with the IX Corps on his right, to the west to examine Jubal Early's defenses. Over the next few days, the VI and II Corps would hold the Confederates in front of them in place by demonstrating against their line, then would slip around behind the Union army to take up a position on the left.

Casting his eyes in the same direction, while remaining aware of other developments on the field, Lee saw a possible opportunity to regain the initiative. It appeared that elements of the Union VI Corps, in front of his left flank, were already beginning to withdraw. In addition, not only was Warren's V Corps active on his right, but it was reported that Sheridan's cavalry was massing on that flank. Certainly, Lee needed to prepare his army for an attack on his right. However, he was also in a good spot to catch the Federals off guard. If he could occupy the enemy cavalry, he could throw Early's corps east toward Warren's V Corps, the only Union force south of Totopotomoy Creek. Warren's isolated force presented a good opportunity to take out a major piece of the Army of the Potomac.

Two of Warren's four divisions, Charles Griffin's and Lysander Cutler's, kept moving west on the Shady Grove Road, eventually coming up to the main Confederate line. They encountered a familiar sight—heavy defensive works in their front, unassailable without assistance. As for that assistance, Warren had not been happy with what was given to him. On his left, Phil Sheridan's cavalry had been tasked with watching that flank, but they never appeared. On the right, Burnside's IX Corps had not been able to keep pace with Warren, falling far behind and eventually asking Warren to fall back so that the two lines could rejoin. Warren was not one to move backward if he didn't have to, but for now, he had two divisions precariously extended in front of the rest of the army.

While Henry Lockwood's division remained in reserve at the Via Farm, Samuel Crawford's division split up. One brigade, Martin Hardin's, would work its way west on Old Church Road, while the other two remained behind in a position to support if necessary. This isolated brigade would be the first target of Jubal Early's attack on the Union V Corps. Beginning at 2 PM, Early began moving Robert Rodes's division, followed by Stephen Ramseur's, south to Old Church Road, where they could attack the isolated Federal brigade. John Brown Gordon's division would remain behind, but could assist if needed. Richard Anderson's corps, being held in reserve, would simultaneously attack Warren's two divisions on Shady Grove Church Road in front of the Confederate line. Warren would be facing fire from front and flank, and with a little luck, the Confederates might be able to crush the Union V Corps.

Your location here at the corner of this busy intersection was the former location of Bethesda Church. If you turn your back to the front of the school, you will be facing north up what is now Walnut Grove Road. This is the road that Hardin's brigade moved south on, toward your position, then turned right (to your left) to move along Old Church Road, now US 360, at 3 PM on May 30.

Now look to your left, down US 360, the former Old Church Road. Hardin's men moved a short distance, then after erecting earthworks, sent a small party westward to scout the road. Hardin's brigade was made up of the famous Pennsylvania Reserves, commonly known as the "Bucktails" for their distinctive headgear. The three-year enlistment period for these men ended the next day, May 31, and although many would reenlist, the thoughts of many of them were in places other than Virginia. The result was a half-hearted effort at constructing a proper earthwork and defensive line, as well as less-than-vigilant patrolling of their front. So when Robert Rodes's Confederates came tearing down the road, only steps behind Hardin's scouting party, they were not exactly ready for combat. Their position was quickly overrun, and the Bucktails were routed. Most of them went back the way they came, turning left at Bethesda Church and heading north toward Shady Grove Road.

Rodes, with Ramseur right behind, had stampeded Hardin's brigade. Now they were in a position to help Anderson take the rest of the Union V Corps. But before they could go anywhere, they had to sort out their own lines, which had become hopelessly mixed during the rapid advance on the Bucktails. The Confederate delay here at Bethesda would be a costly one.

⟩ *From the school parking lot, pull out to your right onto Walnut Grove Road (SR 615). Drive 1 mile, recrossing US 360 and proceeding to the intersection with Pole Green Road (SR 627). Turn right on Pole Green Road, then drive a short distance to the end of the tree line on your left and carefully pull over. Stay in your vehicle.*

You are now on the former Shady Grove Road, now called Pole Green Road. If you look to the right through the open fields, you are looking down the former site of the road, now replaced with the modern Walnut Grove Road. The former road used to come to a T at your current position, and you would have been looking down the road to the south toward Bethesda Church, with Hardin's Federals running in a panic toward your position.

At 4 PM, after sending a message to headquarters from the Via House that Hardin had been overrun, Warren rode to the area, forming a new Union line facing south toward the Confederates, who would be advancing at any moment. Putting Hardin's rallied brigade at the T-intersection facing south, as you are now, Warren placed Crawford's other two brigades on each side of Hardin, but just south of Shady Grove Road, with their flanks turned in slightly and on high ground. With this arrangement, Crawford's division had formed a large area of converging fire around the road from Bethesda Church.

In addition, Griffin moved part of his Federal division, who was now facing Richard Anderson farther west down Shady Grove Road, to help Crawford cover the intersection. (Griffin would have moved from behind you in your direction.) Robert Lockwood's reserve division was also in the area, and they were also called up to Shady Grove Road. Even Cutler's division would eventually come to the area, ready to pitch in if needed. The entire V Corps was now present to meet the Confederate advance.

At 6 PM, a brigade from Stephen Ramseur's division finally advanced toward the Federals, intent on silencing their artillery. Crawford waited until the rebels had reached a point just 200 yards to your right, and then gave the order to fire. Caught in a three-way crossfire from musketry and canister, the Confederates were mowed down mercilessly, yet were able to advance all the way to the Union line. By that point, though, they could go no farther, and those who were not cut down surrendered, not wishing to run the field of fire back to their starting point.

Soon it was dark and the firing stopped. Anderson, who was supposed to have assaulted Griffin from the west down the Shady Grove Road, did virtually nothing, and Early's assaults with Rodes and Ramseur were for naught. The Confederates had lost about 450 men, almost all of them in the fields to your right, to the Union's 417.

OLD CHURCH/MATADEQUIN CREEK

❭ *From your point on Shady Grove Road, drive forward (east) 2.1 miles on Pole Green Road (SR 627). Turn left onto the Mechanicsville Turnpike (US 360) and drive 1.2 miles to Old Church Road (VA 606). Drive 1.4 miles to the intersection with McClellan Road (SR 628). If you are able, find a place to pull over; otherwise, turn right here and continue down McClellan Road to your next stop.*

As mentioned previously, Gouverneur Warren had been asking all day for the cavalry that was supposed to protect his left flank. Sheridan was busy enough, though. The Federal cavalry was tasked with clearing a path for the arrival of Baldy Smith's XVIII Corps, which would be landing at White House shortly and joining the Army of the Potomac. Eventually, Warren's complaints got louder, and Sheridan asked Alfred Torbert to send a brigade of cavalry to Warren's left. Torbert chose Thomas Devin's men, camped at Old Church with the rest of the division, for the task.

Old Church hasn't changed a whole lot over the years. The old church has been gone since before the battle here. On your left, north of the intersection, the large white home was once known as the Old Church Hotel, which served as a temporary headquarters for Sheridan.

Because of some misunderstanding in orders, instead of heading west to the position of the V Corps, Devin turned his men south down the Bottoms Bridge Road (now McClellan Road). He was mistakenly heading to an intersection known as Old Cold Harbor.

❭ *From the crossroads at Old Church, turn left onto McClellan Road (SR 628) and drive 0.9 mile. You will cross a small bridge; this is Matadequin Creek. Proceed past the bridge 0.1 mile to Wood Valley Road, and then pull over. During the battle, most of this area was open farmland, so you may want to instead keep driving forward to a more open area.*

Devin stopped his cavalry brigade in the area of Matadequin Creek, recognizing that it provided a good defensive position. He then sent a small party farther down the road to the intersection of Bottoms Bridge Road (now McClellan Road) and Cold Harbor Road. These men held the crossroads, under orders from Devin to fall back to the creek should any Confederates appear.

In the early afternoon, they did. The lead elements of Matthew Butler's brigade arrived at the crossroads at about 2 PM, sending Devin's advance force back to Matadequin Creek. At 3 PM, Butler attacked the Union position, sending them all to the north bank of the creek. Devin called up his reserve regiments from Old Church, forming a defensive line across Bottoms Bridge Road. Torbert soon arrived as well, and seeing the situation, called up the rest of his division.

Butler's Confederates lined up across the road south of the creek and pushed forward, making their way through several steep ravines before reaching the Union line. Devin attempted to hold his ground, but the rebels were too strong. His line was beginning to weaken when Wesley Merritt's Federal brigade came up from behind, replacing some of Devin's men who were already out of ammunition. Merritt's men helped stabilize the line, but could not gain any advantage over Butler's cavalrymen.

After some heavy fighting, Custer's brigade appeared from Old Church. Custer sent two regiments forward, one on each side of the road, and a third in a roundabout movement to the enemy's left flank. This flanking movement was successful, causing the rebels on the left to begin to fall back, with the rest of their line falling back in turn. Soon it was a rout, and the dismounted Confederates went streaming for the rear, only to find that the men who were holding their horses had fled.

Although it was a small action, the fight at Matadequin Creek on May 30 was yet another decisive victory for the Union cavalry, which, at the moment, seemed almost unstoppable. It would not be until the next day, however, that the Federals realized just how important the consequences of their victory here were.

COLD HARBOR

Old Cold Harbor Crossroads

⟩ *From Wood Valley Road, pull out to the right on McClellan Road (SR 628) and drive 0.6 mile to Crown Hill Road (SR 632). Turn right on Crown Hill Road and drive 3.6 miles. You will come to a five-way intersection; park in the gravel area in the middle.*

After the fight at Matadequin Creek, Butler's fought-out cavalry fell back several miles to the crossroads at Old Cold Harbor. Robert E. Lee saw early that the crossroads were important. From Old Cold Harbor, roads led southeast to both Mechanicsville and Richmond. Roads also led to the rear of Lee's lines. If the Federals were to gain the crossroads, the Confederate army would have to leave its very comfortable

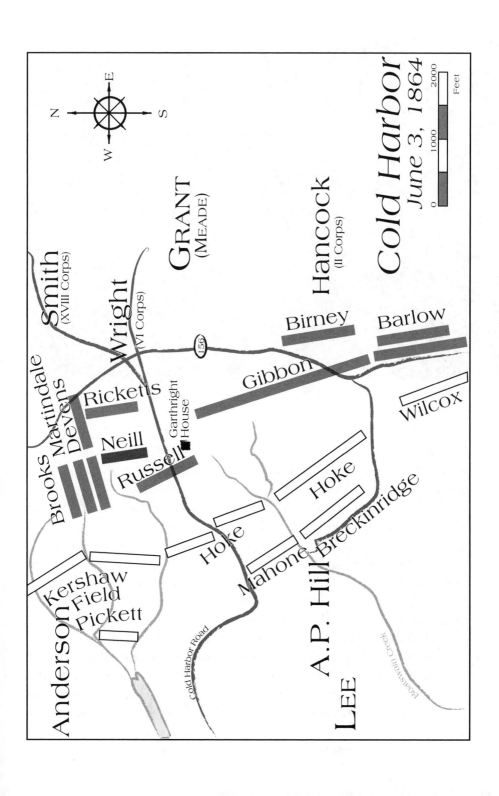

Cold Harbor
June 3, 1864

The Confederate earthworks at Cold Harbor, only a shadow of what they once were, are still impressive today.

lines behind Totopotomoy Creek. Therefore, to relieve Butler's troops, Lee sent Fitzhugh Lee's cavalry to the crossroads to ensure that it would remain secure. They arrived about noon and sent Butler's grateful troopers to the rear.

Thus far, the Federals, though they certainly wanted Lee out of those lines, did not seem very inclined to force him out of them on May 31. The Union infantry, still lined up across from the Confederates on the north bank of the creek, conducted probing attacks all along the line, and did not move from its position. The Federals' main concern was to speed up the arrival of Baldy Smith's XVIII Corps, who had arrived by boat at White House the night before. The addition of an entire corps of infantry would mean big things for the Union army.

The Federal cavalry was responsible for making sure that Smith had a clear march to join the Army of the Potomac. Only one Union division was on the army's left flank to ensure that—Alfred Torbert's. Torbert, wanting a little bit of extra security, decided to attack the Old Cold Harbor crossroads, giving the Union left and Baldy Smith some breathing room. Torbert, along with Custer, devised a plan that would approach the crossroads from two of the five roads that met there. Gaining Sheridan's approval, Torbert set the attack time for 3 PM.

The Union army was not the only one receiving reinforcements on May 31. Lee knew that Smith's Union corps had left Bermuda Hundred, and had sent a desperate plea to Richmond for more troops. Soon, Robert Hoke's division of 6,800 men was headed for Mechanicsville from the Howlett Line at Bermuda Hundred. Unfortunately, Braxton Bragg, Jefferson Davis's military adviser, put the troops on trains headed for Atlee Station. Lee did not need reinforcements there, however, so he forced the train with Hoke's lead brigade, Thomas Clingman, to stop and unload. Hoke's other three brigades would have to make the march from Richmond to Mechanicsville.

Merritt's Union cavalry brigade, followed by Custer's, approached Old Cold Harbor from the northeast on Cold Harbor Road, while Torbert's third brigade, Thomas Devin's, took an alternate route from the east, Black Creek Church Road. Merritt and Custer were to take the rebels by direct assault, while Devin ran around their right and outflanked them. Merritt soon alerted Confederate pickets, who informed Lee of their approach. Knowing that Clingman's infantry was only 3 miles away, Fitz Lee requested that he be reinforced. His uncle, the general commanding, soon sent Clingman to the crossroads.

When Merritt and Devin each reached the crossroads from their respective routes, they found that the enemy had been expecting them. Strong earth and log barricades stretched across both roads. Although the Federals were able to push back the initial resistance, they were stopped cold at the main Confederate line. Meanwhile, as Lee's cavalry held back the assault firmly, Clingman filed in to the left of the cavalry. Almost simultaneously, Custer brought his Federals up, filling the gap between the other two Union brigades. Still, the Confederates would not be budged from their strong position.

To break the stalemate, Torbert reversed his original plan. Originally, Devin's brigade, facing Williams Wickham's men, was to outflank the Confederate right, but that was not possible with the defenses they faced. Now Torbert would send Merritt's brigade around Clingman's troops on the Confederate left. Merritt moved immediately, swinging wide around Clingman's left and taking rebels' flank. As the infantrymen fell back, Lunsford Lomax, whose troopers had been fighting Merritt and Custer in their front, now had his brigade's left exposed. Custer and Devin saw that Merritt was successful and renewed their attack on the front, and the Confederates, outflanked and under pressure, were forced to abandon their position, falling back about 1 mile. The Federals held the Cold Harbor crossroads.

Remarkably, they did not seem to care. Sheridan, hearing from his scouts that additional infantry was joining Lee and Clingman down the road, did not think he could hold the crossroads. Further, according to everything he had been told, the crossroads held little importance. So, after maintaining their position for several hours, Sheridan's men left Old Cold Harbor at 10 PM, leaving it up for grabs.

Well before this time, reports had been coming in to Union headquarters that

Richard Anderson's corps, which had been holding the Confederate left, was now marching behind the rest of his army, moving south to the Confederate right. The confirmed appearance of troops from the Bermuda Hundred line indicated that Lee had been reinforced. The rebels seemed to be massing on the Union left, where Baldy Smith's corps was headed and where there was, at the moment, little Federal presence. All of a sudden, Old Cold Harbor became a strategic necessity.

Lee already realized this and had sent Anderson's corps around 4 PM after learning that the crossroads was threatened. Hoke's division would also be directed to the Confederate right. When the Union high command realized what was happening, Meade ordered Horatio Wright's VI Corps, which now had no Confederates in front of it, to counter Lee's move, marching around the rear of the army from the Union right to the left. Baldy Smith's XVIII Corps, 9 miles to the east, would also be placed there. Sheridan, seemingly the last to know, rushed Torbert's division back to Old Cold Harbor, this time to hold it at all costs. The Union cavalry's capture of the crossroads, seemingly meaningless at the time, had set off a chain reaction of events that would lead to one of the most infamous battles of the Civil War.

Cold Harbor Unit, Richmond National Battlefield Park

> *Pull out of the gravel to your right onto Cold Harbor Road (VA 156). Drive 1 mile to the park road for the Cold Harbor Unit of Richmond National Battlefield Park, then pull into the parking lot for the visitor center.*

By the time the sun was up on June 1, both armies were in a flurry of activity. Robert Hoke's Confederate division had now arrived, and had formed a line running north to south across Cold Harbor Road, west of the crossroads. To their left, Anderson's corps was filing in, first Joseph Kershaw's division, then George Pickett's. Hoke placed two brigades south of the road, while the remaining two, as well as Anderson's two divisions, ran to the north.

Your position here at the Cold Harbor Battlefield visitor center is right along the Confederate line of June 1. The field in front of you is similar to what the soldiers would have seen in 1864, and Cold Harbor ran just as it still does to your left. The center here is small, but inside you will find an electric map program that will take you through the battles for Cold Harbor, including the action immediately before and after. It's a great introduction to help you interpret what you're about to see as you take your tour. Also behind the visitor center is the beginning of a 1-mile loop trail through the battlefield. Although some of the trail is covered by the park road, doing both the trail and the driving tour will give you very good interpretation of a deceptively simple battle. If you wish, there is also an extended 2-mile trail that goes deeper into the park.

While the Confederates were getting their line together, one major piece of the

Union army was stuck because of a clerical error. Baldy Smith, who had been holding his XVIII Corps at a farm to the east, did not have any up-to-date orders to follow. When he finally received a communiqué late on May 31, he followed it to the letter. The order, as it should have read, directed Smith to proceed to Cold Harbor and line up to the left of Horatio Wright's VI Corps. However, instead of "Cold Harbor," the aide who had written the order instead wrote "New Castle Ferry." Not only were these two places nowhere near each other, but it actually pulled Smith's corps in the wrong direction. Smith found New Castle Ferry devoid of any Union presence whatsoever, and requested clarification of his orders. It would not be until around 10 AM that the XVIII Corps would leave New Castle Ferry.

The other major piece that was to be added to the Union left, the VI Corps, was still on the march. While the lead division had left their position at 10:30 PM, the last was not able to withdraw until 4:30 AM on June 1. Sheridan, knowing that the Confederates were gathering west of Old Cold Harbor, grew more anxious by the minute. Kershaw did eventually send a brigade to capture the crossroads, but by this time Torbert's cavalry had strengthened its defenses, and by 8:30 AM the attack was over, Kershaw's men returning to their lines. At around 9 AM, Sheridan finally received word that the VI Corps was approaching, and before long the cavalry was finally relieved of its duties at the intersection. The last troops of the VI Corps reached the Union left at 2:30 PM, and shortly afterward, Smith's XVIII Corps filed into line, finally finishing around 5:30 PM.

By this time, Grant had decided to change his game plan. Initially, his movements to Cold Harbor had been defensive. But Lee's men were also in motion, and had not had a significant amount of time to perfect their defenses. Most significantly, Grant had come to the conclusion that Lee's army was on its last legs. Since the armies left Spotsylvania Court House, the Confederates had had several opportunities to attack the Union lines, but did not. Unless they were behind extremely strong defenses, the rebels did not seem willing to fight. With all of this in mind, Grant decided that the time was right for a large-scale assault. Now that he had an additional corps, and Lee was backed up to Richmond, Grant hoped that his Army of the Potomac—weary, but still confident of victory—could finally strike the final blow to the Confederates.

❭ *Pull out from the visitor center and proceed down the park road 0.4 mile to the parking area at the Confederate earthworks. As you make your way along the road, you will see earthworks to both sides of the road. Also, about 0.2 mile into your drive, you will cross a stream with a small interpretive sign. This is the stream known as "Bloody Run."*

In front of you are some of the wonderfully preserved earthworks here at Cold Harbor battlefield—more than just a slight mound. You can see that even after years of erosion, these works are still formidable. These are such unique examples of earthworks that temptation is there to crawl in them and get an idea of what it felt like to look across the open pine woods (similar to what you see today) toward the Union line, only a few hundred yards to the east. (Because these earthworks are so well preserved, *do not* give in to that temptation, and view them from a distance.)

By 6 PM on June 1, all pieces were in place for a Union assault, and the Confederates were more than ready to receive them. These earthworks were held by Kershaw's division of Anderson's corps. As you stand facing east, Pickett's line would have extended well north of you. Robert Hoke's division was to the south, still in the position it took in the morning. It was between these two divisions that the Confederates, for a time, courted disaster.

On your drive to this position, you crossed a small stream now known as Bloody Run. This creek was one of three that crossed the Confederate line, and this one, the farthest south of the three, happened to form the boundary between Hoke's and Kershaw's division. Johnson Hagood's brigade, of Hoke's division, was covering the run. However, after Thomas Neill's division extended the Union flank past Hoke's right, Hoke thought that he needed to extend his line as well. To do so, he removed Hagood from the run and put his brigade on the army's right.

From south to north, the Union line began with the divisions of Wright's VI Corps—Thomas Neill's to the south, then David Russell's, then James Ricketts's. To their right were Smith's XVIII Corps divisions—Charles Devens's, William Brooks's, and John Martindale's. Because of a wide gap between the north end of Smith's corps and Warren's V Corps, Martindale's division was turned to face north, discouraging a Confederate flank attack. On the south end, Neill did the same thing, refusing the Union left flank with two brigades. The Federal position across the field from you would have been Devens's division, just north of Bloody Run.

After a two-hour artillery barrage that began at 4 PM, the Union line finally advanced. Along most of the line, the results were the same. The soldiers, already good targets because of the proximity of the lines, were hit almost as soon as they left their field works. Most advanced through the storm of musketry and artillery, but stopped somewhere short of the Confederate line, forming an intermediate line and quickly throwing up an earthen barricade to protect themselves from enemy fire.

One brigade, from David Russell's division, had higher expectations than most, and it met them. Emory Upton had been the young officer who had designed the attack on Doles's Salient at Spotsylvania Court House. Now wearing a general's stars, Upton advanced his brigade steadily from just north of the Garthright House across the fields toward the Confederates. Upton gave his men the same instructions he had given his troops at Spotsylvania: advance upon the enemy's works as quickly as possible, without stopping to fire, reload, or aide a wounded comrade, and once inside the works, hit them with everything possible.

A marker commemorates the charge of the 2nd Connecticut Heavy Artillery at Cold Harbor.

Upton's brigade, with the 2nd Connecticut Heavy Artillery leading the charge, made their way toward Clingman's Confederates, just south of Bloody Run. The brigade made it to the obstructions before the line, but no farther. Upton, near the front as usual, commanded his men to lie down, hoping to be supported on his flanks.

No support would be coming from his left; Henry Eustis's brigade had met the same fate as most of the other charging Union regiments. However, on Upton's right were James Ricketts's two brigades—and Bloody Run. The first brigade on Upton's right was William Truex's, and it advanced steadily, trying to keep up with Upton. As the men moved, however, they found that they quickly overran the first line of Confederate works. That was because Hagood's brigade had been removed by Hoke. Ricketts's other brigade, Benjamin Smith's, was forced to fall behind Truex because of a marsh in their front and the slow advance of Devens's division to their right. This caused Truex's men to shift to the left, right into the Bloody Run ravine.

Clingman's Confederates, south of the ravine, and William Wofford's, to the north, did not know that Hagood's brigade had been withdrawn, so when Ricketts's men approached down the ravine, it was not immediately clear whether they were friend or foe. By the time they did find out, the Federals were almost on top of them. Breaking the first number of Confederates, Truex soon swung his men to face south and began enfilading Clingman's line. After he was able to drive two rebel regiments and was working on the third, Emory Upton was able to throw his men back into the fight. The Confederates were now being attacked front and flank south of Bloody Run.

Results to the north of the run were similar. Smith's brigade wheeled to face north, then began to move along the Confederate line. When Devens's two brigades arrived there, they were pleased to see that they were already beginning to break for the rear. After Devens's men pitched in, they began to break even faster. Continuing to work on their opening in two directions, the Federals were in the process of opening a half-mile gap in the Confederate works.

The works you are looking at were from Wofford's brigade. As you look down the line to the right, Smith's Federals would have been working their way toward your position, while Deven's division would have been coming at your front.

Only one active division remained north of Devens's, and that was Brooks's. Unfortunately for the Federals on the field, Brooks ran into the same fierce fire that had stopped the other units short. After advancing a short distance, his troops dug in short of their objective. This left Devens's right flank open, and before long, his men were pinned down in the field, no longer able to assist with Truex's work moving along the Confederate line.

At 7:30 PM, Horatio Wright reported to headquarters. The attack was going well, he said. The Union had suffered many casualties but had also taken many prisoners. Most critically, though, Wright knew that to exploit the break in the Confederate line, particularly before dark, he must have reinforcements. The Federals, however, had not learned from their previous successful breakthroughs at Doles's Salient and the Mule Shoe at Spotsylvania. The nearest reasonable reserves were miles away, and they would not be there in time.

The Confederates did not have the same problem. Before night came on, several units arrived and plugged the gap created by the Federals, successfully counter-charging the already-spent Union soldiers. In addition, Alfred Colquitt's soldiers, who had been in line next to Clingman, turned to face north and began to pummel Upton's and Truex's brigades. Although the Federals made a brave stand, they were driven back to the advance rebel lines that they had captured. By dark, the large gap in the Confederate line, one that could have possibly led directly to Richmond had it been exploited, was sealed.

〉 *Continue down the park road another 0.2 mile to another parking area on your right for the Union entrenchments.*

This position was occupied by Ricketts's division of the Union VI Corps during the major assaults at Cold Harbor on June 1 and 3. You are not looking at the main Union line; rather, the advanced lines that Devens's brigade was able to secure during the evening assault of June 1. Having taken heavy casualties during that assault, Baldy Smith elected to remove his division, and Horatio Wright filled the hole with Neill's division, move north from the left flank. The main Confederate line, the stop you just left, is about 200 yards to your front, as you look at the interpretive sign here; with some binoculars (or a decent pair of eyes), you should be able to see it easily—just look for the interpretive signs at that position.

After the Confederate breach was sealed, both armies reacted swiftly. Wright began to report that the rebels were beginning to extend their lines south toward the Chickahominy River, which would bring them past the Union left. Almost immediately, Meade ordered Winfield Hancock to move his II Corps from the Union right all the way to the its left to fill this gap, similar to what Wright's corps had done the previous night. As soon as Hancock was in place the next day, June 2, the Federals would renew the assault.

This time, though, Grant's assault would not be limited to the two Federal corps on the south end of the line. This would be, hopefully, the assault to end the war. The entire Union line would advance, pressing Lee along his entire line. Still convinced that the Confederates were fought out, there would be a weakness somewhere, and when it was found, the Federals would try to end this terrible war.

It was hoped that Hancock would be in place so that the assault could be launched early on June 2. However, the track record of the Army of the Potomac for successful night marches was not very good. The lead elements of the II Corps did not reach Cold Harbor until 6 AM, and the rest of the corps was well behind. Meade rescheduled the attack for 5 PM to allow Hancock's men to get into place and get some rest. In preparation for an army-wide assault, Burnside's IX Corps, now holding the Union right, and Warren's V Corps shifted position slightly to hold a stronger line and be better able to take part in the assault. This placed the entire Army of the Potomac south of Totopotomoy Creek, with its right near Bethesda Church.

As soon as Hancock's troops began to leave their lines on the night of June 1, Robert E. Lee was aware of it, and he knew where they were going. Lee had already been considering shifting troops south; now, with much of his northern flank unopposed, his thoughts were confirmed. John Breckinridge's force was immediately sent to the Confederate right to extend the line to the Chickahominy River. Shortly afterward, two of Jubal Early's three divisions were also sent south, leaving only Henry Heth's division. Never one to pass up an opportunity, Lee realized that he now overlapped the Union right, and that it was held by Burnside. Heth, along with A. P. Hill's corps, launched a ferocious attack against Burnside's men in the late afternoon, with most of the combat happening west and north of Bethesda Church (including the same ground you visited earlier on Shady Grove Road).

Lee, in sending three divisions south, extended his right flank to the Chickahominy River in strength. He was also able to gain the high ground farthest south at Turkey Hill, site of the battle of Gaines's Mill two years earlier. The natural strength of Lee's line was impressive, and on those portions of the line that had been held for several days, his men now had time to improve their earthworks even further.

A very hard rain began around 4 PM, and given the weather conditions, the attack on the Union right, and the fatigue of the Federals, the attack was again postponed. The new jump-off time was set for 4:30 AM, June 3.

❯ *Drive another 0.3 mile on the park road. Pull into the parking area near the monument to the 2nd Connecticut Heavy Artillery.*

Soon after taking his new position as Lieutenant General, Grant made it policy that no soldier would stand idle duty if he could be used at the front. While the Union army was still at Spotsylvania, some of these soldiers began to trickle in as reinforcements, most of them previously manning the defenses at Washington, D.C. A good number of these new regiments were recruited for and trained in the use of heavy artillery, such as those that protected the capital, but when they joined the Army of the Potomac, they were converted into infantrymen, manning the front lines with the rest of the soldiers.

Many of these artillerymen resented the fact that they had been trained for one duty and asked to do another, but it was nothing compared to the reception they got from their new comrades in arms. The Union veterans derided the new arrivals as "bandbox soldiers" who knew nothing about real fighting, and although they had the least experience and training on the field, these units were often asked to perform some of the worst tasks. With their clean uniforms and martial bearing, the "heavies," as they were called, would need to accomplish extraordinary feats to earn the trust and respect of their fellow soldiers.

They did, and often. In fact, many of these units would go out of their way to take these assignments, eager to show that they were not "bandbox soldiers." At Spotsylvania, at Cold Harbor, and at Petersburg, the heavies would prove their courage time and time again, often charging formations that a veteran infantryman would not dare approach—partly out of inexperience, partly out of bravery. In fact, a close look at the casualty numbers of the Overland campaign, particularly from Spotsylvania onward, reveals that the heavies took a disproportionate amount of casualties, mostly because they were learning on the job (for example, standing and shooting rather than hitting the ground and digging a small earthwork). In any case, it was not long before the heavies proved themselves as capable as any other unit on the field.

Before you is a monument to the 2nd Connecticut Heavy Artillery. During the assault of June 1, the 2nd Connecticut, commanded by Col. Elisha Kellogg, was part of

Emory Upton's brigade. Fighting with conspicuous bravery, his soldiers took part in the advance south down the Confederate line before a lack of support forced them back. Kellogg, who was a veteran fighter, was killed early in the action as he tried to lead them over the Confederate works. The inscription on the monument says it all— these men, once ridiculed, had proven their worth.

Garthright House/Hanover County
Cold Harbor Battlefield Park

❭ *Drive to the end of the park road, then turn left onto Cold Harbor Road. Drive 0.2 mile to the Garthright House and the park on your right.*

When the appointed time came on the morning of June 3, most of the units all along the line did as they were ordered and advanced toward the Confederate line. What resulted was an absolute disaster for the Union forces. On the southern end of the line, south of Cold Harbor Road, Winfield Hancock's II Corps advanced across the open fields to its front and was absolutely slaughtered. Although several units actually did briefly break a weak spot in the Confederate line between Breckinridge and Hoke, the rebels had reserves behind this point and were able to countercharge and drive the Federals back.

The house you see here is the Garthright House, witness to both the June 1 and

The Garthright House still stands just behind the Union line at Cold Harbor.

June 3 assaults at Cold Harbor. Around the house, John Gibbon's division of Hancock's II Corps prepared for what it knew would be a very bloody affair. Turn so that the house is on your left and you are looking southwest down Cold Harbor Road, to your right. Gibbon's men advanced into the fields in front of you, south of the road. On the opposite end of the field, on high ground, was Hoke's division, waiting eagerly for what it also knew would be a death trap for the Union soldiers. It was Hoke's men who were also across this field during the June 1 assault.

While the Garthright House itself is maintained by the National Park Service, just behind you is Hanover County Cold Harbor Battlefield Park, maintained locally. Although it is a walking tour rather than driving, it is a short walk, only a mile, and the earthworks it protects are near pristine, similar to the works in the National Park sector.

On the other side of Cold Harbor Road, to your right, was Horatio Wright's VI Corps. Wright's men, whose line extended all the way through the woods to your stop at the Union entrenchments, knew that an assault here on June 3 would be a replay of the attack two days ago. As a result, most of the units made only a half-hearted attempt at an assault, while the others made no attempt at all. Those who were able to move forward did not move far, and they quickly resorted to erecting earthworks.

Next in the Union line to the north was Baldy Smith's XVIII Corps. Like Wright's men, they had already been through the horror of an assault across these grounds. Unlike Wright's men, they saw an opportunity for success, with what seemed to be a large gap in the Confederate line to their front. With his two available divisions— including Martindale's fresh soldiers—Smith advanced into the gap. It was a trap; the gap was the ravine surrounding the middle stream of the three that cut through the Confederate line. The rebels had created an inverted formation around the mouth of the gap, hoping that the Federals would walk right into what would be a devastating crossfire. The leading brigades of Smith's corps did enter the mouth of the gap and paid a heavy price, but before long, Smith called off the assault, lessening his casualties as much as possible.

By 5:30 AM, less than hour after the beginning of the assault, it was all over. The Union casualties, almost entirely in the II and XVIII Corps, were staggering for an hour's work—approximately 3,500 casualties, five times the Confederates' 700. Casualties for Cold Harbor are often reported much higher than these numbers, and there is dispute over the num-

---

CASUALTIES—
COLD HARBOR
CAMPAIGN,
MAY 26–JUNE 3

Confederate: killed, wounded, missing, or captured: 6,000 (estimated)

Union: killed, wounded, missing, or captured: 12,788 (official)

Total Casualties: 18,788

bers, but with poor recordkeeping and the often combined casualty returns that may or may not include the fighting of June 1, Totopotomoy Creek, and/or Bethesda Church, the hard numbers are almost impossible to determine.

For critics of Ulysses S. Grant, the final assault at Cold Harbor is often pointed to as an example of his lack of military skill and/or the lack of concern he had for wasting his men's lives. However, when considering the information Grant had at the time, the decision makes a bit more sense. The Union army had just been reinforced. The Confederates seemed to be waning. The Chickahominy River was at their backs, limiting their escape options. The rebels' capital was only 10 miles behind the Confederate line. Perhaps most pertinent of all, the only alternative to attack was another withdrawal to maneuver around Lee's army. Grant knew that there was a chance the assault would fail. He also thought that the attack could succeed, well within the realm of possibility given the Union's success on June 1. If it did succeed, the Federals could possibly march right into Richmond. The risk, in Grant's mind, in the mind of his staffers, and in the mind of most of his generals, was worth the reward.

As for the Confederates, June 3 could barely even be called a battle. Although there were some more offensive actions after the main assault, for the most part, the Confederates had been able to stay behind their earthworks and simply mow down the Union soldiers. The greater burden—and one that the Federal soldiers would have to bear as well—came over the next two days, as the thousands of men trapped between the lines suffered, cried out for water, and died, with no terms of truce being agreed to between the armies. For both sides, the agony of the men left to die in no-man's-land tore at the soul, blue or gray.

In any case, the charge here early on June 3 led to not only disastrous Federal losses but yet another stalemate between the two armies. The Union Army of the Potomac was as close to Richmond as it had ever been, yet it still remained out of reach. The Confederate position here at Cold Harbor was the strongest they had held thus far, and they could hold this line as long as Grant wanted to keep trying to attack it. The two armies were in a familiar position. Lee could not make a move until the Federals did; the options for the latter were limited to repeated attacks or maneuver. Grant's decisions over the next few days would be critical ones. His grand assault here at Cold Harbor had failed miserably. He now had to come up with a new solution for destroying the Army of Northern Virginia and ending the war.

OPTIONAL STOP—TREVILIAN STATION

> *The battle of Trevilian Station occurred on June 11–12, 1864, just after the main assaults at Cold Harbor, and the directions given here are from your last stop at Cold Harbor. However, the site of the Trevilian Station battlefield is closer to the*

beginning of your tour at the North Anna, so you may wish to navigate from there to the intersection of Courthouse Square and Main Street (US 33) in Louisa, Virginia.

From Hanover County Cold Harbor Battlefield Park, pull out to your left onto Cold Harbor Road (VA 156) and drive 2.5 miles to Creighton Road (SR 615). Turn left on Creighton Road and drive 0.7 mile, then take the entrance ramp onto I-295 West. Follow I-295 West for 18.3 miles to exit 53A, then merge onto I-64 West. Continue on I-64 West for 34.4 miles to exit 143. Take the exit onto Courthouse Road (VA 208 East) and drive 8.3 miles. When you reach Elm Avenue in downtown Louisa, turn left and drive 0.4 mile, then turn right onto Courthouse Square and park.

After the battles at Cold Harbor had resulted in another stalemate, Grant decided to head south of the James River to Petersburg. Maneuvering away from Lee undetected would be a tricky affair, so Grant decided to send Phil Sheridan on another grand cavalry raid—this time to the west, toward Charlottesville. Most of the bounty of the "Breadbasket of the Confederacy," the Shenandoah Valley, came through the rail center at Charlottesville, and tearing up the railroad center there had been in

The Confederate wagon train at Trevilian Station was located in the open fields across the road. This was the site of what came to be known as Custer's First Last Stand.

Grant's mind as a target for months. Furthermore, David Hunter's force in the Shenandoah was just beyond Charlottesville. If Sheridan could join Hunter, their combined force could approach Richmond from the west. The primary mission, though, was to hopefully pull Lee's cavalry away from the main army, lessening the chances of the Confederates detecting the upcoming Union withdrawal.

Sheridan took two of his three divisions, Alfred Torbert's and David Gregg's, and left for Charlottesville on June 7 with 9,400 troopers. As hoped, the Confederate cavalry pursued, with both Wade Hampton's and Fitzhugh Lee's divisions following two days later. A more direct route, however, allowed them to catch up to Sheridan's army quickly. On the night of June 10, while Sheridan's men camped at Clayton's Store, the Confederates camped near Louisa Court House and Trevilian Station on the Virginia Central Railroad, planning to surprise the Federals the next morning by attacking from two directions. In all, Hampton's cavalry numbered 6,400 men.

This is Louisa Court House. While the edifice you see here does not date back to the battle, other buildings here on the square do. Fitz Lee's cavalry camped in this area on the night of June 10. If you are standing in front of the courthouse, turn so that it is on your left. You are now roughly facing west; if you were to follow the road on your right, Hampton's division would have been in camp at Trevilian Station, approximately 4 miles to your front. If you turn to face the road, the Union camp at Clayton's Store is a little more than 5 miles to your north.

⟩ *From Courthouse Square, turn left onto Main Street (US 33) and drive 0.2 mile. Bear right onto Ellisville Drive (SR 669) and drive 1.1 miles. Pull into the gravel area at the auto shop and park near the Civil War Trails sign.*

The two Confederate divisions, Hampton's and Lee's, had direct routes to the Union camp at Clayton's Store. The advantage of this was that they could converge on the camp from two directions. However, between those two roads was (and, as you can see, still is) filled with very thick forest, making communication between the two divisions nearly impossible.

Early on the morning on June 11, both the Federals and the Confederates rose early and proceeded down the two roads from opposite ends, not knowing that they were headed for a collision. In this spot, on the road just north of Nunn's Creek, one regiment of Custer's brigade met Williams Wickham's brigade just after daybreak. After about 45 minutes of hard skirmishing, Custer sent in another brigade, and the Virginians withdrew back to Louisa Court House. Their withdrawal allowed Custer to use a farm lane to cut across the thick forest between the Marquis Road and the Fredericksburg Road, eventually emerging on the Gordonsville Road between Louisa Court House and Trevilian Station.

The road passing by you is the former Marquis Road, now known as Ellisville Drive. Turn and face the road. Custer's men came from your left, while Wickham's came from your right. Nunn's Creek is easily visible from this spot, only a few hundred feet to your right. The Fredericksburg Road is now behind you, through the thick forest.

〉 *From the auto shop, pull out to your left onto Ellisville Drive and drive 3.8 miles. Pull into the gravel area to your right where Ellisville Drive intersects with Oakland Road.*

This is Clayton's Store, location of the Union camp on the night of June 10. The crossroads here was the epicenter of the camp, with Sheridan's headquarters nearby. Union cavalry was camped in the fields around you, as well as down the Marquis and Fredericksburg Roads.

Turn to face the road. You will see two roads to your left. The one closest to you (the one you drove here on) is the old Marquis Road, now Ellisville Road, where Lee's Confederates met Custer's men. The far road is the former Fredericksburg Road, now called Oakland Road, from which Hampton's cavalry approached. Sheridan had planned on moving through Trevilian Station the next morning to continue his move to Charlottesville using both roads, catching Hampton's cavalry before they could reach the camp.

〉 *From the gravel area, pull out onto Oakland Road (SR 613), across from you, and drive 2.8 miles. Pull into the parking lot at Ebenezer United Methodist Church on your left.*

It was near this spot where Wesley Merritt's Union cavalry brigade met two brigades of Wade Hampton's division, Matthew Butler's and Gilbert Wright's, moving north up the Fredericksburg Road. Merritt was outnumbered, and soon received some assistance from Thomas Devin's brigade, but the Confederates were steadily putting heavy pressure on the Federal line.

However, after Custer had driven off Fitz Lee's cavalry on the Marquis Road and cut through the woods, he emerged in Hampton's rear and immediately headed for the Confederate supply train. Once Hampton heard Custer's attack behind him, he began to pull his two brigades back, making preparations not only to protect his supply trains but possibly catch Custer in the process.

From your location at the church, face the road. The Union cavalry would have come from your right and come across your front toward the Confederates, who came from your left. Most of the fighting here would have been to your left, with the Federals taking a relatively strong position along a ridge running across the Fredericksburg Road.

❯ *From the church parking lot, pull out to your left and drive 2 miles on Oakland Road. On your left will be a gravel pull-off, with a sign marking the property of the Trevilian Station Battlefield Foundation. Pull into the gravel road, but take extreme caution; the area is still undeveloped, and turning around is almost impossible. Until the area is developed, your best bet is probably to keep your vehicle close to Oakland Road and backing out when you are finished.*

With the Union troopers in their front in pursuit, Wright's and Butler's brigades had to conduct a fighting withdrawal as they moved rearward toward their camp and the supply wagons. The Federals conducted several assaults against the Confederate line along the way. Some of the heaviest fighting was in this area, near what was then the Poindexter House. (The house still stands, but it is on private property and is fairly obscured by the woods.) Because of the thick forest and narrow roads you see here, the fighting was generally at close quarters. The Confederates were able to make a stand here, and after Hampton successfully leaded a countercharge to save a Confederate battery, the main fight shifted to the location of Hampton's camp near Trevilian Station.

A good portion of the land in this area is now owned by the Trevilian Station Battlefield Foundation. Although not developed for visitors yet, it is good to know that this piece of land is preserved for further study and enjoyment. The foundation is working to make this piece of land, the center of the battlefield, a prime Civil War destination for the future.

❯ *From the Trevilian Station site, drive south on Oakland Road 1 mile to Louisa Road (US 33). Turn right on Louisa Road and drive 0.5 mile; you will see a store parking lot with two Civil War Trails signs near the road.*

You are now in the town of Trevilians, formerly Trevilian Station. The station itself would have been in this general area, and if you are facing the road, the railroad itself is only a few hundred feet behind you. In front of you, in the open fields across the road, Wade Hampton's cavalry had set up its camp, including its important wagon train.

Although the two sides had already been fighting for several hours, it was still early morning when George Custer's brigade turned west onto the Gordonsville Road. Seeing Hampton's wagon train in front of them, the troopers gleefully rushed forward, quickly capturing most of the wagons. However, by this time, Hampton was well aware that the Federals were in his rear, and had sent Thomas Rosser's Laurel Brigade to attack them. Before Custer's charge had even been completed, Rosser surprised the Federals from the west, pushing them eastward toward Louisa Court House. Also in that direction was Fitz Lee's cavalry division, who began to attack from the east. Not long after, Butler's and Wright's brigades, which had been fighting on the Fredericksburg Road, arrived from the northwest. Custer's entire brigade soon found itself completely surrounded. Still, the Federals fought on, conducting several countercharges and holding the Confederates back.

As they fought on, the Confederates were able to recapture not only their own wagons, but also most of Custer's, including his headquarters wagon. It wasn't until after noon that Sheridan got word that Custer was surrounded at Trevilian Station. He immediately sent Torbert's division to the rescue. Torbert charged from the north with three brigades, not only giving Custer a chance to break out but also persuading the Confederates to fall back, Fitz Lee moving east to Louisa Court House and Hampton west toward Charlottesville.

There was additional fighting during the day—Rosser, notably, was seriously wounded during a rebel assault—but by sundown, the Federals held the field at Trevilian Station. They had lost the wagons they had captured, but they had also driven the Confederates away and averted a surprise morning attack. Their goal of Charlottesville, however, lay to the west, and Wade Hampton's division was still in their path.

> *From the parking lot, pull out to your right onto Louisa Road and drive 0.2 mile, then bear right onto Spotswood Trail (US 33 West). Follow Spotswood Trail for 1.4 miles; pull into the gravel area with the Civil War Trails signs on your right.*

On the night of June 11, Hampton's cavalry pulled back to a position near here, setting up an L-shaped defensive line. One side of the L ran along the Virginia Central Railroad, while the other crossed the railroad and the Gordonsville Road (now Spotswood Trail). Your position here near the interpretive sign is roughly where the angle of the L was, later known as Hampton's Bloody Angle. As you face the road, one of the lines ran roughly outward from where you stand (possibly along the farm road you see to your front left), while the other ran along the tracks to your right rear.

The farm road you see is the former farm road for the Ogg Farm, the farmhouse of which is still standing in the distance. On the morning of June 12, after destroying Trevilian Station and the surrounding railroad track in the morning, Sheridan's troopers attempted to break the Confederate lines, charging both across the Ogg Farm from your far left and across the fields behind you, toward your position at the railroad tracks. The Confederates were able to successfully repulse seven Union assaults.

Turn to your right so that you are facing northwest down Spotswood Trail. During the final assault, Lunsford Lomax's brigade, from Fitzhugh Lee's division, found its way around the battlefield and placed itself northwest of the fighting, well to your front. Lomax then came down directly on the Union right flank, sending the Federal cavalry streaming for the rear. Sheridan's men regrouped at Trevilian Station. Because they were unable to continue their mission toward Charlottesville, Sheridan decided to turn back for the Army of the Potomac that night. Although the casualties were roughly equal—955 for the Union, 813 for the Confederates—the fact that the latter were able to stop the destruction of the rail depots at Gordonsville and Charlottesville provided Lee with a critical line of supply just when he needed it, as the two armies were about to settle into the siege at Petersburg.

The Last Invasion: Jubal Early's Raid on Washington

BACK IN THE SPRING OF 1862, when the Union Army of the Potomac was approaching Richmond, Robert E. Lee had taken a gamble to relieve pressure on the capital. Stonewall Jackson, whose troops would be needed at Richmond, was in the Shenandoah Valley. In the face of overwhelming numbers, rather than recall him immediately, Lee ordered Jackson to stay where he was and create havoc, hopefully delaying Union troops there and in other parts of Northern Virginia from joining the assault on Richmond. Using a combination of stealth, intense marching, and tactical mastery, Jackson was more than effective. Not only did he keep the enemy troops occupied, but the rumors surrounding his arrival at Richmond (some true, some not) were enough to cause the Federals to back away and end their campaign. Stonewall Jackson's Shenandoah Valley campaign of 1862 has since become one of the most storied, studied, and debated campaigns in military history.

Two years later, in June 1864, Robert E. Lee found himself in a similar situation between the Confederate capital and the Army of the Potomac. His army was at Cold Harbor, only a stone's throw away from the old battlefield at Gaines's Mill. It had been after this 1862 battle (also known as the first battle of Cold Harbor) that the Union army had been notified that it would be withdrawing from the outskirts of Richmond. Federal troops were again in the Shenandoah Valley, preparing to threaten Lee's army.

However, there were certainly some major differences to consider. Stonewall Jackson

---

Jubal Early now lies at rest atop the hill from which he commanded Confederate forces at Lynchburg.

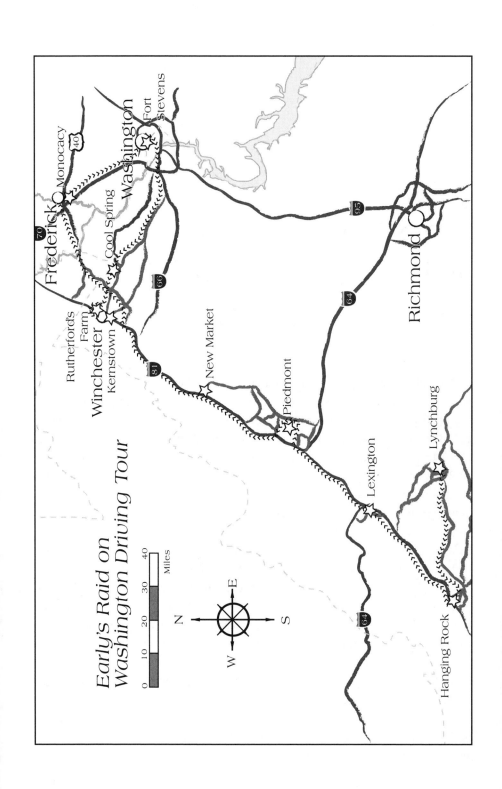

Early's Raid on
Washington Driving Tour

was dead, and although his performance after his arrival at Richmond was questionable, it was still an immeasurable loss. On the other side of the field, the commander had also changed. George B. McClellan, famously diagnosed with "the slows" by Abraham Lincoln for his lack of aggressiveness, was long gone, and aggressive did not even begin to describe Lee's current opponent, Ulysses S. Grant. The Confederate Army of Northern Virginia was in much worse condition than it had been two years earlier, and sparing men for any venture could be fatal. Finally, the present Union troops in the Shenandoah Valley seemed to be much more active than their predecessors, and were on the verge of severing the vital railroads coming to Richmond from the west.

The stakes were now much higher than they were in 1862, but the situation was also becoming more desperate. There was also one very enticing element: While the Federals had been overly concerned with the defense of Washington in 1862, the capital works were now well known to be severely undermanned, with every available soldier being sent to Grant. Lee had already proven himself an able gambler, usually coming out on top after his riskiest moves. So on June 12, 1864—three days after the "Old Men and Young Boys" had successfully deflected the first attack on Petersburg, and three days before the main Union assault—Lee summoned the proven and capable Jubal Early to his Cold Harbor headquarters. Early was to lead the Confederate Second Corps—Jackson's corps—to Lynchburg, then into the Shenandoah Valley. And, if circumstances permitted, Early would have the authority to attempt one of the most daring and unexpected exploits of the Civil War—an attack on Washington, D.C.

BEFORE YOU GO

» PLANNING YOUR TRIP

Although your tour will begin in Lynchburg, Virginia, where the Confederates first encountered the Union troops of the valley, the story of the campaign actually begins almost a month earlier with the May 15, 1864, battle of New Market. This battle, as well as the battle of Piedmont and the events in must-see Lexington, occurred before Early arrived in Lynchburg, but they are critical to the story of the campaign. While you can start at New Market and follow the sites chronologically, it probably won't add to your understanding of the campaign and may not be worth the extra miles.

If you're short on time, you may also want to consider splitting the tour into two. The recommended way will take you through the Shenandoah Valley, a drive that should never be passed up. However, there is a somewhat large gap between some of the sites. Just be sure not to skip those sites to the south—they are all

> **EARLY'S RAID**
> **Number of sites: 10**
> **Total miles: 475**
> **Estimated time: 3–5 days**

great visits. (If you do decide to split up the tour, Lynchburg is very close to Appomattox; it might make sense to add these sites to the tour laid out in chapter 8.)

» RECOMMENDATIONS

Lodging sites abound at the two bookends of the tour, Lynchburg and Washington, D.C. You will also find plenty of places in Frederick, Maryland, and Lexington, Virginia. However, as you drive through the valley, your choices get a bit thinner. There are still plenty of places to stay, but if you're overly picky about your accommodations you may want to plan where you're going to stay ahead of time. Besides hotels, you will find many bed & breakfasts along the way.

The Shenandoah Valley is a wonderful place, with a rich history and beautiful scenery. Try not to get too caught up in your Civil War fervor and be sure to enjoy your drive. There are plenty of great stops, including Natural Bridge, and several of the towns along the way—particularly Lexington, Harrisonburg, and Winchester—offer much more than just their Civil War ties, making them good visits for the whole family. Finally, if you are able, visit Shenandoah National Park, which rides along the Blue Ridge Mountains east of the valley floor. You may want to consider stopping here for at least one night, either in a lodge or using one of its numerous campsites.

THE CAMPAIGN TOUR

LYNCHBURG

Historic Sandusky

⟩ *Begin your tour at Historic Sandusky, 757 Sandusky Drive, Lynchburg.*

The meeting between Robert E. Lee and Jubal Early on June 12, 1864, did indeed lay out a very grand finale at Washington, D.C. However, at the moment, a much more pressing matter needed to be addressed in the Shenandoah Valley—one that would require one quarter of Lee's entire force.

In mid-May, after Franz Sigel's Union forces were soundly defeated at New Market, a command change was made in the Valley. Sigel was replaced as commander of the Department of West Virginia by David Hunter. Hunter's objective was the same as Sigel's: to destroy the Virginia Central Railroad, which supplied the Confederacy with food from the Shenandoah Valley and supplies from points west. "Black Dave" led 8,500 men south toward Staunton, Virginia, quickly capturing it on June 8 and laying waste to the railroad warehouses there. While at Staunton, his force grew by 10,000 men when he was joined by George Crook's Army of Western Virginia and William Averell's cavalry division. By June 11, Hunter had reached Lexington, where

IN DEPTH

B. F. Cooling—*Jubal Early's Raid on Washington, 1864*
Marc Leepson—*Desperate Engagement: How a Little-Known Civil War Battle Saved Washington, D.C. and Changed American History*
Frank Vandiver—*Jubal's Raid: General Early's Famous Attack on Washington in 1864*

"Leepson's captivating narrative is the most recent work. Cooling provides a fine examination of the personalities and fighting men involved, and Vandiver's book is a dramatic narrative by a great historian."

—Tom Trescott, Abraham Lincoln Book Shop, Chicago

he committed even more serious acts of destruction and plunder. By June 14, he was headed for Lynchburg, a major railroad hub, manufacturing center, and Confederate hospital center.

During the lull that occurred while Hunter sat at Lexington, Early had received his orders and was already on his way to Lexington. Leaving at 2 AM on June 13, 8,000 men of the Confederate Second Corps began a 70-mile forced march to Charlottesville, where they started to arrive in the wee morning hours of June 16. After a very brief rest, the men commenced to board trains for Lynchburg, with the first of Early's soldiers reaching the city at 1 PM on June 17. Already in the town were two brigades of infantry and one of cavalry, commanded by John Breckinridge, former vice president of the United States in the Buchanan administration. Just to the southwest of Lynchburg, arriving at approximately the same time as Early, was Hunter's army. Lynchburg was a 45-mile march from Lexington, which the Union forces had entered six days before. For no very good reason, the Federals were just now reaching their objective, just as the Confederates began to pour into the city's defenses.

General David Hunter was not unknown to Southerners, and where he was known, he was universally reviled. Earlier in the war, he had abolished slavery in South Carolina, Georgia, and Florida. He had no authority to do this, and Lincoln made him rescind the proclamation, but this nevertheless earned him the wrath of Southerners everywhere. When he began his campaign up the Shenandoah Valley, the wanton destruction that occurred under his direction had riled even some of his own subordinates, including George Crook and William Averell, who protested several of his actions during the campaign. Mysteriously, though, upon reaching the outskirts of Lynchburg, the audacity and air of invincibility that had fueled the early part of Hunter's campaign disappeared upon learning of the arrival of the veteran Confederate Second Corps. The citizens of Lynchburg felt this, too, as the atmosphere quickly transformed from panic and despair to one of pride and defiance.

When Hunter reached the city on June 17, he took his headquarters here at Sandusky, one of the finest homes in the area. Built in 1808, its owner was a friend and neighbor of Thomas Jefferson, who stayed at the house. Two other presidents also stayed here—Rutherford B. Hayes and William McKinley—both on Hunter's staff, and in fact, they may have even shared the same bed. The home is open for tours by appointment, and also occasionally for special events. From the roof, Hunter and his staff were able to observe the battle. They could also hear, on the other side of the city, numerous trains entering the depot on the evening of June 17 (actually one engine and empty boxcars, run back and forth to fool the Federals into thinking that more reinforcements were arriving). It was Jubal Early's men, just in time to meet Hunter's invaders.

Quaker Meeting House

⟩ *From Sandusky, pull out to your left, then turn right on Sandusky Drive and drive 0.5 mile. Pull into the parking lot across the intersection.*

First contact was made here on June 17, as Hunter's Federals pressed John Imboden and John McCausland's Confederate cavalry toward the city of Lynchburg. The road in front of you, now Fort Avenue, was then the Salem Turnpike, the main route into the city from the south. On your right is the old Quaker Meeting House, dating

This stone wall at the Quaker Meeting House in Lynchburg was used as a defensive position by the Confederates.

The formidable and well-preserved Fort Early, south of Lynchburg.

to 1798. The Confederates took a stand on this ridge, holding back the Federals for two hours as Early's trains entered the city. The wall around the cemetery, present at the time of the fight, was used as a defensive position. When Early did arrive in the city, he quickly rode up to this position and ordered Imboden and McCausland to fall back to the outer defenses of Lynchburg.

Fort Early/Early Monument

❯ *From the parking lot, turn right onto Fort Avenue and drive 1.6 miles. Turn left onto Vermont Avenue, then pull over and park on the street.*

This is Fort Early, constructed well before the battle to protect the important Salem Turnpike approach into the city. When the Confederates arrive on June 17, this fort and two others were the only defenses outside the city proper, and most of the ground around was open field. Overnight, Early had his men form a loose outer defense ring that stretched to the west and south of Lynchburg to complement the inner works that had already been constructed.

At 11 AM on June 17, the Federals opened the battle with an artillery bombardment, quickly answered by the Confederates. Hunter advanced his infantry up the

Salem Turnpike cautiously, remembering the sounds of the trains entering the city overnight and expecting to meet an overwhelming number of rebels. George Crook's division was sent east to try to outflank the Union position, but he soon returned, slowed by the hilly terrain.

Hunter's attack was feeble, and Early knew just what to do with it. At 1 PM, the Confederates launched a counterattack, driving Jeremiah Sullivan's division back down the turnpike, but Crook's men arrived from their earlier foray shortly after, sending the enemy back to its main defensive line. Hunter attacked again at 3 PM, briefly breaking the Confederates, but soon the lines had returned to their original positions.

As you can see, Fort Early (as it was later known) is a massive earthwork, easily able to command the open ground around and below it. It is a public park, and the grounds, well maintained and walkable, are open daily. The building inside the fort and the brick wall surrounding it were built long after the battle. Across the street from the gates to the fort, you will find a monument to Jubal Early, commemorating his defense of the city. As you stand at the gates facing the monument, Hunter's Federals would have been coming up the hill from your right, while the Confederates faced down the slope.

Fort McCausland

⟩ *Continue forward on Vermont Avenue and take the first right onto Richmond Avenue, then another right onto Oakridge Boulevard. Drive 0.1 mile and turn left onto Memorial Avenue. Drive 1.3 miles on Memorial Avenue to Langhorne Road. Turn left onto Langhorne Road and drive 1.3 miles. Pull into the entrance for the synagogue on your left.*

Fort McCausland, like Fort Early, was built as one of the three fortifications guarding the approaches to the city—in this case, the Virginia & Tennessee Railroad, and particularly its bridge over Ivy Creek. The road running next to the fort was then part of Forest Road (which continues to the west), and is now Langhorne Road. Walk up to the interpretive sign and face the road. On your right, the large earth formation is what remains of Fort McCausland. Also to your right, 2 miles beyond, is Lynchburg. To your left, you are looking toward David Hunter's Union cavalry, coming at you up the hill.

Alfred Duffié's two brigades of cavalry approached Fort McCausland in the early afternoon, coordinating their assault with Hunter's advance near Fort Early. Duffié first drove back rebel skirmishers at Ivy Creek, then continued up the hill toward the fort. Confederate artillery slowed the Union cavalry, and Duffié ordered one regiment to advance to attempt to break the stalemate, but they were quickly driven back by the enemy guns. Duffié chose not to renew the attack, holding his position until 10 PM.

Old City Cemetery/Inner Defensive Works

❭ *From the Synagogue, turn right onto Langhorne Road and drive 1.3 miles back to Memorial Avenue. Turn left on Memorial Avenue and drive 0.6 mile, staying with it as it becomes 5th Street. Turn left on Taylor Street; pull into the cemetery entrance in front of you.*

Old City Cemetery, dating back to 1806, was located on the inner defense line of Richmond. Soon after you enter, you will find, on your left, the Confederate section of the cemetery, with a large monument to its soldiers of every state who gave their lives here. Enter this section and walk through the stone gate to the stone fence at the rear. In this area, the cadets of the Virginia Military Institute, whose school had recently been burned down by Hunter, spent the night on the inner defense line, using the wall as a defense and hoping to get a shot or two off at Hunter's attacking army. However, the Federal advance made it this far.

As you drive around the cemetery, you will find a museum chronicling the cemetery's (and the city's) history, as well as the Pest House Medical Museum, Lynchburg's first hospital. On your way out, you will also see a horse hospital, one of four established by the Confederate armies. The work done here studying horse disease became widely known, providing a valuable contribution to the development of veterinary medicine.

Spring Hill Cemetery/Early's Hilltop

❭ *From the Old City Cemetery exit, drive forward to 5th Street and turn right. Drive 0.6 mile to Langhorne Road. Turn left onto Langhorne Road and drive 0.4 mile to Fort Avenue. Turn right onto Fort Avenue and drive 0.7 mile to the entrance for Spring Hill Cemetery on your left.*

Within Spring Hill Cemetery, one of the highest points below the city, Jubal Early watched as the battle of Lynchburg unfolded. After you enter the cemetery, if you drive to the far right corner, you will be at the hilltop from which Early observed the fighting. Although the view is somewhat more obstructed today, you can get an idea of just how good an observation point this was.

After you've taken in the view, you can meet the man himself. Resting in peace atop this hill is Jubal Anderson Early, who was born in the countryside surrounding Lynchburg and made it his home. His monument is a large obelisk of a somewhat darker stone. Also buried nearby are two other prominent Confederate generals, both horsemen, of the Eastern Theater. James Dearing, the last Confederate general mortally wounded on the battlefield, has a large monument nearby. Thomas Dearing, whose white marker is strikingly humble, also lies in the area.

HANGING ROCK

❭ *From the exit at Spring Hill Cemetery, drive straight onto Oakley Avenue for 0.8 mile. Turn left onto US 221 South (Lakeside Drive) and continue for 21.7 miles. In the town of Bedford, you will turn right onto Main Street to continue following US 221 South for another 27.3 miles. Take the entrance ramp onto I-581 North and drive 5.2 miles. Take exit 1S to enter I-81 South and drive 2.6 miles. Take exit 141 for VA 419. Turn left onto VA 419 North (Electric Road) at the bottom of the exit ramp. Drive 0.3 miles to Dutch Oven Road and turn right. Drive 0.1 mile on Dutch Oven Road to the parking area for Hanging Rock Battlefield Trail on your left.*

On the night of June 18, Hunter decided to withdraw his men, citing the large enemy force in his front. The always aggressive Early was not about to let him get away, and pursued Hunter down several paths. One of these went through Roanoke, and on June 21, just beyond the city, John McCausland's cavalry caught Hunter's re-treating troops near a formation known as Hanging Rock. Hunter had been slowed attempting to get his army through and around the narrow rock formations and mountain passes here, giving McCausland a perfect opportunity to pounce. McCaus-land's small force was driven off when Federal reinforcements arrived, but the rebel cavalry had done a fair amount of damage to the Union wagon train.

The Hanging Rock Battlefield Trail is another great rails-to-trails project. The trail is 1.6 miles and is one-way, but it is an easy walk on a gravel path. Through most of it, you will be walking through a peaceful forest surrounded by some amazing rock formations. However, before you begin your hike, please read this carefully. Shortly after you begin at the north trail head, the path appears to go straight onto a dirt path. This is *not* the hiking trail, and it will take you through some rather rugged terrain. The path actually goes up the hillside to your right, taking you across a stream and through a gas station parking lot, after which the gravel path continues. The signs are not very clear about this, so be sure you know where you are at all times, because the surrounding area has much more potential for injury. That said, the trail is very well done, and the interpretation here is good. You will also find interpretive material, as well as several statues and memorials, at the north trail head.

LEXINGTON

Virginia Military Institute

❭ *Turn right from the parking area and drive 0.4 mile to VA 419. Turn left onto VA 419 and drive 0.5 mile, then take the entrance ramp for I-81 North. Drive 47.3 miles on I-81 North and take the exit for US 60 West. Drive 3.2 miles on US 60 West, then turn right onto South Main Street. Drive 0.6 mile on Main Street, then bear left onto*

VMI Parade Ground Road. Follow the road around the VMI Parade Ground for 0.6 mile and park.

After a day of rest on June 22, Old Jube Early's triumphant Confederates arrived in Lexington with mixed emotions. With Hunter's force out of the picture, they had entered the town knowing that there would be absolutely no Union resistance in their journey down the valley. Certainly, the people of Lexington were overjoyed to see them. Unfortunately, this had a lot to do their previous occupier. Black Dave Hunter had done his worst in Lexington.

After bombarding the town upon the Union force's arrival on June 11, Hunter set out on a spree of destruction that would not soon be forgotten. The most visible scar was left the next day, June 12, when the Federals had burned the Virginia Military Institute. The institution had been a source of great pride for the town, and was also well known as the place where Stonewall Jackson had taught. Now, despite the protests of several of his lieutenants, Hunter ordered Jackson's beloved VMI burned. In theory, it may have been a legitimate military target—cadets from the institute had mustered in and fought at New Market—but the action was seen by most as nothing more than large-scale vandalism.

The barracks at the Virginia Military Institute. Stonewall Jackson instructed cadets in the use of artillery with the undersized pieces seen here.

After the war, the VMI rose from the ashes, recovering much of the old barracks, and as you can see, it's grown a great deal since then. The old school is understandably proud of its prestigious history, and you'll find much of it here. Walking the parade ground, you are likely to find cadets either drilling or playing football, depending on what time of day you arrive, and you will find yourself shocked if one of them in uniform does not go out of his or her way to greet you. In front of the old barracks is the VMI Cadet Battery, four guns named Matthew, Mark, Luke, and John by the VMI's former artillery instructor, Stonewall Jackson. Jackson is everywhere here, from the plaque denoting his second-floor classroom to his famous horse, Little Sorrel, buried in front of the battery. You'll find more of Little Sorrel at the VMI Museum—his hide, stretched over a synthetic skeleton. (More of the horse had been mounted in the museum, but it was eventually buried.) You'll also find Jackson's saddle, desk, uniform,

and the raincoat he was wearing when he was mortally wounded at Chancellorsville. The museum also tells the story of the Patton family, one of whom served under Jackson, and another of whom went on to fame in World War II. Above the museum is Jackson Memorial Hall, with a massive mural of the VMI cadets at the battle of New Market. A few buildings down, guarded by the statue *Virginia Mourning Her Dead*, those cadets who were killed in the battle lay at rest. There is a lot to see here, so you may want to go to the experts—cadets give guided tours daily.

Lee Chapel

❯ *Take a U-turn on VMI Parade Ground Road and drive 0.2 mile, then turn right on Letcher Avenue. Drive 0.2 mile on Letcher Avenue, then turn right onto North Jefferson Street. Pull into the parking area for Lee Chapel on your right.*

Lee Chapel, final resting place of Robert E. Lee and family, Washington and Lee University.

Within a short drive or a moderate walk of the VMI Museum, on the adjacent campus of Washington and Lee University, is the Lee Memorial Chapel. After the

Civil War, Robert E. Lee was offered a position as president of Washington University. After his death, his name was added to the university's. On the lower floor of the chapel, you'll find Lee's office, allegedly untouched since his death, as well as a very fine museum with a great collection. Also downstairs is the Lee family crypt, final resting place of the famous general, as well as his wife, several of his sons and daughters (including Civil War generals Custis and W. H. F. "Rooney" Lee), and his father, Henry "Light Horse Harry" Lee, hero of the Revolutionary War. Just outside the door to the crypt lie the remains of Lee's famous horse, Traveler.

Upstairs, in the chapel, you will find the famous sculpture of Lee at rest. The sculpture was initially supposed to be Lee's tomb, but was eventually placed here. Interestingly, by Mrs. Lee's request, the sculpture does not depict Lee on his deathbed, but taking a nap; look for Lee's crossed feet at the end of the bed. The fine detail on the sculpture is amazing, and is worth taking a few minutes to scrutinize.

Stonewall Jackson House

⟩ *From the parking area, turn right onto Jefferson Avenue and take the second left onto West Washington Street. Drive through the first intersection on Washington Street, then park on the street.*

The only house that Stonewall Jackson ever owned is here in Lexington, and it is almost certain that some of Jackson's former soldiers came by the home during their

The only home that Stonewall Jackson ever owned, Lexington, Virginia.

stop in Lexington. Renovated in 2004, the home is open for tours, and the garden and grounds behind the house offer a "cell phone tour," where you can simply punch the appropriate number to learn about what you're looking at. The house is now part of the VMI Museum system, providing it a secure base for the future.

Stonewall Jackson Cemetery

⟩ *From the Stonewall Jackson House, continue to the next intersection and turn right onto South Randolph Street, then take the first right onto East Nelson Street. Drive two blocks to South Jefferson Street and turn left. Drive 0.3 mile on Jefferson Street to White Street. Turn left onto White Street, and then left again onto South Main Street. The cemetery will be on your right; park on the street.*

Lexington was also the final resting place of Stonewall himself. After he was mortally wounded at Chancellorsville, Jackson was taken to a farm near the rail depot at Guinea Station, Virginia, where he eventually died. Thus, most of the men who had served under and so revered him had not been able to give their commander a final farewell, as is often the case in war. But the war had now taken them to Lexington, and thousands of Jackson's former soldiers filed past his grave in silent tribute to their fallen leader.

Today the cemetery is known as Stonewall Jackson Memorial Cemetery. Clearly, Jackson takes center stage in the town's history, and that is well demonstrated here at this small but lovely cemetery. Along with Jackson's grave (Hint: It's the big one in the center) are his original grave site (which still bears a tombstone), as well as the graves

Stonewall Jackson Cemetery, burial site of several notables in Virginia's rich history.

of several other Confederate generals and other notable officers, two former governors of Virginia (including John Letcher, whose home was put to the torch by Hunter's men), several senators and congressmen, and 144 Confederate veterans of the Civil War.

PIEDMONT

> *From the cemetery, continue 1.3 miles on Main Street (US 11). Turn right to continue on US 11 for another 0.9 mile, then take the entrance ramp onto I-64 East/I-81 North. Continue on I-81 North for 37.1 miles to exit 227. At the bottom of the ramp, turn right onto Laurel Hill Road (SR 612) and drive 5.2 miles. Turn left onto Battlefield Road (SR 608) and drive 1.5 miles. Park at the New Hope Community Center on your right.*

On June 5, 1864, two days after the final charge at Cold Harbor to the east, David Hunter fought the first battle of his campaign in the Shenandoah Valley. With Breckinridge's force reinforcing Lee, it would be William "Grumble" Jones's 6,000 infantry and cavalry left to face Hunter's 12,000-man force.

Your position here at the New Hope Community Center is well behind the Confederate line, but there is no good place to stop near the battlefield, although a marker does exist there. What you will find here is a Civil War Trails sign that will help you orient yourself to the land as you drive north to the battlefield. The road here, then known as the East Road, served as the axis for the battle, with the Confederates moving north on this road, then retreating south after their line collapsed.

> *Turn right onto Battlefield Road and drive 1.3 miles. If safe, pull over next to the historic marker on the ground on your right and turn your hazard lights on; if not, keep driving.*

This is the location of the Confederate line. Jones formed his men along this ridge on both sides of the road, facing north. At the time of the battle, the ridge (barely discernible now, if the corn in the field to your right is in season) was mostly wooded, with open field to your front. Hunter opened the battle around noon, conducting several assaults that were repulsed by the Confederate artillery. However, a gap developed on the left side of Jones's line. Hunter saw his opportunity and sent a brigade in that direction. The Confederate left flank broke, and all hope of a rebel rally was lost when Jones was killed on the field. Hunter scooped up a good number of prisoners, then resumed his march, heading for Lexington.

There is a marker here on the east (right) side of the road, and it is supposedly near the spot where Grumble Jones fell. It is a bit hard to spot; keep your eyes peeled for it just before the curve in the road.

NEW MARKET BATTLEFIELD

❭ *Continue 4.1 miles on Battlefield Road to Weyers Cave Road (VA 256). Turn left onto Weyers Cave Road and drive 4.3 miles, and then take the entrance ramp onto I-81 North. Drive 29.6 miles on I-81 North and then take the exit for West Old Cross Road. Turn left onto Old Cross Road and drive 0.2 mile, and then turn left onto George R. Collins Parkway. Continue 1 mile to the entrance for New Market Battlefield State Historical Park.*

When Ulysses S. Grant laid out his grand strategy for winning the Civil War, conquering the Shenandoah Valley—or more accurately, cutting the supply lines that came from within it—was part of the plan. It was not, however, one of the strategy's major points. Initially, Grant considered the Valley a minor theater of the war. This is perhaps best shown by the fact that he put Franz Sigel in charge of the operation.

Throughout the war, Sigel had performed at best satisfactorily, and at worst, terribly. However, he did bring other pluses to the table. A German immigrant with military experience, Sigel played a large part in recruiting other Germans to join the Union effort, which they did in droves, many of them only recently coming to America to escape oppression and war in Germany. Politically, Franz Sigel had great value, and the Lincoln administration was not about to let him go.

In May 1864, the five pieces of Grant's strategy began to move almost simultaneously. Sigel's primary task was to advance to Charlottesville and Gordonsville, occupying the two railroad centers and cutting the supply lines feeding Robert E. Lee's Army of Northern Virginia. His 10,000 men were more than enough to do the job. Further, there were not many obstacles in his path, and almost no Confederates.

Hearing of Sigel's approach, John Breckinridge begged and scraped for every fighting man that he could get, eventually pulling together a force of 4,500 men. This included cadets from the Virginia Military Institute, who marched up from Lexington and were used as reserves. Here at New Market, on May 15, Breckinridge boldly stood in Sigel's path, forcing him to fight.

New Market Battlefield State Historical Park preserves the ground on which Breckinridge's small force repulsed Grant's first attempt at the Shenandoah Valley. Before you tour the battlefield, visit the Virginia Museum of the Civil War. A sister site to the VMI's main museum in Lexington, you will find the story of the VMI cadets retold in great detail, as well as a few impressive works of art. You can also observe the battlefield from here, if you wish, through a large panoramic window providing some guidance to the landmarks of the battlefield.

At 11 AM, the Confederates formed in line of battle and began to move forward toward Sigel's men. The Federals took a position on a ridge to the north, west of the Valley Pike (today's US 11), ultimately putting up a heavy resistance to Breckinridge's

The Virginia Museum of the Civil War at New Market. The white markers around the path are the former headstones of the Virginia Military Institute cadets killed in the battle.

advance. As you observe the battlefield from the museum, it looks similar to its 1864 appearance, when it was mostly the farm of Jacob Bushong. However, the other half of the battlefield—on the other side of the interstate, and not visible from this point— is very different, a rugged, rocky, brush-covered landscape. This part of the field is also preserved, and there is a tunnel that will take you under the interstate to explore it. The museum has created a very detailed tour of up to 20 stops, depending on how much of the field you would like to see. You may also drive along the battlefield on this side of the interstate. The main walking trail is a 1-mile loop, while visiting the portion on the other side of the interstate will add another half-mile or so.

Breckinridge advanced his men to the Bushong Farm, which you see preserved to your front. Here the Confederates became bogged down, and Federal artillery, on the ridge to your front where you can see the pieces currently posted, tore through the rebel line. Left with no other choice, Breckinridge brought up the 257 cadets, lining them up along the rail fence on the north side of the farm. The wheat field in front of them, soaked with several days' rain, was so muddy that it was afterward known as the Field of Lost Shoes.

The cadets made a valiant effort, but Sigel sensed an opportunity with the unco-ordinated Confederate attack. He decided to counterattack across the same field,

The battlefield at New Market. The Bushong Farm sits in the distance.

silencing his artillery as the Federal infantry moved forward. It was a critical mistake; the Union attack was also uncoordinated, and Breckinridge, a much more capable field commander than Sigel, pounced on the opportunity. At 2:30 PM, the rebels launched an all-out assault, breaking the Union line. By 3 PM, the Confederates held the field and more, pursuing the fleeing Federals for a mile.

In the big picture of the Civil War, Sigel's defeat at New Market was significant. Not only would Grant have to resort to other means to take control of the Shenandoah Valley, but rail service from the fertile valley would remain uninterrupted until Phil Sheridan entered the valley four months later. However, most Virginians will always remember New Market for the charge of the Corps of Cadets, which took losses of 10 dead and 57 wounded serving their native state.

THE MARCH OF THE ARMY OF THE VALLEY

〉 *The majority of Early's Confederate Army of the Valley marched north on the Valley Turnpike. Today, US 11 almost exactly follows the route of the old pike. From Lexington or New Market to Winchester, Virginia or Martinsburg, West Virginia, you can follow US 11 the entire way (130–150 miles) until you decide to turn east toward Frederick, Maryland. Although this is the road less traveled, the towns you will pass through along the way are wonderful, so take this route if you have the time.*

If you don't have the time and just want to drive through the valley, I-81 parallels US 11 through its length. Although the distance and the scenery are the same, you will make better time.

Knowing full well that the degree of his success would depend on speed and surprise, Early began to move his army on June 23, heading north down the Valley Turnpike, the major artery through the Shenandoah Valley. The soldiers reached Staunton on June 26 and stopped again, but for a very good reason. John Breckinridge's force met Early in Staunton, bringing the army's total manpower to 16,000 grizzled veterans.

Although John Breckinridge had a political background, he was no stranger to the battlefield. The Kentuckian had served as a major in the Mexican War and was appointed Brigadier General at the outset of the war. Before long he was a major general, and he had led men at many of the war's most significant battles in both the Eastern and Western Theaters. Early transferred an additional division—John Brown Gordon's—to Breckinridge's command, a significant gesture for a general who was known for his mistrust of both subordinates and peers.

While adding men, Early also lightened up his army in Staunton. Shedding most of his wagons and some of his artillery, the Confederates left Staunton on June 28, reaching New Market on June 30 and Winchester on July 2. For a force of 16,000 men, this was an impressive achievement, made all the more remarkable by the supply problems that the rebels had to deal with during the march. Stretching his supply lines to the max, Early's men were short of food, clothing, and shoes, the latter of which were quickly worn out from the blistering pace of the march.

GIVE HIM SOME CREDIT

One of the most controversial and least-liked personalities of the Civil War was General Braxton Bragg. Bragg had commanded the Confederate Army of Tennessee at the battles of Perryville, Stones River, and Chattanooga, and although he scored a major victory at Chickamauga, he was almost universally despised by the officers and men who served under him. Only his strong relationship with Jefferson Davis kept him on the battlefield.

While Bragg was undeniably a poor field commander and leader of men, as a military tactician, he had few equals. After being relieved of command, Davis brought him to Richmond to serve as military adviser. While Lee's sending a force to counter David Hunter in the Shenandoah Valley was under consideration, it was Bragg who suggested that Hunter's defeat would provide an opportunity for a raid on Washington. It was ultimately Lee who took the gamble and Early who determined its course; however, credit the reviled Braxton Bragg for having had the idea.

North of Winchester, in Martinsburg, West Virginia, Franz Sigel heard that Confederates were moving north through the valley. Sigel had been demoted after his loss at New Market to command the reserves of the Department of West Virginia, and had 5,000 soldiers with him. Details were very sketchy about the size of the rebel force, but hearing that it might be three divisions, Sigel was taking no chances. On July 3, he moved his entire command to Harpers Ferry, abandoning the massive amount of supplies, along with the critical Baltimore & Ohio Railroad, which he had been ordered to defend at Martinsburg.

Sigel was correct in that there were three units headed for Martinsburg, but his estimation of their size was grossly incorrect. They were brigades, not divisions, of cavalry, not infantry, detached by Early while in Winchester. The Confederate cavalry entered the town just as the Federals were leaving, and they easily took possession of Martinsburg. Early quickly brought the rest of his army from Winchester to Martinsburg, where they feasted and resupplied thanks to Sigel's quick retreat.

The Confederates were soon taking separate tracks to head east across to Maryland, the third time a rebel army had ventured north of the Potomac River. While several units were dispatched to various cities in the area for ransom—demanding payment in gold or cash in return for not burning the town—the infantry crossed into Maryland at Shepherdstown, Williamsport, and Harpers Ferry. (Although for the most part the soldiers obeyed orders not to plunder the property of the citizens of Maryland, many took their own direction for David Hunter's earlier work in the Upper Valley, exacting revenge where they could.)

On the night of July 5, as much of the Army of the Valley went into camp near the old Antietam battlefield, Jubal Early received a very important courier into his tent. The message was so top secret that the sender had entrusted it only to his own son— Robert E. Lee Jr.—and had him memorize its content in the event that he needed to destroy it. After conferring with Jefferson Davis, Lee was upping the ante on his great gamble. Before raiding Washington, D.C., Early was to aid a joint task force that would liberate Confederate prisoners at Point Lookout, Maryland. Successfully freeing the prisoners at this camp would, in effect, add the strength of an entire corps to Lee's dwindling army. Early sent out additional cavalry forces to prepare for the breakout, then headed for Frederick, Maryland, where he would go into camp on July 8.

On June 3, Franz Sigel, holed up at Harpers Ferry, had wired the War Department that Richard Ewell (Early's predecessor in command) had his entire corps in the Shenandoah Valley, numbering 20,000 to 30,000 men. While Sigel may have been more concerned for his own personal safety, and the corps commander had changed, his report would provide a small service. Despite the fact that there had been rumors and small indications that some part of the Army of Northern Virginia might not be in the lines at Petersburg, it was not until this day that serious suspicions began to arise that Lee may have detached his entire Second Corps. By any measure, Early's march had been a great success.

As for the Federal forces at Harpers Ferry, the Confederates simply marched around them.

MONOCACY NATIONAL BATTLEFIELD

> *From New Market Battlefield, drive 1 mile to return to Old Cross Road. Turn left on Old Cross Road, drive 0.2 mile and take the entrance ramp onto I-81 North. Drive 88.3 miles on I-81 to exit 4 for I-70 East. Keep right onto I-70 East and drive 29 miles. Take exit 54 and drive 0.5 mile, merging onto MD 85. Turn left onto Urbana Pike (MD 355 South) and drive 1.5 miles. Pull into the visitor center for Monocacy National Battlefield on your left.*

Jubal Early's Confederates certainly deserve a great deal of credit for stealing a march on Ulysses S. Grant and the entire Union army. One cannot, however, discount the massive intelligence failure that occurred on the part of the Federals. By the time the Union finally realized the existence and magnitude of the potential threat to its capital, the Confederate Second Corps was within only a few days march of Washington. In fact, it was due primarily to the efforts of two men—one committed to his country, the other to his business—that Washington was saved from what could have been a significant disaster.

The first reports that something might be going on occurred as early as June 17. Union chief of staff Henry Halleck wired Grant in Petersburg that 13,000 Confederates under George Pickett and John Breckinridge were reported to have passed through Gordonsville ten days before. Grant, in turn, passed on intelligence from Benjamin Butler that several enemy units were headed to Lynchburg. In any

Monument to the 87th Pennsylvania Infantry, Monocacy National Battlefield.

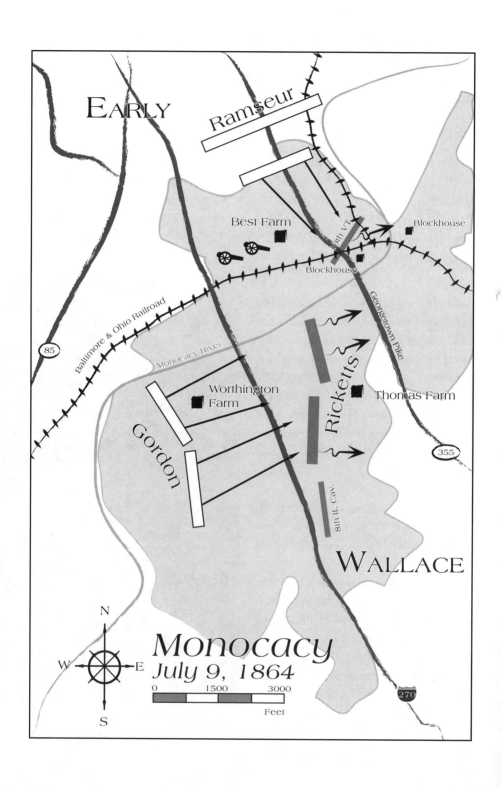

EARLY

Ramseur

Best Farm

Blockhouse

30th VT.

Blockhouse

Baltimore & Ohio Railroad

Georgetown Pike

85

Monocacy River

Worthington
Farm

Ricketts

Thomas Farm

Gordon

355

8th IL. Cav.

WALLACE

N

W ✦ E

S

Monocacy
July 9, 1864

0   1500   3000

Feet

270

case, Grant was not worried, certain that David Hunter would take care of whatever small force the rebels placed in front of him.

With Sigel's report in hand, Grant wired Halleck on July 4, saying that it was possible that a Confederate force was in the Shenandoah Valley, and it was possible that they might be heading for Washington. The next day, July 5, a flurry of indecisive messages was sent between Petersburg and Washington. Several rebel deserters had now confirmed Early's departure, but with no other evidence, Grant still had faith in Hunter. Halleck, meanwhile, vacillated between demanding that Grant send troops to the capital to aid its defense and telling Grant that he was confident that Washington, Baltimore, and Harpers Ferry were safe. (Harpers Ferry had actually fallen the day before; Sigel and his force were on Maryland's Heights, overlooking the town.) By the end of the day, Grant was convinced that the Second Corps was no longer in his front, and he arranged for part of James Ricketts's 3rd Division from the Army of the Potomac's VI Corps to join the still-absent David Hunter in Washington.

Had the Union intelligence kept its ear to the ground, they may have had a bit more notice about the Confederate advance on Washington. On June 29, reliable and accurate intelligence was provided by John W. Garrett, president of the Baltimore & Ohio Railroad. Garrett, who despite his Southern sympathies was rightly concerned about the condition of his railroad and its continued operation, had his workers reporting any and all Confederate activity they were aware of. Naturally, this information was shared with Federal intelligence, as the Union army needed the railroad to remain open. Garrett had wired Henry Halleck directly, reporting that Richard Ewell's corps, along with John Breckenridge's force, was heading down the Shenandoah Valley. Nothing came of it.

Frustrated with the lack of response, Garrett personally went to the Baltimore headquarters of the Middle Atlantic Department, commanded by Lew Wallace, in early July. Wallace had seen some significant actions during the war, but fallout from the near disaster at Shiloh in April 1862 unfairly placed much of the blame on his shoulders. With a few notable exceptions, Wallace was largely watching from the sidelines, due in large part to his poor relationship with Henry Halleck. The jurisdiction of his department covered the state of Delaware and eastern Maryland as far as the Monocacy River, which ran just east of Frederick. Although he had gained the favor of Abraham Lincoln and Secretary of War Edwin Stanton for suppressing Confederate sympathizers in his district, his current command kept him far from the war.

Garrett's surprising report caught Wallace off guard. He had heard no reports of Confederate activity in the area, particularly as far north and east as Garrett was reporting. Still, his intelligence seemed to be reliable, and Wallace pledged to do what he could to protect the railroad. Wallace had two major obstacles, however. The first was his jurisdictional restriction—he was technically not permitted to operate west of the Monocacy River (this was David Hunter's department). Second, he had very few troops at his disposal, and absolutely no cavalry. He sent what he could spare toward Frederick, Erastus B. Tyler's brigade of 2,300 green troops.

At midnight on July 5, Wallace and one of his aides rode a specially arranged locomotive west from Baltimore to Monocacy Junction, where the Baltimore & Ohio Railroad had not only the junction but also an iron bridge crossing the Monocacy River. (The visit was not reported to Halleck, as Wallace suspected that he would find some issue with the action and disallow it.) Arriving early on June 6, more intelligence about Confederate activity had already come in. Reports of rebel cavalry in virtually every moderate-size town in western Maryland were now creeping into the War Department, as well as John Garrett's office. Wallace considered this information and decided that he had to remain at Monocacy Junction.

The position around the junction chosen for the Union stand was ideal. Not only was it a strong defensive position, it was also strategically sound. At this point, whether the Confederates would be heading for Washington or Baltimore was still unknown. Here at Monocacy Junction, the convergence of the National Road and the Georgetown Pike gave the Federals the option to cover either or both of the primary approaches to both cities. The few fords of the Monocacy River were to their front, with large open fields beyond it, providing a clear view of the passes over South Mountain, which the Confederates would have to cross.

Gathering an additional 600 cavalrymen and six pieces of artillery, Wallace set his outnumbered troops and waited. (The 8th Illinois Cavalry had been operating in the area, and Wallace asked Halleck for permission to use those troops; receiving no response, he took them without authorization.) The next day, July 7, he was surprised to learn of the arrival of James Ricketts's division by steamship at Baltimore. The first train with Ricketts's division stopped at Monocacy Junction before sunrise on July 8, much to the surprise and relief of Wallace's men. Wallace asked to see the commanding officer, and a puzzled Col. William Henry was led to him. Henry was as surprised to see Wallace as Wallace's men were to see him. He had not expected to be stopped at Monocacy Junction; his orders were to report to Franz Sigel at Harpers Ferry.

As Wallace tried to convince Henry that he was needed at Monocacy Junction, and as wires were received from Sigel on Maryland Heights asking Wallace to come to his aid, Erastus Tyler spotted Confederate cavalry making its way down the eastern face of South Mountain. There had already been some contact with rebel cavalry west of Frederick the day before, and Wallace, although it was technically out of his jurisdiction, felt the need to send some infantry to support the 8th Illinois. At 4 PM, however, three unmistakable columns of enemy infantry were seen crossing the mountain. Wallace withdrew his force from Frederick and into their defensive positions at Monocacy

Junction, and then wired Washington that he was covering the road to Washington with the Confederates approaching.

At 10:30 PM on July 8, Henry Halleck finally got it. He wired Grant, saying that based on intelligence gathered from scouts, prisoners, citizens, Franz Sigel, and David Couch, commander of the Department of Pennsylvania, a large number of Confederates had crossed the Monocacy River—which they had not. (Halleck did not cite Lew Wallace as a source of intelligence. The degree of disdain Halleck had for Wallace can be deduced by the fact that he did credit Sigel, which is remarkable since he had relieved him of command the day before for incompetence.) Halleck begged Grant to send troops from Petersburg to defend the capital, adding that David Hunter was nowhere to be found. The first signs of desperation and panic began to show with the enemy only 40 miles from the outskirts of Washington.

Monocacy National Battlefield has recently constructed a new visitor center that is a tremendous improvement over the former site. There are many interactive exhibits that will not only teach you about the battle and Early's campaign but also demonstrate very well some of the day-to-day happenings of both soldier and civilian life. Younger visitors will have plenty to keep them busy here. Almost all of the center's exhibits are on the second floor, where you will also find a nice overlook of the battlefield which points out the major features of the landscape. (There is also an enclosed section of the overlook so that it can be used on cold or rainy days.)

One note: The battlefield park has a no-trash policy, meaning that whatever you bring into the park, you are expected to take out. If you are looking for garbage cans, you won't find any, so keep this in mind as you tour.

❭ *Turn right onto Urbana Pike and drive 0.5 mile to MD 85 North. Turn right onto MD 85 and drive 0.3 miles, and then take the entrance ramp for I-70 East. Drive 1.1 miles on I-70 to exit 56 for MD 144 East. Turn left onto MD 144 and drive 0.9 mile to Linganore Road. Turn left onto Linganore Road, then take the next left onto Dr. Baxter Road. Drive to the end of the road and park.*

At 1 AM on July 9, a train with the rest of James Ricketts's 3rd Division of the VI Corps, along with the general himself, arrived at Monocacy Junction. Ricketts was also surprised to see the gathering of Federals at the junction, but a briefing from Wallace about the situation in his front was more than enough to convince him to stay. The addition of Ricketts's men brought the Union strength to 5,800—still far fewer than Early's Confederates, but enough to put up a good fight.

Ricketts's veteran fighters were placed where it was thought the main assault would come, the left of the Union line. The division deployed on high ground overlooking the farms of C. Keefer Thomas and John Worthington, as well as Monocacy

THE MISSING BRIGADE

The appearance of the Union 3rd Division of the VI Corps certainly boosted the odds of a successful battle for Lew Wallace. However, not all of the troops made it to the battlefield. The 2nd Brigade of the 3rd Division, commanded by Col. John Staunton, was mysteriously delayed in the town of Monrovia, 8 miles east of the battle. At least 1,000 Union soldiers spent the day in Monrovia on the day of the battle. Afterward, Col. Staunton reported that the brigade had been slowed by poor transportation, and that is the explanation that appears in the official records. However, neither Wallace nor Ricketts were buying it. Staunton was court-martialed and relieved of command on July 10, the day after the battle, and the 2nd Brigade was long afterward tagged with the unfortunate label of "The Missing Brigade."

Junction itself. Two additional units—the 10th Vermont and the 1st Potomac Home Brigade, recent recruits from Maryland—were placed around the junction itself, somewhat isolated on the west side of the river but with the additional protection of two blockhouses built to protect the iron railroad bridge. Also located near the junction was a 250-foot-long wooden bridge, the Georgetown Pike crossing of the river. To the right of the bridge, Erastus Tyler spread his brigade across a wide front, concentrating at the Stone Bridge, better known as the Jug Bridge, where the Baltimore Pike crossed the Monocacy River.

The Federals did not need to wait very long for the Confederates to approach them, because Jubal Early was in a hurry. He did not want to fight a battle. He wanted to continue his march to Point Lookout and then Washington without delay. In addition, his men were exhausted. They had been on the march for almost a month and were not exactly fresh for battle. But there were too many of the enemy to ignore here, and he was forced to attack. Early placed John McCausland's cavalry brigade on the south end of the line facing Ricketts's Federals, with John Brown Gordon's infantry division to his rear. To his left in the center of the line facing Monocacy Junction was Stephen Dodson "Dod" Ramseur's division. On the Confederate left, Robert Rodes's division was sent down the Baltimore Pike to face the Union right.

The battle opened at approximately 6 AM when the skirmish lines of Rodes's Confederates and Tyler's Federals met just west of Jug Bridge on the Baltimore Pike. The action here, compared to the rest of the battle, was fairly brief. The two units fought for approximately two hours, and then the fighting died down. The lack of action here helped to convince Wallace that the Confederate target was indeed Washington and not Baltimore. Still, Tyler's men would remain here for the length of the battle to guard the Union right. It was not until Rodes attacked again at around 6 PM that further action occurred at Jug Bridge.

The Jug Bridge is mostly gone now, having been replaced by the interstate bridge. However, there are still signs of it. If you follow the directions above, you will eventually come to the dead end of the road. At that point, you can take a short walk down a narrow asphalt lane (do not drive on it, even if not barricaded) and you will eventually come to a very narrow dirt path leading into some thick forest. From this point on, it will be up to you whether or not to continue. The path is very short, but is partially overgrown and eventually becomes very steep. Walking in only a few feet will bring you to some of the remnants of the old bridge on your right side, a small gem of the old Baltimore Pike lying hidden in the forest. Shortly after this point, you will find a very steep slope with a rope leading down to the riverbank. Take great caution if you choose this path. If you climb down the slope, you will be rewarded with a view of the stone abutments of the old bridge, still visible in the Monocacy River. Before you go, though, remember that getting down is the easy part, and you will have to climb back up. Further information on the site and its conditions can be obtained at the visitor center.

〉 *Drive back down Dr. Baxter Road and turn right on Langanore Road to return to MD 144. Turn right onto MD 144 West and drive 2.7 miles to East Street. Turn left onto East Street and drive 0.7 mile to Monocacy Boulevard. Turn right onto Monocacy Boulevard and continue 0.4 mile, and then turn left onto Urbana Pike (MD 355 South). Drive 2.2 miles on Urbana Pike; turn right at the entrance for the Best Farm and drive 0.4 mile to the parking area.*

Shortly after fighting broke out at Jug Bridge, Ramseur's skirmish line met Ricketts's Federals just west of Monocacy Junction. While Ramseur's division would keep advancing down the Georgetown Pike, Confederate artillery was placed in and around the farm of David Best. After the Federals' six cannons and one howitzer fired on the Confederates around 10 AM, Early's nine batteries—36 guns—responded in kind, inflicting heavy damage on the Union men.

Also placing himself at the Best Farm during was Jubal Early, who set his headquarters here. Early did not reach the battlefield until late in the morning. He had spent the previous four hours negotiating with the mayor and city council of Frederick. Early's demands were $200,000 cash and food for his men; the city government argued that such a sum from a city of 8,000 people was impossible. After stalling to see what the outcome of the battle might be, the city handed over the cash, most of which was returned to Frederick after it was spent in the city by the Confederates.

Best Farm, like the other farms in the park, is still a working farm, but the old farmhouse remains. Also recently created is a short interpretive trail that examines slavery on the site. Several interpretive signs here explain how the artillery (as well as Confederate sharpshooters) factored into the battle, and how Early came to his decision to avoid a direct assault on the Union center using the Georgetown Pike.

❭ *From Best Farm, turn right onto Urbana Pike and drive 0.3 mile. Pull into the parking area on your right.*

You are now at the site of one of the crucial strategic points of the battle—Monocacy Junction. Not only did two lines of the Baltimore & Ohio Railroad diverge here, but this is also the location of the railroad's iron bridge over the Monocacy River. This bridge was one of John Garrett's biggest concerns when he pled his case for stopping the Confederates to Lew Wallace. Also here was the large wooden covered bridge of the Georgetown Pike.

The heaviest part of the fighting at Monocacy happened on the south end of the field, but the action here at Monocacy Junction was not without high drama. Skirmishing and artillery fire lasted throughout much of the morning here, with Ramseur's division holding its place in the center against a very small number of Union soldiers. Neither Early nor Ramseur wanted to risk a direct assault, even with the few defenders present, because of the strength of the position, particularly the two blockhouses.

At 12:30 PM, Wallace ordered the burning of the wooden bridge, thinking that he could shift these troops to the Union left, the area of heaviest fighting. In doing so, however, approximately 275 soldiers were left at the junction on the west side of the river. Seeing his opportunity, Ramseur launched an attack, but the Union soldiers, taking advantage of the blockhouse on their side of the Monocacy, held their position for three hours.

Around 3:30 PM, as the conclusion of the battle was nearing, the 200 men of the 1st Potomac Home Brigade evacuated their position, crossing the river over the iron railroad bridge. This left 75 men of the 10th Vermont. Amazingly, these stalwart soldiers held their position for another full hour, finally making their own withdrawal across the railroad bridge at 4:30 PM, taking heavy casualties.

The tour stop at Monocacy Junction is a small one, but it is enough to demonstrate the story. The old railroad tracks of the Orange & Alexandria are easily visible. If you walk toward the bridge you just drove over, you will see the junction itself as the railroad splits off in two directions. You will see an iron bridge over the Monocacy River just past the parking area. This bridge, which you will drive over to get to your next stop, is in the same location as the old covered bridge was. The open space around you is where the small group of Federal soldiers made their stand against Ramseur's division, holding their ground to the very end.

❭ *Turn right onto Urbana Pike and drive 0.3 mile to Araby Church Road. Drive 0.5 mile on Araby Church Road, then turn right onto Baker Valley Road. On your way, you will pass several monuments along the Araby Church Road; if you choose to pull over and see them, be sure to select a safe place—there are several sharp bends in the road here that could prevent other drivers from seeing your car. Drive 0.6 mile on Baker Valley Road to the entrance for Worthington Farm on your right, then drive 0.8 mile to the parking area.*

John McCausland, who had been accompanying his brigade of cavalry from town to town demanding ransom, crossed the Monocacy River just after 10 AM. McCausland's four regiments, about 1,000 cavalrymen, used the Worthington-McKinney Ford, just behind the Worthington Farm House in front of you. (The Worthington family by this time was hiding in the cellar, and remained there throughout the battle. The Thomas family did the same in their home.) After driving away the 8th Illinois cavalry, who had been watching the ford, McCausland's men dismounted and arranged their battle lines in the fields of the Worthington Farm.

As you can see, the Worthington Farm is still a working farm today, under agricultural lease by the National Park Service. The 1.6-mile Ford Loop Trail will take you

The Worthington House at Monocacy National Battlefield.

around part of the farm, and will bring you right to the ford, as well as the fields where the brief cavalry skirmish took place and where McCausland prepared his men for the advance. For now, the Worthington House itself remains closed to the public.

As you look around the Worthington Farm and walk the trail, keep in mind that at the time of the battle, most of the trees around you were not present. The Worthington fields were filled mostly with corn—July corn, approximately waist high. Also not present, of course, was the interstate running between the Worthington and Thomas farms. The primary dividing line between the two farms was a rail fence, and James Ricketts made the most of this feature.

The dismounted Confederate cavalry advanced on the Union line around 10:30 AM, the troops trying their best to maintain their lines as they crossed the cornfields. Ricketts, who had placed his main force to the rear, had posted a heavy skirmish line behind the rail fence, with instructions to hold their fire until directed. When the rebels came within 125 yards of the fence, Ricketts gave the order, and the Federals rose from behind the fence to deliver a devastating volley of musketry. As the Confederates fell into the surrounding corn, the effect was so complete that one of Wallace's aides is said to have remarked, "My God . . . they are all killed!" The elated Federals followed their success by pursuing the enemy troopers, driving them back past the Worthington House, but it was not long before they had been pushed back to their original position at the rail fence.

If you walk to Stop 5 of the Ford Loop Trail, not very far from the parking area, you will see a narrow line of trees. These mark the position of the southern end of the rail fence. If you are looking with your back to the parking area, the fence extended slightly to your right into the trees and then to the northeast, passing through the interstate to your left and running almost all the way to the river, through the fields we will see at your next stop, the Thomas Farm.

⟩ *From the parking area, return to Baker Valley Road and turn left. Drive 0.3 mile to the Thomas Farm on your left.*

By 2:30 PM, McCausland had rallied his men and began a second advance toward the Union left. This time, the assault had the support of the Confederate artillery, which performed exceptionally well on this day. Learning from his earlier disaster, McCausland shifted his line 200 yards to the right, bypassing the skirmishers at the rail fence and moving directly toward the main Federal line at the Thomas Farm, to focus on Araby, the Thomas House.

The Thomas House is still here, just north of the parking area, although it did suffer significant damage during the battle, mostly from artillery fire. Please note that the home is still occupied, so stay on the park's designated paths and do not approach it. After the battle, on August 5, the house continued to make Civil War history. It was

The Thomas Farm, site of the worst fighting during the battle of Monocacy.

in one of the house's upper rooms that Lieutenant General Ulysses S. Grant met with several of his generals to plan what would be Phil Sheridan's Shenandoah Valley campaign. You will find Sheridan's campaign, a direct result of Jubal Early's raid on Washington, outlined in chapter 6.

McCausland's line overlapped the left flank of the Union line, and although the surprised James Ricketts attempted to counter the movement, the Confederates eventually pushed through the Union position around the Thomas House. McCausland held the area around the Thomas House until 3 PM, when Wallace directed two other regiments to reinforce Ricketts's left. The Federals regained the ground around the House, sending the Confederate cavalry back to the Worthington Farm.

Walking the 1.75-mile Thomas Farm Loop Trail will probably give you the best opportunity to see what's left of the southern portion of the Monocacy battlefield. The trail not only covers the Thomas House and most of the Thomas Farm, but also includes much of the former location of the rail fence that proved so critical early in the battle. This is located at Stop 3 on the trail; if you have the interstate to your left, the fence ran along the trees in front of you. Just as you found at the Worthington Farm, almost none of the trees you now see were present at the time of the battle, and one would have been able to view the Monocacy River clearly. It was only the rail fence that marked the division between the two properties.

One other note: Depending on when you visit the farm, the height of the corn may present an obstacle to viewing the terrain. If you're going near the anniversary of the battle, it should still be short enough to see the entire field, but if you visit in August or September before the harvest, it may prevent you from seeing the entire field at once. It certainly shouldn't stop you from visiting, but it might be something to consider in your planning.

Throughout the battle, John Brown Gordon's division lay west of the Monocacy River, enjoying the uncommon opportunity to rest. With arms stacked, some of the men napped, while others watched Ramseur's and McCausland's assaults. Finally, the order came: The Confederate infantry would take McCausland's place and would assault the Union left. Gordon marched his men to the Worthington-McKinney Ford to cross, then rode ahead to observe the field from near the Worthington house. Gordon, a talented general who had been through many a hard fight, noted all of the obstacles his men would meet, including the ones that had contributed to McCausland's failure. Gordon saw that maintaining his lines would be difficult as they passed through the fields, crisscrossed with fences and dotted with heavy stacks of grain.

Knowing it would be a tough advance, Gordon brought four guns up to the Worthington Farm to support his infantry, and then set his battle line. The division consisted of three brigades, a total of 3,600 men. Seven Georgia regiments under Clement Evans formed the Confederate right, Zebulon York's five Louisiana regiments took the center, and William Terry's Virginians, consolidations of several regiments including the remnants of the old Stonewall Brigade, advanced on the left.

Evans's brigade moved first at 3:30 PM, directing its march toward the Thomas House. Taking advantage of the obstacles in their path, the Federals began firing as soon as the Confederates reached their first fence. Many of the Georgians, along with Evans, became casualties as they approached the Union left. Within 15 minutes, though, York's Louisianans came up on the left of the Georgians, pressing the Federal center and aiding their comrades on the left. Terry's Virginians, personally led by Gordon, stepped off around 4 PM, and by that time the weight of numbers was pressing the Federals back through the Thomas Farm toward the Georgetown Pike to their rear. The Confederates did not expect the fight they received, however. The intelligence that they had was that they would be fighting green soldiers, troops who had enlisted for 100 days' service. It was quite a rude awakening when they reached the Union line to find that they were actually fighting the men of the veteran VI Corps of the Army of the Potomac.

The loop trail here at the Thomas Farm winds along the area of the most severe fighting of the day. Stop 1 on the trail, near the Thomas House, would have been the Union left, where McCausland's second assault and the right of Gordon's line met the Federals. Walking along the trail to Stop 2 will essentially take you along the front of

Ricketts's line, with the trail stop very close to the Union right. Although the Federals were pushed back to the Georgetown Pike (now the Urbana Pike), the fighting here on the Thomas Farm in the late afternoon at times became hand to hand, with Wallace desperately forcing the Confederates to stand and fight when they did not want to.

Facing the tree line along the river will point you toward the Best Farm, with the Union line running from your front to your rear. While Gordon had moved a few pieces to the Worthington Farm, most of the Confederate artillery was still at the Best Farm. In addition to the pressure from the infantry in their front, the Federals were also taking heavy artillery fire en enfilade (from the side), shot and shell tearing down their line.

At approximately 4:20 PM, with Ricketts's line crumbling on the right and Ramseur's division pushing the last of the 10th Vermont across the Monocacy River, Lew Wallace finally sounded the retreat. Tyler's brigade, holding the Jug Bridge until 6 PM, served as a rear guard (along with the ever-present 8th Illinois Cavalry) as the Federals split onto several country roads and made their way toward the Baltimore Pike. As for the exhausted Confederates, they made their camp on the field, with Jubal Early placing his headquarters on the east side of the river.

The result was decisive. The Confederates held the field, taking 800 casualties to do so. Wallace's Federals had been driven off, taking 1,300 casualties of their own. But Wallace's ultimate goal had been accomplished. It was not immediately appreciated; when Halleck received official word from Wallace at 11:40 PM, he relayed the message to Grant, spitefully dismissing its accuracy. In Washington, Wallace was blamed by both Halleck and Stanton for the loss and was relieved of his command. Within a matter of days, however, the importance of what Wallace had done became clearer. Not only was he given his position back (over the objections of a steaming Henry Halleck) but he was nationally praised as a hero. Lew Wallace had pulled together a makeshift group of mostly green troops and delayed the Confederate Army of the Valley District for almost ten critical hours. His stand here at Monocacy Junction would go down in history with an alternate name: "The Battle that Saved Washington."

As for John Garrett of the Baltimore & Ohio Railroad, he didn't have to worry about his iron bridge after all. While the rest of Early's army departed the next morning, Dod Ramseur's division remained behind to destroy the bridge, but they didn't have enough gunpowder to blow it up. The bridge did take some damage, but within eight days the railroad had completed their repairs. The total cost: $13,000.

FORT STEVENS

⟩ *From Thomas Farm, turn right onto Baker Valley Road and drive 1.9 miles. Turn left onto Fingerboard Road (MD 80 East) and drive 2.7 miles. Take the entrance ramp onto I-270 South and drive 26.1 miles. Merge onto I-495 and continue another*

3.7 miles, then take exit 31B for MD 97 South (Georgia Avenue). Drive 3.8 miles on Georgia Avenue, and then turn right onto Quackenbos Street NW. Pull into the entrance for Fort Stevens past the church on your right.

By the time the news of the battle at Monocacy Junction reached the citizens of Baltimore and Washington, both cities were in a near panic. It was fairly evident that Washington was the target—Early would have otherwise pursued Wallace to Baltimore—but rumors abounded about the size, intentions, and makeup of the Confederate force. Under Grant's orders, every able-bodied man in Baltimore was pressed into military service. In addition, more widespread reports of Confederate cavalry began to float in front points north and south of Baltimore and Washington. Telegraph wires were cut, stores looted, trains stopped, and bridges burned. Also burned was the home of Maryland governor Augustus W. Bradford, retaliation for David Hunter's burning of Virginia former governor Letcher's home in Lexington. The Confederates even took possession of, and appropriately consumed, several wagonloads of ice cream headed for Baltimore.

All of this was a ruse. Jubal Early had one objective in mind: the prison camp at Point Lookout, Maryland. Incredibly, though, the grand plan for the prison break appeared in the Richmond, Virginia newspapers, and after several other missteps occurred, it was decided that the raid would be called off. This led to Early recalling most

The partially reconstructed works at Fort Stevens. The boulder to the left marks Abraham Lincoln's spot when he was fired upon by a Confederate sharpshooter.

of his cavalry to rejoin the infantry, which was headed southeast on the Georgetown Pike, straight for Washington, D.C.

The morning after the battle, July 10, Early began marching toward Washington down the Georgetown Pike, with McCausland's cavalry in the lead. The heat was stifling, and men fell out along the march regularly. By that evening, Early camped along the pike between Gaithersburg and Rockville, his army stretched out for 5 miles. After marching so far and so long and then fighting a pitched battle, the Confederate troops were exhausted. The next two days, equally hot, dry, and dusty, would not help matters as they made their final march toward the Union capital.

Around the city of Washington, the army and other government departments scrambled to put up an adequate defense. Not only were the defenses manned by only a skeleton crew of soldiers, but those who were on the watch were not all up to the task. Many had been placed in their positions simply because someone had to do it. In some cases, crews who had never fired a cannon were in charge of artillery emplacements. Further, much of the works were manned by the Veteran Reserve Corps, formerly named the Invalid Corps and made up of veterans who could no longer fight on the battlefield. The 10,000 men ready to receive the Confederate assault were being placed into defenses designed to hold 34,125 soldiers.

One advantage for the Union was that those defenses were formidable and intimidating. The construction of the first fortifications had begun in May 1861, and improvements had been occurring ever since. When completed, 68 forts protected a 37-mile perimeter around Washington, filled with almost 100 batteries of artillery. While not all of the forts were created equal, most included some combination of blockhouses, artillery emplacements, parapets for musket fire, and barracks. All of the forts were interconnected by rifle pits running along the heights around the city.

The northernmost of these fortifications was Fort Stevens, a three-sided fortification along the 7th Street Pike, the main road leading into Washington from the north. The ground in front of the fort was farmland, providing a relatively open field of fire toward any oncoming attacker. Heavy artillery at the fort added to its firepower. Other forts such as Fort DeRussy, Fort Totten, and Fort Reno lay to the east and west of Fort Stevens, able to provide support if needed. Still, someone had to man these positions.

You are now standing within what's left of Fort Stevens, a partial reconstruction of the northern wall of the fort. You will find a bronze marker with a model of the fort's former construction that will help you envision the rest of it. Besides the rampart in front of you, a bombproof also still remains in the center of the grounds. Walking up to the rampart and peering over the wall (in the direction of the Confederate approach) will give you an idea of just how massive the Washington defenses were. Remember that what you now see is only a small piece of a massive system of defenses that formed a ring around the entire city. Also note the size of the artillery;

FATHER ABRAHAM

Fort Stevens was built on the grounds of Emory Methodist Church (still here and located right next to Fort Stevens Battlefield Park) and on the home of Elizabeth Thomas, a free black woman who lived in the neighborhood known as Vinegar Hill, now called Brightwood. When Thomas was evicted from her home, she received no notice and no compensation, and when she tried to communicate with the soldiers so that she could at least remove some of the belongings from her home, she found that most of them were German and spoke little English. Despondent, Thomas sat beneath a tree and wept as she watched the Union soldiers destroy her home. A tall stranger came by, put his hand on her shoulder, and assured her that things would be all right. It was Abraham Lincoln himself. Thomas would live in Fort Stevens for the remainder of her life, and although she was never compensated for her loss, she never forgot the kindness shown that day by the commander in chief who necessarily authorized the destruction of her home.

these are not the 12-pounder Napoleon cannon you have seen on most battlefields, but are much heavier and designed specifically for defensive action.

Manning the earthworks was a more difficult task than it should have been. Henry Halleck, the highest-ranking general in the capital, would not take command, and simply relayed Grant's advice, even though he was far away at Petersburg. Resourcefulness and courage, however, brought the Union defenses together. Edwin Stanton pleaded for all government employees who could help to come to the works, and they came by the thousands. The Reserve Corps, eager to prove their worth, proudly shouldered their arms. Grant did his part by not only loading the remaining two divisions of the VI Corps (besides Ricketts, already with Lew Wallace) onto steamboats, but also redirecting the XIX Corps, returning from the Red River campaign in Louisiana, to land in Washington instead of Petersburg. The first of these units arrived shortly after noon on July 11 and immediately began heading to the northernmost defenses of the city.

While the Federal reinforcements were unloading at the city docks, Jubal Early's army appeared on the horizon north of the city. Robert Rodes's division had begun his march at 6:20 AM, almost three hours behind schedule. The short march in the oppressive heat again took its toll, and by the time the Confederates reached the outskirts or Washington, his infantry was down to 8,000 effectives—almost 3,000 fewer than he had begun with. Rapid marches, heat, and the battle at Monocacy had taken their toll on the Army of the Valley.

Early quickly drove the few Union pickets back to their main defense line, then stopped to wait for the rest of his army, strung out along the roadway, to catch up. It was a slow process, and under the conditions, the men were not at their best. Upon their arrival, Early could see that the works, particularly Fort Stevens in his front, were lightly manned. However, as the Confederate infantry formed, great clouds of dust arose behind the Federal earthworks, portending a coming storm. It was the VI and XIX Corps, and they immediately began to fill the works at and around Fort Stevens. While they could not fill them to capacity, the mere presence of veteran troops in Early's front—and there was no confusion about the soldiers he faced this time—was enough to change the whole game.

Almost instantly, Federal artillery fire from all of the nearby forts, at first wildly ineffective, began to hit their targets with deadly precision. Rodes's division, whose pickets had come within 300 yards of Fort Stevens, was forced to pull back. When John Brown Gordon's division arrived at 3 PM, the Confederates moved to the side and stacked their arms, having no orders. Early would not attack this day. The never-ending stream of blue had stopped the usually aggressive Early in his tracks. Although artillery fire and some musketry would continue for the rest of the day, there was no assault on the works.

That night, Early held a council of war with his division commanders to determine what to do. A direct assault would be deadly, but if successful would mean that, at least temporarily, the rebels would be within the Washington works. All knew that the city could not be held, but the mere presence of a Confederate army within the capital, even temporarily, would have enormous repercussions. Simply entering Washington and destroying a few buildings would force Grant to relieve the pressure on Petersburg, and perhaps more important, demoralize Northern citizens in this critically important election year of 1864. At this moment, the probability of Abraham Lincoln's reelection was low, and the Confederate capture of Washington could seal his exit, bringing in a president who would come to peaceful terms with the South. A victory here could win the war for the Confederacy.

On the other hand, if the Confederates did not succeed, or if they stayed too long, the odds of Early escaping with his command intact would be very low. The looming defenses of Washington, along with the veterans now manning the works, could mean the destruction of his army, even if it were to break through the Union line.

None of Early's subordinates (including Gordon, who had earlier urged an attack) supported the idea of an attack. Additional intelligence gathered during the night seemed to support this, with the confirmation of at least two full corps of Federal infantry now present. Still, Early wanted to attack. It was only later in the evening that he decided to view the defenses in the morning and make his decision.

The next morning, July 12, as his troops stood in line for battle, Early again surveyed the works. The parapets were now fully lined with Union troops. It was against every fiber of Jubal Early's being to call off an attack. He had led the Army of the Valley hundreds of miles to the gates of the Federal capital, and was on the brink of possibly turning the tide of the war. But Early had seen enough. He called off the assault, deciding that the Confederates would hold their position until dark, then withdraw during the night. Although there would be fighting throughout the day, and the Union actually did launch an attack around 4 PM that was repulsed, the battle of Fort Stevens would ultimately end in a stalemate. The Federals lost 370 men, while the Confederates suffered about 500 casualties.

It is difficult to imagine this area as a battleground today. Even when atop the fortifications, staring over the parapet into the surrounding neighborhood, picturing the vast open fields that were present 150 years ago is a challenge. In a sense, however, your view of the battlefield at Fort Stevens is exactly the same as that of both the Union and Confederate armies—confused. In later years, the Federals who stood where you now do were not only certain that there would be an attack, but were also certain that the rebels would break through the still lightly defended works with ease. On the other side of the field, the Confederates who viewed the massive earthworks from the distance were just as certain that they could not succeed. The enemy defenses were only one obstacle; a greater one lay with the fatigue of the men. The rebels were simply too exhausted to continue much farther, let alone launch an assault on a heavily fortified position. Which side was right will be argued as long as the Civil War is studied, but no one will ever know the true answer.

While here, you surely noticed the marker referencing Abraham Lincoln's role in the battle at Fort Stevens. It is an often retold story, and although usually embellished slightly, it is mostly true. Lincoln visited Fort Stevens on July 11 with his wife as he toured most of the city's defenses. The next day, July 12, he could not resist making a return visit. The president, with his conspicuous black suit and his stovepipe hat extending his tall frame, began to draw fire from Confederate sharpshooters. Remarkably, Lincoln seemed to pay little mind until a surgeon standing next to him was shot in the general location of the marker. General Horatio Wright, commander of the VI Corps, finally firmly ordered Lincoln to come down off the rampart. It is the only time in United States history that a sitting president came under enemy fire. (Often included in the story is a reference to Private Oliver Wendell Holmes, future Supreme Court Justice, who is said to have yanked the president off the rampart, shouting something to the effect of, "Get down you damned fool!" Although almost certainly not true, it does put an interesting twist on the tale.)

❯ *Turn left onto Quackenbos Street NW, then turn left onto Georgia Avenue. Drive 0.3 mile on Georgia Avenue; park on the street in front of the cemetery on your right.*

With only 45 burials, Battleground National Cemetery is the second-smallest national cemetery in the United States. (The smallest is Ball's Bluff National Cemetery in Leesburg, Virginia, just east of Washington.) Dedicated by President Lincoln himself in 1864, the only soldiers that the cemetery holds are those who were killed during the battle of Fort Stevens. There are an additional four graves for the family of one of the cemetery's former caretakers. Also on the grounds, an orchard at the time of the battle and right in the thick of the fighting, are monuments to several of the regiments and companies who fought here. The cemetery is small and well kept, and although on a major street in Washington is still a quiet, respectful place.

Perhaps the most interesting piece on the property is an interpretive sign that lists personal details about those who are buried here—name, age, rank, company, and where they were from—all under the regimental flag (or, in some cases, the United States flag) under which they entered the battle. These are details necessarily lost in most national cemeteries, where the origins of thousands of graves cannot be so easily presented, but in this small and solemn spot, it is a wonderful touch that makes each headstone more than just a slab of marble.

The tiny but still humbling Battleground National Cemetery on the Fort Stevens battlefield.

❭ *Continue 0.4 mile on Georgia Avenue to the entrance for Walter Reed Hospital on your left. Stop at the entrance gate and let the security guard know that you are there to see the Lincoln Sharpshooter Tree. After the gate, turn left onto Dahlia Road and drive 0.3 mile to Butternut Street. Turn right on Butternut Street and park on the street. As you enter and leave the hospital grounds, note that there are many one way streets, so be careful where you are going.*

The monument you see here commemorates the location of a tulip tree used by Confederate sharpshooters during the battle of Fort Stevens. It has been said that this was the tree from which a sharpshooter came so close to hitting Abraham Lincoln, and it is possible, but not probable. In any case, even though the tree is long gone now, it is a wonderful hidden gem of the battle, and will also give you a sense, judging by the drive you took to get here, of just how large the battlefield was.

COOL SPRING

〉 *From the sharpshooter tree marker, make a U-turn and exit the hospital grounds from Butternut Street. Turn left onto Georgia Avenue and drive 3 mile. Take the entrance ramp for I-495 West to Northern Virginia. Drive 13.5 miles on I-495 West to exit 45A for VA 267 West toward Dulles Airport. Drive 25.4 miles on VA 267 West to exit 1A for VA 7 West. Drive 21.3 miles on VA 7 West; just after you cross the Shenandoah River, turn right onto Castleman Road (SR 603). Drive 1.2 miles on Castleman Road to Cool Spring Lane, the entrance for Holy Cross Abbey. Drive 0.8 mile on Cool Spring Lane and park at the abbey's welcome center and gift shop.*

After dark on July 12, Jubal Early took his army away from the Washington defenses and headed west, crossing the Potomac back into Virginia near Leesburg at White's Ford. A frustrated Abraham Lincoln watched again—this time with his own eyes—as a Confederate army seemed to escape with ease. Lincoln had wanted the army to pursue, and Grant had actually ordered Horatio Wright to do just that, but the order did not reach Washington until it was too late. In any case, the disorganization in Washington caused by throwing a last-minute defensive force together delayed an organized pursuit for a full day. Most, including Lincoln and Grant, blamed Halleck for not taking command.

Fortunately for the Federals, however, another army unexpectedly appeared. David Hunter's forces from the Department of Western Virginia, not seen or heard from since its flight from the battle at Hanging Rock, crossed the Potomac on July 15. Still with Hunter's force was George Crook's Army of West Virginia, who advanced in front of Hunter and united with Wright on July 16. Early, though, was already leading his Confederates into the Shenandoah Valley, setting his headquarters at Berryville and taking a defensive position. Knowing that the Federals were on his tail, Early urged his commanders to be wary of any activity to the east.

At 4 AM on July 18, Crook took his army and headed for Snicker's Gap, a passage through the Blue Ridge Mountains just east of Berryville. From there, Crook was to cross the Shenandoah River, if possible, and attack the Confederates. The VI and XIX Corps, Wright assured him, would right behind him. Besides, no battle was expected. Virtually all of the Union command assumed that Early was still moving toward the valley and escape.

By 11:30 AM, with Crook's lone division at the river and the VI Corps only on the other side of the gap, Wright and Crook, after surveying the ground across the river, decided to make the crossing. They could see the Confederates, but could not tell how many there were, and thought that it was probably only Early's rear guard. Crook ordered Joseph Thoburn's division to cross the river at Island Ford, 2 miles north of the Berryville Turnpike, and to then move south, pushing the rebels away from Snicker's Ford, where the rest of the Union force intended to cross.

The Confederates on the west bank of the Shenandoah River were hardly a rear guard. In fact, John Brown Gordon's entire division was at Snicker's Ford, and Robert Rodes's and Gabriel Wharton's divisions were near Island Ford. When Thoburn crossed the river at 3:30 PM, Confederate prisoners captured by the skirmish line soon revealed that the Confederates were present in force. Thoburn decided not to continue his advance and deployed his three brigades along the river, sending word to Crook that help would be needed. With his back to the river, Thoburn set his left on Cool Spring Run and formed two lines, setting the first behind a small rise a quarter-mile inland and the second, his reserve line, behind a stone wall along an old towpath near the river.

Within 30 minutes, the rebels were on their way to Island Ford to contest the crossing. Wharton's division (of Breckinridge's corps) formed the Confederate right, facing the Federals, while Rodes's division took the left, overlapping the Union flank. With most of the enemy movements concealed by the ridges and surrounding trees, the Federals were soon surprised with skirmish fire in their front and heavy pressure on their right from Rodes. The Confederate fire on their right soon caused the Union flank to crumble, with regiments either retreating to the cover of the stone wall or entirely across the shallow river.

With the aid of Union artillery fire from the east bank, Thoburn was able to slow the Confederate advance, but not stop it. Ricketts's division arrived around 6 PM, but Wright ordered that it stay on the east bank, not wanting to add to the disaster. It was only Thoburn's leadership, rallying many of his men in the towpath, which had averted his entire division from being lost. The stone wall provided excellent defensive cover, and the Federals were able to hold their second line until darkness enabled them to cross back to the east bank of the river safely. In fact, their stand was so effective that in the end, the casualty numbers—419 Union and around 400 Confederate—were roughly equal. Further, the Union army now knew that Jubal Early would not be retreating up the valley, and that his entire army was ready to fight.

The battlefield is now part of Holy Cross Abbey, a monastery of the Cistercian Order. The abbey welcomes visitors, but most of the battlefield grounds are leased to local farmers, meaning that walking the field is usually not permitted. There is a wonderful gift shop at the abbey, and the brothers are actually quite knowledgeable about the battle, selling several books about the area's history and even showcasing a display of some of the artifacts found on the property. The small museum is located in Cool Spring, the abbey, which dates back to 1784 and was not far behind the Confederate line.

Most of the abbey is off limits, but if you turn just before the gift shop and drive toward the Retreat House, you will be able to easily discern the ridge from the landscape. The river is not far behind, but is not visible. When you visit, though, be sure not to disturb the residents or guests on the grounds, who are there to take advantage of its beauty and solitude.

RUTHERFORD'S FARM

⟩ *From the parking area, turn left onto Cool Spring Road and drive 0.8 mile to the entrance for the abbey. Turn left onto Castleman Road and drive 1.2 mile to VA 7 West. Drive 14 miles on VA 7 West and then take the entrance ramp for I-81 North. Drive 2.1 miles on I-81 North to exit 317 for US 11. Turn right onto US 11 and drive 0.3 mile; there will be a parking area next to a set of historical markers on your left past the shopping mall entrance.*

With the rest of Hunter's army moving south from Harpers Ferry and Wright applying pressure to the Confederate left, Jubal Early was forced to withdraw farther into the Shenandoah Valley. Beginning his movement south late on July 19 and fighting several small battles along the way, Early sent Stephen Ramseur's division to Winchester to act as rear guard while the rest of the Confederates moved up the Valley Pike. Ramseur's men reached the northern outskirts of Winchester early on July 20, stopping near Fort Collier, an earthwork along the pike. Also in the area, 2 miles to the north, were two brigades of Confederate cavalry under John C. Vaughn and William "Mudwall" Jackson.

In addition to David Hunter's, George Crook's, and Horatio Wright's Union commands was William Averell's, a combined force of infantry and cavalry, along with 12 guns in two batteries. Averell had been marching south up the Valley Pike and was also approaching Winchester, reaching Stephenson's Depot around 11 AM and skirmishing with Vaughn's cavalry. Vaughn quickly sent a report to Ramseur describing the size of the Federal force, but Ramseur, who had 3,300 men under his command, initially dismissed the Union party.

The first fighting involved only cavalry, with the rebels dismounted and formed on a small rise between the farms of John Rutherford and Susan Carter. Four of the Confederate guns were soon brought to the front and the fight remained stalemated for some time until Averell decided to bring his infantry and artillery forward. Although the infantry paused behind a small ridge, soon the Union guns were driving Vaughn's men off the field and to the rear.

Vaughn, who had not distinguished himself during the war, was nevertheless a veteran, having fought in the Mexican War. He proposed a plan to Ramseur that involved slowly withdrawing his own cavalry, leading the Federals into a trap. Ramseur, who had been ordered by Early to fight only on the defensive (as a rear guard is supposed to do), agreed to the plan and prepared to advance his infantry.

As the Confederate infantry neared the field, Averell was ready to continue his own advance. The Union soldiers rose from their position on the Carter Farm and resumed their movement toward Winchester across the Rutherford Farm. The field in front of them was clear for 800 yards, where a grove of trees stood at the south edge of the farm. It was behind these trees that the Confederates began to form, unseen by the Federals.

Because of the rush to battle, Ramseur did not properly reconnoiter the ground, and did not realize that the wood line in which he formed, as well as a turn in the Valley Pike, threw the left side of his line well in advance of the rest. In addition, the Confederate skirmish line was placed so close to the line that it could provide little warning of a Union attack. Vaughn's cavalry covered the Confederate left while Jackson's protected the right, and the rebel artillery unlimbered along the woods east of the pike.

The small wayside exhibit where you now stand was on the Rutherford Farm, as you can easily see from the name of the shopping center that now occupies most of the ground. The farms and the rise in the ground are now long gone, but still here, as always, is the Valley Turnpike, US 11. It is mostly the same position that it was during the war, and can usually be relied upon to place your position on the battlefield. You are currently standing in between the infantry lines, almost directly in the center of the fighting. As you face the road and look to your left, you are looking in the direction of the Carter Farm, while Rutherford's Farm would have been to your right.

The fighting resumed with the cavalry, this time on the flanks of the armies, as the Federals advanced. As they approached the woods, however, Ramseur's infantry stepped forward and unleashed a deadly volley, stopping the advance. This, along with success by the cavalry on both ends of the line, gave the rebels the upper hand at the beginning of the battle, badly damaging the Union left. However, the fact that the Confederate left was so badly arranged would not give them enough time to take any advantage of the situation. Averell's men on this side of the line resumed their advance, scattering first Vaughn's cavalry and then hitting the flank of the Confederate infantry.

Ramseur tried desperately to maintain the fight, sending two guns to his left and attempting to rally his left, but it was no use. With the Confederate flank wide open, the line crumbled left to right, unit by unit. The Federal pursuit continued through Rutherford's Woods, and although a few of the enemy regiments stopped to make a stand, in the end, Union troops captured many of the fleeing men, as well as four pieces of artillery. A countercharge by Vaughn's cavalry finally stopped the Union pursuit. Confederate casualties numbered near 450, mostly captured, while the Federals lost 211 men. Ramseur's defeat at Rutherford's Farm was the only black mark on what had otherwise been an outstanding campaign.

KERNSTOWN BATTLEFIELD PARK

> *From the parking area, turn left onto US 11 and drive 0.4 mile, and then turn left onto the entrance ramp for I-81 South. Drive 3.9 miles on I-81 South to exit 313B. At the end of the exit ramp, turn right, and then bear left onto East Jubal Early Drive. Drive 1.1 miles on Jubal Early to US 11. Turn left onto US 11 and drive 1.8 miles; just past a car dealership, turn right onto Battle Park Drive. Drive 0.1 mile to the entrance for Kernstown Battlefield Park.*

For the Federals, all signs pointed to the withdrawal of Jubal Early's Army of the Valley. His men were needed at Petersburg, and he had been moving almost continuously into the Shenandoah Valley since the battle at Fort Stevens. Horatio Wright, therefore, wanted to take advantage of Robert E. Lee's besieged army before Early rejoined him, and decided on July 20 that he would withdraw the VI and XIX Corps from the Shenandoah Valley and head for Petersburg himself to join in Grant's assault there. With one swift decision, Union strength in the lower valley shrank from 25,000 men to only the 12,000 of George Crook's Army of West Virginia, along with William Averell's detached division.

Jubal Early had other plans. His army once again outnumbered the Federals, and he knew it, having learned about Wright's departure from Union prisoners. Just as Stonewall Jackson had fooled the enemy into thinking he had left to join Lee in 1862, Early would also stay and hopefully keep soldiers away from the front at Petersburg. From his headquarters at Strasburg, Early sent cavalry scouting northward on July 23 toward Winchester, where Crook had set his headquarters. Although Union cavalry south of the city at Kernstown reported 3,000 Confederate horsemen (an accurate account), Crook left only one infantry division and one brigade of cavalry to guard against a Confederate approach from the south.

Besides the fact that they were the only division there, the single division that Crook left near Kernstown was the smallest and newest in his army, belonging to Col. James Mulligan. Crook had had only two divisions, commanded by James Thoburn and Isaac Duval, but Mulligan's independent brigade arrived just in time for the battle at Cool Spring on July 18. Mulligan had begun the war as commander of the 23rd Illinois Infantry and outranked both Thoburn and Duval, so on July 22 Crook reorganized his army, giving Mulligan his own division of two brigades.

The Confederates were on the move from Strasburg at 4 AM, and by 7 AM first contact was made on the Valley Pike between Union and Confederate cavalry. In fact, the Confederate cavalry, which Early had neither trusted nor used much, was spearing the advance toward Kernstown on four different roads: The Back Road, farthest west; the Middle Road; the Valley Pike; and the Front Royal Road, farthest east. Just as they had the previous day, the rebel horsemen had shown in full force, and just as he had done then, George Crook dismissed the Confederate action as a mere cavalry skirmish. Although he did reinforce Mulligan's infantry division with Thoburn's, the furthest thing from his imagination was that the entire Confederate army was just behind that cavalry.

While Thoburn took position on the Union right near the prominent Sandy Ridge, Mulligan placed his artillery atop the commanding Pritchard's Hill and moved his infantry in front to support them. Around 10 AM, seeing his cavalry scuffling with the Confederates to its front, Crook ordered Mulligan to move forward to support the artillery, then left the field and returned to Winchester, thinking the situation under control.

From here atop Pritchard's Hill, you can see virtually the entire battlefield. Mulligan's reasons for choosing this hill for an artillery position is evident, just as it was to previous Federal commanders during the battles of First Kernstown and Second

The high ground around the Pritchard home at Kernstown. Union soldiers lined up behind the stone wall along the Pritchard farm lane.

Winchester. Facing toward the Pritchard House and other farm buildings, Sandy Ridge is the large tree-lined prominence to your right. In the distance, slightly left of center, you can see the steeple of Opequon Church, which you will approach shortly.

Mulligan sent one brigade forward toward Opequon Church to support the Federal cavalry while keeping the other in reserve. At almost the same time, Confederate infantry and artillery reached the field, out of view of the Union lines. The first division to arrive was John Brown Gordon's, and he immediately began moving his men through a ravine running through Barton's Woods, west of the Valley Pike and south of Opequon Church. Shortly after, John Breckinridge's other division, commanded by Gabriel Wharton, moved undetected to high ground east of the pike. As the pressure mounted, Mulligan sent word to Crook that more reinforcements would be needed than Crook had realized.

Initially denying Mulligan's request, Crook eventually did send reinforcements, Isaac Duval's division, and rode to the front to see what was going on for himself. Seeing the rebel infantry in his front, he planned an assault on both Confederate flanks while Mulligan held the center. Thoburn was already in position on Sandy Ridge to the right, and Rutherford B. Hayes's brigade would come up on Mulligan's left.

Thoburn, however, became one of many Union commanders on the field that day that would see what George Crook would not. Confederate cavalry was moving beyond Sandy Ridge, were making room for the third rebel infantry division, Stephen Ramseur's, which was about to form on the Confederate left next to Gordon's division. Ramseur anchored his left on Sandy Ridge and sent his sharpshooters in front of the line.

At 3 PM, Mulligan advanced, with Hayes and Thoburn moving with him. Forming the center of the line, Mulligan's division reached Opequon Church, but the brigades on either side of him did not have as much luck. Thoburn's brigades were stopped by Ramseur's sharpshooters in their front and could not keep up, forming a large gap in the Union line. At the same time, the Union left, Hayes's brigade, passed directly in front of Wharton's concealed Confederates. As soon as the Federals passed the center of their position, the rebels unleashed a devastating fire, with artillery to their front and musketry to their flank. The brigade could not absorb the shock, and soon the Union left was in retreat.

Today's Opequon Church is not the same building that it was during the battle, but it is in the same place, and the meadow you just strolled through is the Pritchard Meadow, the same one that the Federals advanced through that morning. A quick look at the cemetery here will tell you that it was also here at the time of the battle, which raged in and around it. Mulligan's line advanced to this area, but found itself with both flanks exposed, and they were soon forced to retreat back across the Pritchard Meadow.

Follow the path from Opequon Church and walk back toward the Pritchard Farm, stopping at the interpretive sign near the creek. Withdrawing in relative order, Mulligan's men first found shelter in the small ravine, known as Hoge's Run. At the time of the battle it was dry, but you can see that it now holds quite a bit of water. The Federals were soon forced out of this position and back to the stone wall along the Pritchard Lane, just ahead of you. The Confederates of Gordon's and Ramseur's divisions, who pursued the Union troops across the meadow, took position in the run after the Federals had left it, setting themselves in a sheltered position only 200 yards from the Union line.

Now, walk to and along the stone wall near the Pritchard House. This was the Pritchard farm lane at the time of the battle, and what was left of Mulligan's brigade used the shelter of this wall to their advantage. Able to hold their position, Federal cavalry was able to swoop in on the Confederate right, temporarily stopping some of the flanking fire from Wharton's division. These horsemen were soon forced back, though, and before long, one of only two Federal units left on the field was the 23rd Illinois, the Chicagoans with whom Mulligan had entered the war at its outset. By all accounts, the 23rd fought well, and Mulligan was a picture of inspiration, urging his men to keep fighting. Shortly after he finally gave the order to withdraw, Mulligan was shot through the thigh and dismounted, and his men tried to carry him to safety. First admonishing one of his officers for swearing and then ordering his men to leave him and save the colors, Mulligan was shot two more times in quick succession. Mulligan would die several days later in the Pritchard House, having gained the admiration of not only the Union soldiers who saw him that day, but also the Confederates.

The other Union regiment on the field was the 13th West Virginia, still fighting in what was their first battle. Hayes, who would later be the 19th president of the United States, saw the West Virginians from the top of Pritchard Hill, and sent his aide and future 25th president, Major William McKinley, to order them to withdraw. Another timely Union cavalry charge was enough to allow the rest of the Federals to leave the field in order.

The Union Army of West Virginia had been completely routed. It had taken 1,185 casualties while inflicting only 300 on the Confederates. Jubal Early's victory could not have been more timely or effective. Horatio Wright's VI Corps and the XIX Corps were immediately returned to the Shenandoah Valley, exactly as both Early and Robert E. Lee had hoped.

Unfortunately for the Confederates, their sound victory would yield an unwelcome side effect. Tiring of the rebel dominance of the Shenandoah Valley, particularly in an election year, Abraham Lincoln wanted something done once and for all. In complete agreement was Ulysses S. Grant, who would no longer view the Shenandoah Valley as a sideshow to the other theaters of the war. Taking and holding the valley was now a major priority, and he could only give the task to someone who he could wholly trust to do the job thoroughly. He would give the job to Phil Sheridan.

The Burning: Sheridan in the Shenandoah Valley

SHORTLY AFTER HIS VICTORY at Kernstown on July 24, 1864, Jubal Early directed John McCausland to take his brigade of Confederate cavalry north, across the Potomac and through Maryland, to the town of Chambersburg, Pennsylvania. Reaching Chambersburg on July 30, McCausland demanded $100,000 in gold or $500,000 cash from the town. The citizens defiantly refused to pay. As they had promised to do in such an event, McCausland's raiders torched the town, burning over 400 buildings, including 274 private homes.

Union cavalry caught up with and soundly defeated McCausland's cavalry at Moorefield, West Virginia, on August 7, but for Abraham Lincoln, the burning of Chambersburg was an exclamation point on what had already been a terrible month. The Confederate Army of the Valley had marched virtually undetected to the nation's capital, routed George Crook's force at Kernstown, and burned a Northern city within the span of only a few weeks. To most Northerners, the Confederate army appeared to have quite a bit of fight left in it, even though it was pinned down at Petersburg and being driven to Atlanta. The chances of Lincoln's prevailing in the election, only a few shorts months away, seemed slim, and his defeat could very well mean the dissolution of the Union he had fought so hard to save.

Lincoln and Union commander Ulysses S. Grant met in Virginia at Fort Monroe

This marker commemorates the death of young Confederate General Stephen Ramseur, mortally wounded at Cedar Creek.

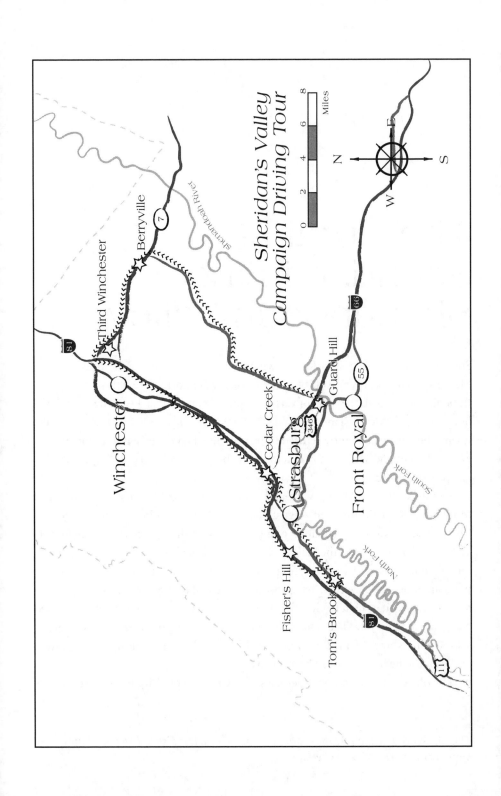

Sheridan's Valley
Campaign Driving Tour

Miles
0   2   4   6   8

N E
W ⊕
S

Shenandoah River

Berryville

Third Winchester

Winchester

Cedar Creek

Strasburg

Guard Hill

Front Royal

South Fork

Fisher's Hill

Tom's Brook

North Fork

on July 31 and August 1 to discuss the situation. Four military departments—of West Virginia, the Susquehanna, and Washington, along with the Middle Department—were creating a bureaucratic mess, and Grant and Lincoln agreed that they should be combined under one commander. Determining who that should be was a more difficult decision. Several names were considered and rejected—William Franklin, George Meade, even George B. McClellan, whom Lincoln would run against in November. In the end, though, it came down to only two names. One was already in the lower valley, while the other would be put on standby.

On August 4, Grant unexpectedly visited the Union forces gathered around Frederick, Maryland, and spoke with David Hunter, commander of the Department of West Virginia. Grant asked him where the Confederates were, and Hunter could not give an answer. Grant then asked if Hunter, who would remain in charge of the new department if he wished, would give field command to Philip Sheridan, who had been sent to Washington to await orders. Hunter replied that if Sheridan could do a better job than he, then he should have the entire department. Accepting what he considered a very gracious and patriotic offer from Hunter, Grant wired Sheridan to come to Frederick immediately. When Sheridan arrived to assume command on August 6, he and Grant met very briefly at Araby, the Thomas House, which had been in the middle of the battle of Monocacy only a month before. Within two hours, Grant had boarded a train to return to the front. Lincoln, Secretary of War Edwin Stanton, and Chief of Staff Henry Halleck were all unsure about Sheridan, but Grant had seen him on the field and trusted him.

Sheridan's orders were simple. He and his newly created Army of the Shenandoah were to first find Jubal Early's troops and drive them out of the Shenandoah Valley. After the Confederates were gone, Sheridan was to leave them no reason to return. The valley, the "Breadbasket of the Confederacy," had provided Robert E. Lee's army with a reliable food supply since the beginning of the war. That would change with Sheridan's arrival, and he was to destroy any and all resources in the valley that could possibly be used to aid the rebels.

The Shenandoah Valley had belonged to the Confederates since the beginning of the war. This decisive move by Grant—along with ruthless execution by Sheridan—would finally put a Union army in charge in the valley. The repercussions of this would be felt by all who witnessed it for decades to come.

BEFORE YOU GO

» PLANNING YOUR TRIP

All of the action you will see here is in the lower Shenandoah Valley, and all of the locations are within a fairly short drive of one another. Although you will still spend a

SHERIDAN'S 1864
SHENANDOAH
VALLEY CAMPAIGN

Number of sites: 6

Total miles: 103

Estimated time: 1–3 days

good amount of your time in your car, you will probably want to pick one place to stay and return there every night, rather than pack up and move between hotels. Don't let the small number of sites fool you, either; there will be plenty enough to see to fill your days.

One thing you should know, though, is that much of the action is best (or only) seen on foot. The Third Winchester, Fisher's Hill, and Cedar Creek battlefields have both short and long trails associated with them, and they cover some of the most critical ground of each fight. While all of the trails are excellent, come prepared to hike if you want to truly get to where the action was.

» RECOMMENDATIONS

Staying in Winchester is an easy option. There are dozens of hotels and restaurants that will satisfy any lodging need, along with plenty of other resources that may be more difficult to come by in other parts of the valley. However, don't let that discourage you from staying at Front Royal, Strasburg, or any of the other towns in the area. The sites are all so close together that making sure you select lodging that fits you will be more important than getting the perfect location.

With everything the Shenandoah Valley has to offer, you may want to choose something a little quieter for this trip. Bed & breakfasts abound here, some with historic ties, and if you haven't tried the B&B approach before, this is as perfect a place as any to give it a shot, particularly since you're likely to be sleeping in the same bed every night. No matter how far you hike or how long you drive, a nice quiet spot anywhere

IN DEPTH

Dennis E. Frye, Martin F. Graham, and George F. Skoch, eds.—*The James E. Taylor Sketchbook—With Sheridan up the Shenandoah Valley in 1864: Leaves from a Special Artist's Sketchbook and Diary*

Jeffry D. Wert—*From Winchester to Cedar Creek: The Shenandoah campaign of 1864*

"Taylor, a young special artist for Frank Leslie's Illustrated Newspaper who accompanied Sheridan's army, provides an amazing collection of skillfully done illustrations and maps. Wert's book is an excellent analysis of the duel between 'Old Jube' and 'Little Phil,' and the definitive book on the campaign."

—*Tom Trescott, Abraham Lincoln Book Shop, Chicago*

in this peaceful valley will be sure to refresh you. Of course, as mentioned in the previous chapter, you also have Shenandoah National Park, which offers several choices for lodging to suit any need.

THE CAMPAIGN TOUR

GUARD HILL

⟩ *Begin your tour in the city of Front Royal at the intersection of Winchester Road (US 340) and Guard Hill Road. Park in the gravel area just off Guard Hill Road next to the interpretive signs.*

Immediately upon taking command, Sheridan, a man of action, began to put his forces on the move. His force consisted of Horatio Wright's VI Corps (formerly the second-largest corps in the Army of the Potomac), William Emory's XIX Corps (having come from the Department of the Gulf), George Crook's Army of West Virginia, and three divisions of cavalry, which Sheridan would quickly organize into a corpslike structure of its own. All 35,000 of his infantry and his 8,000 cavalry had already begun to head west to Harpers Ferry by the time Sheridan arrived on August 6. By the next evening he knew that the Confederates were at Bunker Hill north of Winchester, and on August 9 he issued his marching orders. Never wasteful of anything, including time, Sheridan would not wait for the enemy to come to him.

Sheridan surmised that by moving to the town of Berryville, the Confederates

Historic markers at Guard Hill, just north of Front Royal, Virginia.

would see a threat to their supply lines, and he was correct. Jubal Early, with the Federals in his right rear, pulled his army toward Winchester, camping there on August 10. This maneuvering would continue through the next two days, with occasional cavalry skirmishes, until the evening of April 12. The rebels had taken a position on Fisher's Hill, a prominent east–west ridge often referred to as the "Gibraltar of the Shenandoah" because of its defensive strength. The Union line stretched along Cedar Creek, 4 miles to the north.

For the next three days, both armies would hold these lines. The Confederates did not need to go anywhere, even outmanned three to one; their position at Fisher's Hill was virtually impregnable. The Union army, though, had stopped because of a rumor, and it was one worth heeding. The rumor was that James Longstreet's corps was now in the Shenandoah Valley and coming to Early's assistance.

The rumor was mostly true. Robert E. Lee, upon hearing that more Union troops were headed for the valley, had conferred with Jefferson Davis and Richard Anderson, who was commanding Longstreet's corps while he recovered from the wound he received at the Wilderness. It was decided that Anderson would send Joseph Kershaw's division of infantry, under Anderson's command, as well as Fitzhugh Lee's division of cavalry. They would travel first to Culpeper, then to Front Royal, attempting to get in the left rear of Sheridan's army. Anderson's division reached Front Royal on August 14, camping there for the night.

After Grant confirmed that two Confederate divisions were no longer at the Petersburg front, Sheridan planned a withdrawal from the Cedar Creek line. At 11 PM on August 15, the XIX Corps left for Halltown, just outside of Harpers Ferry. The next day, while cavalry was sent toward Front Royal to reconnoiter, Sheridan withdrew the rest of his army at 8 PM. As they moved north on the Valley Pike toward Winchester, the Union troops could hear the sounds of battle coming from the east, toward Front Royal.

The fight was between Wesley Merritt's Federal cavalry and Anderson's division, occurring on a rise north of Front Royal known as Guard Hill., Not yet knowing what was going on west of Massanutten Mountain, where the two armies faced each other, Anderson had not left Front Royal. When the Confederates finally moved on August 16, Merritt's cavalry swooped down on them from Guard Hill as they crossed the Shenandoah River, catching them off guard and capturing 300 rebels. The rebels were able to mount a counterstrike and pushed the Federals back up the hill, then north toward Cedarville until darkness fell.

You are now standing on Guard Hill, towering over the Shenandoah River below. Front Royal is at the confluence of the North and South Forks of the Shenandoah River, and as you look toward the town of Front Royal, you can see the bridge that crosses the two forks just before they join. The deep valley below you is where the Confederates were caught midstream. They pursued the Union troopers back up the

THE EXECUTIONS

Here at the historical markers, you will read of an ugly event that began here between Union and Confederate cavalry on September 23. John Singleton Mosby's men, officially the 43rd Virginia Battalion, had all but owned the northern counties of Virginia, which came to be called "Mosby's Confederacy." His Rangers, who would stay with Confederate sympathizers and collect at a moment's notice only to disappear as soon as they had done their worst damage, had been a thorn in the side of Federal commanders for months.

A group of Mosby's men had attempted to capture what they thought was an unguarded wagon train south of Front Royal. Not seeing the reserve brigade in the rear, the Confederates were quickly routed, and in the melee, Lt. Charles McMaster of the 2nd U.S. Cavalry was killed. It appeared to the Federals that McMaster had been trying to surrender, though this was probably not true. The Union troopers wanted revenge, and Wesley Merritt, whose men were just behind the reserve brigade, ordered the execution of the six prisoners they held. These orders were carried out without mercy. Four of the prisoners were dragged out and immediately shot, including one who was not even part of the Rangers but had ridden along as an excited seventeen-year-old; he was killed in front of his protesting mother. The other two, after refusing to give up the location of Mosby's headquarters, were hung, one of them wearing a sign reading, "Such is the fate of all of Mosby's men."

Mosby blamed the executions on George Armstrong Custer, and when a group of Custer's men were captured on October 6, Mosby executed a like number, but with far more dignity, drawing straws and even exchanging one when it was found that a drummer boy had been selected. On November 11, Mosby wrote to Sheridan suggesting that this breach from regular warfare be stopped, and no further incidents occurred.

hill toward your position, eventually placing artillery here as they attempted to chase them down.

Guard Hill was only the first of several actions to occur over the next several days. Early and Anderson both advanced on August 17 and fought several cavalry actions as they followed the Federals north. Slowed by heavy rain, the Union army was in its lines at Halltown on August 22. The Confederates, meanwhile, took possession of Charles Towne, and small battles occurred in this area for the next several days while Sheridan tried to confirm the wide range of intelligence that was coming in. On August 27, Early moved back to Bunker Hill while Sheridan reoccupied Charles Towne. August 28 found both armies on the exact same ground they had possessed before Sheridan began his movement almost three weeks before.

BERRYVILLE

❭ *From Guard Hill, turn left onto US 340 and drive 8.2 miles. Turn right to continue on US 340 and follow it for another 11.7 miles, then turn left onto West Main Street (SR 7 Business). Drive 1.1 miles to Westwood Road; park in the school parking lot on your left.*

On September 3, Sheridan moved his Union army to Berryville, just east of Winchester, hoping that a movement similar to the one he had performed before would result in another Confederate withdrawal south. As the Federals came into camp, Richard Anderson's Confederates were passing through, having been ordered back to Petersburg by Robert E. Lee. Anderson surprised George Crook's Army of West Virginia as they went into camp along the Berryville Pike, just west of the town.

Although Kershaw had some initial success, the arrival of the rest of the Federals stopped the attack, and Kershaw withdrew. Early brought up the rest of his army that night, but the Union soldiers had dug in, forming an 8-mile line running north to Summit Point, West Virginia. Early decided not to attack, moving his army west to Winchester. Anderson would remain with Early for the time being, but would again depart for Petersburg on September 15.

The marker you are now standing near is the southwest corner of the intersection. If you turn east to look toward the fields across the road on both sides, you will be facing in the direction of the Confederate attack. Most of the fighting happened on the fields around the new high school, on the northeast corner of the intersection. An additional historic marker here, one of ten placed by the J. E. B. Stuart Camp of Confederate Veterans back in 1914, was located here, and has been promised a new home once the construction of the school is finished. Information on these markers can be found at the Clarke County Historical Association Museum, just a short ride away in Berryville.

THIRD WINCHESTER (OPEQUON)

❭ *Turn left onto West Main Street and drive 0.6 mile, and then turn left onto Berryville Pike (VA 7). Drive 6 miles on Berryville Pike; as you drive, you will enter Berryville Canyon. Notice just how steep the walls become as you make your way through toward Winchester. Turn left onto Greenwood Road (SR 656) and drive 0.1 mile, then pull into the church parking lot on your left.*

Beginning on September 6, a hard rain began to fall that would not let up until September 18. Both armies were holding defensive positions at this point, although Sheridan's was not out of necessity. He knew that Anderson's division would be leaving Early's army soon, and he could wait patiently until that happened.

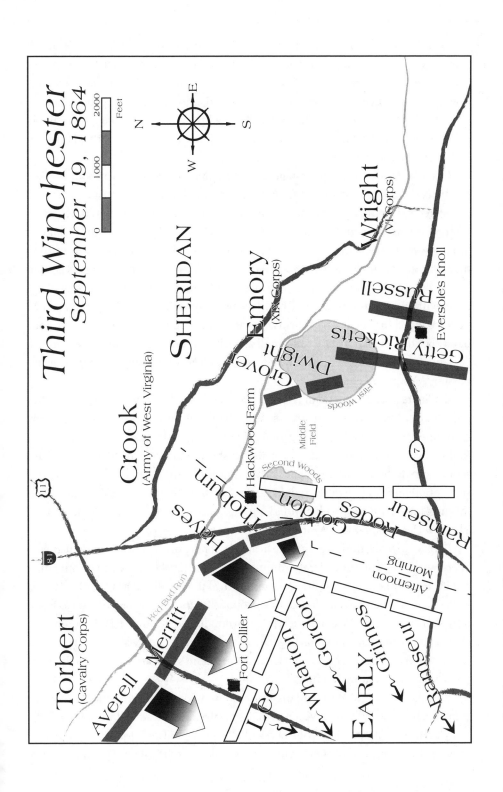

Third Winchester
September 19, 1864

Feet
0   1000   2000

Torbert
(Cavalry Corps)

Crook
(Army of West Virginia)

SHERIDAN

Emory
(XIX Corps)

Wright
(VI Corps)

Eversole's Knoll

Russell

Getty Ricketts

Dwight

Grover

First Woods

Hackwood Farm

Middle Field

Second Woods

Thoburn

Hayes

Gordon

Rodes

Ramseur

Averell

Merritt

Red Bud Run

Fort Collier

Lee

Wharton

Gordon

Grimes

Ramseur

Afternoon

Morning

EARLY

7

11

81

Sheridan had formed a small intelligence network during the downtime, and it soon paid off. A Unionist living in Winchester, a Quaker schoolteacher named Rebecca Wright, had heard from a Confederate officer that Anderson was gone. Receiving the information on September 16, Sheridan immediately began plans for a move to Newtown, south of Winchester. Putting his army here would cut the supply and communication lines of the Confederates, forcing them into battle. However, Sheridan had a surprise visitor: Grant.

Grant had been receiving messages from Washington over concern about the Baltimore & Ohio Railroad, one of Early's primary and favorite targets, and it was for this stated reason that he went to see Sheridan. But Grant had another, much more important reason. He did not want to wait any longer for Sheridan to attack, and he did not want these orders softened, changed, or otherwise mangled by transmitting them through Henry Halleck in Washington. In fact, he had attack plans in his pocket.

He did not need them. When Sheridan met Grant in Charles Towne that afternoon with his new information, Grant listened as he animatedly described his own plan for attacking Jubal Early's army. Grant asked if Sheridan could attack in four days; Sheridan replied that he could, and probably in three. Grant simply responded, "Go in," then went to visit his family in New Jersey before returning to Petersburg, bypassing Washington entirely.

On September 18, Sheridan issued marching orders for 3 PM that afternoon, but quickly countermanded those orders. New intelligence had arrived that Jubal Early committed what could be a fatal mistake. Early had heard a false report that a B&O Railroad crew would be working near Martinsburg. Most commanders would have sent cavalry to harass the crew, but Early did not trust his cavalry. He sent two divisions of infantry to Martinsburg instead, leaving the other two in Winchester. With this new information, Sheridan would not wait until the Confederates could reunite. The new Union target was Winchester.

Early was in Martinsburg when he heard the report that Ulysses S. Grant had paid Sheridan a visit. The Confederate commander immediately realized that something significant may be happening and countermarched the two divisions with him, Robert Rodes's and John Brown Gordon's. Rodes stopped for the night at Stephenson's Depot, only slightly north of Winchester, while Gordon halted at Bunker Hill. Among the Confederate camps, nervous talk began to spread about Grant's visit, and very similar conversations were being held in the Union tents. Grant's appearance could only signal that a very hard fight was coming.

Sheridan had decided to send his entire column down the Berryville Pike toward Winchester. James Wilson's division of 3,300 cavalry would lead and would watch the army's left once it emerged from Berryville Canyon. Wilson's job was to seize the ground at the west end of the narrow canyon, allowing the following units to move through. Setting out at 2 AM, Wilson crossed Opequon Creek at 3:30 AM and made his way through the canyon to find one regiment of Confederate infantry from Stephen Ramseur's division. Had Ramseur placed his infantry close to the mouth of the canyon, he could have easily stopped it up, but he did not, and Wilson was able to seize the ground easily. By 6 AM, Ramseur had two of his brigades on the Berryville Pike, facing off against Wilson's horsemen.

Wesley Merritt's division of cavalry followed Wilson out of the canyon, but turned north, detaching from the main force. Following Merritt was supposed to be the Union infantry, but the only soldier to come out of the canyon was Philip Sheridan, who set his headquarters on Eversole's Knoll, where you are now standing. Although Sheridan was steaming about his infantry's slow progress, he had no one to blame but himself. Instead of using one or more of the other roads approaching Winchester, he had chosen the Berryville Pike, running through a narrow canyon. Before long, the wagons of the VI Corps were stopping up the entire road, and the soldiers chose to make their way along the sides of the canyon. Further, Emory's XIX Corps, which was to follow the VI Corps, was ordered by Horatio Wright that it had to wait until the VI Corps finished its passage through the canyon, and then when these men tried, they, too, had to use the sides, working their way around not only the wagons but the growing number of wounded. It would be 8 AM before the first infantry would emerge from Berryville Canyon, and 10 AM by the time the XIX Corps had finished its passage.

Phil Sheridan's view of the battlefield at Third Winchester from Eversole's Knoll.

The delay in the deployment of the Union infantry would virtually ruin Sheridan's chance of destroying the rebels in pieces. By 6 AM, Early already had all of his divisions moving toward the Federals, and before Ramseur's isolated division could be destroyed, Rodes's and Gordon's men were already on the field, taking their place to Ramseur's left. Jubal Early had needed time, and Sheridan had granted it. Now the two armies would have to stand toe to toe.

Your view here from Eversole's Knoll has changed slightly since the battle, but the key features of the battlefield are still easy to pick out. The first, of course, is the knoll itself, giving you a wide view of the area around you. As you stand in the parking lot of the church and face the Berryville Pike, the battlefield is the ground to your left front. Although the high school complex covers much of the ground today, there is still a good portion of the battlefield left, which begins with the trees in the distance. To your right is the opening of Berryville Canyon, and although the view from here may not give you a complete idea of how narrow it is, your drive through it from Berryville should have given you a pretty good idea of what the Union infantry had to contend with. On your way, you crossed Opequon Creek at a place known as Spout Spring; the battle of Third Winchester is also often referred as the battle of Opequon (pronounced Oh-PEK-un). To your far left, on the pike, is where Ramseur's division held its ground for almost five hours while waiting for the rest of the Confederate infantry to arrive. Note also that the pike makes a noticeable turn to the left, which would become a critical factor during the battle.

❭ *From the church parking lot, turn right onto Greenwood Road and drive 0.3 mile, continuing through the intersection as it becomes First Woods Drive. Turn left here, then follow the road all the way around the high school (about 0.5 mile) to the trailhead for the Third Winchester Battlefield.*

The Confederates set the right of their line, Ramseur's division, on Abraham's Creek, just south of the Berryville Pike, and ran north along the edge of a plateau to Red Bud Run, a small creek to the north. Left of Ramseur's division and forming the Confederate center was Rodes, while Gordon held the left flank. In front of them was a mostly open slope, although it was occasionally broken up here and there by trees, ridges, farm fields, boulders, and other natural features. It was a good defensive position, and the rebels could afford to wait for Sheridan to attack. It also kept both Rodes's and Gordon's divisions out of view of the Federals.

The Union troops, delayed by the mess in the canyon, deployed much more slowly. Wilson's cavalry, breaking off from the fight with Ramseur, went toward Abraham's Creek to protect the Federal left flank. The first infantry division to arrive, George Getty's, turned south to hold the left, running from the creek to the pike. James Ricketts's division anchored itself on the north side of the pike. The last VI

Red Bud Run presented a formidable obstacle to the Federal flanking movement at Third Winchester.

Corps division, David Russell's, would be behind Getty and Ricketts, able to support either one if necessary. When the XIX Corps appeared, Cuvier Grover's division formed at an angle on Ricketts's right in a set of woods, while William Dwight's division lined up to the right rear of Grover, finally forming the Union right. These woods would be known after the battle as the First Woods.

Today, much of the ground where Ramseur and Getty fought has been lost, and the high school covers the middle part of the field. The Third Winchester battlefield trail, though, will take you through where much of the action occurred. Although the tree line has changed a bit over the years, the forest you see at the trailhead is in the same rough position as the First Woods. The total length of the loop trail is 5 miles, but with two different trailheads and several intersections, it does not have to be tackled in one piece. Some parts of the trail are uphill, but for the most part, it is a very easy walk. You are certain to find some of the locals using the trail for recreational purposes, either taking a run or walking their dogs through the park. You will also find several benches and other creative shaded spots to take a break.

The trail will take you through the First Woods, the Middle Field, and the Second Woods, all critical pieces of the battlefield. It will also take you across Red Bud Run to the northern part of the field, as well as to the Confederate line. The signs along the trail are very well done, always letting you know not only where you are but what the field looked like during the battle. For a battlefield that was critically endangered only a few short years ago, the groups that worked to preserve it, such as the Civil War Trust and the Shenandoah Valley Battlefields Foundation, have made this an exceptional place to visit.

At 11:40 AM, Union artillery fired a signal gun that prompted an advance along the entire line. Getty and Ricketts, who were guiding along the Berryville Pike as ordered, followed the turn in the pike, which put their two divisions facing slightly southeast rather than east. This maneuver presented the Federals with two problems, both of which the Confederates took full advantage of. The first was the Ricketts's right was now exposed at an angle to the rebels, and his division took a devastating fire in that flank. The second was that the link between Ricketts's right and Cuvier Grover's right was now broken, creating a massive gap in the Union line.

Robert Rodes's men emerged from the woods and adjusted their line to occupy the obvious gap in the Union center. Rodes ordered Cullen Battle's brigade to charge the gap, and although both Rodes and Battle were killed, the Confederates broke Ricketts's right. The line crumbled all the way down to Getty's division, who was also forced back. Reacting quickly, Sheridan sent David Russell's division into the gap to stop the enemy. The two lines would fight hard, at times hand to hand, for 30 minutes. Russell's stand would cost him his life, as he was killed on the field, but would buy the Federals time and spare a rout of the Union army.

While Getty and Ricketts pressed Stephen Ramseur's division along the pike, Grover's division emerged from the First Woods. In front of it was 600 yards of open ground, now called the Middle Field, with a small tree lot, the Second Woods, behind it. As the Federals crossed the field, Confederate artillery opened up on their right flank, with the fire directed by cavalry commander Fitzhugh Lee. Because of this and other factors (including a drunken staff officer shouting ridiculous orders), Grover's division charged the Second Woods, quickly knocking back the brigade of Georgians holding the ground. The Federals celebrated their gain and kept moving, only to run into more Confederate artillery north of the Hackwood Farm Lane (the now-shaded lane along the trail. Meanwhile, John Brown Gordon brought up his other two brigades, and the two Union divisions were soon forced to withdraw to the First Woods. Dwight's division followed with a similar result, and although several charges were made, the Confederates repulsed every attack. Only the 12th Connecticut and the 8th Vermont would remain on the field, under cover of a very slight ridge line.

While Russell's division made its stand, Emory Upton's Union brigade, which had formed in the First Woods, advanced on the left flank of Rodes's division, now commanded by Bryan Grimes. With this action, the Confederates were finally forced back to their original line, and the Federals were able to withdraw. It was now 1 PM, and the armies were back where they had started. Both were bloodied, but the rebels, whose objective was simply to hold their ground, held the upper hand.

As the firing died down, Sheridan summoned his good friend and West Point roommate George Crook, whose Army of West Virginia had been held in reserve. Sheridan ordered Crook to send his two divisions to the right of Emory's XIX Corps. The 6,000 men under Crook's command hurried to the Union right from Berryville Canyon, where they had been stuck, and it would not be until almost 3 PM that Crook was in position. On the way, Emory asked for one of Crook's divisions, Joseph Thoburn's, to strengthen his line in the First Woods. This left Isaac Duval's division, along with Crook's 18 pieces of artillery, to form on the Union right, extending just beyond the Confederate left.

Whether it was Crook or Sheridan who planned what happened next is not exactly known, but no matter which of the two originated the idea, it was effective. Duval's division formed north of Red Bud Run, a wide, mossy stream that provided quite an obstacle. North of the run, the Confederates had placed the artillery that had so mauled the right flank Emory's men earlier in the day, but that artillery had now

BEST FRIENDS, TO A POINT

Phil Sheridan and George Crook had been roommates at West Point, and remained very close after graduation. Both were talented commanders; still in their midthirties, each led an army in the United States military. Sheridan often confided in Crook, who he knew he could trust. He was also ambitious, however, which later drove a permanent wedge between the two good friends, at least according to a few fairly credible witnesses.

After the war, Sheridan freely claimed credit for the flank attack on the Confederate left at Third Winchester. Almost immediately, several Union officers spoke up and said that the idea had belonged entirely to Crook, whom they had witnessed send a fairly reliable member of his staff—Capt. William McKinley, future president of the United States—to relay the message to Sheridan that he would be making the flanking movement.

A similar occurrence would take place only two days later, when a proposal by Sheridan to turn the Confederate right at Fisher's Hill was flatly rejected by his lieutenants. Crook then presented a plan for turning the left flank instead. Sheridan approved, but wanted to hear the opinions of Crook's two division commanders, both of whom supported the plan. When Sheridan later claimed the idea, it was again discredited by those present, including one of those division commanders—Rutherford B. Hayes, another future president of the United States.

been removed from its commanding hilltop. Crook placed his own artillery there and placed Duval's division at an angle, putting the Federals in position to smash the Confederate left flank.

At 3 PM, a signal gun fired. Thoburn's division attacked the rebels in the Second Woods from the front, while Duval's division approached from the left. Duval himself was wounded, and his men quickly became stuck in the thick mud in and around the run. They also soon found that Gordon had refused his left flank, meaning that the Federals had unexpected guns facing their assault. The combined pressure from the two divisions forced Gordon out of the Second Woods, but they soon found that Grimes's men had also formed a line to face them. As soon as the Federals began to emerge from the Second Woods, they immediately took fire from their front and left, a combination from Gordon's, Grimes's, and Gabriel Wharton's division, which was now on the field.

After being pinned down for an hour, Emory Upton, who had taken command of David Russell's division, began to press the Confederate front, while Ricketts and Getty advanced toward the Confederate right. The rebels withdrew to a more consolidated position north and east of the town, but were still not showing any signs of breaking. Taking advantage of rock ledges, stone walls, and fences, they fiercely defended their position.

As you advance to the Confederate flank portion of the Third Winchester trail, you will come to and cross Red Bud Run. It's a beautiful setting, and it hasn't changed much since the battle—the trees you see on both banks were there, and the marsh was just as it is today. You can also see that for a charging division, the run would present quite a challenge. Following the trail a bit farther will take you to the hilltop where Fitz Lee had placed the Confederate artillery, and where Duval's division lined up before its entry into the battle.

At this point, all signs pointed to the battle becoming a slugfest, with the lines continuing to hammer each other until daylight. Only a sudden shock would change the stalemate. Sheridan, though, had been keeping just such a shock up his sleeve.

⟩ *Drive 0.5 miles back to Berryville Pike, bearing right as you come back around the school. Turn right on Berryville Pike and drive 0.7 mile, and then take the ramp onto I-81 North. Drive 2.1 miles on I-81 to exit 317 for US 11; take the exit and turn right onto US 11 North. Drive 1.5 miles on US 11 to Old Charles Town Road (SR 761). Turn right on Old Charles Town Road and drive 0.4 mile, then turn right onto Milburn Road (SR 662) and pull over at the interpretive signs on the right.*

Earlier in the day, two divisions of Union cavalry had advanced far north of the battlefield, with orders to get in the Confederate rear as soon as possible. Alfred Torbert, in charge of the army's horsemen, had gone with the two divisions, Wesley

Merritt's and William Averell's, to oversee the operation. The cavalry had crossed Opequon Creek at two different points, easily driving back the rebel pickets guarding the fords. However, the Federals soon ran into slightly stronger opposition— Confederate infantry, Wharton's division, who had not yet moved to the battlefield. It would not be until after 11:40 AM when the infantry left for the main Confederate line that the Union cavalry would advance south toward Winchester. Around 12:30 PM, Averell, who was moving on the Valley Pike, and Merritt, east of the pike, ran into three brigades of Fitz Lee's cavalry at Stephenson's Depot. The Federals charged at 1:30 PM, and the two sides charged and countercharged until the rebels were finally forced to retreat. Merritt and Averell took the opportunity to compact their forces, forming a line across the turnpike with Merritt on the left and Averell on the right. Lee would attack again at 3 PM, and although the Confederates did some damage, they were again forced to retreat. Worse, perhaps, Fitzhugh Lee was seriously wounded and taken out of action.

The fields around you are where the major cavalry fight occurred, and it was also in this area that the two Federal cavalry divisions formed their powerful formation that would ultimately make the difference at Third Winchester. As you look at the signs, the Valley Pike (US 11) is only a few hundred yards in front you. Stephenson's Depot itself is now long gone, but at the time of the battle it was a well-known point on the map, and both armies used these fields to camp throughout the war.

⟩ *Turn around on Milburn Road and return to Old Charles Town Road and turn left. Drive 0.4 mile to US 11, then turn left and drive 3.1 miles on US 11 South. Turn left onto Brooke Road (SR 1322), then cross the railroad tracks and turn left into the parking area for Fort Collier.*

For many years, the role of cavalry was very clearly defined. It gathered intelligence, screened an army's movements, and protected an army's flanks during battle. Conventional thinking was that cavalry should not be used to assault infantry, particularly in this war, in which quickly advancing technology made combat so deadly.

Phil Sheridan was not a conventional commander, and he did not view his cavalry as merely a supplement to his army. Whereas Jubal Early viewed his cavalry almost as a necessary evil, Sheridan went to the other extreme. He viewed cavalry as another weapon, truly on a parallel with infantry and artillery, and for the times, he was largely alone in this line of thinking. Sheridan's effective use of cavalry as a powerful strike force during a major battle, the "shock and awe" of its day, would not only change the role that horsemen played in warfare, but would extend itself to the use of tanks and other mechanized armor when they later replaced cavalry on the battlefield. The first major battlefield where Sheridan demonstrated the power cavalry could hold was here at Winchester.

The earthworks at Fort Collier, scene of the devastating Union cavalry charge at Third Winchester.

By 5 PM, Sheridan was riding along the front lines of his infantry, encouraging them to fight on. Even though the Federals were taking a beating, he was there to keep them moving, and his men loved him for it. While he had his limitations as a tactician, no one doubted the influence Sheridan had in the midst of a battle. The most common descriptor of his battlefield presence, then and now, has always been "electrifying." Thus he rode among his men, virtually promising that the Confederates were going to break.

At the same time, the Union cavalry had received Sheridan's order to charge. Alfred Torbert arranged his two divisions across the Valley Pike near Stephenson's Depot—Averell's west of the pike, and Merritt's to the east—with the brigade of George Armstrong Custer centering the massive line. The horses started simultaneously at a trot and increased speed until they were at a full gallop. The Confederate infantry to their front had been removed, leaving little in their front that could stop them.

Merritt's division struck the enemy line here at Fort Collier, an earthwork along the Valley Pike that had been built by Jackson's forces years before. The shocked rebels were quickly driven out of the works. Custer's division hit the earthwork directly, along with the left flank of the Confederate infantry, part of Wharton's division. The brigade to Custer's left, Charles Lowell's, took on elements of Wharton's and Gordon's Confederates, while the leftmost brigade, Thomas Devin's, scored a direct hit on the angle of the line. The Confederates were soon breaking for the rear. Ironically, Col. George Patton, commander of a brigade in Wharton's division, was mortally wounded. Patton's grandson would go on to fame as a general in World War II, due in large part to his development of the United States Army's use of armor.

With two divisions routed, Jubal Early attempted to get the next in line, Bryan Grimes's, to refuse his left and face the attackers, but the line was already beginning to break by the time Early reached the front. Ramseur's division held for a little while longer, and he would eventually form the Confederate rear guard, but with the Federals now at his front, left, and rear, he had no choice but to withdraw.

Fort Collier has held up well over the years, particularly considering the growth around it. As you visit, it may seem a bit odd, with the fort surrounding a very nice-looking home. Although this 1867 home only barely postdates the war, there actually was a house in the middle of the fort during the war. These are among the best-preserved earthworks in this part of Virginia, and as part of the Shenandoah Valley Battlefield Foundation, they will remain that way. You will find several interpretive markers around the fort describing how and why it was built, as well as its role during Third Winchester.

⟩ *Turn right from Fort Collier, then left onto US 11 South (Loudoun Street). Drive 0.5 mile on US 11 South, and then turn right onto Commercial Drive and drive 0.2 mile. Turn right onto Fairmont Avenue (US 511 North) and drive 0.7 mile, then turn right onto Fortress Drive. Drive 0.2 mile and pull over next to Star Fort.*

While Merritt's cavalry division hit the left side of the Confederate infantry, William Averell's division had a much more difficult fight on its hands. In front of it was two brigades of Confederate cavalry; to the soldiers' left was Star Fort, another heavy earthwork. Here, the first Federal charge was not successful, and Thomas Munford's Confederates repulsed the Union horsemen. The second charge was more successful, although it was far from the rout that had come with the infantry. Heavy fighting occurred within the Star Fort, becoming hand to hand, until the Confederates, with no support on their flanks, were forced to withdraw.

Star Fort today is easy to get to and, like Fort Collier, is fairly well preserved. However, for various reasons, you must gain special permission from the Shenandoah Valley Battlefield Foundation to enter the area—at least for the moment. The organization is working to interpret the area and make it safe for visitors so that all can enjoy it in the near future. It lies in the middle of a very nice neighborhood, and the residents keep a watchful eye over the property, so be sure to respect its boundaries. The interpretive signs are more limited than they are at Fort Collier, but even from the outside looking in, it is worth a visit.

By the time the dust had settled, the Confederates were already far along on their retreat south. Sheridan's army held the town, but they had taken too much of a beating to pursue. Their victory was not without great cost. The Federals had suffered 5,018 casualties, making this the bloodiest battle of the valley's history. The Confederates had lost far less in number—approximately 2,000—but they also could not afford to lose the 23 percent of their army that they did.

In the end, Jubal Early had fought a good fight. His decisions were sound, his men had fought well, and he had come close at several points to actually winning the contest. Sheridan's adjustments on the field, though, when accompanied by a three-to-one advantage in manpower, had won the day. Despite the Confederates' extraordinary effort, the most memorable thing about this battle to most people would be that for the first time, the Second Corps of the Army of Northern Virginia— Jackson's corps—had not only been driven from a defensive position, but it had happened, of all places, in the Shenandoah Valley.

FISHER'S HILL

❯ *Turn around and drive 0.2 mile on Fortress Drive to return to Frederick Pike (US 522). Turn right onto Frederick Pike and drive 1 mile, then turn left to take the ramp onto VA 37 South. Drive on VA 37 South for 7 miles, and then exit onto I-81 South and drive 13.2 miles. Take exit 296 and turn right onto John Marshall Highway (US 48 West). Drive 2.2 miles on John Marshall Highway, and then turn left onto Back Road (SR 623) and drive 3.7 miles to Battlefield Road (SR 601). Turn left onto Battlefield Road and drive 0.9 mile to Tumbling Run Lane. Turn right, drive 0.4 mile, and pull over.*

The Federals' stop to rest after the battle of Third Winchester was a brief one. Sheridan could smell blood in the water, and was eager to move in for the kill. Starting out at 5 AM on September 20, Union troops moved as far as Strasburg, 20 miles, setting their line across the Valley Pike facing south toward Fisher's Hill.

The Confederates had immediately and instinctively known where to go after their defeat. Fisher's Hill, the Gibraltar of the Shenandoah, is somewhat of an aberration in the valley, running roughly east to west across for about 4 miles across the valley floor rather than along it. Abutting the east side of the hill is the large, islandlike Massanutten Mountain that separates the main valley from the Luray or Page Valley. On the west, the hill falls just short of Little North Mountain, part of the Allegheny Mountain Range that forms the valley's western boundary. Finally, to its front was a small creek, Tumbling Run, in front of which were several small but prominent positions. The steep, rocky, wooded hill was the strongest defensive point in the entire Shenandoah. It had deterred the Federals from advancing once, and Jubal Early was hoping that it would do so again.

Looking south across the crest of Fisher's Hill.

There was one major difference between this line and the earlier one. The Confederates were now a much smaller force than they had been only a few months ago. Even with its strong defenses, properly defending the position with only 10,000 men would be a very difficult proposition. Early would have to use all of its features and the strengths of his army to his advantage. Unfortunately for the Confederates, he did not do that, and again, his distrust of cavalry was partly to blame.

The east side of Fisher's Hill, where the rebel right lay, was the steepest part of the hill, running along a bend of the North Fork of the Shenandoah River. The position was virtually impregnable, and both the Union and Confederate leaders knew it. Still, rather than defend this flank with a light force (such as cavalry), Early chose to place Gabriel Wharton's division here, along with one battery of artillery. To be sure, its commanding view of the entire valley to his front made this artillery placement ideal, but it was a major overcommitment of manpower.

To Wharton's left was Gordon's division, straddled across the Valley Pike. To his left was the former division of Stephen Ramseur, now commanded by John Pegram. With the death of Robert Rodes the day before, Early needed to shuffle command, and Pegram was rewarded. Forming the left of the infantry line was Rodes's old division, now commanded by Ramseur, extending to the Middle Road. North of Tumbling Run, Early placed sharpshooters along the entire front. The Confederate left was protected by the rebel cavalry, dismounted and acting as infantry, covering the small, open slope from the Middle Road to the base of Little North Mountain. This was the most vulnerable part of the Confederate line.

That is not to say that the line was weak. It was still atop the commanding hill, and the view that they had in front of them virtually assured that they would detect any Federal movement well before it met their lines. Knowing this, the Union commanders, holding a council of war on the evening of September 20, immediately ruled out a frontal assault on the Confederate position. The rebels would have to be outflanked. Sheridan initially wanted to flank their right, but the strength of that position led to its quick dismissal. A movement on the left would be almost impossible unless it could somehow be made undetected.

There would be another controversy after the war as to whose idea the assault was, as Sheridan claimed the credit, but it was likely George Crook's. The plan required the utmost speed, secrecy, and discipline among the entire army to be successful. Crook's Army of West Virginia would need to move immediately, while it was still dark, to get to the west face of Little North Mountain, out of view of the enemy. The men would then have to wait out the next day, concealing their presence as best they could. The VI and XIX Corps would then form a line closer to the Confederate front. While these forces occupied the rebels' attention in their front, Crook's men would bear down swiftly on the Confederate left flank, taking them by surprise. To top off the plan, Wesley Merritt's and James Wilson's divisions of cavalry would ride to Front Royal to pass through the Luray Valley, crossing the Luray Gap at New Market and blocking the enemy's escape route. Success on all fronts would mean the capture or destruction of the Confederate Army of the Valley.

Crook's men moved north of Cedar Creek that night, then stayed under the cover of trees all through September 21. In the afternoon, the VI and XIX Corps advanced on several points, taking a few of the hilltops in front of the Confederate line. The most prominent of these was Flint Hill, a rise with an obstructed view of what would be the battlefield. The Union line now stretched for 2 miles west of Strasburg. When darkness fell, William Emory's XIX Corps moved east of the Manassas Gap Railroad, while Horatio Wright's VI Corps sidled westward to extend their line. Artillery was massed on and around Flint Hill. Shortly after daybreak, Crook's men wound their way around to Little North Mountain, reaching their position on the western slope in the afternoon. William Averell's cavalry division also positioned itself on the Back Road, across from the Confederate left, screening Crook's movement.

On September 22, at 11:30 AM, the Federals began to build pressure all along the Confederate front. Emory's men rushed forward and took more of the rebel works at 12:45 PM, placing themselves only 500 yards away from the enemy line. Around 1:30

PM, James Ricketts's division, holding the Union right, began to press hard on the Confederate left.

Early, watching from atop Fisher's Hill, had not seen Crook's column moving to Little North Mountain, but he had seen enough. He knew that his line was far too thin and that he could only hold his position for so long. Around 2 PM, he issued orders to his commanders, outlining a withdrawal as soon as darkness fell. The Confederates had not given ground yet, but with the small force he had left, it was only a matter of time. Unfortunately for them, Early's orders came too late to make a difference.

At about the same time, Crook's Federals were slowly making their way down the mountain to the small valley across from the Confederate left flank. Advancing to within 200 yards of the rebel pickets, each of the two divisions halted to form two lines, stacking their brigades only 15 to 20 yards apart. It was only just as they finished that the 5,500 Union soldiers of the Army of West Virginia began to take artillery fire. In front of them were Lunsford Lomax's dismounted Confederate cavalrymen and the left flank of the rebel line.

At 4 PM, Crook gave the order. The Federals, as brigade commander Rutherford B. Hayes put it, rushed at the Confederates with "no line, nor order, all yelling like madmen." The surprise could not have been more complete. Lomax's cavalrymen made little attempt at holding its ground, quickly breaking for the rear. The Union charge kept up its momentum as it ascended the western slope of what would afterward be known as Ramseur's Hill.

You are now in a small valley that broke the Confederate line slightly. To your west, Little North Mountain is only a short distance away, and it was from here that Crook's assault began. Turn and face north so that the mountain is at your left. You are now facing the same direction the Confederates were, toward the main Union line, with Crook coming at you from your left side. Lomax's dismounted horsemen ran through this valley, with Crook's Federals only slightly behind them, making their way up the tree-covered hill to your right, atop which the Confederate left flank was perched.

❭ *Turn around on Tumbling Run and drive 0.4 mile to return to Battlefield Drive. Turn right and drive 0.3 mile, and then pull into the parking area for Fisher's Hill battlefield on your right.*

After you pull up to the small parking area at the Fisher's Hill Battlefield, cared for by the Shenandoah Valley Battlefields Foundation, walk to your left and cross the bridge over the small stream. This stream is Tumbling Run, running along the base of Fisher's Hill. Fisher's Hill is, more accurately, a series of ridges, and the one in front of you is Ramseur's Hill, where the Confederate left flank was left hanging. The trail here is a 1-mile loop, and although it does go up the hill and back down, it is not overly strenuous, and the foundation does a good job of maintaining the path, which is mown grass throughout its length.

From your position here at the bottom of the hill, you are looking from the direction of James Ricketts's Union division, just before it made its assault up the hill. Crook's flank attack came from your right. Walk up the trail until you get to the second trail marker (a wooden post marked "2"), about halfway up the hill, then turn and face the roadway.

When Stephen Ramseur realized that the Federals were streaming rapidly toward his left flank, he moved his closest brigade, Cullen Battle's, to meet the threat head on, while also turning his artillery to the left. The Federals were slowed but not stopped, and the Union rank approached to within 60 yards of Battle's front. Ramseur sent a second brigade to aid him, but remarkably, William Cox's Confederates became lost in the woods and passed right by the Union force.

At nearly the same time, Rutherford B. Hayes's Union brigade moved to its right, passing around the end of the Confederates. Ramseur's division was now taking fire from the left and the rear of the main enemy line. Things quickly worsened when James Ricketts's division of the VI Corps charged down from their position, through Tumbling Run, and up Fisher's Hill toward the rebels. Now being hit on three sides, the Confederates began to break for the rear, one regiment at a time. After Battle's brigade went Bryan Grimes's, then Philip Cook's, finishing off Ramseur's division. The Federals went down the line with their assault, working on the next Confederate

BETWEEN A ROCK AND A HARD PLACE

Some military commanders lead by example. Others inspire. The best do both of these and more, using almost any means necessary to motivate their soldiers to answer the call of duty. At times, this might mean taking some tough action. At Fisher's Hill, both Cullen Battle and George Crook were forced to resort to this last method to keep their men in place.

Battle, attempting to hold the Confederate left flank so the rest of the army could meet the Union attack, stormed up and down his line, cursing any rebel soldier who dared to turn and run. When more harsh means were necessary, he brandished his preferred tool, a large cedar stick, and administered a punishing whack.

Crook was forced to improvise. As the Confederates fiercely resisted the Union assault, some of his men turned back for the safety of the woods they had left. As they attempted to pass their commander, a furious Crook began picking up rocks and firing them at the offenders. Most, it is said, returned to the line rather than receive Crook's embarrassing reprimand.

division to their left, John Pegram's, by sending George Getty's Federals up the hill, while the rest of the Federals kept pushing down the Confederate left flank. Jubal Early tried to send Gabriel Wharton's division to the left to stop the Union wave, but it was already far too late.

Looking across the roadway, the large hill somewhat to your right front is Flint Hill. To your far right, east, is towering Massanutten Mountain. You can now look down the hill and see just how naturally strong Fisher's Hill was as a defensive position, and what the Federals had to overcome to reach this point. Ricketts's division would have made their assault from your front.

Moving farther along the trail, you will come to an interpretive sign alongside an old, large tree. (There is also a bench here in case you need to take a break from your climb.) This is approximately where Ramseur refused his left and sent Cullen Battle's brigade to stop the Federals. The area around you probably saw the heaviest action of the battle. As you face the sign, the small valley from your last stop is not far beyond the trees to your left. The tree was used as a Confederate signal station while the rebels were manning the hill. Turn and face the tree, and you can try to imagine what Battle's Confederates had to try to stop—most of Crook's men would have come from your front, while you also took enfilading fire from your left side, Hayes's brigade, and your right, Ricketts's division.

Complete the loop around the battlefield. The views from atop Fisher's Hill as you walk around are fantastic, so take your time with this stroll and enjoy the scenery.

> ❯ *Pull out to the right on Battlefield Road and drive 1 mile to Copp Road (SR 757). Turn right onto Copp Road and drive 0.6 mile, and then turn left onto Locust Grove Road (SR 641) and drive 0.4 mile. Safely pull over close to the railroad tracks.*

Carefully exit your car and face to the northeast, the wooded grove on the hilltop. This was the position of John Brown Gordon's division, the next Confederate division in the line. The Federals kept pushing east, with Frank Wheaton's division now pushing the Confederate front. Gordon's men, like the rest, soon began streaming backward across where you now stand. The railroad here is in the same spot as the old Manassas Gap Railroad, present at the time of the battle.

Gordon's men were the last Confederates west of the Valley Pike. Wharton's reinforcements, originally east of the pike, had no one to support, and began falling back with the rest of the rebels, with Emory's XIX Corps taking its position on Fisher's Hill. The Union troops pursued Early's men down the Valley Turnpike until after dark, capturing many. What was left of the Army of the Valley moved throughout a stormy night, finally coming to a stop at Mount Jackson.

After the battle was finished, both commanders took the time to wire their commanders. Early notified Robert E. Lee at 4 AM the next morning of the dreadful loss:

1,235 casualties, almost 1,000 of which were missing or captured, along with 14 guns. He also asked for Lee to return Joseph Kershaw's division of Robert Anderson's corps to the valley. Sheridan, who had gone up Fisher's Hill with the VI Corps, was quicker to pass on his good news: Early's army had been destroyed, at a cost of 456 casualties.

As sound a defeat as this was, it could have been worse for the Confederates. Sheridan's cavalry, which was supposed to block the escape, did not make it through the Luray Gap, being held up by enemy cavalry. More important, Sheridan's intimation that the Confederate Army of the Valley was finished was somewhat premature. The rebels eventually withdrew all the way to Brown's Gap, near Port Republic, reaching the gap on September 25. The next day, Joseph Kershaw's division joined Early at the gap, along with 12 pieces of artillery. The Federals had stopped their pursuit at Harrisonburg the same day. Despite pressure to relieve Jubal Early from command, Lee would not and could not let go of his "Bad Old Man." There was nobody better, for one, and Early had performed well. And he was not done yet.

The next chapter, though, in the Shenandoah Valley campaign of 1864 did not involve the Confederates, although they were still present. Sheridan was certain that the first part of his mission, to destroy Early's army, was complete. Now it was time to move on to the second part: the destruction of the valley.

TOM'S BROOK AND THE BURNING

> *Continue on Locust Grove Road 0.4 mile, then turn right onto US 11 South. Drive 3.4 miles on US 11 to the entrance for Shenandoah County Park on your left. Turn left onto Park Road and drive 0.2 mile; pull around the tennis courts on your left and park, then walk to the interpretive sign.*

The Union Army of the Shenandoah reached Harrisonburg on September 26. Phil Sheridan did not want to push farther; his lines were already stretched thin. But there was work to be done. Sheridan sent out his men, mostly cavalry, to begin the next phase of the campaign. For the next ten days, the Federals proceeded to burn, confiscate, or use every piece of property in the valley that could possibly aid the Confederate cause. Barns full of the fall's harvest went up in flames, as did flour mills. Livestock was driven off to be used by the Union army. Private homes, for the most part, were left alone, but anything else that was part of making the Shenandoah Valley the "Breadbasket of the Confederacy" was destroyed.

Beginning their work from Harrisonburg, the Union army turned the Shenandoah into a virtual wall of fire. Sheridan's orders had been to oversee the destruction of the valley's war making capacity. Complete did not even begin to describe it. The Shenandoah Valley was turned into a wasteland. On October 5, Sheridan's men slowly began to move north down the valley, performing the same destructive work from

Harrisonburg all the way to Strasburg. Sheridan's final estimates included burning more than 2,000 barns, over 70 mills, confiscating 4,000 head of livestock, butchering 3,000 sheep for the army, and taking numerous horses from the farms of the valley. As a result, thousands of refugees—farmers, slaves, Mennonites, many of them Unionist—fled the area and abandoned their farms. From a distance, the rebel soldiers watched helplessly and angrily.

One thing that Jubal Early could do was harass the enemy as it went about on its destructive mission, and for that he would need his own cavalry. Acquiring additional horsemen from Robert E. Lee, Early sent them north on October 6 to follow the Federals as they moved from Harrisonburg to Strasburg. His new division commander, Thomas Rosser, took his men along the Back Road, on the west side of the valley, while Lunsford Lomax used the Valley Pike.

Only a few days into their mission, the two cavalry divisions went into camp along the Valley Pike on October 8—Rosser at Tom's Brook, to your west, and Lomax at Woodstock, the ground you are now standing on. Only a few miles north of both divisions were the Union cavalry, wrapping up their work in the area. In fact, Wesley Merritt's troopers were only 3 miles north of the Confederates, while George Armstrong Custer's division was not far from Rosser's men.

George Custer had only been commanding a division for less than a month. His promotion came partly because of a command reshuffle made necessary after Sheridan relieved William Averell. Sheridan believed Averell had not pursued the Confederates vigorously enough after Fisher's Hill, and if there was anything that raised Little Phil's ire, it was laziness, real, perceived, or otherwise. Now, his cavalry had allowed the rebels to pursue them for three days without a challenge, and this did not sit well. He ordered his chief of cavalry, Alfred Torbert, to attack the two Confederate divisions at daylight. To further emphasize his expectations, he let Torbert know that he would personally be watching the attack from Round Top Mountain.

Merritt's and Custer's divisions, totaling 4,000 men, began moving early, Custer on the Back Road and Merritt on the pike. First contact occurred around 7 AM, when Merritt met Lomax's skirmishers, to your front as you face the sign. The small ridge you stand on was where Lomax had placed his line, with the rebel camp behind you. After the Union assault began to pressure the Confederate line, Lomax thrust forward in a countercharge, driving the Federal brigade to his front back toward Strasburg.

Unfortunately for the Confederates, Lomax had pushed far enough that Thomas Devin's brigade now had an easy shot at their left. Turning his men only slightly, Devin slammed into Lomax's now exposed flank, driving him back to his original line.

On the Back Road, Custer had a more difficult time with Rosser's troops, but after a long stalemate launched a charge against the Confederate left. Rosser's men broke, and Custer's division chased them for 2 miles to Pugh's Run. Hearing the commotion,

Merritt ordered another Union advance. Lomax had heard the fighting, too, and was already pulling back to open ground to your rear. When Merritt finally called the charge, Lomax's line was split into two, and both Confederate divisions were breaking rearward.

Merritt and Custer pursued their prey for 26 miles, rounding up many prisoners along the way. Also part of the spoils were 45 wagons, four cannons, and 68 horses and mules. The battle at Tom's Brook would also be known as the "Woodstock Races" for the haste with which the rebels left their position. As far as Sheridan was concerned, this was further proof that the Confederates in the Shenandoah Valley had been broken.

With no more Confederates and the Burning coming to its end, Sheridan considered his mission accomplished. As his army went into camp north and south of Cedar Creek, Sheridan wired Grant, telling him that his work was done here, and that he was sending the VI Corps back to the Army of the Potomac. (Sheridan was one of those rare commanders that only wanted exactly as many men as he needed, no more and no less, so that his soldiers could do good elsewhere if needed.) Although he later countermanded his order, he expected that he would not be in the valley much longer. There was simply nothing left for him here, and he could not stand to sit still while there was a war going on. He needn't have worried. Jubal Early was about to give Phil Sheridan plenty to do.

CEDAR CREEK

❭ *Drive 0.2 mile on Park Road to return to US 11 and turn right. Drive 6.6 miles on US 11, and then turn left to continue on US 11 as it changes to North Massanutten Street. Continue on US 11 for 1 mile, then enter the parking area for Hupp's Hill on your left.*

Robert E. Lee had sent Jubal Early and the Confederate Second Corps to the Shenandoah Valley to take pressure off his army at Petersburg. Early's successes had been brilliant, and his losses, though decisive, had not been a result of poor generalship but instead being badly outnumbered. Lee had resisted every call to take Early away from his army, but the pressure around Petersburg was growing by the day. Lee understood better than most others that Early had been performing valuable service. Even now, while the Army of the Valley was truly on its last legs, Lee would ask Early to help him take one more gamble. More trouble in the valley, before the November elections and before the armies went into winter camp, meant fewer Union troops at Petersburg. Lee asked his beloved lieutenant for one more victory in the Shenandoah Valley, and Early would do his best to give it to him.

From New Market on October 11, the Confederates slowly began to move north toward the Federals. On October 13, forming a line at Hupp's Hill near Strasburg, their artillery lobbed a few shells into the Union camps while simultaneously performing a

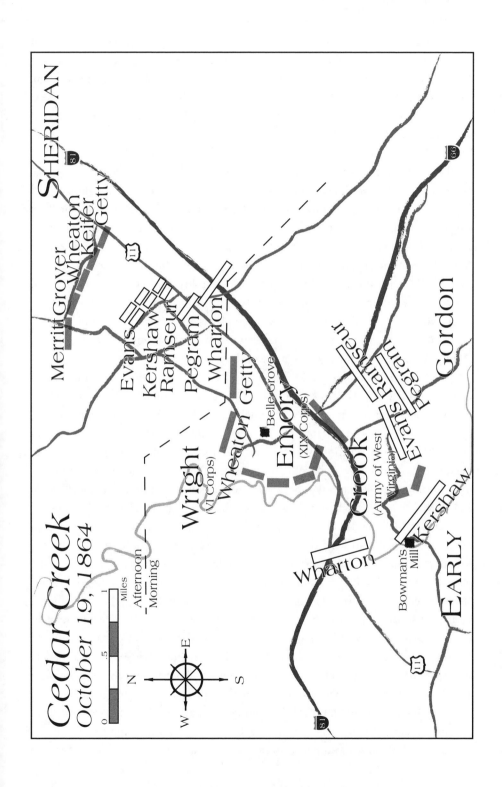

Cedar Creek
October 19, 1864

SHERIDAN

Merritt
Grover
Wheaton
Keifer
Getty

Evans
Kershaw
Ramseur
Pegram
Wharton

Wright
(VI Corps)

Wheaton
Getty

Belle Grove

Emory
(XIX Corps)

Ramseur

Evans
Pegram

Crook
(Army of West Virginia)

Wharton

Bowman's
Mill

Kershaw

Gordon

EARLY

N
E
S
W

Miles
0   .5   1

Afternoon
Morning

forced reconnaissance near Cedar Creek. It was this small but informative action that caused Sheridan to countermand the order sending the Union VI Corps away. The rebels had not gone away, and although there did not seem to be very many of them, Sheridan grew cautious.

When summoned to Washington the next day by Edwin Stanton, Sheridan first made sure that the Confederates were not moving, and only then agreed to the visit. Besides, his army, although scattered by the many ridges in the area, was in a position good enough to beat the rebels back even if they did attack. The army was on a large plain north of Cedar Creek, just south of Strasburg. Sheridan's best men, the VI Corps, were camped near his line's most vulnerable point, his right, around the Belle Grove mansion. A Confederate advance on the Union left was almost unthinkable because of the terrain and the fact that it was roughly (very roughly) anchored on the North Fork of the Shenandoah River and Massanutten Mountain. Accordingly, the Union XIX Corps and George Crook's Army of West Virginia were camped in isolated spots, and only minor earthworks, if any, were constructed. The likelihood of the enemy's attacking the Federal line, on an open plain with almost no possibility of surprise, was slim. So Sheridan and his staff left for Washington on October 15, placing Horatio Wright in temporary command of the Army of the Shenandoah.

While Sheridan was meeting Stanton and Grant on October 17, John Brown Gordon and Jedediah Hotchkiss, part of Early's staff and Stonewall Jackson's famous cartographer, climbed Massanutten Mountain to survey the Federal position. Gordon surveyed the position while Hotchkiss sketched, getting as many details as they could about the Union disposition. What the two men saw was an army at rest, leisurely making the transition from hard fighting to camp life. They also saw weaknesses—many weaknesses—in the Union position. Coming down from the mountain, Gordon and Hotchkiss went straight to Early to pass on their findings and plan the rebel assault.

October 18 was a day of planning for the Confederates, with Early gathering all of his subordinates to hear their ideas. Having seen the terrain and making the soundest argument, John Brown Gordon was the one who presented the ultimate plan. It was risky, but if successful could possibly earn the victory that Lee so desperately needed. Gordon would lead his men on a night march along the base of Massanutten Mountain toward the Union left, while the other rebel divisions readied themselves for an early morning assault. The Federal divisions were all isolated to some extent, and with a coordinated effort and surprise on their side, the Confederates might be able to take them apart piece by piece. All present approved of the plan, and preparations were made to move that night. The attack would begin at 5 AM.

You are standing on Hupp's Hill. Looking down at the town of Strasburg (or in any direction, for that matter), you can see that this is a commanding rise, and it was occupied by both armies numerous times as they made their way up and down the valley. The hill is now home to the Hupp's Hill Cedar Creek Museum, a new visitor's center operated by the Cedar Creek Battlefield Foundation. Although still developing, the museum now contains excellent exhibits on not only the battle of Cedar Creek but all the events in the Shenandoah Valley. There is an excellent diorama of the entire Cedar Creek battlefield that will help you interpret what you're going to see. The displays here, along with a small theater showing two different films about the battle, are already great, but there are already plans to increase the amount of exhibits in the large space. In front of the museum building, you will also find a nice walking trail that will take you past some Civil War earthworks—built after the battle at Cedar Creek, but well preserved nonetheless. Formerly the Stonewall Jackson Museum, it has been upgraded nicely, and the new center promises a bright future for the interpretation of the battlefield.

> *Turn right onto US 11 and drive 0.9 mile, then turn left onto East Washington Street. Drive 0.6 mile, and then continue left onto Bowmans Mill Road (SR 635) and drive another 1.2 miles. Cross the small bridge and pull over.*

After sundown on October 18, Early's entire army—there would be no reserves anymore, at least not by design—was on the move. The first to move were Confederate engineers, preceding the Confederate forces to ensure that the trails were marked clearly enough for a night march. The infantry left at 8 PM, headed for several different crossing points of the North Fork of the Shenandoah River. While the exact route of the march is not known for certain, it is known that the rebels were forced to move along a very tight passage along the base of Massanutten Mountain, so tight as to require single-file marching. Also required was complete silence; there was no talking, and any equipment that would make noise—canteens, cartridge boxes—were either muffled or left behind.

Gabriel Wharton's division stayed on the Valley Pike, moving to Hupp's Hill with the artillery and waiting there to move as the situation dictated. The Confederate Second Corps—Gordon's, Pegram's, and Ramseur's divisions—crossed using fords to the east, while Joseph Kershaw's division crossed here, at Bowman's Mill Ford. In front of them, atop the hill you are now facing, was the isolated position of Joseph Thoburn's division of the Army of West Virginia, still sound asleep.

The bridge you just crossed over is in the area of the ford used by Kershaw's men. Jubal Early was also among them, making sure that Kershaw knew exactly where to attack by pointing out the glow of the Union campfires, then moving on to accompany Wharton's division. The Confederates crossed the ford and then formed into battle lines, waiting for the moment of the attack to come.

> *Continue 0.2 mile on Bowmans Mill Road, then turn right onto Long Meadow Road. Drive 1.6 mile on Long Meadow Road and pull over just after the curve in the road.*

Gordon's division, commanded by Clement Evans while Gordon assumed command of the Second Corps, crossed at Bowman's Ford (not to be confused with Bowman's Mill Ford, where Kershaw crossed), with Stephen Ramseur's and John Pegram's divisions following. After crossing (the ford is located behind the private property to your right rear), Gordon advanced on this road a mile and a half to the Cooley House, well to the left of Thoburn's Federals, to put themselves in position to hit the other division of Crook's Army of West Virginia, Rutherford B. Hayes.' At that point, the entire division turned to the left (west), they too waiting for 5 AM to arrive.

> Continue 0.8 mile on Long Meadow Road, then turn left onto Bowmans Mill Road (SR 635). Drive 1.3 miles and pull over near the gate on your right.

The pending Confederate attack was actually detected far before the 5 AM start time. It began with the pickets of the XIX Corps, who had noticed that they were no longer receiving signals from the pickets of Thoburn's division. Around 4 AM, some firing was heard in the direction of Bowman's Mill Ford, but it was easily explained. Horatio Wright, temporary commander of the army in Sheridan's absence, had arranged for a reconnaissance to begin at daylight. Almost every report of firing, marching, and other noises was dismissed out of hand.

While many of Joseph Thoburn's soldiers who were awake before 5 AM heard suspicious sounds coming from the darkness, virtually all of Joseph Kershaw's Confederates heard the enemy. They had crept up so close to the Federal position that the voices of those Union men who were already awake could be heard clearly. However, they could not see them. A heavy fog entered the low areas of the valley around 4 AM, and would stay throughout much of the morning. This fog would be both a blessing and a curse to both sides throughout the early part of the battle.

The road that you drove in on to get to this position, State Route 635, roughly follows the line of earthworks that Thoburn's Federals had established. The Union line would have been to your right side as you went along the road, and extended past the sharp angle you see here. Some of those earthworks remain, and as you face the gate here, the open space in front of you has been preserved by the Shenandoah Valley Battlefields Foundation. While it is not yet open for interpretation, hopefully you will one day be able to walk these grounds.

Thoburn's position here was almost completely isolated from the rest of the Union army, which was scattered in different pieces north of Cedar Creek. That, along with the scant earthworks put up by the Confederates, gives some indication about just how unlikely the Federals thought would be a rebel attack on their left. It was an extremely unwise placement of troops, as Kershaw's men were about to demonstrate. Most of the trees you see beyond the field were not present at the time of the battle.

Hayes's division, in camp about a half-mile away to your right, would have been clearly visible, although they had not formed any defensive works. .

Turn around so that the gate is at your back. Looking downhill, the Confederates would have been lined up about a half-mile to your right front. Kershaw had ordered his men not to fire until they reached the Union line, which they obeyed with relative ease, hidden by the fog. At almost precisely 5 AM—the Confederate commanders had all synchronized their watches so that the attack would come simultaneously—Kershaw's lead brigade charged up the hill. Unfortunately, the other three brigades were not yet prepared to move, but it mattered little. The Confederates hit Thoburn's line almost exactly where its two brigades met, and the rebels poured into the tiny gap. Advancing in both directions down the line, the men of both brigades were either captured, killed, or were running north toward the position of the XIX Corps. The fall of Thoburn's position took approximately 15 minutes.

Gabriel Wharton's division, moving along the pike, had only slightly less success, but success nonetheless. North of Thoburn's infantry, Henry DuPont's three batteries of Union artillery were set on a ridge overlooking the bridge over Cedar Creek. DuPont's men were already up with their guns ready, and although the first battery was overrun without being able to fire a single round, the second battery unleashed a volley of canister into the fog, directing their fire only by the sound of the rebel yell. Immediately afterward, DuPont ordered that the guns been withdrawn, then rode to the third battery, where he split his fire toward both Wharton's and Kershaw's troops. Although many of DuPont's artillery was captured (at least for the moment), his batteries' fire was enough to slightly slow the Confederate advance, and he would receive the Congressional Medal of Honor for his actions here.

John Brown Gordon's men began their assault on Rutherford B. Hayes's position at 5:20 AM. Hayes's men had already been made aware that something was going on, mostly by the scattered Union soldiers running through their camp. However, the fog prevented them from seeing what was coming, and they had only slightly more warning than Thoburn's men had had. Evans's and Ramseur's divisions hit the enemy camp directly while most of the Federals were still lining up for battle, and what little resistance there had been quickly dissolved into a rout. In little more than a half an hour, the entire Army of West Virginia had been swept away, taken piecemeal just as designed. Next in line was William Emory's XIX Corps, whose left flank had just been completely exposed.

It was around this time, though, that one of the Confederates' primary weaknesses, one that had plagued them throughout the war, would have a direct effect on the ultimate outcome of the day's fight. Supply problems had dogged not only Jubal Early's campaign but virtually every campaign in the Eastern Theater. As the rebels streamed through the abandoned Union camps, many eyes began to wander to things left behind that they did not have—simple things, such as shoes, clothing, blankets, and, of course, food, some of which had already been prepared just in time for breakfast. It was not long before the Confederate ranks began to thin out not due to enemy fire but instead to their own empty stomachs and bare feet.

⟩ *Carefully turn around and drive 1.3 miles on Bowmans Mill Road to return to Long Meadow Road. Turn left and drive 0.1 mile to Water Plant Road, and then drive 1.1 miles to US 11. Turn right onto US 11, then immediately pull into the gravel area with the large monument on your left.*

By the time the rebels began to approach William Emory's XIX Corps line, he had at least been able to arrange some sort of defense. It was Emory's men who were scheduled to conduct a reconnaissance at daylight, and they were already awake, fed, and ready to move. Although it was not long before Confederate artillery placed on Hupp's Hill began shelling the Union line, Emory had enough time to shift some regiments to his left, refusing his flank and lining it up along the Valley Pike. He also sent the 8th Vermont and the 12th Connecticut, the same two regiments that had held so bravely at Winchester a month earlier, to form in the woods east of the pike along with the 160th New York and face the fire coming down on their flank. As Clement Evans's Confederates bore down on the Union left, these three regiments would take over 350 casualties in only 10 minutes.

Belle Grove, Union headquarters before and after the battle of Cedar Creek.

As Wharton's division pressed from the southwest and Evans's and Ramseur's divisions approached from the east, Emory, along with some rallied elements of Crook's men, held the Confederates at bay. The fighting became hand to hand. Joseph Thoburn was mortally wounded during the fight. It was not long until Horatio Wright came riding up from Union headquarters at Belle Grove mansion, north and slightly east of Emory's position. It was decided that Emory must make his stand here, and it was a critical one. Just beyond Belle Grove, where the Union VI Corps was getting ready for action, were the army's wagons and livestock. They were already moving to safety, but they needed time. The outnumbered XIX Corps was eventually pushed northwest across a small stream, Meadow Brook, but they held long enough, almost a full hour, to enable the Federal supplies from falling into enemy hands.

The monument here commemorates the actions of the 128th New York infantry, who held what was originally the Union left flank of the XIX Corps but eventually became the point of the angle formed when Emory deployed units along the Valley Pike. Just past the monument, there is a nicely interpreted and recently updated walking trail that will take you along the XIX Corps entrenchments overlooking Cedar Creek. The trail is just under a mile long, but it is not a loop, so you will have to hike back. Still, the trail is of the best-preserved features of the battle.

> *Pull out to your left onto US 11 and drive 0.9 mile to the Cedar Creek Battlefield Foundation on your right.*

Site of the final Confederate line at Cedar Creek.

This is the original home of the Cedar Creek Battlefield Foundation, the group behind some extraordinary preservation efforts during its relatively short existence. When compared to its new center at Hupp's Hill, this building may seem like a bit of a shack, but there is an excellent shop inside, along with a knowledgeable and helpful staff. The center also still houses some exhibits and artifacts pertaining to the battle, so if you catch it during its open hours, be sure to stop in.

The ground that the center sits on along the Valley Pike would have been near where Stephen Ramseur's division overlapped the Union left, eventually pushing and pursuing the rest of the XIX Corps across the fields across from the center. In the distance, the large mansion of Belle Grove, Union headquarters and a centerpiece of the battle, can easily be seen. As you face the road, you are looking northwest in the direction of Ramseur's advance, with Emory's right and the rallied but fragile elements of Crook's Army of West Virginia retreating in your front toward Belle Grove.

⟩ *Pull out to your left onto US 11 and drive 0.2 mile, then turn left onto Belle Grove Road. Follow the road 0.5 mile to the parking area for Belle Grove.*

Between 6:30 and 7 AM, the Confederates were pushing the XIX Corps through the grounds around Belle Grove. Belle Grove had been the headquarters for the Union Army of the Shenandoah since the soldiers went into camp here, and taking a quick look at the home and the grounds, it's no wonder. Both in its day and today, Belle Grove and the surrounding countryside is one of the most beautiful mansions in the entire Shenandoah Valley. Unfortunately, on October 19, 1864, it also found itself in the midst of a major battle.

Belle Grove was completed in 1797, and its first residents were practically royalty. Isaac Hite, a member of the Shenandoah Valley's wealthiest and most well-known family, had taken the hand of Nelly Conway Madison, sister of founding father and future president James Madison. The architect of the house was recommended by none other than Thomas Jefferson, who also made numerous visits to the home. The manor was not only the center of a massive grain plantation of 7,500 acres, but also the valley's social scene, as the Hites and their descendants held spectacular galas in the home.

While you are here, take a walk onto the front lawn of the manor. Looking away from the house and to your left, you will see the Valley Pike in the distance, along with the fields over which the Federal line was pushed by Early's army. If you turn to face the house, the Union VI Corps, as well as what was left of William Emory's XIX Corps, were forming defensive lines just a short distance away. Also, if you come just a bit closer to the home, look to the right of the columned porch on the second story, just to the right of the closest window. You will find that a large chunk has been taken out of the finished granite facing the home. This is the result of a Confederate cannonball that dealt a glancing blow to the home. It is a wonder that the home did not suffer more damage in the fight, but the two armies passed through the grounds relatively quickly.

The National Park Service, one of several partners operating Cedar Creek and Belle Grove National Historical Park, now conducts several programs about the battle here at Belle Grove. You may also tour the mansion itself to hear about not only the battle but also the remarkable stories of the families and people who lived and died here. The tour is very well done, and the knowledge of the guides here is remarkable. As you go through the home, pay particular attention to the nursery, as it will play a further part in the story of the battle.

❭ *Turn right onto Belle Grove Road and drive 0.2 mile, then park in the church parking lot on your left.*

With Horatio Wright in command of the army while Sheridan was in Washington, James Ricketts had assumed temporary command of the VI Corps, which was already up and moving well before the XIX Corps and George Crook's men began streaming through their camps in retreat. Ricketts moved his three divisions into line on high ground just to the west of Meadow Brook. George Getty's division was placed on the left, with Frank Wheaton's just to his right. To Wheaton's right was Ricketts's division, temporarily commanded by Col. Warren Keifer. As Emory's men crossed Meadow Brook, those troops that he could rally were placed along the brook to the right of the VI Corps.

Already trying to deal with the chaos caused by a surprise attack, the fog obscuring the field, and thousands of soldiers fleeing through their lines, a further confounding factor was presented to the VI Corps. Just as the lines were being set, its commander, James Ricketts, was wounded and taken from the field. The next officer in line for command was George Getty, but there was no time to inform him. The Confederates were already in front of them.

Kershaw's men were met with a heavy volley of canister and musketry as soon as they approached the Union line, and the enemy followed this up with a surprising counterattack that, for the first time this day, stopped the Confederate advance. The Union position was on the first of a series of rises known as Red Hill. A second thrust by the rebels was also unsuccessful, although by this time John Brown Gordon (again in command of his own division) and Stephen Ramseur were bringing their division up, overlapping the Union left. The VI Corps fought hard at and around Red Hill for almost an hour before being forced back, and when it did withdraw, it did so fighting, greatly slowing the Confederate advance. Keifer and Wheaton withdrew their troops to the northeast. George Getty's moved only slightly. They had not yet been brought into the fight.

Walk to where the railroad tracks cross the road and look away from the church. The rise to your front left is Red Hill, where the VI Corps and, for a time, the XIX Corps finally slowed the Confederate juggernaut. Just beyond the tracks is Meadow

Brook, not a large stream but enough to hamper the deployment of the VI Corps to aid the other pieces of the Union army.

⟩ *From the church parking lot, turn right onto Belle Grove Road, then left onto Meadow Mills Road (SR 624). Drive 0.8 mile to Veterans Road (SR 625). As you drive, the fields to your left held the Union wagons at the beginning of the battle, and it was over these fields that the Confederates continued to push the Union lines from ridge to ridge. Turn left on Veterans Road and drive 0.6 mile to 3rd Street. Turn right onto 3rd Street and drive 0.2 mile to the entrance for Middletown Cemetery.*

This is Middletown Cemetery, now part of Mount Carmel Cemetery. Getty's Federals were already in this vicinity when the Confederates attacked, and as the other two VI Corps divisions withdrew, Getty formed his men around the crown of this hilltop, facing east and south. This division was the largest in the Army of the Shenandoah, and with the battle now almost three hours old, Getty's men were fresh, alert, and prepared for what was coming their way. By 8 AM, they were the only operating and intact Union command on the field.

Although the view is somewhat obstructed today, standing on the hilltop here in the center of the cemetery will give you an idea of the strength of this position. Most of the trees on the hill were not present during the battle, and Getty's men would have seen the first Confederate division to approach—John Pegram's.

Pegram had not had much to do with the battle up to this point, and even today, this is somewhat of a mystery. His division was always present on the Confederate left, but at no point did any unit of his division launch an assault until, possibly, this battle at Red Hill. Pegram approached the right side of the Union line, passing through the ravine at Meadow Brook and appearing from the south. As the 1,600 Confederates approached the Federals, Getty ordered his men to wait until the enemy was only 30 yards away. When Pegram's division reached that point, the Union line of 4,000 let forth a devastating volley, followed by a counterattack that drove the Confederates back across Meadow Brook. The Federals returned to their position on the hill and waited for the next assault.

That assault would be launched by a brigade of Stephen Ramseur's division, Bryan Grimes's. Grimes had the assistance of Confederate artillery that had by now been placed on the Valley Pike, 1,000 yards to the southeast. As the second assault on the Union line was made, this time to the left center, the rebels briefly found a gap and attempted to exploit it, but ultimately, the result was the same. They were again sent back in a hurry.

At this point, Jubal Early met with Ramseur and Pegram. Both had seen that Getty's right flank was up in the air, and if the Confederates could take advantage of it, they would finally dislodge the final Union position on the field. Early made a somewhat controversial decision, sending Gabriel Wharton's division to the left to attack Getty's flank. Wharton's assignment had been to stick to the Valley Pike, denying its use to the enemy. The pike was the lifeline of the Shenandoah Valley; its macadamized surface enabled quick movement, and taking it away from the Federals slowed them down considerably. Now Early had decided to abandon this strategy. To add to the controversy, the assault made no difference. Wharton attacked directly against the center of the Union line, essentially following the same path of attack. Wharton, too, was repulsed.

It was not until Gordon's and Kershaw's men were sent west to swing far around the Union right that Getty's division withdrew. They had held the position until 9:30 AM, enabling the rest of the enemy infantry to escape past Middletown and far to the north.

⟩ *From the cemetery, pull out to your right onto 3rd Street/High Street and drive 0.3 mile. Turn right onto Chapel Road (SR 627), then immediately turn left onto Mineral Street (SR 635). Pull over near the intersection with Cougill Road on your left.*

As the Union units left the field, Early paused his troops to reorganize their units and form a new line. By this point, the rebels had lost up to an entire third of their army to plundering, and because of the rapid advances, many of the units had scattered. Now dealing with Confederate cavalry who had appeared in their front, along with a large amount of prisoners, Early sent Pegram's and Wharton's divisions north of Middletown around the Valley Pike. The rest of the infantry lined up to their left, with Ramseur's right flank on Meadow Brook, Kershaw to his left, and Gordon's division on the far left. Later, around 1 PM, these three divisions advanced to the Miller Farm, lining up behind a farm lane on the property and facing northeast toward what was left of the Union army. The Confederates would not go any farther than this point.

At 10 AM, Jubal Early made another decision that would later be pointed to as controversial, to say the very least. Although the exact words of the conversation have varied in their retelling, John Brown Gordon approached him to discuss the next part of the Confederate attack. Early's reply, at least as most versions of the story go, was that the soldiers had had "glory enough for one day." Gordon said that he had already told his men that they would be attacking, delivering the death blow to the Union army. Early replied that the Federals would be leaving soon anyway, apparently believing that they had already been destroyed. Gordon argued that the men they faced were the VI Corps of the Army of the Potomac, and that they weren't going to go anywhere until they were forced to. His argument failed to sway Early's decision. Gordon, who did not like Jubal Early, would later call this "the fatal halt."

If you have not yet pulled around the corner onto what is now Cougill Road, turn to your left. You are looking at the Miller Farm. The original farmhouse is still here, a bit difficult to see behind the trees but still standing. (The land is still privately owned, so be sure not to trespass.) Now drive around the corner onto Cougill Road.

This road was formerly the Miller Farm lane, and the Confederates would be lined up on your left shortly after 1 PM. As you drive along the road, Stephen Ramseur's division would be first, followed by Kershaw's, and then Gordon's, extending only slightly past the T at the end of the road.

> *Continue straight on Mineral Street, and then follow the curve to the left onto Cougill Road. Drive 0.8 mile on Cougill Road, then turn right onto Hites Road (SR 625). Drive 0.9 mile to the intersection with Klines Mill Road. Turn right onto Klines Mill Road and pull over.*

The Union units, bloodied but not completely scattered, formed a defensive line along the road you are about to travel on. Before you turn right and drive along Klines Mill Road, take a look at the open ground to your left front. In this area, George Armstrong Custer's cavalry would be sent to form. The right flank of the Union infantry would be very near the intersection you're at, and after you turn onto Klines Mill Road, the line would stretch roughly parallel to the road on your right side. When the Federals were ready to advance, it would extend all the way to the Valley Pike, anchoring its left there, with Merritt's cavalry division east of the pike.

> *Continue 0.9 mile on Klines Mill Road; pull over when you reach the small stream.*

Upon completing his meeting in Washington, Philip Sheridan immediately boarded a train and headed back toward his army. Getting off the train late on October 17 in Martinsburg, he spent the night there, and then rode to Winchester to spend the next night there.

Around 6 AM on October 19, Sheridan was wakened by a member of his staff, who reported an irregular amount of fire to the south of Winchester. Sheridan sent the aide away, saying that it was only part of the planned reconnaissance of the XIX Corps, and went back to sleep. It would not be until 8:30 AM that Sheridan would begin to ride south on the Valley Pike toward his army. Shortly after leaving Winchester, he himself heard the firing, and for the first time began to worry. He hurriedly gathered his cavalry escort and quickly began to ride south. It was not long before he realized what had happened.

Only a half-mile south of the town, Sheridan began to see the escaped Union wagons, gathered in a jam on the pike. The teamsters driving the wagons told Sheridan that his army had been destroyed and that his headquarters had been captured. Hearing this information flipped the internal switch inside of Phil Sheridan, the one that got his blood flowing and turned him into one of the most remarkable commanders ever to take the field of battle. Immediately, he began issuing orders for the wagons to block the pike and stop the retreat of any Federal soldiers who came their way. He then turned his horse, Rienzi, and raced for the front, 10 miles away.

Along the way, Sheridan encountered many stragglers from his army. More than a few of them had thought that if he had been present, they would never have been put in the position they were in, stumbling rearward in defeat. But as soon as their commander came racing by, asking for them to return to the front and fight, many of the men performed an immediate about-face and headed back toward the enemy. As he passed, Sheridan shouted that if they didn't want to fight, they could come and watch, and that they would be back in their camps by 4 PM.

By 10:30 AM, just as Horatio Wright was reforming the shattered Union line, Sheridan rode up. The news that Sheridan was back on the field spread like wildfire. Finding Wright, Crook, Emory, and Alfred Torbert gathered, trying to devise a plan, Sheridan dismounted to get a briefing on the situation. When told that the commanders were discussing whether they should attempt to hold their position or withdraw, Sheridan cursed and told them that they would do neither. They would attack.

The race to the front and the rallying of his men to the attack would go down in history simply as "Sheridan's Ride." It was somewhere near this location that Sheridan established his command post and immediately began preparations for the Union assault. It was suggested by several of the officers present that he should ride up and down the line to let his men know that he was here. He did just that, roughly along the path you just drove, and his men cheered him loudly. You are now at the left-center of the Union line, with the Federals still to your right as you face down the road. The Confederates are also to your right, lined up in the distance at Miller's Lane.

❯ *Continue 0.5 mile on Klines Mill Road to US 11 (Valley Pike). Turn right onto US 11 and drive 1.3 miles. Turn left into the campus of Lord Fairfax Community College; drive around to the parking lot on your right.*

Sheridan's appearance, though electrifying to his troops, did not mean that the shattered army was instantaneously ready for an assault. Preparations still needed to be made. In fact, he was expecting the Confederates to attack—just as John Brown Gordon wanted to do—but he planned an assault anyway, focusing on the Confederate left, Gordon's position.

When the line formed, there was no thought given to defensive preparation, and given the success the soldiers had met that day, this is not surprising. It was not a good defensive position at all; the divisions had simply gotten in line next to each other as they had arrived. The 1 PM advance to the Miller Farm lane was done simply to test the Federal strength. Other than this movement and some light skirmishing around it, along with some small cavalry actions, the lull after the Confederate "fatal halt" would last for almost six hours. Furthermore, the line was thin, the Confederates having lost many of their men to plundering.

As the day grew late and the Federals formed their battle lines in the trees, there was only one thing holding Sheridan back. The same rumor that had caused him to be cautious in front of Fisher's Hill in August, that James Longstreet's corps was in the vicinity, had again floated up. Although he didn't believe it, he wanted it confirmed, so he asked Wesley Merritt to capture some Confederate prisoners. Merritt ordered Charles Lowell's brigade to charge a rebel battery and take some, which it did. All of the men who were seized confirmed the same intelligence: Kershaw's division had returned to Early's army, but that was all. With that, the Federals were ready. (Lowell would be killed later that day.)

Beginning at the Valley Pike and leading eastward were the VI Corps divisions, which would assault the Confederate center, followed by the XIX Corps, which would outflank the enemy left. In addition, George Custer's cavalry would be on the far right of the line, waiting for the right moment. The bugles sounded at 4 PM, and the Union infantry, rabid from a combination of Sheridan's appearance and revenge, went forward in a rush.

The Confederates, surprised but patient, waited as the Federals approached, then took them head on. In the front of the line, the Union VI Corps was stopped, and the two lines beat on each other for almost 30 minutes. On the Confederate left flank, though, the Union troops, overlapping their line, were able to bend it back, gaining some ground on Gordon's division. Sheridan, in his excitement, rode over to the small crest they had taken and celebrated with them, cheering them on. This was William Dwight's division of the XIX Corps, and they were about to aid in the action that would ultimately win the day for the Union.

At 4:30 PM, Custer ordered his division, which had been screened from the Confederate line, to charge at full speed. Just as it had done at Winchester, the Union cavalry completely surprised the enemy defenders. Just as Custer arrived, Dwight began to wheel his brigade to the right, perpendicular to the Confederate line, and proceed to roll it up. The rebels had seen this twice in the last month, at both Winchester and Fisher's Hill, and they were not about to stick around to see it again. All three of Gordon's brigades broke for the rear one by one, followed swiftly by Kershaw's and Ramseur's.

The Confederate commanders tried valiantly to rally their men. Ramseur, who had been slightly wounded earlier in the day, lost a horse. He quickly found another mount, but soon it, too, was killed. As he was searching for a third horse, Stephen Ramseur was shot in the chest, with the bullet passing through both lungs. The rebels placed him in an ambulance and headed for the rear with the rest of the army.

From your vantage point here at the college, look west across the Valley Pike. Almost directly in front of you, just a short distance away, is the Miller Farm, and you are practically looking down the Miller Farm lane. The Union left remained anchored on the pike, and would have advanced from your far right to a point right in front of you, where the men began their sharp fight with the Confederates. The Union flank attack began at the far end of the line and pressed toward your position. Ramseur was one of the last to leave the field, and he was wounded somewhere near the Miller Farm.

❯ *Exit the Community College parking area and turn left onto US 11. Drive 2.3 miles on US 11 to the intersection with Belle Grove Road; turn right onto the road and carefully pull over near the monument on the corner.*

The Confederates poured south through Middletown and all the way past Cedar Creek, with the Federals in close pursuit. Darkness came at around 5:30 PM, and by that time the battle was over. Just as Sheridan had promised, the Union soldiers would sleep in their own camps that night.

Federal cavalry had raced in front of the fleeing Confederates, blocking the escape path of their wagons and their artillery. The Union had lost 24 guns in the morning's fight, but now recaptured all 24 of them, plus an additional 24. Also captured was the ambulance carrying Confederate general Stephen Dodson Ramseur.

At Belle Grove that night, which was once again Union headquarters, the officers of the Army of the Shenandoah built a massive bonfire and celebrated their victory into the night. There was no question about it now: The Confederate Army of the Valley was finished.

In the mansion's nursery, Stephen Ramseur, a major general at 27, lay dying. Having discovered his ambulance, the Union command had him brought to the mansion to pass in comfort. Throughout the night, many of the men he fought against that day, who also happened to be friends and former classmates, visited him to provide what comfort they could. Henry DuPont and George Custer, particularly good friends since West Point, were among these. Ramseur would die the next morning.

The monument here commemorates Ramseur's death, and in practicality, the hopes of the Confederacy in the Shenandoah Valley, which had come very close to a fantastic victory. A difficult battle plan had been executed almost perfectly, and the Union army was attacked piecemeal as designed. But through a combination of factors, some of which were not under their control, the rebels were ultimately brushed away, and with authority. The Union casualty total of 5,665 almost doubled that of the Confederates, who had lost 2,910 men. But the Federals could afford loss, whereas the rebels could not. Further, the Confederates had lost the valley, a crushing psychological blow to the South. Jubal Early, from the time he had left Lee's side at Gaines Mill in June until his defeat at Cedar Creek, had outgeneraled his opponent at virtually every one of his battles. In the end, though, he could not overcome insurmountable odds, and he was found guilty in the court of public opinion simply of not being Stonewall Jackson. The gamble Lee had taken and that Early had carried out had paid off for a time, but not for long enough. The focus in the Eastern Theater, from this point on, would be solely on Petersburg.

MAINE.
FIRST HEAVY ARTILLERY

IN MEMORY OF
604 BRAVE MEMBERS WHO FELL
CHARGING HERE
JUNE 18, 1864

MAINE — UNION / PEACE — VIRGINIA

The Longest Battle: Petersburg Under Siege

WHEN THE DUST SETTLED at Cold Harbor on June 3, the stark reality of the situation could not be denied. The field was littered with thousands of dead and wounded Union soldiers, while the Confederates, comparatively, had barely received a scratch. As long as the latter could fight from behind protective works such as these, or those at the North Anna, or Spotsylvania, or the Wilderness, or Mine Run, there was no reason for them to move. No matter how many reinforcements the Federals could bring to the field, the rebels could stay within their entrenched positions and fire at charging bluecoats for a long, long time.

Ulysses S. Grant knew this already; the only reason he had tried a direct assault at Cold Harbor was because he thought the enemy was played out. But he could no longer waste the lives of his men this way, not for absolutely no gain. He had to find another way.

For the last month, Grant had maneuvered Lee out of every position, only to have him find another. Lee's Army of Northern Virginia was still the objective, not capturing the capital at Richmond, but he could use the capital to accomplish what he needed. Lee would protect the capital, and if the capital was threatened, he would move his army. Lee's army could survive without it, but it would be a tough prospect. All of the food and supplies the army needed came through Richmond. If that did not happen, Lee would have difficulty finding another source for those goods. So Grant

---

This marker commemorates the valiant charge of the First Maine Heavy Artillery Regiment during the initial Union assault at Petersburg.

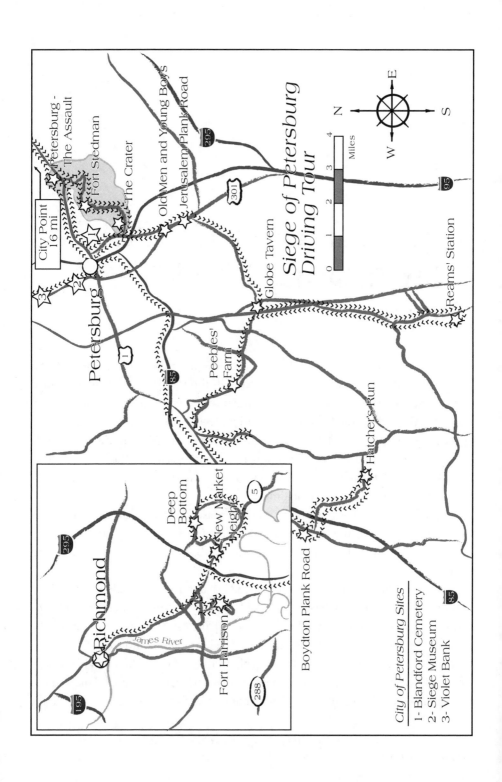

Siege of Petersburg Driving Tour

City Point 16 mi

Petersburg - The Assault
Fort Stedman
The Crater
Old Men and Young Boys
Jerusalem Plank Road
Petersburg
Globe Tavern
Peebles' Farm
Reams' Station
Hatcher's Run

295
301
95
1
85

Miles
0   1   2   3   4

Richmond
Deep Bottom
New Market Heights
Fort Harrison
James River
Boydton Plank Road

295
195
288
5
85

City of Petersburg Sites
1 - Blandford Cemetery
2 - Siege Museum
3 - Violet Bank

resolved to cut the supplies to Richmond, thereby cutting the supplies to Lee's army. To do that, the Union army needed to capture the vital rail center at Petersburg.

It has been said by some historians that Petersburg was not a true siege; rather, one long battle—one that lasted ten months. Petersburg was never fully invested, and had virtually the entire north and west sides open for escape, if necessary. The rebels, though, knew that the fall of Richmond would likely mean the destruction of Lee's army, and perhaps of the Confederacy itself. Lee knew as much long before the armies reached Petersburg. In a conversation with Second Corps commander Jubal Early, Lee stated it quite plainly. "We must destroy this army of Grant's before he gets to the James River. If he gets there, it will become a siege, and then it will be a mere question of time."

Grant would get to the James, and by nothing short of a miracle, Petersburg did not fall immediately, and the siege Lee had predicted began. Far from remaining idle behind their works, though, the strategies and tactics the armies adopted would turn into the first large-scale trench warfare, directly leading to the horrors of World War I over fifty years later. During these ten months, the armies did not simply hammer away at each other as they had previously, but they would employ tactics that would combine active combat with traditional siege warfare. Petersburg was more than just the beginning of the end for the Confederacy. Only one out of many conspicuous changes to how wars were fought, the siege at Petersburg was perhaps the hallmark event that distinguished America's Civil War as the world's first modern war.

BEFORE YOU GO

»PLANNING YOUR TRIP

The battleground at Petersburg is a large one, and in the ten months of combat here, the events that shaped the siege are numerous and unique. From the rise and fall of some of the Civil War's most familiar personalities to the explosion at the Crater, this site is replete with great history, great drama, and great stories. For the most part, the progression of events is remarkably orderly, as the Union line stretched to the west and the Confederates did the same to try to counter the movement. However, when there were disruptions in that movement, they were big ones. Therefore, to fully understand the extent of the combat here, you may find yourself backtracking over ground you've already passed once or twice. Don't cheat yourself; this is the last act of possibly the most important event in

> **PETERSBURG**
>
> **Number of sites:** 16
> **Total miles:** 130
> **Estimated time:** 3–5 days

IN DEPTH

Earl J. Hess—*Into the Crater: The Mine Attack at Petersburg; In the Trenches at Petersburg: Field Fortifications and Confederate Defeat*
John Horn—*The Petersburg Campaign: June 1864–April 1865*
Richard J. Sommers—*Richmond Redeemed: The Siege at Petersburg*
Noah Andre Trudeau—*The Last Citadel: Petersburg, Virginia, June 1864–April 1865*

"There is not as much to choose from as there should be. Hess does an outstanding job on an infamous moment, and on how the siege was conducted and defended, while Sommers focuses on Grant's Fifth Offensive. Horn's and Trudeau's books are excellent sources."

—*Tom Trescott, Abraham Lincoln Book Shop, Chicago*

American history, so take your time and try to fully understand how the events relate to one another.

Keeping that in mind, the siege at Petersburg was also conducted north of the James River. Those sites, all relatively close to each other, are grouped together as a separate part of your tour. This also includes a few of the many sites in Richmond, the capital of the Confederate States of America and as historically rich as any city in America. The battles at Fort Harrison, New Market Heights, and Deep Bottom play a critical part here, but it's easy to forget their importance when taken out of the context of the overall siege, so try to keep this in mind when you tour them.

»RECOMMENDATIONS

For quite a while, Petersburg was stuck in a bit of an economic rut, one that actually began even before the war came to its doorstep. However, in recent years, the city has seen some nice developments. Petersburg National Military Park is obviously a large part of the city and its identity, and Petersburg has done a great job in recent years of trying to atone for some past preservation sins and preserve more of the battlefield. The downtown area in particular is making a nice comeback, and you'll find that it is a great place to have lunch, take a walk, and explore. Perhaps best of all, Petersburg still retains all of its original charm, and does not have the least hint of being a tourist trap.

The other part of Petersburg's modern identity is the massive Fort Lee, still undergoing a major expansion of its facilities. As a result, Petersburg has become very visitor-friendly, not just for tourists but also to serve the many needs of the base. There are lodging options in Petersburg, but you will also find a lot of nice options in Colonial Heights, just north of the city. You'll find a lot of accommodations here.

THE CAMPAIGN TOUR

THE BATTLE OF OLD MEN AND YOUNG BOYS

⟩ *Begin your tour at the corner of Crater Road (southbound) and Oakland Street in Petersburg. Park in the large parking lot, then walk across Oakland Street to the small monument on the corner.*

Since the Army of the James landed at Bermuda Hundred, Benjamin Butler had wanted to assault Petersburg. Several attempts were begun but aborted, even after the Confederate Howlett Line had bottled up his forces on the peninsula. A pontoon bridge reaching from the Federal camp at Point of Rocks north of the James crossed the Appomattox River northeast of the city, enabling a Union force to move around the city and attack from the south. On June 8, as Grant's massive Army of the Potomac prepared for its own movement south, Butler saw an opportunity to give the capture of Petersburg one last shot.

P. G. T. Beauregard had been steadily informing Richmond that Petersburg was about to be attacked for quite some time. He had done the same when the city was

Site of the Confederate stand during the battle of Old Men and Young Boys at Petersburg.

threatened by Butler's landing, and it was only at the last minute that anyone in Richmond seemed to realize that Beauregard had not been simply crying wolf. Soon after the major fighting of the Bermuda Hundred campaign was over, however, Beauregard went back to his old ways, warning of the imminent fall of the city, and thereby the fall of Richmond and the Confederacy. The cries became louder as June 9 approached, but as before, few paid attention.

The assault of Petersburg that occurred on June 9, 1864, is remembered mostly for two things. One is that the first men to meet the advancing Federals were an impromptu Petersburg home guard, 125 citizens of the town ranging in age from 14 to 61. As for the other, the inspiring story of these citizens sometimes overshadows that, had Butler's force tried just a little bit, it is likely that it could have captured Petersburg before the siege began, possibly avoiding it altogether.

Butler arranged for two units to attack the city. Augustus Kautz would lead the main force, 1,300 cavalrymen who would approach the city from the south. An infantry force of 5,300 troops, led personally by Union X Corps commander Quincy Gillmore, would also cross the river and approach the city from the northeast as a diversion.

To say that Gillmore's force tried to cause a diversion is generous. Not long after the infantry crossed the Appomattox, it came upon Petersburg's formidable earthworks and encountered a feeble resistance. Gillmore, convinced that a much stronger force was manning the works, pulled back and did little. Had the infantry advanced, it likely would have met only a handful of soldiers to its front, as the entire city was, at that time, defended by only about 1,000 men.

South of the city, however, the situation seemed much more threatening for the Confederates. Kautz's cavalry force approached the city along the Jerusalem Plank Road (now Crater Road), hitting the defensive line where it crossed the road at an artillery position tagged as Battery 27. In the works were Maj. Fletcher Archer and 125 members of the Home Guard. The "Old Men and Young Boys," as they would be known, did not hold long, especially after Kautz got his forces together for a coordinated assault at 1:15 PM. However, the time bought by Archer's men enabled Henry Wise, a former governor of Virginia and commander of the Petersburg defenses, to summon infantry and artillery from Port Walthall Junction, to the north, and from the eastern part of the line (where Gillmore was not keeping them very busy.

There is a memorial here to the Home Guard, near the site of the former Battery 27. If you face Crater Road, Kautz's cavalry would have been attacking from your right. The Home Guard was no match for Kautz's troopers, and there was no question what the result would be, but its brave stand here (along with a few stumbles on the Union side) may have saved the city. To many, the assault of Petersburg occurred on June 15, but if you were to ask any resident of Petersburg, you would be firmly told (and rightfully so) that it was the stand of the Old Men and Young Boys on June 9.

> *Pull out to the left onto Crater Road and drive 0.8 mile north to Graham Road. Turn left on Graham Road and drive 0.6 mile. Pull over next to the Virginia Civil War Trails marker on your right.*

After breaking through the Home Guard's line, Kautz split his force, sending two companies north on Jerusalem Plank Road and one to the west on New Road (now Graham Road, which you drove in on). Here, he ran into a defensive line commanded by James Dearing, who had rushed south from Bermuda Hundred with cavalry and artillery.

Turn so that the road is to your left. Kautz's men approached from behind you, while the Confederates formed their line just to your front. To your left, you can see that there is a large rise of ground. Dearing placed Edward Graham's battery on this high ground, as well as on the other side of the road. When Kautz approached, Graham's artillery opened fire, and Dearing followed with a cavalry charge. His horsemen on the Jerusalem Plank Road also met resistance from Confederate infantry. Kautz's losses were not heavy, but hearing no news from Gillmore, he decided to withdraw.

Had Kautz pressed his attack, he may or may not have gotten through the small force; whether he could have held the city is also open for debate. More important though, had Gillmore not already been on his way back to camp by the time Kautz attacked, the tiny defensive force in Petersburg would have been completely overwhelmed. The Union assault of Petersburg on June 9 would go down as another prime opportunity missed for the Federals.

THE ASSAULT OF PETERSBURG

> *You will now be entering the Eastern Front Unit of Petersburg National Battlefield. When you enter the park, you will be asked to pay a small entrance fee; keep your receipt, as you will need to show it when you re-enter. The receipt is good for one week.*
> *From Dearing's defensive line, pull out to your left and drive 0.6 mile to Crater Road. Turn left onto Crater Road and drive 1.2 miles to Wythe Street, then turn right. Follow Wythe Street, and then East Washington Street, for 2.2 miles to the entrance of Petersburg National Battlefield. Take the exit ramp to the park, then drive 0.5 mile to the park's visitor center, stopping to pay your entrance fee along the way.*

It did not take Ulysses S. Grant long to realize that he had to remove his army from the front at Cold Harbor. By June 5, only two days after the disastrous frontal assault there, he began making plans to withdraw his entire army south of the James River to assault the city of Petersburg.

Petersburg, located only 20 miles south of the capital at Richmond, was Virginia's second-largest city at the time of the war. The Richmond & Petersburg Railroad was

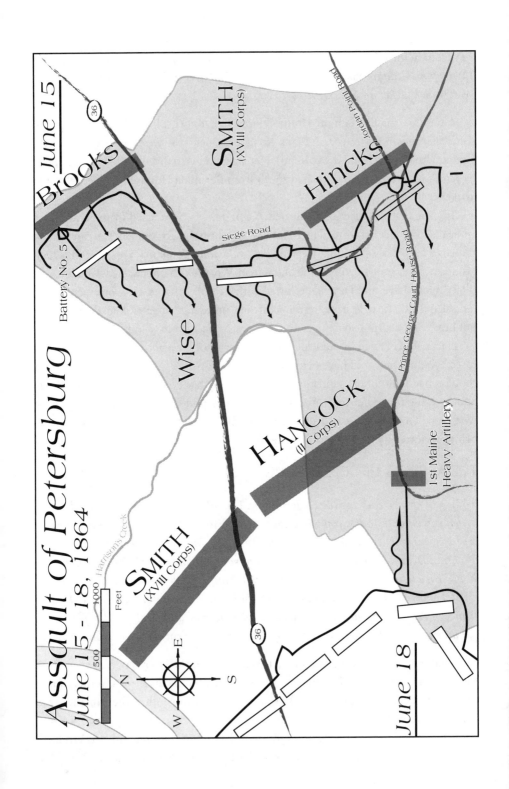

Assault of Petersburg
June 15 - 18, 1864

June 15

Brooks

SMITH
(XVIII Corps)

Battery No. 5

Wise

Hincks

Siege Road

Jordan Point Road

Prince George Court House Road

HANCOCK
(II Corps)

1st Maine
Heavy Artillery

SMITH
(XVIII Corps)

Harrison's Creek

June 18

Feet
0   500   1000

N
E
W   S

the vital link between the two cities, connecting them with only a single track. Petersburg, however, had four additional lines running to it, making it essentially the railroad center for the capital. From the northeast was the City Point Railroad, which ran only a short distance but connected Petersburg with the deep water access at City Point. Running south east was the Norfolk & Petersburg Railroad, providing convenient access to the Atlantic but of little value to the Confederate, as the Union held the city of Norfolk. To the south was the Petersburg & Weldon Railroad, linking the city to Weldon, North Carolina, and, more important, one of the south's largest ports in Wilmington. Running west was the South Side Railroad, extending to another critical rail hub at Lynchburg, which fanned out to central Virginia, the Shenandoah Valley, and the Carolinas. Cutting these important railroad lines into Petersburg was equivalent to cutting rail traffic to Richmond.

Pulling his army from Lee's front would not be easy, nor would it be easy to move the entire army—across a long distance over several road networks, through the swamps of the Chickahominy, across the James and Appomattox Rivers, and to the outskirts of Petersburg—without Lee's attacking the Union columns as they moved. The Federals had, by this point, already stolen several marches on the Confederates, but this one would by far be the most difficult.

Attempting to draw the nosy enemy cavalry away from his lines, Grant sent Sheridan with two of his three cavalry divisions on a mission west to destroy the rail centers at Gordonsville and Charlottesville on July 7, leaving only James Wilson's division behind to screen the army's movements. (Sheridan's raid would end at the battle of Trevilian Station, which you can read about in chapter 4.) He also instructed his engineers to construct a defensive line behind the current line at Cold Harbor, enabling the Federals to provide cover for each Union corps as it withdrew. After the line was completed, the movement was scheduled for the next evening, June 12.

Robert E. Lee knew that the enemy would be moving from Cold Harbor, and shortly after the June 3 assault he began to prepare his men for their response. Always looking for a chance to take the initiative, he longed for a chance to attack the Federals when they were most vulnerable, and attacking while they withdrew would be their best opportunity. Knowing only that they would likely be moving south again, Lee elected to hit the Union troops as they crossed the Chickahominy. Timing would be critical, and he urged his corps commanders to remain vigilant, looking for any indication that the enemy was on the move.

At 6 PM on June 12, Gouverneur Warren's V Corps left its works, masked by the sounds of many of the Union army's regimental bands. Samuel Crawford's division swung slightly to the west and began building earthworks, providing an excellent diversion as the rest of the corps prepared for their mission of protecting the Union right flank. After dark, the rest of the army moved. William "Baldy" Smith's XVIII Corps moved east to White House to board boats bound for Bermuda Hundred. Winfield Hancock's II Corps and Horatio Wright's VI Corps moved to the fallback line created by the engineers, and then began to head south to cross the Chickahominy at two different points. Last to leave was Ambrose Burnside's IX Corps, which would follow its VI Corps companions.

When a furious Robert E. Lee was told on the morning of June 13 that the Federal works were completely empty, he immediately moved his army south to protect the capital. It was the best he could do, as he had no idea where the enemy was. Most of his cavalry was engaged with Sheridan's troopers at Trevilian Station, depriving him of most of his intelligence-gathering arm. It would not be until the afternoon of June 14 that Lee would decide that Grant must be heading for Petersburg.

Lee also further felt the ramifications of a critical decision he had made the day before. Union forces were making another advance in the Shenandoah Valley, threatening to cut off rail supplies from the west. After considering the matter, he decided to rush Jubal Early's corps to Lynchburg to meet the Federals. From there, Early would elect to follow discretionary orders given to him by Lee and move into the Shenandoah Valley, then advance on Washington, D.C. (This is the campaign covered in chapter 5.) The valley was too important and it warranted, in Lee's eyes, the subtraction of an entire corps to protect it. Now well on their way, having left at 2 AM, these soldiers would not be coming back.

After the Federals made their way across the Chickahominy River, they encountered a much more formidable obstacle: the James River. While the II Corps started its crossing, using ferry boats, Union engineers began work on a pontoon bridge spanning the river at Wyanoke Neck, just south of Charles City Court House and well downriver of the Confederates. Construction of the half-mile-long bridge began at 4 PM on June 14, and by 3 AM the following day, only eleven hours later, the wagons and artillery of the IX Corps began crossing. It was nothing short of an engineering wonder; the bridge was able to compensate for a four-foot tidal difference, and also contained a removable center span to allow boats to pass through. The crossing remained unmolested, and by June 17 the entire army was south of the James River. The Union withdrawal could not have gone any better.

At midday on June 14, while the engineers were preparing for their task, Baldy Smith's XVIII Corps arrived at Bermuda Hundred. It had taken a day and a half for its river transports to make their way down the York River, around the end of the Virginia Peninsula, and up the York River, but the men were now poised to take the city of Petersburg as the rest of the army moved. Smith's attack was set to begin at 2 AM the next day, June 15.

Smith's three divisions, along with August Kautz's 2,500-strong cavalry, crossed the pontoon bridge at Point of Rocks and began heading for Petersburg, a relatively short march along the City Point Railroad. However, it was not long before the Federals ran into a Confederate position at Baylor's Farm, 2 miles northeast of the Petersburg defenses. Smith fought here for nearly two hours, with Edward Hincks's all-black division (one of two in the army) making the final assault and capturing the works. Having previously been told that he would meet little resistance, Smith became extraordinarily cautious, covering the final 2 miles in roughly five hours, and then taking another four to examine the Confederate positions and deciding whether and when he should assault the works.

Smith's information had been correct. The rebel force defending the entire city of Petersburg on the morning of June 15 was only 2,200 strong. Even with the attack on June 9 and Beauregard's persistent warnings, the Confederates had not chosen to reinforce Petersburg. At 7 AM, Beauregard informed Richmond of Smith's arrival, and within hours reports were sent detailing the Federals' movements. Before long, Beauregard made a command decision that would finally get the Confederate focus shifted southward. With Robert Hoke's division having been returned to him from Lee's command to man the Howlett Line at Bermuda Hundred, Beauregard informed the capital that he could not hold both Bermuda Hundred and Petersburg, and that he was shifting Hoke's division south to man the works at Petersburg.

The Petersburg defenses were known as the Dimmock Line, named after the Confederate engineer who had constructed them in 1862. They stretched 10 miles around the city, encircling it on the south with both flanks resting on the Appomattox River. The line contained 55 battery positions, numbered from east to west, and was designed to hold 25,000 defenders. Clearly, Beauregard's 2,200 would not do.

Beauregard threw his entire force to the 4 miles of the Dimmock Line facing east toward the oncoming Federals, then watched and waited as Smith pondered his options. Finally concluding that the lines were not strongly held, Smith decided on a direct assault across a wide front. The attack began shortly before 7 PM, and within two hours, the Federals had captured over 2 miles of the Dimmock Line, consisting of Batteries 4 through 9. Beauregard, who arrived in Petersburg only just before the assault, watched his men streaming westward as the Federals eliminated one-third of the Confederate defenses in one swift stroke.

The primary visitor center for Petersburg National Battlefield sits just behind the former Dimmock Line, adjacent to Confederate Battery 5, still in excellent condition. In front of the visitor center is a display of the wide variety of artillery used during the war, along with an explanation of what each was used for. (This significant improvement was just completed in 2011; the guns had previously been lined up on the ground along a trail.) Inside the center, you will find a museum regarding the siege, as well as a film telling the story of Petersburg.

Confederate Battery No. 5, part of the original Dimmock Line at Petersburg.

The massive Union mortar known as the Dictator.

THE CHANGING LANDSCAPE

As you tour the sites of Petersburg, there is an important difference between the landscape you see today and the one the Union and Confederate armies saw in 1864. Many of the areas around Petersburg are now heavily wooded. During the war, however, this was not the case. In many areas of the siege, and particularly on the Eastern Front, the landscape was nearly devoid of trees. Those few that did exist did not last long, eventually becoming part of an earthwork. From almost any point as you drive through this portion of the park, the city of Petersburg, almost 2 miles west of you, was clearly visible. Also visible to all of the soldiers here were the enemy's lines; the no-man's-land in between did not have the obstructed views that you will find here. Today, many of these trees serve to screen out some of the surrounding industry, but as you try to visualize the fighting, try to remove most of the trees from the picture.

Behind the center is a short walking trail. The entire loop trail is 0.6 mile, taking you through Battery 5 and around to the location of a massive Union mortar known as the Dictator, which dropped heavy rounds onto the city of Petersburg for three months with remarkably little effect. If you take the entire loop, be aware that beyond Battery 5, there is a steep descent to the trail that may be difficult for some. You can, however, view Battery 5, then backtrack and go around the battery to see the Dictator on a much less strenuous path.

At the very least, take the very short walk to Battery 5. This battery, one of the largest on the Dimmock Line, was one of the centerpieces of the June 15 assault. The preserved earthwork here, though still reduced from its former self by time and erosion, will begin to give you an idea of just how formidable the works around Petersburg became. Walking around to the Dictator and seeing the battery from that low ground will further emphasize the position's power.

Also note that on June 15, Battery 5 was not the enclosed work you see today. The Confederates had only built the portion of the battery that faces east, away from the city. After the Federals took possession, they immediately began "refacing" the work so that it faced west toward the enemy. You will see several examples of this as you tour the Petersburg earthworks.

Finally, as you walk back to your vehicle, note the strip of unmown grass in the field to your left. This grass denotes the former location of the rest of the defenses, which stretched for miles. The park has resorted to this unobtrusive method of indicating the lines in several places, so keep this in mind as you continue your tour.

> Exit the parking lot and drive 1 mile on Siege Road, bearing left to remain on the park road. Pull into the park's Tour Stop 3 for Battery 9.

The old roadbed of the Prince George Court House Road, near Confederate Battery No. 9.

This is the location of Battery 9 of the Confederate Dimmock Line. This portion of the line was assaulted by Edward Hincks's division. Hincks's men would have to prove themselves repeatedly to their white fellow soldiers, but they always did, and they did not disappoint on the night of June 15.

There is a short loop trail of 0.6 mile that will take you down two former roadbeds—the Prince George Court House Road, which forks off to your left, and the Jordan Point Road, to the right. Both of these were important routes to Petersburg at the time of the siege. Following the trail will eventually bring you to Meade Station, a former rail stop on the U.S. Military Railroad that Grant would construct after the siege began. You will also find a memorial to all of the black soldiers who served during the siege.

Also on the grounds here is a nice example of reconstructed earthworks from the siege of Petersburg. The display created by the park contains examples of not only the construction of the trenches, but also some of the various obstacles that were typically placed in front of them.

At 9 PM on June 15, Smith returned to his headquarters to find Winfield Hancock, who had been struggling to bring his II Corps up to assist Smith in his assault. Hancock reported his men ready to aid in the continued assault, but Smith declined. It was too late in the day, he said, and he asked Hancock to relieve the men in his lines and be ready to resume the assault in the morning. Benjamin Butler issued peremptory orders for the assault to be renewed immediately, but Smith, who did not want to be disturbed, could not be found until the next morning. This delay would provide Beauregard enough time to pull his men west to form a new defensive line, a strong position on the west bank of Harrison Creek.

〉 *Continue 0.6 mile along Siege Road to the crossing of Harrison Creek. Pull into Tour Stop 4 for the park.*

The next morning, June 16, the Union II Corps was able to capture more of the Dimmock Line, but that was due mostly to the fact that the enemy had left it. Their new line on the west bank of Harrison Creek, though not quite as formidable, would still provide an adequate defense as Beauregard continued to press for Confederate reinforcements. Before the next evening, the size of the rebel force in Petersburg had swelled from 2,200 to 14,000. These soldiers were still outnumbered approximately three to one, but there was no doubt that they had gotten off easy. Had Wright pressed the attack of the XVIII Corps the night before (or started hours earlier than he did), he almost certainly would have walked into Petersburg and captured it.

After realizing where the Confederate position was, it was not until 6 PM that the Federals launched their main assault of the day. The II Corps pushed westward, but the men were not able to break the new Harrison Creek Line. The fighting went on into the night, but the rebels held.

The next morning, June 17, saw more troops coming to the field. By 3 AM, Ambrose Burnside's IX Corps had now extended the Union line westward. Their movement screened by a ravine, Burnside's men surprised the Confederates and destroyed the Harrison Creek line south of the Jordan Point Road. Although Warren's V Corps was soon lining up on Burnside's left, the IX Corps did not follow up its attack until early afternoon, gaining little, and a later evening had the same result.

The Confederates had survived another day, but Beauregard knew that he was pressing his luck. During the day, his engineers began laying out another defensive position to the west, almost a half-mile behind his present location at Harrison Creek. The left of the line was anchored on the Appomattox River and ran south, where it rejoined the Dimmock Line formations near Battery 27 at the Jerusalem Plank Road. After midnight, his men quietly slipped rearward to their new line.

Here at Harrison's Creek, you can see that the western bank upon which Beauregard formed his defense is quite a natural obstacle. The Jordan Point Road is not mostly gone, but Siege Road, which you have been driving on, follows the old road from your last stop at Battery 9 to your next stop at Colquitt's Salient. From this area, the Harrison Creek Trail extends in two directions. Not far beyond the road on either

Harrison's Creek, where the Confederates made a stand during the initial Union assault of Petersburg.

side, the trails branch out into part of a wide network crisscrossing the Eastern Front area of the park. The trails are a fantastic way to see the terrain, but before you go, be sure you are prepared, as there are quite a few of them and they extend for miles.

> ❯ *Continue 0.3 mile on Siege Road to Tour Stop 5.*

Just as the Union II and IX Corps were advancing to find empty enemy trenches on the morning of June 18, Robert E. Lee's Army of Northern Virginia finally began to arrive in Petersburg. As they arrived, they filed into the new Confederate defenses, only a short distance from the city. The Union army had been given three days to take the city of Petersburg, and it could have done so. This was a golden opportunity to perhaps end the war, and they had blown it.

George Meade was not quite ready to give up. It had been Meade who had been largely directing the attacks of the last two days, and during that time he had found it difficult to impossible to coordinate the efforts of his army. An assault by all four corps present was planned for noon, but only pieces of the II and XVIII Corps went forward, all of their attacks easily repulsed. Meade tried to get his men to move throughout the afternoon, but to no avail. After a late assault by the II Corps met with disaster, Meade finally gave the order to entrench at 6:30 PM.

From the parking area, you will first see a large earthen fort to your left. This is Fort Stedman, which we will revisit at the end of your tour. There is a 0.5 mile loop trail that will take you through the scene of the last fighting on June 18, the charge of the 1st Maine Heavy Artillery. Note that this trail is not completely open for part of the year, as it is a nesting area for eagles, but you will be able to follow the charge of the 1st Maine Heavies for its entirety.

Continue down the path past the fort. On your right is a small hill with an interpretive

> ### CASUALTIES— THE ASSAULT OF PETERSBURG
> **Confederate:** total: 4,000 (estimated)
>
> **Union:** killed and wounded, 8,150; missing or captured, 1,814; total: 9,964
>
> **Total Casualties (estimated): 14,000**

sign at the crest. This is Hare House Hill, a critical rise fronting a bulge in the Confederate line now known as Colquitt's Salient. The salient is about 300 yards to your front, and if you continue down the trail, you will come upon its earthworks. At 6 PM on June 18, the 1st Maine heavies charged the salient, largely unsupported, and took dreadful casualties. Of the 900 men of the regiment that charged that day, 632 of them were killed or wounded, the highest regimental casualty total of the entire war.

THE TRAGEDY OF THE 1ST MAINE HEAVY ARTILLERY

By the time the Union army reached Petersburg, most of the men—particularly the veterans—had become quite disillusioned with making frontal assaults against Confederate earthworks. When the order came down from David Birney, temporarily commanding the II Corps, for three veteran regiments from New York and Pennsylvania to charge Colquitt's Salient, the veterans refused, and suggested that the 1st Maine Heavy Artillery—relatively green "bandbox soldiers" who had come from the Washington defenses—make the charge instead.

Remarkably, the veterans' wish was granted, which spelled disaster for the 1st Maine heavies. When the assault began at 6 PM, not only did the artillerymen rush toward the salient into a wall of flame, but the supporting units on either side of them—many of them the veterans who had refused to charge—did not advance. In less than 30 minutes, Lee's veterans had inflicted 632 casualties on the regiment.

Upon their return to the lines, the few survivors were met with taunting jeers by the veterans for making the charge. Birney, now at the scene, rode up to the regimental commander, Col. Daniel Chaplin, and asked him where his regiment was. His face covered with tears, Chaplin's response was scathing. "There they are, out on that field where your tried veterans dared not go. Here, you can take my sword; I have no use for it now."

Continuing down the path will bring you to a large monument commemorating their fateful charge.

THE CRATER

> *Continue 0.9 miles on Siege Road to Tour Stop 7.*

The story of the battle of the Crater is one of the most unique and fantastic of the entire Civil War. The very idea of digging a tunnel under the enemy's works and blowing them up in spectacular fashion sounds like the stuff of Hollywood. But like any good story, there is much more to the Crater than just the explosion of the mine. The events leading up to and following the battle also hold heavy drama. Had the Federals followed the script, the architects of the battle likely would have gone down in history as brilliant. Instead, the Union army's failure at the Crater resulted in disaster, congressional inquiries, courts-martial, and the downfall of several of the army's most prominent figures.

After the initial assaults at Petersburg had failed, Grant resigned to the fact that the only way to destroy Lee's army without the terrible bloodletting of the previous six weeks was to starve them out of their lines. Grant was aggressive but he was not a

Union IX Corps commander Ambrose Burnside observed the battle of the Crater, on the opposite rise, from here at Fort Morton.

monster, and although a siege would take time, the disparity in resources between the Union and the Confederacy would virtually ensure the destruction of Lee's armies.

While the army began its strategy of extending the siege westward to stretch the Confederate line thinner and thinner, a novel idea was proposed by members of the 48th Pennsylvania Infantry. The men of the regiment came from mining country and more than half of them were miners, including their leader, Lt. Col. Henry Pleasants. Pleasants noticed a shallow section just in front of a salient in the Confederate line held by Stephen Elliott's brigade, and his engineer's eye saw an opportunity for his miners to tunnel underneath the line, pack the tunnel with explosives, and blow it up, causing a massive breach in the rebel works. Pleasants approached his division commander, Robert Potter, with the idea, who then brought it to the attention of IX Corps commander Ambrose Burnside. Both Potter and Burnside loved the idea and immediately made preparations for it, notifying headquarters of their plan.

Opinions of the mine operation outside of the IX Corps were not very favorable. Mining operations like these were not new to warfare; some had been successful, others not. Many questioned the length of the tunnel, saying that the 500 feet the Pennsylvanians proposed to dig was too long to be properly ventilated. It was quickly decided that the Union high command did not want anything to do with Burnside's

The entrance to the Union mine at the Crater.

Oyster shells denote the position of the advanced Union line during the battle of the Crater at Petersburg National Battlefield.

operation, but did not prohibit his men from proceeding with their work, either. Still, many requests for simple supplies, such as wheelbarrows and picks, and engineering instruments needed to construct the mine were refused. Potter and Burnside often had to go through other channels to obtain them, and many of the necessary tools were constructed by the men.

Digging began on June 25 at noon. The experienced miners maintained a good pace, and it was almost pleasant work for them, relieving them of many of their normal military duties and bringing a piece of home to the battlefield. The ventilation issue was solved quickly, with the miners constructing a ventilation shaft and system for the tunnel. Although they did encounter a few obstacles along the way, the main tunnel, roughly 510.8 feet in length, according to engineer Pleasants, was completed on July 17. Two 40-foot branches were then dug on either side, creating three corridors underneath the enemy that could be packed with gunpowder.

The Confederates were not completely oblivious to the miners' activity. Chief of Artillery E. Porter Alexander suspected a mining operation late in June in front of Elliott's Salient. Soon afterward, the rebels began to dig countermines of their own, attempting not only to head off the Union operation before it could reach their lines but also to listen, underground, to the miners' activities. None of these operations were successful.

While the miners dug, the assault troops were readied for the operation, which would certainly be a unique one. Three weeks before the operation, Burnside selected Edward Ferrero's division, consisting entirely of black troops, to conduct the main assault. Ferrero's men rehearsed the attack for weeks and talked about what to expect with the explosion, as it would certainly provoke a great deal of awe if not prepared for it. The attack would consist of three columns. Two of the columns, one on each side of the crater, would immediately advance and begin to work their way down the Confederate line, widening the opening. The third column was to advance past the line and take the high ground behind the crater at the Jerusalem Plank Road. Only a short distance west of this position was the city of Petersburg.

Ferrero's men also discussed, in detail, what *not* to do. The primary subject here was the crater itself. The large, gaping hole would create a large bowl. If the men were to charge into the crater, the Confederates could simply line up along the edge and fire downward into the massive hole, like shooting fish in a barrel. The crater was a potential death trap and was to be avoided.

As preparations were completed, Grant made preparations for an additional assault to occur north of the James River at a location known as Deep Bottom. In conjunction, Grant ordered Meade to proceed with the mine operation. On July 27, the mine was packed with 8,000 pounds of gunpowder (4,000 less than the miners asked for), and the fuse was laid. The miners had requested a very specific type of fuse for the operation. Inexplicably, not only were they given common blasting fuse instead of the premium fuse they had asked for, but the fuse had also been cut into lengths of only 10 feet. The miners were forced to splice each of these together to create the hundreds of feet required for the detonation.

The next day, July 28, with all preparations made, the Union high command made a decision that would virtually guarantee that the mine operation would fail. Meade informed Burnside that day that the plan of attack did not meet his approval, and that the troops should head directly for the crest behind the crater rather than going to the sides. Further, instead of Ferrero's troops, who were inexperienced, Burnside should use troops who had been more exposed to combat. In reality, the decision to remove Ferrero's troops was entirely political; if the assault failed (and it was expected to fail miserably), Meade and Grant would have to answer to charges that they had sacrificed black troops for an assault they knew would not work.

Meade's orders created several large problems. First, of course, was that the troops who had spent weeks preparing for a special operation were to be replaced with new troops less than two days before the assault. Second, the troops would be ordered to charge directly, potentially trapping them in the crater. Finally, after much debate between Burnside's remaining three division commanders, they resorted to drawing straws to see who would lead the attack. The man who drew the short straw was James

The Crater. The person standing to the left gives some sense of scale.

Ledlie, who had nearly wiped out his previous brigade at the North Anna because he was too drunk to command.

You are at the site of Fort Morton, where 14 pieces of artillery were placed directly across from Elliott's Salient. Walk toward the cannons in the field. As you saw earlier at Confederate Battery 5, the tall grass represents the former location of the Confederate earthworks. It is from Fort Morton that Ambrose Burnside watched anxiously as the explosion of the mine and the battle of the Crater occurred.

As you walk up to the guns, you can see a large, gently sloped depression in front of you. Atop the rise on the opposite side is Elliott's Salient and the crater. Between the two are the Norfolk & Petersburg Railroad and Poor Creek. The Union advance lines were on the far side of both of these, with covered walkways taking advantage of the ridges and ravines in your front. The entrance to the mine is also on the far side, on the slope and to the right of the crater.

> *Continue 0.6 miles on Siege Road to Tour Stop 8.*

Exit your vehicle and take the path to your right. As you walk, you will see the guns of Fort Morton, the railroad, and Poor Creek to your right. The Confederate line was on the high ground to your left. You will also see white lines of oyster shells on the ground around you; these denote the advance Union lines, and the location where Ledlie's men lined up for the assault. Keep walking until you reach the entrance to the mine.

This is the entrance to the mine, reconstructed but still very much intact. Many sections of the mine have collapsed through the years, but some remain. On July 30 at 3:30 AM, as Ledlie's division lay in the covered earthworks just in front of the Confederate lines, Henry Pleasants entered the mine and lit the fuse, then ran out and waited. Nothing happened. Messages began to pour into Burnside's headquarters, asking why the explosion hadn't occurred, and to attack regardless of whether the mine could be detonated or not. After a bit of time, two of Pleasants's miners entered the mine and discovered the problem. The inferior fuse bad become wet at one of the splicing points. Rushing back out to get the appropriate tools, the miners repaired the fuse, then relit it.

The explosion finally occurred at 4:44 AM. By all accounts, it was stunning, even to the Federals who knew the blast was coming. Accounts describe a shaking of the ground, then an eruption of soil, followed by a deafening blast accompanied by a sheet of flame reaching skyward, and finally a rise and fall of earth, weapons, and men. As soon as those who witnessed it regained their senses, 164 Federal cannons and mortars opened on Elliott's Salient, and Ledlie's division leapt up from its position and charged toward the chaos. James Ledlie was not with them.

If you haven't already, climb down to the mine entrance to take a look, then continue on the path around the mine. The path, for the most part, follows alongside the Union mine, which is on your left side. Easily discernible are several areas where the mine has collapsed. You will also eventually come to the mine's ventilation shaft, just behind the Union position marked by the oyster shells. It was from behind these shells that Ledlie's men emerged and made their way up the hill, as you are now. Continue on until you have reached the crater.

The crater you see today is not what it once was, and certainly nothing compared to its July 30, 1864, appearance. The crater was, for a short time, used as a mass grave. After the war, the grave was excavated, and the site became a popular tourist attraction. At one point, when this portion of the battlefield was part of a golf course, the crater was America's most famous sand trap. Thankfully, the park service eventually acquired it and preserved it as you see today. The original crater was probably close to 200 feet long, 60 feet wide, and 30 feet deep. What you can see, looking down into the hole, are small rises in the ground. These are the locations of the three sections of the mine that the Federals filled with powder.

Of the 330 Confederates who were in the blast area, 278 were killed or wounded. The scene was one of absolute confusion. The rebels were trying to figure out what had just happened. The Union soldiers, meanwhile, were trying to figure out what to do. Most of Ledlie's men charged right into the crater and stopped. Some began to gather prisoners and send them rearward. Others succumbed to human nature and tried to dig away at exposed, writhing limbs. Still others were in absolute shock. In any case, those that did try to advance past the hole soon found that making their way up the steep wall of the crater on the Confederate side was extremely difficult, a long climb on sandy soil.

The Federals in the crater were able to direct concentrated fire at several units, who were driven backward. However, it was not long before other Confederate units began to make their way to the rim of the crater, their artillery soon adding to the punishment of the Union troops. Other brigades of the IX Corps also made their way toward the crater. Within an hour, 7,500 men, Union and Confederate, were packed into the small space where the explosion had occurred.

While the Union soldiers remained leaderless in and around the crater, their leader, James Ledlie, was getting drunk. Ledlie, along with Ferrero, who was supposed to lead the original attack, were in a bombproof well behind the Union lines. A surgeon, preparing for the expected mass casualties, entered the bombproof to find the two generals sharing a bottle of alcohol.

At 8 AM, Ferrero's division was ordered to advance into the crater, despite warnings to Burnside from his aides that the crater was already too packed and confusing. Many of the men never made it to the crater, cut down during their run across no-man's-land by Confederate canister fire. Once they did reach the crater, they found only a confusing mass of men. The black soldiers, in their first significant combat of the war, fought bravely but suffered heavy casualties. (It was later reported that many of these men were killed while trying to surrender.)

Northwest of the crater, three brigades of William Mahone's division were gathering in a sheltered ravine, several hundred yards away. (This area is now obscured by trees.) Mahone was positioned to the south of the crater when Lee asked him to send his men to help seal the breach. Just before 9 AM, one of Mahone's brigades charged from the ravine on a run, just as several of the Union brigades were beginning to advance past the crater. The two collided in the area just northwest of the crater, with the Federals being driven back after fierce fighting.

Over the rest of the morning and early afternoon, Mahone's other brigades were sent in. The Union troops clung desperately to their hold at the crater, most not wanting to risk crossing back over no-man's-land to return to their line.

> ### CASUALTIES— THE CRATER
>
> **Confederate:** killed, 361; wounded, 727; missing or captured, 403; total: 1,491
>
> **Union:** killed, 504; wounded, 1,881; missing or captured, 1,413; total: 3,798
>
> **Total Casualties: 5,289**

By 3 PM, the fight was over, and the Confederates had complete possession of the area around the crater.

Take the path that loops around the crater and view some of the monuments. You will find one to Mahone, a Petersburg native, who is buried nearby at Blandford Cemetery. You will also find one to the South Carolina soldiers who perished in the initial blast, as well as the Pennsylvania men who created it. Just north of the crater, you will also see remnants of the Confederate countermines.

The disaster at the crater begged for blame. In the end, a court of inquiry found that the assault had failed from, among other things, poor disposition of troops and a lack of leadership at the front. Ambrose Burnside, a former commander of the Army of the Potomac, went on furlough but was never called back to duty, and the Union IX Corps fell to John Parke. James Ledlie likewise went on a four-month-long sick leave and never came back. Edward Ferrero retained his command, and Grant submitted that had Ferrero's men led the assault as planned, they likely would have succeeded, but that he had agreed with Meade's decision. He referred to the battle of the Crater as "the saddest affair I ever witnessed in the war."

JERUSALEM PLANK ROAD

> *Pull out from the parking area and continue 0.4 miles on Siege Road, exiting the park at Crater Road. Turn left onto Crater Road and drive 1.9 miles to Flank Road. Turn right onto Flank Road and park near the interpretive signs for Fort Davis.*

Shortly after the initial assault on Petersburg but prior to the battle at the Crater, Grant, having decided on a siege, developed his strategy. It was based on simple math. The Union army had more men and supplies than the Confederates did, and could replenish each quickly. The rebels relied on the railroads coming into Petersburg. By extending the Federal line westward, Grant would not only cut off the routes of supply to Richmond and Lee's army, but would also stretch the Confederate line to the breaking point. Either Lee would eventually be forced to abandon the capital, an unlikely proposition, or he would simply have to continue weakening his line until he did not have enough men to keep the Federals back.

Grant ordered Wright's VI Corps and Hancock's II Corps to initiate this movement, stretching the line westward to cut off the Weldon & Petersburg Railroad. Before the movement even began, however, the Federals suffered a major casualty. Winfield Hancock's Gettysburg wound, bordering on unbearable for the last few months, finally became incapacitating. Unable to leave his tent, Hancock relinquished command of the II Corps to division commander David Birney.

Hancock would not be the only change in corps commanders, but the others would not be temporary. After blowing the initial assault against Petersburg on June 9, Quincy Gillmore was relieved of command of the Union X Corps, Army of the James, although he stuck around long enough to irritate his former commander, Benjamin Butler. Soon afterward, the other corps commander in Butler's army, Baldy Smith, was also dismissed. Shortly after his June 15 assault of Petersburg, Smith requested to be removed from Butler's command. Grant first attempted to mollify both Smith and Butler, giving Smith command of the troops of the army while Butler controlled administrative affairs. After receiving the order, Smith went by Grant's tent to thank him before taking a 10-day leave. During their conversation, Smith went on to freely criticize both Butler and George Meade liberally. As Smith went on his way, Grant rescinded his order and relieved Smith of command. Grant thought Smith an excellent general, and three months earlier had considered giving him command of the Army of the Potomac. But he could not have that kind of negative influence in the army. The X Corps was given temporarily to Alfred Terry, while Edward O. C. Ord took command of the XVIII Corps.

Gouverneur Warren's V Corps held the Union left near the Jerusalem Plank Road. Birney and Wright would connect with the V Corps and line up alongside the road, facing west. Then, with the connection to the V Corps as the hinge, the entire line would swing to face north, extending across the Weldon Railroad to the west. The movement was simple enough, although Wright's VI Corps, on the outside, would have to keep pace.

From the start, the line broke repeatedly, particularly in the sector of the VI Corps. From Confederate skirmishers to bad terrain, Wright's men seemed to run into every conceivable obstacle, and could only be advanced with heavy prodding, which Wright was not prone to do. By 10 AM, Birney ordered Francis Barlow, whose division was on the left of the II Corps and was supposed to maintain a link with Wright's corps, was ordered to leave him behind. Soon, Birney's men were in their assigned position, facing north, while Wright's VI Corps floated off to the west, creating an ever-widening gap in the line.

Fort Davis was, for some time, the largest earthwork in the entire Union line at Petersburg. However, the fort had not been built at the time of the battle of Jerusalem Plank Road. One of the outcomes of the battle was that the Federals did gain control of the road, and were able to extend their lines somewhat farther to the west, though not as far as they had hoped. Fort Davis was built to maintain possession of the road. Now maintained by the City of Petersburg, it was rescued only recently after years of neglect; you can now enter the fort and explore its interior.

❯ *Continue 0.9 miles on Flank Road. Pull off into the paved area on your right near the Virginia Civil War Trails Sign.*

Across from the Federals of the II Corps, the divisions of William Mahone and Cadmus Wilcox watched as the Union extended its lines. They had attempted to take this ground the previous day, and were doing what they could to slow the enemy advance, but in reality there was little else they could do. Mahone, though, had an ace up his sleeve.

A Petersburg native, Mahone knew of a ravine to the west that would be screened from the Federals. If he could bring even a small force here, he could come down hard on the Union left and roll it up. Mahone selected three brigades to move behind the Confederate lines and enter the ravine, while informing Wilcox of his plan so that he could press the attack as the flanking force came across. By 3 PM, the rebels were ready to go.

The small earthwork you see here was part of Fort Hays, which, like Fort Davis, had not been built by June 22. It was in this area, though, that Mahone's men emerged from the ravine, just in front of you, and bore down into the gap between the two Union corps, behind the exposed left flank of Barlow's division. Barlow could do nothing to stop the advance, and soon his division was breaking east for the Jerusalem Plank Road. Gershom Mott's and John Gibbon's divisions, next in line, were compelled to do the same. Birney's II Corps had been completely thrown back.

A. P. Hill had commanded Wilcox to add to the attack, but his men were slowed by the same thick vegetation that the Union VI Corps had encountered. Surprisingly, Wright's troops were barely involved, but they also fell back to the Jerusalem Plank Road.

It was a decisive rebel victory. The rebels had lost only 572 casualties to the Federals' 2,542, the vast majority of those being captured. In fact, the primary reason that Mahone's attack slowed was because the men were gathering prisoners. More important, the Confederates had prevented the Union from gaining the Weldon Railroad—at least for the time being.

GLOBE TAVERN

> *Continue west on for 2.3 miles to the intersection with Halifax Road. Turn right on Halifax Road, then pull into the parking area on your left. This is Tour Stop 1 for Petersburg National Battlefield's Western Front Driving Tour.*

In early August, Grant sent one of his most trusted subordinates, Phil Sheridan, north to drive the Confederates out of the Shenandoah Valley. The initial assignment had been given to Franz Sigel in May, but within a month, he had suffered an embarrassing defeat at New Market. Shortly afterward, David Hunter had achieved some progress in the valley, but he was quickly run off when Robert E. Lee sent Jubal Early's corps from the Army of Northern Virginia to Lynchburg. Early then proceeded to take his army, now called the Army of the Valley District, north to Winchester, across Maryland, and to the gates of Washington. Having decided enough was enough, Sheridan got the assignment of clearing the valley, and Grant was confident that he would be successful.

However, soon after his departure, rumors began to swirl. When Early had left, it had taken several weeks to determine just how many Confederates Lee had sent to Lynchburg, let alone which units they were. Now, with Sheridan ready to pounce on the rebels, prisoners had been captured giving details about forces of all sizes leaving to join Early in the valley. If the rumors were true, Sheridan might be marching into more than he could handle.

Lee had indeed sent more troops to the Shenandoah Valley, but the number actually on their way had been greatly exaggerated. This was by design. Lee's hope was that Grant would hear that sizeable numbers were moving to join Early, and would send more of his own troops; Lee could then counter by sending much of his army in the face of the weakened Union force, shifting the war back toward the Potomac. In reality, though, he had sent one division, Joseph Kershaw's of Richard Anderson's corps, with Anderson taking personal command. Soon afterward, Wade Hampton took a division of cavalry in the same direction.

Just before the battle of the Crater, Grant had launched an assault north of the river at Deep Bottom, prompting Lee to send many of his troops north, away from the mine, to defend the direct line to Richmond. Grant now considered the idea again, with the idea that he could either keep Lee from sending more men north or to recall those he had already sent. Therefore, late on August 13, the X Corps, now under the command of David Birney, and Winfield Hancock's II Corps crossed the river at Deep Bottom and began pressing their way toward the Confederate defenses. The assaults themselves were not very successful, but Grant was able to determine, by taking an account of the units that the captured prisoners belonged to, that Lee had sent only one division north. Further, he now knew that Lee had also weakened his Petersburg lines considerably. It had been almost two months since the Federals had unsuccessfully tried to hit the critical Weldon Railroad; perhaps now would be a good time to try again.

On August 18 at 5 AM, Gouverneur Warren's V Corps marched west from the Jerusalem Plank Road, still the westernmost point held by the Union line, toward the Weldon Railroad, 3 miles to the east. By 9 AM, Warren's lead division, Charles Griffin's, met the railroad at Globe Tavern, a large inn along the tracks. As the other divisions closed up behind him, Griffin immediately began tearing up the railroad. By 11 AM, the other three divisions were up, and they began to form lines around the position as Griffin worked. Romeyn Ayres's division lined up across the Halifax Road, facing north, and began to slowly march toward Petersburg, determined to find out where the Confederates were.

They were not far. P. G. T. Beauregard first received word that the Federals were at the Weldon Railroad about 10 AM. Notifying Lee north of the James, he began to scratch together a defensive force of three brigades to drive off what he thought was a Union raiding party. Henry Heth would lead them.

As Ayres advanced, Samuel Crawford's division began to line up on his right, while Lysander Cutler's formed behind him. Ayres, by this time, was almost a mile and a half north of Globe Tavern. Before Crawford and Cutler could get into position, Heth launched a counterattack from the north, surprising Ayres's lead brigades and driving them back. They were not able to push the Federals far, though, as Cutler was able to bring his men up from behind and stop them. Heth, now seeing that he was outnumbered considerably, withdrew back to the Petersburg defensive line, where he reported to Beauregard that if he were to drive off the enemy, he would need a bigger force.

Much of the battlefield of the battle of Globe Tavern, also known as the battle of Weldon Railroad, has either been lost or forested over, so try to orient yourself to the landscape as best you can. First, Fort Wadsworth, surrounding you, was not present during the battle, but was built shortly afterward. It does, however, sit in the middle of the battlefield, particularly that of the last day's fighting. Turn to face Halifax Road, the road you drove in on. As you face the road, you may have noticed (if a train happened to come by) that there is a railroad behind you. Please don't let these get you mixed up. The Halifax Road you see today is actually where the Petersburg & Weldon Railroad ran; it sits right atop the former railroad bed. Halifax Road was also present at the time, but was originally a bit behind you. The site of Globe Tavern, long gone, was to your right, a half-mile down the current road.

On the night of August 18, both sides arranged for reinforcements. Meade and Grant saw that the V Corps was isolated, and also saw an opportunity to possibly do more than just wreck the Weldon Railroad. One of Hancock's divisions was ordered to move from the battlefield at Deep Bottom to Warren's right. John Parke's IX Corps, which held the left of the Union line at Jerusalem Plank Road, was asked to extend westward as much possible, while a reserve unit of Edward Ord's XVIII Corps took its place in the line. The Confederates, still not aware that an entire Union corps had gathered around Globe Tavern, gave Henry Heth an additional two brigades, as well as three additional brigades to be led by William Mahone as a flanking force. Mahone would use the same ravine he had used to attack the Jerusalem Plank Road, but instead of swinging east, this time he would swing west.

Warren spent the rainy morning of August 19 improving his defenses. He had received new orders, and in the face of several disappointing performances, he was eager to prove himself to the Union high command. Instead of just wrecking the railroad, as previously ordered, he was now to attempt to hold his position, extending the Federal line westward to permanently close the Weldon Railroad to the Confederates. It was a big job, and Warren was up to it.

Griffin's men lined up along the railroad, facing west, while Ayres's, Crawford's, and Cutler's faced north. Cutler held the Union right, closest to where the Confederate flank attack would occur. Griffin's right flank was approximately in your location, and his line extended down the road; however, most of the battle on August 19 occurred about a half-mile to your north and northwest, most of which is now wooded over.

Around 5 PM, Heth advanced from the Union front, challenging Ayres's and Crawford's divisions. Shortly afterward, Mahone emerged from the west, surprising Cutler's troops and quickly rolling up their right flank, capturing two regiments nearly intact. Mahone's men kept working their way west against Mahone's division, who was now receiving fire from front and flank. By this time, however, Warren had Orlando Willcox's division of the IX Corps ready to move, and he sent them to support Crawford; Julius White's IX Corps division followed. Mahone's three brigades were simply not enough to take on three Union divisions, and he was forced to withdraw. Once again, the V Corps, with a little help, had held.

August 20 saw more rain, and little action between the two armies. Beauregard spent almost the entire day organizing enough troops to dislodge the Federal hold on the Weldon Railroad. Warren, meanwhile, decided to strengthen his lines by condensing them, pulling them back toward Globe Tavern. His men spent the day digging in. The Union formation was a strong L-shaped line, with Ayres's division holding the angle of the L around the Blick House, next to the railroad. Warren's men stretched southward along the railroad, while three divisions of the IX Corps—Willcox's, White's, and Robert Potter's—faced north, stretching almost a mile east across the Johnson Road.

Where you now stand is approximately where Warren formed the angle of his line.

Halifax Road, the former bed of the Weldon & Petersburg Railroad, at Reams's Station. The sunken railroad presented an obstacle for Union forces behind their own lines.

Still facing the road, Ayres's division would have been crowded in the space around you. The rest of the V Corps would have been lined up along the railroad (i.e., the current Halifax Road) to your right, while the line of the IX Corps would have extended out from your front.

August 21 brought another rainy morning and a new Confederate assault. The new rebel force was not only larger but consisted of fresh troops. Heth would again lead the attack from the north with four brigades, while Mahone would take the other four brigades against the Union left.

Turn around so that you are now facing away from the Halifax Road. Mahone marched along the Vaughn Road, just over a half-mile to your front, and then turned his men to face east, toward you. At 9 AM the Confederate artillery opened, and shortly afterward the infantry advanced against the Union lines. The Federals had cleared the field of fire in front of them, and their artillery was placed for maximum effect against approaching troops. As soon as they were within range, both Mahone's and Heth's men were mown down, taking heavy casualties. Mahone attempted to find the Union left for some time, but could not remain in front of the incoming fire for very long, eventually withdrawing his men. Mahone's advance came from your front, while Heth's came from your right.

One notable exception was Johnson Hagood's Confederate brigade. As the rest of Mahone's men were withdrawing, Hagood's were still advancing. They eventually charged the Union line and became trapped. It was only by a small miracle that Hagood was able to pull his brigade out, but not without taking heavy casualties. The monument you see to your left, along the Halifax Road, was placed in memory of Hagood's Brigade.

By 10:30 AM, Warren was wiring Union headquarters that he had successfully held the Weldon Railroad. Within days, the Federals would begin heavily fortifying this position—resulting in Fort Wentworth, surrounding you—as well as a line from your position west to the Jerusalem Plank Road and including Fort Hays, which you visited on your previous stop. The Union victory had severed yet another of the Confederacy's few remaining lifelines.

REAMS'S STATION

⟩ *From Fort Wentworth, pull out of the parking area to your right onto Halifax Road. Drive 5.3 miles on Halifax Road; for the entire length of the road, you are driving atop the former bed of the Petersburg & Weldon Railroad. At Reams Drive (SR 606), turn right, then drive 0.1 mile to the parking area on your right.*

The loss of the Weldon Railroad at Globe Tavern was a major blow to the Confederates. The railroad had been the primary supply line leading to the city. Considering his options, Robert E. Lee decided to organize a fleet of wagons to bring supplies from the closest open station on the railroad, Stony Creek Depot, to Petersburg using the Boydton Plank Road, west of the present Union position. The distance the wagons would have to cover in this roundabout route would be 30 miles, but the line was too important to give up.

As Warren solidified the Union hold on the railroad, Meade ordered Hancock's II Corps to proceed down the tracks and destroy them, making the railroad unusable should the position be lost. The men had just completed a night march from Deep Bottom and were exhausted, but after a short amount of rest made their way to the tracks, working their way south. By 1 PM August 23, the Federals had gained control of Reams's Station, one stop north of Stony Creek Depot on the Weldon line. By the next day, Hancock's two available divisions—Francis Barlow's and John Gibbon's—would be supplemented by David Gregg's cavalry. Barlow, though, who had been ill since before the fight at Deep Bottom, would go on sick leave, leaving Nelson Miles in command of the division.

There were other horsemen coming to the field. Wade Hampton, recalled from his mission to reinforce Jubal Early in the Shenandoah Valley, had by now taken a good look at the enemy operations around Reams's Station. Here was almost an entire

Union corps, completely isolated with almost no support. Hampton reported to Lee that he believed a decent-size infantry force might be able to bag the entire II Corps. Although it weakened his lines, the opportunity was too good to pass up. Lee assigned eight hand-picked brigades to A. P. Hill, and the infantry force left Petersburg at 4 PM on August 24, swinging wide around the Union line.

Late that evening, Hancock received reports from Meade that a large infantry force was seen moving west, probably to attack either his position or Warren's at Globe Tavern. It would not be until 1 AM that Hancock found out what "large" meant; 8,000 to 10,000 infantry, larger than what he had present at Reams's Station. The next morning, Hancock sent out cavalry patrols to the south and west to look for the Confederates, but finding none, ordered Gibbon to resume his work along the railroad.

At 5 AM on August 25, Hampton and Hill, at Holly Point Church to the west, conferred one final time about their plan of attack. Hampton would ride around the Federals and attack from the south, while Hill would march east with the infantry. Hampton and his troopers left immediately, coming into contact with the first Union cavalry patrol at 8 AM.

You are now standing on two battlefields. This ground had previously been fought over on June 29, when a cavalry raid led by James Wilson and Augustus Kautz almost ended in disaster here. Wilson had been surrounded by Confederate horsemen and was only barely able to make his escape. When Hancock's II Corps arrived at Reams's Station, some of the earthworks from that fight remained. However, they were not substantial to begin with, and the heavy rains of the previous days had diminished them significantly.

Begin to walk the short trail here at Reams's Station Battlefield, preserved by the Civil War Trust. The signs here interpret the second battle that involved Hancock's II Corps. As you proceed, you will pass a monument to the five North Carolina brigades that fought here. You will then turn left along the trail, with the Halifax Road to your right. As you walk, you can see the remnants of the Union earthworks on your left. Remember that the road is the former location of the railroad. There are two important things to note here. The first is how deep the road is when compared to the field. The railroad bed was equally as deep at the time of the battle. Not only was it extremely difficult to protect any defensive position running across the railroad, but anything that had to move from one side of the tracks to the other, be it troops or artillery shells, would need to be carried down one side and hauled up the other. The other thing to notice is that the distance between the earthworks and the railroad (the road) is very narrow. Maneuvering in this small area, particularly with the steep drop behind the line, is difficult for regiments and brigades; getting artillery into place, or removing it, was almost impossible to do quickly.

Now turn to face the field, so that your back is to the road. While Hampton slowly pushed the Federals back south of Reams's Station, eventually reaching Gibbon's men working on the track, A. P. Hill prepared to launch his attack from the west (your front). The first Confederate infantry was detected around noon, and over the next few hours, their opponents prepared to meet them, Hancock sending repeated telegrams to Meade regarding his situation. Meade responded that he would send more troops, but it would be hours before any of them could cover the distance between the II Corps and the rest of the Union army.

Hancock formed his men into a U-shaped line. The bottom of the U, using the old Union earthworks in front of you, faced directly west along the railroad, while the two upper portions of the U slanted to the southeast. Hill's first assault was against the base of the U at around 2 PM. The open field you see here, along with the tree line, is not very different from its 1864 appearance. The Confederates had about 200 yards of open ground to cover, and their first assault was beaten back with heavy casualties. Hill attacked again at 4 PM and 5 PM, all with the same result. It is this open field where most of the Confederate casualties occurred.

Finally, a fourth rebel assault, aimed squarely at the northern angle of the U, broke the Union line at the railroad bed. The Federals began stream rearward toward Oak Grove Church, just east of the tracks. Nelson Miles, whose division held this part of the U, along with Hancock, tried in vain to stop their men and hold against the enemy, and although some units tried to hold on, it was not enough. Soon, the base of the U had been shattered. The line to the north held for a time, while the line to the south (Gibbon's men, facing Hampton's dismounted cavalry) did the same, and Hancock began to organize a counterattack. Gibbon, however, said that his men could not do it, and David Gregg's cavalry was reporting that the roads running to the east, Hampton's escape route, were in danger of becoming closed off. Left with little choice, Hancock ordered his men to withdraw at 8 PM, humiliated at his defeat. While the Federals had destroyed the Weldon Railroad practically beyond repair, necessitating the Confederate wagon trains to continue rolling, Hampton had lost 2,602 men, with over 2,000 of these missing or captured, along with nine guns, trapped west of and along the railroad cut. The Confederates were beaten too badly to pursue the Federals—they had taken 814 casualties, with the total killed and wounded about even with the Union tally—but they had inflicted a severe blow to Hancock and the II Corps. Once the most revered corps in the Army of the Potomac, the II Corps had been repeatedly called upon to do the army's hardest fighting. Now the corps, along with its commander, was a shell of its former self.

〉 *Pull out to your left onto Reams Drive and drive 0.1 mile. Drive through Halifax Road, but turn left immediately beyond it onto Acorn Drive (SR 1101). Drive 0.2 mile and park in the church parking lot on your right.*

This is the location of Oak Grove Methodist Church, rebuilt on its original foundation. The church was at the center of the action for both battles at Reams's Station, and was used as headquarters, hospital, and rally point for both sides. During the second battle, after the base of the U collapsed, it was over the ground that you see here that much of the Confederate rout of the II Corps occurred. The road in front of the church is part of the old Halifax Road, now long since gone. You will also find interpretive signs here that tell the story of the June 29, 1864, cavalry battle that also ran across these fields.

PEEBLES'S FARM

❭ *From the church parking lot, turn right onto Acorn Drive and drive 0.1 mile to the T-intersection with Oak Grove Road (SR 606). Turn left, and then immediately turn right onto Halifax Road (SR 604). Drive 5 miles on Halifax Road, and then turn left onto Flank Road (immediately after your previous stop at Fort Wadsworth). Drive 2.3 miles on Flank Road, staying with it as it becomes SR 676. Pull into the parking area for Fort Fisher on your right, just before the intersection with Church Road (SR 672).*

With his gain of the Weldon Railroad, Grant had cut off a critical supply line to Lee's army. The next railroad, and the only one still running directly into Petersburg except from Richmond, was the South Side Railroad, still quite a distance away. Grant, though, still wanted to stretch the Confederate line as thin as possible. His strategy of attacking both north and south of the James River had had good effects each time. So he decided to try it again. The larger assault would occur north of the James against the Confederate lines protecting Richmond. South of the James, Warren's V Corps, along with some additional help, would move west to try to extend the Union line west to the Boydton Plank Road.

On September 29, the X and XVIII Corps of the Army of the James attacked at New Market Heights and Fort Harrison, not only scoring victories but gaining much respect for the significant contributions of black troops during the battles, particularly at New Market Heights. The next day, Union infantry marched from Fort Wadsworth toward an advanced defensive line that the enemy had erected along Squirrel Level Road. The line was thinly manned, with much of the rebel infantry having shifted north of the James. At the southern end of the line, near the Peebles's farm, was a large Confederate earthwork called Fort Archer.

Warren did not launch his attack until 1 PM, but when he did, it was decisive. His men overran Fort Archer, sending the scratched-together Confederate defensive line east toward their main line, just east of the Boydton Plank Road. For the rest of that day and all of the next, October 1, the Federals began to throw up earthworks westward from Fort Wadsworth to their newly gained ground. Fort Archer, which had

Fort Fisher, the largest earthwork on the Union line at Petersburg.

been facing east, and the former Confederate line around it were refaced to the west, and the fort was rechristened Fort Wheaton.

You are now at Fort Fisher, the largest fort on the entire Union line. Fort Fisher, as well as the other forts along the western front, was a result of the ground gained at the battle of Peebles's Farm, and did not exist at the time of the battle. As you walk around the fort, you will come to several wooden elevated platforms. Find the one along Church Road, and look across the road to the southwest. It was through this area that the Confederates were driven after the initial assault on September 30. Later that day and again on October 1, they conducted counterattacks but had little success. Fort Archer/Fort Wheaton is still intact, but it is not accessible. If you are facing Church Road, it lies about a half-mile to your left. Peebles's Farm is just beyond to the south.

❭ *From Fort Fisher, pull up to the intersection and turn right onto Church Road. Drive 0.8 mile to Hofheimer Road. Turn left onto Hofheimer Road and drive 0.9 mile to Boydton Plank Road (US 1). Turn left and drive 0.3 mile to Duncan Road, then turn left and drive 1.1 miles. Pull into the gravel area on your left, a gated road that leads into Pamplin Park.*

This road, Duncan Road, was also called Harmon Road at the time of the battle of Peebles's Farm. As you stand alongside the road and look down it, you are facing southeast, and turning just a bit to your left will point you to the area of Fort Archer. The main Confederate line, protecting the Boydton Plank Road, was just behind you. The fields to your left were part of the Hart Farm.

On the night of October 1, Gershom Mott's division of the II Corps was transported by the U.S. Military Railroad to join the V and IX Corps at Peebles Farm. On October 2, Mott marched his men up the Harmon Road, toward you, from the south. Henry Heth's division was in the works behind you, and challenged the Federals as they moved through the fields around you. Mott's men poked at the Confederate lines, and although they traded fire for several hours, they never launched a serious attack. Mott withdrew his men back toward Peebles's Farm, where the Union line was still growing.

If you wish to walk the fields of the Hart Farm, you may do so by visiting Pamplin Historical Park. There is a short trail that leads to the farm, and you will find some interpretation regarding the closing action of the battle of Peebles's Farm. The park protects much of the battlefield of April 2, 1865, which will be a major stop in your next chapter; you can enter by backtracking to the Boydton Plank Road, where you will see the entrance to the right.

BOYDTON PLANK ROAD/BURGESS'S MILL

> *From the gravel area, turn around and head back on Duncan Road for 1.1 miles to Boydton Plank Road. Turn left on Boydton Plank Road and drive 3.5 miles. Pull into the gravel area on your right with the historical marker next to the lake.*

In yet another left-right combination, Grant decided to assault the Confederate lines at Richmond with the Army of the James, and simultaneously to send the Army of the Potomac to attack the rebels south of Petersburg along the Boydton Plank Road. While Butler's men attacked along the Charles City and Williamsburg Roads east of Richmond, three Union corps were assigned to a task that would hopefully break the final intact Confederate lifeline at the South Side Railroad. John Parke's IX Corps would head west from Fort Fisher along Duncan Road to attack the enemy line along the Boydton Plank Road. Gouverneur Warren's V Corps would cross the stream of Hatcher's Run to the south, near the old Dabney saw mill. Winfield Hancock's II Corps would swing well south of both corps, emerging on the Boydton Plank Road far beyond the Confederate right.

The Confederate lines along Boydton Plank Road were thought to be fairly weak and not fully developed. Therefore, Parke, if he broke through the rebel line, would swing north up the Boydton Plank Road to cut the railroad. If Parke could not accomplish this, Hancock would move toward the railroad farther west. Warren would support whichever of the two corps was designated as the main attack column, depending on Parke's success.

That success was minimal. Contrary to Union intelligence, the Confederates had established a very strong line along Boydton Plank Road. Henry Heth was in charge of this sector, with A. P. Hill once again too ill to command, and his men were up to the task. The decision to shift support to the II Corps was made by 9 AM, with the V Corps ordered to support them.

Hancock's march went fairly smoothly, considering that his corps had the longest distance to march. He also had the help of David Gregg's cavalry division, protecting his open left flank. Starting their march at 3 AM, the Federals reached the Boydton Plank Road around 10:30 AM and immediately met Confederate resistance. Gregg also ran into the enemy to Hampton's south, but was able to break through and join Hancock. Hancock, only now receiving word that Parke was not able to break through, was ordered wait for Warren. Hancock halted his men near the intersection of Boydton Plank Road and White Oak Road, just south of Burgess's Mill.

Prowling around the area were two divisions of Wade Hampton's cavalry, one commanded by himself and the other by W. H. F. "Rooney" Lee. Hampton, quickly recognizing that the Union II Corps was becoming isolated, began to form a trap. Rooney Lee's cavalry was to their south, and would approach from that direction along the Boydton Plank Road. At the same time, Hampton would lead his horsemen from the west along White Oak Road. Heth, to the north, would send one brigade of cavalry and one of infantry down the road, while William Mahone's division, operating in the area, was sent to approach the Federals from the northwest.

If Warren could not join with Hancock in time, the entire Union II Corps would be virtually surrounded. Grant, though, had been at the front and spoken with Hancock, and had been assured that Samuel Crawford's division of the V Corps was on its way. Satisfied, at 4 PM, Grant, Meade, and their staff left Hancock and his men at the Boydton Plank Road.

The small bridge where you are standing is where the Boydton Plank Road crosses Hatcher's Run. The now large lake next to you was the former mill pond for Burgess's Mill, which once stood at this site. The northern end of Hancock's position was approximately here and extended well past the White Oak Road intersection, only a quarter-mile south of you. If you stand with the lake on your left, you are facing north. Rooney Lee would have been riding up from behind you, with Gregg's cavalry

A monument marks the spot where Confederate General John Pegram was killed at Hatcher's Run Battlefield.

facing south toward them. Hampton's cavalry would have come from your left-rear, south of the pond. Heth's men would have been coming toward your front, with Mahone's division coming in from the woods in your right front.

Samuel Crawford's V Corps division left for Hancock's position at 11:45 AM, but they were slowed by undergrowth, swamps, and poor weather conditions, and by 4:30 PM had still not made their way to Hancock's position. The Confederates would not wait for them. Mahone's men came first, surprising the Federals in the northeast corner of Hampton's defensive formation and driving them back. At almost the same time, Lee, Hampton, and Heth all made their advance. It was a furious fight, but a short one. Gregg's troopers were able to hold Lee, while Hancock organized a party to drive Mahone back out of the works. Sundown brought an end to the battle, and the II Corps slipped away in the darkness.

The Federals had lost 1,758 men, while the Confederates took about 1,300 casualties in their attempt to bag the II Corps. Among the latter casualties were two of Wade Hampton's sons, both of whom were serving on his staff. Lost to the Army of the Potomac, after a string of unfortunate defeats, was Winfield Hancock. In addition to his near-crippling Gettysburg wound, his spirit had simply been broken, and he handed command of the II Corps to Andrew Humphreys, Meade's chief of staff.

The Confederates, meanwhile, regained one of their most valuable commanders. James Longstreet had recovered from the wound he received at the Wilderness and returned to active service on October 19. It was he who was in command of the forces north of the James River, and easily repulsed Benjamin Butler's Federals.

HATCHER'S RUN

⟩ *From the gravel area at Burgess's Mill, pull out and continue south on Boydton Plank Road for 0.7 mile. Turn left onto Dabney Mill Road (SR 613) and drive 2.9 miles, following it winds, to Duncan Road (SR 670). Turn left onto Duncan Road and drive 0.3 mile. On your left, just after you cross a small bridge over Hatcher's Run, you will see a large pond. Find a safe place to make a U-turn and then return to this spot.*

While rifles and artillery continued incessantly along the entire Petersburg line, on the flanks of the two armies, where all of the action had been, the winter of 1864/1865 was relatively quiet, as it usually was. Poor roads and weather conditions ground active operations to a halt. One notable exception to this occurred December 7 through 11, when the Union V Corps headed south to destroy the Weldon Railroad beyond Reams's Station. Later known as the "Applejack Raid" because of the large stores of fermented apple cider that were found and consumed by the Federals, the Union troops succeeded in destroying another 16 miles of track, making Lee's fleet of wagons travel even farther south, to Hicksford, to pick up their supplies.

Ideally, of course, the Union army wished to shut of access to the Weldon Railroad together, which meant gaining possession of the Boydton Plank Road. On February 5, after a good break in the weather, Andrew Humphreys's II Corps and Warren's V Corps, along with Gregg's cavalry division, moved west to gain the road or, at the very least, capture a good portion of the Confederate supply wagons. The V Corps was to be the primary operator, south of Hatcher's Run, while the II Corps acted as a screen north of the stream.

As the V Corps moved into position, Humphreys took possession of two critical crossings of Hatcher's Run, the bridges at the Vaughn Road and at Armstrong's Mill. A defensive line was set up around the mill. Thomas Smyth's brigade formed a line facing west along the Duncan Road, with the mill and Hatcher's Run serving as its left flank. Half a mile north of the mill, Smyth's line turned, crossing the road and facing east. Gershom Mott's division formed farther to the east off Smyth's right flank. Soon, Humphreys noticed that a 300-yard gap lay between Smyth and Mott. At 4 PM, before he correct it, the Confederates, whose defensive line lay less than a half-mile to the north, attacked.

Henry Heth's division manned the lines at this point, with John Pegram's division of Gordon's corps forming the far right of the Confederate line. An additional division of Gordon's, Clement Evans's, was also brought up. While Pegram's moved south toward Dabney's Saw Mill, Heth's and Evans's struck the Federals from the north. Just as the rebels approached, however, Robert McAllister's Union brigade began to fill the gap. Three assaults were made on the Union line, but the Confederates, now outnumbered and taking converging fire, were forced to fall back. When the fighting ended at 5:30 PM, the line of the Federal II Corps was still intact.

While most of the land where the fighting of February 5 took place is currently inaccessible, much of the area is preserved by the Civil War Trust, just waiting for the proper funding to develop the site for visitors. The pond you see to your right is Armstrong's Mill Pond. The original mill sat just north of Hatcher's Run, very close to your current position. The Union line would have stretched from your position along the road behind you, and then turned to the east after approximately a half-mile.

〉 *Continue 0.3 mile to return to Dabney Mill Road. Turn left onto Dabney Mill Road and drive 0.6 mile, and then pull into the gravel parking area for Hatcher's Run Battlefield.*

As a result of the fighting at Armstrong's Mill and the lack of Confederate wagons found, the Union V Corps withdrew during the night of February 5. Warren halted his men near the Vaughn Road late that night. The next afternoon, February 6, Meade ordered Warren to probe westward to see if the rebels were active. Sam Crawford's division was chosen to head west toward Dabney's Saw Mill.

From the other direction, John Pegram's soldiers were on a similar mission, searching to the east to determine whether or not the Federals were still near the Boydton Plank Road. Pegram passed Dabney's Saw Mill around 1 PM. An hour later, Pegram and Crawford would collide to the east, south of Hatcher's Run.

Both sides were soon pouring reinforcements into the fight. Crawford's troops pushed Pegram back all the way to Dabney Mill, but Evans's division formed to the left of Pegram and pushed back. Crawford soon had support of his own from Romeyn Ayres's division, who again pushed the rebels rearward. During this action around the abandoned saw mill, the Federals were able to gain possession of what they first thought was a fortification, only to find that it was a huge pile of sawdust. William Mahone's division of A. P. Hill's corps was the next Confederate unit to arrive, just as Crawford's and Ayres's men were running out of ammunition. With this extra push, the Union line began to waver and eventually to break. But as the V Corps was retreating to the east, the VI Corps, sent by a worried George Meade, made its way to the field. Forming a line and making a final stand, the Federals were finally able to hold their position when night came.

Although the Confederate attack was largely successful, lost in the action was John Pegram, a good commander who was much beloved by his men. Pegram had been married only three weeks when he was killed at Hatcher's Run. Here at the Civil War Trust's Hatcher's Run Battlefield, you will find a monument to Pegram near the spot where he fell. Several interpretive signs are also located here to tell the story of the battle and help you orient yourself. If you walk up to the road and turn to the left, the site of Dabney's Saw Mill is to your front about a quarter-mile, just beyond the bend in the road. The Confederates would have attacked from your front, while the Federals approached from your rear.

There was some action the next day, with Crawford's division reforming and pushing west toward the mill. They withdrew that night, but not before they had started extending their line farther west, taking advantage of the position that Humphreys had held on February 5. Although they did not have the Boydton Plank Road, Lee was again forced to extend the Confederate right.

CITY POINT

❯ *From Hatcher's Run Battlefield, pull out left onto Dabney Mill Road and drive 2.3 miles to Boydton Plank Road (US 1). Turn right and drive 5 miles on Boydton Plank Road, and then take the ramp for I-85 North/US 460 East. Drive 4.7 miles. Follow the ramp for I-95 North, but after only 0.4 mile, keep right to continue to Wythe Street. Turn right on East Wythe Street and drive a total of 8.5 miles, staying with the road as it becomes VA 36. At East Randolph Road (VA 10), turn left and drive 0.4 mile to Terminal Street. Turn right on Terminal Street and drive 0.1 mile; turn right onto South Hopewell Street, then immediately turn left onto Station Street. Drive 0.7 mile on Station Street/Ramsey Avenue, then turn left onto Water Street. Drive 0.4 mile and enter the parking lot to your left across from the park.*

City Point was first occupied by Benjamin Butler's Army of the James at the beginning of the Bermuda Hundred campaign. When the Army of the Potomac came into the picture in mid-June 1864, the small prominence that marked where the Appomattox River met the James took on an all-new importance not only as the headquarters for the Union high command but also as the nerve center for the entire Federal force in the region.

Almost instantly upon their arrival, engineers began building warehouses, extending and improving wharves, setting up hospitals, and erecting tent cities that housed everything from blacksmiths to sutlers to barbers to the press. A bakery was built, providing the army with over 120,000 loaves of bread per day. A prison, known

Grant's headquarters cabin at City Point, Petersburg National Battlefield.

commonly as the "Bull Pen," housed both Confederate prisoners of war and Union criminals. With the deep-water James River to the north and east, it was estimated that City Point could see up to 40 steamboats, 75 sailing ships, and 100 barges per day. Before the war, City Point had seen its fortunes decline, and there was not much here except for a few small houses and the large Eppes Manor. After the army arrived, however, City Point was transformed into the busiest port in the world almost overnight.

The long pier you see here in the park is in the location of the City Point wharf. The wharf stretched along the eastern side of the peninsula for as far as you can see, with laborers constantly unloading supplies, mail, passengers, and everything else Grant's massive force would need during its stay outside of Petersburg. It was also approximately in this spot that Confederate secret agents were able to slip a bomb onto one of the ships. Its cargo happened to be ammunition, and when the bomb exploded, the incredible explosion instantly destroyed much of the wharf, the warehouses, and any surrounding buildings. Although the official total was 43 dead, it was most certainly higher than that, because most of the laborers on the docks were recently freed slaves who had never registered with anyone, and they simply disappeared. Remarkably, operations at City Point were slowed only slightly, and were soon back to normal.

Next to the wharf, along where the road now currently sits and running to the south, was the terminus of the City Point Railroad, which Grant soon appropriated as the U.S. Military Railroad. Union engineers soon extended the line to run behind almost the entire length of the Union line at Petersburg, delivering food, supplies, and men from the supply center at City Point. Fifteen trains per day delivered to stations all along the front, keeping the Union soldiers well fed and well supplied, something that their counterparts across no-man's-land were not able to accomplish easily.

❭ *Pull out to your left and round the corner onto Pecan Avenue. Drive 0.2 mile and turn left onto Cedar Lane, then pull into the parking lot on your right.*

The large home in front of you is "Appomattox," the estate of the Eppes family. The Eppeses left in 1862, when George McClellan's Peninsula campaign made Union gunboats a common sight from the back porch. When the Federals landed at City Point in 1864, the home was soon occupied by Union quartermaster Rufus Ingalls, who oversaw the vast operations at the supply base. The mansion is now the headquarters for Petersburg National Battlefield's City Point Unit. You will find several

Reconstructed entrenchments at Petersburg National Battlefield.

exhibits and a short film on City Point here, as well as the park staff, available to answer any of your questions.

Behind the home, you will find a wonderful view of the water. The James River is to your front and flows across your view to your right. To your left, the Appomattox River joins the James. The land to your left, between the two rivers, is the Bermuda Hundred peninsula.

As you walk the grounds, you will come to a small wooden cabin. Reconstructed from the original materials, this was Grant's headquarters, a stark contrast to the massive house to the west. Grant used his headquarters tent until November 1864, when the cold weather prompted him to seek cozier accommodations. Inside are two small rooms, one with a fireplace and table, the other with a small cot, similar to the one he slept on. The grounds around the cabin were once covered with similar structures, but Grant's cabin is all that is left today.

FORT STEDMAN

〉 *Pull out to your right onto Cedar Lane and drive 0.4 mile to East Broadway Avenue. Turn right on East Broadway Avenue and drive 0.6 mile, and then turn left onto East Randolph Road. Drive 0.6 mile on East Randolph Road to Winston Churchill Drive (VA 156) and turn right. Continue on VA 156 for 6 miles, keeping with it as it changes to VA 36. Enter Petersburg National Battlefield using the exit for Siege Road; remember that the receipt you received when you visited earlier is still good for entry. Follow Siege Road for 1 mile until you reach the park's Tour Stop 2, Confederate Battery 8.*

The spring of 1865 was quickly approaching. Good weather and, with it, the campaign season, would soon be here, and Robert E. Lee knew that he had critical decisions to make. His army was little more than 50,000 strong, and they were hungry. Elsewhere in the country, although some armies remained in the field, the situation for the Confederates was dire. John Bell Hood's army had been destroyed at Nashville. Phil Sheridan had laid waste to the Shenandoah Valley. Perhaps of most importance to Lee, William Tecumseh Sherman had taken Atlanta, then marched to the sea and through the Carolinas to claim Savannah, Charleston, and Wilmington. Now, although he still faced Joseph Johnston in North Carolina, Sherman was within a short march of joining Grant to deal the Army of Northern Virginia a death blow. The combined Union force, if the armies united, would be over 200,000 men, all of them ready to end the war.

Lee knew that the end was likely near. Perhaps Jefferson Davis did, too, but if he did, he would not admit it. Davis was committed to fighting for the Confederacy to the death, and no matter how painful it would be, Lee would do his duty and follow his orders. It left him with two options. The first would be to evacuate Petersburg and

Richmond, and hopefully join Johnston's army, but withdrawing from the Federal front without being mauled would be difficult. The second was to attack and somehow wound the enemy enough that the Confederates could buy time or, better yet, make a withdrawal without Union harassment. Either way, action needed to be taken before Sherman arrived.

Lee came to the conclusion that the only way to save his army to fight another day was to attack. He tasked John Brown Gordon, now commanding the Confederate II Corps while Jubal Early remained in the valley, with creating the attack plan on March 20. Lee approved Gordon's plan on March 23, and the moment of attack was set for March 25.

The earthwork you see here was originally Battery 8 on the Confederate Dimmock Line. When the Federals overtook the line in June 1864, they refaced this battery to face west and renamed it Fort Friend, after the nearby Friend House. Fort Friend is a little less than a mile northeast of Fort Stedman, and at the time of the rebel attack on Fort Stedman was a secondary Union defensive position. The artillery posted here would take part in the counterattack against the Confederates, and capturing the position, although it saw no other action, was actually a critical part of Gordon's original attack plan.

> *Continue on Siege Road for 1.2 miles to Fort Stedman, where you earlier visited Colquitt's Salient—Tour Stop 5, Fort Stedman, on the park tour map.*

Earlier in your tour, you visited this stop to see where the 1st Maine Heavy Artillery made its fateful charge on June 18, 1864, during the initial Union assault on Petersburg. It would also be here that the Confederates would try to end the siege.

From the parking area, Fort Stedman is the large earthwork to your right. For now, as you did before, proceed down the trail past the fort. As you proceed, you will see a rise to your right. This is Hare House Hill, and was the location of Union Battery X, also known as the Hare House Battery. Continuing on the path will lead you to Colquitt's Salient, a large bulge on the main Confederate defensive line. The trail forms a loop through the area, but the trail is closed for much of the year, due to eagles' nesting in the area. Keep walking until you reach Colquitt's Salient.

In the early hours of March 25, Gordon quietly gathered 11,500 Confederates, mostly from his corps but also from Bushrod Johnson's division of Richard Anderson's corps, behind Colquitt's Salient. Another 1,700 men of Cadmus Wilcox's division remained in reserve. Gordon's ultimate goal was the City Point Railroad, quite a distance from the Confederate line. However, less than 300 yards separated Colquitt's Salient from Fort Stedman. If they could cut the railroad here, the Union left would be isolated. Gordon's plan contained several intricate parts, and success would mean that all of them had to work, but if it did, it could mean a brilliant victory.

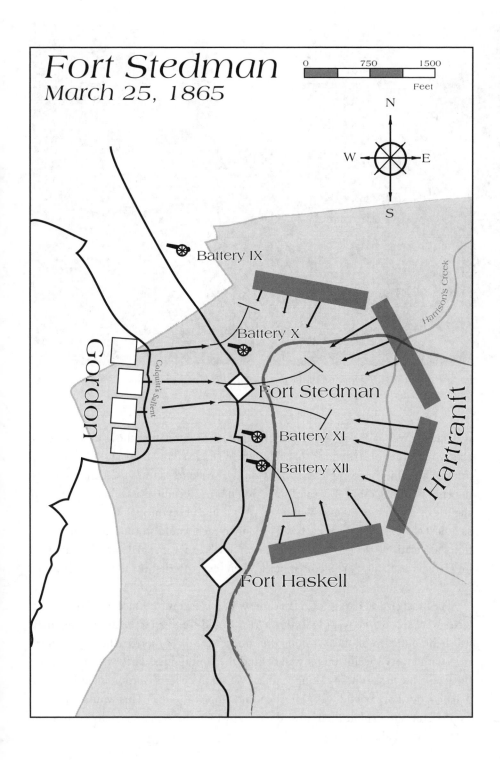

Fort Stedman
March 25, 1865

0   750   1500
Feet

N
W ⊕ E
S

Battery IX

Harrison's Creek

Battery X

Gordon

Colquitt's Salient

Fort Stedman

Hartranft

Battery XI

Battery XII

Fort Haskell

Fort Stedman sits atop the rise in the distance in this view from Colquitt's Salient on the Confederate line.

Under cover of darkness, the first group of men would be sent out to remove the abatis and other obstructions that filled the no-man's-land between the two main lines. When this was complete, a ruse would be used to capture the Union pickets, hopefully without a shot. The third wave would bring the initial assault. Preceded only slightly by a group of 50 men with axes, who would chop through the Union fraises as quickly as possible, three parties of 100 men each would storm four Union positions, all relatively close to each other. From north to south, one would be Battery X on Hare House Hill; Fort Stedman itself; then two batteries just to the south of the fort, Batteries XI and XII.

The most critical part of the plan came with the next wave. Once the fort and batteries were secure, the rest of Gordon's men would come up to begin pushing their way behind the Union lines. Among this group were three more parties of 100 men, each with a very specific target well behind the Union lines: They were to take out three separate forts running along a ridge. (Which three forts Gordon intended is still debated, but Fort Friend was almost certainly one of them.) This would allow the Confederates to exploit their advantage and widen the gap, eventually cutting the enemy line in half.

THE UNWRITTEN RULES OF WAR

While the large-scale war was a fierce one, war on the picket lines was, usually, decidedly friendlier. Pickets often exchanged jabs and jokes, as well as newspapers, tobacco, and other goods.

At Fort Stedman, several Confederates had crossed the picket line pretending to surrender, then turned their guns on their captors. Later, when a Union picket shouted out that he was hearing noises and warned his rebel counterparts that he was about to shoot, a quick-thinking Confederate replied that they were only gathering corn, and to go back to sleep.

That same Confederate was the man who was to fire the signal shot that would begin the rebel attack. When John Brown Gordon ordered the man to fire, the soldier hesitated, not wanting to betray the trust of the Union pickets. After Gordon ordered him again, the picket first shouted, "Hello, Yank! Wake up; we are going to shell the woods. Look out, we are coming." He then fired the shot, content that he had satisfied the unwritten rules of the picket line.

At 3:30 AM, with the obstructions cleared from their front, the first wave of Confederate attackers, along with the axmen assigned to them, dashed across no-man's-land in the dark. Apparently, one of the Federal pickets had not been picked up by the earlier mission, and he ran back toward the Union line, shouting for his comrades to wake up and meet the rebels. It was not enough.

From Colquitt's Salient, turn around and face toward the fort. Notice the relatively short distance between your position and Fort Stedman, then walk back toward the parking lot, but veer to your left to reach the site of Battery X at Hare House Hill. This battery held only two guns. When you reach the interpretive, again get your bearings. Note again the very short distance, less than 100 yards, between your current position at Battery X and Fort Stedman. Batteries XI and XII are just beyond the fort, out of your view. Remember, also, that almost all of the trees around would not be present.

This part of the Union line was manned by John Parke's IX Corps. Even before the debacle at the Crater, the IX Corps had not had a very distinguished run since the Overland campaign began almost a year before, but on this day, it would have its chance to redeem itself.

Grant had been telling his men all along the line to keep a very watchful eye for the past month. Like Lee, he knew that the enemy would soon be out of options. His commanders were put on alert for a Confederate attack, as well as the more likely scenario of a Confederate withdrawal. In either case, the Federals were to inflict as much damage as possible. Artillery on the front line was ordered to be loaded and at the ready at all times. The secondary defensive line, necessary to stem a rebel breakthrough, was also put on alert. This included the three forts that Gordon needed to capture to achieve victory.

Having been signaled by a single shot, the Confederates raced into the designated positions, completely surprising the Union soldiers manning the works. Battery X was able to fire its two guns, but was overrun before they could be reloaded. Battery XI, south of the fort, did not get a shot off. The much larger Fort Stedman required a bit more time, but it was not long before it was completely under enemy control. By 4:15 AM, the Confederates not only had their breakthrough, but were attacking the camps in the Union rear, finding most of the Federals still asleep.

Now walk over to Fort Stedman. As Union troops were hurriedly organized into a defense, the rebels continued to widen their gap. Gordon had wisely arranged for artillerymen to accompany the main wave of attackers, and soon they had turned Fort Stedman's guns around, using them against the Federals. In addition, Confederate artillery on the main line also opened up. The rebels pushed southward and took Battery XII, and although Union soldiers quickly counterattacked and took it back, they could not hold it for long. It appeared, for the moment, that the Confederates were in complete control of the situation. They had created a deep gouge in the union position, radiating out from Fort Stedman, at the center, and growing by the minute.

〉 *Continue on Siege Road for 0.4 miles to park Tour Stop 6, Fort Haskell.*

As Union infantry scrambled to mount a defense, Federal artillery roared into action. Once they had received word of the Confederate attack, the guns of Batteries VII and IX and Fort McGilvery to the north, Fort Friend and the Dunn House Battery to the east, and Fort Haskell to the south concentrated their fire on Fort Stedman and the advancing enemy. Gordon's men pushed their way toward these positions, but as they grew nearer, the men of Parke's IX Corps began to form up. Many of the Union regiments were set into motion by division commander John Hartranft, who would later receive much credit for his actions this day. Meanwhile, John Parke went to notify George Meade of the Confederate breakthrough, only to find that Meade was absent and that Parke was in temporary command of the Army of the Potomac.

This is Fort Haskell, scene of some of the most defiant Union defense. Fort Haskell repulsed several Confederate attacks, and it was here, with their left resting on the fort, that units of the IX Corps, hastily thrown together, began to push the enemy back. Cross the small bridge to enter the fort, turn to your right so that you are facing the direction from which you came, and then walk toward the edge of the fort. The rebels would have been charging toward you, with the Union cannons all pouring fire into their lines. The Federal infantry, once organized, would have lined up in the forest to your left, which was not here at the time of the battle.

By 5 AM, Gordon received distressing news. All three parties whose mission it was to take out the three Union forts on the secondary defense line had not been able to find their objectives. Further, Federal artillery was now taking its toll, and Union infantry was beginning to mount not only an organized resistance but possibly a counterattack. The Confederate position, essentially an inward bulge on the Union line, now meant that all of the men within that bulge were taking heavy fire from three sides. As he saw the resistance growing around him, Gordon sent word to Lee that the day was lost. Later, Gordon said that it was the resistance here at Fort Haskell that convinced him to withdraw.

It was about 7:45 AM when Hartranft had formed a completely sealed line around Fort Stedman and the batteries the Confederates had captured. While the Federals were going on the attack, the rebels were already on the run, attempting to cross back over no-man's-land and reach the safety of Colquitt's Salient. By 8 AM, it was all over. The last Confederate offensive operation of the war had failed, and Fort Stedman was firmly in Union hands.

> **CASUALTIES—FORT STEDMAN (INCLUDING OTHER ACTION OF MARCH 25)**
>
> **Confederate:** killed, wounded, missing, or captured: 4,000 (estimated)
>
> **Union:** killed, wounded, missing, or captured: 2,100
>
> **Total Casualties: 6,100 (estimated)**

Along other parts of the line, the Union II and VI Corps, deducing that the line must have been weakened, began to attack to their front, gaining some ground but not much. All told, the Confederates had almost nothing to show for the operation but 4,000 casualties and a few prisoners. For the Federals, Fort Stedman was a clear signal. It was time to finish this war.

PETERSBURG

Blandford Church and Cemetery

> *Continue on Siege Road for 1.4 miles until you reach the end of the park at Crater Road. Turn right on Crater Road and drive 0.6 mile to the entrance for Blandford Cemetery.*

Cemetery Hill, atop which Blandford Church sits, was one of the Union army's objectives during the Crater assault on July 30. The church and cemetery date back to 1735, and their rich history includes notable events and burials from the Colonial period as well as the American Revolution. By the time the Civil War came around,

Old Blandford Church, site of the nation's first Memorial Day celebrations.

however, the church was no longer being used for services, and was quickly turned into a field hospital.

Restored in 1901 as a memorial to the 30,000 Confederate dead in Blandford Cemetery, the interior of the chapel is stunning. Fifteen Tiffany stained-glass windows, each donated by one of the states that fought for the Confederacy (including some that didn't secede), fill the otherwise drab chapel with a glorious light. There are also memorials on the walls, and particularly distinct are the mentions of the Old Men and Young Boys who defended the city on June 9, 1864, and there is an annual remembrance at the church on that date to honor them. Among the notables in the cemetery are Confederate generals Cullen Battle and David Weisiger, as well as William Mahone, who led several memorable charges during the siege of Petersburg, including the one at the Crater, just beyond the trees from where he lies today.

The Siege Museum

❭ *From Blandford Cemetery, pull out to your right onto Crater Road. Drive 0.3 mile to East Washington Street. Turn left onto East Washington Street and drive 0.9 mile*

The Siege Museum at Petersburg.

to *North Market Street, then turn right and drive 0.3 mile. Turn right onto West Bank Street and drive 0.1 mile. A parking area is available behind the museum on your left.*

Remarkably, for all the shelling Petersburg took from Union artillery, quite a few beautiful old buildings survived and continue to grace the city today. One of them, the former Exchange Building, now houses the Siege Museum. Focused mainly on how Petersburg's citizens were affected by 10 months of warfare surrounding them, the museum boasts a noteworthy collection, ranging from simple period items and small personal effects and letters to industrial equipment, the former spire of one of the town's churches, and the headquarters wagon of General George Thomas. There is also an introductory film that provides a nice overview of wartime Petersburg, though both the film and its views are bit dated. Regardless, you are bound to find something inside that leaves an impression, making this museum a very personal experience.

Violet Bank

❯ *From the Siege Museum, pull out to your left onto Bank Street and drive 0.2 mile. Turn left onto US 1/US 301 (2nd Street) and drive 0.7 mile, crossing the Appomattox*

Violet Bank, Petersburg headquarters of Robert E. Lee.

River. Turn right onto Arlington Avenue; Violet Bank will be the house to your front at the T-intersection with Virginia Avenue. Find parking on the streets around the house.

Only a portion of the once massive Violet Bank house still remains, but like much of Petersburg, it has seen more than its share of history. The original home served as Lafayette's headquarters during the revolution, and when it burned down in 1810, the new house was built on top of the former foundation. Its tie to the Civil War comes from none other than Robert E. Lee, who used the house as his headquarters from the beginning of the Petersburg siege until late October. President Jefferson Davis also visited Lee in the home to talk strategy.

The home's basement houses several unique items, including Stonewall Jackson's field desk. The magnificent cucumber tree in front of the house, reportedly the world's largest, may have been planted by the original owner of the house. The real treasure, though, is the house itself. The City of Colonial Heights is dedicated to completing restoration and repair of the building, which has served as everything from town library to American Legion post. What's left of the home is small, but the history here looms large.

DEEP BOTTOM

⟩ *From the T-intersection, follow Arlington Avenue back to US 1/US 301 and turn right. Drive 1.3 miles to VA 144 (Temple Avenue). Turn right onto VA 144 South and drive 4.6 miles to VA 36. Turn left onto VA 36 and drive 1 mile, then take the ramp for I-295 North. Drive 12.7 miles on I-295 to exit 22A for VA 5/New Market Road. Take the exit and merge onto New Market Road, driving 1.7 miles to Kingsland Road. Follow Kingsland Road for 0.7 mile, then turn left onto Deep Bottom Road. Follow Deep Bottom Road for 1.3 miles to the public park and boat launch.*

Two battles occurred north of Deep Bottom, site of the northern bridgehead of a pontoon bridge linking Bermuda Hundred to the north side of the James River. The park here is near the site of the bridge, which the Federals used several times to quickly mass troops north of the James for various operations.

Walk down to the small pier at the river. As you face the water, the pontoon bridge crossed the river just to the left of the boat ramp. The area around Deep Bottom has not changed much—swamps, thick forests, and other obstacles that made movement through the area difficult, but it was the shortest and easiest route for the Union army to move here, and the Federals maintained their hold on this important bridgehead throughout the siege.

A public boat launch at Deep Bottom Landing. The Federal bridgehead and pontoon bridge here served as the starting point for many of the Union assaults north of the James River.

> Leave the parking area and drive 1.3 miles on Deep Bottom Road, then turn right onto Kingsland Road and drive 0.7 mile. Turn right onto New Market Road (VA 5) and drive 0.4 mile to Long Bridge Road, then turn left and drive 0.8 mile. Turn left onto Yahley Mill Road.

From this point on, the route will run through the heart of the battlefield. Please read below before you go any farther so that you can recognize some of the things you see along the way.

> Continue 1.5 miles north on Yahley Mill Road, then turn right onto Darbytown Road. Drive 0.4 mile on Darbytown Road to Fussell's Ridge Drive, where you will see a historic marker. Turn right here, then turn around and return to the intersection.

There isn't much left to see, at least at the moment, of either the First or Second Deep Bottom battlefields, but the Civil War Trust has been successful in acquiring some land here and is working to gain more. Much of the ground of the two battles overlaps each other, and one of the more important landmarks in both battles was Fussell's Mill.

As you drive north along Yahley Mill Road, you are headed toward the mill pond, out of view but not far to your front. During the first battle, Winfield Hancock's II Corps set a line to the southwest of the pond (along Long Bridge Road), while David Gregg's cavalry formed to the east of it. The main assault occurred on July 28, 1864, as a prelude to the battle of the Crater, with Grant again trying to draw Lee's forces north. Gregg's horsemen fought Joseph Kershaw's division, well to your right (east) through the forest.

The battle of Second Deep Bottom was intended to be an attack along the Richmond lines to prevent more Confederates from joining Jubal Early in the Shenandoah Valley, but the attention it attracted resulted in much greater gains for the Federals south of the James, as it enabled them to capture the Weldon Railroad. The II and X Corps, led by David Birney, crossed the pontoon bridge at Deep Bottom on the night of August 13, and both Hancock and Birney made their first attacks on August 14. You will come to a great bend in the road; the II Corps was in the portion south of the bend (i.e., south of the mill pond), while the X Corps was far to the west at New Market Heights. The rebels were able to repulse every attack. By the time fighting renewed on August 16, the X Corps had swung all the way around the line to the Union right. Alfred Terry's division of the X Corps was briefly able to break the Confederate line only to be driven back, though, to their approximate starting point, near the historic marker you see here at the end of your route. Confederate general John Chambliss was killed in the action. The Union troops did not withdraw until the night of August 20.

NEW MARKET HEIGHTS

❯ *From Fussell's Ridge Drive, turn left onto Darbytown Road and drive 1 mile to Turner Road. Turn left onto Turner Road and drive 1.8 mile, then turn right onto New Market Road (VA 5). Drive 0.3 mile on New Market Road; you will see a historic marker on your right. Carefully pull over, if possible; if not, continue driving.*

On the evening of September 28, the two corps of the Army of the James, David Birney's X Corps and Edward Ord's XVIII, crossed the James River at Deep Bottom to launch another assault against the Richmond defenses. Ord moved toward the heavily fortified Confederate line at Chaffin's Farm, while Birney headed north toward the naturally strong rebel position to the north at New Market Heights. The enemy was atop a steep slope that was covered with thick undergrowth, making an assault slow and dangerous.

Only 1,800 men manned these defenses, but the Confederates put up a stiff resistance. However, within an hour, they abandoned their position, moving west to aid in the defense of Chaffin's Bluff. Even though it was a relatively short battle, the Union victory was significant in several ways. For one, the Federals had taken a key position on the way to Richmond. More important, the assault had been conducted by Charles Paine's division of the XVIII Corps, selected to move along with Birney during the assault. Paine's division consisted entirely of black soldiers. Benjamin Butler, commander of the army, was determined to show the fighting ability of black soldiers. Paine's men suffered 800 casualties, but all who observed the action agreed that their skill and valor had been impressive. During the entire Civil War, sixteen Medals of Honor were awarded to black infantrymen; fourteen of those medals were earned here at New Market Heights.

None of the battlefield at New Market Heights is preserved. Here near the historic marker, you can look to your right (north) and see that the Confederate position was quite formidable. The Union attack occurred along much of the ridge to your north, with the rebels lined up just behind the New Market Road, between I-295 to the west and Long Bridge Road to the east.

FORT HARRISON

❯ *Continue 3.5 miles on New Market Road to Battlefield Park Road. Turn left onto Battlefield Park Road. Drive 2.3 miles to Fort Harrison; along the way, you will see excellent examples of the Richmond Confederate defensive line, much of it interpreted by the National Park Service. There will be several areas to stop and explore, so be sure not to rush through it.*

While the X Corps assaulted New Market Heights on September 29, Ord's XVIII Corps swung to the west to take Lee's defensive line at Chaffin's Bluff head on. The line began at the James River and then headed north, covering the three main roads from Richmond to the peninsula. The New Market Road was farthest south; in the middle was the Darbytown Road; and the northernmost road was the Charles City Road. Just like the rest of their line, with the Federals working constantly to lengthen their own earthworks, the rebels were stretched thin trying to defend their position.

Ord directed his assault toward the largest fort on the Confederate line, Fort Harrison, which, situated on high ground, provided an unobstructed view to the James River (which has obviously been lost now to the surrounding trees). Only 200 men held Fort Harrison, so when Ord launched his assault, the enemy was quickly overrun. However, fire from the other rebel forts on the line both north and south began to pour fire into Fort Harrison. The Federals were able to hold the fort, but they were prevented from moving down the line and capturing more of the works. Lee launched a strong counterattack the next day, but the Federals held, having been reinforced by the X Corps after their victory at New Market Heights. Further Union attempts to capture other Confederate fortifications on September 30 were unsuccessful.

Fort Harrison is extremely well preserved, as is much of the Confederate line from the James River north to New Market Road. In fact, after a private citizen's group donated the land to the state of Virginia and then the National Park Service, the first headquarters of the park were here at Fort Harrison, and they stayed here for 23 years, overseeing this gem of an earthwork. The visitor center here was recently reopened, and though it is only open regularly during the summer, it is also opened for special occasions, including the anniversary of the battle. You will notice that Fort Harrison is enclosed; like its counterparts south of the river, the fort used to face to the east only, and then was refaced to the west almost immediately upon its capture by the Federals, who renamed it Fort Burnham, after General Hiram Burnham, who was killed in the assault. There is an excellent nine-stop walking tour of the huge fort covering both the battle and the nature of the fortifications on the Confederate line. While you're here, drive or walk down Hoke-Brady Road and take a look at a few of the other fortifications, all of which were held by the Confederates not only during the attacks of September 29 and 30, but until the evacuation of Richmond. The interpretation and preservation of these works merit it much more frequent visitation than it usually receives.

RICHMOND

Tredegar Iron Works

⟩ *If you wish to continue exploring the Confederate earthworks, Battlefield Road continues all the way to Fort Brady at the James River, a distance of 3.6 miles.*

Otherwise, from Fort Harrison, pull out to your right and drive 2.3 mile, then turn left onto New Market Road (VA 5 West). Continue on VA 5 West for 5.3 miles. Turn left onto Wharf Street and continue as it becomes Dock Street, driving 1.4 miles total. Turn right onto South 14th Street, then take the next left onto East Canal Street and drive 0.3 mile. Turn left onto South 10th Street and drive 0.4 mile; when you come to the large traffic circle, continue straight onto Tredegar Street and drive another 0.2 mile. Parking for Tredegar Iron Works will be on your right.

In the last year of the Civil War, as Ulysses S. Grant began to move south and Phil Sheridan's cavalry raids increasingly threatened the city, Richmond went through several periods of panic. Still, everyday life went on in the city as best it could, even through the siege, as Richmond was not only the capital of the Confederacy but also a major industrial city. The remnants of one of the behemoths of Richmond's industry loom before you, the famous Tredegar Iron Works.

The story of Richmond during the war is best interpreted here at Richmond National Battlefield Park's main visitor center. The old iron works that now house the visitor center produced artillery and shells for the Confederates throughout the war and survived long after as an iron foundry. Walking the grounds to see the remnants

The ruins of the massive Tredegar Iron Works serves as headquarters for Richmond National Battlefield Park.

of the furnaces and mill runs and reading the interpretive signs about the foundry's history and operations provide a glimpse into Richmond's past, a large city of industrial might that was a center of Southern culture. Although these still stand true today, the city has changed a great deal since (and because of) the Civil War.

There are two interpretive centers on the site. One is operated by the National Park Service, and is free to visit. The center contains numerous maps, signs, and exhibits to help you interpret and decipher the swirl of activity that surrounded Richmond during the war. This is also the place to go to learn about any park programs happening either here or at the park's other units and visitors centers. The other museum, the American Civil War Center at Tredegar, is privately run. Its collection is very good, but the real strength of this museum is helping visitors understand the Civil War as a whole, presenting as many viewpoints as possible and putting you in the place of the people who had to make some very tough decisions during the period. The center's focus is highly interactive and makes a determined effort to interpret sensitive and not necessarily politically correct issues as historical conditions and debated viewpoints rather than as indisputable facts. Although there is a charge for the museum, it is an hour or two well spent, and children will enjoy the exhibits.

Hollywood Cemetery

⟩ *Turn left onto Tredegar Street and drive 0.1 mile to South 5th Street. Turn left onto 5th Street and drive 0.3 mile to East Canal Street. Turn left onto East Canal Street and drive 0.6 mile, continuing as it changes to Columbus Street. (Be sure to bear right, and do not take any of the exit ramps.) Turn left onto South Laurel Street and drive 0.2 mile to Albemarle Street, then turn right. Continue for one block; the cemetery entrance will be on your left.*

Not long before the Civil War began, Hollywood Cemetery was opened to provide some long-term relief for the many small cemeteries scattered around Richmond. Built in the then new garden style, the cemetery's lush landscape and beautiful view of the James River promised to be a peaceful place for many years to come. With the coming of the war, however, the cemetery took on a much more critical role.

Today, Hollywood Cemetery, still active, maintains that beautiful, peaceful feeling, but its inhabitants include some of the most well-known names of the Confederacy, including President Jefferson Davis. Cavalry legend J. E. B. Stuart is also here, as are Fitzhugh Lee and George Pickett. In addition, two United States presidents, James Monroe and John Tyler, also rest here. Certainly the most humbling memorial, though, is the Pyramid, a 90-foot granite monument placed amid 18,000 Confederate soldiers, a good many of whom are unknown. Dozens of other famous interments are here, so if you visit, be sure to set aside ample time.

This pyramid at Hollywood Cemetery in Richmond memorializes the 18,000 Confederate dead here, most of them unknown.

Virginia State Capitol

> *From the cemetery gates, pull out to your right, then turn left onto South Cherry Street. Take the next right onto Idlewood Avenue; continue for 0.9 mile as it changes to Byrd Street. Turn left onto South 9th Street and drive 0.3 mile. Turn left onto Bank Street. The entrance to the capitol is on Bank Street, but you will likely want to walk the capitol grounds. You can find street parking nearby.*

Every state capitol is somewhat unique, although viewed from a distance they may not seem to be. The Virginia State Capitol, however, really takes the cake, not only because of the history associated with it, but because most of the other state capitols that followed it somehow tried to emulate it. In total effect, none have equaled it.

The capitol was designed by Thomas Jefferson while he was in France, which inspired its templelike design, and construction was completed in 1788. The rotunda is also special, featuring all eight of Virginia's presidents, including the original marble sculpture of George Washington by Jean-Antoine Houdon, considered to be the finest likeness of our first president. The massive paintings that grace the walls of the various chambers are like a giant American history picture book—Jamestown, Yorktown, and,

The Virginia State Capitol Building, seat of the Confederate Congress from 1861–1865.

of course, the Civil War. The Confederate Congress met in the Old Hall of the House of Delegates, and it was here that Robert E. Lee was given command of the armies of Virginia. Along these walls are the likenesses and remembrances of Virginia's heroes, many of them household names. Infamy also comes with the territory; former vice president Aaron Burr was tried for treason in this same room. The grounds of the capitol are equally magnificent, large, sprawling, and dotted with both massive and humble memorials, all of them impressive.

After a massive restoration that took several years, the Virginia State Capitol is now once again open to tourists. It is open most days, and free guided tours are given hourly Monday through Saturday. The grounds are also open to the public.

Museum of the Confederacy

⟩ *From the intersection of Bank Street and 9th Street, turn right (north) onto 9th Street and continue 0.4 mile to East Leigh Street. Turn right on East Leigh Street and drive 0.2 mile. Turn right onto North 12th Street. The museum is just ahead 0.1 mile, but there is very limited street parking here. Your best bet is to park in the parking garage to your left just after you turn onto 12th Street. Parking here is free for museum visitors; just be sure to take your parking ticket with you to get it validated at the museum.*

While the siege drew on, Jefferson Davis, like much of the Confederacy, was holding on to hope. Unwilling to move the government, Davis would maintain both the capital and his home here in Richmond while Lee's army and the country withered away before his eyes. It was not until the end of the siege that the Confederate government was evacuated.

Although he did travel to the capitol building down the street, for the most part, Davis did his business and conferred with the generals of his army here at his home, dubbed the "White House of the Confederacy," now part of the collection of the Museum of the Confederacy. Hailing from Mississippi, this is the home that the Davis family used during its stay in Richmond. Besides the obvious strain of the war, the Davises suffered personal tragedy here as well, including the loss of a child, Joseph, who died after an accident at the mansion.

The guided tours of the home are conducted by well-trained staff that seems to have an answer for every question, whether it be about the Davis family or the origins of the wallpaper in each room. The tours are very entertaining and the stories told are both historically and personally intriguing. Tickets for the tour are obtained at the museum.

The Museum of the Confederacy is a true treasure trove of the history of this

The Museum of the Confederacy in Richmond boasts a spectacular collection, including the Confederate White House itself.

short-lived but world-changing nation. If the Confederate States of America had anything comparable to the Smithsonian, this is it. The museum is not exceedingly large (though its collection is), and you may find it fairly easy to get through quickly, but you will more likely catch yourself gaping at some of the artifacts you see. While most museums seem to display only one or two truly significant pieces, it seems that this museum carries at least one in every single display. For instance, that's not just any anchor sitting out in front of the museum; it's the CSS *Virginia*'s, along with her propeller shaft. That tent on display? It's Robert E. Lee's headquarters tent. Those leather riding gloves? Stonewall Jackson's. That plumed hat? Yes, it's the one made famous by J. E. B. Stuart, sitting on his field desk. It seems that personal effects of virtually every significant Confederate commander, east to west, have made their way here. (To showcase its massive collection, the Museum of the Confederacy is opening a satellite museum at Appomattox, providing visitors there with another great reason to make the drive west.) Be sure to buy the combination ticket to see both the museum and the White House; this place is a must-see.

Checkmate: The Appomattox Campaign

It was obvious to most in early 1865 that the Army of Northern Virginia could not remain in Petersburg for very much longer. While the Confederate supply lines of the South Side Railroad and the Boydton Plank Road were still open, other outside factors were now also coming into play. Phil Sheridan's Army of the Shenandoah, by now consisting of only cavalry but still almost 10,000 strong, would soon be rejoining the Army of the Potomac. Also near, and drawing closer every day, was William Tecumseh Sherman's combined force of the Army of the Tennessee and the Army of Georgia. Joseph E. Johnston's Confederate Army of Tennessee tried in vain to slow them down, but Sherman's breakneck pace through the Carolina swamplands led Johnston to remark that "there had been no such army in existence since the days of Julius Caesar."

Things accelerated further in late March. On March 19 to 21, Sherman defeated Johnston at Bentonville, North Carolina, brushing away one of the final obstacles that could have prevented him from moving north to join Grant. Also on March 19, Sheridan's troopers pulled into White House, Virginia, just northeast of Richmond. Grant was on the verge of having four Union armies—the armies of the Potomac, James, Shenandoah, and Tennessee—ready to complete the destruction of Lee's forces. To compound matters, the assault on Fort Stedman on March 25, a direct result of Jefferson Davis's reluctance to give up the fight, further weakened the Confederate army and signaled that Lee was now in a very desperate situation. The rebels still had

---

Inside the new Five Forks Visitor Center, Petersburg National Battlefield.

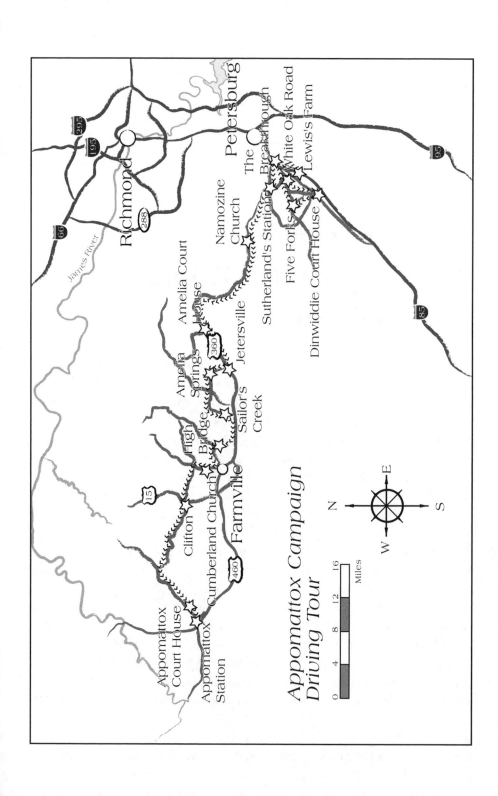

*Appomattox Campaign
Driving Tour*

plenty of fight left in them, but soon, the band of just over 50,000 men would be surrounded by a horde of 200,000 Federals.

Lee had already decided that he would have no choice but to pull out of Petersburg and abandon the capital as soon as Sherman crossed the Roanoke River, 60 miles to the south. Grant, however, did not want to leave that decision up to his opponent. He had avoided letting the Confederate commander take the initiative since he took the field at the Wilderness, and he was not about to give it up now. Grant surmised that Sherman's crossing of the Roanoke would be the trigger for the rebels to withdraw, with their only hope being to unite with Johnston's army to the south. He did not want to wait for Lee and Johnston to make plans to unite. He wanted to be the one to trigger the enemy withdrawal, putting the Army of Northern Virginia to flight, and hopefully, catching them in the open before they could find Johnston.

The Union and Confederate soldiers who had been hammering at each other for over four years were still face to face when the sun rose on March 29, 1865. Less than two weeks later, after a dizzying blur of events, these two great armies would finally take their rest. While other rebel forces remained in the field across the divided nation, Lee's surrender at Appomattox meant that the bloodshed was over. After four long years, the men would finally go home, and they would do so under the same flag.

BEFORE YOU GO

»PLANNING YOUR TRIP

Following the Appomattox campaign is, for the most part, a fairly straightforward journey. However, things can get a bit complicated. For instance, parts of the Confederate army, after it left the Petersburg lines, was occasionally separated—sometimes by design, sometimes not. The Union army also took multiple paths in its pursuit, not only following the enemy but also trying to get in front of it, all while also preventing the rebels from moving south to join Joe Johnston's army in North Carolina. It's not a difficult campaign to understand, by any means, but there is more to explore here than meets the eye at first glance.

Keeping that in mind, this tour will take you on the primary path of the Confederate retreat, taking you to all of the major battle sites, the towns where the rebels stopped, and then finally to the scene of the surrender, Appomattox Court House. If you do want to study the campaign in very great detail, you can find some of the lesser-known sites on the Lee's Retreat route. Developed in the early 1990s, the Virginia Civil War Trails folks, along with a

> **APPOMATTOX CAMPAIGN**
>
> **Number of sites:** 19
>
> **Total miles:** 160
>
> **Estimated time:** 2–3 days

number of very dedicated individuals, have thoroughly researched every aspect of this campaign. In addition to the trail brochure that you can pick up at many rest stops and other locations along the way, there is also a guide to the trail written by Chris Calkins, perhaps the foremost expert on the campaign. Even if you choose to visit only the sites listed here, Calkins's guide, filled with detailed maps and eyewitness accounts, will prove a valuable companion to your tour. In fact, depending on time, you may want to follow the main route presented here to Appomattox, then hit some of those smaller sites on your way back to Petersburg or Richmond.

» RECOMMENDATIONS

As noted, this tour is a one-way tour from Petersburg to Appomattox. Taken as a straight shot with no stops, the distance can be driven in less than two hours. You, of course, will be stopping along the way. Therefore, you should be aware that as far as restaurants, hotels, and other amenities go, there isn't a whole lot between the two cities. Further, you will mostly be driving on state and county roads off the main highway. Farmville, approximately in the middle, is the one exception, having a number of restaurants and gas stations, but other than that, the pickings will be slim. You should certainly take advantage of the opportunity to stop at some of the smaller restaurants and visit with the locals, but you may also want to stock up on some "road food" or other snacks before you set out. You may also want to consider a long picnic stop at Sailor's Creek Battlefield Historical State Park, about midway through your journey.

You will spend the first half of your tour in and around Petersburg, keeping you close to many choices for food and lodging. However, after you've made the drive out to Appomattox, that two-hour drive back may seem longer than it really is. If, however, you'd like to stay near the end point of your tour, Lynchburg, 20 miles beyond Appomattox, has plenty of hotels and restaurants, not to mention a good deal of Civil War history of its own.

THE CAMPAIGN TOUR

LEWIS'S FARM

> *Your tour begins on Quaker Road, southwest of Petersburg. From the intersection of Boydton Plank Road and Quaker Road, drive 0.8 mile south on Quaker Road to a historical marker on your left. Make a U-turn and come back to the marker.*

When the Confederates launched their attack east of Petersburg at Fort Stedman on March 25, they had faced the Union IX Corps. After they were repulsed, the II and V Corps, west of Petersburg, had launched their own attacks, knowing that Lee must have weakened his line to support the large assault. The assumption was correct, so by the end of the day, the Federals had captured much of the Confederate picket line, bringing the two lines closer together.

Just to the Union left, the Boydton Plank Road, Lee's wagon supply line to the terminus of the Weldon Railroad, still remained in Confederate hands. The Federals had tried on several occasions to take the road, but came up short each time. Grant, however, needed that road, and the South Side Railroad beyond it, to force the rebels out of Petersburg. Accordingly, orders went out for an assault by Andrew A. Humphrey's II Corps, Gouverneur Warren's V Corps, and Phil Sheridan's Army of the Shenandoah, to take both the road and, if possible, the railroad beyond it. Their place on the main Union line would be filled by divisions from Edward Ord's Army of the James, was brought down from Bermuda Hundred on the night on March 27.

The first movement was made early on March 29, only four days after Lee's Fort Stedman assault. While Sheridan rode southwest to Dinwiddie Court House in an attempt to outflank the Confederates, Warren and Humphreys left the trenches and began to move west and then north, up the Quaker Road toward the Boydton Plank Road.

In their front, less than 2 miles away, was the main Confederate line, stretching across the Boydton Plank Road just south of Burgess's Mill, near its intersection with White Oak Road. A. P. Hill's corps manned the works here, facing south, and Richard Anderson's corps, only one division strong, was lined up to their right.

You are now at the site of the Lewis Farm, where the first heavy action of Grant's plan occurred. Look down the road with the historical marker to your right. (The farm is private property, so remain in your vehicle.) The Lewis Farm was in the fields to your left. The Federals advanced from behind you, with the II Corps on your right and the V Corps on your left. After meeting skirmishers in your rear at the Quaker Road's crossing of Gravelly Run, the lead elements of Warren's V Corps—Joshua Lawrence Chamberlain's brigade—found Henry Wise's Confederate brigade, sent forward from Bushrod Johnson's division of Anderson's corps. The rebels were to your front, facing you.

Most of the battle occurred in the area to the left of the road. Chamberlain's men pushed the enemy back three-quarters of a mile to the Boydton Plank Road, but Anderson then sent in two more brigades and launched a counterattack. After a fierce fight, Chamberlain, with his left beginning to fold, asked for reinforcements, which were soon on their way. Once Anderson saw that more Federals were coming, he withdrew his troops to Confederate entrenchments along the White Oak Road. The rest of the V Corps moved up and formed their line directly across the Boydton Plank Road, finally cutting off Lee's supply line from the Weldon Railroad, far to the south.

WHITE OAK ROAD

〉 *From the historic marker, drive forward 0.8 mile to Boydton Plank Road; this is the same direction that the battle of Lewis's Farm progressed. Turn right onto Boydton Plank Road (US 1) and drive 0.9 mile to White Oak Road (SR 613). Turn left onto White Oak Road and drive 1.7 miles to the intersection with Claiborne Road. A parking area for White Oak Road Battlefield will be on your right.*

As soon as the Federals had possession of the Boydton Plank Road, they made preparations to hold it. On March 30, Humphreys's II Corps sidled to the left to cover the road, while Warren's V Corps moved its entire force to the west and prepared to meet the Confederates to their front. Warren slowly and cautiously moved north and found Richard Anderson's men lined up along the White Oak Road. The Union troops began to dig in and some skirmishing took place, but no major action occurred.

Robert E. Lee, by this time, knew that Phil Sheridan was moving to Dinwiddie Court House. Sheridan's cavalry was preparing to perform a grand sweep around the Confederate right, and Lee knew that he needed to protect the South Side Railroad at all costs. Lee instructed Anderson and Bushrod Johnson, commanding the only division in Anderson's corps, to strengthen their position along White Oak Road and sent George Pickett's division of Longstreet's corps toward Dinwiddie Court House, hoping to intercept Sheridan and drive him off.

The Federals also knew about Pickett. If Anderson and Pickett were able to join forces, either Sheridan or the V Corps could be endangered. Therefore, Grant ordered Warren to attack along Anderson's front, holding him in place at the very least and, hopefully, driving him back and cutting him off from Pickett entirely. The best way to do this was to close off the White Oak Road west of the Confederate position.

Lee knew that Anderson was outnumbered, but as he had often done in the past, he would not wait for the Federals to attack him. Riding to Anderson's position, Lee was told that the Union left, across the road, was "up in the air," not anchored on any strong position or bent backwards to receive an attack, and was therefore vulnerable to an attack on its flank. Lee saw his chance.

You are on the White Oak Road Battlefield, protected by the Civil War Trust. There is a 0.6-mile trail here with interpretive signs that will take you along the Confederate entrenchments. The trail is a nice easy walk on a good path, and the woods here are isolated and peaceful, so this one is definitely worth taking the time for. However, please be aware that the trail crosses White Oak Road twice. Traffic can move rather swiftly along this road, and the drivers won't often be expecting a pedestrian out here in the woods and farms, so take extreme caution as you walk across.

Before you take the trail, orient yourself to the terrain around you. The intersection here at the parking area is where Claiborne Road meets White Oak Road. The Confederate right angled around the intersection, with the right side of its line along Claiborne Road. Early on March 31, before the Federals across from them were ready to move, Lee prepared to send four brigades from this area to attack the Union left. A brigade from Romeyn Ayres's division, on Warren's left, was already feeling its way toward the enemy line when the Confederates attacked. The Federals were completely surprised and quickly began to fall back. Before long, the units of Ayres's division were being routed. To their left rear and next in line was Samuel Crawford's division. As Ayres's men became entangled in their column, they, too, became disorganized and began to retreat in disorder. Both Federal divisions fell back to a position south of Gravelly Run, where Warren's last division, Charles Griffin's, was being held in reserve.

Walk to the intersection and face across White Oak Road toward the open fields, which were much larger at the time of the battle. It was in this field that the Confederates first struck Ayres's division, driving them back in confusion, and farther in the distance and to the left is where Crawford's Federals were hit. When the two Union divisions fell back, they moved to the southeast behind Gravelly Run. The rebels, realizing that they could not the position they had chased the enemy to, fell back slightly to the low earthworks that the Federals had held earlier.

Now, take the trail along the Confederate works. You will find that much of the line here is very well preserved, with the earthworks still substantial. Along the path, you will find a large artillery position. It was from this position that Lee, along with Johnson, watched the Union troops reform and begin their counterattack at 2:30 PM. (Remember that these were open fields 150 years ago.) Warren took his time organizing the movement, but once it began, it was overwhelming—or, at least, should have been. This time, Griffin's Federals led the attack, supported by Nelson Miles's men of the II Corps, while Ayres and Crawford supported them. After about an hour of heavy fighting, the rebels withdrew back to their original defensive line. Griffin, meanwhile, swung to the west to wrap around the Confederate right and finally cut off the White Oak Road. Although it had taken all day, Warren had succeeded in keeping Richard Anderson's and George Pickett's forces from uniting.

When the Federals reached the Confederate defenses, Warren stopped his men, thinking the rebel works too strong for an assault. It may have been a reasonable decision; Warren had achieved his objective, and the works were indeed strong. However, he had also taken an inordinate amount of time, and he outnumbered the enemy by a considerable margin. By the end of the next day, April 1, his decision not to continue the attack here, coupled along with many similar incidents, would come back to haunt him.

DINWIDDIE COURT HOUSE

❯ *From the parking area, turn right onto White Oak Road and drive 1.7 miles to Boisseau Road (SR 661). Turn left onto Boisseau Road and drive 2.4 miles to Courthouse Road (SR 627) and turn left. Drive 1.4 miles on Courthouse Road, and then turn right onto Wilkinson Road (SR 611). Drive 1.2 miles on Wilkinson Road; you will cross a small bridge with wooden guardrails. Cross the bridge, make a U-turn when safe, and return to the bridge.*

While Gouverneur Warren had his hands full with Bushrod Johnson's division at White Oak Road on March 31, Phil Sheridan was trying to get past the Confederates that Lee had sent with George Pickett. Lee had guessed that Sheridan would have to move through Dinwiddie Court House, and he was right. Lee sent the cavalry commanded by his nephew and son—Fitzhugh Lee and W. H. F. "Rooney" Lee—to support Pickett, as well as another division of cavalry under Thomas Rosser. Pickett led his combined group from the intersection known as Five Forks south toward Dinwiddie Court House at 10 AM.

Not long after Pickett moved, Phil Sheridan was just leaving Dinwiddie Court House, with Five Forks, a key intersection on his approach to the South Side Railroad, as his objective. As Sheridan headed north on Dinwiddie Court House Road, Pickett was to the west on the other side of a swampy creek known as Chamberlain's Bed. Pickett used both of the two primary crossings across the creek: Danse's Ford, to the north, and Fitzgerald's Ford to the south. Sheridan, wanting to protect his left flank as he moved north, also sent men to both fords, one brigade each.

You are now at Fitzgerald's Ford. Here, Charles Smith's Union cavalry brigade found two Confederate cavalry divisions, one commanded by Rooney Lee and the other by Thomas Rosser, which would have come from your rear, crossing across the wetlands here, while Smith was coming toward you on what was then the Ford Station Road. To the north (your left), Henry Davies's Federals were met at Danse's Ford by Pickett's infantry, who soon pushed the Union cavalry back. This had a direct effect on Smith's stand here, as Davies's retreat opened Smith's flank to Pickett's men. With Confederate cavalry in his front and infantry on his right, Smith was forced to withdraw back down the Ford Station Road toward Dinwiddie Court House Road.

Dinwiddie Court House, looking very much as it did in 1865.

> ❯ *Continue forward on Wilkinson Road 1.2 miles to return to Courthouse Road.*
> *Turn right on Courthouse Road and drive 0.9 mile to Boydton Plank Road (US 1).*
> *Turn right on Boydton Plank Road and drive 0.2 mile, then park near the court-*
> *house on your left.*

Sheridan sent an additional two brigades of cavalry to reinforce Davies, but it was not enough to hold back Pickett's infantrymen. The Federals were pushed back from Danse's Ford and then south on Dinwiddie Court House Road. Pickett pressed south, eventually joining Lee's cavalry coming from Fitzgerald's Ford. However, during the fight, more Union cavalry was arriving at Dinwiddie Court House. Two brigades from George Custer's division who had been guarding the wagon train arrived at 5:30 PM, and the Federals formed a line across Dinwiddie Court House Road north of the town. Pickett and Lee's reunion happened too late for the Confederates to continue the attack, and the Federals held their position until nightfall.

The courthouse you see here is the same one that Sheridan's cavalry camped around on the nights of March 30 and 31. There is a monument here commemorating the participants of both sides of the battle of Dinwiddie Court House, as well as the other Civil War battles that occurred in the county. You will also find a large monument to the county's Confederate sons. If you walk to Courthouse Road and turn so that the courthouse is to your right, you will be looking northeast up the Boydton Plank Road. The Union defensive line was across the Dinwiddie Court House Road, about a half-mile to the north.

At 5 PM, as Sheridan was still fighting off Pickett, Gouverneur Warren received a message from George Meade to send a division to Dinwiddie Court House in the hopes of trapping Pickett's men. However, because of the heavy rains that had fallen in the previous days, Romeyn Ayres's division was stalled at Gravelly Run, and would not join Sheridan until the next morning. In reality, there was little Warren could do about it, but in Sheridan's eyes, it was just another strike against the commander of the V Corps.

George Pickett also received a message. Intending to camp outside Dinwiddie Court House and resume the attack in the morning, Pickett found out that Warren was moving in his left rear. Rather than become squeezed by two large Federal forces, Pickett withdrew, prompting a note from a displeased Robert E. Lee: "Hold Five Forks at all hazards . . . and prevent Union forces from striking the Southside Railroad. Regret exceedingly your forced withdrawal, and your inability to hold the advantage you had gained." Lee had put the fate of the army in Pickett's hands before, on July 3, 1863, on the field at Gettysburg. On that day, overwhelming odds had prevented him from succeeding, and there was little that he could have done to change the result. Now Pickett would have another opportunity, and this time, responsibility for the outcome would sit squarely and undeniably on his shoulders.

FIVE FORKS

> *From the courthouse, turn right onto Boydton Plank Road and drive 0.2 mile, then turn left onto Courthouse Road (SR 627). Drive 4.7 miles on Courthouse Road; pull into Petersburg National Battlefield's Five Forks visitor center on your left.*

By early morning on April 1, Pickett had withdrawn his infantry back to Five Forks, with Fitz Lee's cavalry screening the movement. The Confederates immediately began to dig in, improving on earthworks they had dug the previous day. Their defensive line ran for almost 2 miles along the north side of White Oak Road, facing south, and was centered on a five-way intersection known as Five Forks. White Oak Road ran to the east and west of the crossing, while two other roads ran to the south (Scott's Road) and southeast (Dinwiddie Court House Road). To the north, Ford's Road stretched to the South Side Railroad, less than 3 miles beyond.

Pickett's force was sizeable, and dislodging them from the heavily wooded area around the intersection would be difficult. Three brigades of infantry and one of cavalry,

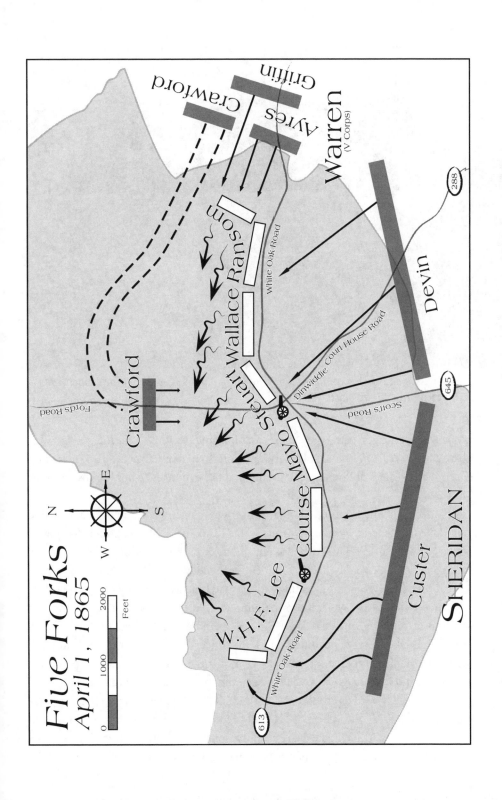

Five Forks
April 1, 1865

Feet
0   1000   2000

N
E
S
W

Warren
(V Corps)

Crawford
Griffin
Ayres

Ransom
Wallace
Steuart
Course Mayo
W.H.F. Lee

Crawford

White Oak Road
Dinwiddie Court House Road
Fords Road
Scott's Road
White Oak Road

288
645
613

Devin

Custer

SHERIDAN

The star-shaped Five Forks intersection. The cannon marks the spot of the Confederate artillery position at the northwest corner.

along with a four-gun battery, lay to the east of the intersection. At the intersection were three guns of William Pegram's artillery battalion. To the west, two more brigades of infantry, two brigades of Rooney Lee's cavalry, and three more of Pegram's guns ran along the road.

North of the intersection, Thomas Rosser's cavalry brigade had been assigned to guard the Confederate wagons. Normally, this would be of little consequence, but its impact on the battle at Five Forks was enormous. Rosser and one of his fellow officers had gone fishing two days before, and chose this day, April 1, 1865, to host a shad bake, which involved not only eating a lot of shad but also drinking a lot of bourbon. Pickett, ordered by the general commanding to hold Five Forks at all costs, thought this was a fine idea, and decided to attend, as did Fitzhugh Lee. Just after noon, thinking their defensive position sound, the officers rode north to join in Rosser's tempting picnic. In their haste, neither one of them told anyone where they were going, nor did they assign anyone to take command in their absence.

In those heavy woods around Five Forks, Phil Sheridan was making final preparations for an assault. As Robert E. Lee had predicted, Sheridan's cavalry, along with Warren's V Corps, would make their run at the South Side Railroad through Five Forks.

The Five Forks Unit of Petersburg National Battlefield captures a large part of the area encompassing the battle. There are several trails running through, and while most are recreational, some will take you through parts of the Confederate lines. You can pick up information on the battle and the trails here at the new Five Forks visitor center, opened in 2009. You will find a few artifacts here, along with a film about the battle and park service employees who can answer any and all of your questions. A far cry better than the previous center (a small shack which had been at the Five Forks intersection), the new center has brought a new and long-overdue light to this critical piece of the story of the Civil War.

❭ *From the visitor center, turn right onto Courthouse Road. Drive 0.1 mile and pull into the parking area to your left.*

Sheridan's plan for capturing the intersection placed most of the burden on the infantry. Cavalry, though, would also play an active part. While Warren moved the V Corps from the east and attacked the Confederate left, Union cavalry would attack the Confederate front, keeping the rebels occupied so that they could not reinforce their beleaguered flank. As Warren moved across, the cavalry was to join in the attack, rolling up the enemy line from east to west. Also part of the plan was elements of George Custer's cavalry division making a feint toward the Confederate right flank.

Your location here is approximately where the Union cavalry formed to make its assault. Thomas Devin's division lined up across the road here, while Custer's brigades formed west of Scott's Road on the Union left. Wesley Merritt was in overall command of the cavalry during the battle, while Sheridan chose to ride with Warren and the infantry. Little Phil was always one to command from the front and put himself where the action was, but today it was for an entirely different reason. Sheridan did not trust Gouverneur Warren with this attack, and for reasons known to only a few, wanted to keep a very close eye on him during this action.

❭ *From the parking area, pull out to your right onto Courthouse Road. Drive 0.6 mile to the Five Forks intersection, then turn right onto White Oak Road. Drive 0.7 mile on White Oak Road and pull into the parking area on your left.*

Despite his best efforts, this would not be a good day for Gouverneur Warren. Sheridan's orders for the V Corps were very clear. Warren was to bring his men north along Gravelly Run Church Road to its intersection with the White Oak Road, where the left flank of the Confederate defensive line was located. From there, his three divisions would wheel to the left, hitting the rebels' flank squarely and driving it back. Warren received his orders at 1 PM and immediately went on the march. Upon reaching White Oak Road, he swung around to hit the rebels as ordered, only to find that they were not there.

The problem lay with poor reconnaissance and faulty maps, a responsibility that lay directly with Phil Sheridan and his staff. Sheridan had committed similar sins in the past, and they had cost him. Today, though, Sheridan would not hear of excuses, even if they came about under his watch. His attack had been delayed, and it was critical that it took place before the sun went down.

Having discovered that the enemy was not where it was supposed to be, Warren promptly marched his men westward until the rebel line was found. Ayres's division was on the left and Crawford's on the right, with Griffin's behind in support. The Federals would march three-quarters of a mile through the thick woods before they would find the Confederate flank. By that time, Crawford's division had careened to the right and lost contact with the rest of the corps, actually passing behind the rebel line. While Warren went to redirect them, Sheridan stayed with Ayres and led the assault.

In Sheridan's eyes, the delay, along with what he believed was Warren's relaxed attitude in getting his men on track, was enough to act on a discretionary order given to him earlier in the day. Ulysses S. Grant, like Sheridan, was not fond of Warren's command style. He authorized Sheridan to relieve Warren of command of the V Corps if, in his judgment, Warren performed poorly. If Sheridan's mind was not already made up as soon as he received the order (and it may have been), at least he now had what he saw as a reasonable excuse.

Both Confederate flanks had been refused, meaning that a right angle had been formed on each end of the line to defend against a flanking attack. Here on the Confederate left, where you now stand, the rebel flank stretched into these woods 150 yards, while the main line ran along White Oak Road. Matthew Ransom's brigade held this portion of the line, including the angle, supported by four cannon. However, one brigade and 150 yards would not slow the Union advance. Ayres's division hit the angle and kept right on moving down the line, driving west and rolling up first Ransom's men, then William Wallace's. Sheridan rode at the front, where he was always at his best, leading his men through the attack and driving them forward. Behind Ayres, Griffin's division continued the push as Ayres slowed to gather prisoners.

There is a short trail here that will take you into the woods and along what remains of the Confederate earthworks here at "the Angle," the rebels' left flank. Standing with White Oak Road on your left, you are facing west toward Five Forks. The main Confederate line extended in front of you, facing south, while the refused flank stretched to your right, facing toward you (east). The Federals came from behind you, steamrolling their way through your position and forging ahead toward the intersection.

❯ *From the parking area, pull out to your right onto White Oak Road. Drive 0.7 mile on White Oak Road and pass through the Five Forks intersection, then pull into the parking area on your left.*

This is Five Forks, the critical intersection that the Confederates needed to hold to prevent the Federals from approaching the South Side Railroad. Across from where you parked are a few interpretive signs, along with some artillery; carefully cross the road so that you can orient yourself.

Stand next to the artillery here and face in the direction it is firing, as though you were firing it yourself. This was the position of three guns of William Pegram's artillery battalion. From your left, the Union V Corps would be making its way toward you along the White Oak Road, which is also directly in front of you. Union cavalry was attacking this position from the south along the two roads to your front, Scott's Road (now Wheeler's Pond Road) and Dinwiddie Court House Road (now Courthouse Road). The monument you see across the intersection is between these two roads. It would have been Thomas Devin's Federal cavalry attacking you, while Custer's horsemen would have been to your right, closer to the Confederate right flank. Behind you, Ford's Road stretched to the north, toward the railroad and the infamous shad bake.

Willie Pegram was 23 years old when the battle of Five Forks occurred. Less than two months earlier, his brother, John Pegram, had been killed leading a Confederate division at Hatcher's Run. This day, it would be Willie who would fall, mortally wounded, near the spot where you now stand. His artillery repulsed several attempts by the Union cavalry to gain the crossroads. Pegram would die the next day.

⟩ *From the parking area, pull out to your left onto White Oak Road. Drive 1 mile on White Oak Road, then pull into the parking area on your left.*

On the western half of the Confederate line, the battlefield was dominated by cavalry action. Custer's orders were to feint toward the enemy's right, keeping Fitzhugh Lee's cavalry, which held this flank, from assisting in the defense of Warren's attack on the left.

The field in front of you is the Gilliam Field. One Union brigade attacked the front of the Confederate line, meeting Rooney Lee's rebel horsemen in the fields in front of you and to your right. Custer, however, did not just want to feint an attack, and took his other two brigades far to the left, attempting to swing around Lee's cavalry and get in their rear. The rebel horsemen were able to mount a stalwart defense, keeping Custer in check and holding their position on the right flank.

This position would become important for the infantry as well. Behind you, to the north, was a farm road leading to the north. As the Confederate soldiers were pushed to the west, they eventually made their final stand here in Gilliam's Field, just to your front left. The farm road would prove to be their only escape as the rest of the Federals converged to destroy Pickett's force.

⟩ *From the parking area, pull out to your right onto White Oak Road. Drive 1 mile on White Oak Road back to the Five Forks intersection, then turn left onto Courthouse Road. Drive 0.5 mile on Courthouse Road, then pull into the parking area on your right.*

Ayres's and Griffin's divisions continue their push from the east toward Five Forks until only one Confederate brigade, George Steuart's, remained between them and the intersection. Steuart had enough time to form a new line facing east toward the Federals, slowing the Union advance. Men of Joseph Mayo's brigade, west of the intersection, also rushed to assist Steuart in holding back the Union assault from the east. Soon, however, they had a bigger problem.

George Pickett had been thoroughly been enjoying Thomas Rosser's shad bake while the battle of Five Forks raged only a few miles to the south. No one at the bake could hear the commotion, mostly due to the thick forest covering the ground in between. Finally, Pickett received a message that roused his attention enough to head south and check on his now crumbling line.

As he rode south along Ford's Road, Pickett began to encounter Union troops, emerging from the woods to his left. Realizing quickly that it was more than a few, Pickett spurred his horse, racing through the Federals toward Five Forks, only a short distance ahead.

The Union troops were the men of Crawford's division of the V Corps. After Crawford became detached from the rest of the corps and drifted to the north, Gouverneur Warren caught up to them and guided them into position to emerge on Ford's Road, then attack Five Forks from the north. The Confederates already had Union soldiers attacking their left, right, and front. Now they would have an entire division attacking them in the rear.

Your position here is where Crawford's Federals began to emerge from the woods and swing to the south, surrounding the Confederates and cutting off their main route of retreat. Turn so that the road is on your right. You are now facing south toward Five Forks. The Union troops would have advance from here toward the intersection, not only bearing down on the line created by Steuart's and Mayo's rebels but also gathering up the many Confederates sent to flight by the rest of the V Corps.

As Crawford approached Five Forks, Mayo faced his brigade north to meet them, but it was not enough. The Confederate infantry, under

---

CASUALTIES— FIVE FORKS

Confederate: killed and wounded, 545; missing or captured, 2,400; total: 2,945

Union: killed, 103; wounded, 670; missing or captured: 57; total, 830

Total Casualties: 3,800

WHERE DID EVERYBODY GO?

You may have noticed that during the relatively short period of time covered in chapters 7 and 8, many of the corps and division commanders in both armies had changed. There were a number of reasons for this; generals were killed or wounded, returned after recovering from wounds, or went on special assignments or missions. In some cases, a simple reorganization was needed, and in December 1864, the Union army did a complete restructuring of the Army of the James. Parts of the X and XVIII Corps were reorganized into the XXIV Corps, while the XXV Corps combined all of the black units from both armies together as one unit.

Here are some of the more significant command changes that were made between June 1864 and April 1865:

Previous	New
Union II Corps:	
Winfield S. Hancock	Andrew A. Humphreys
Union V Corps:	
Gouverneur Warren	Charles Griffin
Union IX Corps:	
Ambrose Burnside	John Parke
Army of the James:	
Benjamin Butler	Edward C. Ord
Union X Corps/XXIV Corps:	
Quincy Gillmore	John Gibbon
Union XVIII/XXV Corps:	
William "Baldy" Smith	Godfrey Weitzel
Confederate First Corps:	
Richard Anderson	James Longstreet
Confederate Second Corps:	
Richard S. Ewell	Jubal Early, John Brown Gordon
Confederate Fourth Corps:	
(none)	Richard Anderson

attack from three directions, was pressed into the Gilliam Fields to make a final stand. Only Rooney Lee's determined cavalry stand enabled any of the rebels to escape, as they found their way to the farm road and headed north.

The Union victory at Five Forks was complete. In less than two hours, the Federals had completely swept George Pickett's leaderless Confederates from the field. The road to the South Side Railroad was now wide open, and the V Corps moved in that direction to begin its destruction that night.

Having little time to bask in the glow of victory, Gouverneur Warren, whose direction of Crawford's division had been not only appropriate but inventive, received a note from Sheridan. He had been relieved of command of the Union V Corps, and he was to report to Grant immediately. Charles Griffin would take the corps. Warren was stunned, and went to Sheridan, asking him to reconsider, to which Sheridan sharply replied that he would not. Although he was given other responsibilities in the army, Gouverneur Warren would demand a court of inquiry, which he would not be granted until 1879. The court would find that Sheridan's dismissal of Warren was inappropriate, and the reasons presented by Sheridan were insufficient for his actions. Their report would be submitted in November 1882, three months after Gouverneur Warren, the hero of Gettysburg, died and was buried in civilian dress with no military honors.

At 9 PM that evening, Grant, who had moved his headquarters to Dabney's Saw Mill near the old Hatcher's Run battlefield, received a full report on the action at Five Forks. Grant then walked to his tent, returning only minutes later with several slips of paper. Grant handed out the papers to his staff, explaining, "I have ordered a general assault along the lines."

PETERSBURG—THE BREAKTHROUGH

⟩ *From the parking area, pull onto Courthouse Road to your left and drive 0.5 mile to the Five Forks intersection. Turn left onto White Oak Road and drive 6.1 miles. Turn left onto Boydton Plank Road and drive 3.6 miles to the entrance for Pamplin Historical Park on your left.*

Since learning the harsh lessons of the Wilderness, Spotsylvania, and Cold Harbor, Ulysses S. Grant had largely avoided direct assaults. His last major attempt at Cold Harbor, where he had calculated that the Confederates had lost their fight, resulted in disaster. This time, though, the game was different. The final supply line to Petersburg was about to be severed. Sherman was approaching. It did not take a military tactician to know that if Robert E. Lee wanted to save his army, he had to leave Petersburg and attempt to join Joseph E. Johnston's army in North Carolina. If Grant gave Lee the opportunity to do so, he just might succeed. In fact, Grant almost had no choice but to launch his assault immediately, before the Confederates could react.

The Federals would not even wait for the sun. Immediately after issuing his orders, pieces of the three Union armies began to move into position for a 4 AM assault on April 2. John Parke's IX Corps would mostly remain in place east and south of Petersburg, but would throw its weight into an attack along the Jerusalem Plank Road. On its left was Horatio Wright's VI Corps, and then, farther west; Andrew Humphreys's II Corps; they would attack from the advanced positions they had gained after the Confederate attack at Fort Stedman on March 25. Also in the area was one of the two

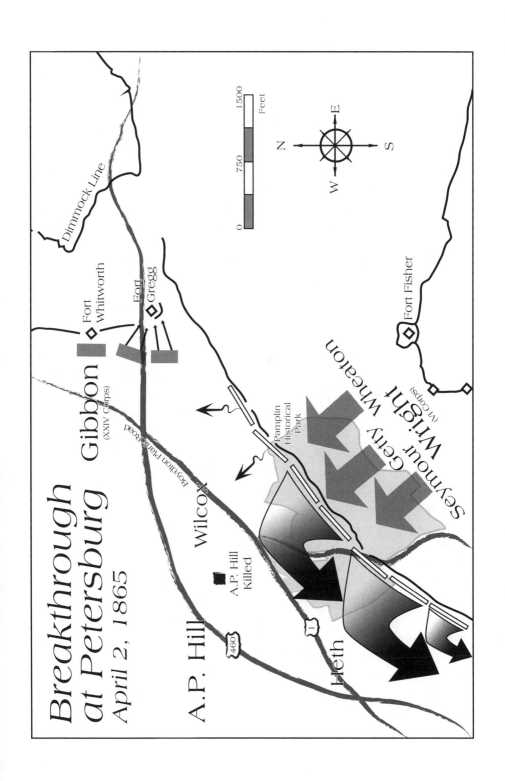

Breakthrough
at Petersburg
April 2, 1865

Dimmock Line

Fort
Whitworth

Fort
Gregg

Gibbon
(XXIV Corps)

Boydton Plank Road

460

A.P. Hill

Wilcox

A.P. Hill
Killed

Pamplin
Historical
Park

1

Heth

Seymour
Getty Wheaton
Wright
(VI Corps)

Fort Fisher

Feet

1500

750

0

N
E
W
S

recently reformed corps of Edward Ord's Army of the James—the XXIV Corps, commanded by John Gibbon, which would support the attacks of the II and VI Corps. The V Corps, now under Charles Griffin's command, along with Sheridan's Army of the Shenandoah, would continue toward the South Side Railroad to officially carry out the act of cutting Lee's final lifeline.

The IX Corps would begin the assault, slightly behind schedule, along the Jerusalem Plank Road. Two divisions, Robert Potter's and John Hartranft's, lined up behind Union Fort Sedgwick, each augmented by one brigade. Less than a half-mile to their front was a slight bulge in the Confederate line known as Rives's Salient, containing Confederate batteries 26 through 30, including the infamous Fort Mahone (Battery 27). The close proximity of Forts Mahone and Sedgwick, as well as the unceasing fighting between the two during the siege, led men on both sides of the line to rename them: "Fort Damnation" for Fort Mahone, and "Fort Hell" for Fort Sedgwick. Although these names were the source of many jokes by those who did their work while caught between the two, their stiff defenses and the bloody fighting around them had rendered them fitting.

Parke attacked at 4:30 AM. As the Federals moved forward, Rives's Salient erupted in canister fire, knocking large holes in the Union line. The swift assault had caught the Confederates off guard, however, and soon Union troops had rushed past both picket lines and were at the base of the rebel entrenchments. On the Confederate line was John Brown Gordon's corps, remnants of the corps that Jubal Early had taken to the Shenandoah Valley the previous summer. These were hard men, veterans all, and they resisted the enemy with everything they had. Hand-to-hand fighting raged everywhere throughout the day. Although the Federals had quickly taken Batteries 25, 27, and 28, Gordon began to launch organized counterattacks at 11 AM, attempting to take the works back one traverse at a time. By the time the fighting stopped here at sundown, the IX Corps held onto most of the ground it had gained, but it had not broken through. Gordon's troops had held.

To the west, Wright's VI Corps was massed on the ground they had won a week earlier in front of Union Forts Fisher and Welch. Here, too, the Federals had approximately a half-mile of ground to cover, and it was filled with obstructions—abatis, fraise, and everything else the Confederates could think to throw in front of their works. But Wright had a plan that he hoped would allow his men to slice through the obstructions and allow his three divisions—17,000 men—to pierce the Confederate line.

Opposing the Union attack would be the divisions of Henry Heth and Cadmus Wilcox, both from A. P. Hill's corps. The line here had been built to defend the Boydton Plank Road, and it had done so successfully until only four days before. Now, six brigades were stretched thin across 6 miles of excellent but undermanned defensive works.

The memorable sculpture The Bivouac *provides a fitting introduction to* The National Museum of the Civil War Soldier *at Pamplin Historical Park.*

Hill, like other Confederate commanders this day, had not slept well and would be up early. Robert E. Lee and James Longstreet were both also stirring, and by 4 AM, the three had found one another and were already discussing the strategy for the day. It was while they were together that a signal gun, fired from Fort Fisher at 4:40 AM, would launch the attack of the Union VI Corps.

The ground over which Wright's Federals rushed to meet Hill's Confederates is preserved here in Pamplin Historical Park. Developed privately through generous donations, the park tells the story of the siege of Petersburg, and its end, through preservation, demonstration, and imagination. Your first stop at the park will be the National Museum of the Civil War Soldier. At its entrance are stones representing each of the states whose men fought in the war; seeing the number of those who served, along with those who died, is humbling. Inside, once you've made your way past its impressive bookstore (a tough task for some), the museum presents the everyday life of a Civil War soldier on the front line. Of course, the history is unavoidable, but the focus is very much on the men in the trenches. Many of the exhibits are interactive, and a guided audio tour will let you learn as much as you'd like about every item you see in the displays. There are also plenty of age-appropriate activities for younger visitors,

The excellent reconstructed earthworks at Pamplin Historical Park give visitors an idea of what Petersburg looked like during the siege.

and the museum does a wonderful job of teaching history while still providing the "wow" factor that will keep kids interested.

Exiting the museum will first take you through the restored Tudor Hall, an 1812 plantation that stood just behind the Confederate line. Along with the mansion, reconstructed slave quarters and the exhibits inside them help to dissect the various viewpoints on slavery before the war. Also here are plenty of farm animals, again more than enough to keep the kids busy.

As you walk toward the battlefield, you will pass the most impressive set of entrenchments you've ever seen. It's a reconstruction, of course, but its illustration of exactly what the soldiers were up against is as good as you'll see anywhere. Here, you will be able to walk right up to the breastwork and peer out, then walk around to the front of the earthwork to see the moat, abatis and other obstructions, right down to the tree stumps from a cleared field of fire. You will likely learn more here just by observing these simulated works for 10 minutes than you could in a lifetime's worth of reading.

Finally, you will reach the battlefield itself. The Battlefield Center will help you orient yourself, and it shows an excellent film about the battle at Petersburg on April 2, 1865. Also present are interactive maps and exhibits about what you will find when you venture out onto the field. Perhaps most important, you can use the center to help you decide between the many options for walking the battlefield.

You will have several trails to choose from, all of which loop back to the Battlefield Center. The shortest is a 0.3-mile tour of the main Confederate works, whereas an intermediate trail of 0.7 mile will give you a better explanation of the battle and the line. If you are able, though, choose at least the main trail, about 1.3 miles in length. The trail contains the same views of the main Confederate line, but will also take you out to the rebels' picket line, which contains some nicely preserved rifle pits and other features. The trail will then bring you back along the route of the Union assault, and the numerous interpretive signs along the way will ensure that you know exactly where you are on the battlefield. Although there are a few climbs and dips, the trails are well laid with gravel and are very walkable. Additional trails, if you wish, will take you out to the Hart Farm—covering part of the battlefield of Peebles's Farm—or deeper into the now peaceful woods around the works. The state of preservation of these earthworks is outstanding, so no matter which trail you choose, you're bound to leave impressed.

Wright had arranged his corps in a wedge-shaped formation. George Getty's division took the point of the wedge and would trigger the others to move. To his right rear was Frank Wheaton's division, with the greatest concentration of power next to Getty. On the left rear of the wedge was Truman Seymour's division. In front of each

Confederate artillery on the Petersburg line, Pamplin Historical Park.

The winding path past the massive Confederate works at the site of the Union breakthrough, Pamplin Historical Park.

division, a group of men were armed with axes to clear the path for the charging Federals. Learning from past assaults in which the lines had quickly dissolved through forests and other obstructions, the men were commanded not to stop until they had carried the works, then to halt and reform, going no farther until the corps was ready to move again as a unit.

After Getty had been signaled to move, the formation quietly rushed across the field, then ran into the Confederate pickets, who quickly returned to the main line. The Union men hacked away at the obstructions while those behind provided the best covering fire they could. Soon all three divisions hit the Confederate line, vaulting the works and pouring fire into the enemy. Although the combat in the trenches was initially brutal, the rebels were soon streaming to the rear. Within 20 minutes, the Federals had solidly pierced the Confederate line.

Along the trail, you will find markers where each Union divisions achieved its breakthrough, as well as the stories of the men who fought here (several of whom claimed the honor of being the first man into the works). As the Federals achieved their breakthrough, it was more difficult than anticipated to keep the Union line together. Every man of the VI Corps who charged that morning seemed to realize the significance of what had just happened, and they went forth, entering the Confederate camps and spreading out to gobble up as much of the enemy as he could.

By 9 AM, Wright had most of his command back together and was moving south toward Hatcher's Run, rolling up the Confederate line to his left. Soon meeting Humphreys's II Corps, Wright saw that the rest of the line, which had collapsed quickly, did not need his attention, and he swung his men back around to move north toward the city of Petersburg. They soon found Gibbon's XXIV Corps, which had followed them over the ground they had claimed, following up on the Union gains. It had taken almost 10 months, but at last, the breakthrough everyone had been waiting for had occurred. The siege of Petersburg was over.

⟩ *From Pamplin Park, turn right onto Boydton Plank Road and drive 0.1 mile, then turn left onto A. P. Hill Drive. Follow A. P. Hill Drive as it turns to Sentry Hill Court for 0.3 mile. Pull over at the side of the road, then walk down the short trail to the stone marker.*

Shortly after the breakthrough, broken Confederates were streaming past Robert E. Lee's headquarters, where he was still conferring with Longstreet, and A. P. Hill. Informed of the danger by one of Lee's staff, Hill raced to his horse and galloped toward his troops. Two couriers and one of Lee's staff, raced after Hill, one of the men carrying a message from Lee that Hill should not expose himself to enemy fire.

After a short distance, the group ran into two Union soldiers who had separated from the rest of the army. After capturing them, one of the couriers led the men back as prisoners. It was soon apparent that Hill's line had been completely scattered, and there were Federal soldiers all around them. They soon found a Confederate battery of artillery, and Hill ordered Lee's aide to set the artillery to slow the Union troops. He then rode farther into what was now enemy territory, accompanied now only by a lone courier.

The courier was the first to spot two more Union soldiers slightly ahead of them. The soldiers saw them at about the same time and ducked behind a tree for cover, both aiming their rifles squarely at the two Confederates. Hill and his companion rushed forward and demanded the surrender of the men, now only 10 yards in front of them. The Union soldiers first paused, wary of other Confederates possibly in the area, then decided to fire. One of them missed; the other did not. The bullet tore off Hill's thumb, then passed through his heart—and he was dead on the spot.

A short walk from this suburban street will bring you to the spot where A. P. Hill was killed. A simple stone marks the spot, although you will often also find wreaths,

A small marker in a secluded spot denotes where Confederate General A. P. Hill fell.

trinkets, and other tributes to the general. The marker and the ground around it are maintained by the Civil War Trust.

〉 *Drive 0.3 mile to return to Boydton Plank Road, then turn left. Drive 0.7 mile on Boydton Plank Road. Take right turn, then an immediate left, on VA 142 (Simpson Road). Drive 0.7 mile on Simpson Road to 7th Avenue. Turn left on 7th Avenue and drive 0.1 mile, then pull into the parking area on your right.*

John Gibbon had been a division commander in the Army of the Potomac for much of the war, and when he was offered command of the newly formed XXIV Corps of the Army of the James, he was quick to accept. However, when it was time for the final assault, Gibbon marched two of his divisions south of the Appomattox River to temporarily rejoin the Army of the Potomac, filing his men behind the VI and II Corps on the Union line.

At 6:50 AM on April 2, Gibbon received the order to move forward and support the VI Corps. The men advanced through the gap and turned to the right, mopping up the aftermath of the breakthrough and extinguishing any remaining small pockets of resistance. By noon, they were within only a short distance of Petersburg's inner defensive line. To reach it, however, they would have to pass two Confederate fortifications: Fort Gregg and Fort Whitworth.

The Confederate defensive line was the last hope of at least stalling the Federal occupation of Petersburg, and these two forts were the last hope they had of getting enough men to that line to defend the city. James Longstreet's corps, which had been manning the Richmond defenses, was on its way south to Petersburg, but they needed time. Nathaniel Harris's brigade, which had been manning the Howlett line at Bermuda Hundred, was sent early on April 2, and by this time had already taken position in the forts. Also present was part of James Lane's brigade, which had been scattered by the VI Corps breakthrough and had now taken a position in the earthworks. Lane wished to enter the Petersburg defenses, but his division commander, Cadmus Wilcox, ordered him to stay, adding to his force by giving him part of Edward Thomas's brigade.

To reach Fort Gregg, you will have to walk over the fields to your front. The fort is facing south; you are walking east. Gibbon launched his attack on Fort Gregg from both directions. Once you get closer to the fort, you will quickly see that it is a fairly substantial earthwork, with high earthen walls and a deep moat. You will find interpretive signs here, along with a single small historical marker. One notable item that you will not find is the rear wall of the fort. Originally, a wall of logs, stuck vertically into the ground, ran across the rear of the fort, making Fort Gregg a virtually enclosed work.

The relatively small but critically important Fort Gregg, the last Confederate earthwork in front of Petersburg.

The Federals began their assault of Fort Gregg at 1 PM. Four brigades were able to reach the moat, but climbing up the steep, slippery walls of the fort was another matter. The fighting was incredibly hot, but the Confederates were able to hold off the first Union assault. Gibbon was forced to pull his men back and reform his lines. At 2 PM, the attack was renewed with additional Federal troops, and this time it was just too much. The fort was overrun, although the Confederates held it for nearly half an hour.

The fighting inside the fort continued until those rebels still standing were finally compelled to either surrender or retreat to the walls of the inner defenses of Petersburg.

The Confederate loss at Fort Gregg was dreadful; however, the forces had accomplished their mission. Shortly before the fort fell, Lee had ordered its evacuation. Longstreet was now on the line, and would be able to hold any assault against the city from the west. In addition, John Brown Gordon still held the entire eastern front, keeping the Union IX Corps from advancing to the Confederate inner works. Although the Federal army had achieved its breakthrough and the South Side Railroad had been cut, the city of Petersburg, at least for a few more hours, still belonged to the rebels.

> ### CASUALTIES— PETERSBURG BREAKTHROUGH
>
> **Confederate:** killed, wounded, and missing or captured: 4,252
>
> **Union:** killed, 511; wounded, 2,868; missing or captured: 125; total, 3,504
>
> **Total Casualties: 7,756**

⟩ *Turn right onto 7th Avenue and drive 0.3 mile. Park in the area to your right.*

This is Fort Whitworth, sister fort to Fort Gregg. While Gibbon had concentrated his attack on Fort Gregg, Fort Whitworth (which, at the time, was not separated by an interstate highway) aided in its defense by directing its artillery fire southward. That prompted Gibbon to launch a simultaneous attack against this fort, which was defended by only two regiments of Harris's Confederate brigade. They held their ground in the face of four Union regiments. However, after Fort Gregg fell, the two regiments received their orders to evacuate Whitworth, falling back into Petersburg.

This large, enclosed work is still very much discernible and is now a public park. You will find only some interpretation of the fort and the battle here.

SUTHERLAND STATION

⟩ *Continue 0.1 mile on 7th Avenue to Albemarle Street. Turn left on Albemarle Street and drive 0.4 mile, then turn left on Boydton Plank Road and drive 0.2 mile to the entrance ramp for I-85 South. Drive 1.8 miles on I-85 South, then take exit 61 for US 460 West. Drive on US 460 West for 4.3 miles to Namozine Road. Turn right on Namozine Road (SR 708) and pull into the parking area on your left.*

While the rest of the Union army was preparing for the grand assault, Nelson Miles's division of the II Corps was marching. He had been camped south of White Oak Road, when word came late on April 1 that he should move west to aid Phil Sheridan at Five Forks. Arriving at 1 AM, Miles was told that his men were not needed, and after a short rest, they turned around to return to their former position. When they got there, they found that Henry Heth's troops, who had been holding the intersection of White Oak Road and Claiborne Road, were gone. Miles's new orders were to march north along Claiborne Road toward Sutherland Station on the South Side Railroad.

Heth had begun to move toward Sutherland Station shortly after hearing of the breakthrough, leaving only an hour before Miles's arrival at 8 AM. Soon, however, Heth was informed of A. P. Hill's death, putting him in command of Hill's III Corps. Heth gave command to John Cooke and raced for Petersburg.

As the Federals moved north along Claiborne Road, they pushed through the Confederate rear guard until finally reaching the station at 10 AM. The four rebel brigades were entrenched along the Cox Road from Sutherland's Tavern, on their right, to Ocran Methodist Church, a distance of about a half-mile. Their position was strong, on a small ridge overlooking a small stream.

The large white building you see here is the former Sutherland's Tavern and was present at the time of the battle. Turn to face the highway. In front of you is US 460, which roughly follows the path of the old Cox Road. Claiborne Road is to your front, and it is from that direction that the Federals would make their first attacks. Your position here is

The Confederate stand at Sutherland Station was the final Union obstacle to gaining the South Side Railroad.

on the Confederate right. As you look to your left, Cooke's four brigades would be lined up along the road on the opposite side. Almost directly behind you is the railroad. It's difficult to see, but there's a more than fair chance that a train will run by while you're here at this stop.

The first Union assault occurred at 11 AM, when Miles sent one brigade against the Confederate line. That attack would come against the part of the line to your front left, and was easily repulsed. A second attack was made at 12:30 PM, farther to your left, and again the Federals were beaten back. It was not until Miles moved his remaining brigade through the dense woods and emerged to the east of the Confederate line. This attack, at 2:45 PM, finally dislodged the rebels, hitting them squarely on their left flank. As the line was rolled up, Miles's other troops attacked from the front, and soon Sutherland Station—and, officially, the South Side Railroad—was theirs.

NAMOZINE CHURCH

> *Pull out to your left onto Namozine Road and drive 10.5 miles. At the intersection with Mill Quarter Road (SR 622), pull into the gravel area in front of Namozine Church on your left.*

For several weeks, Robert E. Lee had been warning Richmond about the impending danger, telling Jefferson Davis as plainly as he could that he could probably

Namozine Church, witness to a fierce cavalry fight during the Appomattox Campaign.

THE GREAT EMANCIPATOR

Abraham Lincoln had arrived at City Point late on March 24, seeking a respite from the Washington grind. He was present for the Confederate attack at Fort Stedman the next day, and he stayed for the finale of the breakthrough at Petersburg. The next day, April 3, Lincoln entered the city a little after 10 AM, along with a contingent that included a cavalry bodyguard squad and two of his sons, the young Tad and the older Robert, an aide on Grant's staff.

Stopping at Fort Mahone, where the aftermath of the struggle was still visible, Lincoln wept as he was reminded of the great cost of the war. The party then continued into the city, where the president was cheered by Union soldiers, if not the citizens.

The next day, Lincoln went to Richmond, where he saw the smoldering ruins of the city, visited the capitol building, and sat in the chair in Jefferson Davis's study. However, none who witnessed Lincoln's reception from the black men, women, and children of Richmond would ever forget it. Almost as soon as the party landed, the president was surrounded by them, some shouting, some singing, some weeping, others silent. One old man threw himself at Lincoln's feet, to which Lincoln responded, "That is not right. You must kneel to God only, and thank Him for the liberty you will enjoy hereafter." Still, for decades afterward, Lincoln remained the Great Emancipator to black citizens all over the nation.

not hold the city. Now, on April 2, Lee's messages were finally being listened to. The government of the Confederate States of America began to evacuate its capital, with Davis and his cabinet departing for Danville by rail at 11 PM.

Lee had a much larger task of coordination on his hands. He had troops north of the James, at Bermuda Hundred, in Petersburg, and west toward Five Forks and Sutherland Station. While he managed the various disasters on the battlefield, his engineers laid out several routes of retreat, all of them leading to Amelia Court House. The town was located 35 to 40 miles west of both Petersburg and Richmond, and the Richmond & Danville Railroad, which was still operating, had a station there. The army was equipped to move light, leaving and spiking their heavy artillery, and only ammunition was taken; food would be waiting for them at Amelia Court House. Beginning at 8 PM, the Confederates began to slip from their lines, withdrawing on their various routes and setting fire to prearranged piles of the two most valuable commodities in Richmond and Petersburg: tobacco and cotton.

Early on April 3, Union soldiers entered both cities, attempting to arrange surrender and restore order as quickly as possible. This was a fairly simple matter in Petersburg. By 4:28 AM, the Stars and Stripes were flying over the courthouse spire that Union troops had been viewing from a distance for months. Although its citizens were certainly in a dejected state, by afternoon, most of the public domain was fairly secure. Some of the citizens began to cooperate with the soldiers and even have some light conversation with them. Fires were brought under control in cooperation, and many of the locals seemed particularly impressed with the appearance and demeanor of the black Union soldiers marching through the city.

The situation in Richmond was much worse. Richard Ewell, in command of the defense of Richmond, set fire to the stores as he had been ordered to do, but these fires were soon raging out of control, quickly engulfing much of the now former Confederate capital. Rather than assist the citizens of Richmond, Ewell thought it militarily necessary to burn the last bridge out of town and leave the city burning. When Union troops began to march into the surrendered city at 8:15 AM, they immediately began to work at putting out the fires, as well as stop an outbreak of looting that had begun with it.

As the Federals began to organize their pursuit, which would begin that night, the Confederates used April 3 to get a head start, making fairly good progress. For the most part, they ran into little or no resistance. The most significant action of the day came here, at the intersection in front of Namozine Church.

The small, white country church is the same one that witnessed the battle, dating back to 1847. Early on April 3, Richard Anderson, whose infantry was already moving with Fitz Lee's cavalry, used this church as his headquarters. While here, he received Lee's orders to proceed to Amelia Court House and join the rest of the army.

There was one element of the pursuing Union army that got a head start on the rest. Phil Sheridan's cavalry, already west of most of the action, almost immediately began to attempt to locate the Confederates. Early on April 3, George Custer's division, leading Sheridan's column, found Fitz Lee's rear guard, quickly scattering the men. They fell back to this position around Namozine church, where they dismounted and dug in. Three North Carolina cavalry regiments—the 1st, 2nd, and 5th—formed around the intersection under the command of Rufus Barringer.

Custer first sent two regiments forward to break the Confederate hold on the intersection, but the rebels were slow to fall back. When a third regiment was added to the weight of the attack, the enemy could not hold, and was forced to fall back to the east. Barringer was able to escape, but was captured later that night when he rode up to a group of cavalry he thought were "friendlies." He was mistaken, and was taken as a prisoner of war.

Walk up to the narrow V of land at the intersection in front of the church, and stand with the church at your back. The road running along your left and curving out of sight in the distance is today's Namozine Road. However, it is the portion of the road you can't see, around the bend, on which Custer's Federals approached Namozine Church. Your location here at the church was the Confederate right, and the line stretched across the Namozine Road behind you, then curved around your left rear and in front of you. Two of Barringer's regiments were placed on the left side of the road stretching in front of you, past the intersection and facing across the road from left to right. The Confederate escape was along Green's Road, the road leading from the intersection off to your left, and Cousin's Road, now the continuation of Namozine Road that runs behind you and to your left.

AMELIA COURT HOUSE

❯ *From the gravel area in front of Namozine Church, pull out to your left onto Namozine Road (SR 708). Drive 9.6 miles on Namozine Road, being sure to stick with it as you join with SR 612 about 6 miles along the way. Turn left on Military Road (VA 153) and drive 3 miles to VA 38 (Five Forks Road). Turn left on VA 38 and drive 5.9 miles, then turn right and continue to follow it for another 0.9 mile. Turn left onto Church Street, then take the first right onto Washington Street. You will now drive around the courthouse square, taking the next left turn onto Court Street. Park on Court Street and walk to the square.*

Amelia Court House was an ideal location to gather up the pieces of the scattered Confederate Army of Northern Virginia. Not only was it equidistant from Petersburg and Richmond, but its location on the Richmond & Danville Railroad, still operating, meant that the troops could resupply while on the march. From the town, the rebels could then follow the railroad southwest to Danville, then quickly cross into North Carolina and join with Joseph Johnston's army.

Lee rode into Amelia Court House on the morning of April 4 and went immediately to the railroad. Two days before, he had ordered 350,000 rations to be delivered here to meet his hungry and tired army. Unfortunately for the Confederates, the trains were there, but the food was not. Somehow, in all the confusion of April 2, Lee's orders had been miscarried, and instead of rations, the Confederates had been supplied with boxcar after boxcar of ammunition.

Taking action immediately, Lee sent a courier to Danville with an order to send 200,000 rations to Amelia Court House. Lee also sent a note to the citizens of Amelia County, explaining that his army needed food and begging for anything they could spare. Ultimately, the citizens had little they could offer, and unbeknownst to him, the courier carrying his order for rations was captured by Sheridan's cavalry.

Amelia County had been formed in 1734, and had a population of only 40 at the time of the Civil War. As you can see here from the courthouse square, it's grown a bit since then, but still retains its small-town charm. The courthouse in front of you does not date back to the time when Lee's army reunited here, but the Coehorn mortar, on a monument in the square, does, and as you can read here, this particular one was

A monument to the Confederate dead of Amelia County, Virginia, at Amelia Court House.

used in the battle of the Crater the previous summer. (It was captured just down the road during the retreat.) Also on the square is a monument to the county's Confederate dead. If you stand facing the courthouse, the critical railroad runs only about 400 yards behind you, then curves south to your right at about the same distance.

Phil Sheridan's cavalry, approaching the Confederates from several different directions, had now pinned down Amelia Court House as the destination of the entire rebel army. Although he did have most of the V Corps with him, Sheridan alone could not attack the Confederates; he would have to wait for the rest of the army. What he could do, though, was block the routes to the south, preventing Lee from joining Johnston. The Union high command had already determined that Lee would follow the railroad, and the II, V, VI, XXIV, and XXV Corps were all on their way. As long as Sheridan could prevent the Confederates from moving south, he could hold them until the rest of the infantry caught up.

JETERSVILLE

❭ *Continue on Court Street for 0.1 mile, then turn left onto Amelia Avenue (SR 656). Turn left onto US 360 West (Patrick Henry Highway) and drive 7.1 miles to Amelia Springs Road. Turn left onto Amelia Springs Road (SR 642) and drive 0.2 mile to the intersection with Jetersville Road (SR 671). Pull into the gravel parking area on your right just before the intersection.*

While Lee waited for food at Amelia Court House, Sheridan and the V Corps moved north toward Jetersville, the next stop south on the Richmond & Danville Railroad. On the evening of April 4, they began to entrench, forming a line squarely across the railroad.

Finally giving up hope that food would be delivered to his army in time, Lee began to withdraw from Amelia Court House at 1 PM on April 5, moving south along the railroad with James Longstreet's corps in the lead. Soon, several reports came in that Federal cavalry was blocking the road ahead, and that infantry might be present as well. Lee rode to the front to assess the situation. The enemy force appeared to be large, but it was far from being the entire Union army.

For a moment, Lee had a choice, and anyone who knew Robert E. Lee knew what his ultimate answer would be. He would attack, break through the Federal line, and keep moving for North Carolina. However, within minutes, the situation changed for the worse. Rooney Lee reported that the Union II Corps began to arrive at 2:30 PM, filing in on the left of the V Corps. In addition, the VI Corps was right behind it, and when these soldiers arrived at 6 PM, they formed to the right. The Union line, when finished, would be almost 4 miles long.

Ultimately, Lee would elect to march around the Federals. Countermarching

Longstreet's corps and redirecting the other parts of his army, Lee forced his men and their empty stomachs to conduct a night march. The new objective was Farmville, a 23-mile march to the west. The Confederates would move through the resort town of Amelia Springs, over the Appomattox River at High Bridge, then into Farmville, where Lee was informed that 80,000 rations would be waiting for his men. It would be later argued that had Lee not waited for rations at Amelia Court House, giving the Union army over a day to catch up with him, he may have had at least a fair chance of breaking through Sheridan's line and heading south. Whether he would have made it very much farther is another matter.

It was in this area that Sheridan formed his defensive line, facing northeast and perpendicular to the Richmond & Danville Railroad. If you walk to the intersection and put Jetersville Road on your right, you will be facing the same direction as the Federals did, hoping Lee would come into the open and attack their line. If you look to your right and just to your rear, you will see a STOP sign across a small field; that sign is only a few yards from the railroad.

AMELIA SPRINGS

❭ *From the gravel parking area, turn left onto Amelia Springs Road. Drive 3.3 miles on Amelia Springs Road, then pull into the gravel area on your right.*

It's probably a bit difficult to picture now, but the area around you was once a very popular resort. At the time of the Civil War, mineral hot springs were all the rage, and Amelia Sulphur Springs was a well-known retreat. The resort was a whopping 1,300 acres, with over 20 buildings, and Lee spent the night of April 5 in one of these.

From the gravel area, with your left to the road, the resort would have been in the large fields to your right (you may have to inch forward a bit to see past the trees). Less than a quarter-mile in front of you is one of the few remains of the era—the bed of the former Zion Church Road, which you will see on your right just before you turn left onto St. James Road. It was on this road that the Confederate army marched the night of April 5. Longstreet, commanding both his corps and A. P. Hill's former corps at this point, led the march. Behind Longstreet was Richard Anderson's corps, then Richard Ewell's reserve corps, the former Richmond defensive force. Behind Ewell was the main Confederate wagon train, followed by John Brown Gordon's corps.

SAILOR'S CREEK

❭ *Pull out to your right onto Amelia Springs Road. Drive 0.2 mile, then turn left onto St. James Road; remember to look for the trace of the old Zion Church Road on your right just before you turn. Drive 3 miles on St. James Road to Genito Road. Turn left on Genito Road and drive 0.4 mile to East Sayler's Creek Road (SR 617).*

Turn right on East Sayler's Creek Road and drive 3.2 miles. Cross the intersection with James Town Road (SR 618) and pull over to your left.

The next destination for the rebels on their way to Farmville was Rice's Depot, a stop on the South Side Railroad. On the way, their long column passed through this crossroads, known as Holt's Corner, on the morning and afternoon of April 6. The Confederate wagon trains, along with John Brown Gordon's corps, took a detour here, turning onto the Jamestown Road. The rest of the men continued on the Deatonsville Road (now East Sayler's Creek Road).

As the column progressed, George Crook's division of Union cavalry attacked here at Holt's Corner. Richard Anderson's corps was the Confederate unit passing through at the time, and Anderson had his men quickly throw up breastworks to defend their position. The attack did not last long, but it was long enough to provide the Federal army with a golden opportunity.

Lee and Longstreet, at the head of the Confederate column, were already pulling into Rice's Depot, 6 miles distant, when Crook attacked at 11 AM. Anderson resumed his march after the danger had passed, but the delay was enough to create a large gap in the column between Longstreet and Anderson. It also allowed converging units of the Union army to position itself to cause major damage to the Army of Northern Virginia.

The battle of Sailor's Creek would emerge as three separate battles, all of which would be disastrous for the Confederates. It was here at Holt's Corner that the beginning of what many in the old Confederacy call "Black Thursday" began. After visiting two of the battles, you will return to Holt's Corner to follow the path of the third.

One other note: You are likely to encounter multiple spellings of "Sailor's"— Saylor, Sayler's, and Sailer's. Chris Calkins, in his book *The Appomattox Campaign* (highlighted as recommended reading at the beginning of the chapter), gives a very thorough breakdown of where these names originated and how they're used, solving what is still a mystery to many Civil War buffs. Bottom line, when referring to the battle, the proper term is "Sailor's Creek."

Union Attack—Ewell's Reserve Corps

❯ *Continue 0.9 mile on East Sayler's Creek Road. You are now entering Sailor's Creek Battlefield State Historical Park; pull into the parking area for the Hillsman House on your left.*

As you pull into the parking area for the Hillsman House, you may notice a yellow flag with a large *H* on it. During the war, this flag designated a building or camp as a hospital site, meaning that it was off-limits for attack. The Hillsman House, which dates to 1770, served just such a purpose during the battle of Sailor's Creek. During

The Hillsman House, site of the Union artillery at Sailor's Creek and a hospital after the battle.

certain parts of the year, you may enter the house. If you have the chance, be sure to check it out; otherwise, walk around to the rear of the building.

Walk over to the cannon and benches behind the house. You will notice that you are on a large rise overlooking a broad valley. This is the valley of Little Sailor's Creek. The creek is located in the tree line at the bottom of the ravine, less than half a mile to your front. On the other side of the creek, the ravine sweeps back up to a similar elevation, although the trees, most of which weren't present at the time of the battle, make this a bit difficult to see. In fact, except for a small tree line at the creek, the battlefield was mostly open field in 1865.

Ewell's rear guard was the first to form here, taking position while the rebels advanced down the road. However, while Ewell was conferring with Richard Anderson farther up the column, these units were attacked by Horatio Wright's VI Corps, which had been trailing the Confederate column. The small band of rebels quickly scampered across the creek to join the rest of the column.

Phil Sheridan was riding with the VI Corps and took overall command of the field. Wright was able to bring two of his three divisions up before Sheridan called for the attack to begin. Truman Seymour's division formed to the right of Deatonsville Road and Frank Wheaton's to the left, while Wright massed his artillery—20 guns— on the ridge behind the Hillsman House. Ewell, seeing the Federals forming, brought his reserves into line on the crest on the opposite side of the valley. The Union artillery opened at 5:30 PM, and at 6 PM, the infantry advanced to Little Sailor's Creek. The creek presented quite an obstacle, flooded to a depth of 4 feet in places, but once the Federals were able to cross, they reformed their lines and prepared to attack.

⟩ *Pull out to your left onto East Sayler's Creek Road and drive 0.8 mile to the parking area for the Confederate Overlook on your left. On your way, you will cross over Little Sailor's Creek.*

Ewell formed his line here, only 300 yards southwest of Little Sailor's Creek. Ewell had two divisions, Custis Lee's (Robert E. Lee's son) to the left and Joseph Kershaw's to the right, a total of 5,200 men to hold off Wright's 7,000. He did not, however, have any artillery, as it had gone with Gordon and the wagon train. Had he had some, Sailor's Creek might have been a much hotter and bloodier battle.

First take a look down toward the creek from the parking area, then walk across the road to the monument and benches in the field in front of you. This would have been Custis Lee's position during the battle. When you get there, turn to your right and again look downhill toward Little Sailor's Creek. From both of these areas, you would have been able to see across the valley to the Hillsman House at the time of the battle.

Wheaton's Union division, to your right from this position, was the first to emerge

Union soldiers, advancing from Sailor's Creek in the tree line, forced their way up this hill and captured Richard Ewell's Confederate Reserve Corps.

from the tree line at the creek, and when it did, the soldiers were greeted with a heavy volley of musketry. Wheaton began to push up the slope, but several of the units began to break, and before long, most of Wheaton's division was headed back for the creek. A few of Lee's units counterattacked, making sure that the repulse was complete. The fighting along the creek became hand to hand at times, and ultimately, Wheaton's men were forced back across the creek.

However, when Seymour's division appeared, and Wheaton's had been rallied, they rushed the short distance up the ravine, this time outstretching both Confederate flanks and overwhelming the enemy. The fighting was again fierce, this time in the area around you atop the ridge, but the Federals had the upper hand. The rebels had no choice but to surrender en masse, although many escaped to fight another day. Of the 5,200 men that Ewell had brought to the fight, 3,400 of them surrendered, including Ewell, Kershaw, Lee, and three other generals.

⟩ *Pull out to your left onto East Sayler's Creek Road and drive 0.4 mile to the parking area for the Sailor's Creek visitor center.*

This is the new visitor center for Sailor's Creek Battlefield State Historical Park. The center opened in 2009, and this new modern facility is a great improvement over the former center at Hillsman House. Thanks to a very dedicated staff, the park is often conducting tours and lectures about the battlefield, as well as natural and cultural programs. The center's exhibits not only feature the battle here but also its important place in the entire Appomattox campaign. There is a gift shop here, as well as outstanding picnic facilities and back porch that provide a great place to stop, take a breath, and enjoy the beauty of the area.

After Ewell's line collapsed, many of the Confederates streamed south toward Richard Anderson's corps. The Federals followed, capturing as many of them as they could. Allegedly captured here, in the area around the visitor center, was Richard Ewell himself.

Union Attack—Anderson's Corps

⟩ *Pull out to your left onto East Sayler's Creek Road and drive 0.1 mile. Pull into the paved area on your right before the intersection.*

While Richard Ewell was attempting to fend off the Union VI Corps to the rear of Richard Anderson's corps, Anderson faced another dilemma to his front. Custer's division of Union cavalry had discovered the gap in the Confederate column between Anderson and Longstreet around 2 PM, and after initially skirmishing with Anderson's lead elements, fell back to wait for the rest of the Federal cavalry to arrive. Anderson and Ewell were now almost back to back.

East Saylor's Creek Road, which you drove in on, was the Deatonsville-Rice Road at the time of the battle. Anderson lined up his two divisions along the road, facing an open field to the south and southeast. (The road curves beyond the intersection to face south.) George Pickett's division was here, across the intersection, while Bushrod Johnson's was farther down the road to his right. If you walk to the intersection, put the parking area at your back, and look across East Saylor's Creek Road, you will put yourself in the position of Pickett's men, facing the oncoming brigades of George Armstrong Custer.

Wesley Merritt arrived to take overall command of the Federals, who now had three divisions of cavalry present. George Crook's division lined up on the left, assigned to attack the enemy right, while the other two, Thomas Devin and Custer, attacked at center and left. Crook dismounted his leftmost brigade and soon overran the Confederate flank. While Anderson's flank began to crumble, Custer made several charges against Pickett's line, finally breaking through. Anderson's entire corps broke, and although many were able to escape, 2,600 Confederates, along with two more generals, were captured here at Marshall's Crossroads.

Union Attack—Gordon's Corps/Confederate Wagon Train

❯ *From the intersection (or the parking area), pull out to your left onto East Sayler's Creek Road and drive 2.2 miles, making your way back through the park. Turn left onto James Town Road (SR 618) and drive 2 miles, staying with it as it becomes CR 618. Turn left onto CR 619 and drive 0.6 mile, then pull into the gravel area on your right.*

While Horatio Wright's VI Corps pursued Ewell, Andrew Humphreys's II Corps was hot on the trail of John Brown Gordon's corps and the all-important Confederate wagon train. Gordon had been fighting off the Federals in a running battle that lasted for fourteen miles. At 4:30 PM, Humphreys passed through Holt's Corner and pursued Gordon down the James Town Road toward a crossing at the confluence of Big and Little Sailor's Creek known as Double Bridges.

At 5 PM, Humphreys formed a line here around the Lockett House, the white house across the road from you. Please note that this is private property, so do not trespass. If you put the road to your left, you will be looking west toward the Confederates. Down the road to your front is the valley of Sailor's Creek. Gordon pulled his men across the creek and formed on the high ground on the opposite bank. Régis de Trobriand (commanding the division of Gershom Mott, who had been wounded earlier) and Nelson Miles pushed their divisions south from this point to attempt to bring Gordon to battle before the sun went down.

Across the road, you will find a monument to the battle, erected in 1928 and

The Lockett House, where the Federals prepared to advance to the crossing of Sailor's Creek at Double Bridges.

containing three major errors in its 22 words. The Lockett House dates to 1858, and a good pair of eyes will see that the front of the house is still pockmarked with bullet holes.

❯ *Continue 0.8 mile on CR 619. Pull into the gravel area on your left.*

Although much of the area here is now wooded, enough remains visible of the battlefield to interpret what happened here. Just in front of you is a bridge over Sailor's Creek, and Gordon's men were formed on the opposite side. Across the road from you, barely visible through the brush, is an open field through which the Federals advanced. Also visible, on your side of the road, are the famous Double Bridges, two single-lane bridges crossing each of the two branches of the creek, which come together here.

With sundown approaching, the Federals made their final advance on Gordon's men and the Confederate wagon train. Had darkness not ended the fighting, the results may have been

> ### CASUALTIES— SAILOR'S CREEK
>
> **Confederate:** killed, wounded, missing, or captured: 7,700
>
> **Union:** killed, 114; wounded, 486; missing or captured: 550; total, 1,150
>
> **Total Casualties: 8,850**

Double Bridges at Sailor's Creek. An old iron railing in the center of the picture marks one of the two bridges here.

worse for the rebels, but as it was, it was not a good result. Several of their lines broke in the face of the overwhelming Union force. While not as complete as their victories at the Hillsman Farm or Marshall's Crossroads, the Federals still picked up 1,700 Confederate prisoners, along with 300 wagons and 70 ambulances.

The Confederate army, split in half because of the gap in its long column, had courted disaster, and three separate elements of the Union army jumped at the opportunity to provide it. As Anderson's broken corps began to find its way to Rice's Depot in pieces, Lee was heard to remark, in disbelief, "My God! Has the army been dissolved?" The fighting in the valleys of Sailor's Creek had cost Lee almost one-fifth of his army.

FARMVILLE

❯ *From the Double Bridges parking area, continue on CR 619 for 4.9 miles. Turn right onto US 460 West and drive 3.9 miles, then take the exit onto US 460 Business West and drive another 2.6 miles. Turn right on North Main Street (VA 45) and drive 0.3 mile. Pull into the parking lot on your left next to the large brick warehouses (now a furniture store).*

After the Confederate disaster at Sailor's Creek, Lee concluded that he had no other choice but to conduct another night march. The Federals were too close, and he could not afford to miss the rations waiting for him at Farmville. Longstreet's men, leading the way, marched into Farmville at 9 AM on April 7, receiving their rations and then quickly crossing to the north side of the Appomattox River to prepare them. What was left of Gordon's and Anderson's corps trailed Longstreet's, tasked with destroying the massive and critical High Bridge, a railroad bridge spanning the Appomattox River.

From the parking lot here at the furniture store and restaurant, you can see the Appomattox River winding past you. Walk over to the roadway and turn so the road is to your right. The former site of the Farmville railroad station is just behind you, and it was in this area that Lee's men waited hungrily for their rations. To your front, you can see where Main Street crosses the Appomattox River. Looking just a bit to your right, you can also see the former railroad bridge across the river. After Lee had his army on the north side of the Appomattox, he ordered both of these bridges burned to stall the Union pursuit. He had not realized that the parties left to burn the bridges had not been able to accomplish their mission, and he was now stuck north of the Appomattox River. The next crossing was at Appomattox Station, a 28-mile march for his army. For the Federals, south of the river, it was a much more direct route of only 20 miles.

HIGH BRIDGE

> *From the parking lot, turn left onto North Main Street. Drive 0.2 mile, then turn left onto River Road (CR 600). Drive 3.1 miles and pull into the parking area for High Bridge Trail State Park.*

Longstreet's corps crossed here at High Bridge earlier in the morning, with his rear guard fighting off George Crook's Union cavalry the entire time. Behind Crook, Federal infantry of the Army of the James followed, ready to lend support if needed.

At 7 AM, Humphreys's II Corps reached High Bridge, whose far end was only just beginning to burn. The Federals quickly pushed forward to try to save both bridges, and although five spans of High Bridge were lost to the flames, the wagon bridge below was still intact.

William Mahone, whose division had made up the rear of the Confederate column, sent troops back to retake the bridge and destroy it. Mahone's men were only barely holding when Francis Barlow's division was joined by that of Nelson Miles. Mahone's men had no choice but to fall back.

John Brown Gordon, wishing to further stall the Union advance, began to try to hold back Barlow's men from reaching Farmville. However, it soon became apparent

The crossing of the Appomattox River at High Bridge, in the distance at the center of the photo.

that the Confederate rations, no matter how badly they were needed, would have to be sent away. Lee, meanwhile, ordered his entire army to gather around Cumberland Heights, north of the city. Only half of his men would be fed, and it was hardly sufficient to sustain them on an extended march. The Union army had full possession of Farmville by 1:30 PM on April 7.

High Bridge was an engineering marvel of its time, possibly the largest bridge in the world when the combined factors of length (2,400 feet) and height (160 feet) are put together. For many years, except by rail, the famous bridge could only be seen from a distance. Now, thanks to Virginia State Parks and several local organizations, you can not only hike to the bridge, but also across it. High Bridge has been included in High Bridge Trail State Park, a rails-to-trails project that currently runs 31 miles and is still growing. There are several trailheads, but this one is the closest to the bridge itself, approximately 1 mile (one-way). The path is well taken care of, and the hike is easy. However, if you choose to go, please note that there are no facilities along the way, so be sure that you are prepared for a good hike before you go. That said, once you get there, you will have a spectacular view of the Appomattox River Valley, not to mention a rare view of a great piece of history.

> For those who do not wish to take the trail but still want to see the bridge from a distance, pull out onto River Road to your left and drive 0.7 mile, then carefully pull to the side of the road. If you choose to exit your vehicle, put your hazard lights on and make sure you are stopped in a place where cars can see you from both directions.

With the road to your left, turn right and look in the distance across the fields. This is the mighty High Bridge, and you are viewing it from approximately 1.25 miles. Still impressive, the bridge now has its future virtually ensured for a long time now that it is part of the Virginia State Park System.

CUMBERLAND CHURCH

> From the overlook of High Bridge, make a safe U-turn, return to this spot, and continue 3.8 miles on River Road. (If you're leaving from the trailhead, pull out to your right; the distance will be 3.1 miles.) Turn right onto VA 45 North (East Main Street) and drive 2.8 miles. Pull into the parking area on your left just before Cumberland Church.

Mahone moved his division from the fight northwest of High Bridge directly to Cumberland Heights, a good defensive position with command of most of the ground around it. In the middle of the heights, as well as Mahone's defensive line, was Cumberland Church. Nelson Miles's division of the Union II Corps followed him here, and combat began at 1 PM, but before long the rest of the Confederate army was filing in next to Mahone, first Gordon's corps, then Longstreet's, then Fitz Lee's cavalry.

Miles had placed himself opposite the Confederate left, north of the formation, and was under the impression that the VI Corps was present to the south. He was mistaken; the VI Corps had been held up at Farmville by the bridges Lee had burned there. Hearing gunfire to the south at 4:15 PM, Mahone ordered the charge, and the brigade he had sent in was repulsed easily. The firing he had heard was from an attack on a Confederate wagon train by J. Irvin Gregg's brigade of George Crook's cavalry division. Gregg soon found that the train was very well protected, and not only were his men repulsed with heavy loss, but many of them, including Gregg, were captured.

Ulysses S. Grant spent the night of April 7 in Farmville, staying in the same hotel (and, allegedly, the same room) that Robert E. Lee had slept in the night before.

By sundown, the rest of Humphreys's II Corps was entrenched across from the Confederates, and after nightfall, the VI Corps marched north to join them. The two divisions of the Army of the James camped near Farmville that night, while the V Corps, along with two of Sheridan's three cavalry divisions, moved farther west to Prince George Court House.

The Cumberland Church you see in your rear is the original building and was

Farmville, April 7, 1865, 5:00 PM

General:

The results of the last week must convince you of the hopelessness of further resistance on the part of the Army of Northern Virginia in this struggle. I feel that it is so, and regard it as my duty to shift from myself the responsibility of any further effusion of blood, by asking of you the surrender of that portion of the C.S. Army known as the Army of Northern Virginia.

Very respectfully, your obedient servant,
U.S. GRANT, Lieutenant General,
Commanding Armies of the United States.

Cumberland Church, April 7, 10:00 PM

Genl

I have recd your note of this date. Though not entertaining the opinion you express of the hopelessness of further resistance on the part of the Army of N. Va. I reciprocate your desire to avoid useless effusion of blood, & therefore before considering your proposition, ask the terms you will offer on condition of its surrender.

Very respy your obt Svt
R. E. LEE, Genl

Robert E. Lee's final field headquarters near Appomattox Court House.

present during the battle. Lee used the church as his headquarters during the short time the Confederates were here. Standing with the church at your back, their line swept in a wide semicircle around you, facing east, while the II Corps line began at their left and ran opposite but stopped almost directly in front of you. Miles's attack occurred about a quarter-mile to your left, well to the left of the roadway.

Realizing that he could be caught in a trap between the James River to the north and the Appomattox River to the south, Lee reluctantly called upon his men to make a third consecutive night march. At 11 PM, the Confederates quietly began to pull out of their lines and march toward their next objective: Appomattox Station.

CLIFTON

> *Pull out to your left onto VA 45 North and drive 1.6 miles. Turn left onto CR 636 (Raines's Tavern Road) and continue as it becomes SR 636 (Stage Coach Road) for a total of 6.9 miles. Shortly after the intersection with US 15, near your destination, is a parking area on your right; you may want to stop here, because you will not be able to stop at Clifton. It is private property. The estate will be on your left as you drive by.*

The large white house on the left is Clifton, a privately owned property, so do not trespass. You will only very briefly see the estate through the gate as you drive past, but it is very clearly marked "Clifton" just outside the entrance. While part of the army moved west along the South Side Railroad, south of the Appomattox, Grant chose this path, trailing the Confederates, to be more readily able to answer any offers of surrender from Lee. Grant spent the evening of April 8 here, establishing his temporary headquarters and sharing a bed with his chief of staff, John Rawlins.

During the day of April 8, Grant had sent another note to Lee. It was here at Clifton that Grant would receive Lee's reply to his second note, and while Grant was keen on accepting the meeting Lee proposed, Rawlins vehemently and persuasively argued against it, primarily on the grounds that Grant lacked the authority to do so under Lee's proposed terms, but also because it seemed that Lee was asking for less than a full surrender. Although Grant was convinced he would leave the meeting with a full surrender from Lee, he accepted Rawlins's argument.

LEE'S LAST HEADQUARTERS

> *From Clifton, continue on SR 636 for 13.4 miles. Turn left onto VA 24 West and drive 8.2 miles. You are now within the boundaries of Appomattox Court House National Historical Park. Pull into the parking area on your left.*

On the road, April 8, 1865, morning, to Robert E. Lee:

Peace being my great desire, there is but one condition I would insist upon—namely, that the men and officers surrendered shall be disqualified for taking up arms against the Government of the United States until properly exchanged. I will meet you, or will designate officers to meet any officers you may name for the same purpose, at any point agreeable to you, for the purpose of arranging definitely the terms upon which the surrender of the Army of Northern Virginia will be received.

U.S. GRANT

Near Appomattox Court House, April 8, 1865, evening, to U.S. Grant:

I did not intend to propose the surrender of the Army of N. Va., but to ask the terms of your proposition. To be frank, I do not think the emergency has arisen to call for surrender of this Army, but as the restoration of peace should be the sole subject of all, I desired to know whether your proposals would lead to that end. I cannot therefore meet you with a view to surrender the Army of N. Va.; but as far as your proposal may affect the C. S. forces under my command, and tend to the restoration of peace, I shall be pleased to meet you at 10 A.M. tomorrow on the old stage road to Richmond, between the picket lines of the two armies.

R.E. LEE

There is some disagreement about exactly what happened when at the location on this tour stop, and it's a bit out of the timeline of our tour, but you don't want to miss it. If you park and walk down the very short trail to the site, you will come to a small clearing with a marker and a bench.

This was, as the sign indicates, Lee's last headquarters, and there is little to dispute that. What is unclear is when this headquarters was established, which makes a big difference when trying to recount the last moments of the Army of Northern Virginia. For years, the consensus was that this was the location where Lee held his last council of war, and when his final breakthrough attempt failed, where he came to the painful decision to surrender. However, other evidence indicates that Lee's council of war occurred elsewhere on the evening of April 8, and that Lee did not even see this location until after he was actually returning from the surrender.

More certain is that Lee's famous farewell address to the Army of Northern Virginia was written here, although it was likely written by his secretary, Lt. Col. Charles Marshall. Regardless, it's a wonderful and hopeful address, and it was written on a field desk right here in this small clearing.

APPOMATTOX STATION

⟩ *From the parking area, pull out to your left onto VA 24 West. Drive 3.9 miles, crossing over the interstate and proceeding through the town of Appomattox. Turn left onto Confederate Boulevard and drive 0.1 mile, then take the next right onto North Court Street. Drive 0.6 mile on North Court Street to Main Street, then turn left. Drive 0.1 mile to the Appomattox Visitor Information Center on your right.*

When the Union II and VI Corps woke up on April 8 to find that the Confederates had vacated their lines at Cumberland Church, they immediately set off in pursuit. In effect, the rebels had only two remaining corps at this point: Longstreet's, as he had taken command of A. P. Hill's remaining men, and Gordon's. The two corps took separate paths from Cumberland Church and rejoined down the road, the VI Corps following Longstreet and the II Corps following Gordon. Along the way, because their commands had been decimated to the point of no longer having a command (and, probably, partly because of their performance at Sailor's Creek), Lee relieved Richard Anderson, George Pickett, and Bushrod Johnson of their remaining duties with the army. (Pickett and Johnson stayed anyway, while Anderson went home.)

Site of Appomattox Station. Three Confederate supply trains would have been located here along these tracks when the Union cavalry arrived.

To the south, Phil Sheridan was driving his cavalry to Appomattox Court House. Although he had a shorter route than the enemy did, he was not about to take any chances. Grant did not want to simply pursue the Confederates. He wanted to cut them off, to leave them no alternative but to surrender. Following Sheridan was Ord's Army of the James, along with Charles Griffin's V Corps.

Before reaching Appomattox Station, the Union troopers came through Pamplin's Depot, where they found the Confederate supply trains that had attempted to fee Lee's army at Farmville. Taking possession, they quickly moved on to Appomattox Station, where even more supplies were waiting—three full trains (a fourth had been scared off), containing 300,000 rations, shoes, clothing, blankets, medical supplies, and other items that the rebel army needed badly. Custer's and Devin's divisions quickly and easily secured the trains at 4 PM, and then directed their attention to Confederate activity on the hillside above the town.

The old railroad station you see here was not around during the Civil War. However, the railroad tracks next to it are where the three supply trains were parked, 51 cars in all. If you face the tracks and look to your right, the original Appomattox Station was just down the tracks, just past the next road. While you're here, you might want to stop in at the visitor center and check out some of the other things to see in the area.

❭ *From the visitor information center, continue on Main Street, then take the next left turn onto North Church Street. Drive 0.4 mile on North Church Street to Patricia Anne Lane. Turn left on Patricia Anne Lane, then take the second right turn onto Patterson Street (SR 1009). Continue on SR 1009 for 0.2 mile; you will see a home on a ridge to your left. Drive past the home, make a U-turn, and return to this spot. NOTE: All the land in this area is private property, so do not leave your vehicle.*

Lindsay Walker's Confederate artillery reserve—about 100 guns—had been riding ahead of the rest of the army, along with part of the wagon train, intending to stop at Appomattox Station that night. Walker, who also had a brigade of cavalry with him, began to go into camp on a rise just to the north when he realized that Federal cavalry was present.

Both Walker and Custer fought cautiously at first, neither knowing just how large the respective enemy forces were. Walker, though, had enough time to arrange his artillery on a ridge in a semicircle directed south, with cavalry on his flanks. The ridge you see here is approximately where he set his guns. The thick growth you see in the area is similar to what was present at the time of the battle, although most of the field is privately owned today.

Custer launched several attacks at Walker's line without success, continuing on

Union artillery position during the final battle of the campaign at Appomattox Court House.

into the night. The final Union attack at 8 PM finally broke what remained of the rebels. The Federals captured with 30 pieces of artillery, almost 200 wagons, and just short of 1,000 Confederate soldiers. More important, they had not only stopped Lee from getting to his supply trains, but also blocked his route to the south.

That evening of April 8, the weary Confederates finally went into camp along the Richmond Stage Road just northeast of Appomattox Court House. Shortly after nightfall, Custer would send a scouting party toward the town, alerting them that, once again, Union troopers were in their front.

That night, Lee held a council of war to weigh his options. He knew that two corps of enemy infantry were to his rear and that Federal cavalry was to his front. He also knew that his army, after three consecutive night marches and little to no rations, was not only exhausted but shrinking, with large numbers of stragglers and, by this time, a growing number of deserters who sensed that the end was near. It was decided that the next morning, the Confederates would attempt a breakthrough to the south. If only Union cavalry was to their front, the chances of success were good, and they could keep moving. If, however, Union infantry was also present, his soldiers were trapped, leaving them with only one alternative.

MUSEUM OF THE CONFEDERACY—APPOMATTOX

❭ *Continue forward on SR 1009 for 0.2 mile to Patricia Anne Lane. Turn right and drive another 0.2 mile and turn right onto Confederate Boulevard. Drive 0.4 mile on Confederate Boulevard, then turn right onto Old Courthouse Road. Drive 0.8 mile on Old Courthouse Road, crossing over the highway, to SR 656. Turn left onto SR 656, then take another immediate left onto F 1011. Pull into the parking lot for the museum.*

In April 2012, the Museum of the Confederacy, running out of room at the Richmond campus to display its vast collection of amazing artifacts, opened a sister site at Appomattox. The quality of the museum here is every bit as good as at the main facility in Richmond, but the experience at this museum is quite different. Geared more toward interpretation and the story of what led up to Appomattox, the surrenders ending the war, and their immediate aftermath, the museum features high-tech displays, with interactive features that invite participation, adding to the museum's normal display of "the real stuff." A state-of-the-art classroom and learning center has also been built to host presentations and lectures. As the museum develops further, it will prove to be an excellent companion piece to the historical park, making Appomattox even more attractive as a prime destination.

APPOMATTOX COURT HOUSE

❭ *Return to Old Courthouse Road (VA 24 East) and turn left. Drive 1.1 miles and pull into the parking lot to your left at the cemetery.*

The battle plan was simple. John Brown Gordon's infantry, 2,000 strong, would form a line west of Appomattox Court House, facing southwest. Fitz Lee's 2,400 cavalrymen would guard the flanks of the line, and artillery placed in the small town would hammer away during the attack. At dawn on April 9, the entire line moved, sweeping down the Richmond-Lynchburg Stage Road and pivoting to the south to face the small Union cavalry force in its front, Charles Smith's brigade of George Crook's division.

Smith did his best to buy time for the Union infantry and cavalry to come up in support, having his men fire their 7- and 16-shot repeating carbines repeatedly to fool the Confederates into thinking a larger force was present. Soon, though, Smith was forced rearward, as were Crook's other two brigades sent in support.

Your position here at the Confederate cemetery is approximately where Smith's pickets, as well as two pieces of artillery, defiantly faced Gordon's corps as it wheeled toward them. Running near the cemetery is a split-rail fence; turn so this fence is at your left, with the modern road on your right. The fence marks the former location of the Richmond-Lynchburg Stage Road, the main route through Appomattox Court House. You are looking toward the town, and the Confederates would have been coming toward you from your left front, with the entire line wheeling over the left flank of the advance Union position.

Now, turn around so that the fence is on your right. After the rebels pushed Smith and his reinforcements back, they advanced in the direction you are now facing, moving from ridge to ridge and easily overwhelming the Union horsemen. Fitz Lee, in an attempt to attack the Union rear, sent two of his three divisions on a wide sweep to the north, while Rooney Lee's division stayed here to help press the attack. Soon, the entire Confederate line had finished its sweep and was facing south, across the modern road to your left and into the trees, which were not present at the time of the battle.

Clifton, April 9, 1865, dawn, to General Robert E. Lee:

Your note of yesterday is received. I have no authority to treat on the subject of peace; the meeting proposed for 10 A.M. today could lead to no good. I will state, however, General, that I am equally anxious for peace with yourself, and the whole North entertains the same feeling. The terms upon which peace can be had are well understood. By the South laying down their arms they will hasten that most desirable event, save thousands of human lives, and hundreds of millions of property not yet destroyed. Seriously hoping that all our difficulties may be settled without the loss of another life, I subscribe myself, &c., U.S. GRANT, Lieutenant General.

East of Appomattox Court House, April 9, 1865, 8:30 AM

General:
I received your note of this morning on the picket line, whither I had come to meet you and ascertain definitely what terms were embraced in your proposal of yesterday with reference to the surrender of this army. I now request an interview, in accordance with the offer contained in your letter of yesterday, for that purpose.
Very respectfully, Your obt servt
R. E. LEE.

On the road to Appomattox Court House, April 9, 11:50 AM, to Robert E. Lee:

. . . will push forward to the front for the purpose of meeting you. Notice sent to me on this road where you wish the interview to take place will meet you.
U.S. GRANT

With the enemy line facing this direction, only the unit on the right—William Cox's brigade—could see what was coming from the west. John Gibbon's XXIV Corps of the Army of the James, followed closely by elements of the XXV Corps, appeared to your front, completely blocking the Richmond-Lynchburg Stage Road. Although Cox repulsed several attacks, there would be no escape westward for the Confederates.

With no roads leading north and the Union II and VI Corps to the east, the only remaining option was to move south, and the Confederates were making steady progress. More Federal cavalry, Thomas Devin's division, had shown up to slow the Confederates, and was holding a ridge to the south. As the Confederates watched in dismay, Devin was soon joined by Custer's cavalry, and directly behind the Union horsemen, the infantry of the Union V Corps began approaching over the rise. Gordon, now certain that he could not break out, pulled his line back through Appomattox Court House, with the Federals in pursuit. Although the two divisions of cavalry sent earlier were able to escape, Lee, who had watched the battle, was now certain that the rest of his men would not be able to fight their way out of Appomattox Court House.

❭ *Pull out to your left onto Old Courthouse Road and drive 0.3 mile, then pull into the main parking area for Appomattox Court House National Historical Park on your left.*

Telling his staff that he "would rather die a thousand deaths," Lee directed his staff to arrange for couriers to present flags of truce along the line, and after 10 AM the firing began to cease. Lee rode east toward Andrew Humphreys's II Corps, reaching the line at 8:30 AM. It was here that Lee received Grant's earlier note proposing surrender, and quickly wrote out a response. Lee had thought Grant would be on this front, but he was actually riding toward Sheridan's, to the south. However, George Meade was present, and suggested that he send a copy in that direction as well. Lee and Meade agreed on a temporary cease-fire, and Lee went back to await Grant's response.

Grant and his staff were southeast of Appomattox Court House when they received Lee's message just before noon. Grant had been suffering from a terrible headache since the previous day, but as he recounted later, "The instant I saw the contents of the note I was cured." While several of his party openly wept at the news, Grant scribbled a note to Lee telling him that he was on his way.

Lee received Grant's final note at about 1 PM and began to make his way toward Appomattox Court House, sending two of his aides ahead to find a suitable location for the meeting. They ultimately decided on the home of Wilbur McLean, whose previous residence in Manassas had been Confederate headquarters during the first battle of Bull Run. McLean had moved to Appomattox to escape the war, but it had caught up to him nonetheless.

This is Appomattox Court House, many of its original buildings still standing. Unless you visit on a particularly busy day, you may find yourself quickly drawn back in time 150 years or so. The first building you will notice, on your right, is the court-house, a reproduction of the original that now serves as headquarters for Appomattox Court House National Battlefield Park. Inside you will find the main visitor center, as well as exhibits and a film. Stop here first and get a map of the town, and find out which tours and programs are scheduled for the day. After you have seen the exhibits, come back outside and reorient yourself.

Stand so that the entrance to the courthouse is to your back. The Richmond-Lynchburg Stage Road ran right by the courthouse, and you are now looking west down the same road. There are several buildings to stop and visit, so take your time; you're sure to find that the peaceful setting of the park is unique. Keep moving down the road until you reach a large white home on your left. This is the Wilbur McLean House, reconstructed from its original materials after it had been dismantled, shipped across the country as an exhibition, then left as a pile of rubble after the exhibition company went bankrupt. The accomplishment of the National Park Service in re-building and restoring this home is nothing short of miraculous.

The reconstructed McLean House, site of the famous meeting between Grant and Lee.

Lee and his small staff arrived shortly after 1 PM and waited in McLean's parlor for Grant to arrive. At 1:30 PM, Grant, along with a considerably larger entourage, dismounted in the front yard and made his way into the house. If you climb up the steps to the porch, you can either enter the home for your brief tour or take a rest on the McLean's front porch. Inside, the parlor has been restored to its April 9, 1865, appearance.

After Grant had initiated a bit of small talk, Lee cut straight to the matter, obviously not wanting to extend the event any longer than it needed to be. Having been expecting this ceremony, Lee had been wearing his best dress uniform since 1 AM; Grant, who had just ridden cross country and forded a river, was dressed in his usual common military overcoat, with only the stars on his shoulder indicating his rank.

Lee suggested that Grant write the terms of surrender, to which Lee would respond. Grant wrote out the terms and handed them to his secretary for review, who then handed them to Lee. These were not the sort of terms that "unconditional surrender" Grant had been known for; in fact, they were quite generous. This was in accordance with the wishes of Abraham Lincoln, who had spoken with Grant several times regarding his plan to heal the country after the war had ended. Officers were allowed to keep their sidearms, meaning that no swords would be surrendered, skipping a customary but humiliatingly submissive part of the surrender ceremony. The Confederate soldiers would be paroled, free to go home and return to the lives they knew before, provided they did not take up arms against the United States government again. Finding the terms more than agreeable, Lee did ask for one more favor. Cavalry and artillerymen were required to supply their own mounts, meaning that most had brought their own horses from their farms. Realizing that they would need these horses to go back to their previous living, Grant readily acceded that the men could keep them. Also, knowing that Lee's men were hungry, Grant offered to provide rations for the rebel troops, a gesture that Lee gratefully accepted.

The conference ended at 3 PM, although the generals' staffs would remain to work out the formalities. Lee mounted his horse, and the two generals saluted each other. With that, on Palm Sunday, April 9, 1865, the two great armies that had pushed themselves through four years of the most terrible warfare ever seen would battle no more. The Civil War in the Eastern Theater, and in effect the entire nation, was over.

Leave the McLean House to explore the rest of the town. You will find a bookstore, the former tavern, and various other homes and buildings, along with park rangers scattered throughout the village. Be sure to make your way past the courthouse on your return, continuing down the old Richmond-Lynchburg Stage Road. On your right, you will pass the Peers House. Confederate artillery placed in front of the house was active in the morning battle of April 9, and a marker here denotes that these were the last shots fired by the artillery of the Army of Northern Virginia.

Keep moving down the road. To your left, in the open fields along the road, Lee's army camped from April 8 to 12, waiting through the formal surrender. On April 10, after Grant and Lee had met at the McLean House, the two met for a final time here along the road at 10 AM, having a small conversation about the proceedings that were about to begin. Grant also requested that Lee use his influence to persuade the other armies of the Confederacy to lay down their arms, to which Lee replied he must first consult with Jefferson Davis. Lee then returned to his headquarters, while Grant headed east for City Point, his work complete.

This stretch of the road is where the official surrender activities took place. The Confederate cavalry surrendered on April 10, the artillery on April 11, and finally the infantry on April 12. Through the days of the surrender, the Federals were under very strict orders from Grant not to demean or humiliate their foes; there would be no cheers, no bands, no celebrations. This went a long way with many of the Confederates, who while devastated by their defeat, were ready to go home and resume their lives as citizens. Joshua Lawrence Chamberlain, ordered to take charge of the proceedings, very deliberately saluted John Brown Gordon's infantry, and Gordon had his men return the salute.

The old Richmond Stage Road, scene of the tearful surrender of the Army of Northern Virginia.

Less than a week later, on Good Friday, Abraham Lincoln was assassinated in Washington at Ford's Theater. Many of the policies that the president had wished to enact regarding the reconstruction of the country were scuttled, and hard times remained for the South for many decades after the war. However, between the soldiers who held the lines, who did the heavy lifting, who had seen the worst of the worst waging this Civil War, it was over. There was honor in defeat and a respect for the enemy that would last through the years, thanks largely to gestures like those made by Grant, Lee, and their soldiers at Appomattox. Although the repercussions of this great conflict are felt even today, the Civil War between the soldiers ended at Appomattox Court House.

Site Information

CHAPTER 1—INTERLUDE: THE BRISTOE AND MINE RUN CAMPAIGNS

Jack's Shop
Jack's Shop
Intersection of VA-231 and Shelby Road,
Aroda, VA 22709
Latitude: –78.273567
Longitude: 38.308819

Brandy Station
Stuart and Kilpatrick
15148 State Police Road, Culpeper,
VA 22701
Phone: 540-727-7718
Website:
www.brandystationfoundation.com
Latitude: –77.926430
Longitude: 38.493740

Fleetwood Hill
On Fleetwood Heights Road, 0.5 mile
west of Alanthus Road, Brandy Station,
VA 22714
Latitude: –77.886467
Longitude: 38.506351

Auburn
First Battle
Intersection of Old Auburn Road and
Rogues Road, Warrenton, VA 20187
Latitude: –77.701859
Longitude: 38.702106

Stuart's Hideout
Intersection of Taylor Road and Marshall
Gardens Court, Catlett, VA 20119
Latitude: –77.693352
Longitude: 38.706127

Coffee Hill
Intersection of Old Auburn Road and
Rogues Road, Warrenton, VA 20187
Latitude: –77.701256
Longitude: 38.703194

Bristoe Station
Bristoe Station Battlefield Heritage Park
10708 Bristow Road, Bristow, VA 20136
Phone: 703-792-5546
Website: www.pwcgov.org/bristoe
Latitude: –77.544144
Longitude: 38.727055

Break in Union Line
Intersection of Bristow Road and Milford
Road, Bristow, VA 20136
Latitude: –77.536613
Longitude: 38.723286

Buckland Races
Broad Run
On Lee Highway East, 0.1 mile west of
Buckland Mill Road, Gainesville, VA
20155
Latitude: −77.6747
Longitude: 38.779719999999998

Chestnut Hill
Intersection of Lee Highway and Colonial
Road, Warrenton, VA 20187
Latitude: −77.767990
Longitude: 38.738571

Kelly's Ford
Kelly's Ford
Intersection of Kelly's Ford Road and
Stones Mill Road, Elkwood, VA 22718
Latitude: −77.780716
Longitude: 38.477009

Rappahannock Station
Union Approach
104 South James Madison Street,
Remington, VA 22734
Latitude: −77.809237
Longitude: 38.531967
Pontoon Bridge Site
On Remington Road, 0.5 mile east of
James Madison Highway, Remington,
VA 22734

Latitude: −77.813759
Longitude: 38.529922

Mine Run
New Hope Church
On Old Plank Road, 0.4 mile west of
Gold Dale Road, Locust Grove, VA
22508
Latitude: −77.811790
Longitude: 38.264408

Robinson's Tavern
Intersection of Gold Dale Road and
Constitution Highway, Locust Grove, VA
22508
Latitude: −77.810539
Longitude: 38.304554

Widow Morris Farm
Intersection of Indiantown Road and
Russel Road, Locust Grove, VA 22508
Latitude: −77.825478
Longitude: 38.351650

Payne's Farm
On Zoar Road, 0.2 mile east of In-
diantown Road, Locust Grove, VA
22508
Latitude: −77.828476
Longitude: 38.332321

CHAPTER 2—BERMUDA HUNDRED CAMPAIGN

Bermuda Hundred Landing
Bermuda Hundred Landing
4719 Bermuda Hundred Road, Chester,
VA 23836
Latitude: −77.271568
Longitude: 37.341572

Enon Church
Enon Church
13607 North Enon Church Road, Chester,
VA 23836
Latitude: −77.323441
Longitude: 37.343559

Point of Rocks
Point of Rocks
201 North Enon Church Road, Chester,
VA 23836
Latitude: −77.354691
Longitude: 37.321609

Port Walthall Junction
Port Walthall Junction
2126 Ruffin Mill Road, Colonial Heights,
VA 23834
Latitude: −77.391945
Longitude: 37.311249

Swift Creek

Arrowhead Church
17201 Jefferson Davis Highway, Colonial
    Heights, VA 23834
Latitude: −77.410835
Longitude: 37.285538

Swift Creek
17401 Jefferson Davis Highway, Colonial
    Heights, VA 23834
Latitude: −77.412064
Longitude: 37.283733

Fort Clifton
Intersection of Conduit Road and Brock-
    well Lane, Colonial Heights, VA 23834
Latitude: −77.367462
Longitude: 37.280506

Chester Station

Chester Station
3301 West Hundred Road, Chester, VA
    23831
Latitude: −77.421738
Longitude: 37.356472

Woodbridge Hill

Woodbridge Hill
0.2 mile north of intersection of Centralia
    Road and Hopkins Road, Chester, VA
    23831
Latitude: −77.460037
Longitude: 37.384651

Drewry's Bluff

Drewry's Bluff
7600 Fort Darling Road, Richmond, VA
    23237
Phone: 804-226-1981
Website: www.nps.gov/rich
Latitude: −77.424561
Longitude: 37.421059

Fort Stevens

Fort Stevens
8900 Pams Avenue, Richmond, VA
    23237
Latitude: −77.429283
Longitude: 37.403938

Half-Way House

Half-Way House
10301 Jefferson Davis Highway,
    Richmond, VA 23237
Latitude: −77.424538
Longitude: 37.385559

Howlett Line

Battery Dantzler
1820 Battery Dantzler Road, Chester, VA
    23836
Latitude: −77.392227
Longitude: 37.357903

Parker's Battery
1801 Ware Bottom Spring Road, Chester,
    VA 23831
Phone: 804-226-1981
Website: www.nps.gov/rich
Latitude: −77.395195
Longitude: 37.350258

Ware Bottom Church Battlefield
Intersection of Old Bermuda Hundred
    Road and Lawing Drive, Chester, VA
    23836
Latitude: −77.389061
Longitude: 37.342567

Howlett Line Park
On Howlett Line Drive, 0.3 mile south of
    intersection with Woods Edge Road,
    Colonial Heights, VA 23834
Latitude: −77.381714
Longitude: 37.333255

Wilson's Wharf

Sherwood Forest Plantation
14501 John Tyler Memorial Highway,
    Charles City, VA 23030
Phone: 804-829-5377
Website: www.sherwoodforest.org
Latitude: −76.994720
Longitude: 37.306370

CHAPTER 3—THE OVERLAND CAMPAIGN, PART I: THE WILDERNESS AND SPOTSYLVANIA COURT HOUSE

Germanna Ford

Germanna Ford
2062 Germanna Highway, Locust Grove, VA 22508
Latitude: −77.781960
Longitude: 38.377075

Ely's Ford

Ely's Ford
On Ely's Ford Road, 0.1 mile south of Rapidan River, Fredericksburg, VA 22407
Latitude: −77.685173
Longitude: 38.357998

Wilderness

Chancellorsville
Intersection of Ely's Ford Road and Plank Road, Fredericksburg, VA 22407
Latitude: −77.634468
Longitude: 38.309498

Chancellorsville Visitor Center
9001 Plank Road, Fredericksburg, VA 22407
Phone: 540-786-2880
Website: www.nps.gov/frsp/wilder.htm
Latitude: −77.649483
Longitude: 38.311424

Wilderness Tavern
Intersection of Lyons Lane and Plank Road, Spotsylvania, VA 22551
Latitude: −77.722885
Longitude: 38.324680

Grant's HQ
On Constitution Highway, 0.4 mile south of intersection with Plank Road, Locust Grove, VA 22508
Latitude: −77.734062
Longitude: 38.322224

Lacy House (Friends of Wilderness Battlefield)
36380 Constitution Highway (Route 20), Locust Grove, VA 22508
Website: www.fowb.org/ellwood
Latitude: −77.732437
Longitude: 38.319469

Saunders Field
On Constitution Highway, 0.2 mile east of intersection with Hill Ewell Drive, Locust Grove, VA 22508
Latitude: −77.756393
Longitude: 38.317249

Ewell's Line
Intersection of Constitution Highway and Hill Ewell Drive, Locust Grove, VA 22508
Latitude: −77.759354
Longitude: 38.316044

Higgerson Farm
On Hill Ewell Drive, 0.8 mile south of Constitution Highway, Locust Grove, VA 22508
Latitude: −77.749817
Longitude: 38.308662

Chewning Farm Trailhead/Old Parker's Store Road
On Hill Ewell Drive, 1.9 mile south of Constitution Highway, Spotsylvania, VA 22551
Latitude: −77.744362
Longitude: 38.296032

Parker's Store Site
Intersection of Orange Plank Road and Windy Acres Lane, Locust Grove, VA 22508
Latitude: −77.759361
Longitude: 38.274761

Brock Road/Orange Plank Road
Intersection
Intersection of Brock Road and Orange
Plank Road, Spotsylvania, VA 22553
Latitude: −77.709709
Longitude: 38.300800

Widow Tapp Farm
On Orange Plank Road, 0.5 mile west of
Hill Ewell Drive, Spotsylvania, VA
22551
Latitude: −77.726509
Longitude: 38.288597

Longstreet's Wounding
Intersection of Orange Plank Road and
Forest Walk Drive, Spotsylvania, VA
22551
Latitude: −77.714592
Longitude: 38.297977

Todd's Tavern

Tavern Site
Intersection of Brock Road and Catharpin
Road, Spotsylvania, VA 22551
Latitude: −77.668694
Longitude: 38.247509

Corbin's Bridge
On Catharpin Road, 0.1 mile south of
Corbin Road, Spotsylvania, VA 22551
Latitude: −77.700851
Longitude: 38.232586

Piney Branch Church Site
Intersection of Brock Road and Piney
Branch Church Road, Spotsylvania, VA
22553
Latitude: −77.635361
Longitude: 38.230530

Spotsylvania

Alsop Farm Site
Intersection of Brock Road and Gordon
Road, Spotsylvania, VA 22553
Latitude: −77.626068
Longitude: 38.226547

Block House Bridge
On Robert E. Lee Drive, 0.3 mile west of
River Valley Lane, Spotsylvania, VA
22551
Latitude: −77.633385
Longitude: 38.204769

Exhibit Shelter
On Grant Drive, 0.1 mile north of Brock
Road, Spotsylvania, VA 22553
Website: www.nps.gov/frsp/spot.htm
Latitude: −77.614143
Longitude: 38.219105

Union Line—Spindle Field
On Hancock Drive, 0.2 mile south of
Brock Road, Spotsylvania, VA 22553
Latitude: −77.616859
Longitude: 38.216564

Confederate Line—Spindle Field
On Pritchett Road, 0.1 mile west of Block
House Road, Spotsylvania, VA 22551
Latitude: −77.615150
Longitude: 38.211697

Sedgwick Monument
Intersection of Brock Road and Grant
Drive, Spotsylvania, VA 22553
Latitude: −77.614738
Longitude: 38.218155

Upton's Farm Road
On Grant Drive, 0.7 mile north of Brock
Road, Spotsylvania, VA 22553
Latitude: −77.606384
Longitude: 38.223671

Doles's Salient
On Anderson Drive, 0.2 mile south of
Grant Drive, Spotsylvania, VA 22553
Latitude: −77.603333
Longitude: 38.221207

Reconstructed Entrenchments
On Anderson Drive, 0.3 mile south of
Gordon Road, Spotsylvania, VA 22553
Latitude: −77.607719
Longitude: 38.214310

McCoull House Site/Ramseur Monument
On park road, 0.2 mile north of Gordon
Drive, Spotsylvania, VA 22553
Latitude: −77.600212
Longitude: 38.219975

Bloody Angle Trail
Intersection of Grant Drive and Anderson
Drive, Spotsylvania, VA 22553
Latitude: −77.601372
Longitude: 38.223381

Harrison House/Lee's Second Line
Intersection of Anderson Drive and
Gordon Drive, Spotsylvania, VA 22553
Latitude: −77.603004
Longitude: 38.217514

East Angle Trail
Intersection of Gordon Drive and Grant
Drive East, Spotsylvania, VA 22553
Latitude: −77.593605
Longitude: 38.220585

Heth's Salient
On Burnside Drive, 0.5 mile south of
Gordon Drive, Spotsylvania, VA 22553
Latitude: −77.591148
Longitude: 38.215248

Gayle Farm/IX Corps on Fredericksburg
Road
On Courthouse Road, 0.3 mile north of
Tremont Lane, Spotsylvania, VA 22553
Latitude: −77.568687
Longitude: 38.219654

Spotsylvania Court House
Intersection of Courthouse Road and
Brock Road, Spotsylvania, VA 22553
Latitude: −77.589111
Longitude: 38.201557

Zion Methodist Church
Zion Methodist Church
8700 Courthouse Rd., Spotsylvania, VA
22553
Latitude: −77.586510
Longitude: 38.194035

Massaponax Church
Massaponax Church
5101 Massaponax Church Road, Freder-
icksburg, VA 22407
Latitude: −77.509995
Longitude: 38.193081

CHAPTER 4—THE OVERLAND CAMPAIGN PART II: NORTH ANNA TO COLD HARBOR

North Anna
Mount Carmel Church
24320 Jefferson Davis Highway,
Ruther Glen, VA 22546
Latitude: −77.480217
Longitude: 37.929722

Long Creek
On Jefferson Davis Highway, 0.2 mile
north of Oxford Road, Ruther Glen, VA
22546
Latitude: −77.467514
Longitude: 37.895248

Henagan's Redoubt/Telegraph Road
On Oxford Road, 0.3 mile west of
Jefferson Davis Highway, Ruther Glen,
VA 22546
Latitude: −77.470985
Longitude: 37.890709

Fight at Jericho Mills
On Noel Road, 0.2 mile north of Verdon
Road, Doswell, VA 23047
Latitude: −77.542145
Longitude: 37.907028

North Anna Battlefield Park
12075 Verdon Rd., Doswell, VA 23047
Latitude: -77.498856
Longitude: 37.881187

Yellow Tavern

Tavern Site
Intersection of Brook Road and Mountain
  Road, Glen Allen, VA 23060
Latitude: -77.459404
Longitude: 37.639484

Telegraph Road
Intersection of Telegraph Road and
  Stonemeadow Drive, Glen Allen, VA
  23060
Latitude: -77.454124
Longitude: 37.656525

Lomax's Line
Intersection of Telegraph Road and
  Maryland Drive, Glen Allen, VA 23060
Latitude: -77.456024
Longitude: 37.650616

Mountain Road/Union Line
Intersection of Greenwood Road and
  Mountain Road, Glen Allen, VA 23060
Latitude: -77.469086
Longitude: 37.651024

Confederate Ridgeline
Intersection of Battlefield Road and
  Harmony Road, Glen Allen, VA 23059
Latitude: -77.456894
Longitude: 37.660545

Stuart Memorial
Intersection of Telegraph Road and
  Towering Road, Glen Allen, VA 23059
Latitude: -77.453445
Longitude: 37.661739

Meadow Bridge

Richmond Outer Defense Line
On Brook Road in Brook Run Shopping
  Center, Richmond, VA 23227
Latitude: -77.458832
Longitude: 37.611153

Meadow Bridge
On Richmond Henrico Turnpike, 0.8 mile
  northeast of Azalea Avenue, Richmond,
  VA 23227
Latitude: -77.412476
Longitude: 37.608673

Nelson's Bridge

Crossing
On Nelson Bridge Road, 0.3 mile north-
  east of River Road, Hanover, VA 23069
Latitude: -77.289246
Longitude: 37.715534

Cavalry Fight
Intersection of Nelson Bridge Road and
  River Road, Hanover, VA 23069
Latitude: -77.291801
Longitude: 37.710968

Enon Church

Enon Church
6156 Studley Road, Mechanicsville, VA
  23116
Latitude: -77.310921
Longitude: 37.676144

Totopotomoy Creek

Totopotomoy Creek Battlefield
7273 Studley Road, Mechanicsville, VA
  23116
Phone: 804-226-1981
Website: www.nps.gov/rich
Latitude: -77.346367
Longitude: 37.661613

Polegreen Church
Intersection of Rural Point Road and
  Heatherwood Drive, Mechanicsville, VA
  23116
Latitude: -77.330788
Longitude: 37.645702

Bethesda Church

Bethesda Church Site
Intersection of Mechanicsville Turnpike
  and Walnut Grove Road,
  Mechanicsville, VA 23111
Latitude: -77.296883
Longitude: 37.626606

Union Defensive Line
Intersection of Walnut Grove Road and
Pole Green Road, Mechanicsville, VA
23116
Latitude: −77.299011
Longitude: 37.639633

Old Church/Matedequin Creek

Old Church
Intersection of Old Church Road and Mc-
Clellan Road, Mechanicsville, VA
23111
Latitude: −77.221268
Longitude: 37.644615

Matadequin Creek
Intersection of McClellan Road and
Spillway Lane, Mechanicsville, VA
23111
Latitude: −77.223396
Longitude: 37.631721

Cold Harbor

Cold Harbor Crossroads
Intersection of Cold Harbor Road and
Crown Hill Road, Mechanicsville, VA
23111
Latitude: −77.271049
Longitude: 37.591110

Cold Harbor Battlefield
5515 Anderson-Wright Drive,
Mechanicsville, VA 23111
Phone: 804-226-1981
Website: www.nps.gov/rich
Latitude: −77.287094
Longitude: 37.585423

Garthright House and Cold Harbor
County Park
6005 Cold Harbor Road, Mechanicsville,
VA 23111
Latitude: −77.278580
Longitude: 37.589298

Trevilian Station

Louisa Court House
Intersection of Main Street and
Courthouse Square, Louisa, VA 23093
Website: www.trevilianstation.org
Latitude: −78.003082
Longitude: 38.024319

Lee and Custer
845 Ellisville Drive, Louisa, VA 23093
Latitude: −78.004898
Longitude: 38.042725

Clayton's Store
Intersection of Ellisville Road and
Oakland Road, Louisa, VA 23093
Latitude: −77.998764
Longitude: 38.094902

Hampton and Merritt
On Oakland Road, 0.1 mile west of
SR 692, Louisa, VA 23093
Latitude: −78.047424
Longitude: 38.087429

Hampton's Charge
On Oakland Road, 1.1 miles north of
Louisa Road, Louisa, VA 23093
Latitude: −78.058739
Longitude: 38.060612

Confederate Wagons
Intersection of Louisa Road and Danne
Road, Louisa, VA 23093
Latitude: −78.074059
Longitude: 38.050762

Ogg Farm
On Spotswood Trail, 1.3 miles north of
Louisa Road, Louisa, VA 23093
Latitude: −78.093231
Longitude: 38.068016

CHAPTER 5—EARLY'S RAID ON WASHINGTON

Lynchburg

Sandusky
757 Sandusky Drive, Lynchburg, VA 24502
Phone: 434-832-0162
Website: www.historicsandusky.org
Latitude: −79.196922
Longitude: 37.379707

Quaker Meeting House
5810 Fort Avenue, Lynchburg, VA 24502
Latitude: −79.192299
Longitude: 37.372772

Fort Early/Early Monument
3511 Memorial Avenue, Lynchburg, VA 24502
Latitude: −79.173363
Longitude: 37.389935

Fort McCausland
2055 Langhorne Road, Lynchburg, VA 24501
Latitude: −79.184647
Longitude: 37.412991

Old City Cemetery/Inner Works
401 Taylor Street, Lynchburg, VA 24501
Phone: 434-847-1465
Website: www.gravegarden.org
Latitude: −79.157173
Longitude: 37.415054

Spring Hill Cemetery—Early's Hilltop
3000 Fort Avenue, Lynchburg, VA 24501
Phone: 434-846-0801
Latitude: −79.164261
Longitude: 37.393654

Hanging Rock

Hanging Rock Battlefield Trail
Intersection of Dutch Oven Road and Timberview Road, Roanoke, VA 24019
Latitude: −80.040207
Longitude: 37.327942

Lexington

Virginia Military Institute
512 Letcher Avenue, Lexington, VA 24450
Phone: 540-464-7212
Website: www.vmi.edu
Latitude: −79.435799
Longitude: 37.790142

Lee Chapel
100 North Jefferson Street, Lexington, VA 24450
Phone: 540-458-8768
Website: leechapel.wlu.edu
Latitude: −79.441933
Longitude: 37.786591

Stonewall Jackson House
8 East Washington Street, Lexington, VA 24450
Phone: 540-463-2552
Website: www.stonewalljackson.org
Latitude: −79.441452
Longitude: 37.784737

Stonewall Jackson Cemetery
Intersection of Main Street and McDowell Street, Lexington, VA 24450
Latitude: −79.445778
Longitude: 37.781593

Piedmont

Civil War Trails Marker
691 Battlefield Road, Fort Defiance, VA 24437
Latitude: −78.904144
Longitude: 38.201099

Confederate Line
On Battlefield Road, 0.3 mile north of Patterson Mill Road, Grottoes, VA 24441
Latitude: −78.897186
Longitude: 38.218681

New Market

New Market Battlefield State Historical
Park
8895 George R Collins Parkway, New
Market, VA 22844
Phone: 866-515-1864
Website: www2.vmi.edu/museum/nm
Latitude: −78.670723
Longitude: 38.661526

Monocacy

Monocacy National Battlefield Visitor
Center
5201 Urbana Pike, Frederick, MD 21704
Phone: 301-662-3515
Website: www.nps.gov/mono
Latitude: −77.397438
Longitude: 39.377525

Jug Bridge
Intersection of Dr Baxter Road and
Linganore Road, Frederick, MD 21704
Latitude: −77.368317
Longitude: 39.398819

Best Farm
On Urbana Pike, 0.3 mile south of New
Technology Way, Frederick, MD 21704
Latitude: −77.398499
Longitude: 39.370777

Monocacy Junction
On Urbana Pike, 0.2 mile north of Araby
Church Road, Frederick, MD 21704
Latitude: −77.392113
Longitude: 39.370846

Worthington Farm
On Baker Valley Road, 0.3 mile west of
Araby Church Road, Frederick, MD
21704
Latitude: −77.400551
Longitude: 39.361897

Thomas Farm
On Baker Valley Road, 0.6 mile west of
Araby Church Road, Frederick, MD
21704
Latitude: −77.390709
Longitude: 39.356979

Fort Stevens

Fort Stevens—Rock Creek Park
Intersection of 13th Street NW and
Quackenbox Street NW, Washington,
D.C. 20011
Phone: 202-895-6015
Website: www.nps.gov/cwdw
Latitude: −77.029526
Longitude: 38.964115

Battleground National Cemetery
6625 Georgia Avenue NW, Washington,
D.C. 20012
Phone: 202-895-6000
Latitude: −77.027145
Longitude: 38.970814

Lincoln Sharpshooter Tree Marker
Walter Reed Hospital, Washington, D.C.
20307
Latitude: −77.027863
Longitude: 38.973621

Cool Spring

Holy Cross Abbey
901 Cool Spring Lane, Berryville, VA
22611
Phone: 540-955-4383
Website: www.hcava.org/index.html
Latitude: −77.876541
Longitude: 39.144733

Rutherford's Farm

Rutherford's Farm
Intersection of US 11 and Nulton Lane,
Winchester, VA 22603
Latitude: −78.131958
Longitude: 39.219917

Second Kernstown

Kernstown Battlefield
610 Battle Park Drive, Winchester, VA
22601
Website: www.kernstownbattle.org
Latitude: −78.197311
Longitude: 39.143009

CHAPTER 6—SHERIDAN'S VALLEY CAMPAIGN

Guard Hill

Guard Hill
Intersection of Winchester Road and
Guard Hill Road, Front Royal, VA 22630
Latitude: -78.200294
Longitude: 38.952999

Berryville

Berryville
Intersection of West Main Street and
Westwood Road, Berryville, VA 22611
Latitude: -77.997566
Longitude: 39.161911

Third Winchester

Eversole's Knoll
143 Greenwood Road, Winchester, VA
22602
Latitude: -78.113243
Longitude: 39.186687

Third Winchester Battlefield
251 First Woods Drive, Winchester, VA
22603
Latitude: -78.115662
Longitude: 39.193459

Stephenson's Depot
Intersection of Old Charles Town Road
and Milburn Road, Stephenson, VA
22656
Latitude: -78.109924
Longitude: 39.229767

Fort Collier
Intersection of Brook Road and Brick Kiln
Road, Winchester, VA 22601
Latitude: -78.155228
Longitude: 39.200516

Star Fort
On Fortress Drive, 0.1 mile north of Fred-
erick Pike, Winchester, VA 22603
Latitude: -78.164543
Longitude: 39.206715

Fisher's Hill

Crook's Attack
On Tumbling Run Lane, 0.4 mile west of
Battlefield Road, Strasburg, VA 22657
Latitude: -78.427559
Longitude: 38.989437

Fisher's Hill Battlefield
On Battlefield Road, 1 mile west of Copp
Road, Strasburg, VA 22657
Latitude: -78.414825
Longitude: 38.989738

View of Gordon's Position
On Locust Grove Road, 0.4 mile north of
Valley Pike, Strasburg, VA 22657
Latitude: -78.408676
Longitude: 38.974400

Tom's Brook

Tom's Brook
Intersection of Valley Pike and Park Lane,
Maurertown, VA 22644
Latitude: -78.453079
Longitude: 38.934811

Cedar Creek

Hupp's Hill Visitor Center
33229 Old Valley Pike, Strasburg, VA
22641
Phone: 540-465-5884
Website: www.ccbf.us
Latitude: -78.348373
Longitude: 38.999241

Bowman's Mill Ford
On Bowman Mill Road, 0.1 mile north of
Pouts Hill Road, Strasburg, VA 22657
Latitude: -78.328140
Longitude: 38.991005

Gordon's March
On Long Meadow Road, 0.8 mile south of
Bowmans Mill Road, Middletown, VA
22645
Latitude: -78.303337
Longitude: 38.984966

Thoburn's Position
On Bowmans Mill Road, 1.3 miles west of
Long Meadow Road, Middletown, VA
22645
Latitude: −78.319649
Longitude: 38.998840

XIX Corps Left/NY Monument
Intersection of Valley Pike and Water
Plant Road, Middletown, VA 22645
Latitude: −78.309799
Longitude: 39.008713

Cedar Creek Battlefield Foundation
8437 Valley Pike, Middletown, VA
22645
Phone: 540-869-2064
Latitude: −78.297455
Longitude: 39.016701

Belle Grove
336 Belle Grove Road, Middletown, VA
22645
Phone: 540-869-2028
Website: www.bellegrove.org
Latitude: −78.304588
Longitude: 39.021049

Meadow Brook
Intersection of Belle Grove Road and
Meadow Mills Road, Middletown, VA
22645
Latitude: −78.305870
Longitude: 39.023388

Middletown Cemetery
Intersection of 3rd Street and Commerce
Street, Middletown, VA 22645
Latitude: −78.286247
Longitude: 39.032681

Miller's Lane
Intersection of Mineral Street and Cougill
Road, Middletown, VA 22645
Latitude: −78.273392
Longitude: 39.038502

Union Line
Intersection in Hites Road and Klines Mill
Road, Middletown, VA 22645
Latitude: −78.277397
Longitude: 39.057968

Sheridan's Ride
On Klines Mill Road, 0.5 mile west of
Valley Pike, Middletown, VA 22645
Latitude: −78.262962
Longitude: 39.052982

Union Advance
173 Skirmisher Lane, Middletown, VA
22645
Latitude: −78.269394
Longitude: 39.036404

Ramseur Monument
Intersection of Valley Pike and Belle
Grove Road, Middletown, VA 22645
Latitude: −78.301231
Longitude: 39.014851

CHAPTER 7—THE SIEGE OF PETERSBURG

Battle of Old Men and Young Boys
Battery 27
Intersection of Crater Road and Oakland Street, Petersburg, VA 23805
Latitude: −77.382095
Longitude: 37.204292

Dearing's Line
425 Graham Road, Petersburg, VA 23805
Latitude: −77.393433
Longitude: 37.218105

Assault of Petersburg
Visitor Center/Battery No. 5
5001 Siege Road, Petersburg, VA 23803
Phone: 804-732-3531
Website: www.nps.gov/pete
Latitude: −77.356110
Longitude: 37.243927

Battery 9
On Siege Road, Petersburg NB, Petersburg, VA 23803
Latitude: −77.354431
Longitude: 37.233112

Harrison's Creek
On Siege Road, Petersburg NB, Petersburg, VA 23803
Latitude: −77.363991
Longitude: 37.232735

Hare House/Colquitt's Salient
On Siege Road, Petersburg NB, Petersburg, VA 23803
Latitude: −77.369125
Longitude: 37.231842

The Crater
Fort Morton
On Siege Road, Petersburg NB, Petersburg, VA 23803
Latitude: −77.369576
Longitude: 37.219749

The Crater
On Siege Road, Petersburg NB, Petersburg, VA 23803
Latitude: −77.377121
Longitude: 37.216930

Jerusalem Plank Road
Fort Davis
Intersection of Crater Road and Flank Road, Petersburg, VA 23803
Latitude: −77.376060
Longitude: 37.193230

Fort Hays
On Flank Road, 0.1 mile north of Fort Hays Drive, Petersburg, VA 23805
Latitude: −77.381973
Longitude: 37.181328

Globe Tavern/Weldon Railroad
Weldon Railroad Battle Site
Intersection of Flank Road and Halifax Road, Petersburg, VA 23805
Latitude: −77.416000
Longitude: 37.167210

Reams's Station
Reams' Station Battlefield
Intersection of Halifax Road and Reams Drive, Petersburg, VA 23805
Latitude: −77.423691
Longitude: 37.093620

Oak Grove Methodist Church
12715 Acorn Drive, Petersburg, VA 23805
Latitude: −77.420769
Longitude: 37.096069

Peebles's Farm
Fort Fisher
Intersection of Church Road and Flank Road, Petersburg, VA 23804
Latitude: −77.453674
Longitude: 37.174294

Duncan Road
Intersection of Duncan Road and Rabbit
Drive, Petersburg, VA 23803
Latitude: −77.477188
Longitude: 37.174622

Boydton Plank Road/Burgess's Mill

Boydton Plank Road/Burgess's Mill
On Boydton Plank Road, 0.3 mile north of
White Oak Road, Petersburg, VA 23803
Latitude: −77.517227
Longitude: 37.153004

Hatcher's Run

Armstrong's Mill Site
On Duncan Road, 0.3 mile north of
Dabney Mill Road, Petersburg, VA
23803
Latitude: −77.487221
Longitude: 37.130306

Hatcher's Run Battlefield
On Dabney Mill Road, 0.6 mile west of
Duncan Road, Petersburg, VA 23803
Latitude: −77.497025
Longitude: 37.124886

City Point

City Point Wharf
Intersection of Pecan Avenue and Water
Street, Hopewell, VA 23860
Latitude: −77.273354
Longitude: 37.315914

Eppes Manor/Grant's Headquarters
1001 Pecan Avenue, Hopewell, VA 23860
Phone: 804-458-9504
Website: www.nps.gov/pete
Latitude: −77.277016
Longitude: 37.315018

Fort Stedman

Fort Friend
On Siege Road, Petersburg NB, Peters-
burg, VA 23803
Latitude: −77.357910
Longitude: 37.236240

Fort Stedman
On Siege Road, Petersburg NB,
Petersburg, VA 23803
Latitude: −77.369125
Longitude: 37.231834

Fort Haskell
On Siege Road, Petersburg NB,
Petersburg, VA 23803
Latitude: −77.369888
Longitude: 37.225899

Petersburg

Blandford Church and Cemetery
319 South Crater Road, Petersburg, VA
23803
Phone: 804-733-2396
Website: www.hbcf.us
Latitude: −77.388596
Longitude: 37.226341

The Siege Museum
15 West Bank Street, Petersburg, VA
23803
Phone: 804-733-2404
Website: www.petersburg-
va.org/tourism/siege.asp
Latitude: −77.405380
Longitude: 37.231812

Violet Bank
326 Royal Oak Avenue, Colonial Heights,
VA 23834
Phone: 804-520-9395
Website: www.colonial-heights.com/
RecParksVioletBank.htm
Latitude: −77.405472
Longitude: 37.241596

Deep Bottom

Deep Bottom Landing
9525 Deep Bottom Road, Richmond, VA
23231
Latitude: −77.304985
Longitude: 37.407692

Deep Bottom Battlefield
Intersection of Darbytown Road and
  Fussell's Mill Drive, Richmond, VA
  23231
Latitude: −77.282509
Longitude: 37.450272

New Market Heights

New Market Heights
Intersection of New Market Road and
  New Market Heights Lane, Richmond,
  VA 23231
Latitude: −77.317917
Longitude: 37.431114

Fort Harrison

Fort Harrison
8621 Battlefield Park Road, Richmond,
  VA 23231
Phone: 804-226-1981
Website: www.nps.gov/rich
Latitude: −77.373535
Longitude: 37.428791

Richmond

Tredegar Iron Works
470 Tredegar Street, Richmond, VA
  23219
Phone: 804-771-2145
Website: www.nps.gov/rich

Latitude: −77.445442
Longitude: 37.534794

Hollywood Cemetery
412 South Cherry Street, Richmond, VA
  23220
Phone: 804-648-8501
Website: www.hollywoodcemetery.org
Latitude: −77.452988
Longitude: 37.540440

Virginia State Capitol
910 Capitol Street, Richmond, VA 23219
Phone: 804-698-1788
Website: www.virginiacapitol.gov
Latitude: −77.434837
Longitude: 37.538216

Museum of the Confederacy
1201 E. Clay Street, Richmond, VA
  23219
Phone: 855-649-1861
Website: www.moc.org
Latitude: −77.429588
Longitude: 37.540970

CHAPTER 8—THE APPOMATTOX CAMPAIGN

Lewis' Farm

Lewis' Farm
On Quaker Road, 0.8 mile south of Boy-
  dton Plank Road, Dinwiddie, VA 23841
Latitude: −77.528427
Longitude: 37.125561

White Oak Road

White Oak Road
Intersection of White Oak Road and Clai-
  borne Road, Petersburg, VA 23803
Latitude: −77.549622
Longitude: 37.151981

Dinwiddie Court House

Fitzgerald's Ford
Intersection of Wilkinson Road and Whip-
  porwill Lane, Dinwiddie, VA 23841
Latitude: −77.608688
Longitude: 37.093590

Court House
Intersection of Boydton Plank Road and
  Courthouse Road, Dinwiddie, VA 23841
Latitude: −77.587425
Longitude: 37.077461

Five Forks

Visitor Center
9840 Courthouse Road, Dinwiddie, VA 23841
Phone: 804-469-4093
Website: www.nps.gov/pete
Latitude: −77.617645
Longitude: 37.135349

Initial Assault
On Courthouse Road, 0.5 mile southeast of White Oak Road, Dinwiddie, VA 23841
Latitude: −77.615585
Longitude: 37.134312

The Angle/V Corps Attack
On White Oak Road, 0.7 mile east of Courthouse Road, Dinwiddie, VA 23841
Latitude: −77.610535
Longitude: 37.139904

Five Forks Intersection
Intersection of White Oak Road and Courthouse Road, Dinwiddie, VA 23841
Latitude: −77.623077
Longitude: 37.139515

Confederate Right
On White Oak Road, 1 mile west of Courthouse Road, Dinwiddie, VA 23841
Latitude: −77.639305
Longitude: 37.140232

Crawford's Attack
On Courthouse Road, 0.5 mile north of White Oak Road, Dinwiddie, VA 23841
Latitude: −77.623146
Longitude: 37.146736

Breakthrough at Petersburg

Pamplin Park
6125 Boydton Plank Road, Petersburg, VA 23803
Phone: 804-861-2408
Website: www.pamplinpark.org/
Latitude: −77.479019
Longitude: 37.187691

Death of A. P. Hill
Sentry Hill Court, Petersburg, VA 23803
Latitude: −77.480270
Longitude: 37.192245

Fort Gregg
On 7th Avenue, 0.1 mile north of Simpson Road, Petersburg, VA 23803
Latitude: −77.454384
Longitude: 37.198006

Fort Whitworth
On 7th Avenue, 0.1 mile south of Albemarle Street, Petersburg, VA 23803
Latitude: −77.454269
Longitude: 37.202328

Sutherland's Station

Sutherland's Station
Intersection of US 460 and Namozine Road, Sutherland, VA 23885
Latitude: −77.564354
Longitude: 37.196796

Namozine Church

Namozine Church
Intersection of Namozine Road and Mill Quarter Road, Sutherland, VA 23833
Latitude: −77.724953
Longitude: 37.249626

Amelia Court House

Amelia Court House
Intersection of Court Street and Virginia Street, Amelia Court House, VA 23002
Latitude: −77.980988
Longitude: 37.342407

Jetersville

Jetersville
Intersection of Jetersville Road and Amelia Springs Road, Jetersville, VA 23083
Latitude: −78.096397
Longitude: 37.294300

Amelia Springs

Amelia Springs
On Amelia Springs Road, 0.2 mile south
of St James Road, Jetersville, VA
23083
Latitude: −78.108208
Longitude: 37.333424

Sailor's Creek

Holt's Corner
Intersection of Sayler's Creek Road and
Jamestown Road, Rice, VA 23966
Latitude: −78.212524
Longitude: 37.321049

Hillsman House/Union Position
On Sayler's Creek Road, 0.9 mile south of
Jamestown Road, Rice, VA 23966
Latitude: −78.221756
Longitude: 37.310310

Confederate Position
On Sayler's Creek Road, 0.5 mile north of
Morisetts Mill Road, Rice, VA 23966
Latitude: −78.227219
Longitude: 37.302784

Visitor Center
6541 Saylers Creek Road, Rice, VA
23966
Phone: 804-561-7510
Website:
http://dcr.virginia.gov/state_parks/
sai.shtml
Latitude: −78.229980
Longitude: 37.297882

Marshall's Crossroads
Intersection of Sayler's Creek Road and
Morisetts Mill Road, Rice, VA 23966
Latitude: −78.230904
Longitude: 37.296509

Lockett House
On CR 619, 0.6 mile south of CR 618,
Rice, VA 23966
Latitude: −78.248291
Longitude: 37.330357

Double Bridges
On CR 619, 1.4 mile south of CR 618,
Rice, VA 23966
Latitude: −78.258568
Longitude: 37.326763

Farmville

Farmville
Intersection of North Main Street and Elm
Street, Farmville, VA 23901
Latitude: −78.390190
Longitude: 37.305706

High Bridge

Trailhead
On River Road, 0.2 mile west of
Jamestown Road, Farmville, VA 23901
Phone: 434-315-0457
Website:
dcr.virginia.gov/state_parks/hig.shtml
Latitude: −78.336807
Longitude: 37.323891

Viewpoint
On River Road, 0.6 mile east of
Jamestown Road, Farmville, VA 23901
Latitude: −78.324799
Longitude: 37.325123

Cumberland Church

Cumberland Church
Intersection of Cumberland Road and
Churchview Estate, Farmville, VA 23901
Latitude: −78.385307
Longitude: 37.345432

Clifton

Clifton
On Francisco Road, 0.2 mile west of US
15, Farmville, VA 23901
Latitude: −78.488754
Longitude: 37.391636

Lee's Last Headquarters

Lee's Last Headquarters
Intersection of Courthouse Road and SR
656, Appomattox, VA 24522
Latitude: −78.783653
Longitude: 37.391701

Appomattox Station

Railroad
214 Main Street, Appomattox, VA 24522
Latitude: −78.827995
Longitude: 37.353645

Confederate Position
On Patterson Street, 0.2 mile north of
   Patricia Anne Lane, Appomattox, VA
   24522
Latitude: −78.823418
Longitude: 37.361698

Appomattox Court House

Museum of the Confederacy—
   Appomattox
Intersection of SR 656 and F 1011,
   Appomattox, VA 24522
Website: www.moc.org
Latitude: −78.824326
Longitude: 37.370815

Battlefield/Confederate Cemetery
On Old Courthouse Road, 0.7 mile west
   of SR 627, Appomattox, VA 24522
Latitude: −78.803284
Longitude: 37.375771

Appomattox Court House National
   Historical Park
On Old Courthouse Road, 0.4 mile west
   of SR 627, Appomattox, VA 24522
Phone: 434-352-8987
Website: www.nps.gov/apco
Latitude: −78.798317
Longitude: 37.374760

Abbreviated Orders of Battle

BRISTOE STATION AND MINE RUN CAMPAIGNS

OCTOBER AND NOVEMBER 1863

UNION

ARMY OF THE POTOMAC
Maj. Gen. George G. Meade

FIRST CORPS
Maj. Gen. John Newton
First Division: Brig. Gen. Lysander Cutler, Brig. Gen. Solomon Meredith
Second Division: Brig. Gen. John C. Robinson
Third Division: Brig. Gen. John R. Kelly

SECOND CORPS
Maj. Gen. Gouverneur K. Warren
First Division: Brig. Gen. John C. Caldwell
Second Division: Brig. Gen. Alexander S. Webb
Third Division: Brig. Gen. Alexander Hays

THIRD CORPS
Maj. Gen. William H. French
First Division: Maj. Gen. David B. Birney
Second Division: Brig. Gen. Henry Prince
Third Division: Brig. Gen. Joseph B. Carr

FIFTH CORPS
Maj. Gen. George Sykes
First Division: Brig. Gen. Charles Griffin, Joseph J. Bartlett
Second Division: Brig. Gen. Romeyn B. Ayres
Third Division: Col. William McCandless, Samuel W. Crawford

SIXTH CORPS
Maj. Gen. John Sedgwick
First Division: Brig. Gen. Horatio G. Wright, Brig. Gen. David Russell
Second Division: Brig. Gen. Albion P. Howe
Third Division: Brig. Gen. Henry D. Terry

CAVALRY CORPS
Maj. Gen. Alfred Pleasonton
First Division: Brig. Gen. John Buford
Second Division: Brig. Gen. David McM. Gregg
Third Division: Brig. Gen. H. Judson Kilpatrick

ARTILLERY
Brig. Gen. Henry J. Hunt

CONFEDERATE

ARMY OF NORTHERN VIRGINIA
Gen. Robert E. Lee

SECOND CORPS
Lt. Gen. Richard S. Ewell
Early's Division: Maj. Gen. Jubal A. Early
Johnson's Division: Maj. Gen. Edward "Allegheny" Johnson
Rodes's Division: Maj. Gen. Robert E. Rodes

THIRD CORPS
Lt. Gen. Ambrose Powell Hill
Anderson's Division: Maj. Gen. Richard H. Anderson
Heth's Division: Maj. Gen. Henry Heth
Wilcox's Division: Maj. Gen. Cadmus M. Wilcox

CAVALRY CORPS
Maj. Gen. J. E. B. Stuart
Hampton's Division: Maj. Gen. J. E. B. Stuart
Lee's Brigade: Maj. Gen. Fitzhugh Lee

ARTILLERY
Brig. Gen. William N. Pendleton

BERMUDA HUNDRED CAMPAIGN

MAY 1864

UNION

ARMY OF THE JAMES
Maj. Gen. Benjamin F. Butler

TENTH CORPS
Maj. Gen. Quincy A. Gillmore
First Division: Brig. Gen. Alfred H. Terry
Second Division: Brig. Gen. John W. Turner
Third Division: Brig. Gen. Adelbert Ames

EIGHTEENTH CORPS
Maj. Gen. William F. Smith
First Division: Brig. Gen. William T. H. Brooks
Second Division: Brig. Gen. Godfrey Weitzel
Third Division: Brig. Gen. Edward W. Hincks

CAVALRY DIVISION
Maj. Gen. Augustus V. Kautz

CONFEDERATE

BEAUREGARD'S FORCES AT RICHMOND AND PETERSBURG
Gen. Pierre Gustave Toutant Beauregard
Ransom's Division: Maj. Gen. Robert Ransom
Hoke's Division: Maj. Gen. Robert F. Hoke
Colquitt's Division: Brig. Gen. Alfred H. Colquitt
Whiting's Division: Maj. Gen. William H. Chase Whiting

DEPARTMENT OF NORTH CAROLINA
Maj. Gen. George E. Pickett

OVERLAND CAMPAIGN

MAY–JUNE 1864

UNION

ARMY OF THE POTOMAC

Maj. Gen. George G. Meade

SECOND CORPS

Maj. Gen. Winfield S. Hancock

First Division: Brig. Gen. Francis C. Barlow
Second Division: Brig. Gen. John Gibbon
Third Division: Brig. Gen. David B. Birney
Fourth Division: Brig. Gen. Gershom Mott, Brig. Gen. Robert O. Tyler

FIFTH CORPS

Maj. Gen. Gouverneur K. Warren

First Division: Brig. Gen. Charles Griffin
Second Division: Brig. Gen. John C. Robinson, Brig. Gen. Henry H. Lockwood
Third Division: Samuel W. Crawford
Fourth Division: Brig. Gen. James S. Wadsworth (k), Brig. Gen. Lysander Cutler

SIXTH CORPS

Maj. Gen. John Sedgwick (k); Brig. Gen. Horatio G. Wright

First Division: Brig. Gen. Horatio G. Wright, Brig. Gen. David A. Russell
Second Division: Brig. Gen. George W. Getty (w), Brig. Gen. Thomas H. Neill
Third Division: Brig. Gen. James B. Ricketts

CAVALRY CORPS

Maj. Gen. Philip H. Sheridan

First Division: Brig. Gen. Alfred T. A. Torbert, Brig. Gen. Wesley Merritt
Second Division: Brig. Gen. David McM. Gregg
Third Division: Brig. Gen. James H. Wilson

ARTILLERY

Brig. Gen. Henry J. Hunt

NINTH CORPS (INDEPENDENT; INCORPORATED INTO ARMY OF THE POTOMAC MAY 24)

Maj. Gen. Ambrose E. Burnside

First Division: Brig. Gen. Thomas G. Stevenson (k); Brig. Gen. Thomas L. Crittenden
Second Division: Brig. Gen. Robert B. Potter
Third Division: Brig. Gen. Orlando B. Willcox
Fourth Division: Brig. Gen. Edward Ferrero

EIGHTEENTH CORPS (INCORPORATED INTO ARMY OF THE POTOMAC MAY 31)

Maj. Gen. William F. "Baldy" Smith

First Division: Brig. Gen. William T. H. Brooks
Second Division: Brig. Gen. John H. Martindale
Third Division: Brig. Gen. Charles Devens

CONFEDERATE

ARMY OF NORTHERN VIRGINIA

Gen. Robert E. Lee

FIRST CORPS

Lt. Gen. James Longstreet (w), Maj. Gen. Richard H. Anderson

Kershaw's Division: Brig. Gen. Joseph B. Kershaw
Field's Division: Maj. Gen. Charles W. Field
Pickett's Division: Maj. Gen. George E. Pickett (May 21)

SECOND CORPS

Lt. Gen. Richard S. Ewell, Maj. Gen. Jubal A. Early

Early's Division: Maj. Gen. Jubal A. Early, Brig. Gen. John B. Gordon
Johnson's Division: Maj. Gen. Edward "Allegheny" Johnson (capt.)
Rodes's Division: Maj. Gen. Robert E. Rodes
Ramseur's Division: Maj. Gen. Stephen D. Ramseur

THIRD CORPS

Lt. Gen. Ambrose P. Hill

Anderson's Division: Maj. Gen. Richard H. Anderson, Brig. Gen. William Mahone
Heth's Division: Maj. Gen. Henry Heth
Wilcox's Division: Maj. Gen. Cadmus M. Wilcox

BRECKINRIDGE'S DIVISION

Maj. Gen. John C. Breckinridge

HOKE'S DIVISION

Maj. Gen. Robert F. Hoke

CAVALRY CORPS

Maj. Gen. James Ewell Brown Stuart (k), Maj. Gen. Wade Hampton

Hampton's Division: Maj. Gen. J. E. B. Stuart, Maj. Gen. Wade Hampton
Fitzhugh Lee's Division: Maj. Gen. Fitzhugh Lee
William H. F. Lee's Division: Maj. Gen. William H. F. "Rooney" Lee

ARTILLERY

Brig. Gen. William N. Pendleton

EARLY'S RAID ON WASHINGTON—
BATTLE OF MONOCACY

JULY 9, 1864

UNION

WALLACE'S DEFENSIVE FORCE

Maj. Gen. Lew Wallace

Middle Department: Brig. Gen. Erastus B. Tyler
Cavalry Force: Lt. Col. David R. Clendenin
Third Division, Sixth Corps: Brig. Gen. James B. Ricketts

CONFEDERATE

ARMY OF THE VALLEY DISTRICT

Lt. Gen. Jubal A. Early

BRECKINRIDGE'S CORPS

Maj. Gen. John C. Breckinridge

Gordon's Division: Maj. Gen. John B. Gordon
Breckinridge's Division: Brig. Gen. John Echols

EARLY'S CORPS

Lt. Gen. Jubal A. Early

Rodes's Division: Maj. Gen. Robert E. Rodes
Early's Division: Maj. Gen. Stephen D. Ramseur

CAVALRY CORPS

Maj. Gen. Robert Ransom

CHIEF OF ARTILLERY

Brig. Gen. Armistead L. Long

SHERIDAN'S VALLEY CAMPAIGN

SEPTEMBER–OCTOBER 1864

UNION

ARMY OF THE SHENANDOAH

Maj. Gen. Philip H. Sheridan, Maj. Gen. Horatio G. Wright

SIXTH CORPS

**Maj. Gen. Horatio G. Wright, Brig. Gen. James B. Ricketts,
Brig. Gen. George W. Getty**

First Division: Brig. Gen. David A. Russell (k), Brig. Gen. Emory Upton (w),
Col. Oliver Edwards, Brig. Gen. Frank Wheaton
Second Division: Brig. Gen. George W. Getty, Brig. Gen. Lewis A. Grant
Third Division: Brig. Gen. James B. Ricketts, Col. J. Warren Keifer

NINETEENTH CORPS

Maj. Gen. William H. Emory

First Division: Brig. Gen. William Dwight, Brig. Gen. James W. McMillan
Second Division: Brig. Gen. Cuvier Grover, Brig. Gen. Henry W. Birge

ARMY OF WEST VIRGINIA

Maj. Gen. George Crook

First Division: Col. Joseph Thoburn, Col. Thomas M. Harris
Second Division: Col. Isaac H. Duval (w), Col. Rutherford B. Hayes

CAVALRY

Maj. Gen. Alfred T. A. Torbert

First Division: Brig. Gen. Wesley Merritt
Second Division: Brig. Gen. William W. Averell, Brig. Gen. George A. Custer,
Col. William H. Powell
Third Division: Brig. Gen. James H. Wilson, Brig. Gen. George A. Custer

CONFEDERATE

ARMY OF THE VALLEY DISTRICT

Lt. Gen. Jubal A. Early

BRECKINRIDGE'S CORPS

Maj. Gen. John C. Breckinridge

Gordon's Division: Maj. Gen. John B. Gordon, Brig. Gen. Clement A. Evans
Breckinridge's Division: Brig. Gen. John Echols, Brig. Gen. Gabriel C. Wharton

EARLY'S CORPS

Lt. Gen. Jubal A. Early

Rodes's Division: Maj. Gen. Robert E. Rodes (k), Maj. Gen. Stephen D. Ramseur
Ramseur's Division: Maj. Gen. Stephen D. Ramseur (mw), Brig. Gen. John Pegram
Wharton's Division: Brig. Gen. Gabriel C. Wharton
Kershaw's Division: Maj. Gen. Joseph B. Kershaw

CAVALRY CORPS

Maj. Gen. Fitzhugh Lee

Lomax's Division: Maj. Gen. Lunsford L. Lomax
Lee's Division: Maj. Gen. Fitzhugh Lee (w), Brig. Gen. Williams C. Wickham,
Brig. Gen. Thomas C. Rosser

CHIEF OF ARTILLERY

Brig. Gen. Armistead L. Long, Col. Thomas H. Carter

SIEGE OF PETERSBURG

JUNE 1864–DECEMBER 2, 1864

UNION

ARMY OF THE POTOMAC

Maj. Gen. George G. Meade

SECOND CORPS

Maj. Gen. Winfield S. Hancock, Maj. Gen. Andrew A. Humphreys

First Division: Brig. Gen. Francis C. Barlow, Brig. Gen. Nelson A. Miles
Second Division: Maj. Gen. John Gibbon
Third Division: Brig. Gen. David B. Birney, Brig. Gen. Gershom Mott

FIFTH CORPS

Maj. Gen. Gouverneur K. Warren

First Division: Brig. Gen. Charles Griffin
Second Division: Brig. Gen. Romeyn B. Ayres
Third Division: Samuel W. Crawford
Fourth Division: Brig. Gen. Lysander Cutler

SIXTH CORPS

Brig. Gen. Horatio G. Wright

First Division: Brig. Gen. David A. Russell
Second Division: Brig. Gen. Thomas H. Neill, Brig. Gen. George W. Getty
Third Division: Brig. Gen. James B. Ricketts

NINTH CORPS

Maj. Gen. Ambrose E. Burnside, Maj. Gen. John G. Parke

First Division: Brig. Gen. James H. Ledlie, Brig. Gen. Julius White,
Brig. Gen. Orlando B. Willcox
Second Division: Brig. Gen. Robert B. Potter
Third Division: Brig. Gen. Orlando B. Willcox, Brig. Gen. Edward Ferrero
Fourth Division: Brig. Gen. Edward Ferrero

CAVALRY CORPS
Maj. Gen. Philip H. Sheridan
Second Division: Brig. Gen. David McM. Gregg

ARTILLERY
Brig. Gen. Henry J. Hunt

ARMY OF THE JAMES
Maj. Gen. Benjamin F. Butler

TENTH CORPS
Maj. Gen. Alfred H. Terry, Brig. Gen. William Brooks, Maj. Gen. David B. Birney
First Division: Brig. Gen. Robert S. Foster, Brig. Gen. Alfred H. Terry,
Brig. Gen. Adelbert Ames
Second Division: Brig. Gen. Adelbert Ames, Brig. Gen. John W. Turner,
Brig. Gen. Robert S. Foster
Third Division: Brig. Gen. Orris S, Ferrey, Brig. Gen. William Birney,
Brig. Gen. Joseph R. Hawley

EIGHTEENTH CORPS
**Maj. Gen. William F. "Baldy" Smith, Maj. Gen. Edward O. C. Ward,
Maj. Gen. Godfrey Weitzel**
First Division: Brig. Gen. George F. Stannard, Brig. Gen. Hiram Burnham,
Brig. Gen. Gilman Marston
Second Division: Brig. Gen. John H. Martindale, Brig. Gen. Adelbert Ames,
Brig. Gen. Charles A. Heckman, Brig. Gen. George J. Stannard
Third Division: Brig. Gen. Edward W. Hincks, Brig. Gen. Joseph B. Carr,
Brig. Gen. Charles J. Paine
Cavalry Division: Brig. Gen. August V. Kautz, Col. Robert M. West

CONFEDERATE

ARMY OF NORTHERN VIRGINIA
Gen. Robert E. Lee

FIRST CORPS
Lt. Gen. Richard H. Anderson, Lt. Gen. James Longstreet
Kershaw's Division: Brig. Gen. Joseph B. Kershaw
Field's Division: Maj. Gen. Charles W. Field
Pickett's Division: Maj. Gen. George E. Pickett

SECOND CORPS
Lt. Gen. Jubal A. Early, Maj. Gen. John B. Gordon
Gordon's Division: Brig. Gen. Clement A. Evans
Grimes's Division: Maj. Gen. Bryan Grimes
Early's Division: Brig. Gen. John Pegram, Brig. Gen. John A. Walker

THIRD CORPS
Lt. Gen. Ambrose P. Hill (k), Maj. Gen. Henry Heth
Mahone's Division: Maj. Gen. William Mahone
Heth's Division: Maj. Gen. Henry Heth, Brig. Gen. John R. Cooke
Wilcox's Division: Maj. Gen. Cadmus M. Wilcox

CAVALRY CORPS
Maj. Gen. Wade Hampton
Butler's Division: Maj. Gen. M. C. Butler
Fitzhugh Lee's Division: Maj. Gen. Fitzhugh Lee
William H. F. Lee's Division: Maj. Gen. William H. F. "Rooney" Lee

ARTILLERY
Brig. Gen. William N. Pendleton

PETERSBURG DEFENSIVE FORCE
Gen. Pierre Gustave Toutant Beauregard
Johnson's Division: Maj. Gen. Bushrod R. Johnson
Hoke's Division: Maj. Gen. Robert F. Hoke

RICHMOND DEFENSIVE FORCE
Lt. Gen. Richard S. Ewell, Brig. Gen. Henry A. Wise

SIEGE OF PETERSBURG AND APPOMATTOX CAMPAIGN

DECEMBER 2, 1864–APRIL 1865

UNION

ARMY OF THE POTOMAC
Maj. Gen. George G. Meade

SECOND CORPS
Maj. Gen. Andrew A. Humphreys
First Division: Maj. Gen. Nelson A. Miles
Second Division: Maj. Gen. John Gibbon, Brig. Gen. Thomas A. Smyth
Third Division: Brig. Gen. Gershom Mott

FIFTH CORPS
Maj. Gen. Gouverneur K. Warren, Maj. Gen. Charles Griffin
First Division: Brig. Gen. Charles Griffin, Maj. Gen. Joseph J. Bartlett
Second Division: Maj. Gen. Romeyn B. Ayres
Third Division: Maj. Gen. Samuel W. Crawford

SIXTH CORPS
Brig. Gen. Horatio G. Wright
First Division: Maj. Gen. Frank Wheaton
Second Division: Maj. Gen. George W. Getty
Third Division: Brig. Gen. Truman Seymour

NINTH CORPS
Maj. Gen. John G. Parke
First Division: Brig. Gen. Orlando B. Willcox
Second Division: Brig. Gen. Robert B. Potter
Third Division: Maj. Gen. John F. Hartranft
Fourth Division: Brig. Gen. Edward Ferrero

ARMY OF THE SHENANDOAH
Maj. Gen. Philip H. Sheridan, Maj. Gen. Wesley Merritt
First Division: Brig. Gen. Thomas C. Devin
Second Division: Brig. Gen. David McM. Gregg, Maj. Gen. George Crook
Third Division: Maj. Gen. George A. Custer

ARMY OF THE JAMES
Maj. Gen. Benjamin F. Butler, Maj. Gen. Edward O. C. Ord

TWENTY-FOURTH CORPS
Maj. Gen. Edward O. C. Ord, Maj. Gen. John Gibbon
First Division: Brig. Gen. Robert S. Foster
Third Division: Brig. Gen. Charles Devens
Independent Division: Maj. Gen. Thomas M. Harris, Maj. Gen. John W. Turner

TWENTY-FIFTH CORPS
Maj. Gen. Godfrey Weitzel
First Division: Brig. Gen. Charles J. Paine, Brig. Gen. Edward A. Wild,
Maj. Gen. August V. Kautz
Second Division: Brig. Gen. William Birney
Third Division: Brig. Gen. Edward A. Wild
Cavalry Division: Brig. Gen. August V. Kautz, Brig. Gen. Ranald S. Mackenzie

ARTILLERY
Brig. Gen. Henry J. Hunt

BERMUDA HUNDRED DEFENSIVE FORCE
Maj. Gen. Edward Ferrero

CONFEDERATE

ARMY OF NORTHERN VIRGINIA
Gen. Robert E. Lee

FIRST CORPS
Lt. Gen. James Longstreet
Kershaw's Division: Brig. Gen. Joseph B. Kershaw
Field's Division: Maj. Gen. Charles W. Field
Pickett's Division: Maj. Gen. George E. Pickett

SECOND CORPS
Maj. Gen. John B. Gordon
Gordon's Division: Brig. Gen. Clement A. Evans
Grimes's Division: Maj. Gen. Bryan Grimes
Early's Division: Brig. Gen. John Pegram, Brig. Gen. John A. Walker

THIRD CORPS
Lt. Gen. Ambrose P. Hill (k), Maj. Gen. Henry Heth
Mahone's Division: Maj. Gen. William Mahone
Heth's Division: Maj. Gen. Henry Heth, Brig. Gen. John R. Cooke
Wilcox's Division: Maj. Gen. Cadmus M. Wilcox

FOURTH CORPS
Lt. Gen. Richard H. Anderson
Johnson's Division: Maj. Gen. Bushrod R. Johnson
Mahone's Division: Maj. Gen. William Mahone
Heth's Division: Maj. Gen. Henry Heth, Brig. Gen. John R. Cooke
Wilcox's Division: Maj. Gen. Cadmus M. Wilcox

CAVALRY CORPS
Maj. Gen. Fitzhugh Lee
Rosser's Division: Maj. Gen. Thomas L. Rosser
Fitzhugh Lee's Division: Brig. Gen. Thomas T. Munford
William H. F. Lee's Division: Maj. Gen. William H. F. "Rooney" Lee

ARTILLERY
Brig. Gen. William N. Pendleton

RICHMOND DEFENSIVE FORCE
Lt. Gen. Richard S. Ewell
G. W. C. Lee's Division: Maj. Gen. G. W. Custis Lee

ACKNOWLEDGMENTS

THE MORE I VISIT AND REVISIT HISTORIC SITES, the more I am amazed by the dedication and sacrifice of the people and organizations that work so hard to preserve our history and to help us understand it. Discovering these sites for oneself is rewarding; having a helping hand ready and willing to guide you through them is priceless. I cannot possibly thank them all individually in one volume. Many thanks to all the park rangers, guides, volunteers, and enthusiasts I have encountered for having the passion, care, and zeal to tell the same story time and time again and still love every minute of it. In particular, thanks to Ed Bearss, A. Wilson Greene at Pamplin Historical Park, and Waite Rawls at the Museum of the Confederacy for providing guidance and information that I could not have possibly learned in any book.

Special thanks also to the employees and volunteers of the National Park Service, whose passion for these sites never wanes despite being consistently underpaid for not only taking care of "America's Best Idea" but also helping us all enjoy and learn from them. Thanks also to the Civil War Trust, a group that has preserved tens of thousands of acres of hallowed ground for future generations to experience and continues to remind us of the importance of these places.

The Civil War Round Table of Chicago has been an endless source of enjoyment and information for me. Thank you to all of my fellow members for their interest, support, and good times.

The guidance provided by the Abraham Lincoln Book Shop in Chicago, both for myself and the readers of this book, continues to be simply the best. Thanks to Tom Trescott, Bjorn Skaptson, and Daniel Weinberg, who have always given their support and put me on the right path.

Aaron Porter's work on the maps for both volumes of this project has been nothing short of amazing. Thank you again for your long hours and for understanding and demanding that the work is first rate.

The Countryman Press has now provided a good home for me for almost four years, and I am eternally grateful for their guidance, commitment, effort, and patience. To Kermit Hummel, Lisa Sacks, and Tom Haushalter, thank you, guys, for your continued support, great ideas, and willingness to listen. Also, many thanks to Iris Bass, who polished the final manuscript into something I could not have imagined.

Finally, endless thanks to my wife, Charlotte, who has continued to make sacrifices and patiently endure yet another of my endless projects only because she knows it's important to me. I love you very much.

BIBLIOGRAPHY

EXCEPT FOR THE CRITICAL EXAMPLES listed here, much of the information presented in this book was gleaned from interpretive signs, faded highway markers, pamphlets, brochures, internet sites, wandering exploration, and, most important, the many wonderful volunteers who take care of the sites listed in this book. Contact, site, and location information for each historical site are provided in the text and in appendix A, and should be considered references.

In addition, the following were used as sources:

Battlefield America: Fredericksburg and Spotsylvania National Military Park. A Civil War Map Series. Aurora, CO: Trailhead Graphics, 2007.

Battlefield America: The Petersburg Campaign, Including Petersburg National Battlefield and Pamplin Historical Park. A Civil War Map Series. Aurora, CO: Trailhead Graphics, 2007.

Brown, Joel F. "The Charge of the Heavy Artillery." The Maine Bugle, January 1894.

Calkins, Chris. "The Battle of Weldon Railroad (or Globe Tavern), August 18–19 and 21, 1864." *Blue & Gray Magazine,* Winter 2007.

_____. *Blue & Gray Magazine's History and Tour Guide of Five Forks, Hatcher's Run and Namozine Church, Including the Battles of Lewis' Farm, White Oak Road, and Dinwiddie Court House.* Columbus, OH: Blue & Gray Enterprises, 2003.

_____. *Great Campaigns: The Appomattox Campaign, March 29–April 9, 1865.* Conshohocken, PA: Combined Books, 1997.

_____. *Lee's Retreat: A History and Field Guide.* Page One History Publications, Richmond, Virginia, 2000.

Civil War Sites Advisory Commission Report on the Nation's Civil War Battlefields. Prepared for the United States Senate Committee on Energy and Natural Resources, the United States House of Representatives Committee on Natural

Resources, and the Secretary of the Interior. National Park Service, Civil War Sites Advisory Commission, Washington, D.C., 1993.

Civil War Trust. "Civil War Maps." civilwar.org, http://www.civilwar.org/maps/.

Davis, Major George B.; Perry, Leslie J.; and Kirkley, Joseph W. *The Official Military Atlas of the Civil War.* New York: Arno Press, 1978.

Eicher, David. *Civil War Battlefields: A Touring Guide.* Dallas, TX: Taylor Publishing Company, 1995.

Esposito, Brigadier General Vincent J., ed. *The West Point Atlas of War: The Civil War.* New York: Tess Press, 1995.

Foote, Shelby. *The Civil War: A Narrative* (3 vols.). New York: Random House, 1963.

Forman, Maj. (Ret.) Robert J., et al. *Bermuda Hundred Campaign Tour Guide.* Chesterfield, VA: Chesterfield Historical Society, 2010.

Freeman, Douglas Southall. *Lee's Lieutenants: A Study in Command,* Vol. 3: *Gettysburg to Appomattox.* New York: Charles Scribner's Sons, 1944.

Gallagher, Gary W., Finkelman, Paul, and Wagner, Margaret E. *The Library of Congress Civil War Desk Reference.* New York: Simon & Schuster, 2002.

Graham, Martin F. and Skoch, George F. *Mine Run: A Campaign of Lost Opportunities, October 21, 1863–May 1, 1864.* The Virginia Civil War Battles and Leaders Series. Lynchburg, VA; H. E. Howard, Inc., 1987.

Humphreys, Andrew A. From *Gettysburg to the Rapidan: The Army of the Potomac, July, 1863, to April, 1864.* New York: Charles Scribner's Sons, 1883.

Kennedy, Frances H., ed. *The Civil War Battlefield Guide.* 2nd Ed. New York: Houghton Mifflin, 1998.

Leepson, Marc. *Desperate Engagement: How a Little-Known Civil War Battle Saved Washington, D.C., and Changed American History.* New York: Thomas Dunne Books, 2007.

Mackowski, Chris, and White, Kristopher D. "The Battle of the Bloody Angle, or 'Mule Shoe,' Spotsylvania Court House, May 12, 1864." *Blue & Gray Magazine* 26, no. 1, (2009).

_____. "Maneuver and Mud: The Battle of Spotsylvania Court House, May 13–20, 1864." *Blue & Gray Magazine* 27, no. 6 (2011).

Marvel, William. "Retreat to Appomattox." *Blue & Gray Magazine,* April 2001.

Mertz, Gregory A. "General Gouverneur K. Warren and the Fighting at Laurel Hill During the Battle of Spotsylvania Court House, May 1864." *Blue & Gray Magazine,* Summer 2004.

_____. "Upton's Attack and the Defense of Doles' Salient, Spotsylvania Court House, Va., May 10, 1864." *Blue & Gray Magazine,* August 2001.

Miller, J. Michael. "The Battles of Bristoe Station." *Blue & Gray Magazine* 26, no. 2 (2009).

Patchan, Scott C. "The Battle of Cedar Creek, October 22, 1864." *Blue & Gray Magazine* 26, no. 1 (2007).

_____. "The Battle of Fisher's Hill, September 22, 1864." *Blue & Gray Magazine,* Winter 2008.

_____. "Opequon Creek: The Third Battle of Winchester, September 19, 1864." *Blue & Gray Magazine* 27, no. 2 (2010).

_____. *Shenandoah Summer: The 1864 Valley Campaign.* Lincoln, NE: University of Nebraska Press, 2007.

_____. "The Shenandoah Valley, July 1864: Grant and Lincoln Realize the Need for a New Commander in the Valley." *Blue & Gray Magazine,* Summer 2006.

Rhea, Gordon C. *The Battle of the Wilderness, May 5–6, 1864.* Louisiana State University Press, Baton Rouge, Louisiana, 1994.

_____. *The Battles for Spotsylvania Court House and the Road to Yellow Tavern, May 7–12, 1864.* Baton Rouge, LA: Louisiana State University Press, 1997.

_____. *Cold Harbor: Grant and Lee, May 26–June 3, 1864.* Baton Rouge, LA: Louisiana State University Press, 2002.

_____. *To the North Anna River: Grant and Lee, May 13–25, 1864.* Baton Rouge, LA: Baton Rouge, LA: Louisiana State University Press, 2000.

Robertson, William Glenn. *Back Door to Richmond: The Bermuda Hundred Campaign April–June 1864.* Baton Rouge, LA: Louisiana State University Press, 1987.

Schiller, Herbert M. *The Bermuda Hundred Campaign.* Dayton, OH: Morningside Press, 1988.

Tighe, Adrian G. *The Bristoe Campaign: General Lee's Last Strategic Offensive with the Army of Northern Virginia, October 1863.* LaVergne, TN: Xlibris, 2011.

Trudeau, Noah Andre. *Bloody Roads South: The Wilderness to Cold Harbor, May–June 1864.* Boston: Little, Brown and Company, 1989.

_____. *The Last Citadel: Petersburg, Virginia, June 1864–April 1865.* Baton Rouge, LA: Louisiana State University Press, 1991.

Venter, Bruce M. "Hancock the (Not So) Superb: The Second Battle of Reams' Station, August 25, 1864." *Blue & Gray Magazine,* Winter 2007.

Warner, Ezra J. *Generals in Blue: Lives of the Union Commanders.* Baton Rouge, LA: Louisiana State University Press, 1964.

_____. *Generals in Gray: Lives of the Confederate Commanders.* Baton Rouge, LA: Louisiana State University Press, 1959.

Weeks, Michael. *The Complete Civil War Road Trip Guide: More than 400 Civil War Sites, from Antietam to Zagonyi's Charge.* Woodstock, VT: The Countryman Press, 2009.

_____. *Civil War Road Trip: A Guide to Northern Virginia, Maryland, & Pennsylvania, 1861–1863—First Manassas to Gettysburg.* Woodstock, VT: The Countryman Press, 2011.

Wert, Jeffry D. *From Winchester to Cedar Creek: The Shenandoah Campaign of 1864* (2010 edition). Carbondale, IL: Southern Illinois University Press, 1987.

Wittenberg, Eric J. "Sheridan's Second Raid and The Battle of Trevilian Station, June 7–25, 1864." *Blue & Gray Magazine,* Winter 2002.

Wyrick, William C. "Lee's Last Offensive: The Attack on Fort Stedman, March 25, 1865." *Blue & Gray Magazine* 25, no. 1 (2008).

INDEX